# American
# Writers

ELIZABETH H. OAKES

■® Facts On File, Inc.

**Note on Photos**

Many of the illustrations and photographs used in this book are old, historical images. The quality of the prints is not always up to current standards, as in some cases the originals are from old or poor quality negatives or are damaged. The content of the illustrations, however, made their inclusion important despite problems in reproduction.

Facts On File, Inc.
132 West 31st Street
New York NY 10001

**Library of Congress Cataloging-in-Publication Data**

Oakes, Elizabeth H., 1964–
    American writers / Elizabeth H. Oakes.
        p. cm. — (American biographies)
    Includes bibliographical references (p.    ) and indexes.
    ISBN 0-8160-5158-5 (acid-free paper)
    1. American Literature—Bio-bibliography—Dictionaries. 2. Authors, American—
        Biography—Dictionaries. 3. American literature—Dictionaries. I. Title. II. Series.
    PS129.O34    2004
    810.9'0003—dc22

Facts On File books are available at special discounts when purchased in bulk quantities for businesses, associations, institutions, or sales promotions. Please call our Special Sales Department in New York at (212) 967-8800 or (800) 322-8755.

You can find Facts On File on the World Wide Web at http://www.factsonfile.com

Text design by Joan M. Toro
Cover design by Cathy Rincon

Printed in the United States of America

VB FOF 10 9 8 7 6 5 4 3 2 1

This book is printed on acid-free paper.

# CONTENTS

# LIST OF ENTRIES

Welty, Eudora
West, Nathanael
Wharton, Edith
Wheatley, Phillis
Whitman, Walt
Wideman, John Edgar

Wilder, Thornton
Williams, Tennessee
Williams, Terry Tempest
Williams, William Carlos
Wilson, August
Wolfe, Thomas

Wouk, Herman
Wright, Charles
Wright, James
Wright, Richard
Young Bear, Ray Anthony
Zitkala-Sa

# AUTHOR'S NOTE

American Writers is a book of vast scope, much like America itself. Within these pages one will find the early Puritan visionaries, leaders of the American Renaissance, realists and naturalists, the Lost Generation, the modernists, the Fugitives and agrarians, the Beats, the Black Mountain writers, postmodernists, and more. What brings them all together is the literary merit of their writing. Whether novelists, short story writers, poets, dramatists, essayists, or nonfiction writers, they are all judged by history and/or their contemporaries to be writers whose work has helped to create "American literature."

American Writers includes all the major literary genres to provide biographical profiles of writers from colonial times to the present and from all major literary movements. Emphasis is placed on reflecting the diverse ethnic backgrounds of America's literary greats, with special effort made to include writers who have not often been represented in major reference works of this kind.

Although it cannot claim to be comprehensive, this book aims to be representative of the diversity of American writers in both literary genre and ethnicity. While it does not attempt to profile writers from all genres, and will not include writers who are best known for their work in some other field, the book stands out among competitors for its expanded coverage of multiethnic writers and its attention to contemporary writers.

This reference brings together a diverse group of more than 250 American writers, providing basic biographical details about their lives. Its focus, however, is on the literary achievements of each writer. Although most writers profiled in this book are considered literary "greats," some are contemporaries whose work is just verging on greatness. Within these pages are a handful of writers born in the 1960s who have not been previously represented in a book such as this. Also this book contains many writers of diverse ethnic backgrounds. Although they are U.S. or Canadian citizens, their lives and their work reflect a deep interest in and connection to another culture.

Entries are arranged alphabetically by surname, using the name by which the writer is most commonly known. You will therefore find Mark Twain under "T" for Twain instead of under "C" for Clemens, his surname at birth. Each essay contains basic biographical information, including date and place of birth and death when known; family information; educational background; positions held; prizes won; and more. Each essay focuses on the writer's literary career, with attention given specifically to the educational, work, and travel experiences that shaped the writer's life and art. Effort is made to place the writer in context, revealing any relevant information on his or her role in literary movements or schools.

In addition to the alphabetical list of writers, readers searching for names of individuals who wrote in specific genres can consult the appendix in the back of the book, which indexes writers by genre. Entries by Year of Birth lists entrants by the period of their birth. The main index provides page references for writers and literary terms used in the book.

# ACKNOWLEDGMENTS

I am particularly grateful to Cindy Shiner and Elizabeth Rowe, whose contributions to this book were invaluable. For assistance with photographs, I thank those writers and publishers who generously responded to my requests. Finally, for patience and support on the home front, heartfelt thanks to Millie Dorsey, Courtney Zeller, and my littlest readers, Colter and Ella.

# INTRODUCTION

## COLONIAL LITERATURE TO 1776

Although American literature actually began with the oral myths and traditional stories of Native American cultures, there was no written literature among the more then 500 different Indian cultures before the first Europeans arrived. Written American literature, which forms the subject of this book, dates back to the times of early European colonists.

Many of the Puritans who settled in the northeastern United States in the later 17th century were university graduates. They desired education to understand God, and their literature reflects their religious commitment. Whether they were writing metaphysical poetry, mundane daily journals, or religious dogma, their focus was on worshipping God and avoiding the dangers presented to the soul here on Earth. The Puritans placed great emphasis on stewardship; they tended to believe that material success was a sign of spiritual health. Advancing one's individual profit and the community's well-being was seen as serving God.

ANNE BRADSTREET's (1612–72) book of poems, *The Tenth Muse Lately Sprung Up in America*, was one of the first poets to write English verse in the American colonies as well as the first American book published by a woman. Due to the lack of printing presses in the American colonies, the book was published in England. Bradstreet's long religious poems, inspired by English metaphysical poets such as Edmund Spenser and John Donne, exemplify the work of early colonial writers and exhibit her mastery of the metaphysical style, which relied heavily on the use of extended conceits and metaphors. Bradstreet also wrote shorter, witty poems on more pedestrian subjects, as well as love poems for her husband and children.

MARY ROWLANDSON's (ca. 1635–78) captivity narrative, describing the 11 weeks she spent with Indian Americans following an attack on her village, is the earliest prose writing of note by an American woman. Its simplicity of style stands in contrast to Bradstreet's more educated work. Writings such as this captivity narrative by Rowlandson were not uncommon during the early colonial period and were often extremely popular with readers.

The zealous Puritan spirit, ready to conquer the American wilderness in God's name, is typified in the work of COTTON MATHER (1663–1728). A prolific and educated writer from a long line of early colonists in Massachusetts Bay, he wrote more than 500 books and pamphlets, many of them histories and biographies that form the cornerstone of New England colonial literature.

## REVOLUTIONARY LITERATURE, 1776–1820

Although the triumph of America in the Revolutionary War heralded to many the promise of a great new literature, there was little literature of significance in the first years following the war except for outstanding political writing. The poet PHILIP FRENEAU (1752–1832) was one of the few exceptions. He stood out among his contemporaries for his passionately democratic spirit. Although he came from the same educated and aristocratic background as other writers of the time, he embraced liberal and democratic causes and opposed the other writers' tendencies to support the monarchy. In addition to his poetry, Freneau became a well-known newspaper editor, crusading for democratic ideals and establishing a tradition later followed by WILLIAM CULLEN BRYANT (1794–1878) and H. L. MENCKEN (1880–1956), among others.

A slave who was brought to Boston, Massachusetts, from Africa when she was seven, PHILLIS WHEATLEY (1753–84) became one of the most notable poets of her age and the first African-American writer of note. Her poetry resembles Freneau's in its religious subject matter and neoclassical style.

With the turn of the 18th century, American intellectuals became obsessed with the search for a native literature, something that would loosen the apron springs of attachment to the cultural and literary models of England. Such cultural independence cannot be won with the speed of a military revolution. Only time and shared experience contribute to the eventual expression of the heart of a place by its people.

Practical reasons also delayed the development of American literature. With no tradition to imitate, American writers of the Revolutionary period had only their forebears to look to for inspiration. American writers continued to anticipate and imitate new writing from England, as did American readers. In addition, with America growing so quickly, talented and educated people found rewarding work in politics, diplomacy, and law. These professions brought fame as well as fortune, while writing paid little or nothing. The publishing industry was slow to establish itself in America, and without publishers, there was no ready audience. Until about 1825, most writers paid printers to publish their own work, which meant that most published writing came from the wealthy, who could afford such a luxury. Another issue hampering the American literary scene was the lack of copyright laws protecting American writers. JAMES FENIMORE COOPER (1789–1851), one of the pioneers of America's fledgling literature, saw his first successful novel, *The Spy,* pirated by four different printers within a month of its publication. The high point of piracy, around 1815, coincided with the lowest point in the output of American writers. By 1825, however,

America's first great works of literature were on the horizon.

WASHINGTON IRVING (1789–1859) was born and educated in a well-to-do family and would likely have chosen some profession other than writing had it not been for friends who helped him to publish his *Sketch Book* in America and England simultaneously, obtaining copyright and payment in both countries, making his publishing venture more profitable than was common at the time. Irving is remembered for famous stories such as "Rip Van Winkle" and "The Legend of Sleepy Hollow" and for helping to instill a sense of history and wonder among Americans for their new home.

While Irving endowed the American landscape with a history and personality that its settlers could grasp, he did it by reinventing the stories and myths of the motherland. Cooper, however, understood the essential irony at the heart of the American identity—that the attraction of America's wilderness would lead to its destruction. His renowned literary character, Natty Bumppo, was the forerunner of numerous other legendary American heroes, including HERMAN MELVILLE's Billy Budd and MARK TWAIN's Huck Finn. Cooper's *Leather-Stocking Tales* created the first distinctively American settings, characters, and themes.

## ROMANTIC PERIOD, 1820–1860

The romantic movement arrived in the United States around 1820, coinciding with the nation's discovery of its distinctive artistic voice. The excitement of this discovery was fueled by the idealism and passion of romanticism, resulting in the great works of the American renaissance by such writers as RALPH WALDO EMERSON, HENRY DAVID THOREAU, WALT WHITMAN, HERMAN MELVILLE, MARGARET FULLER, and others.

Romanticism was well suited to the fledgling American literature. It affirmed the democratic ideals of individualism, found value in the common person, and looked to the imagination for inspiration. Romanticism found a natural home in the transcendentalists of New England. The transcendentalist movement was based on a fundamental belief in the unity of the world and God. Transcendentalists vowed that each soul was a microcosm of the world itself and thus the doctrine of self-reliance and individualism, associated so strongly with this movement, were born and nurtured by the prevailing romantic spirit.

Concord, Massachusetts, was the first rural artists' colony in America and the home of transcendentalism. Here the core writers associated with this movement met for conversation, published their magazine, *The Dial*, wrote great books, planned reform movements, and gardened. Great emphasis was placed on individual expression and on discovering an authentic literary form and voice. The sheer number of literary masterpieces created between the 1830s and 1860s, when the Civil War captured everyone's attention, attests to the richness of America's literary culture during this period.

The major texts of the transcendentalist movement included Emerson's (1803–82) essay *Nature*, Thoreau's (1817–62) masterpiece *Walden, Or Life in the Woods*, and Walt Whitman's (1819–92) *Leaves of Grass*.

Emerson is remembered for his insistence on the creation of an American individualism inspired by nature. The central figure in the transcendentalist movement, Emerson had a spiritual mission, with much of his insight inspired by his readings in Hinduism, Confucianism, Taoism, and Sufism. He was also a great prose poet, whose work had significant influence on Whitman, as well as on poets of subsequent generations, including HART CRANE, WALLACE STEVENS, and ROBERT FROST.

Thoreau's experiments in living independently and in accordance with his principles became the subject of his writings. *Walden*, his book about the time he spent living in a cabin that he built at Walden Pond, is considered to be the first American work of literature about self-discovery. In the book, Thoreau admonishes the reader to live life authentically. *Walden* remains very popular with modern readers due to its ecological consciousness, its theories of civil disobedience, and its commitment to basic civil rights.

A carpenter by trade and free spirit by nature, Walt Whitman tapped into America's democratic spirit with his book *Leaves of Grass*. The poems, including the famous "Song of Myself," rose from the romantic and transcendentalist ideal of oneness with nature and celebrated the notion of creation

itself. Both innovative and energetic, the poems spoke without inhibition, creating their own history and embodying the American epic that generations of literary critics had been searching for.

The Boston Brahmins exercised yet another influence in this period. Composed of scholar-poets such as HENRY WADSWORTH LONGFELLOW (1807–82), this group sought to infuse American literature with a bit of refined European culture. Longfellow, for example, wrote three long narrative poems in European forms that popularized Native American legends. These included "Evangeline" and "The Song of Hiawatha." He also wrote a travel narrative that retold European legends. Although the Brahmin poets meant to educate the American reader, their efforts served in part to retard the recognition of the immensely innovative and genuinely American talents of Walt Whitman, EDGAR ALLAN POE, HERMAN MELVILLE, and other writers of the Romantic period.

EMILY DICKINSON (1830–86) was ahead of her time in many ways. Writing at the end of the transcendentalist period in New England, Dickinson loved nature and studied the birds and plants in her surroundings, which often found their way into her poems. She was also a loner and an extreme individualist, all of which made the principles of transcendentalism appealing to her. But unlike the writers of that period, Dickinson wrote poems that were extremely modern in their reliance on images and their insistence on brevity. Hers was a chiseled and mystical style that captivates modern literary critics.

The novelists and fiction writers most associated with the Romantic period include NATHANIEL HAWTHORNE, Edgar Allan Poe, and Herman Melville, writers who were more interested in the larger-than-life characteristics of their protagonists than they were in presenting realistic figures. Characters like Ahab in *Moby Dick* and Hester Prynne in *The Scarlet Letter* struggle with their own anguished souls in the mystery of life that rises from the dark and unknown unconscious. The drama is centered in the human interior. The loners of early American literature reflected the lack of tradition in early American culture. Communities were not as settled as in Europe, and society was relatively classless compared to that of England. The constantly changing American frontier was reflected in the literary landscape, where the novelist had both the freedom and burden of inventing and defining the democratic American society in which he or she lived.

Nathaniel Hawthorne (1804–64) wrote the classic novel of Puritan America, *The Scarlet Letter*, which was published in 1850 and treats issues that were usually suppressed at the time, such as the influence of democratic ideals on individual behavior, especially sexual and religious freedom. His work is notable for its portrayal of broken, dysfunctional families and its emphasis on the individual alone in tragic circumstances.

A sailor who turned his interest and knowledge of the sea and exploration into classic novels, Herman Melville (1819–91) is best remembered as the author of the great novel *Moby Dick*. More realistic and philosophical than some of the other books of this period, the novel is still tragic, with its mighty protagonist, Ahab, doomed in the end to be consumed by the great white whale he intends to know and conquer. *Moby Dick* is also notable for its modern tendency to be reflexive. Melville is often compelled in the course of the novel to comment on the act of writing, reading, and understanding—explorations of the mind, another ultimately unknowable, unconquerable terrain. An epic of the natural world, like Thoreau's *Walden* before it and Twain's *Huckleberry Finn* after it, *Moby Dick* dramatizes the human spirit in its struggle with nature. It finds the greatest power of life in the hidden and wild depths of the human spirit, not in the organized and ranked urban world.

Edgar Allan Poe (1809–49) shared an interest in the metaphysical world with the other writers of this period, but his writing incorporated elements of the strange and exotic to produce tales unlike most other writers of the time. He exercised tremendous influence over future American writers of science fiction, horror, and fantasy. Poe's interest in themes of death-in-life, especially being buried alive or returning to life from the grave, appear in many of his stories and poems, including "The Cask of Amontillado" and "The Fall of the House of Usher." Although these themes carry great dramatic weight, they also reflect the disturbed unconscious of his characters. Like Hawthorne and Melville, Poe finds exploration of the human psyche to be the most compelling form of adventure.

Ultimately, the writers of the romantic period exposed the dark underside of the American dream. Their stories, novels, and poems revealed the loneliness, alienation, and psychic distress that came with excessive competition and individualism.

Reform movements gained momentum during the idealistic decades of romanticism. Many writers found their voice in the struggle to improve society. The feminist MARGARET FULLER (1810–50), for example, was an exceptional essayist and the first professional woman journalist in America. Her popular book, *Woman in the Nineteenth Century*, explores woman's role in society and uses transcendentalist principles to analyze the difficulties faced by women.

Other reformers included HARRIET BEECHER STOWE (1811–96), whose sentimental novel *Uncle Tom's Cabin* was the most popular novel of the 19th century. It appealed to the reader's emotions and dramatized the contentious social issues surrounding slavery that led the country into civil war. Abolitionism and other social reform issues were at the heart of the women's literary movement. SOJOURNER TRUTH (ca. 1797–1883) represented this movement as well, and though she was illiterate her entire life, her *Narrative of Sojourner Truth*, transcribed by the editor Oliver Gilbert, tells the remarkable story of her work as a charismatic women's rights advocate.

## THE RISE OF REALISM, 1860–1914

With the Civil War (1861–65) came significant change in America's vision of itself. Where idealists had focused on the abolition of slavery and on promoting human rights prior to the war, they increasingly looked toward economic progress and materialism afterward. Great industries were founded, and business boomed. Railroads crossed the country, and with them the telegraph, linking town to town and America to the world. The population of the country moved from the countryside to the city. Immigrants flooded harbors on both coasts, providing cheap labor, as well as a wealth of diversity.

The Age of Realism (1860–1914) took hold as American writers began to grapple with the dehumanizing forces of the capitalist economy. As industry and cities grew larger, the individual seemed to matter less. Literature of this period illustrates the harm done to the weak and vulnerable in such a competitive and impersonal society. Triumph comes in realist fiction through hard work and kindness.

Mark Twain's (1835–1910) *Huckleberry Finn* is the classic realist tale. Other offshoots of realism include the naturalist novels of THEODORE DREISER (1871–1945) and JACK LONDON; the investigative journalism of UPTON SINCLAIR; Western writers like BRET HARTE and WILLA CATHER; (1873–1947) cosmopolitan realists EDITH WHARTON (1862–1937) and HENRY JAMES (1843–1916); and Chicago poets EDGAR LEE MASTERS, (1868–1950) VACHEL LINDSAY (1879–1931), and CARL SANDBURG (1878–1967).

Mark Twain's realism was unconventional, arriving as it did at the tail end of romanticism. It was a fresh way to speak the truth and get society's attention. *Huckleberry Finn* dramatizes Twain's vision of a harmonious community and restores the open road and the American wilderness as the ultimate destination, in opposition to the already established American myth of success in the material world. Twain's frontier humor and regional sketches represented literary currents that became prevalent in the late 19th century.

Although numerous writers prior to this time were interested in specific regions, the regionalists, or local colorists as they have sometimes been called, were interested exclusively in portraying a particular place as realistically as possible.

Bret Harte was an extremely popular author of western tales, portraying the mining frontier. MARY WILKINS FREEMAN (1852–1930), Harriet Beecher Stowe (1811–96), and SARAH ORNE JEWETT (1849–1909) all depicted New England with intimate detail. Later in this period, the novelists ELLEN GLASGOW (1873–1945) and Willa Cather explored women's lives and their own regions—Richmond, Virginia, for Glasgow and the Nebraska prairie for Cather—in novels that resist categorization due to their exceptional ability to speak universally.

Henry James and Edith Wharton were both brought up in wealthy, educated New York families who spent much of their time in Europe. Consequently, the novelists often contrasted Europeans and Americans. Their novels frequently focused on the gulf between the inner reality of individuals and the social conventions surrounding them.

Naturalist writers like Theodore Dreiser insistently probed the increasingly industrial age. Naturalism developed as an extension of realism and was concerned primarily with depicting life as accurately as possible, without artificial distortions brought about by literary conventions or philosophical ideals. The characters in naturalist novels were helpless victims of environmental and biological forces beyond their control. *An American Tragedy*, Dreiser's best-known novel, is a scathing portrait of the American success myth gone awry. It reflects the dissatisfaction and despair of the poor and dispossessed at the bottom of America's social structure.

The investigative journalism of the muckrakers came about in response to these social ills and gave rise to writers like Upton Sinclair, whose literary work played a significant role in instigating social change. *The Jungle*, Sinclair's famous portrayal of the Chicago meat-packing industry, caught the attention of the American public as well as the political elite, creating a hotbed of discourse that ultimately led to new laws and more protection for the general population.

The Chicago Renaissance, led by Edgar Lee Masters, Vachel Lindsay, and Carl Sandburg, concerned itself with portraying the common people, using colloquial language, and openly dealing with taboo subjects such as sex. It was the voice of the Midwest, rising up to meet the East Coast literary establishment on its own terms.

Sandburg, often thought of as a latter day Walt Whitman, sang the song of the Midwest in everyday, ebullient language that captured the heart of Americans across the land. Lindsay foreshadowed the Beats with his love of public readings and his populist spirit. Edgar Lee Masters is remembered for his daring and original *Spoon River Anthology*, which presented Master's collection of epitaphs on the 250 people buried in a fictitious small country village cemetery.

## RISE OF AFRICAN-AMERICAN LITERATURE

The literary achievements of African Americans in post–Civil War America were astounding. Beginning with autobiography, protest literature, sermons, and poetry, the roots of black writing established themselves with writers such as BOOKER T. WASHINGTON (1856–1915), JAMES WELDON JOHNSON (1871–1938), and W. E. B. DU BOIS, who became the central figure in the Harlem Renaissance of the 1920s.

Booker T. Washington's autobiography, *Up from Slavery*, tells the story of his struggle to better himself. Eventually one of the most powerful black men in the nation, Washington worked relentlessly to improve the lives of African Americans and is remembered for his controversial accomodationist policy toward whites.

The poet James Weldon Johnson was of mixed white and black ancestry and explored issues of identity in his fictional book *Autobiography of an Ex-Colored Man*. His poems showed the influence of African-American spirituals.

The Harlem Renaissance in New York City in the 1920s had an intensity that sent shock waves throughout the nation. Black artists, musicians, dancers, and writers found new appreciation for their work. A wide range of styles and visions existed within Harlem's literary community, but the common thread for all black writers of this period was the advent of a cultural identity that included both the sufferings and injustices of the African-American experience as well as the creative triumphs and rich communal history.

Many African-American writers, such as ZORA NEALE HURSTON (1903–60) and LANGSTON HUGHES (1902–67) broke with tradition in favor of writing in the style and idiom of their own communities. Others continued to incorporate traditional forms and themes into their writing, believing that art should not be defined by race. Among these writers were COUNTEE CULLEN (1903–46), who was briefly married to W. E. B. Du Bois's daughter. An accomplished writer of formal verse, Cullen believed that race should not dictate the subject or style of a poem. JEAN TOOMER (1894–1967) also believed in a vision of America in which race did not define people and chose to employ traditional poetic forms in his writing.

Characteristic works by writers who embraced the creation of a new black aesthetic include Zora Neale Hurston's *Their Eyes Were Watching God*, RICHARD WRIGHT's (1908–60) *Native Son*, and Langston Hughes's jazz-inspired poetry.

## MODERNISM, 1920–1945

The modernist movement began to take hold in the period between the two world wars. Although spirits soared, the economy boomed, and modern conveniences eased the drudgery of daily tasks for the growing middle class, a general disillusionment settled over the country. GERTRUDE STEIN (1874–1946) aptly named young Americans of the 1920s "the lost generation." For despite the growth and success of this period, the loss of traditional values and social structures resulted in a personal identity crisis for many.

Numerous works of literature evoke the excesses and ennui of this period, especially ERNEST HEMINGWAY's (1899–1961) *The Sun Also Rises* and F. SCOTT FITZGERALD's (1896–1940) *This Side of Paradise*. T. S. ELIOT (1888–1965) captured the spiritual emptiness felt by this generation in his famous long poem *The Waste Land*.

Innovative writers such as Gertrude Stein, EZRA POUND (1885–1972), and WALLACE STEVENS (1879–1955) mirrored the breakdown of traditional society in writing that played fast and loose with conventional notions of time, space, and consciousness. Modern life was faster and more technological, and modernist literature addressed these changes by choosing the fragmented over the unified and the abstract over the concrete. Traditional devices of narrative and plot were discarded. Point of view in the novel became as important as the story itself. While writers such as Henry James, WILLIAM FAULKNER (1897–1962), and others experimented with fictional points of view, no longer satisfied with the simple first-person or third-person narrative, they also wrote in a more realistic style, carrying the tradition of American realism into the 20th century.

Socially conscious writers of this period who carried on in the tradition of the naturalists and muckrakers included JOHN DOS PASSOS

(1896–1970), JOHN STEINBECK (1930–  ), and CLIFFORD ODETS (1906–1963).

Several literary currents developed during the years between the two wars that would have a major impact on the development of American literature in the 20th century. The first was the creation of the New Criticism, which was a new theoretical approach to literature. The name was taken from the title of a book published by JOHN CROWE RANSOM (1888–1974) in 1941. Ransom, a leading writer of the Southern Renaissance, was associated with the Fugitives, a literary group centered at Vanderbilt University. His book laid out a critical approach to literature that was based not on the history and biography of the writer but on elements of the text itself. The New Criticism became the dominant American critical approach in the mid-20th century.

The Fugitives, of which Ransom was the leader, included the poets ALLEN TATE (1899–1979) and ROBERT PENN WARREN (1905–89), among others. This southern literary school called for a return to traditional values that its proponents thought could still be found in the South and a rejection of the urban, commercial values that dominated the North.

The modernist period was really the beginning of a truly American theater. Prior to the 1920s, American dramatists routinely looked to Europe for inspiration. But with modernism, playwrights such as EUGENE O'NEILL (1888–1953), THORNTON WILDER (1897–1975), and Clifford Odets began to play with tradition and locate a uniquely American dramatic voice.

## LITERATURE SINCE 1945

The sense of dislocation that pervaded modernist literature carried over into the postwar period, encouraged by the Holocaust of World War II, an increase in materialism, the protest movements of the 1960s, the cold war, and the Vietnam War, among other events. Perhaps greatest of all the influences, however, was the development of a pervasive mass media culture.

In poetry, the shift away from traditional forms and ideas produced a myriad of styles that are quite varied and numerous. Poets who carried on or revitalized traditions include the Fugitive poets JOHN CROWE RANSOM, ALLEN TATE, and ROBERT PENN WARREN, LOUISE BOGAN (1897–1970), ROBERT LOWELL (1917–77), JAMES MERRILL (1926–95), and WENDELL BERRY (1934–  ), among others. These poets were not shy about using poetic diction, meter, and rhyme, though they often reinterpreted a traditional form by applying a modern twist.

Other poets shaped their own unique styles. Although they may have drawn on tradition, they ultimately differentiated themselves as wholly contemporary. The poets of the confessional school fell into this category. JOHN BERRYMAN (1914–72), SYLVIA PLATH (1932–63), and ANNE SEXTON (1928–74) expressed a direct relationship to poetic traditions in many of their earlier poems but went on to write in their own unique, idiosyncratic styles. Other poets whose relationship to tradition was similar include THEODORE ROETHKE (1908–63), ELIZABETH BISHOP (1911–79), ADRIENNE RICH (1929–  ), PHILIP LEVINE (1928–  ), and JAMES DICKEY (1923–97).

A number of experimental schools of poetry emerged in the 1950s and 1960s. These included the Black Mountain school, the New York school, the Beats, and the surrealist and existentialist poets. The poets associated with these schools tended to be outspoken and independent of mainstream intellectual communities at universities. Their poetry was daring, sometimes shocking, and generally committed to the spontaneous and organic.

Some of the notable writers of these movements include the Black Mountain poets ROBERT CREELEY (1926–  ) and DENISE LEVERTOV (1923–  ), whose minimalist styles reflect the philosophy of projective verse that was the theoretical focus of their movement.

Apolitical and disinterested in moral questions, poets of the New York school, including KENNETH KOCH (1925–2002) and JOHN ASHBERY, (1927–  ), became known for their reliance on hallucinatory images and mysterious prose written in experimental forms. Their verbal puzzles often seemed to hold little meaning, existing only for themselves. Absurdity and abstraction, with a self-mocking tone, defined the poets of the New York school, who became known by this name because of their location and their many references to the city.

San Francisco poets, such as GARY SNYDER (1930– ) and LAWRENCE FERLINGHETTI (1919– ) merged with the Beat poets of the 1950s since they were all centered in San Francisco. Snyder's poems exhibit traits characteristic of the San Francisco school, including an indebtedness to Eastern philosophy and religion, as well as a reliance on the natural world for poetic inspiration.

The Beat poets were distinguished by their interest in oral poetry and their audacity in the face of convention. It was the most anti-establishment literary movement in America, but the focus of Beat poets such as ALLEN GINSBERG (1926–97) and ANNE WALDMAN (1945– ) was not on negation and protest so much as it was on affirmation and celebration.

Although the modernist poets introduced symbolist techniques into American poetry in the 1920s, surrealism did not take root in the United States until the 1960s, when poets such as ROBERT BLY (1926– ), CHARLES SIMIC (1938– ), CHARLES WRIGHT (1935– ), MARK STRAND (1934– ), and others began to incorporate archetypal images and existentialist themes.

Another trend in poetry since 1945 has been the increase in poetry by women and ethnic minorities. Distinguished women poets of the past half-century included RITA DOVE (1952– ), LOUISE GLÜCK (1943– ), AUDRE LORDE (1934–92), and MARY OLIVER (1935– ), among many others. Writers brought into the spotlight by the renaissance in multiethnic literature included Hispanic Americans such as DENISE CHAVEZ (1948– ), Asian Americans such as MARILYN CHIN (1955– ), Native Americans such as LESLIE MARMON SILKO (1948– ) and SIMON ORTIZ (1941– ) and African Americans such as AMIRI BARAKA (1934– ).

Fiction since 1945 has been as various and difficult to categorize as poetry during the same period. Stimulated by international literary influences, such as magic realism from Latin America and European existentialism, American fiction has also been profoundly affected by the computer age. Popular symbols and subjects handed down through the mass media pop up regularly in the literature of serious writers. It is not at all unusual to find THOMAS PYNCHON (1937– ), JOYCE CAROL OATES (1938– ) or ALICE WALKER (1932– ), for example, commenting on Hollywood films, popular music, or even the fashion industry.

In addition, the experimentation with point of view that characterized realist fiction between the world wars has been taken one step further. The postmodern novel is highly reflexive, always keeping one eye on itself and commenting on what it sees there. Post–World War II novelists of note are linked by the subject matter handed down to them. NORMAN MAILER (1923– ), THOMAS PYNCHON (1937– ), HERMAN WOUK (1915– ), and KURT VONNEGUT (1922– ), among others, wrote masterful novels set during World War II.

The Southern Renaissance continued to produce new talent among fiction writers in the 1940s with EUDORA WELTY (1909–2001), TENNESSEE WILLIAMS (1914–83), and KATHERINE ANNE PORTER (1890–1980) among them. Fiction of the 1950s was characterized by a sense of alienation and stress amidst abundance. JOHN CHEEVER (1912–82), JOHN UPDIKE (1932– ), ARTHUR MILLER (1915– ), and PHILIP ROTH (1933– ) were some of the writers whose work explored the dark side of material abundance and corporate success.

SAUL BELLOW (1915– ), BERNARD MALAMUD (1914–86), and ISAAC BASHEVIS SINGER (1904–91) led the way for Jewish American writers, whose significant contributions helped shape American literature to include Jewish experience both in America and in the Old World.

A blurring of lines between fiction and non-fiction has characterized many works of literature since the 1960s. This trend began with TRUMAN CAPOTE's (1924–84) *In Cold Blood*, which appeared in 1966. A highly suspenseful analysis of a brutal mass murder, the book read like a detective novel. Other books that pushed the boundaries between the two genres included Norman Mailer's *The Executioner's Song* which was published in 1979.

Realism began to make a return in the 1970s with novels by John Gardner (1933–1982), TONI MORRISON (1931– ) and ALICE WALKER (1944– ), among others. At the same time, literature by ethnic minorities became a significant component of the literary scene. Dramatists AUGUST WILSON (1945– ) and DAVID HENRY HWANG (1957– )

and novelists MAXINE HONG KINGSTON (1940– ), AMY TAN (1952– ), OSCAR HIJUELOS (1951– ), and SANDRA CISNEROS (1954– ) have captured the interest of American readers and critics within their own ethnic communities and beyond.

Although an interest in portraying a sense of place in literature has always been part of the American tradition, regionalism experienced a decline during the early and mid-20th century. The turn of the 21st century, however, witnessed a return to regionalism as one of the defining traits of American fiction.

From STEPHEN KING's (1947– ) thrillers set in Maine to ANNE TYLER's (1941– ) domestic novels set in Baltimore, Maryland, writers have delved into the places they know best to offer readers all across the country an insider's view. Other writers whose works portray a strong sense of place include KAYE GIBBONS (1960– ) and REYNOLDS PRICE (1933– ), both of whom set most of their fiction in North Carolina; WENDELL BERRY (1934– )

whose agrarian fiction is set in rural Kentucky; JANE SMILEY (1949– ) whose novels unfold in the vast American heartland; BARBARA KINGSOLVER (1955– ), CORMAC MCCARTHY (1933– ), and LESLIE MARMON SILKO (1948– ), all of whom chronicle the American Southwest; WALLACE STEGNER (1909–93) whose region was California and the West Coast; and RAYMOND CARVER (1939–88), whose stories brought to life the small towns of the Pacific Northwest. Dramatists like Chicago's DAVID MAMET (1947– ) have also contributed to this literary trend.

From colonial times to the present, writers have followed a circuitous path in helping to map America's identity, for a country's literature is no less than its own vast autobiography, its story of itself. Shaped by history, by ancestors, by the tremendous technological and scientific advances of the last 400 years, and by the varied influences brought to bear in the global age, the American story is rich with both tradition and possibility.

## Abbey, Edward
### (Edward Paul Abbey)
(1927–1989) *essayist, novelist, nature writer*

Labeled by many as an environmental radical, Edward Abbey preferred to think of himself as just a writer. His essays, novels, letters, and speeches form one of the most persuasive and well-known bodies of work in defense of the American West. In more than four decades of writing, he authored 21 books, including *Desert Solitaire, The Monkey Wrench Gang, The Brave Cowboy,* and *The Fool's Progress.* "Resist much, obey little," a quote from WALT WHITMAN, became the title for one of Abbey's books, as well as a motto to live by. In 1987, Abbey was offered a major award by the American Academy of Arts and Letters. He declined the honor, saying that he had plans to run a river in Idaho the week of the award ceremony.

Edward Abbey was born in the town of Indiana, Pennsylvania, on January 29, 1927, the oldest of five children in a Scottish-German family. His father was a trapper and logger with marxist leanings; his religious mother was a schoolteacher. As a child, Abbey wrote his own comic books. After graduating from high school in 1945, he hitchhiked west for the first time. He served in the U.S. Army from 1945 to 1947 as a motorcycle MP (military police officer) in Naples, Italy.

Upon returning home from Italy, he attended Indiana University of Pennsylvania for one year. In 1948, at age 21, Abbey left home again, hitchhiking across the Midwest and the Rockies to the West

Coast, then returning by way of the Southwest. It was during this trip that Abbey first fell in love with the desert. He entered the University of New Mexico that year and eventually earned his undergraduate and graduate degrees there. The thesis for his master's degree in philosophy was titled "Anarchism and the Morality of Violence." He served as the editor of *The Thunderbird,* the student literary magazine, and began the commitment to writing that would last the rest of his life.

In addition to a prolific writing career, Abbey worked for 15 years, until he was well into his forties, as a part-time ranger and fire lookout at several different national parks. The two seasons he spent as a ranger at Arches National Monument (later a national park) in Utah inspired him to write *Desert Solitaire.*

First published in 1968, this nonfiction account of Abbey's two summers in Utah's canyonlands earned Abbey his reputation as an environmentalist and nature writer. Praised as both poetic and fiercely combative, *Desert Solitaire* became essential reading for defenders of nature everywhere. But it was *The Monkey Wrench Gang,* published in 1975, that has been credited with inspiring an entire generation of environmental activists. This fictional account of four "environmental warriors" who travel the Southwest, "liberating" parts of Utah and Arizona from evil road-builders, miners, and rubes, introduced "monkey-wrenching," or acts of sabotage intended to save wilderness, as viable political action. Organizations such as Earth First! continue the fight. Other novels by Abbey received higher literary praise, but it was *The Monkey Wrench Gang* that secured Abbey's place as an underground cult hero. *Hayduke Lives!*, a sequel to *The Monkey Wrench Gang* and Abbey's last novel, was published after his death. It resurrects the Monkey Wrench Gang to continue its battle against Goliath, a giant earth-moving machine that walks.

Abbey's other novels include *The Brave Cowboy* (1956), *Good News* (1980), and *The Fool's Progress* (1988). His works of nonfiction, in addition to *Desert Solitaire*, include *Appalachian Wilderness* (1970), *The Cactus Country* (1973), *The Journey Home* (1977), *Beyond the Wall* (1984), and *One Life at a Time, Please* (1988). In addition to his collections of essays and articles and his novels, Abbey published one book of poetry, *Earth Apples* (1994), and contributed to numerous anthologies and other works.

Abbey was married five times and had five children. He married his final wife, Clarke Cartwright, in 1982. He died on March 14, 1989, at his home in "Fort Llatikcuf" near Tucson, Arizona, after four days of esophageal hemorrhaging, a complication from surgery. He was 62.

Although he was popular during his lifetime, Abbey has become even more of a legend since his death. Perhaps some of this legend-building has been fueled by the mysterious circumstances surrounding his burial. It has been reported that Abbey requested to be buried in the desert, without the interference of undertakers, embalming, or coffins, and that he wanted to be transported to his burial site in the back of a pickup truck. In the message he left his wife with details about his burial, he said, "I want my body to help fertilize the growth of a cactus or cliff rose or sagebrush or tree." Abbey was buried according to his wishes, somewhere in the Cabeza Prieta Desert in southern Arizona. Fans have been looking for the gravesite ever since, for one more chance to pay homage to the man whose books have been praised by fellow writer WENDELL BERRY as "indispensable solace" and "antidotes to despair."

## Further Reading

Bishop, James, Jr. *Epitaph for a Desert Anarchist: The Life and Legacy of Edward Abbey.* New York: Atheneum, 1994.

Cahalan, James M. *Edward Abbey: A Life.* Phoenix: University of Arizona Press, 2001.

Peacock, Doug. "Chasing Abbey," *Outside Magazine.* August 1997. Available online. URL: http://web.outsideonline.com/magazine/0897/9708abbey.html. Downloaded March 13, 2003.

## Abu-Jaber, Diana
(1959–   ) *novelist, food writer*

Diana Abu-Jaber's writing is known for its skillful treatment of the Arab-American immigrant experience. In addition, several reviewers of her work have commented on its contribution to dispelling traditional stereotypes of Arabs in America. Jean Grant suggested in a review of *Arabian Jazz* published in the *Washington Report on Middle East Affairs* in 1993 that "Abu-Jaber's novel will probably do more to convince readers to abandon what media analyst Jack Shaheen calls America's 'abhorrence of the Arab' than any number of speeches or publicity gambits."

Abu-Jaber was born in 1959 in Syracuse, New York, to a Jordanian father, a hospital administrator whose passion is cooking, and an American mother of Irish-German descent, who worked for many years as a reading teacher before retiring to spend more time on her painting. She has two younger sisters, Suzy and Monica. The family moved to Jordan when she was seven, and Abu-Jaber has lived in both Jordan and the United States ever since. "I feel that in many ways I grew up *between* Jordan and America," Abu-Jaber has said, "even through we mostly lived in the States." When questioned about the effects of this cross-cultural life on her writing, Abu-Jaber replied, "My father always wanted to return to Jordan (he still sometimes does) and he raised us to think of ourselves as Arab women, instilled with Arab values and beliefs. This was frequently a confusing, frustrating, and mysterious way to be raised, but it always offered lots of interesting material and great food. And it was also, frequently, a lot of fun. I still have a 'divided' sense of self and I try to visit Jordan and my friends and family there whenever possible."

In 1981 Abu-Jaber received a B.A. degree in English from the State University of New York at

Oswego. She completed her M.A. degree in English in 1982 at the University of Windsor. She has taught literature and creative writing at the University of Oregon, the University of California at Los Angeles, the University of Michigan, and Portland (Oregon) State University.

Arabian Jazz, Abu-Jaber's first novel, was published in 1993 to critical acclaim. It won the Oregon Book Award and was a finalist for the National PEN/Hemingway Award. It was praised for its sensitive treatment of the Arab immigrant experience and its effort to shed light on Arab culture. Set in upstate New York, where Abu-Jaber grew up, the book follows the first generation Arab-American Ramoud family as it attempts to navigate between the expectations of highly individualized American culture and those of the traditional extended Arab family.

Arab-American writer Diana Abu-Jaber's first novel was Arabian Jazz. (Photo by Eric Feinblatt. Courtesy of Diana Abu-Jaber.)

Her second novel, Crescent, was published by W. W. Norton in April 2003. Asked about the subject of this new novel, Abu-Jaber said it is "set in an Arabic café in Los Angeles and it's all about a love affair between an Arab-American chef and an Iraqi linguistics professor at UCLA." Abu-Jaber is currently at work on a nonfiction book called The Language of Baklava, which she describes as "a sort of life-story told through food—all about my experience with growing up in a multicultural, food-obsessed family." Another novel-in-progress, Memories of Birth, won a National Endowment for the Arts grant. In addition to these works, Abu-Jaber has published numerous short stories online and in literary magazines such as Ploughshares, Story, and North American Review.

She is currently writer-in-residence at Portland State University, where she teaches in the graduate fiction program. She also enjoys teaching film studies and postcolonial literature. She wrote film reviews for The Oregonian for years and explained that she divides her "'day job' pretty evenly between teaching and writing journalism. I do regular food writing for The Oregonian and other publications and publish a fair amount of personal essays—I've written for Salon.com, Gourmet, Good Housekeeping, Saveur, and More Magazine, among others. I'm particularly drawn to examining the intersections between cultural and personal identity, especially with regard to linking my own experience as the child of an Arab immigrant to my American identity."

## Further Reading

Innes, Charlotte. "A Chef in Love." The Nation, June 16, 2003, p. 46.

De Haven, Tom. "Arabian Jazz," New York Times Book Review, July 18, 1993, p. 9.

Web Del Sol. "Diana Abu-Jaber." Available online. URL: http://webdelsol.com/LITARTS/abujaber. Downloaded February 12, 2003.

## Ackerman, Diane
(1948–   ) poet, essayist, nature writer

Ackerman described herself best when she said, "People don't know how to describe me usually, so

Author of *A Natural History of the Senses,* Diane Ackerman writes about nature and human nature and, as she says, "that twilight zone where the two meet and have something they can teach each other." *(Photo by Toshi Otsuki. Courtesy of* Victoria Magazine*)*

Diane Ackerman was born in 1948 in Waukegan, Illinois, just outside of Chicago. She graduated from Pennsylvania State University and later received an M.F.A. and a Ph.D. from Cornell University. She published three books of poetry before leaving Cornell. Ackerman calls her first book, *The Planets: A Cosmic Pastoral,* a collection of "scientifically accurate poems on the planets." The famous astronomer Carl Sagan sat on her doctoral committee, and she spent lots of time going out to the Jet Propulsion Laboratory and working with the space sciences department at Cornell. Her next two books of poems were *Wife of Light,* which she has characterized as more "normal" poems, and *Lady Faustus.* Then came Ackerman's first book of prose, *Twilight of the Tenderfoot,* written about her experience of the different seasons of the year on a New Mexico cattle ranch. Her other books include the best-selling *A Natural History of the Senses; Jaguar to Sweet Laughter: New and Selected Poems; The Moon by Whale Light, and Other Adventures Among Bats, Crocodilians, Penguins and Whales; A Natural History of Love; Monk Seal Hideaway; Deep Play;* and *The Senses of Animal.*

Ackerman has been praised as an exceptionally gifted lyric poet, and her prose has benefited from this poetic skill, although she has said that she does not think about the rhythm of prose the way one thinks about rhythm in poetry. "When I write prose, I don't fret about the prose rhythm of the whole chapter. I don't think in large structures like that, although I know fiction writers who do. I understand the general architecture of the book—I outline the book so I do know what I'm going to be writing. But I write it tiny piece by tiny piece and worry about how each word will fit. I think that my structures are smaller."

Ackerman is married to fiction writer Paul West, with whom she has lived for more than three decades. Since her first book publications in the 1970s, she has written prolifically and traveled often. Although her work has often taken her on far-flung expeditions where she conducts research for upcoming books, she has always returned to the small town of Ithaca, New York, which she described as a "latter-day hippie community that consists largely of therapists and artists, with a few massage people thrown in." Ackerman praises the

what they do is say, 'Poet, essayist and naturalist,' because they're not sure what I am." When pressed to describe her writing more specifically, Ackerman continued, "I write about nature and human nature. And most often about that twilight zone where the two meet and have something they can teach each other. I like that best." Her diverse bibliography includes nine books of adult nonfiction, seven books of poetry, three books of juvenile nonfiction, and numerous shorter pieces in anthologies and periodicals. Her book *A Natural History of the Senses* was adapted for television and became the five-hour PBS *Nova* series called *Mystery of the Senses. On Extended Wings,* another nonfiction book, was adapted for the stage.

sense of neighborliness in Ithaca and has written about her experience there as a suicide prevention counselor in *A Slender Thread*, which was published in 1997. She has also done volunteer work at an Ithaca hospice. About this work, she said, "I grew up in the 70s with the idea that an individual not only could make a difference, but had it as a duty to try."

Ackerman has received the Academy of American Poets' Lavan Award as well as grants from the National Endowment for the Arts and the Rockefeller Foundation. In 1999, a molecule, "dianeackerone," was named after her.

## Further Reading

Ackerman, Diane. "Taking Time for the Marvelous." *Victoria*, January 1997, pp. 29–33.

Cornell Writers: "Diane Ackerman." Available online. URL: http://www.writers.cornell.edu/ackerman.html. Downloaded February 23, 2003.

Zinsser, William, ed. *Going on Faith: Writing as Spiritual Quest*. New York: Marlowe & Co., 1999.

## Agee, James
(1909–1955) *poet, novelist, screenwriter, journalist, letter writer, literary critic, nonfiction writer*

James Agee has been described by literary critic Kenneth Seib as a "versatile and accomplished artist whose mind played freely over all possible media of expression and whose ability with the English language was exceeded by none of his contemporaries." Agee wrote the text for *Let Us Now Praise Famous Men* (1941), which details the lives of depression-era sharecroppers. He also wrote the screenplays for *The African Queen* (1951) and *Night of the Hunter* (1955) and the Pulitzer Prize–winning novel *A Death in the Family* (1957), as well as poetry and film criticism.

James Agee was born on November 27, 1909, in Knoxville, Tennessee. His Father, a postal worker, was killed in an automobile accident when Agee was six years old, an event that shaped Agee's life and inspired the novel for which he is most famous, *A Death in the Family*. Following the death of his father, Agee was sent to Saint Andrews Seminary, an Episcopal boarding school in the Appalachian Mountains. Although he found comfort in the academic life he established there, he also suffered a sense of abandonment due to this early separation from his mother, which followed his father's death so closely. Agee's mentor at Saint Andrews, Father Flye, became a surrogate parent and would remain his closest friend in the years after he left Saint Andrews. It was Flye who first perceived Agee's intellectual gifts and introduced him to classical literature and music. He also helped him gain acceptance to the prestigious Phillips Exeter Academy in New Hampshire and then Harvard University. Agee graduated from Harvard in 1932 and published his first and only volume of poetry in 1934—*Permit Me Voyage*, which was chosen for publication by the Yale Series of Younger Poets. A collection of Agee's poems was published posthumously in 1968, as was *Letters of James Agee to Father Flye*.

Following his graduation from Harvard, Agee worked as a staff journalist for several prominent magazines, including *Time*, *The Nation*, and *Fortune*. In 1936, while employed by *Fortune*, Agee and photographer Walker Evans spent a summer living with sharecroppers in Alabama to report on the plight of the tenant farmer. Their work led to the 1941 publication of *Let Us Now Praise Famous Men*. Although the book was not particularly well received by wartime audiences, it won popular and critical acclaim following the war. Its partly fictional accounts of southern farm life accompanied by Evans's candid photographs became a classic text on social injustice in America. Agee's experience during his work on *Let Us Now Praise Famous Men* helped him connect with his southern roots and resulted eventually in his writing *The Morning Watch* (1951) and *Knoxville Summer 1915*, both of which depict the struggles of a Tennessee boy.

Although enjoying great success in his career, Agee grew restless. His leftist leanings led him to become involved with a radical journal, *The New Masses*, after leaving *Fortune* in 1939. He was extremely uncomfortable with U.S. involvement in World War II, and his smoking and drinking became more of a problem, contributing to his heart disease. In addition, Agee's first two marriages dissolved. He married a third time, but this union was also troubled.

During these troubled times, Agee sought new outlets for his writing. Like F. SCOTT FITZGERALD and others, he looked to Hollywood. Agee pioneered the art of film criticism, writing for *The Nation* and *Time,* and then worked on several screenplays, including the film adaptation of *The African Queen* in 1951. His work on *The African Queen* earned both Agee and coauthor John Huston the Oscar for best screenplay adaptation in 1952. In 1953, Agee wrote a screenplay and acted in a film short based on STEPHEN CRANE's *The Bride Comes to Yellow Sky.* He also worked on his novel, *A Death in the Family,* during this period; it was based on Agee's life story and published posthumously in 1957.

Agee's health had begun to deteriorate rapidly in the mid-1950s. He experienced daily problems with his heart, and on May 16, 1955, he died of a heart attack in a New York City taxicab, while on the way to a doctor's appointment. He was 46 years old. Ironically, Agee's death occurred on the same day and month as his father's had many years before. In 1957, Agee was posthumously awarded the Pulitzer Prize for *A Death in the Family.*

## Further Reading

Behar, Jack. "James Agee: Notes on the Man and the Work." *Denver Quarterly* 13, no. 1 (1978): 3–15.

Madden, David, and Jeffrey J. Folks. eds. *Remembering James Agee.* Athens: University of Georgia Press, 1997.

Steinhardt, Georgia. "Agee." Available online, URL: http://athena.english.vt.edu/~appalach/writersA/agee.html. Downloaded February 10, 2003.

# Ai
## (Florence Anthony)
## (1947–   ) *poet*

Although reviewers often refer to her as a black poet, Ai calls herself black and Japanese and also claims Irish, Choctaw, and German ancestry. A writer of dramatic monologues whose mixed heritage has greatly shaped her work and life, Ai in her poetry makes a point of calling into question cultural definitions and the very notion of a single ethnic identity. She won the National Book Award for poetry in 1999 for her book *Vice.*

Florence Anthony was born in Albany, Texas, in 1947 to a Japanese father and a mother who was part black, Choctaw, and Irish. About her birth family, she has said, "Since I am the child of a scandalous affair my mother had with a Japanese man she met at a streetcar stop, and I was forced to live a lie for so many years, while my mother concealed my natural father's identity from me, I feel that I should not have to be identified with a man, who was only my stepfather, for all eternity." That is why she would later adopt the name "Ai."

She grew up in Tucson, in a family situation she calls a kind of "half-breed culture," and in Las Vegas and San Francisco. As an undergraduate, she majored in Japanese at the University of Arizona and began writing poetry. It was during these years that she met her mentor, Galway Kinnell, when he came to campus to read his poems. After the reading, Ai occasionally sent her poems to Kinnell for his feedback. He encouraged her to apply to the writing program at the University of California at Irvine. Ai did, and during her second year at Irvine, Kinnell took a copy of Ai's thesis to an editor at Houghton Mifflin. In 1972, Ai's first book, *Cruelty,* was published.

Following the book's publication, Ai received a Bunting Fellowship, which she held in 1975–76. Between 1979 and 1999, she published five volumes of poetry and taught creative writing in a number of universities around the country. The style she honed during these 20 years of writing can best be described as gritty. She has said that she consciously chose to write in the vernacular Wordsworthian tradition.

The speakers in her poems include necrophiliacs, rapists, and scoundrels of various orientations. But the personae of her poems are not always unknown figures. Marilyn Monroe and J. Edgar Hoover, among others, have also made appearances. About her decision to write first-person dramatic monologues, Ai said, "I find it very exciting to become other people. I don't think of them as masks for myself. Some people say that, but to me they're not. They're my characters; they're not me." Ai has begun work on a memoir in recent years, the first time she has written directly about her own background.

Publication and prizes have come readily to Ai. In addition to her Bunting Fellowship in the 1970s, she has won a Guggenheim Fellowship, the Lamont Prize for poetry, an American Book Award, and the latest and greatest of her prizes, the National Book Award. After receiving this award in 1999 for her collection *Vice,* Ai was awarded tenure as a full professor at Oklahoma State University, where she has taught as a visiting professor for several years.

### Further Reading

Harrison, Pat. "The Many Voices of the Poet Ai." *Radcliffe Quarterly,* Spring 2000. Available online. URL: http://www.radcliffe.edu/quarterly/200002/justice-17.html. Downloaded February 3, 2003.

*Modern American Poetry.* "A 1999 PBS Interview with Ai." Available online. URL: http://www.english.uiuc.edu/maps/poets/a_f/ai/pbsinterview.htm. Posted November 18, 1999.

*The Oxford Companion to Women's Writing in the United States.* "Ai." New York: Oxford University Press, 1995.

## Aiken, Conrad
### (Conrad Potter Aiken)
(1889–1973) *poet, short story writer, literary critic, novelist*

Conrad Aiken's poetry is known for its fascination with psychoanalysis and the development of identity. His many influences included Freud, William James, EDGAR ALLAN POE, and the French symbolists. In addition to his accomplished career as a poet, Aiken was also an editor and critic of note. He edited EMILY DICKINSON's *Selected Poems,* which came out in 1924, and is considered largely responsible for establishing her posthumous literary reputation. Aiken was also very well connected to the American literary scene in the early 1900s, sharing classes at Harvard with T. S. ELIOT and graduating in the same era as E. E. CUMMINGS and others. Aiken played a significant role in introducing American poets to the British, as he traveled frequently between England and the United States. Aiken's *Selected Poems* won the Pulitzer Prize in 1930 and

his *Collected Poems* won the National Book Award in 1953.

Conrad Aiken was born in Savannah, Georgia, on August 5, 1889. As a young boy, he was severely traumatized when he discovered the dead bodies of his parents. His father, a physician, had killed Conrad's mother and then committed suicide himself. From the age of 11, Aiken was reared by a great-great-aunt in Massachusetts. He was educated at private schools, including the Middlesex School in Concord, Massachusetts. He went on to study at Harvard University, where he edited the *Advocate,* a literary magazine, with T. S. Eliot. He was also a contributing editor of famed literary journal *The Dial* and befriended its then editor EZRA POUND. Aiken graduated from Harvard in 1912.

Aiken's first collection of poetry, *Earth Triumphant,* was published in 1914 and established his reputation as an important young poet. He subsequently won exemption from service during World War I by claiming that, as a poet, he was part of an "essential industry."

During the 1920s and 1930s, Aiken made many transatlantic journeys and married three times. In 1921 he moved from Massachusetts to Rye, Sussex, England. His first marriage was to Jessie McDonald. Their daughter, Joan Aiken, became a well-known children's book writer whose more than 60 publication include the Wolves of Willoughby Chase series. Aiken then married Clarissa M. Lorenz in 1930. Shortly after their divorce in 1937, he married the artist Mary Hoover while traveling with her in Mexico. The two settled in Rye first but then returned to the United States after the outbreak of World War II.

Most of Aiken's fiction was written during this period. He wrote *Blue Voyage* (1927), *King Coffin* (1934), and two short story collections—*Bring! Bring!* (1925) and *Among the Lost People* (1934)—during this era of many marriages and much travel. His *Selected Poems,* published in 1929, was awarded the Pulitzer Prize in 1930.

The following decades proved somewhat more stable for Aiken. He served as a consultant in poetry at the Library of Congress from 1950 to 1952, and in 1953 he published his *Collected Poems,* which won the National Book Award in poetry. Aiken's critical essays, letters, and autobiographical novel provide significant insight into his life and philosophy. *A Reviewer's ABC*, which came out in 1958, is a compilation of Aiken's critical essays. *The Selected Letters of Conrad Aiken* was published in 1978 and contains his correspondence with other literary greats, such as WALLACE STEVENS, Edmund Wilson, and Harriet Monroe. *Ushant*, an autobiographical novel, was published in 1952. Aiken's bibliography is quite extensive. In addition to the titles listed here, Aiken published many other works, including quite a few novels, several short story and poetry collections, children's books, and a play.

Aiken received the Bollingen Prize in 1956, the Gold Medal in Poetry from the American Academy of Arts and Letters in 1958, and the National Medal for Literature in 1969, as well as the Pulitzer Prize, the National Book Award, and other honors. He died in Savannah on August 17, 1973, where he lived part time in a house adjacent to the one he lived in as a child.

## Further Reading

Lorenz, Clarissa M. *Lorelei Two: My Life with Aiken.* Athens: University of Georgia Press, 1983.

Marten, Harry. *The Art of Knowing: The Poetry and Prose of Conrad Aiken.* St. Louis: University of Missouri Press, 1988.

Seigel, Catharine F. *The Fictive World of Conrad Aiken: A Celebration of Consciousness.* De Kalb: Northern Illinois University Press, 1993.

## Albee, Edward
(1928–   ) *playwright*

Edward Albee is one of the most influential American dramatists of the 20th century. Albee's work can be characterized as a continuous stream of theatrical experimentation. He is probably best known for his play *Who's Afraid of Virginia Woolf?*, which enjoyed great critical and popular acclaim. But Albee has remained immune to commercial pressure and insistent on testing the boundaries of American drama, even when it means negative reviews from the critics or failure at the box office. Albee has said that his plays are "an examination of the American Scene, an attack on the substitution of artificial for real values in our society, a condemnation of complacency, cruelty, and emasculation and vacuity, a stand against the fiction that everything in this slipping land of ours is peachy-keen."

Edward Albee was born on March 12, 1928, in Washington, D.C. Adopted two weeks later by Reed and Frances Albee, he was taken to live in the family home in Westchester County, New York, where he was raised. Reed Albee owned a national chain of vaudeville theaters, which afforded the young Albee plenty of opportunities to experience life around the stage and the colorful personalities who worked in the theater.

As a child, Albee led a privileged life. There were servants, tutors, riding lessons, summers spent sailing, and winters in the warmth of Miami, Florida. Albee attended several private schools during his high school years, including Lawrenceville School and Valley Forge Military Academy. He was dismissed from both of these for failure to attend classes and subsequently enrolled at the prestigious Choate School from 1944 to 1946. His first published play, *Schism*, appeared in the school's literary magazine in 1946. In the fall of 1946, Albee enrolled at Trinity College, a small liberal arts college in Hartford, Connecticut, but his time there was brief. He was dismissed for failure to attend chapel and classes. This was the end of Albee's formal schooling.

In 1948, at the age of 20, Albee moved to Greenwich Village, where he lived on the income he earned at odd jobs and on the proceeds from his grandmother's trust fund, while establishing his life as a writer. During these years he worked as an office boy, record salesman, and Western Union messenger before finally achieving success with *The Zoo Story* in 1959. First produced in Berlin, *The Zoo Story* later appeared in New York in a double bill with Samuel Beckett's *Krapp's Last Tape*. Albee was forever connected to the Theatre of the Absurd as a result of this early association with Beckett. Several of Albee's early works, including *The Zoo Story*, *The Sandbox* (1959), and *The American Dream* (1960), formed the beginnings of absurdist drama in America. Albee was lauded as the leader of this theatrical movement, which emerged in Paris during the late 1940s and early 1950s in the plays of Jean Genet, Eugene Ionesco, and Samuel Beckett, among others. Commonly associated with existentialist thought, absurdist drama often grapples with the anxiety and amazement humans feel in the face of an inexplicable universe. Its literary roots can be traced to the allegorical morality plays of the Middle Ages, the nonsense literature of writers such as Lewis Carroll, and the dream novels of James Joyce and Franz Kafka. He was commended as following in the footsteps of great American playwrights like ARTHUR MILLER, TENNESSEE WILLIAMS, and EUGENE O'NEILL while also incorporating the influence of European playwrights such as Beckett and Harold Pinter.

Albee won the Pulitzer Prize in 1966 for *A Delicate Balance,* in 1975 for *Seascape,* and again in 1994 for *Three Tall Women,* a play based on the life of his adoptive mother, who apparently struggled against Albee's interest in art and intellectuals and his homosexuality. Albee's other plays include the theatrical adaptation of *The Ballad of the Sad Café, Counting the Ways and Listening, The Lady from Dubuque,* the theatrical adaptation of VLADIMIR NABOKOV's *Lolita, Marriage Play,* and *Everything in the Garden,* among others.

The 1980s were difficult years for Albee, whose plays failed to meet with any commercial success. However, *Three Tall Women* won Best Play awards in 1994 from the New York Drama Critics Circle and Outer Critics Circle, as well as the previously mentioned Pulitzer Prize.

Albee remains active, writing and directing his plays, teaching at the University of Houston's School of Theater, and giving lectures on his work at colleges around the country.

## Further Reading

The English Page. "Edward Albee." Available online. URL: http://www.educeth.ch/english/readinglist/albee/index/html. Downloaded February 23, 2003.

Gussow, Mel. *Edward Albee: A Singular Journey: A Biography.* New York: Simon & Schuster, 1999.

Hirsch, Foster. *Who's Afraid of Edward Albee?* Berkeley, Calif.: Creative Arts Book Company, 1978.

PinkMonkey.com. "The Author and His Times." Available online. URL: http://pinkmonkey.com/booknotes/barrons/whoafrd1.asp. Downloaded February 23, 2003.

## Alcott, Louisa May
### (Flora Fairfield)
(1832–1888) *novelist, poet, short story writer, essayist, children's fiction writer, letter writer*

Louisa May Alcott is one of the foremost women writers of the 19th century. Alcott's best-known book, *Little Women,* portrays the lives of four sisters growing up in New England during the Civil War. The novel, based on Alcott's childhood experiences with her sisters, focuses on family relationships and promotes such values as self-reliance and perseverance, traits demonstrated by Alcott as she faced the hardships of her own life. Alcott published more than 30 books and collections of short stories. In addition to her writing, she worked when she was young as a teacher, seamstress, and domestic servant. From 1861 to 1863, during the Civil War, she was a nurse at Union Hospital, Georgetown, in Washington, D.C. She also became editor of the children's magazine *Merry's Museum* in 1867 and was active in various reform movements throughout her life, including the temperance, education, and women's suffrage movements.

Born in Germantown, Pennsylvania, on November 29, 1832, Louisa May Alcott and her three sisters—Anna, Elizabeth, and May—were educated and raised by their father, Bronson Alcott, a prominent transcendentalist and teacher, and their mother, Abigail May Alcott, who was well-known as an abolitionist and suffragist and became the first paid social worker in the state of Massachusetts. American transcendentalism was a philosophical and literary movement that originated as a reform movement in the Unitarian Church and flourished during the mid-19th century. It was based on the belief that the soul of each individual is identical with the soul of the world and contains what the world contains. Transcendentalists believed in the innate goodness of humans and in the power of divine inspiration, especially as derived through contact with the natural world.

Louisa grew up in Boston and later in Concord, Massachusetts, where her parents' circle of friends included other prominent transcendentalists such as the Emersons, Thoreaus, Hawthornes, and

Ripleys. By all accounts, she was a tomboy. She claimed herself that "No boy could be my friend till I had beaten him in a race and no girl if she refused to climb trees, leap fences . . ."

Alcott's passion for writing began when she made up stories for her sisters that the girls would then act out at home, with Louisa always choosing to play the lurid characters. Troubled by the poverty that plagued her family, she determined to make money with her passion for storytelling. She vowed at the age of 15, "I will do something by and by. Don't care what, teach, sew, act, write, anything to help the family; and I'll be rich and famous and happy before I die, see if I won't!" For many years, Louisa did any work she could find in order to help support the family. Her career as an author began when she published poetry and short stories in popular magazines. Her first book, *Flower Fables*, appeared in 1854, when she was 22. She worked as a nurse in Washington, D.C., during the Civil War and published *Hospital Sketches* in 1863, which is based on the letters she wrote home to her family during this time.

When Alcott was 35 years old, Thomas Niles, her publisher in Boston, asked her to write "a book for girls." *Little Women* was written between May and July 1868 at Orchard House, which was the Alcott family home in Concord, Massachusetts, from 1858 to 1877. Jo March, the heroine of the novel, is said to be the first American juvenile heroine to act from her own individuality. *Little Women,* the autobiographical account of four sisters growing up in New England during the Civil War, was published in 1868–69 and immediately established Alcott's reputation as a writer. She published four sequels to *Little Women—Good Wives* (Volume 2 of *Little Women*), *Little Men: Life at Plumfield with Jo's Boys* (1871), *Aunt Jo's Scrap Bag* (1872–82), and *Jo's Boys and How They Turned Out* (1886). Following the publication of these books, Alcott became a celebrity and easily supported her family with her earnings.

RALPH WALDO EMERSON said of Alcott's novels, "She is a natural source of stories. . . . She is and is to be, the poet of children. She knows their angels." In addition to writing for children, Alcott published gothic fiction for adults during the early part of her writing career. These stories were published anony-

mously and pseudonymously in various New England periodicals and provided Alcott with a steady income while she worked on her longer novels. Although the stories of this period have been described as lurid and melodramatic, contemporary critics agree that the characters and plots were well developed. The books Alcott published in the latter part of her career, following the success of the Little Women series, included *A Story of Experience* (1873) and *Rose in Bloom* (1876). These were written at a time when her health was failing and are generally considered to be her weakest works.

By the end of her life, Alcott had sold more than 1 million books and earned more than $200,000 from her writing. Her Little Women series remains popular among young and old readers alike and is regarded as having revolutionized

This wood engraving is titled "The late Louisa May Alcott" and was published in 1888 in *Harper's Weekly,* vol. 32, p. 193. *(Library of Congress, Prints and Photographs Division [LC-USZ61-452])*

the portrayal of adolescents in fiction. Louisa May Alcott died on March 6, 1888, in Boston, Massachusetts, and is buried in Sleepy Hollow Cemetery in Concord, Massachusetts.

## Further Reading

Dawson, Melanie. "A Woman's Power: Alcott's 'Behind a Mask' and the Usefulness of Dramatic Literacies in the Home." *Atq: the american transcendental quarterly* 11, no. 1 (March 1997): 19–41.

Delamar, Gloria T. *Louisa May Alcott and "Little Women": Biography, Critique, Publications, Poems, Songs, and Contemporary Relevance.* Jefferson, N.C.: McFarland, 1990.

Ramsey, Inez. "Louisa May Alcott: Teacher Resource File." Available online. URL: http://falcon.jmu.edu/~ramseyil/alcott.htm#D. Downloaded February 23, 2003.

## Alexie, Sherman
### (Sherman Joseph Alexie, Jr.)
(1966–    ) *novelist, poet, screenwriter*

A prolific novelist, poet, and screenwriter, Sherman Alexie is known for his skill in blending humor with biting social commentary. In all genres, the specifics of his Native American characters' lives mix with what he knows about the universality of human experience to create compelling and original drama. His meteoric rise to fame, first as an author and then as a screenwriter, has given other Native Americans a model for success in literature and film unlike any they have previously seen. Before reaching the age of 30, he had been hailed by the literary journal *Granta* as one of their Best Young American Novelists and was featured in the *New Yorker*'s special issue "Writers for the 21st Century."

Sherman Alexie, an enrolled Spokane/Coeur d'Alene Indian, was born on October 7, 1966. He grew up on the Spokane Indian Reservation in Wellpinit, Washington, about 50 miles northwest of Spokane. Despite complications from being born hydrocephalic (with water on his brain), Alexie learned to read by the age of three and had read JOHN STEINBECK's *The Grapes of Wrath* by the time he turned five. He was a gifted student, often scorned by his classmates for his bookishness. He attended reservation schools until he reached high school at which time he chose to attend school off the reservation in order to get a better education. At Reardan High School, Alexie was the only Indian except for the school mascot, he has said. He excelled in his school as he had in elementary school and was a star player on Reardan's basketball team.

Following his graduation from high school in 1985, Alexie entered Gonzaga College in Spokane on a full scholarship. After two years, he transferred to Washington State University in Pullman. He planned to be a doctor but decided to change his major after fainting three times in an anatomy class. After taking a creative writing class with poetry teacher Alex Kuo, Alexie began to write regularly and to publish in magazines such as *The Beloit Poetry Journal, The Journal of Ethnic Studies, New York Quarterly, Ploughshares,* and *Zyzzyva.* He graduated with a degree in American studies and a commitment to pursuing a career in writing. In 1991, he received the Washington State Arts Commission Poetry Fellowship and in 1992, the National Endowment for the Arts Poetry Fellowship.

*I Would Steal Horses* and *The Business of Fancydancing: Stories and Poems,* Alexie's first published books, appeared in 1992. Alexie, who developed an alcohol problem while in college, has told a story about giving up alcohol for good upon learning that Hanging Loose Press would publish *The Business of Fancydancing.* Several more titles followed in rapid succession, including *The Lone Ranger and Tonto Fistfight in Heaven* (1993), his first book of short stories, which received a PEN/Hemingway Award for best first book of fiction and a Lila Wallace-Reader's Digest Writers' Award. Alexie also won the American Book Award for his novel *Reservation Blues* (1995), and his second novel, *Indian Killer* (1996), was named a *New York Times* Notable Book when it appeared in 1996.

In addition to writing prolifically, Alexie launched a career as a stand-up performer. He has worked with Jim Boyd, a Colville Indian musician, on readings of his work; the two also collaborated on a record album called *Reservation Blues,* which contains the songs from the book of the same name. Boyd and Alexie opened for the Indigo Girls in 1996 at a concert to benefit the Honor the Earth Campaign.

Other performance work includes Alexie's defeating Jimmy Santiago Baca, the reigning champion, in the World Heavyweight Poetry Bout in 1998. (In a poetry bout, poets read poems in early rounds. In the final, they are given a word and must come up with a poem on the spot. The matter is scored by judges.) He went on to win the title for three more consecutive years, making him the first poet to hold the title for four years. Alexie also debuted as a stand-up comedian in 1999 at the Foolproof Northwest Comedy Festival in Seattle, Washington.

His film career began when he collaborated with Chris Eyre, a Cheyenne/Arapaho Indian, on a screenplay based on Alexie's short story "This is What It Means to Say Phoenix, Arizona." The film was titled *Smoke Signals* and was released at the Sundance Film Festival in 1998, where it won the Audience Award and the Filmmaker's Trophy. Miramax Films released *Smoke Signals* later that year. The film went on to win a Christopher Award, presented to creators of artistic works that "affirm the highest values of the human spirit," and to be nominated for the Independent Feature Project/West 1999 Independent Spirit Award for Best First Screenplay. Since finding success with *Smoke Signals*, Alexie has continued to work on screenplays for his novels. In 2002, he released *The Business of Fancydancing*, shot independently in digital video. It has not yet been released by a major distributor but has won notice in the independent film community.

All this success has not slowed Alexie's writing in the least. His latest book publications include *The Toughest Indian in the World* and *One Stick Song*, a collection of poems. In addition to the awards and honors already mentioned, Alexie was a 1999 O. Henry Award juror, a judge for the 2000 inaugural PEN/Amazon.com Short Story Award, and a member of the 2000 Independent Spirit Awards Nominating Committee, which honors independent films. He has received honorary degrees from Columbia College, Chicago, and Seattle University. He lives with his wife and two sons in Seattle.

**Further Reading**

De Ramirez, Brill, and Susan Berry. *Contemporary American Indian Literatures & the Oral Tradition.*

Sherman Alexie, an enrolled member of the Spokane/Coeur d'Alene tribe, enjoyed a meteoric rise to fame following the publication of his first book of short stories, *The Lone Ranger and Tonto Fistfight in Heaven.* (photograph © Rob Casey)

Tucson: University of Arizona Press, 1999, pp. 190–199.

Gillian, Jennifer. "Reservation Home Movies: Sherman Alexie's Poetry." *American Literature* 68 (1996): 91–110.

McFarland, Rom. "'Another Kind of Violence': Sherman Alexie's Poems." *American Indian Quarterly* 21, no. 2 (spring 1997): 251–264.

———. *Studies in American Indian Literatures* 9, no. 4 (1997). Special Sherman Alexie Issue.

# Alger, Horatio
## (Horatio Alger, Jr.)
(1832–1899) *children's fiction writer, poet*

Horatio Alger's name is inextricably bound with the notion of success achieved through honesty, hard work, and independence. In more than 100 books, his boy characters exhibited just these traits, inspiring several generations of readers to pursue similar lives of upright behavior and commitment to excellence in all endeavors. The Horatio Alger Society's Strive and Succeed Award and the Horatio Alger Association's Horatio Alger Award keep his name and his beliefs alive by honoring Americans every year who demonstrate the spirit expressed in Alger's stories.

Horatio Alger, Jr., was born on January 13, 1832, in Chelsea (now Revere), Massachusetts to Reverend Horatio Alger, a Unitarian minister, and Olive (Fenno) Alger, the daughter of a wealthy landowner. He was educated at home by his father and spent, according to him, lots of time reading both educational and entertaining works because his father was often busy with church affairs.

At the age of 12, when Alger and his family moved to Marlborough, he enrolled at the Gates Academy, a college preparatory school. He noted in his Class Book from these years that the education at Gates Academy was heavy on mathematics and the physical sciences, which did not seem to displease him. He graduated from the academy at the age of 15 and enrolled the following year at Harvard.

Alger was employed as a "President's Freshman" at Harvard, running errands for the university president. In addition, he received financial aid from his father's cousin, Cyrus Alger, a wealthy industrialist. A member of the Psi Upsilon fraternity, Horatio Alger enjoyed an active extracurricular life as well as academic success at Harvard. He graduated from Harvard in 1852 at the age of 19 and entered the Harvard Divinity School in the fall of 1853, but he soon left school and went to work as an assistant editor at the *Boston Daily Advertiser*. This position did not last long either, with Alger moving on to work as a tutor, a teacher, and, eventually, a writer.

He wrote all the time, too, and in 1856 his book *Bertha's Christmas Vision*, a collection of previously published stories, was published. *Nothing To Do*, a book-length satirical poem, came out in 1857. Other stories and poems appeared regularly in monthly and weekly publications, but Alger was not yet able to earn a living from his writing and teaching and so returned to the Harvard Divinity School in 1857. He graduated in 1860 and entered the ministry for a short time in Chicopee,

Massachusetts, but soon made plans for a grand tour of Europe, a trip made possible by an unexpected inheritance. During his travels, he submitted travel narratives to the *New York Sun* to help defray his costs. By all reports, he enjoyed nearly a year of travel away from his family before returning to New York.

When Alger returned from his trip, he made a conscious decision to begin writing for children. He contacted a publisher, A. K. Loring, who encouraged Alger to submit the manuscript of a book he had been working on. *Frank's Campaign* was published by Loring at about the same time that Alger took a post as a Unitarian minister, this time in Brewster, Massachusetts. For a time, Alger worked as a minister and wrote stories and novels on the side. His life changed dramatically in 1866 when an investigative committee at the church determined, in response to rumors that were circulating, that Alger had molested two boys. He was charged with pedophilia, which he did not deny. Alger resigned and returned to his parents' home for a while before moving to New York City to be a full-time writer.

Some of Alger's best-loved books include *Ragged Dick* and the series of novels that followed it, all based on the lives of young boys who lived in the streets of New York. Alger eventually became an advocate for homeless children and appealed to his readers often for support of places that provided meals and lodging to homeless children. Alger found success later in his career in writing biographies for a juvenile audience. The first of these was the life of James Garfield, *From Canal Boy to President*, written following the president's death. He later wrote biographies of Daniel Webster (*From Farm Boy to Senator*) and Abraham Lincoln (*Abraham Lincoln, The Backwoods Boy*).

Although Alger found much success in writing for children, he always hoped to write for adults. He did publish several books that appealed to a more mature audience—*Grand'ther Baldwin's Thanksgiving* (1875), a collection of poems, and his novel, *The New Schoolma'am, or A Summer in North Sparta* (1877), but he returned to writing for children and wrote until his health deteriorated in 1895.

In later years, Alger's work came under attack from critics who found it predictable and melodramatic. Although he had written prolifically during most of his career and enjoyed a large readership, Alger's life ended in poverty. He died at his sister's home in Natick, Massachusetts, on July 18, 1899, at the age of 67.

## Further Reading

Bennett, Bob. *A Collector's Guide to the Published Works of Horatio Alger, Jr.* Newark, Del.: MAD Book Company, 1999.

Horatio Alger Association. "General Information." Available online. URL: http://www.horatioalger. com/geninf/geninf.htm#HoratioAlger Award. Downloaded September 23, 2002.

Scharnhorst, Gary, and Jack Bales. *The Lost Life of Horatio Alger, Jr.* Bloomington: Indiana University Press, 1985.

## Algren, Nelson
### (Nelson Algren Abraham)
(1909–1981) *novelist, short story writer, poet, literary critic, screenwriter, nonfiction writer*

Nelson Algren's writing was inspired by life in Chicago, and his characters and situations reflect many of his own experiences. During his lifetime, Algren published four novels, more than 50 short stories, and numerous poems, criticism, and travel books. His fiction depicted the sordid underside of urban life with topics that focused on poverty and crime, drunks, pimps, prostitutes, freaks, drug addicts, prizefighters, corrupt politicians, and hoodlums. He won several awards and two of his books were made into feature films, but his controversial themes often met with harsh criticism and several of his short stories were banned from the Chicago Public Library.

Nelson Algren's full name is Nelson Algren Abraham. He was born in Detroit, Michigan, in 1909, the youngest of three children. In 1913, when Nelson was four years old, the family moved to Chicago where they lived in a poor, immigrant neighborhood on the south side of the city. Nelson's father worked as a machinist and his mother worked in a candy store. When Nelson was 11 years old, the family moved to Chicago's northwest side. Nelson attended Chicago's public schools and studied journalism at the University of Illinois, where he earned his bachelor of arts degree in 1931.

Algren worked to pay his tuition at the University of Illinois and was a reporter for the university newspaper, *The Daily Illini.* Inspired by his success with the paper, Algren tested for certification as a journalist by the Illinois Press Association and passed. After graduating, he hitchhiked throughout the Midwest and for a brief time wrote headlines for the *Minneapolis Journal.*

His travels took him through New Orleans and Texas. Along the way, Algren picked up odd jobs, was a door-to-door salesman, and even worked in a carnival for a short time. He lived with friends in 1933 in an abandoned gas station in Texas. This is where he wrote his first short story, "So Help Me," which was later published in *Story* magazine. This success led to a contract with Vanguard Publishing to write his first novel, for which he received a $100 advance. Algren settled in Alpine, Texas, and lived in a boardinghouse near the Sul Ross State University campus so he could use the school's typing lab to work on his novel. He needed to return to Chicago to continue research for his work, so Algren stole a typewriter from the campus and attempted to mail it to his parents' home in Chicago. He was arrested by local authorities and spent the next four months in jail. After his release, Algren returned to Chicago where he lived with his parents and became an editor for the *New Anvil*, an experimental magazine. During that time, he also worked for the Chicago Board of Health.

Algren's first book, *Somebody in Boots*, was published in 1935. It was based on his experiences while living in Texas. Written in the documentary style of the 1930s, it received mixed reviews and sold only 750 copies. Gravely disappointed, Algren was briefly hospitalized. *Somebody in Boots* contained the locations, characters, and situations that would form the basis for Algren's future novels.

Between 1935 and 1942, Algren wrote short stories and worked on the Works Progress Administration (WPA) Illinois Writers' Project. His second novel, *Never Come Morning*, was published in 1942. It is a realistic story about poverty and crime, depicting a small-time hoodlum and aspiring boxer who cheats and murders and is eventually sentenced to death. Because of its controversial subject matter, the book was banned from the Chicago Public Library.

Algren was stationed in France during World War II, where he served as a medical army corpsman. His later short stories would be based on his army experiences. In 1947, Algren received financial support for his writing through an award from the American Academy of Arts and Letters and a grant from Chicago's Newberry Library. At age 41, Algren published *The Man with the Golden Arm*, a novel about junkies, drunks, and petty thieves. This book received the National Book Award, and a film version directed by Otto Preminger was released in 1956. Algren traveled to Hollywood to write the screenplay, but the entire experience proved to be disastrous for Algren and he later sued Preminger.

In 1951, *Chicago, the City on the Make*, was published. Because of the book's presentation of life as it existed in the back alleys of Chicago and Illinois, it was not well received by the Chicago Chamber of Commerce. Algren sold the film rights to his next novel, *A Walk on the Wild Side*, which was published in 1956. The story depicts a drifter during the Great Depression who gets involved with prostitutes, pimps, and con artists. It received only mixed reviews from the critics. Devastated by the book's cool reception, Algren tried to commit suicide and again was hospitalized for a short time.

Algren taught creative writing at the universities of Iowa and Florida, regularly wrote a column for the Chicago Free Press, and lived a progressively self-destructive lifestyle. His life—filled with heavy drinking, gambling, unsuccessful marriages, and a transatlantic love affair with a controversial French writer—was as varied, and at times as sordid, as the themes about which he wrote. In 1937, he married Amanda Kontowicz and moved to a neighborhood in Chicago not far from his childhood home. The two divorced in 1940, only to remarry and divorce again before finally ending the relationship once and for all in 1956. In 1947, Algren met French writer Simone de Beauvoir, who was Jean-Paul Sartre's lifelong companion and with whom he started an affair that would continue off and on for years. Then in 1965, Algren married

Nelson Algren is shown in this photo holding a copy of his book *A Walk on the Wild Side*. (Photo by Walter Albertin. Library of Congress, Prints and Photographs Division [LC-USZ62-117525])

New York actress Betty Ann Jones; however, this marriage also ended in divorce after just two years.

In 1974, Algren settled in Paterson, New Jersey, where he wrote *The Devil's Stocking*, his fourth novel. It was based on the life of Rubin "Hurricane" Carter, a prizefighter who was wrongly tried and imprisoned for murder. In 1983, John Aldridge noted in an article in *The New York Times* ". . . the character of Carter himself has been transmogrified into Rudy Calhoun, a protagonist who grows in complexity as the action proceeds, until he becomes a fully realized, multi-dimensional tragic personage in a narrative that has all the vital signs of having been produced by a writer still fully confident of his inventive powers." *The Devil's Stocking* was published posthumously in 1983.

In September 1980, Algren moved to Long Island, New York. On May 9, 1981, the morning after attending a party to celebrate his election into the American Academy and Institute of Arts and Letters, Algren died of a heart attack. He was 72 years old. Algren is buried in Sag Harbor Cemetery on Long Island. After his death, the city of Chicago changed the name of West Evergreen Street to West Algren Street, but reversed the decision due to complaints from residents.

## Further Reading

Bruccoli, Matthew J., and J. Braughman. *Nelson Algren: A Descriptive Bibliography.* New Castle, Del.: Oak Knoll Books, 1986.

de Beauvoir, Simone, and Nelson Algren. *A Transatlantic Love Affair: Letters to Nelson Algren.* New York: New Press, 1999.

Donahue, H. E. F. *Conversations with Nelson Algren.* 1964. Reprint, Chicago, Illinois: University of Chicago Press, 2001.

Drew, Bettina. *Nelson Algren: A Life on the Wild Side.* Austin: University of Texas Press, 1991.

Giles, J. R. *Confronting the Horrors: The Novels of Nelson Algren.* Kent, Ohio: Kent State University Press, 1989.

## Allen, Paula Gunn
(1939–   ) *poet, novelist, literary critic*

Paula Gunn Allen, one of the foremost scholars of Native American literature, is also recognized as a major literary critic and teacher. She writes from the perspective of a Laguna Pueblo woman—a culture that holds women in high respect. Allen's novels elaborate on the roles and power of Native American women and are intended to raise the consciousness of Euro-American women. Allen's themes abound with mythic dimensions of women's relationships to the sacred, as well as the plight of contemporary Native American women. Her poems draw on her own multicultural background, using such sources as country-western music, Pueblo corn dances, Catholic masses, Mozart, Italian opera, and Arabic chanting. In her poems, a finely detailed sense of place resonates with landscapes from the city, the reservation, and the interior.

Paula Gunn Allen was born in 1939 in Albuquerque, New Mexico. Her father was Lebanese-American, and her mother was of Laguna, Sioux, and Scotch heritage. Paula grew up in Cubero, New Mexico, a Spanish-Mexican land grant village abutting the Laguna and Acoma reservations and the Cibola National Forest. She attended mission schools in Cubero and San Fidel, but received most of her education at a Sisters of Charity boarding school in Albuquerque. She graduated from high school in 1957. Allen began her college studies at the University of Colorado Women's College, but earned her bachelor's degree in English in 1966 and master of fine arts degree in creative writing in 1968, both from the University of Oregon.

Allen first became interested in writing during high school, when she was introduced to the work of GERTRUDE STEIN. She read Stein's work extensively and also was fond of and strongly influenced by the writings of the romantic poets, Percy Bysshe Shelley and John Keats. Much of Allen's writing focuses on her desire to identify and describe "breeds," which she defines as individuals alien to traditional Native Americans, while also alien among whites. Allen does not restrict her concept of "breeds" to Native Americans, however, but extends it to other groups and, in particular, to herself as an individual—she has always considered herself a "breed" as well.

It was through Allen's positions on the Native American panels of the Modern Language Association and the American Studies Association that she was able to influence those seeking knowledge of the Native American literary community. Her involvement in this field helped her foster a sense of her own breed, which she calls "a breed that enlightens others."

Allen's writing career began in 1974 with the publication of her first book, *Blind Lion Poems.* In her poetry, Allen explored the various "breeds" she encountered in her personal life. While well known as a poet, Allen also has had a strong voice as a writer and critic. In her well-known critical work, *Studies in American Indian Literature: Critical Essays and Course Designs,* published in 1983, as well as her other critical works, Allen concentrated on the reader's perspective. In her critical pieces, Allen stressed that readers of Native American literature not be put into the position of feeling they had to impose European or American expectations or allow preconceptions to interfere with the messages being offered through the writing. *The Sacred Hoop: Recovering the Feminine in American Indian Traditions,* published in 1975, contains Allen's 1986 germinal essay "The Sacred Hoop: A Contemporary Perspective," which was one of the first works to detail the ritual function of Native American literature. In all of her critical works, Allen stresses that Native American culture is real and deserving of open-minded consideration. Underlying all of Allen's work is the theme of how oral tradition embodied in contemporary Native American literature has the power to affect healing, survival, and continuance.

In addition to being one of the foremost scholars of Native American literature, a writer, and a poet, Allen is also a collector and interpreter of Native American mythology. Although she always has had a strong voice as a poet and author, it is her academic work that may have been most significant for Native Americans. Allen has defined ways in which to study Native American writings and culture and has opened doors for herself and for other Native Americans as well.

Throughout the 1990s, Allen's work continued to receive attention, being examined and critiqued in such publications as *The Journal of Homosexuality, The Explicator,* and *Ariel.* In 1996, she cowrote an anthology of nine profiles of Native Americans for young readers entitled *As Long As the Rivers Flow.* In 1998, she produced a series of political, spiritual, and intensely personal essays entitled, *Off the Reservation: Reflection on Boundary-Busting, Border-Crossing Loose Canons.* Allen, who also was a professor of English at the University of California at Los Angeles, retired from her academic position in July 1999.

**Further Reading**

Bredin, Renae Moore. *Guerilla Ethnography (Dissertation Abstracts International (DAI) Degree Granting Institution).* Phoenix: University of Arizona, 1995.

Holford, Vanessa. "Re Membering Ephanie: A Women's Re-creation of Self in Paula Gunn Allen's 'The Woman Who Owned the Shadows.'" *Studies in American Indian Literature: The Journal of the Association for the Study of American Indian Literatures (SAIL)* 6, 1 (spring 1994): 99–113.

Keating, Ann Louise. *Myth Smashers, Myth Makers (Critical Essays: Gay and Lesbian Writers of Color).* New York: Hawthorn Publishers, 1993.

Perry, Donna. *Paula Gunn Allen.* Backtalk: Woman Writers Speak Out. New Brunswick, N.J.: Rutgers University Press, 1993.

Van Dyke, Annette. *Paula Gunn Allen.* Contemporary Lesbian Writers of the United States: A Bio-Bibliographical Critical Sourcebook. Westport, Conn.: Greenwood Publishing, 1993.

# Ammons, A. R.
## (Archie Randolph Ammons)
### (1926–2001) *poet*

A. R. Ammons is probably best known for his book-length poems that explore the connection between singularity and community, between the one and the many. These poems are noted for their incorporation of many different types of text, everything from religious hymns to business memos to jokes overhead on a bus, and for their original use of the colon in punctuating the diverse material. The author of more than 30 books of poems, Ammons has been called a "transcendentalist" by critic Harold Bloom, who compared Ammons's love of nature to ROBERT FROST's, both of whom loved nature too much to sentimentalize it.

Archie Randolph Ammons was born outside Whiteville, North Carolina, on his family's small subsistence farm, in 1926. He grew up during the Great Depression and joined the U.S. Navy when he graduated from high school. He served as a sonar operator aboard the USS *Gunason* during World War II, traveling widely through the South Pacific. Returning to North Carolina, Ammons attended Wake Forest University, from which he received a B.S. degree in 1949. Ammons married Phyllis Plumbo on November 26, 1949, and the couple had one son, John. Ammons worked the following year as principal of Hatteras Elementary School in Cape Hatteras, North Carolina, before heading west to study literature at the University of California at Berkeley, where he remained until 1952.

He published his first book of poems, *Omnateum,* in 1955 with a vanity press (a publishing house that charges authors for printing their books). He had no literary community, and few people took notice of his work. He worked during these years as a real estate salesman and as an editor. Later, he managed his father-in-law's glassware factory in southern New Jersey.

It was not until 1964, at age 38, that Ammons secured a teaching position at Cornell University. By the end of his first 10 years at Cornell, Ammons had begun to receive critical praise for his work as a poet. And in the several decades since that time, he became one of the most interesting and influential figures in American poetry. Despite this success, he always remained a little outside the literary community, protecting his independence and insisting on his own original approach to the literary life he created.

During his career, Ammons wrote close to 30 books of poetry, including six book-length poems. Among his most notable books were *Collected Poems, 1951–1971*, which won the National Book Award; *Sphere* (1974), which won the Bollingen Prize; *A Coast of Trees* (1981), which won the National Book Critics Circle Award for Poetry; *Garbage* (1993), which received the National Book Award and the Rebekah Johnson Bobbitt National Prize for Poetry from the Library of Congress; and *Glare* (1997). His six book-length works are *Sphere, Garbage,* and *Glare,* as well as *Tape for the Turn of the Year* (1965), *The Form of a Motion* (1974), and *The Snow Poems* (1977). Although Ammons easily gravitated toward longer forms, his short poems were collected in *The Really Short Poems of A. R. Ammons* (1990) and attest to his capability with compression as well.

Ammons's many other honors included the Wallace Stevens Award from the American Academy of Poets, the Poetry Society of America's Robert Frost Medal, the Ruth Lilly Prize, and fellowships from the Guggenheim Foundation, the MacArthur Foundation, and the American Academy of Arts and Letters. In 1998, he received the Tanning Prize, a $100,000 award for "outstanding and proven mastery in the art of poetry." In 1990, he was inducted into the National Institute and Academy of Arts and Letters.

Ammons lived in Ithaca, New York, with his wife and taught at Cornell throughout his career. He suffered a massive heart attack in 1989, fol-

lowed by hematoma and brain seizures in 1992. When he retired in 1998, he was Goldwin Smith Professor of Poetry emeritus at Cornell. A. R. Ammons died in Ithaca, New York, on February 25, 2001, at age 75.

**Further Reading**

Bloom, Harold. *A. R. Ammons*. New York: Chelsea House Publishers, 1986.

Goldfarb, David. A. "Critical Distance: The Psychology of Criticism and the Poetry of A. R. Ammons." Available online. URL: http://mosaic.echonyc.com/~goldfarb/distance.htm. Posted February 26, 1993.

Schneider, Steven P., and Cary Nelson. "A. R. Ammons, 1926–2001." Modern American Poetry. Available online. URL: http://www.english.uiuc.edu/maps/poets/af/ammons/ammons.htm. Downloaded March 8, 2003.

## Anderson, Sherwood

(1876–1941) *novelist, poet, short story writer, playwright*

Sherwood Anderson was a naturalist whose work is noted for its poetic realism, psychological insight, sense of the tragic, and use of everyday speech. His stories are all dominated by a similar theme: the conflict between organized industrial society and the subconscious instincts of the individual. While Anderson's unique talent found its best expression in short stories, his novels continued to explore the spiritual and emotional sterility of a success-oriented machine age, but with generally less skill than he demonstrated in his short stories.

Anderson was the third child of Irwin and Emma Smith Anderson. He was born in Camden, Ohio, on September 13, 1876. His parents led a transient life, moving from place to place searching for work. Sherwood attended school intermittently while working at odd jobs to help support his family. At age 17, Anderson moved to Chicago, where he worked as a manual laborer and attended business school at night. In 1898, he enlisted in the U.S. Army to serve in Cuba during the Spanish-American War. After the war, Anderson moved to Springfield, Ohio, to be near his brother and to attend Wittenberg Academy. The next few years found Anderson traveling restlessly around Ohio, finally settling in Chicago, where he worked in advertising. Upon moving back to Chicago, he also joined the Chicago Group, which included such writers as THEODORE DREISER and CARL SANDBURG.

In 1904, Anderson married Cornelia Lane, the daughter of a wealthy Ohio wholesaler. He moved his family from Chicago to northern Ohio in 1906, where he managed a mail-order business and two paint manufacturing firms during the next six years. In today's vernacular, he would have been called a "workaholic," putting in long hours at the office and consuming all of his free time with writing.

His lifestyle took a toll on his health, and in 1912, Anderson suffered a mental breakdown. In later writings, he referred to this as ". . . a conscious break from his materialistic existence." This "conscious break" proved to be a pivotal point in Anderson's career, at which he broke free from the responsibilities of his businesses and began writing circulars for an advertising agency in Chicago. He continued to write feverishly in his free time. In 1914, Sherwood and Cornelia divorced. That same year he married Tennessee Mitchell.

It was not until 1916 that Anderson began publishing his works. His first two novels, *Windy McPherson's Son* (1916) and *Marching Men* (1917), focused on psychological themes and depicted the inhabitants of Midwestern villages in their pursuit of success and disillusionment of attaining that success. His talent was not widely recognized by critics, however, until his collection of stories, *Winesburg, Ohio*, was published in 1919. In this book, Anderson presented 23 thematically related sketches that deal with the instinctive struggle of ordinary people to assert their individuality during the standardization of the machine age. This book received much acclaim and established Anderson as a talented modern American author. *Winesburg, Ohio*, together with Anderson's other collections of short stories, *The Triumph of the Egg* (1921), *Horses and Men* (1932), and *Death in the Woods* (1933), redirected the American short story with their simplistic, consciously naive style.

In 1922, Anderson separated from Mitchell. He married Elizabeth Prall two years later. He published *Many Marriages* in 1921 and *Dark Laughter* in 1925. While vacationing in Virginia in 1927,

Anderson bought property in the Virginia countryside and purchased Marion Publishing Company in Marion, Virginia, where he became the editor of two newspapers. In 1928, his marriage to Prall failed. In 1933 Anderson married Eleanor Copenhaver, a Marion County native. The two traveled extensively throughout the South, touring factories and studying labor conditions, which became the theme of many of his works during the 1930s.

During his lifetime, Anderson authored 27 works, including collections of short stories, seven novels, and several collections of poems. Selected works include *Beyond Desire* (1932); *Death in the Woods and Other Stories* (1933); *Puzzled America*, a book of essays based on his extensive travels throughout the United States (1935); and *Kit Brandon*, a novel (1936). In 1922, Anderson was awarded the first Dial Award for distinguished service to American letters, but he was later ridiculed by the same publication when his popularity declined. His *Memoirs*, published in 1942, and *Letters*, published in 1953, were collected and published together as *The Memoirs of Sherwood Anderson* in 1969.

Anderson had a significant influence on the next generation of authors, both through his writings and acts of personal kindness. He was known to have encouraged WILLIAM FAULKNER and ERNEST HEMINGWAY in their writing aspirations. In fact, it was through his influence that the first books of both were published.

Sherwood Anderson died of peritonitis on March 8, 1941 in Colón, Panama, during an unofficial goodwill tour to South America. He never lost his zest for life, which is reflected in his epitaph in Marion's Round Hill Cemetery, which reads, "Life Not Death, Is The Great Adventure." In his honor, a Sherwood Anderson short story contest is held yearly in Marion, Virginia.

## Further Reading

Abraham, P. A. *Sherwood Anderson and the American Short Story*. Columbia, Mo.: South Asia Books, 1994.

Lewis, Ray. *The Achievements of Sherwood Anderson: Essays in Criticism*. Chapel Hill: University of North Carolina Press, 1966.

Townsend, Kim. *Sherwood Anderson*. Boston: Houghton Mifflin Company, 1987.

Williams, Kenny J. *A Storyteller and a City: Sherwood Anderson's Chicago*. De Kalb: Northern Illinois University Press, 1988.

## Angelou, Maya
## (Marguerite Johnson)
(1928–  ) *novelist, poet, playwright, autobiographer*

Maya Angelou is an internationally respected poet, author, and educator, as well as a historian, playwright, actor, civil rights activist, producer, and director. One of the great voices of contemporary literature, Angelou has been hailed as a Renaissance woman. She has published 10 best-selling books and countless magazine articles and has earned Pulitzer Prize and National Book Award nominations. At the request of President-elect Bill Clinton, Angelou wrote and delivered a poem at his 1993 presidential inauguration.

Maya Angelou's given name at birth was Marguerite Johnson. She was born on April 4, 1928, in Saint Louis, Missouri, the daughter of Bailey and Vivian Johnson. She has one brother, Bailey, who was named after their father. When Johnson was three years old, her parents divorced and she and her brother went to live with their grandparents in Arkansas. Growing up in segregated, rural Arkansas, she quickly found out what it meant to be a black girl in a world where white people set all the boundaries. She felt the sting of humiliation at having to accept and wear hand-me-down clothing from a white woman and being refused treatment by a white dentist. Despite the odds, her grandmother managed to instill pride in both the children.

After five years with their grandmother, the children were sent back to Saint Louis to live with their mother. The move proved to be disastrous for Marguerite, who was raped by her mother's boyfriend. Devastated by the attack, she became mute for nearly five years. She returned to live with her grandmother, but in 1940 was sent back to live with her mother again. Her dysfunctional childhood spent moving back and forth between her mother and grandmother left her struggling to find where she fit in. She gave birth to a son, Guy, at age 16.

Her career began in drama and dance. In her early 20s, after her debut performance as a dancer at the Purple Onion cabaret, she decided to change her name. Her brother had called her Maya, and Angelou was a corruption of her married name (when she was 22, she married Tosh Angelos. She left him after 2 1/2 years). The life and work of Angelou are fully intertwined. In her autobiographies and books of poetry, she shatters the prisms of race and class between reader and subject and captivates audiences. She has written 12 best-selling books, beginning with the volume of her first autobiography, *I Know Why the Caged Bird Sings*, published in 1970, in which she recalls her oftentimes difficult life. In it, she uses lyrical imagery and realism to describe her struggles to overcome the hostile environment of her youth. Her second book, *Gather Together in My Name* (1974), focuses on Angelou's experiences during her late teens and early 20s. She describes her life as a mother, Creole cook, madam, tap dancer, prostitute, and chauffeur. The book ends with a plea to readers for forgiveness for the accounts of her past.

*Singin' and Swingin' and Gettin' Merry Like Christmas*, the third volume of her autobiography, was published in 1976. It spans her life from age 22 to 27, during which time she married, divorced, and toured Europe as a dancer with the production of *Porgy and Bess*. The book focuses primarily on the tour but also describes the guilt she felt over neglecting her son, which nearly drove her to suicide. It is her love of life, dancing, and family that finally brings her home. The title of her fourth memoir, *The Heart of a Woman*, published in 1981, was taken from a poem written by Georgia Douglas Johnson during the Harlem Renaissance. Like her other memoirs, this, too, is a story of Angelou's struggle to find identity and place. Now in her 30s, Angelou reflects on her son, the Civil Rights movement, marriage, and her writing. It is a time in her life when she becomes more committed to her writing and to promoting black civil rights. Published in 1986, Angelou's next book, her fifth autobiography, *All God's Children Need Traveling Shoes*, was dedicated to Julian Mayfield and Malcolm X, who, like Angelou, were both passionately in search of their symbolic homes. This book exemplifies Angelou's sense of connection with her African heritage and describes her visit to Ghana, which she adopted as her own homeland. In her most recent work, *A Song Flung Up to Heaven,* published in 2002, Angelou takes readers along as she returns from Africa in the early 1960s to begin working with Malcolm X. His assassination was devastating to her. When she finally meets Martin Luther King, Jr., he encourages her to become the northern coordinator for the Southern Christian Leadership Conference (SCLC). When he is assassinated, she becomes completely withdrawn from society, completely unable to deal with yet another tragedy. Forced out of isolation by a friend, Angelou attends a dinner party, where she gets the idea to write a book. *A Song Flung Up to Heaven* ends as Angelou begins to write the first sentences of *I Know Why the Caged Bird Sings.*

During a short stay in Cairo, when Angelou was in her 20s, she served as editor of *The Arab Observer,* then the only English-language news weekly in the Middle East. In Ghana, she was feature editor of *The African Review* and taught at the University of Ghana. President Gerald Ford appointed Angelou to the Bicentennial Commission and President Jimmy Carter appointed her to the National Commission on the Observance of International Women's Year. In 1975, she received the Ladies Home Journal Woman of the Year Award in communications. Her inaugural poem, "On the Pulse of Morning," sparked much debate among poets and academics over the role of poetry in our public and private lives. Angelou was the first poet since Robert Frost, who read at John F. Kennedy's inauguration, to read a poem as part of the ceremony.

Angelou's books, essays, poetry, and personal narratives have become a point of consciousness for African-American people, particularly black women seeking to survive masculine prejudice, illogical hatred from whites, and a black lack of power. Her autobiographies, which continue to inspire lively critical response, are widely read and taught in schools and universities. Some critics have referred to her poetry as "too simple" and suggest they are unworthy of inclusion in the estab-lished canon of American poetry. Nevertheless, her poetry remains widely popular.

Maya Angelou's work in scriptwriting and directing, while less well known than her poetry and books, has been groundbreaking for black women in the film industry. She has made hundreds of television appearances, and the autobiographical account of her youth, *I Know Why the Caged Bird Sings,* was made into a two-hour special on CBS. Angelou also has written and produced several prize-winning documentaries, including *Afro-Americans in the Arts,* which was a PBS special for which she received the Golden Eagle Award. She is on the board of the American Film Institute and is one of the few women members of the Directors Guild of America.

Today, Angelou lectures throughout the United States and abroad and is the Reynolds professor of American studies at Wake Forest University in North Carolina.

### Further Reading
Courtney-Clarke, Margaret. *Maya Angelou: The Poetry of Living.* New York: Clarkson N. Potter, 2000.

Harper, Judith E. *Maya Angelou: Journey to Freedom.* Minneapolis: Childs World Publishing, 1999.

Hobbs, Avaneda D. *Dr. Maya Angelou: As Seen through the Eyes of America (Honoring a Woman Full of Life).* London: CAP Publishing and Literary Company, 2000.

McPherson, Dolly Aimee. *Order Out of Chaos: The Autobiographical Works of Maya Angelou.* Studies in African and African-American Culture, Vol. 1. New York: Peter Lang Publishing, 1990.

### Ansay, A. Manette
(1964–   ) *novelist, short story writer, memoirist*

Catapulted into stardom when her first novel, *Vinegar Hill,* was chosen by Oprah Winfrey as her November 1999 book club selection, A. Manette Ansay has since published three more highly acclaimed novels, a collection of short stories, and a memoir. Known for fiction that draws on her own rural Midwestern upbringing among a large extended Catholic family, Ansay has a gift for taking the mundane aspects of life and infusing them with luminous vision.

A. Manette Ansay was born in Lapeer, Michigan, just outside Detroit, in 1964, where she spent the first five years of her life. Then her family moved to Port Washington, Wisconsin, a small town north of Milwaukee, where she grew up surrounded by the more than 200 cousins in her extended Roman Catholic family. Ansay began Suzuki piano lessons with a local teacher, traveled to music camps in the summer, and attended the University of Wisconsin at Milwaukee for lessons while still a student at Port Washington High School. A gifted student from early childhood, she went on to the Peabody Conservatory of Music in 1982 with intentions of becoming a concert pianist. She was forced to leave the conservatory in 1984, however, as a result of the increasing health problems she was experiencing.

By 1985, Ansay was unable to walk and was diagnosed, incorrectly, with multiple sclerosis. For many years, doctors struggled to identify the cause of her illness. In 2001, she was told that she probably had some kind of immune system reaction to a series of inoculations she had received. In the beginning, she was bedridden and lived with her parents throughout the late 1980s, eventually reaching the point where she could get around again on her own with the use of a wheelchair. She began writing as a response to this illness, resolving on New Year's Day of 1988 that she would write for two hours a day, three days a week. Ansay was able to focus the discipline learned in her piano studies on her new endeavors as a writer, and though she had never written much and was not even a particularly avid reader, by her own admission, she persevered with her schedule, determined to find a career that she could manage sitting down. In the summer of 1988, Ansay won a scholarship to the Stonecoast Writer's Conference at the University of Southern Maine. Having completed her undergraduate degree at the University of Maine in Orono, Ansay proceeded with her plans to establish a career as a writer, studying at Cornell University, where she received her M.F.A. degree in creative writing in 1991. She married her husband, Jake Smith, on the Cornell campus in 1990.

Ansay's health stabilized around this time, and she was able to pursue writing and teaching full time following her graduation from Cornell. Her first position was a lectureship at Cornell from 1991 to 92, then from 1992 to 93 she was writer in residence at Phillips Exeter Academy in Exeter, New Hampshire. Between 1993 and 1997, she was an assistant professor at Vanderbilt University in Nashville, Tennessee. *Vinegar Hill* was published in 1994. Her short story collection, *Read This and Tell Me What It Says,* appeared next and is set in the same locale as *Vinegar Hill.* Her other novels include *Sister* (1996), *River Angel* (1998), and *Midnight Champagne* (1999). Ansay has been widely praised for her graceful prose and her gift for choosing the telling domestic details that connect her characters with her readers. In 1997, Ansay resigned from her teaching position in order to write full time and has since taught as a visiting writer at Warren Wilson College in Asheville, North Carolina, and at the University of the South in Sewanee, Tennessee. In spring 2000, Ansay held the Women's Chair in Humanistic Studies at Marquette University in Milwaukee, Wisconsin.

Ansay's latest book, a memoir called *Limbo,* was published in 2001 and tells the story of her illness. Among her numerous awards are the Pushcart Prize, a Friends of American Writers Prize, two Great Lakes Book Awards, the Nelson Algren Award for short fiction from the *Chicago Tribune,* a National Endowment for the Arts grant, a Bread Loaf Writers Conference fellowship, and a Ragdale Foundation residency. She currently lives in Florida with her husband, and is working on a new novel entitled *Blue Water.*

## Further Reading

Renshaw, Camille. "Interview with A. Manette Ansay." Pif Magazine. Available online. URL: http://www. pifmagazine.com/SID/136/?page=1&&PHPSES SID=b605ccee24520def4125669d3edc3ad1. Downloaded February 16, 2003.

Zukerman, Eugenia. "Grace Notes: 'Limbo' by A. Manette Ansay." WashingtonPost.com. Available online. URL: http://www.washingtonpost.com/ac2/wp-dyn? pagename=article&node=&contentI d=A53713-2001Oct25&notFound=true. Posted October 28, 2001.

# Ashbery, John
(1927–   ) *poet, editor, novelist, playwright*

John Ashbery has often been described as one of the most important poets writing today in English. His poems are known for their modern, colloquial voices, but not for their ready accessibility. His work, in his own words, "has a reputation for being aloof and antihuman." Like his professed favorite poet, WALLACE STEVENS, he has made it his concern to write about the workings of the mind, specifically the way the mind shapes reality. He has incorporated what critic David Perkins has described as the language of "contemporary journalism, advertising, bureaucracy, business memos, scientific reports, newspapers, psychology textbooks, and the like." This may sometimes leave the reader cold, but when Ashbery's characteristic irony is sharply honed, his work sparkles with imaginative language and grace.

John Ashbery was born in Rochester, New York, in 1927. He grew up on a fruit farm in upstate New York, near the shores of Lake Ontario. He has said that he was not happy with his father, who was a farmer, so he spent lots of time with his grandparents in Rochester. Ashbery's mother was a biology teacher, and his one younger brother died at age nine. Ashbery attended Deerfield Academy as a boy, where he read the work of W. H. AUDEN, Wallace Stevens, and other early modernists, but Ashbery's first love was painting, and he took weekly art classes at the Art Institute in Rochester between the ages of 13 and 15. After graduating from high school, he went on to Harvard in 1945, where he met and studied with fellow writers FRANK O'HARA, Edward Gorey, ROBERT BLY, DONALD HALL, and KENNETH KOCH.

After graduating from Harvard, Ashbery moved to New York, where he struggled to make a living and to publish his poems. In 1951, Ashbery received a master's degree from Columbia University. He then worked in publishing for a time and published his first volume, *Turandot and Other Poems,* in 1953. By this time, he had become known as a member of the New York school, which included Koch and O'Hara. In the mid-1950s, Ashbery moved to Paris, where he lived for a decade, writing poems and art criticism for the *New York Herald Tribune* and *ARTnews* and living with the French writer Pierre Martory. His second collection of poems, *Some Trees* (1956) was chosen by Auden to be included in the Yale Younger Poets series.

When he returned to the United States in 1965, Ashbery continued to work as an art critic and he served on the editorial board *ARTnews.* He also began to teach creative writing, taking a position at Brooklyn College and later becoming the Charles P. Stevenson, Jr., Professor of Languages and Literature at Bard College. Ashbery served as editor of the *Partisan Review* from 1976 to 1980.

His recognition as a major poet came with the publication in 1975 of *Self-Portrait in a Convex Mirror,* which won the Pulitzer Prize, the National Book Award, and the National Book Critics Circle Award. In all, Ashbery has published more than 20 books, including *The Tennis Court Oath* (1962); *Rivers and Mountains* (1966); *A Wave* (1984); *April Galleons* (1987); *Flow Chart* (1991); *Hotel Lautréamont* (1992); *And the Stars Were Shining* (1994); *Can You Hear, Bird* (1995); *Wakefulness* (1998); *Girls on the Run: A Poem* (1999); *Your Name Here* (2000); and *As Umbrellas Follow Rain* (2001). He has also published a novel, *A Nest of Ninnies* (1969), with James Schuyler; *Reported Sightings* (1989), a book of art criticism; a collection of plays; and *Other Traditions: The Charles Eliot Norton Lectures* (2000). He edited *The Best American Poetry 1988.* His awards are numerous and include, in addition to the ones mentioned above, the American Academy of Arts and Letters Gold Medal for Poetry in 1997; the Poetry Society of America's Robert Frost Award in 1995; a MacArthur fellowship in 1985; and the Bollingen Prize in 1984. During his rise to stardom, Ashbery has continued to teach at Bard College and live in New York City.

## Further Reading

Longenbach, James. "Ashbery and the Individual Talent," *American Literary History* 9, no. 1 (spring 1997): 105.

Norton, Jody. "'Whispers Out of Time': The Syntax of Being in the Poetry of John Ashbery." *Twentieth Century Literature* 41, no. 3 (fall 1995): 281–305.

Schultz, Susan M., ed. *The Tribe of John: Ashbery and Contemporary Poetry.* Tuscaloosa: University of Alabama Press, 1995.

Shoptaw, John. *On the Outside Looking Out: John Ashbery's Poetry.* Cambridge, Mass.: Harvard University Press, 1994.

## Asimov, Isaac
(1920–1992) *novelist, short story writer, nonfiction writer, science fiction writer*

Perhaps one of the greatest science fiction writers of the 20th century, Isaac Asimov was also one of the most prolific writers in American literature. He published more than 500 titles. While Asimov may be best known for his science fiction, his works span almost every major division of the Dewey decimal system, with topics ranging from anatomy, physiology, astronomy, the Bible, biology, chemistry, etymology, geography, Greek mythology, history, humor, mathematics, and physics.

Isaac, the son of Judah and Anna Asimov, was born in Petrovichi, Russia, in 1920. His family moved to the United States when Isaac was three years old and settled in New York City, where his father opened a candy store. It was in his father's candy story that Isaac was first introduced to science fiction magazines. At age eight, Isaac became a citizen of the United States.

Isaac taught himself to read before he started school. Blessed with a near-photographic memory, Isaac excelled academically, which propelled him through school. At age 15, Isaac graduated from high school and went on to study at Columbia University. He earned his bachelor of science degree in chemistry in 1939 and his master of arts degree in 1941. After serving for a short time in the military during World War II, Isaac continued his education and earned his doctorate in 1948. Isaac became a faculty member of Boston University, serving as an associate professor and later full professor of biochemistry at the university's School of Medicine. Asimov's scientific research includes work in kinetics, photochemistry, enzymology, and irradiation.

Asimov published his first short story in 1939 in *Amazing Stories* magazine. He went on to become a regular contributor to *Astounding, Astonishing Stories, Super Science Stories,* and *Galaxy,* other popular magazines of the day. It was not until 1958, however, that Isaac turned to writing as a full-time career. John W. Campbell, editor of *Astounding,* who was known for inspiring his writers with new ideas, was said to have been the inspiration behind Asimov's *Three Laws of Robotics,* which ran first in *Astounding* and then culminated in one of his most brilliant novels, *The Naked Sun* (1956), which was a hybrid of science fiction and detective writing.

Asimov's most famous short story, "Nightfall," which was published in 1941, is based on astronomical phenomena, a very popular subject for science fiction authors in that era. Astronomy also fueled Asimov's most famous work, *The Foundation Trilogy,* which portrays a future galaxy over which a predicted 10,000 years of barbarism is about to descend unless a lowly foundation, established at the end of the galaxy, triumphs. The Foundation series, widely considered one of the most popular science fiction series ever written, earned Asimov approximately two cents a word when first published. Since then, however, the trilogy has been reprinted so many times and now appears in so many countries throughout the world that those few pennies have since turned into several thousand dollars a word.

Despite his vivid imagination and prolific career, Asimov's life was a bit of a paradox—he wrote of travel to the stars, yet would not fly in airplanes; he stayed in the safety of his own home while writing about alien universes and vast galactic civilizations. He worked in an apartment with a view overlooking Central Park but wrote behind drawn shades so as not to be distracted.

Disturbed by changes to the science fiction genre during the 1960s, Asimov put his science fiction publications on hold. He did not begin writing consistently again until the 1980s. His work has been published in *Esquire, Harper's,* the *Saturday Evening Post,* and Atomic Energy Commission pamphlets. Asimov is the recipient of numerous awards, including the American Association for the Advancement of Science Westinghouse Award for excellence in magazine writing and the Hugo Award from the World Science Fiction Convention for his novel *Foundation's Edge,* a sequel to his robot trilogy.

In 1942, Asimov married Gertrude Blugerman. They divorced in 1973 and Asimov later married Janet Opal Jeppson. While Asimov's parents were

Orthodox Jews, according to Asimov's autobiography (1994), he remained without religion simply because no one made an effort to teach him any. Some have speculated that Asimov was an atheist, others refer to him as a humanist (someone who believes that humans alone are responsible for the problems and achievements of society; that neither good nor evil is produced by supernatural beings and that the problems of humankind can be solved without such things). According to Asimov himself, ". . . I am incapable of accepting existence on faith alone." As cited in Corvallis Secular Society in 1997, Asimov summed up his religious views by saying, "I don't have the evidence to prove that God doesn't exist, but I so strongly suspect that he doesn't that I don't want to waste my time." While Asimov does not use religion in abundance in his fictional work, he took a great enough interest in Christianity to publish a two-volume set entitled *Asimov's Guide to the Bible*, which some critics noted "went too far in its secular approach to placing biblical events in a historical context."

Unique and irrepressible, Asimov was an incomparable writer who entertained readers for nearly half a century. Isaac Asimov died on April 6, 1992.

**Further Reading**

Asimov, Isaac. *I, Asimov: A Memoir.* New York: Bantam Spectra Books, 1995.

Boerst, William. *Isaac Asimov: Writer of the Future.* World Writers. Greensboro, N.C.: Morgan Reynolds Publishers. 1999.

Gunn, James. *Isaac Asimov, the Foundations of Science Fiction.* Oxford, England: Oxford University Press, 1992.

Judson, Keren. *Isaac Asimov: Master of Science Fiction.* People to Know. Berkeley Heights, N.J.: Enslow Publishers, 1998.

# Atwood, Margaret
## (Margaret Eleanor Atwood)
(1939–  ) *novelist, poet, children's fiction writer, short story writer*

One of Canada's best-known living writers, Margaret Atwood has published poems, novels, short stories, essays, criticism, and children's literature in her prolific career. Her works have been translated into numerous languages and published in more than 25 countries. She is known for her treatment of contemporary themes, especially feminism, and revered for her ability to work with equal success in diverse literary forms, including, among others, the mystery novel, the historical novel, and science fiction. Her work has earned Atwood 16 honorary degrees and an impressive array of awards. She has a devoted following in North America and around the world.

Margaret Eleanor Atwood was born on November 18, 1939, in Ottawa, Ontario, Canada. She has said of her mother that she was a "tomboy, enticed into marriage with promises of dangerous adventures and no vacuum cleaners." Atwood's father was an entomologist who ran a forest insect research station in northern Quebec, a setting that provided a wealth of experience with the natural world and limited experience with society. Her parents liked it this way. "Both of them liked being as far away from civilization as possible, my mother because she hated housework and tea parties, my father because he liked chopping wood. They also weren't much interested in what the sociologists would call rigid sex-role stereotyping. This was a help to me in later life, and helped me to get a job at summer camp teaching small boys to start fires."

These years were spent living in the forest, in cabins furnished with furniture her father built. Atwood has described how her parents taught her the practical skills necessary for this remote life. She learned to clean a gun and kill a fish quickly— "with a knife blade between the eyes"—all before she turned eight. "My childhood," Atwood has explained, "was divided between the forest, in the warmer parts of the year, and various cities, in the colder parts. I was thus able to develop the rudiments of the double personality so necessary for a poet. I also had lots of time for meditation. In the bush there were no theatres, movies, parades, or very functional radios; there were also not many other people. The result was that I learned to read early—I was lucky enough to have a mother who read out loud, but she couldn't be doing it all the time and you had to amuse yourself with something or other when it rained. I became a reading addict, and have remained so ever since."

When the family left its forest cabin and moved permanently to a Toronto suburb when Atwood was eight, she encountered the complex social structure of little girls, many of whom had no experience in the woods. Some have said that this experience of becoming an outsider at the tender age of eight may have been the beginning of Atwood's life as a writer. She herself has told about the vocation she established for herself, telling horror stories at birthday parties she arranged each year for her sister, who was 12 years her junior. But according to Atwood, she officially became a poet one sunny afternoon in 1956, when a poem, fully formed, appeared in her head as she was walking home from school.

Atwood attended high school in Toronto before entering Victoria College, University of Toronto, where she received her B.A. degree in 1961. From there she went straight to Radcliffe College, in Cambridge, Massachusetts, and received her master's degree in Victorian literature in 1962. She studied at Harvard in 1962–63 and again from 1965 to 1967 before leaving to try out life as a writer. During the late 1960s, she taught literature and composition courses to engineering students and stayed up late at night, "writing verse and novels on leftover exam booklets. I didn't sleep much, had big dark half-moons under my eyes, lived on Kraft dinners and Denny's pancakes, and emitted a pale flickering glow in the dark."

Atwood wrote prolifically during this time and her hard work paid off. She published five collections of poems between 1964 and 1972, including *The Circle Game* (1964), *The Animals in That Country* (1969), and *Procedures for Underground* (1970). In 1969, Atwood's first novel, *The Edible Woman*, was published; and in 1972, she published *Surfacing*, her second novel and a classic of feminist literature, and *Survival: A Thematic Guide to Canadian Literature*, which she has called "my rabble-rousing nationalistic book, still causing academic ulcers." These books brought the young Atwood immediate fame in Canada.

Atwood's first book publication, *The Circle Game*, won her the esteemed Governor General's Award in 1966, an honor she earned a second time, in 1985, for her novel *The Handmaid's Tale*. A dystopic tale about the role of women in society, *The Handmaid's Tale* was also made into a major motion picture, starring Natasha Richardson and Faye Dunaway.

Since the mid-1960s, Atwood has published more than 40 books, including novels, collections of poetry, short story collections, children's books, and volumes of literary criticism. In addition, she has edited a handful of anthologies, written television scripts, and made several audio recordings. Her work has garnered numerous awards, including most recently, the Booker Prize in 2000 for her novel *The Blind Assassin*. She has also won a Guggenheim Fellowship, a Molson Award, the Ida Nudel Humanitarian Award, and a Canada Short Fiction Award. In 1986, *Ms.* magazine named her Woman of the Year. Her many other highly praised titles include *Cat's Eye* (1989), *Wilderness Tips* (1991), *The Robber Bride* (1993), *Alias Grace* (1996), and *Oryx and Crake* (2003).

In addition to being prolific writer, Atwood has lectured at universities around the world, including the University of British Columbia, the University of Toronto, the University of Alabama, New York University, and Macquarie University, Australia, among others. She was president of the Writers' Union of Canada from 1981 to 1982 and of the International PEN, Canadian Centre, from 1984–86.

She has lived with the writer Graeme Gibson since 1974. They make their home with their daughter Jess and a cat in Toronto.

**Further Reading**

Atwood, Margaret. O. W. Toed: The Margaret Atwood Reference Site. Available online. URL: http://www.owtoed.com. Downloaded on April 20, 2003.

Howells, Coral Ann. *Margaret Atwood.* New York: St. Martin's Press, 1996.

Ingersoll, Earl G., ed. *Margaret Atwood: Conversations.* Princeton, N.J.: Ontario Review Press, 1990.

York, Lorraine M., ed. *Various Atwoods: Essays on the Later Poems, Short Fiction, and Novels.* Concord, Ont.: House of Anansi Press, 1995.

# Auden, W. H.
## (Wystan Hugh Auden)
(1907–1973)  *poet*

W. H. Auden is, along with W. B. Yeats and T. S. ELIOT, considered to be one of the most influential English-language poets of the 20th century. His treatment of the central concerns of the human condition has rarely been matched, and the range and variety of his poetry distinguishes him from his counterparts. His best-known works include "In Memory of W. B. Yeats" (1940), "Funeral Blues" (1940), and "The Double Man" (1945).

Wystan Hugh Auden was born in York, England, on February 21, 1907, as the third of three sons of George Augustus Auden, a physician, and Constance Rosalie (Bicknell) Auden, a former nurse. The year after his birth, the family moved to Birmingham, where Auden began to develop his lifelong fascination with urban and industrial landscapes. From 1920 to 1925, Auden attended Gresham's School in Holt, Norfolk, where his principal interests were in science, especially geology and mining. In autumn 1925, Auden became an undergraduate at Christ Church College of Oxford University. He started as a student of natural science, but, after a brief flirtation with politics, economics, and philosophy, settled on English. As the end of his college years approached and adult life loomed before him, Auden began to be concerned about his homosexuality, which was both severely condemned by the standards of his religious upbringing and by British law (at the time, homosexual activity was a criminal offense in England and subject to a prison term). In his attempts to live what he then regarded as a normal life, Auden had a sexual relationship with one woman and later became engaged to another, but he broke off the engagement after several months. (In June 1935, Auden would marry Erika Mann, the daughter of the great German novelist Thomas Mann, but this was done to secure her a British passport and enable her to leave Nazi Germany; although they never lived together as husband and wife, Auden took more than a casual interest in the relationship and dedicated his next book of poetry to her.)

After Auden's college graduation in 1928, his father offered to pay for him to spend a year abroad, which allowed Auden to spend a year in Berlin from 1928 to 1929. In Berlin he was exposed to a less restrictive lifestyle than he had known in England. Auden soon chose to acknowledge his sexual orientation and live accordingly; as a result, he also committed himself to a life of secrecy and public evasion that necessarily involved a degree of alienation from mainstream existence.

Upon his return to England, Auden worked as a tutor in London and in 1930 began a two-year period as a schoolmaster at Larchfield Academy in Helensburgh, Scotland, which was followed by three years at the Downs School in Colwall. Meanwhile, he achieved his first major publication when T. S. Eliot's journal *The Criterion* published his play *Paid on Both Sides,* a "charade" about the destructive consequences of a feud between two families. Later that year, the prestigious firm of Faber & Faber, of which Eliot was an editor, issued Auden's first commercially published volume, *Poems.* Auden's earlier works, powerful and disturbing, were illustrative of the realities of life at the time they were written. Within a short period, he became the most closely watched, controversial, and influential young poet in Britain. In the summer of 1935, he began a six-month stint as a writer and assistant director for the GPO (General Post Office) Film Unit, through which he collaborated on several projects with the young composer Benjamin Britten. With Britten, several years later in the United States, Auden would write his first opera, *Paul Bunyan.* In the late 1930s, Auden began to write in more accessible styles and address issues of social and political engagement more directly. Like many intellectuals and artists of the 1930s, he aligned himself with far-left movements, which he felt represented the most direct and seemingly effective responses to the worldwide economic distress and rising fascist threat.

In January 1939, Auden made the most controversial move of his life when he took up permanent residence in New York. To many in England, his departure represented a flight from danger on the eve of a world war, an unforgivable act of cowardice and betrayal. In late summer of 1939, as Hitler's armies rolled into Poland to commence the deadly conflict, Auden wrote "September 1, 1939," one of his greatest poems, and one of the many first-rate pieces in *Another Time* (1940), which also included "In Memory of W. B. Yeats," "As I Walked Out One Evening," and "Funeral Blues."

Through much of the 1940s, Auden occupied himself with the writing of long poems, including *The Double Man, The Sea and the Mirror,* and *For the Time Being,* which is widely considered to be Auden's greatest technical achievement. From 1946 to 1958, he served as judge and editor of the Yale Series of Younger Poets, which annually publishes the first book of a promising young poet. His selections included a number of poets who went on to major careers, among them ADRIENNE RICH, JOHN ASHBERY, and JAMES WRIGHT.

As Auden settled into middle age, his writing began to lose some of the tightness and intensity that had previously been among its most distinguishing characteristics. Most critics find the poems in Auden's last four books of poetry, published between 1965 and 1974, to be among the weakest parts of his collected work, seeing them as slack and facile in execution, often trivial in theme, and concerned above all with the display of a personality that had grown cozy and somewhat crotchety. Several critics have particularly objected to his tendency to dot these poems with old and disused words, a result of Auden's compulsive reading of the *Oxford English Dictionary.* The works are criticized for being essentially about themselves rather than some larger and more significant subject.

Auden bought a house in Austria in 1958, where he spent six months of every year thereafter. In 1972, in failing health, he permanently left New York to take up residence in a cottage at Christ Church College of Oxford University, his alma mater. On the evening of September 28, 1973, he gave a poetry reading in Vienna, Austria. Later that night in his hotel room, he died in his sleep of heart failure. He was 66 years old.

**Further Reading**

Brophy, James D. *W. H. Auden.* New York: Columbia University Press, 1970.

Carpenter, Humphrey. *W. H. Auden: A Biography.* London: George Allen & Unwin, 1981.

Davenport-Hines, Richard. *Auden.* London: Heinemann, 1995.

Hecht, Anthony. *The Hidden Law: The Poetry of W. H. Auden.* Cambridge, Mass.: Harvard University Press, 1993.

McDiarmid, Lucy. *Auden's Apologies for Poetry.* Princeton, N.J.: Princeton University Press, 1990.

Mendelson, Edward, ed. *W. H. Auden: Collected Poems.* New York: Vintage Books, 1991.

# B

## Baldwin, James
### (James Arthur Baldwin)
(1924–1987) *novelist, essayist, nonfiction writer, poet, playwright*

James Baldwin was a prolific writer who contributed a powerful voice to the struggle of black Americans during the Civil Rights movement. As an openly homosexual man, Baldwin drew on his own personal experiences of prejudice as well as his analysis of social injustice in his novels and essays. His most famous and influential novel, *Go Tell It on the Mountain* (1953), was a partially autobiographical account of his experiences as a child coming of age in poverty in the Harlem neighborhood of New York City. Although Baldwin spent most of his adult life living as an expatriate, he remained committed to the fight for social justice in America and returned to New York City often in his later life. Not always praised by his critics, and often disliked by his audiences, he nevertheless touched a vast number of readers with his sharp examinations of issues of personal identity and political prejudice. Critic and scholar Henry Louis Gates, Jr., said about Baldwin that "He named for me the things you feel but couldn't utter. . . . Jimmy's essays articulated for the first time to white America what it meant to be American and a Black American at the same time."

James Arthur Baldwin was born in Harlem on August 2, 1924, to an unmarried woman named Berdis Jones. As an illegitimate child, he never knew his biological father and was raised in poverty.

He received his surname at three years old, when his mother married an abusive factory worker named David Baldwin. In addition to his factory job, James's new stepfather also acted as a storefront preacher in a small church in Harlem. David involved his stepson in the church at an early age, and James, a voracious reader, published his first story in the church newspaper at age 12. By the time he was 14, he had converted from Catholicism and had become a minister at the small Fireside Pentecostal Church in Harlem. Although James later exchanged his passion for religion with a passion for literature, critics have said that the fiery preachings of the black church are still echoed in his writing. He remained a preacher for three more years, until Harlem race riots, as well as his difficult relationship with his stepfather, drove him to leave home and relocate to Greenwich Village in 1941.

In 1943, at the age of 19, Baldwin quit the last of a series of ill-paying jobs and became a full-time writer. His first book, a collection of essays about the storefront churches in Harlem, was not a success. Publishers repeatedly rejected his work, though he did succeed in publishing numerous book reviews and essays in publications such as *The Nation, The New Leader, Commentary,* and *Partisan Review.* These works won him the Rosenwald Fellowship in 1948.

Later that year, due to sexual identity problems, the suicide of a close friend, and the state of U.S. race relations, Baldwin chose to leave New York and take refuge in Paris. It was there, in 1953, that he published his first novel, *Go Tell It on the*

*Mountain.* Based on his experiences as a teenage preacher in Harlem, *Go Tell It on the Mountain* describes the life of a religious and sensitive young boy named John who struggles with issues of sin, guilt, and self-doubt. The novel won him widespread acclaim and was well received by both literary critics and the public.

Baldwin was to remain in Paris for the next 10 years, though he returned frequently to the United States to lecture or teach. Despite his living abroad, his work continued to have a strong impact on American readers. In 1955, he published a collection of essays entitled *Notes of a*

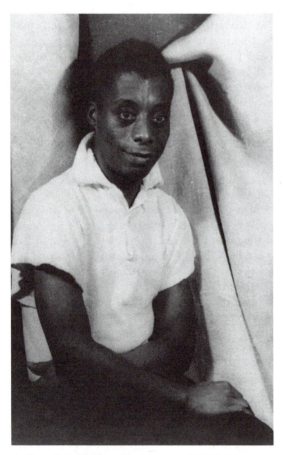

Author of *Go Tell It on the Mountain* (1953), James Baldwin was a powerful figure in the Civil Rights movement in America, though he lived much of his life abroad in Europe. *(Library of Congress, Prints and Photographs Division [LC-USZ62-42481])*

*Native Son,* which provided a powerful description of American racism that succeeded in reaching white American audiences. Following that was a second novel, *Giovanni's Room* (1956), which depicted a white American expatriate attempting to come to terms with his homosexuality. Baldwin published several other essays assessing American racism and prejudice against homosexuality, and he became increasingly outspoken in condemning discrimination against lesbian and gay people. In 1969, he gave up his year-round residence in France and began dividing his time between France and New York.

Though his writings on racial issues were widely read, and reached a wide audience, his inclusion of homosexual themes angered many in the black community. Following the 1962 publication of *Another Country,* a novel about racial and gay sexual tensions among New York intellectuals, Eldridge Cleaver, of the Black Panthers, asserted that Baldwin's writing displayed an "agonizing, total hatred of blacks." Baldwin's analysis of the civil rights activities of the 1960s also earned him a fair amount of negative attention from the U.S. government. Following the 1963 publication of *The Fire Next Time,* in which Baldwin examined the Black Muslims movement and discussed the role that violence would potentially play in the Civil Rights movement, the U.S. Federal Bureau of Investigation (FBI) made him a special target, eventually accumulating a file with more than 1,750 pages chronicling his activities.

James Baldwin's eloquent and honest treatment of civil rights issues made him one of the most influential writers of his time. In addition to the works mentioned above, he also published the plays *The Amen Corner* (1955) and *Blues for Mister Charlie* (1964) and wrote a volume of poetry entitled *Jimmy's Blues* (1983). In addition to the Rosenwald fellowship, Baldwin also received a Eugene F. Saxon Memorial Trust Award, a Guggenheim fellowship, a Partisan Review fellowship, and a Ford Foundation grant. Baldwin was also a professor in the African-American Studies department of the University of Massachusetts at Amherst. He spent the last years of his life in St. Paul de Vence, on the Riviera in France, where he died of stomach cancer on November 30, 1987.

## Further Reading

Balfour, Lawrie. *Evidence of Things Not Said: James Baldwin and the Promise of American Democracy.* Ithaca, N.Y.: Cornell University Press, 2001.

Duberman, Martin B., and Randall Kenan. *James Baldwin.* London: Chelsea House Publishers, 1994.

McBride, Dwight. *James Baldwin Now.* New York: New York University Press, 1999.

Tosse, Lisa, and Carol Bergman. *James Baldwin: Author.* Los Angeles: Holloway House, 1991.

## Bambara, Toni Cade
### (Miltona Mirkin Cade)
*(1939–1995) novelist, short story writer, documentary filmmaker*

Toni Cade Bambara was a civil rights activist who devoted her life to writing about African-American politics and culture and who was deeply committed to improving the lives of African-American women. Born and raised in the Harlem neighborhood of New York City, Bambara in her work spoke to the struggles of African-American life in the racially charged urban America of the 1960s. Initially gaining recognition as a short story writer and later branching out to include other genres, Bambara continued to focus her work on themes of racial awareness and feminist equality. She also had a significant impact on the arts community by organizing and nurturing emerging African-American writers.

She was born in Harlem on March 25, 1939, to Helen Brent Henderson Cade. Named Miltona Mirkin Cade at birth, Miltona opted to shorten her first name to simply "Toni" when she was in kindergarten. She later adopted the name "Bambara" after discovering it as part of a signature on a sketchbook in her great-grandmother's Harlem apartment. Growing up in Harlem was instrumental in forming an important part of her identity, and she later credited the Harlem neighborhood as having a large impact on her writing. It was her mother, however, who was Bambara's greatest influence and inspiration and who instilled in her a rage against the injustices she saw in the treatment of women and the black community.

In 1959, Toni Cade graduated from Queens College with a B.A. degree in theater arts and English. Shortly after her graduation she published her first short story, *Sweet Town,* for which she received the John Golden Award for fiction. Bambara returned to school in 1962 and earned her master's degree while working as an investigator for the New York State Department of Social Welfare. After completing her education she began teaching at the City College of New York, where she stayed until 1970.

During the highly unsettled political atmosphere of the 1960s, Bambara became increasingly involved as a feminist and community activist. In 1970, she edited and published an anthology of fiction, nonfiction, and poetry entitled *The Black Woman.* Bambara contributed three essays to the anthology, and among the other writers were NIKKI GIOVANNI, ALICE WALKER, and AUDRE LORDE. The book was the first major anthology featuring the work of these prominent black feminist authors.

Bambara edited her second anthology in 1971, entitled *Tales and Stories for Black Folks.* The collection revolves around the importance of storytelling and examines how the oral tradition is an inextricable part of African-American heritage. The following year Bambara published *Gorilla, My Love,* the first book composed entirely of her own work. A collection of short stories, *Gorilla* considers the sense of strength and empowerment that can be derived from a community.

Over the following five years, Bambara traveled extensively, visiting Cuba, Vietnam, and the southern United States. In her travels she encountered people and situations that fueled her political voice and strengthened her sense of social injustice. Following her return, Bambara began work on her first novel, *The Salt Eaters.* Published in 1980, *The Salt Eaters* depicts a community of black people seeking the healing properties of salt. In her novel, Bambara "looked for a new kind of narrator . . . a narrator as medium . . . a kind of magnet through which other people tell their stories." This experimental technique won her acclaim with some, but was met with mixed reviews.

Bambara was enraged by Hollywood's portrayal of blacks. Spurred by a desire to challenge the movie industry, Bambara wrote and directed her first documentary film, *The Bombing of Osage*

*Avenue,* in 1986. The film, which centered on the bombing of a black organization in Pennsylvania, won the Academy Award for Best Documentary Feature that year. She wrote several screenplays for other films during her career, but none were as successfully received as *The Bombing of Osage Avenue.*

Bambara's work earned her numerous awards, including the American Book Award in 1981 for *The Salt Eaters,* a literature grant from the National Endowment for the Arts in 1980, and an Honorary Doctorate of Letters from the State University of New York at Albany in 1990. In 1993, at the height of her career, she was diagnosed with colon cancer. She died in Philadelphia on December 9, 1995, at the age of 56.

## Further Reading

Alwes, Derek. "The Burden of Liberty: Choice in Toni Morrison's *Jazz* and Toni Cade Bambara's *The Salt Eaters.*" *African American Review* 30, no. 3 (fall 1996): 353–365.

Evans, Mari, ed. *Black Women Writers.* Garden City, N.J.: Anchor, 1984.

Fleming, Robert. *The African American Writer's Handbook.* New York: Ballantine, 2000.

Griffin, Farah J. "Toni Cade Bambara: Free to Be Anywhere in the Universe." *Callaloo* 19, no. 2 (spring 1996): 229–231.

## Banks, Russell
(1940–   ) *novelist, short story writer, poet*

Russell Banks, originally a poet and short story writer, has become best known for his novels about the hardscrabble, working-class struggles of ordinary people. He explores how "normal" people come to do horrendous things, and though his work is often full of tragedy and the mundane realities of daily life, his books somehow rise above hopelessness with the help of their narrators' sensitivity, humor, and compassion. Banks has published more than a dozen novels, and two of these, *The Sweet Hereafter* and *Affliction,* have been successfully adapted for the screen.

The eldest of four children, Russell Banks was born in Newton, Massachusetts, on March 28, 1940, to Earl and Florence Banks. At age two,

Banks lost the sight in his left eye as a result of abuse from his father, a violent alcoholic who abandoned the family when Banks was 12. Banks grew up in poverty, living in both eastern Massachusetts and New Hampshire. He attended Colgate University for a time, and graduated Phi Beta Kappa in 1967 from the University of North Carolina at Chapel Hill with the help of his mother-in-law at the time, who footed the bill for his tuition.

Between his studies at Colgate and the University of North Carolina, Banks had numerous adventures, including a trip to Cuba to fight for Fidel Castro that ended in south Florida and a six-week drive cross-country in a borrowed car that ended with Banks on the wrong end of a gun barrel in a Tijuana brothel. "Writing in some way saved my life," Banks said in an interview with *Book* magazine. "It brought to my life a kind of order and discipline and an attention to the world outside myself that I don't see how I could have obtained otherwise."

Since his first marriage at the age of 18, Banks has been married three more times, most recently to Chase Twichell in 1989. He has a total of four grown daughters and has lived for 15 years with Twichell, who is a poet and faculty member in the creative writing program at Princeton University, from which Banks retired in 1998.

Although Banks wrote regularly from the time he was a teenager, it was many years before he could support himself with his writing. When asked by an interviewer how he began to write, Banks answered,

> I began as a boy with artistic talent . . . as a visual artist . . . I thought that was what I'd become and in my late teens drifted into reading serious literature. And out of a desire essentially to imitate what I was reading, I began to write, like a clever monkey. By the time I was in my early twenties I had abandoned painting and drawing and had become a beginning poet and fiction writer. Although I still occasionally paint and draw, my life has now been shaped by my writing. But really, it was reading that led me to writing. And in

particular, reading the American classics like Twain who taught me at an early age that ordinary lives of ordinary people can be made into high art.

During the years before he settled into the writing life, he worked as a plumber, shoe salesman, and window trimmer, among other things. Once his writings began to gain recognition, he found work as a teacher and has taught at numerous colleges and universities, including Columbia University, Sarah Lawrence College, New England College, the University of New Hampshire, New York University, and Princeton University.

Banks's numerous novels include *Searching for Survivors* (1975), *Family Life* (1975), *The Book of Jamaica* (1980), *Trailerpark* (1981), *The Relation of My Imprisonment* (1983), *Continental Drift* (1985), *Affliction* (1989), *The Sweet Hereafter* (1991), *Rule of the Bone* (1995), and *Cloudsplitter*. His story collections include *The New World Stories* (1978), *Success Stories* (1986), and *The Angel on the Roof: The Stories of Russell Banks* (2000). He has also contributed poems, stories, and essays to *The Boston Globe Magazine*, *Vanity Fair*, *The New York Times Book Review*, *Esquire*, *Harper's*, and other publications. His works have been widely translated and published in Europe and Asia. The film adaptation of *The Sweet Hereafter* won the Grand Prix and International Critics Prize at the 1997 Cannes Film Festival. *Affliction* was adapted into an Academy Award–winning film.

Banks's work is known for chronicling the lives of people who are often scorned and derided. Most often set in the Northeast, the stories unfold with irony and compassion for their mostly working-class characters. The novels and stories alike have claimed a long and impressive list of literary prizes and awards, including a Guggenheim Fellowship, National Endowment for the Arts Creative Writing Fellowships, the Ingram Merrill Award, the St. Lawrence Award for Short Fiction, the O. Henry and Best American Short Story Award, the John Dos Passos Award, and the Literature Award from the American Academy of Arts and Letters. He is a Fellow of the American Academy of Arts and Sciences. *Continental Drift* and *Cloudsplitter* were both finalists for the Pulitzer Prize, in 1986 and

1998, respectively. *Affliction* was short-listed for both the PEN/Faulkner Fiction Prize and the Irish International Prize.

Banks's film success has led to his latest work on a screenplay adaptation of Jack Kerouac's *On the Road* for Francis Ford Coppola. About the Kerouac project, Banks said, "I turned eighteen the year it was published (1958), and I thought it was about me. But it was about someone from the late '40s, a different generation. My own children read the book and thought it was about them in the '80s. And now kids in Princeton's class of 2003 are reading it and think it's about them. And it is. . . . But it's also about America in that age of innocence."

In early 2001, Banks was elected president of the International Parliament of Writers, a post previously held by Wole Soyinka and Salman Rushdie. In 2002, Banks served as producer and screenwriter for the film adaptations of his novels *Continental Drift* and *Rule of the Bone*.

**Further Reading**

Hasted, Nick. "A Working-Class Hero Is Something to Be." *The Guardian*. Available online. URL: http://books.guardian.co.uk/departments/generalfiction/story/0,6000,388829,00.html. Posted October 28, 2000.

Towers, Robert. "You Can Go Home Again." *The New York Review of Books*. Available online. URL: http://www.nybooks.com/articles/article-preview?article_id=3820. Posted December 7, 1989.

Washington Center for the Book. "A Reading Group Toolbox for the Works of Russell Banks." Audiences for Literature Network. Available online. URL: http://www.wab.org/aln/alnweb/resources/html/grouprgtwcbbanks.html. Downloaded October 15, 2002.

# Baraka, Amiri
## (Everett LeRoy Jones, LeRoi Jones, Imamu Amiri Baraka)
(1934–  ) *novelist, playwright, poet, essayist, autobiographer*

Amiri Baraka was one of the most outspoken and controversial African-American writers of the 20th century. During the course of his career, Baraka went through several different and distinct phases with respect to his political views and his writings. In his early 20s, he married a white woman and lived in Greenwich Village among a loose circle of musicians, artists, and writers. In the following years, he turned his back on his previous life, career, and family and became a white-hating radical Muslim intimately involved in the Black Arts Movement. Known for his extreme views, he was once quoted as saying "We must eliminate the white man before we can draw a free breath on this planet." Then, in yet a third incarnation, Baraka abandoned his spiritual life and became increasingly politically involved. He aligned himself with Marxist-Leninist philosophy and devoted himself to examining the social and psychological role of race in the United States. Throughout his career, Baraka has been best known for his unflinching commitment to the rights and equality of African Americans and has been a powerful spokesperson for radical black literature and theater.

Everett LeRoy Jones was born on October 7, 1934, in Newark, New Jersey, to Colt LeRoy Jones and Anna Lois Jones. He was the product of a middle-class family. His father worked as a postal supervisor and a lift operator and his mother was a social worker. He studied philosophy and religion at Rutgers, Columbia, and Howard Universities, but abandoned his studies in 1952. After dropping out he joined the air force and spent two years as a gunner in Puerto Rico. It was during this period that he began to devote time to writing. He also changed his name to LeRoi, a "Frenchified" version of his father's name. Following his stint in the air force, he returned to the United States and moved to Greenwich Village, in New York City.

Baraka's life can be viewed as containing three distinct periods. The first began with his move to Greenwich Village, where his neighbors and compatriots were mostly white. In 1958 he married a Jewish woman named Hettie Cohen in a Buddhist temple in New York City. The couple had two children together shortly thereafter. He and his wife published *Yugen*, an avant-garde poetry journal, and he coedited a literary newsletter called *Floating Bear*. He also began publishing his own poetry and prose during this period, most of which focused on themes of death, suicide, and self-hatred. His first

published work appeared in 1958, a play entitled *A Good Girl Is Hard to Find*. Although not widely distributed, it received moderately good reviews. His next publication was a volume of poetry, *Preface to a Twenty-Volume Suicide Note* (1961), which was well received and earned him respect and praise as a poet. Following its publication, he traveled to Cuba for several months. The trip had a profound effect on Jones and marked a turning point in his political life.

During the 1960s, Jones began the second major period in his life, becoming increasingly radical and involved with issues of racial and national identity. In 1964, four of his plays were produced, *The Baptism, The Toilet, The Slave,* and *Dutchman. Dutchman*, which depicted a confrontation between a sadistic white woman, Lula, and a naive black college student, Clay, earned him an Obie Award for the Best American Play of 1963–64. His second volume of poetry, *The Dead Lecturer*, was published in 1963. It spoke of his changing allegiances and his desire to leave the white world behind and move toward a black life. In 1965, following the death of Malcolm X, he divorced his white wife and moved uptown to Harlem, where he adopted a separatist, completely African-American lifestyle. He married a black woman named Sylvia Robinson (later Amina Baraka) and turned his back on the "white" life he had lived in Greenwich Village.

Shortly after moving to Harlem, Jones founded the Black Arts Repertory Theatre School. The theater school produced mainly Jones's works, primarily antiwhite plays that were attended exclusively by black audiences. The school taught acting to young African Americans living in Harlem and was a model that inspired black actors and playwrights throughout the country. The theater enjoyed success for a short time after its opening but dissolved only a few months later. Following the dissolution of the Black Arts Repertory in 1967, Jones founded a religious and cultural community theater in Newark, New Jersey, called the Spirit House Players. Like the Black Arts Repertory, the Spirit House Players produced plays primarily containing antiwhite sentiments. Among these were two works focusing on police brutality against blacks: *Police* and *Arm Yourself and Harm Yourself.* Also in 1967, Jones published his Black Nationalist collection of poetry, which explores his painful transition from the white world to the black world.

That same year, during racial riots in Newark, he was severely beaten and then arrested for carrying a concealed weapon. The judge fined him $25,000 and justified the large fine by reading one of Jones's poems, which he considered obscene, aloud in the courtroom. This enraged black communities across the nation, and the fine was paid with the contributions of Jones's supporters. He later successfully appealed the judge's verdict in the case.

In 1968, still deep in his white-hating, Black Nationalist stage, Jones performed his play *Home on the Range* for a benefit for the Black Panther Party. His resentment of the "slave name" Jones led him to drop his birth name and adopt the Muslim name of Imamu Amiri Baraka. "Imamu" is Swahili for "spiritual leader," and "Amiri Baraka" is the Arabic name that he chose for himself. His writings during this period became increasingly political, covering topics such as the development of a black value system and the examination of black political institutions. Among these writings was the essay collection *Raise, Race, Rays, Raze: Essays since 1965*, which was published in 1971.

As a black leader, Baraka was instrumental in organizing the Congress of African Peoples in 1970 and the National Black Political Assembly in 1972. However, by 1974 Baraka had undergone yet another reconsideration of his political and spiritual views. In a surprising turnabout, he renounced Black Nationalism as racist and became a Third World Socialist. He proclaimed himself a Marxist-Leninist, and dropped the "Imamu" from his name for its spiritual implications. During what became known as his "Third World Marxist Period," Baraka produced a number of marxist poetry collections and plays, including *Hard Facts* (1976). Widely considered to be some of his best works, Baraka's socialist/Marxist writings were aimed at the destruction of the capitalist state and the creation of a socialist community. Baraka intended these works primarily for black audiences, as he believed that the black community had the greatest revolutionary potential in America. In 1995 he published *Transbluesency: The Selected Poetry of Amiri Baraka/LeRoi Jones (1961–1995)*.

Baraka was a teacher at the New School for Social Research in New York (1961–64) and a visiting professor at San Francisco State College (1966–67), Yale University (1977–78), and George Washington University (1978–79). He was a professor of African studies at the State University of New York at Stony Brook from 1980 to 2000, when he retired. In 2002, Baraka was appointed poet laureate of New Jersey, but in early 2003 his post was eliminated due to the anti-Semitic views expressed in his poem "Somebody Blew Up America" about the September 11, 2001, terrorist attacks on the country. Through he continues to write, much of Baraka's writings has remained unpublished or has been printed in obscure pamphlets. His many awards include the Guggenheim Fellowship, Rockefeller Foundation Awards for drama, and the National Endowment for the Arts Awards for poetry. Today, Baraka is a critic, poet, playwright, and activist who is still recognized as an outspoken critic and advocate for the rights of African Americans. He frequently tours to make speaking and reading engagements at universities and colleges nationwide.

### Further Reading

Baraka, Amiri. *The Autobiography of LeRoi Jones.* New York: Freundlich Books, 1984.

Harris, William J., ed. *The LeRoi Jones/Amiri Baraka Reader.* New York: Thunder's Mouth Press, 1991.

Lee, A. Robert. "Imamu Amiri Baraka." *American Drama.* Edited by Clive Bloom. New York: St. Martin's Press, 1995, pp. 97–116.

Oliver, Edith "Off Broadway: 'Over the Edge'." *The New Yorker,* April 4, 1964, pp. 78–79.

## Barthelme, Donald
### (Donald Barthelme, Jr.)
(1931–1989) *novelist, short story writer, children's fiction writer*

Donald Barthelme was an influential American writer whose work, with its bizarre subject matter and unique style, stretched and expanded fiction writing. Rejecting traditional use of grammar, plot, and chronology, Barthelme's stories contain an element of the fantastic. His characters often find themselves in strange and surreal situations, which they accept with casual disregard and lack of concern. He both delighted and anguished in popular culture, and frequently wove segments from television advertisements and other odd cultural references into his stories. Called the father of postmodernism, Barthelme was distinguished by his innovation and experimentation and was immensely influential to legions of up-and-coming writers in the 1970s. Though he remained on the fringes of mainstream literature and was not widely read by the public, the originality of his work has ensured him an enduring literary reputation.

Donald Barthelme was born on April 7, 1931, in Philadelphia, Pennsylvania, but moved to Houston, Texas, at age two. His mother, Helen Bechtold, was a devout Catholic, and his father, Donald Barthelme, Sr., was a modernist architect and a professor at the University of Houston. His parents' tastes made them, according to Bechtold, "somewhat of an anomaly in Texas in the '30s." They were well read, and the family library was always well stocked with a wide variety of reading material. Donald Barthelme, Jr., who had decided to become a writer by age 10, was mesmerized by the library's contents from early on and read voraciously every day after returning home from Catholic school.

Barthelme entered the University of Houston in 1949, where he set a precedent by becoming editor in chief of the school newspaper, Cougar, while still a sophomore. In February 1953, while working toward a journalism degree, Barthelme was drafted into the army. During his service he worked as a reporter for an army newspaper. He was sent to Korea, but the war ended two weeks later and he returned to Houston in late 1954. He took a job as a reporter for the Houston Post until 1955, when he began working for Farris Block at the University of Houston News Service. His job at the news service began with writing what he called "poppycock" speeches for the president of the university until, the next year, he succeeded Block as editor in chief of Acta Diurna, a weekly newsletter for University of Houston faculty and staff.

The following year Barthelme founded a student literary journal called Forum, which was composed of articles written by students of a variety of majors. Barthelme, by then a philosophy major, edited the journal until 1960. He subsequently left school without a degree and worked odd jobs until he joined the board of directors at Houston's Contemporary Arts Museum in 1961. He quickly became lead director, and was forced to deal with a wide array of museum issues with which he had little experience. Part of his job at the museum included collecting random cultural artifacts for the exhibits. This experience later manifested itself in his work through his fascination with items from popular culture, and indeed his work during that time began to display some of the characteristic style for which he would become recognized. However, most of what he was writing during this period were "hack" pieces for pulp magazines, usually published under pseudonyms.

Barthelme remained museum director for only one year, at which time he decided to move from Texas to New York and pursue his career as a full-time writer. His first short story, L'Lapse, was published in the New Yorker in 1963. In 1965, he served as editor of Harold Rosenberg and Thomas Hess's art and literature journal, Location, for the two issues that the journal was in publication. In the following years, Barthelme's work began to appear frequently in the New Yorker, and he started branching out from short story writing to work on novels as well. His first book, a collection of stories entitled Come Back, Dr. Caligari, was published in 1964. The book, though not widely distributed, earned him critical acclaim.

During his early years in New York, Barthelme met and married his first wife, Birgit, and the couple had a daughter together, Anne Katherine. They divorced, however, after only a few years of marriage. He later married again, but he and his second wife, Marion, never had children and their relationship also ended in divorce. Many critics have commented that, more than any other theme in his writing, marriage, children, and the problems of family life are topics that frequently appear in his stories.

Barthelme remained in New York for 18 years and continued to work and publish steadily. He published four novels—Snow White (1967), The Dead Father (1975), Paradise (1986), and The King (1990)—and more than 100 short stories, many of which were published in collections such as *Unspeakable Practices, Unnatural Acts* (1968), *City Life* (1970), *Sixty Stories* (1980), and *Forty Stories* (1987). He also published one book of nonfiction, *Guilty Pleasures* (1974), and a large number of short essays and interviews on a wide range of topics. In 1971, he and his daughter wrote his first work of children's fiction, entitled *The Slightly Irregular Fire Engine or the Hithering Thithering Djinn*. The book won the National Book Award for Children's Literature in 1972.

Barthelme lived in New York until 1980, when he returned to Houston to serve as the director of the Creative Writing Program at the University of Houston. In addition to the 1972 National Book Award, Barthelme received numerous other awards for his work, including a Guggenheim Fellowship in 1966, the National Institute of Arts and Letters Zabel Award in 1972, the Rea Short Story Award in 1974, and the Jesse H. Jones Award from Texas Institute of Arts and Letters in 1976. He remained in Houston until his death from throat cancer in 1989 at age 58.

**Further Reading**

Barthelme, Helen Moore. *Donald Barthelme: The Genesis of a Cool Sound*. College Station: Texas A & M University Press, 2001.

Couturier, Maurice, and Regis Durand. *Donald Barthelme*. New York: Methuen, 1982.

Patteson, Richard F., ed. *Critical Essays on Donald Barthelme*. New York: G. K. Hall, 1992.

Roe, Barbara L. *Donald Barthelme: A Study of the Short Fiction*. Boston: Twayne, 1992.

Trachtenberg, Stanley. *Understanding Donald Barthelme*. Columbia: University of South Carolina Press, 1990.

## Baum, L. Frank
### (Lyman Frank Baum)
(1856–1919) *novelist, playwright, children's fiction writer*

Nearly every reader knows L. Frank Baum's most famous and well-loved story, *The Wizard of Oz*. Baum was an exquisite storyteller whose imaginative writings have entranced readers for more than a century. His life was frenetic and nearly as fascinating as his stories, with frequent moves, bankruptcies, and travel. Unfortunately, his health was poor from birth and he suffered frequent illness and hardship. The father of two, Baum devoted his life to feeding children's imaginations and writing fairy tales with positive messages and fewer frightening characters than the average children's stories of the day. Although his work has been criticized, censured, and banned, his stories are still adored by children and adults today.

Lyman Frank Baum was born to Benjamin and Cynthia Ann Stanton Baum on May 15, 1856, in Chittenango, New York. He took his place as the seventh of nine children born to his parents. His father, Benjamin Baum, was a barrel manufacturer until L. Frank was five years old. By that time oil had been discovered nearby, and Benjamin made his fortune in the oil business. Cynthia, a devout Episcopalian of Scotch-Irish descent, schooled her children in observance of the Sabbath and devotion to God. The family's life revolved around friends, family, and church, and they were by all accounts very happy.

Young Frank, who quickly decided to be called by his middle name, was a quiet and imaginative child. He was born with a weak heart that prevented his involvement in sports or other strenuous pursuits. Consequently, he spent much of his childhood reading and daydreaming. This concerned his parents, who enrolled him in the Peekskill Military School in an attempt to toughen up their "soft" and overly sensitive son. This proved to be a disaster, as Frank suffered a mild heart attack after his first week in the school. In 1886, his first book was called *The Book of Hamburgs, A Brief Treatise upon the Mating, Rearing, and Management of Different Varieties of Hamburgs*. He also wrote plays. His parents then decided to foster his interest in writing and storytelling, and when Frank was 14 they bought him a small printing press.

Frank began publishing a small neighborhood newspaper, with modest success. Some local businesses paid to run advertisements, and he and his younger brother were able to produce the paper's content, mainly poetry, stories, and word puzzles.

In 1873, he began a magazine for stamp collectors and a newspaper called *The Empire*. An interest in breeding chickens led to his starting yet another publication—*The Poultry Record.* In 1891, his sister pressured him to meet a friend of hers, Maud Gage, the daughter of a prominent feminist. Baum reluctantly agreed, and the two began dating shortly thereafter. Later that year Frank proposed to Maud, who agreed to marry him despite protests from her family. The two were wed in November 1892.

The year prior to his marriage Baum had written and published a melodrama called *The Maid of Arran.* It enjoyed moderate success with Frank playing the lead character, and the couple toured with the play for a year after getting married. When Maud announced she was pregnant, Frank found another lead actor to take his place and he and Maud settled down in Syracuse, New York. Frank, who had always enjoyed wealth from his father's company, was now facing financial difficulties. He discovered that a clerk had gambled away all of the money his father had left him and he was now facing bankruptcy. Frank took a job as a salesperson to support his family and continued to write on the side.

In May 1893, Baum, his wife, and his infant son moved to Chicago, lured by the upcoming world's fair. They rented a small house and Frank continued to write and work as a traveling salesperson. He also became the father of a second son shortly after the move. He adored his children and spent as much time with them as his schedule would allow, frequently reading them fairy tales and Mother Goose rhymes. It was his children's interest in these poems that inspired him to write *Mother Goose in Prose* in 1897. The book was highly praised and was the most successful children's book written that year. Other books by Baum include *American Fairy Tales, The Life and Adventures of Santa Claus, The Sea Fairies,* and *Sky Island.*

Baum continued to write and publish, but no book became as popular as *The Wizard of Oz.* Published in 1900, the book was immediately embraced by children and adults alike and amazed its readers with its vivid imagery and fantastic story line. Encouraged by the book's success, Baum adapted it to the stage. *Oz,* his musical extravaganza, became hugely popular and toured for nine years. On the urging of his readers, Frank also

wrote 13 sequels to *The Wizard of Oz,* though his writing began to slow as he continued to be plagued by health problems. In addition to his failing heart, he suffered gall bladder complications that left him in constant pain and confined to his bed.

Although his work has been criticized over the years as overly sentimental, racist, and too fantastical, its immense popularity has endured. Several of Baum's books were among the most successful written during his time, and he was tremendously gratified by the outpouring of praise he received from his readers. Perhaps the most enduring product of his imagination is the 1939 film version of *The Wizard of Oz,* directed by Victor Fleming and starring 16-year-old Judy Garland. The film, which won the Academy Award for Best Picture that year, has become a staple in the childhood of nearly every American. Frank Baum continued writing until the day his health finally failed him. Speaking of the imaginary line between Oz and reality, his last words to his wife before he slipped into unconsciousness were "Now we can cross the shifting sands together." He died of a stroke in his home on May 5, 1919.

### Further Reading

Baum, Frank J., and Russell P. McFall. *To Please a Child: A Biography of L. Frank Baum, Royal Historian of Oz.* Chicago: Reilly and Lee, 1961.

Carpenter, Angelica Shirley, and Jean Shirley. *L. Frank Baum: Royal Historian of Oz.* Minneapolis: Lerner Publications Co., 1991.

Hearn, Michael Patrick. *The Annotated Wizard of Oz.* New York: Clarkson N. Potter, 1973.

Riley, Michael O. *Oz and Beyond: The Fantasy World of L. Frank Baum.* Lawrence: University Press of Kansas, 1997.

## Bell, Madison Smartt
(1954–  ) *novelist, short story writer, screenwriter, literary critic*

The author of more than 10 novels and several short story collections, Madison Smartt Bell writes fiction known for its seedy locales, desperate characters, and spiritual quests. He was named one of *Granta* magazine's best novelists under 40 following the publication of his novel *All Souls Rising,* which also was nominated for the National Book Award and a PEN/Faulkner Award. He is also known for an essay he wrote in 1986 for *Harper's* magazine, "Less Is Less: The Dwindling American Short Story," which sharply criticized the growing trend toward minimalist fiction and angered more than a few writers and publishers.

Madison Smartt Bell was born in 1957 in Nashville, Tennessee. His parents, both educated at Vanderbilt University, had purchased a farm outside Nashville shortly before he was born, and this is where Bell spent his entire childhood. He has told stories of using the clippings from horses' hooves as teething rings and of being attached to a papoose board and strapped to his mother's back as an infant so that he could accompany her on her trail rides. Bell's mother taught horseback riding lessons and ran a summer camp. His father was a lawyer in Nashville.

At age four, Bell learned to read. In an autobiographical essay about his childhood, he told how his mother sat him down at the kitchen table, drew the letter "A," and asked him to identify it, which Bell had no trouble doing. She followed this exercise by typing an "a" and asking him to identify that. It was then that he understood the difficulty of learning to read. But the young Bell was determined, and he learned to read so well that by the time he reached first grade, his skills were far ahead of those of his classmates, which set him apart at school. This and living on a farm outside town contributed to his becoming a writer, he believes, because they set him apart a little, which enabled him to see things more clearly. "By the time I was seven," he said, "I thought the writer was the most powerful person in the universe—that's what I wanted to be."

Bell suffered from chronic asthma from the time he was two. He would often have to stay at home, reading books for entertainment, when the asthma was bad. At the end of his senior year in high school, his left lung collapsed. Bell was offered the choice of undergoing surgery or staying in bed for a couple of weeks to see if the lung would heal on its own. The choice was easy, and out of boredom, he said, he wrote his first short story during those weeks.

Bell attended Princeton University, which had an undergraduate creative writing program. There he studied with George Garrett, who became a significant supporter of Bell's work. During his four years at Princeton, Bell won four awards for his fiction and graduated summa cum laude in 1979. He lived in New York briefly, before going on to the creative writing program at Hollins College in Roanoke, Virginia, where he received his M.A. degree in 1981. The Hollins program lasted just one year, but Bell managed to write his first novel, *The Washington Square Ensemble,* while there. It was published by Viking in 1983. Both his first book and his second, *Waiting for the End of the World* (1985), were set in New York. Bell returned there after Hollins and continued to write. *The Year of Silence* (1987), *Soldier's Joy* (1989), *Barking Man* (1990) a collection of short stories, and *Doctor Sleep* (1991) followed in rapid succession.

Madison Smartt Bell's trilogy-in-progress on the Haitian Revolution began with his acclaimed novel, *All Souls Rising. (Photo by Madison Smartt Bell)*

Bell has said that he felt *Doctor Sleep* was the end of a trend in his work. Following its publication, he took a little time off before beginning to write his next novel, *All Souls Rising,* the first book of a trilogy that will eventually cover the entire Haitian revolution, with Toussaint Louverture as the central character. The idea for the novel was actually formed more than a decade prior to its publication, when Bell was researching his first and second novels. When he picked up the idea in the 1990s and began working on it in earnest, he relearned French and learned Creole but was never able to travel to Haiti because of an embargo. He told an interviewer, "I'd never been there, I didn't know any Haitians, and so I was relying entirely on historical records." The novel's success testifies to the success of Bell's research, and in the years since its publication, he has traveled to Haiti nine times. The second volume of the trilogy, *Master of the Crossroads,* appeared in 2000 from Pantheon.

In addition to writing novels, Bell has worked on numerous screenplays based on his novels and is an accomplished guitarist. His screenplay adaptation of *Doctor Sleep* was released in April 2003 as *Hypnotic,* and his first album, a collaboration with friend and poet Wyn Cooper, was due to be released later that year. His work has been translated into many other languages, including French, German, Spanish, Portuguese, and Danish. Bell's essays, book reviews, and nonfiction articles have appeared in numerous magazines, including the *New York Times Book Review, USA Today,* the *Village Voice, Harper's,* and others. He has taught at several universities, including the Iowa Writers' Workshop and the Johns Hopkins Writing Seminars. He and his wife, poet Elizabeth Spires, have one daughter and shared the writer-in-residence position at Goucher College in Baltimore, Maryland, before becoming full professors of English there. Bell was appointed Director of Kratz Center for Creative Writing at Goucher in 1999.

## Further Reading

Bell, Madison Smartt. "One Art." *My Poor Elephant: 27 Male Writers at Work.* Atlanta: Longstreet Press, 1992.

Ghackem, Malick. "Madison Smartt Bell, *All Souls Rising.*" Stanford Electronic Humanities Review 5, no. 2 (1997). Available online. URL: http://www.stanford.edu/group/SHR/5-2/ghachem.html. Updated March 15, 1999.

Henderson, Randi. "Interview with Madison Smartt Bell." *Baltimore Sun,* March 24, 1991, p. E1.

## Bellow, Saul
### (Solomon Bellow)
(1915–  ) *novelist, essayist, short story writer, playwright*

Winner of a 1976 Nobel Prize, a 1975 Pulitzer Prize, and numerous National Book Awards, Saul Bellow is best known for his focus on the Jewish-American experience following World War II. A novelist, playwright, essayist, and short story writer, Bellow creates characters branded with self-doubt, humor, charm, disillusionment, and neurosis who epitomize the modern American way of life, and specifically the chaos that surrounds it. Important themes in Bellow's writing include alienation, moral responsibility, and simply making sense of— and thriving despite—life's confusion. Bellow's characters tend to turn inward to cope with their struggles and are distinguished, almost universally, by their careful optimism.

Solomon Bellow was born in Lachine, Quebec, on June 10, 1915. His parents had emigrated from Russia to Canada in 1913. Bellow was raised until age nine in an impoverished section of Montreal, a neighborhood composed of Russians, Poles, Ukrainians, Greeks, and Italians. Speaking of his childhood, Bellow noted, "My life in Canada was partly frontier, partly the Polish ghetto, partly the Middle Ages . . . I was brought up in a polyglot community." His family moved to Chicago in 1924, following a physical attack on his father, who worked as a bootlegger. Bellow's mother passed away when he was 17. In 1933, he entered the University of Chicago but graduated in 1937 from Northwestern University with degrees in anthropology and sociology. The English department chairman at Northwestern had told Bellow to forget his plans to study the language: "No Jew could really grasp the tradition of English literature."

While pursuing postgraduate studies at the University of Wisconsin, Bellow fell in love, married, and abandoned his studies to become a writer. He returned to Chicago, where he would spend most of his life. There he was close friends with writers Isaac Rosenfeld and Delmore Schwartz and became a permanent member of the University of Chicago's Committee on Social Thought. In Chicago, he also taught at Pestalozzi-Froebel Teachers' College, from 1938 to 1942, and worked for the editorial department of the *Encyclopaedia Britannica* from 1943 to 1944. In 1944–45, he served in the U.S. Merchant Marine, an experience that he would draw from while writing his first novel, *The Dangling Man* (1944). After the war, Bellow returned to teaching and held various professorial posts at universities in Minnesota, New York, Princeton, and Puerto Rico.

Bellow's other early books, *The Victim* (1947), *The Adventures of Augie March* (1953), and *Seize the Day* (1956), articulate postwar malaise. During this stage of his career, Bellow's writing was influenced by Trotskyism and the *Partisan Review* group of intellectuals. He rejected ERNEST HEMINGWAY's "tough guy" model of American fiction and became engaged with a wide range of cultural fields and traditions, including such topics as Nietzsche, the debate surrounding Freud's Oedipal theories, popular culture, and Russian-Jewish heritage. From the beginning of his publishing career, Bellow has dismissed public assumptions that his writing is based closely on his own personal experience. Books narrated in the first person, especially, have often been mistaken for representing Bellow's own thoughts. "No writer can take it for granted that the views of his characters will not be attributed to him personally," he said in a *New York Times* interview in 1994. "It is generally assumed, moreover, that all the events and ideas of a novel are based on the life experiences and the opinions of the novelist himself."

Bellow is the only writer to have won the National Book Award three times: for *The Adventures of Augie March* (1953), *Herzog* (1964), and *Mr. Sammler's Planet* (1970). With *The Adventures of Augie March*, Bellow replaced a more restrictive style of writing with a more loosely flowing one. *Herzog* (1964), Bellow's major novel from the 1960s, centers on a middle-aged Jewish intellectual, Moses E. Herzog, whose life has come to a

standstill. He is on the brink of suicide and writes long letters to Nietzsche, Heidegger, his ex-wife Madeleine, Adlai Stevenson, and God. Moses Herzog, like Augie March, is introspective and troubled, but finally finds that he has many reasons to be content with his life. After pouring all Herzog's thoughts into letters, Bellow notes in the last words of the book: "At this time he had no messages for anyone. Nothing. Not a single word."

In 1975, Bellow visited Israel and recorded his impressions in his first substantial nonfiction book, *To Jerusalem and Back* (1975). Bellow's disenchantment with liberal political theory was reflected in his novel *Mr. Sammler's Planet* (1970), in which Arthur Sammler, an elderly Polish Jew and survivor of the Holocaust, views with his only intact eye the world of revolutionaries and the ill-mannered younger generation. For *Humboldt's Gift* (1975), Bellow won the Pulitzer Prize. The protagonist, Charlie Citrine, is a rich and successful writer, but in his heart he knows that he is a failure. He is under the thumb of a small-time Chicago gangster, ruined by a divorce, and finally abandoned by his mistress. He admires his dead friend, Von Humboldt Fleischer, modeled on the poet Delmore Schwartz (1913–66). Humboldt, a talent wasted, represents for Citrine all that is important in culture. In *Humboldt's Gift*, Bellow continues with his series of defeated and failing characters. Contrary to his other novels though, *Humboldt's Gift* is not gloomy; it attempts instead to reveal humor despite life's tragedies.

Bellow has three sons from his first four marriages. In 1989, he married Janis Freedman. They have one daughter, born in 1999. Bellow has not lost his ability to spark controversy, as his 13th novel *Ravelstein* (2000) proved. It draws a portrait of Abe Ravelstein, a university professor and a closeted homosexual who ultimately dies of AIDS-related illness. Ravelstein's character is modeled on Allan Bloom, Bellow's colleague at the University of Chicago and the author of *The Closing of the American Mind* (1987), who died in 1992. Ravelstein's sexual inclinations were only a small detail in Bellow's book but critics found it most interesting. Of this, Bellow states, "This is a problem that writers of fiction always have to face in this country. People are literal minded, and they say, 'Is it true? If it is true, is it factually accurate? If it isn't factually accurate, why isn't it factually accurate?' Then you tie yourself into knots, because writing a novel in some ways resembles writing a biography, but it really isn't. It is full of invention."

## Further Reading

Cohen, Sarah B. *Saul Bellow's Enigmatic Laughter.* Urbana: University of Illinois Press, 1974.

Cronin, Gloria L. "An Introduction to Saul Bellow." Saul Bellow Society and Journal. Available online. URL: http://engfac.byu.edu/faculty/CroninG/saulb. Posted March 4, 2002.

Goldman, L. H., et al., eds. *Saul Bellow: A Mosaic.* New York: Peter Lang, 1992.

Hyland, Peter. *Saul Bellow.* New York: St. Martin's Press, 1992.

Pifer, Ellen. *Saul Bellow Against the Grain.* Philadelphia: University of Pennsylvania Press, 1990.

## Berry, Wendell
## (Wendell Erdman Berry)
(1934– ) *poet, essayist, novelist, children's fiction writer, nature writer, nonfiction writer*

Called by the *New York Times* the "prophet of rural America," Wendell Berry is a poet, essayist, novelist, farmer, and former professor of English. His books focus on the importance of community, in terms of human and ancestral connections, as well as connections with the land. The author of more than 30 books, he has worked his family's farm since 1965. Perhaps more than the work of any other contemporary writer, Berry's work exemplifies the notion that the personal is political, that what one chooses to do in private existence is inseparable from its impact on the community.

Wendell Erdman Berry was born on August 5, 1934, in Henry County, Kentucky, where he still resides on the farm that has been in his family since the 1800s. Berry is the fifth generation of his father's family and the sixth generation of his mother's to farm in Henry County. He graduated from the University of Kentucky in 1956 with a B.A. degree in English, and in 1957 earned his M.A. degree in English. That same year, he married Tanya Amyx. The couple have two children, a son

and a daughter, both of whom still live in Henry County and both of whom are farmers. Berry has five grandchildren as well.

Wendell Berry began his teaching career at Georgetown University, where he worked for a year before winning a Wallace Stegner Writing Fellowship at Stanford University for the 1958–59 school year. After finishing the fellowship, he taught at New York University for a short time before returning to the University of Kentucky, where he taught from 1964 until 1977, when he left his position to give his full attention to farming and writing. Also in 1977, in association with Rodale Press, Berry served as a contributing editor for *The New Farm,* a magazine devoted to organic farming. His position grew out of Berry's interests, but it also continued an association that had begun years earlier with Berry's father, who was one of the major contributors to the organic farming movement in the 1930s, along with Robert Rodale, son of Rodale Press founder J. I. Rodale. Berry uses nothing but horses to work his land and employs only organic methods of fertilization and pest control. He feels he is living in harmony with nature by not using tractors or chemicals on his farm.

In 1987, Berry returned to the University of Kentucky to teach "Readings in Agriculture," a class he created, and "Composition for Teachers." He has called the teaching of reading and writing "an obligation of major importance." His poetry collections include *The Broken Ground* (1964), *There Is Singing Around Me* (1976), *Clearing* (1977), *Collected Poems 1957–1982* (1985), *Traveling at Home* (1989), *Entries: Poems* (1994), and *A Timbered Choir: The Sabbath Poems 1979–1997* (1997). His novels include *Remembering* (1988), *A World Lost* (1996), *The Memory of Old Jack* (1999), and *Jayber Crow* (2000). Berry is also the author of numerous collections of essays, including *A Continuous Harmony: Essays Cultural and Agricultural* (1972), *The Gift of Good Land* (1981), *Standing on Earth: Selected Essays* (1991), *Sex, Economy, Freedom, and Community* (1993), *Home Economics* (1995), *Another Turn of the Crank* (1995), and *The Unsettling of America: Culture and Agriculture* (1996). He has been called a writer of "brilliant moral imagination." His work is known for its tough-minded and original observations of human ecology and its graceful, classical prose.

Among his honors and awards are fellowships from the Guggenheim and Rockefeller Foundations, a Lannan Foundation Award, and a grant from the National Endowment for the Arts.

### Further Reading

Ditsky, John. "Wendell Berry: Homage to the Apple Tree." *Modern Poetry Studies* 2, no. 1 (1971): 7–15.

Driskell, Leon V. "Wendell Berry." *Dictionary of Literary Biography*. Vol. 5. pp. 62–66.

Ehrlich, Arnold W. "Wendell Berry." *Publishers Weekly* 5 (September 1977): 10–11.

House, Freeman. "Life From Behind a Barber's Chair: Review of *Jayber Crow*." *San Francisco Chronicle*. January 14, 2001. Available online. URL: http://www.sfgate.com/cgi-bin/article.cgi?file=/chronicle/archive/2001/01/14/RV20459.DTL.

Mendes, Guy. *Living by Words*. Lexington: Kentucky Educational Television Video, 2002.

Prunty, Wyatt. "Myth, History, and Myth Again." *The Southern Review* 20 (1984): 958–68.

## Berryman, John
### (John Allyn Smith, Jr.)
(1914–1972) *poet, short story writer, literary critic*

Known as one of the key writers to practice and develop the "confessional" style, John Berryman wrote poems that seemed to turn the interior life of their protagonists inside out for full exposure, revealing painful private experiences and the psychological processes related to them. He experimented with many different personae in his work, the most famous being the blackface minstrel through whom the "dream songs" are told, and twisted ordinary syntax to suit the voices of his speakers. In addition to finding success as a poet, Berryman established an impressive academic career, teaching at Princeton University and the University of Minnesota and publishing critical essays, articles, and books on EZRA POUND, STEPHEN CRANE, Christopher Marlowe, William Shakespeare, WALT WHITMAN, SAUL BELLOW, and THEODORE DREISER, among others. Despite the success he found in

his professional life, Berryman could not escape the childhood shock he experienced at age 12, when his father shot himself outside John's window. Alcoholism, emotional instability, and reckless behavior haunted Berryman's adult life.

John Berryman was born John Allyn Smith, Jr., in McAlester, Oklahoma, in 1914. His father, John Allyn Smith, was a banker; his mother, Martha Little, had been a schoolteacher. The family moved frequently in the first years after young John's birth but finally settled in Tampa, Florida, where John, Sr., speculated unsuccessfully in land. In 1926, when his son was 12, John, Sr., committed suicide. Three months following the suicide, John's mother married John McAlpin Berryman, whose name was given to the son.

The Berryman family relocated to New York City, but life there following the stock market crash of 1929 proved difficult as well. In 1931, young John attempted suicide, but the following year, he began attending Columbia College (now known as Columbia University) and met the prominent academic Mark Van Doren, who became a mentor. Berryman published poems in *Columbia Review* and *The Nation* during his college years and graduated Phi Beta Kappa with a degree in English in 1936. He continued his studies on a fellowship at Cambridge University, where he met W. B. Yeats, T. S. ELIOT, W. H. AUDEN, and Dylan Thomas and continued writing and publishing poems. His first poems appeared in *Five Young American Poets* (1940) and greatly reflected the influence of these poets.

Berryman's career as a teacher began about the same time. In 1939, he taught at Wayne University (later Wayne State University) in Detroit, Michigan and served as poetry editor of *The Nation*. In 1939, he experienced the first of what would be many hospitalizations during his life. These were always brought on by "nervous exhaustion," and by 1958 occurred at least once a year until his death in 1972.

Following his hospitalization in 1939, Berryman went on to teach at Harvard, then at a prep school, before finally landing an instructorship at Princeton University, where he remained for a decade. In 1942, he married Eileen Mulligan. Berryman's teaching was described by PHILIP LEVINE as "brilliant, intense, articulate," and his poems were gaining more recognition. In 1950, he won the American Academy Award for Poetry. In 1956, with the publication of *Homage to Mistress Bradstreet,* Berryman finally won wide acclaim for his poetry. This was followed in 1964 with the publication of his most significant work, *77 Dream Songs,* which firmly secured his position as a unique American poet. By now, his poems had found a wide and adoring readership.

Berryman's private life had fallen into a shambles during these years from which it would never fully recover. In 1953, while a lecturer at the University of Iowa Writers' Workshop, he was arrested for public drunkenness and disturbing the peace. The university dismissed him and he separated from his wife, Eileen, that same year. With the help of friend and fellow poet ALLEN TATE, he was appointed lecturer in 1955 at the University of Minnesota, just 30 miles from his biological father's birthplace. He began *77 Dream Songs,* which won a Pulitzer Prize, while living in Minnesota. Berryman and Eileen divorced in 1956, and two weeks later, he married 24-year-old Anne Levine. The couple had one son before divorcing in 1959. His third marriage, to 22-year-old Kate Donahue, took place in 1961. The couple had two daughters. The youngest was just six months old when Berryman jumped off the Washington Avenue Bridge in Minneapolis to his death in 1972.

John Berryman's books of poems include *The Dispossessed* (1948); *Homage to Mistress Bradstreet* (1956); *77 Dream Songs* (1964); *His Toy, His Dream, His Rest* (1968); *Love and Fame* (1970); and *Collected Poems (1937–1971)* (1989). *The Dream Songs,* published in 1969, ultimately collected 385 poems. His nonpoetry books include *Stephen Crane: A Critical Biography* (1950); *The Arts of Reading* (1960) with Ralph Ross and Allen Tate; *Recovery* (1973), a nonfiction work about his struggles with alcoholism; and *The Freedom of the Poet* (1976), a collection of his essays and short stories.

**Further Reading**

Haffenden, John. *The Life of John Berryman.* Boston: Routledge and Kegan Paul, 1982.

Levine, Philip. "Mine Own John Berryman." *Gettysburg Review* 4, no. 4 (autumn 1991): 78–85.

Mariani, Paul L. *Dream Song: The Life of John Berryman.* New York: William Morrow, 1990.

Stitt, Peter. "The Art of Poetry." *Paris Review* 53 (winter 1972): 43–50.

Weaver, Elizabeth. "Master Poets Pay Homage to Berryman." *Columbia University Record.* February 28, 1997. Available online. URL: http://www.columbia.edu/cu/record/archives/vol22/vol22iss16/record2216.17.html. Downloaded September 23, 2003.

## Bishop, Elizabeth
(1911–1979)  *poet, short story writer*

Frequently referred to as a "poet's poet," Elizabeth Bishop has come to be regarded as one of the premier American poets of the 20th century. Although she published only five slim volumes in her 35-year career, her work has been profoundly influential within the writing community and is increasingly popular with a wide range of readers. She is best known for her poems that examine the physical world in minute detail, simultaneously retaining a feel of objectivity and revealing much of her own emotions. A very patient writer, she would often work on a single poem for years. This unhurried approach resulted in a body of poetry remarkable for its acuity, wisdom, and depth of expression. Amid a life of loves, losses, travels, and illnesses, Bishop created masterpieces that firmly established her as one of the principal poets of her generation.

Elizabeth Bishop was born in Worcester, Massachusetts, on February 8, 1911, the only child of William T. Bishop and Gertrude May (Boomer) Bishop. Elizabeth had a difficult childhood. Her father, a vice president in his father's construction company, suffered from frequent illnesses and died of kidney failure on October 13, 1911. Elizabeth was only eight months old at the time of her father's death. Her mother suffered repeated nervous breakdowns over the following several years. She was permanently institutionalized in 1916, and Elizabeth, who was five years old at the time, never saw her again. Gertrude Bishop died in a sanitarium in Dartmouth, Nova Scotia, in May 1934.

Following her father's death and her mother's institutionalization, Elizabeth went to live with her maternal grandparents in a Nova Scotia town called Great Village. She remained with them until September 1917, when she was forced to move back to Worcester to live with her father's parents. After the move she began suffering from asthma, eczema, and other illnesses. Her grandparents, realizing how unhappy their granddaughter was, allowed her to go live with her mother's sister, Maud Shepherdson, and her husband, George. Elizabeth found happiness and stability in her new home, and later credited her aunt with having saved her life.

In 1927, Bishop left home to attend Walnut Hill School for the Arts, a boarding school in Natick, Massachusetts. She dabbled in creative writing while at Walnut Hill and began publishing stories and poems in the school literary journal, *The Blue Pencil*. She remained in Natick until her graduation in 1930, at which time she became a freshman at Vassar College in Poughkeepsie, New York. She chose English as her major and did well as a student, though some of her professors found her overly proud and aloof. Sometimes forming brief relationships with young men, Bishop showed little inclination toward women, though years later she would have lesbian relationships.

While at Vassar, Bishop and some of her fellow students founded the Vassar literary magazine *Con Spirito*, and she worked as editor of the school yearbook. Prior to her graduation in 1934, she also began publishing her work in more well-known literary journals, some with national circulation. That same year, Bishop met the poet MARIANNE MOORE and the two formed a close friendship. Elizabeth began turning to her new friend for advice and criticism of her writing, and Moore became one of the biggest influences on Elizabeth's life and work.

Following her graduation from Vassar, Bishop moved to New York City and devoted herself to writing full time. Her first book publication occurred in 1936, when a selection of her poems appeared in *Trial Balances*, an anthology of works by new young writers. Despite repeated attempts, however, she did not publish a book of her own poetry for another decade. During that time her work did appear in such noteworthy publications as *Partisan Review*, *New Directions*, and the *New Yorker*.

In 1936 she took her first visit to Europe, a trip that sparked a wanderlust that would shape her life and career for the next several decades. Between 1936 and 1937 she traveled to Paris, London, Italy, Spain, and Morocco. She then discovered Key West, Florida, which impressed her so much that she settled there and made it her home for the next 13 years. In 1942, at the start of U.S. involvement in World War II, she worked briefly for the U.S. Navy. She also visited Mexico that year, where she met Chilean poet Pablo Neruda and Mexican painter David Siqueiros. She also met Lota de Macedo Soares that year, on a trip to New York. A striking young Brazilian woman, Lota would become the love of Elizabeth's life.

In 1945, Bishop successfully published her own book of poetry. Invited by an editor at Houghton Mifflin to submit her work for the annual Houghton Mifflin Poetry Prize Fellowship, Elizabeth agreed and was awarded the prize. The book, entitled *North & South*, was released the following year. Among its contents were some of her most popular and enduring masterpieces, including "Roosters" and "The Fish." The book received favorable reviews from critics and brought her increased recognition as a promising writer. It also earned her a Guggenheim Fellowship in 1947, an appointment as Consultant in Poetry at the Library of Congress in 1949, and an award from the American Academy of Arts and Letters in 1950.

Bishop visited Brazil for the first time in 1951 and decided to move there later that year to live with Lota de Macedo Soares. The move marked the beginning of one of the happiest and most settled periods of Bishop's life. Lota, her friend and lover, helped her to come to terms with her increasing dependence on alcohol, and she also sought help for chronic depression. She devoted much time to writing, and the poems she produced, though there were not many of them, were of high quality. By 1955, a decade after her first book, her publisher was tired of waiting for enough poems for a new publication and decided to rerelease *North & South* in an edition that included the poems from the intervening years. This volume, entitled *Poems: North & South—A Cold Spring*, received excellent reviews and was awarded the Pulitzer Prize for poetry.

It was another decade before Bishop published her next book, *Questions of Travel,* in 1965. This third collection contained 20 poems and the short story "In the Village." It was, overall, well received. There were some criticisms, mainly that the poems' attention to daily routines and personal observations was too trivial, but it was roundly applauded by Bishop's fellow poets for its descriptiveness and simplicity. Her next publication was a collection of previously published poetry that won the National Book Award in 1969.

While her publications were bolstering her literary reputation, her personal life was suffering. She and Lota were having domestic difficulties, and Bishop was torn between her longtime companion and another woman. Lota, who worked in a stressful urban development job in Rio, became the subject of a good deal of criticism, and Bishop, consequently, found herself also caught in a web of negative press. She began spending more time back in the United States, and in 1966 she accepted her first teaching job at the University of Washington in Seattle. The next year, while Bishop was on a trip to New York, Lota flew from Rio to join her. On the first night of her visit, with Elizabeth sleeping in the next room, Lota took an overdose of sleeping pills. She died five days later.

Following the death of her lover, Bishop traveled extensively throughout Asia and Europe. After returning to the United States she taught at several different universities until becoming an English professor at Harvard in 1973. Her last collection of poetry, *Geography III,* was published in 1976 and won the National Book Critics Circle Award. Later that same year she became both the first American and the first woman to win the Books Abroad/ Neustadt Prize for Literature. Having won numerous poetry awards, she retired from Harvard in 1978. She never published another book, and died in Boston of a cerebral aneurysm on October 6, 1979.

**Further Reading**

Doreski, Carole. *Elizabeth Bishop: The Restraints of Language.* New York: Oxford University Press, 1993.

Fountain, Gary, and Peter Brazeau. *Remembering Elizabeth Bishop: An Oral Biography.* Amherst: University Press of Massachusetts, 1994.

Millier, Brett Candlish. *Elizabeth Bishop: Life and the Memory of It.* Berkeley: University of California Press, 1993.

Jarraway, David R. "'O Canada!': The Spectral Lesbian Poetics of Elizabeth Bishop." *PMLA* 113, no. 2 (March 1998): 243–258.

## Bly, Robert
### (Robert Elwood Bly)
(1926– ) *poet, nonfiction writer, essayist, translator, editor*

Famous for inspiring the men's consciousness movement with his best-selling book *Iron John: A Book About Men,* Robert Bly is a poet, translator and editor whose work has had a significant impact on postwar American poetry. He first came to national prominence in the 1960s when he cofounded American Writers Against the Vietnam War and became the leading voice among poets and other writers protesting the war.

Robert Elwood Bly was born to parents of Norwegian ancestry in Madison, Minnesota, on December 23, 1926. He enlisted in the U.S. Navy in 1944 and spent two years in service before attending St. Olaf College. After one year at St. Olaf, he transferred to Harvard University, where he earned his B.A. degree in 1950 and became associated with quite a few other notable writers, including DONALD HALL, ADRIENNE RICH, KENNETH KOCH, and JOHN ASHBERY. After spending some time in New York City, working odd jobs and writing, Bly went to the University of Iowa Writers' Workshop, where his fellow students included the poets W. D. Snodgrass and Donald Justice. In 1955, during his time at Iowa, Bly married Carolyn McLean, who was also a writer. He earned his M.A. degree at Iowa, then traveled to Norway on a Fulbright grant in 1956, where he translated Norwegian poetry into English. For Bly this was a time to trace his lineage and to broaden his experience of poetry in the world. While in Norway, Bly encountered the work of poets such as Pablo Neruda, Cesar Vallejo, Georg Trakl, and Gunnar Ekeloef, who were not well known in the United States but were widely read in Norway. This fueled his interest in translating literature and inspired him to found *The Fifties,* a literary magazine devoted to work in translation. Over the years of its publication, *The Fifties* (later called *The Sixties, The Seventies, The Eighties,* and *The Nineties*) was responsible for bringing the works of many lesser-known international poets to an American audience. Bly was heavily involved in the antiwar movement during the 1960s. He cofounded American Writers Against the Vietnam War in 1966 and led much of the opposition effort among writers. When his 1967 collection of poems, *The Light Around the Body,* won the National Book Award, he donated the prize money to the antiwar movement. A prolific writer, Bly published 15 books of poetry during the 1970s and 1980s, including poetry collections, books of essays, and translations.

The book for which he is best known, *Iron John: A Book About Men* (1992), became an international best-seller and inspired much debate. Translated into many other languages, the book inspired the men's consciousness movement, which has involved Bly in conducting workshops for men and sometimes for men and women together. Since the 1960s and 1970s, the men's movement in America has explored male consciousness and new definitions of masculinity with a focus on supporting men in relation to one another. Bly has also conducted workshops on European fairy tales with his current wife, Ruth.

Bly's edited works included *The Rag and Bone Shop of the Heart* (1993), an anthology of poems coedited with Michael Meade and James Hillman; *The Darkness Around Us Is Deep: Selected Poems of William Stafford* (1993); and *The Soul Is Here for Its Own Joy,* a collection of sacred poetry from many cultures. He also edited the anthology *Best American Poetry 1999.*

Bly has published more than 30 books during his prolific career. Some of his other notable poetry publications include *Loving a Woman in Two Worlds* (1987), *What Have I Ever Lost by Dying: Collected Prose Poems* (1992), *Snowbanks North of the House* (1999), and *The Night Abraham Called to the Stars* (2001). Nonfiction works include *The Spirit Boy and the Insatiable Soul* (1994), *The Sibling Society* (1996), which inspired another round of national debate reminiscent of *Iron John,* and *The Maiden King: The Reunion of Masculine and Feminine* (2000),

a collaboration with Marion Woodman. His books of translations include *Neruda and Vallejo Selected Poems* (1971), *Friends: You Drank Some Darkness: Three Swedish Poets—Martinson, Ekeloef, and Transtroemer* (1975), *The Kabir Book* (1977), *Machado's Times Alone: Selected Poems* (1983), and *Lorca and Jimenez: Selected Poems* (1997).

In addition to the National Book Award, Bly has received Guggenheim, Rockefeller, and National Endowment for the Arts fellowships. He married for a second time in 1980 and lives with his children and his wife, Ruth Ray, on a farm in western Minnesota.

## Further Reading

Davis, William V. *Robert Bly: The Poet and His Critics.* Columbia, S.C.: Camden House, 1994.

———. *Understanding Robert Bly.* Columbia: University of South Carolina Press, 1988.

Harris, Victoria F. *The Incorporative Consciousness of Robert Bly.* Carbondale: Southern Illinois University Press, 1992.

Heep, Hartmut. *A Different Poem: Rainer Maria Rilke's American Translators Randall Jarrell, Robert Lowell, and Robert Bly.* New York: Peter Lang, 1996.

Jones, Richard, and Kate Daniels, eds. *Of Solitude and Silence: Writings on Robert Bly.* Boston: Beacon Press, 1981.

Nelson, Howard. *Robert Bly, an Introduction to the Poetry.* New York: Columbia University Press, 1984.

Sugg, Richard P. *Robert Bly.* Boston: Twayne, 1986.

## Bogan, Louise
(1897–1970)  *poet, literary critic*

Perhaps best known as the poetry reviewer for the *New Yorker,* a position she held from 1931 to 1969, Louise Bogan was also a first-rate poet. Her lyric poems, often short and formal compared to many of the more expansive and highly experimental works of her early modernist peers, addressed the entwined themes of love and grief that seemed to rise intimately from her own life experiences with severe depression.

Louise Bogan was born on August 11, 1897, in Livermore Falls, Maine, to Daniel Joseph Bogan, who worked as a superintendent in the local paper mill, and Mary Helen Murphy Shields Bogan, who was a homemaker. Bogan's parents had an unhappy marriage, and throughout her life she was troubled by her mother's affairs. As a young girl, Louise attended private schools in New Hampshire, and then in Boston, at the Girls' Latin School, which was known for its challenging classical curriculum. She had begun to read *Poetry* magazine and write poetry by the time she graduated from high school in 1915, and although modernism was just beginning to shape the literature of her day, Bogan developed a style that relied heavily on formal elements and traditional metrics. Bogan went on to Boston University in 1915, but completed just one year before marrying an army officer, Curt Alexander, in 1916. The couple soon moved to Panama, where their daughter was born in 1917. Their marriage was not a happy one. After Alexander's death in 1920, Bogan was left with a young child to care for and no reliable source of income. She moved to New York City and supported herself and her daughter by working at bookstores and libraries.

Although financially difficult, these years were exciting for Bogan. She attended literary events in Greenwich Village and met numerous writers, including WILLIAM CARLOS WILLIAMS, MARIANNE MOORE, and CONRAD AIKEN. She also began what was to be one of the most important friendships of her life, with the writer and critic EDMUND WILSON, who became her early mentor. Bogan soon began to publish her work to critical acclaim in the leading journals and magazines of the time, including *Poetry, Vanity Fair,* and *The New Republic.* This recognition led to the publication of her first book, *Body of This Death,* which appeared in 1923. She also, at Wilson's urging, began to publish reviews of literature, which became one of Bogan's lifelong sources of income.

In 1925, Bogan married Raymond Holden, a fellow writer. That marriage also was troubled and did not last. Bogan's private life was full of turmoil during these married years, but this did not prevent her from writing poems. She produced her most significant verse during this time. *Dark Summer* was published in 1929 and *The Sleeping Fury* in 1937. Bogan was not a prolific writer. Her poems came infrequently and with great effort. The remaining books she published during her career were primarily collections of previously published poems with a few new poems added.

When many of Bogan's friends and fellow writers became involved in leftist politics during the 1930s, Bogan insisted that politics had no place in art. Carrying the banner for literary purity, she became somewhat isolated from her circle of literary friends and supporters.

In 1931, Bogan became the poetry critic at the *New Yorker,* a job she would hold until almost the time of her death. Her reviews for the magazine are collected in *A Poet's Alphabet: Reflections on the Literary Art and Vocation* (1970). She was lauded for writing accessible and insightful criticism and is still considered to be one of America's great poetry critics.

As she grew older, she battled severe depression and found writing poetry to be more and more difficult. Consequently, she began to focus more heavily on criticism and education. In addition to writing for periodicals, Bogan found occasional teaching jobs, starting in the 1940s. She also worked as a translator during these years and helped to edit the works of younger writers. In 1951, she was commissioned to write a short history of American poetry, which was published under the title *Achievement in American Poetry, 1900–1950.*

She wrote few new poems during the second half of her life, but her work was collected for book publication several times. *Poems and New Poems* came out in 1941. *Collected Poems, 1923–1953* won a shared Bollingen Prize in 1955, and *The Blue Estuaries: Poems 1923–1968* was released in 1968 and contained 103 poems. These collections received quiet praise, but Bogan felt largely unrecognized as a poet.

The financial burdens that plagued her most of her adulthood finally eased in the last decade of her life. She received a monetary award from the Academy of American Poets in 1959 and one from the National Endowment for the Arts in 1967. Battling depression, she died alone in her apartment in 1970. In the years since her death, interest in her work has gained some momentum, with feminist critics reassessing its role in the tradition of women's writing, and scholars of American modernism examining her work for its adherence to formal structures and tones at a time when her peers had opposite concerns for their work.

## Further Reading

Collins, Martha, ed. *Critical Essays on Louise Bogan.* Boston: G. K. Hall, 1984.

Dodd, Elizabeth. *The Veiled Mirror and the Woman Poet: H. D., Louise Bogan, Elizabeth Bishop, and Louise Glück.* Columbia: University of Missouri Press, 1992.

Frank, Elizabeth. *Louise Bogan: A Portrait.* New York: Columbia University Press, 1985.

Knox, Claire E. *Louise Bogan: A Reference Source.* Lanham, Md.: Rowman & Littlefield, 1991.

Limmer, Ruth, ed. *What the Woman Lived: Selected Letters of Louise Bogan, 1920–1970.* New York: Harcourt Brace Jovanovich, 1973.

Ridgeway, Jacqueline. *Louise Bogan.* Boston: Twayne, 1984.

Upton, Lee. "The Re-Making of a Poet: Louise Bogan." *Centennial Review* 36, no. 3 (fall 1992): 557–572.

## Bontemps, Arna
### (Arna Wendell Bontemps)
(1902–1973) *poet, short story writer, children's writer, playwright, novelist*

A central figure in the Harlem Renaissance, Arna Bontemps was a poet and children's writer as well as a teacher and librarian. He is most often remembered as the close associate of JEAN TOOMER and LANGSTON HUGHES, whose books were published to greater acclaim.

Arna Wendell Bontemps was born to Paul Bismarck and Maria Carolina (Pembroke) Bontemps, both of Creole heritage, on October 13, 1902, in Alexandria, Louisiana, but most of his childhood was spent in the Watts section of Los Angeles, where his family moved when he was three. His father was a skilled brick mason, who encouraged his education but always expected his son to apprentice in the same trade. When the younger Bontemps refused to follow in his footsteps, he was sent to a white boarding school in San Fernando to finish his secondary education. From there, he went on to Pacific Union College in Angwin, California, which later became the University of California at Los Angeles (UCLA), and he graduated in 1923 after just three years of study.

It was during his time in college that Bontemps became interested in writing, especially in poetry. He won many awards early on for his work and began to publish his poems in 1917 in *The Crisis,* the magazine of the National Association for the Advancement of Colored People (NAACP) that was edited by W. E. B. DUBOIS. In 1926, *The Crisis* awarded Bontemps its poetry prize for his poem "A Black Man Talks of Reaping."

Bontemps married Alberta Johnson on August 26, 1916, and they became the parents of six children (Joan Maria, Paul Bismarck, Poppy Alberta, Camille Ruby, Constance Rebecca, and Arna). From 1924 to 1931, Bontemps taught at the Harlem Academy in New York City and wrote poetry, essays, short stories, and children's books. He had hoped to go back to school and study for a Ph.D. in English, but the demands of family life prevented this. Instead, Bontemps wrote and became close to other writers of the Harlem Renaissance, most importantly Jean Toomer and Langston Hughes. He published his first book, the novel *God Sends Sunday,* in 1931, and then moved that same year to Huntsville, Alabama, where he had accepted a teaching position at Oakwood Junior College. *You Can't Pet a Possum* was published in 1934, followed by two historical novels—*Black Thunder* (1936) and *Drums at Dusk* (1939)—and a children's book, *Sad-Faced Boy* (1937). In 1938, he went on a study tour in the Caribbean, supported by a Julius Rosenwald Fund Fellowship.

From 1940 on, his books appeared less frequently. Bontemps had returned to school to receive professional training in librarianship at the University of Chicago Graduate School. When he graduated in 1943, he took a job as the librarian at Fisk University in Nashville, Tennessee, a position he held until 1966. Although he produced less after becoming a librarian, one of his finest books was written during this time. *Story of the Negro,* a book for children, was a 1949 Newbery Honor Book; it also received the Jane Addams Children's Book Award in 1956.

Bontemps wrote two plays during his career. *St. Louis Woman,* an adaptation of Bontemps's first novel, *God Sends Sunday,* was written with COUNTEE CULLEN and performed in 1946. *Free and Easy* was performed in 1949. He also edited several books, including *The Harlem Renaissance Remembered*, which he coedited with Langston Hughes, and *Father of the Blues: An Autobiography* by W. C. Handy.

When he retired from Fisk University, Bontemps served for a year as director of university relations and acting librarian before becoming a professor at the University of Illinois at Chicago. He published *Great Slave Narratives* in 1966, and in 1969 he took a position as lecturer and curator of the James Weldon Johnson Collection at Yale University. In 1971, he returned to Fisk University as writer-in-residence.

In addition to the awards already mentioned, he won an Alexander Pushkin Poetry Prize from *Opportunity* magazine in 1926 and 1927; the Opportunity Magazine Short Story Prize in 1932; Rosenwald Fellowships in 1949 and 1954; Guggenheim Fellowships in 1949 and 1954; and the James L. Dow Award for *Anyplace but Here* in 1967. He was awarded honorary doctorates from Morgan State College in 1969 and from Berea College in 1973. Bontemps died suddenly on June 4, 1973, from a stroke and was interred in Greenwood Cemetery in Nashville.

## Further Reading

Canaday, Nicholas. "Arna Bontemps: The Louisiana Heritage." *Callaloo* (February–October 1981): 163–169.

Flamming, Douglas. "A Westerner in Search of 'Negro-Ness': Region and Race in the Writing of Arna Bontemps." *Over the Edge: Remapping the American West,* edited by Valerie J. Matsumoto and Blake Allmendinger. Berkeley: University of California Press, 1999.

Harris, Violet J. "From Little Black Sambo to Popo and Fifina: Arna Bontemps and the Creation of African-American Children's Literature." *The Lion and the Unicorn* (June 1990): 108–127.

Jones, Kirkland C. "Arna Bontemps." From Trudier Harris and Thadious M. Davis, eds. *Dictionary of Literary Biography: Afro-American Writers from the Harlem Renaissance to 1940.* Detroit: Gale Research Company, 1987.

Reagan, Daniel. "Voices of Silence: The Representation of Orality in Arna Bontemps' Black Thunder." *Studies in American Fiction* (spring 1991): 71–83.

# Boyle, T. Coraghessan
## (T. C. Boyle, Thomas John Boyle)
(1948–  ) *novelist, short story writer*

T. Coraghessan Boyle never intended to become a writer. The six-foot-three eccentric with the bright shock of orange hair and the flamboyant apparel began his college career with aspirations of becoming a musician. He quickly abandoned that goal after taking his first creative writing course and subsequently became a critical and popularly successful novelist. Often beginning with historical events, Boyle goes on to weave imaginative tales that blur the boundaries between fact and fantasy. Now the award-winning author of numerous novels and more than 60 short stories, Boyle's quirky and satirical style has earned him the reputation as one of America's most imaginative contemporary novelists.

Thomas Coraghessan Boyle was born on December 2, 1948, in Peekskill, New York. Named Thomas John Boyle at birth, he was 17 when he adopted the name Coraghessan from the Irish side of his mother's family. Boyle spent his childhood in poverty with his two alcoholic parents. Thomas's mother was from a poor New England family that had lacked the money to send her to college. His father, who had only an eighth-grade education, worked as a bus driver to support his son. Both of his parents died from alcohol abuse when he was young.

In 1964, Boyle entered college at the State University of New York at Potsdam, originally as a sax-playing music major with little talent for it. While still studying music, he enrolled in his first creative writing course on a whim. He took to it immediately and graduated in 1968, at the age 21, with a B.A. degree in English and history. Following graduation, he accepted a teaching position at a local high school to avoid serving in Vietnam. For the next four years, he taught English to students not much younger than himself, many of whom were from violent, drug-laden neighborhoods. He himself has admitted that during this time his main interests were "hanging out" and "taking lots of drugs." He began using heroin and remained addicted for more than two years.

After overcoming his heroin addiction, Boyle applied to the University of Iowa Writers' Workshop. Despite his unimpressive undergraduate academic record (he left Potsdam with a 2.0 grade point average), the workshop accepted him based on writing talent alone. It was while studying there that Boyle finished his first collection of short fiction, *Descent of Man*. Boyle also met and married his wife, Karen Kvashay, while in the Writers' Workshop. He left Iowa with a 4.0 grade point average, an M.F.A. degree in fiction, and a Ph.D. in British literature.

Boyle's first novel, *Water Music*, was published in 1980. A mock Victorian novel about a trip up the Niger River, *Water Music* caught the attention of readers and was moderately well received by literary critics. George Kearns of the *Hudson Review* called the book "a historical novel unlike any other, for the language is simultaneously that of its period (circa 1800) and that of streetwise America (circa 1980)."

Within five years of *Water Music*, Boyle published a second novel, *Budding Prospects: A Pastoral* (1984), and a second collection of short stories, *Greasy Lake and Other Stories* (1985). With the publication of his third novel, *World's End*, in 1987, Boyle's fame began to increase. Based in his native Peekskill, this dark and complex novel recounts 300 years in the intertwining lives of three families. *World's End* earned Boyle the Pen/Faulkner Award in 1988.

Boyle went on to publish other novels and more collections of short fiction. *The Road to Wellville*, Boyle's novel about the real-life Dr. John Harvey Kellogg and his Battle Creek sanitarium, was made into a movie starring Anthony Hopkins and Matthew Broderick in 1994. In addition to the Pen/Faulkner Award, Boyle has received numerous other awards, including a Guggenheim Fellowship in 1988, the O. Henry Award in 1988, the *New York Times* Editor's Choice Award in 1989, and the Howard D. Vursell Memorial Award in 1993. He has been a professor of English at the University of Southern California since 1978 but also writes methodically from 9 A.M. to 1 P.M., seven days a week. He lives near Santa Barbara, California, with his wife; their daughter, Kerrie; and their two sons, Milo and Spencer. His 2003 novel, *Drop City*, was a finalist for the National Book Award.

## Further Reading

Adams, Elizabeth. "An Interview with T. Coraghessan Boyle." *Chicago Review* 37, nos. 2–3 (1991): 51–63.

Appell, David. "Earthquakes, Critics and the 600 Nitro: An Interview with T. C. Boyle." *Hayden's Ferry Review* 18 (spring/summer 1996): 38.

Cheng, Terence, and Anthony Spaeth. "Interview with T. Coraghessan Boyle." *Crazyhorse* 51 (winter 1996): 84–96.

"T. Coraghessan Boyle." *Contemporary Literary Criticism.* Detroit: Gale Group, Volume 36, 1986; Volume 59, 1989, pp. 45–47.

# Bradbury, Ray
## (Ray Douglas Bradbury)
(1920–  ) *novelist, short story writer, essayist, playwright, screenwriter, poet, science fiction writer*

One of the world's best-known science fiction writers, Ray Bradbury is generally considered a creative genius. In addition to his many award-winning novels, stories, and plays, Bradbury has worked as an "idea consultant" on such world-class projects as the United States Pavilion at the 1964 New York World's Fair, Disney's *Spaceship Earth* at Disney's EPCOT Center, and the Orbitron ride at the Disney parks in Paris and Anaheim.

Born in Waukegan, Illinois, on August 22, 1920, Ray Bradbury is the third son of Leonard Spaulding Bradbury and Esther Marie Moberg Bradbury. The Bradburys gave their son the middle name "Douglas" after Douglas Fairbanks, who played swashbuckling adventurers in the early decades of film.

Most of Bradbury's early childhood was spent in Waukegan among his extended family. Beginning in 1926, however, the Bradbury family moved back and forth between Waukegan and Tucson, Arizona. In 1931, the young boy began writing stories on butcher paper (the long rolls of paper used by butchers to wrap meat). In 1934, the family moved permanently to Los Angeles, California, where Bradbury attended Los Angeles High School. There he was active in the drama club and had hopes of becoming an actor. During his teenage years, Bradbury liked to roller-skate through

Hollywood, trying to spot celebrities. He befriended radio and television star George Burns, who eventually paid Bradbury for contributing a joke to the *Burns and Allen Show*.

Bradbury received significant support from high school teachers who recognized his writing talent and became more serious about pursuing writing instead of acting. He joined the Los Angeles Science Fiction League and the Poetry Club at school. Although he did not continue his formal education after graduating from high school, he spent lots of evenings in his local library. When he was not delivering newspapers during the day, he worked on short stories. "Hollerbochen's Dilemma" was his first published short story; it appeared in *Imagination!*, an amateur fan magazine, in 1938. The following year, he published four issues of his own fan magazine, *Futuria Fantasia*. And in 1941, his first paid publication, "Pendulum," appeared in *Super Science Stories*. The next year Bradbury wrote "The Lake," the story that launched his distinctive style, and by 1943, Bradbury had given up his newspaper delivery job to work full time as a writer. His short story "The Big Black and White Game" was selected for inclusion in the *Best American Short Stories of 1945*, the same year that Bradbury hit the road, traveling through Mexico on an assignment to collect American Indian masks for the Los Angeles County Museum.

When he returned from Mexico, Bradbury met Marguerite "Maggie" McClure, a graduate of the University of California at Los Angeles. The couple married on September 27, 1947, in the Church of Good Shepherd, Episcopal, in Los Angeles and have been together ever since. Bradbury's *Dark Carnival*, a collection of short stories, was published in 1947 as well. The publication in 1950 of *The Martian Chronicles* firmly established Bradbury's reputation as science fiction writer. His family was settling in, as well, with the birth of Susan, the first of four daughters, in 1949. Bradbury's other daughters, Ramona, Bettina, and Alexandra, were born in 1951, 1955, and 1958 respectively.

In total Bradbury has published more than 50 books. Some of the best-known publications include *Fahrenheit 451* (1953), *Dandelion Wine* (1957), *The October Country, The Wonderful Ice Cream Suit and Other Plays* (1972), and *The Stories of Ray Bradbury* (1980). He has also been involved in numerous film and television projects. His story "The Fog Horn" was adapted for the screen in a film entitled *The Beast from 20,000 Fathoms* (1952). He also worked on the film version of his novel *Something Wicked This Way Comes* (1983), and on John Huston's film version of *Moby Dick* (1956). *Icarus Montgolfier Wright* (1962), Bradbury's animated film about flight, was nominated for an Academy Award.

Known for his skill with fantasy and futuristic landscapes, Bradbury is also praised for his ability to incorporate social and political themes in ways that inspire readers and provide enlightenment along with the entertainment.

Bradbury has been the recipient of dozens of honors and awards. Some of the more notable include the O. Henry Memorial Award, the Benjamin Franklin Award, the Aviation-Space Writer's Association Award for Best Space Article in an American Magazine, the World Fantasy Award for Lifetime Achievement, and the Grand Master Award from the Science Fiction Writers of America. Bradbury was also awarded the National Book Foundation's 2000 Medal for Distinguished Contribution to American Letters. His work was included in the *Best American Short Stories* collections for 1946, 1948, and 1952, and his book *Dandelion Wine* served as the inspiration for the Apollo astronaut who named Dandelion Crater on the Moon.

Bradbury continues to write daily. He and his wife, Maggie, still live in Los Angeles with their four cats. They have eight grandchildren.

**Further Reading**

Johnson, Wayne L. *Ray Bradbury*. New York: Ungar Publishing Company, 1988.

Miller, Walter James. *Ray Bradbury's 'The Martian Chronicles': A Critical Commentary*. New York: Simon & Schuster, 1987.

Mogen, David. *Ray Bradbury*. Boston: Twayne, 1986.

Reid, Robin Anne. *Ray Bradbury: A Critical Companion*. Westport, Conn.: Greenwood Publishing Group, 2000.

Touponce, William F. *Ray Bradbury and the Poetics of Reverie: Fantasy, Science Fiction, and the Reader*. Detroit: University of Michigan Research Press, 1984.

———. *Ray Bradbury*. London: Borgo Press, 1989.

## Bradstreet, Anne
### (Anne Dudley Bradstreet)
(ca. 1612–1672) *poet*

Anne Bradstreet is regarded by many as one of the most important figures in the history of American literature and is frequently referred to as the first American poet. She crossed the Atlantic with her family at the age of 18, leaving behind her comfortable life of English aristocracy for the harsh realities of the new American frontier. A Puritan wife, she broke the social conventions of her time by writing and publishing poetry about the struggles she encountered in her new land. Her first book, though it does not contain her best work, is historically significant as the first book written by a woman to be published in America. Bradstreet's work, which has long been valued mainly for its historical importance and less for its literary merit, gives a rare voice to the hardships encountered by many new settlers living in colonial times. Though her poetry was largely ignored for more than 200 years, it was rediscovered by 20th-century feminists, who have argued its significant artistic value.

Anne Dudley was born in about 1612, in Northampton, England, to Thomas Dudley and Dorothy Yorke. Her mother was a well-educated gentlewoman of noble heritage, and her father was a former soldier in the Elizabethan army who managed the affairs of the Earl of Lincoln. At age 16, Anne married her childhood sweetheart, Simon Bradstreet. Simon, a 25-year-old assistant in the Massachusetts Bay Company, had been in the Dudleys' care since his father, a Puritan minister, had died in 1618. The couple was very much in love, and judging from Anne's later poems, they remained very happy together for the remainder of their relationship.

In 1630, when Anne was 18, Thomas Dudley packed his family aboard the *Arabella,* one of the first ships to bring Puritans to the New World, in hopes of establishing a plantation colony. The journey proved extremely long and difficult, and many of the passengers did not survive the trip. Anne, who had always been plagued by health problems, was ill suited for such a venture and found the journey very taxing. Upon their arrival things did not improve much. Many more of their fellow settlers

died, and others decided to return to England. Thomas, however, was committed to establishing the new settlement and refused to succumb to hardship. He and his friend John Winthrop founded the government for the Boston settlement, with Thomas Dudley as governor and Simon Bradstreet as chief administrator. Their work kept them frequently away from home, a fact that pained Anne immensely, as she would often worry about her husband's safety. She relied on her faith to help her survive these difficult times and passed the days reading in her father's library.

Anne Bradstreet, who had once endured a smallpox infection, was fated to have a lifetime of poor health. Shortly after the trip from England she suffered from a partial paralysis of her joints. Despite her affliction, however, she managed to lead a productive life, and she and Simon had eight children. She educated the children at home, teaching them what she had learned from her father's library books and from her own schooling back in England. She was especially interested in the study of the English language and loved poetry in particular.

Bradstreet began to write poetry herself when her husband was away on his frequent political trips to neighboring colonies. Intending the poems for only her family and close friends, Bradstreet never planned to have them published. It was frowned upon for women at the time to have intellectual pursuits, particularly to make public their own opinions. One of Bradstreet's closest friends, Anne Hutchinson, had been banished from their community for holding prayer meetings at which women discussed their religious and ethical ideas.

Bradstreet's work might never have been published had it not been for her brother-in-law, John Woodbridge. Without her permission, he secretly copied her earlier, more imitative work and took it back with him on a trip to England. In 1650, he had it published under the title *The Tenth Muse Lately Sprung Up in America, By a Gentlewoman of Those Parts.* It was moderately well received and sold fairly well in England. It was, unfortunately, the only book of her poetry that was published in her lifetime, and it certainly does not contain her best work. Her later writings were of a more private and personal nature and were much more original than her earlier works. Her later journals contain poems written about her fear of childbirth, her love for her husband, and her mixed feeling about her religion.

The bulk of Anne Bradstreet's poetry remained unpublished and unnoticed until the 20th century, when it enjoyed a revival by those who consider Bradstreet to be America's first feminist. Among the recent publications of her poetry are collections entitled *To My Husband and Other Poems* and *The Works of Anne Bradstreet*. There is little evidence about her life beyond that given in her poetry, as she left no portrait or grave-marker, and the Bradstreet home is no longer standing. Anne continued to write until she succumbed to illness and died on September 16, 1672, in Andover, Massachusetts, at the age of 60.

**Further Reading**

Dolle, Raymond. *Anne Bradstreet: A Reference Guide.* Boston: G. K. Hall & Co., 1990.

Nicolay, Theresa Freda. *Gender Roles, Literary Authority, and Three American Women Writers: Anne Dudley Bradstreet, Mercy Otis Warren, Margaret Fuller Ossoli.* New York: Peter Lang Publishing, 1995.

Ostriker, Alicia. *Stealing the Language: The Emergence of Women's Poetry in America.* Boston: Beacon, 1986.

Rosenmeier, Rosamond. *Anne Bradstreet Revisited.* Boston: Twayne Publishers, 1981.

# Brautigan, Richard
## (Richard Gary Brautigan)
(1935–1984) *novelist, short story writer, poet*

With origins in the Beat Generation, Richard Brautigan went from unknown Haight-Ashbury poet to best-selling novelist overnight when his novel *Trout Fishing in America* was published in 1967. Known for his easy-to-read yet idiosyncratic prose style and his often self-deprecating narrators, he has often been described as the writer who best expressed the hippie lifestyle embraced during the 1960s and 1970s. The cult following he developed during those decades grew even more devoted following his suicide in 1984.

Richard Gary Brautigan was born in Tacoma, Washington, on January 30, 1935, to Mary Lou Keho, who was 23, and Bernard F. Brautigan, Jr., a laborer who was 27. Mary Lou and Bernard separated before Richard was born, perhaps even before Mary Lou knew she was pregnant. Accounts of Brautigan's childhood are somewhat sketchy, but it is certain that he lived an itinerant and impoverished life. Mary Lou, a waitress, and her son lived above a candy factory in Tacoma, and Mary Lou frequently left him with others while she worked. Richard's half-sister, Barbara, was born on May 1, 1939, during Mary Lou's relationship with Arthur Martin Titland.

In 1943, Mary Lou married Robert Jeffrey Porterfield, and in 1944 the family settled in Eugene, Oregon. Richard's half-sister, Sandra Jean Porterfield, was born on April 1, 1945. Prior to this time, Mary Lou had moved around the Northwest, probably following Porterfield. Brautigan frequently told a story of being left alone in a hotel room in Great Falls, Montana, with one of his stepfathers (probably Porterfield). According to the story, Brautigan, who was seven, ate meals at his stepfather's place but lived alone in the hotel room. His mother worked mostly as a waitress and barmaid. It is believed that Brautigan met his biological father only twice, both times when he was a young boy, and thought his last name was Porterfield until he graduated from high school.

In 1950, Mary Lou divorced Porterfield and married her third husband, William "Papa" Folston, who taught Richard how to fish and hut. By this time the family was fairly settled in Eugene, but the patterns of abuse and neglect appear to have continued throughout Brautigan's childhood. As a teenager, he fished and hunted frequently, bringing home his catch for the family table. He told stories of pushing a baby stroller with Barbara along the roads looking for glass bottles to recycle for money. He always worked at odd jobs—mowing lawns and carrying a paper route. When he was old enough, he went to work in a cannery, a job he held until he graduated from Eugene High School in 1953.

Brautigan's poem "The Light" was published in the school newspaper in 1952, and his coursework during his senior year included a creative writing class. Barbara recalled that during his last years of high school, he often wrote all night in his unheated bedroom. His parents were not supportive of his writing, but there were other adults in his life who may have been. An English teacher, Juliet Gibson, was likely the first one to introduced Brautigan to the poems of EMILY DICKINSON and WILLIAM CARLOS WILLIAMS, both of whom had a significant influence on Brautigan's work. Pete Webster, his best friend during high school, said "He was a good poet even then, and I loved the sound of his voice." Brautigan often spent time at the Webster home, where Pete's mother, Edna, became a mother figure to Brautigan and Pete's sister, Linda, was his first girlfriend.

By the time of his high school graduation, Brautigan was determined to become a writer. He worked for a time in a pickle factory in Eugene, since there was no money for college tuition and he believed that the education would not do much to further his writing anyway. By the mid-1950s, Brautigan had journeyed to San Francisco several times, attempting to set up a residence there but always failing due to lack of money and ending up back in Eugene. In the fall of 1955, Brautigan began to experience some problems that may have been due to the strain of living in poverty and his confusing love for Linda Webster, who was six years his junior. He ended up throwing a rock through the window of the Eugene police station and being jailed for about a week. Following this, he was committed to the Oregon State Hospital, where he remained for three months. While there, he received shock treatments and was diagnosed as a paranoid schizophrenic. His half-sister Barbara said that the family never visited him and that she did not even know he was there until after he had been released.

In any case, Brautigan left home soon after his release from the hospital. This was the last time he ever saw his mother. At this time, his poetry, was beginning to receive recognition. He published numerous single poems during these days and lived mostly in San Francisco. His first collection of poems, *Lay the Marble Tea,* was published in 1959. On June 8, 1957, he married Virginia Dionne Adler in Reno, Nevada. Their daughter, Ianthe, Brautigan's only child, was born on March 25, 1960. He spent the summer of 1961 camping with his family in Idaho's Stanley Basin and writing *Trout Fishing in America* on a portable typewriter beside the river. *A Confederate General from Big Sur* was published in 1964; *Trout Fishing in America* followed

in 1967. In 1966–67, he was poet-in-residence at the California Institute of Technology, and in 1968 he was awarded a grant from the National Endowment for the Arts.

By 1970, Brautigan was at the height of his career. He was reading his work publicly with other well-known writers such as Gary Snyder and Lawrence Ferlinghetti. His stories were appearing in *Rolling Stone* magazine, and his book publications were frequent and well received by both the critical audience, who hailed him as a fresh, new voice, and an increasingly devoted popular audience. In 1970, *Life* magazine published a feature article on the poet, "Gentle Poet of the Young: A Cult Grows around Richard Brautigan." But things began to go downhill for Brautigan before he had much time to relax and enjoy the fame.

Brautigan and his wife, Virginia, had separated in 1962 and pursued separate lives, with Virginia and Ianthe moving to Salt Lake City with Tony Aste, a friend of Brautigan. The separation was made final when the couple divorced in 1970. He began to experiment with different literary styles, none of which appealed to his critics, and he became increasingly troubled by alcoholism, insomnia, and paranoia. In 1973, he made his first trip to Pine Creek, Montana, where he met writers Tom McGuane and JIM HARRISON, among others. In 1973, Brautigan bought a 43-acre ranch in Pine Creek and established a residence there, just a stone's throw from the Pine Creek Lodge and Store, where he had stayed on his first visit and written *The Hawkline Monster.* In addition to the writers he knew, actor Peter Fonda and his wife Becky lived nearby, as did actor Jeff Bridges, film director Sam Peckinpah, and painter Russell Chatham.

During the early 1970s, Brautigan refused to make many public appearances. He traveled to Japan in 1976, where he met Akiko Nishizawa Yoshimura, whom he married the following year. She was with Brautigan during the writing of *June 30th, June 30th,* published in 1978, and *The Tokyo-Montana Express,* published in 1979. The couple divorced in 1980. Brautigan resumed his schedule of poetry readings and other public appearances, traveled around the country, and worked on his final novel, *An Unfortunate Woman: A Journey.* In

1982, *So the Wind Won't Blow It All Away* was published. It sold poorly and was ignored or dismissed by the critics.

The last two years of his life were uneventful in terms of his career. He was last seen alive on September 14, 1984, when he left San Francisco for his home in Bolinas, California. He had by chance run into his former wife Akiko and a former girlfriend, Marcia Clay, while in San Francisco. On his way home, he stopped at a favorite Japanese restaurant and borrowed a handgun from the owner, Jimmy Sakata. He drank heavily that afternoon. That evening, Clay called Brautigan. They hung up when he said he wanted to go find a piece of writing so that he could read it to her. When Clay called back to hear the writing, Brautigan never answered the phone. Over a period of several weeks, the answering machine picked up all calls. Finally, on October 25, Becky Fonda, the wife of Peter Fonda, called a private investigator in San Francisco to check on Brautigan. His badly decomposed body was found in front of the fireplace, with the handgun nearby on the floor. It is believed that he committed suicide while standing up facing the ocean. He was 49 when he died.

## Further Reading

Abbott, Keith. *Downstream from Trout Fishing in America: A Memoir of Richard Brautigan*. Santa Barbara, Calif.: Capra Press, 1989.

Bishoff, Don. "Author's Life Was Shaped in Eugene." *The Register-Guard*, August 25, 1993, pp. 1B, 2B.

The Brautigan Bibliography. Available online. URL: http://www.eaze.net/~jfbarber/brautigan/index.html. Updated August 14, 2002.

Foster, Edward Halsey. *Richard Brautigan*. Boston: Twayne, 1983.

## Brooks, Gwendolyn
## (Gwendolyn Elizabeth Brooks)
(1917–2000) *poet, essayist*

The author of more than 20 books of poems and the Illinois poet laureate for 32 years, Gwendolyn Brooks wrote about inner-city life, informed by her own years living in racially divided Chicago. Her poems are marked by the compassionate way they illustrate black culture and speak to the importance of inclusiveness among people of all races. She once said, "I believe that we should all know each other, we human carriers of so many pleasurable differences. To not know is to doubt, to shrink from, sidestep or destroy." She was the first African-American poet to win the Pulitzer Prize.

Gwendolyn Elizabeth Brooks was born to David Anderson Brooks, the son of a runaway slave, and Keziah Corinne (Wims) Brooks, on June 7, 1917, in Topeka, Kansas. Her parents had been living in Chicago, but Keziah wanted her baby to be born at her mother's home. The Brooks family returned to Chicago when Gwendolyn was one month old and moved into their longtime residence on Champlin Avenue when she was four years old. It was here that the young Brooks grew up. It is reported that by the time she was seven, Gwendolyn had begun to dabble in rhymes. She published her first poem, "Eventide," at age 13 in a popular children's magazine, *American Childhood*.

Brooks attended several high schools in Chicago. She started at Hyde Park High School, a predominantly white school, in 1932, and later attended Wendell Phillips High School, an all-black school, and finally Englewood High School, which was integrated. While in high school, she continued to write poems and met some influential poets. JAMES WELDON JOHNSON suggested that she read some of the modernists who were writing at the time, poets such as T. S. ELIOT and E. E. CUMMINGS.

She also met LANGSTON HUGHES, who encouraged her work as a poet and who offered her more tangible assistance early in her career when he wrote about her several times in his weekly newspaper column in the *Chicago Defender*. When she was 17, she began submitting poems to the *Chicago Defender*'s poetry column, which was called "Lights and Shadows." The *Defender* was an African-American newspaper, and Brooks continued to publish poems there for several years, while she attended Wilson Junior College. After she graduated from Wilson in 1936, Brooks attempted to get a permanent position working for the paper. When it was clear that the paper had no intention of hiring her, Brooks found work as a typist. Her poems appeared in two anthologies in 1937, and in 1939

Brooks married Henry Blakely II, who was also a poet and writer. The couple had a son the following year, Henry Blakely III. A daughter, Nora Brooks Blakely, was born in 1951.

Brooks and her husband enrolled in 1941 in a poetry workshop taught by Inez Cunningham Stark which critics have suggested was a crucial turning point in Brook's writing. She also became involved with the group of writers associated with Harriet Monroe's *Poetry: A Magazine of Verse.* Two years later, she won an award from the Midwestern Writer's Conference. Her first book, *A Street in Bronzeville,* appeared in 1945, and *Mademoiselle* named her one of its "Ten Young Women of the Year." She won a Guggenheim Fellowship the following year as well an Academy of American Arts and Letters award for $1,000. She was just 29 years old. Brooks went on to win the Pulitzer Prize for poetry in 1950 for her second book of poems, *Annie Allen,* making her the first African-American poet to receive this award.

Her career became more public starting in the early 1960s. President John Kennedy invited her to read at a Library of Congress poetry festival in 1962, and in 1963 she began her first teaching job at Columbia College (Chicago). She eventually taught at many different colleges and universities, including Northeastern Illinois University, Elmhurst College, Columbia University, Clay College of New York, and the University of Wisconsin.

In 1967, Brooks became more conscious of her role as a black artist and got involved with the Black Arts movement after attending the Fisk University Black Writers' Conference. Her many unforgettable characters were drawn from black neighborhoods where life was often difficult and resources limited, but they were not victims in Brooks's poems. They were ordinary individuals, living one day at a time, coping as best they could with what life offered up, finding both joy and sadness. Her unique style blended street talk with African-American urban vernacular in such poems as "We Real Cool," which has been frequently anthologized.

In 1985, Brooks was appointed poetry consultant to the Library of Congress, and in 1994, the National Endowment for the Humanities appoint-

ed her as the Jefferson Lecturer, the greatest distinction in the humanities given by the federal government. In her roles as the Illinois poet laureate and as the poetry consultant to the Library of Congress, Brooks was exceptionally active. She saw her position as an opportunity to make poetry more accessible to the general public and was quite involved in teaching workshops and conducting poetry contests for young people, with the hope that she might help inner-city children discover the value of poems.

Brooks was a prolific writer. Some of her best-known works include *A Street in Bronzeville* (1945); *Annie Allen* (1949); *Bronzeville Boys and Girls* (1956); *The Bean Eaters, Poems* (1960); *Jump Bad: A New Chicago Anthology* (1971); *Primer for Blacks* (1980); *Young Poet's Primer* (1981); *Mayor Harold Washington and Chicago, the I Will City* (1983); and *Blacks* (1987). She also wrote collections of poetry for children and published reviews and essays.

The recipient of more than 50 honorary doctorates from universities around the country, Brooks died in her Chicago home on Sunday, December 3, 2000, at age 83, from cancer.

## Further Reading

Kent, George E. *A Life of Gwendolyn Brooks.* Lexington: University Press of Kentucky, 1990.

Kufrin, Joan. "Gwendolyn Brooks." *Uncommon Women.* Piscataway, N.J.: New Century Publishers, 1981, pp. 35–51.

Madhubuti, Haki R. ed. *Say That the River Turns: The Impact of Gwendolyn Brooks.* Chicago: Third World Press, 1987.

Shaw, Harry B. *Gwendolyn Brooks.* Boston: Twayne, 1980.

Wright, Stephen Caldwell. *On Gwendolyn Brooks: Reliant Contemplation.* Ann Arbor: University of Michigan Press, 1996.

## Bruchac, Joseph
### (Joseph E. Bruchac III)
(1942–   ) *poet, novelist, autobiographer, children's fiction writer, editor*

Joseph Bruchac has authored more than 70 books for adults and children. His poems, articles, and stories have appeared in more than 500 publications, including *American Poetry Review, Cricket and Aboriginal Voices, National Geographic, Parabola,* and *Smithsonian Magazine.* He is known as a storyteller whose work, both oral and written, draws extensively on the rich history of his Abenaki ancestry.

Born on October 16, 1942, in Saratoga Springs, New York, to Joseph E. Bruchac II, a taxidermist, and Flora (Bowman) Bruchac, Joseph Bruchac III was raised by his maternal grandparents in Greenfield Center, a village in the foothills of the Adirondack Mountains. As a child, Bruchac has said that he learned to read books from his grandmother, a graduate of Skidmore College, and to read the world from his grandfather, an Abenaki Indian who could barely read or write. As a child he was taught that his ancestors were Scotch-Irish, although many of the elders in his community had the same dark skin as his grandfather. It was not until Bruchac was a grown man that he discovered the truth about his Abenaki heritage.

Bruchac was always a good student, excelling especially in literature and science courses. When he had free time, he liked to wander into the woods by himself and read books for hours at a time, surrounded by the two things he has always loved most—books and nature. After completing his secondary education, Bruchac attended Cornell University, where he studied English. In 1964, while a student, he married Carol Worthen, a kindred soul in the love of literature. Bruchac graduated from Cornell with a B.A. degree in 1965 and immediately entered a graduate program in English at Syracuse University. He received his M.A. degree in 1966.

Bruchac always wanted to be a writer, but the first thing he did after leaving Syracuse University was move to Ghana, West Africa, to teach English and literature at Keta Secondary School. He returned to the United States to teach African and black literatures and creative writing at Skidmore College in Saratoga Springs, New York. He also continued his graduate education at the State University of New York (SUNY) at Albany and eventually earned his Ph.D. at Union Graduate School in 1975.

During his graduate studies at SUNY-Albany, Bruchac established and taught creative writing workshops in prisons throughout the country.

Working with little or no outside financial support, Bruchac offered practical tips about marketing manuscripts, as well as artistic encouragement to many writers serving time. In 1975, he was awarded a National Endowment for the Arts grant for his efforts in serving the prison population. With this funding, Bruchac was able to expand his program of workshops and launch a newsletter, *Prison Project Newsletter,* which served a network of thousands of prison writers and instructors across the country.

Bruchac's success with the prison workshops was only the beginning of his career as a publisher. In 1970, he founded Greenfield Review Press. The *Greenfield Review* literary magazine was the press's first effort to establish itself in the world of literary publishing. It showcased poetry and fiction from a variety of cultures and featured interviews with important Native American writers. Bruchac and his wife, Carol, published the magazine for 17 years. Meanwhile, Greenfield Review Press developed an impressive list of multicultural books.

Although he has done much to foster the careers of other writers as a publisher and teacher, Bruchac is best known for his own writing and storytelling. His first book of poems, *Indian Mountain and Other Poems,* appeared in 1971, with subsequent collections following almost every year. It was not until 1992 that he began to write short fiction, a genre with which he has found much success.

*Turtle Meat and Other Stories,* a book for young adults, was his first book of fiction. Bruchac's bestselling series of children's books, coauthored by Michael J. Caduto, an internationally known author and ecologist, have been his most successful efforts to share his Abenaki heritage with the general public. The Keepers series—*Keepers of the Earth* (1998) and *Keepers of the Animals* (1991)— has more than 500,000 books and tapes in print. It received the 1990 Art and Literary Award from the New York State Outdoor Education Association and an Association of Children's Booksellers 1992 Choice Award.

Other notable books by Bruchac include *The First Strawberries; Tell Me a Tale; When the Chenoo Howls* (co-authored with his son James); his autobiography, *Bowman's Store* and such novels as *Dawn Land, The Waters Between, Arrow Over the Door,* and *The Heart of a Chief.* He has edited numerous anthologies of contemporary poetry and fiction, including *Songs from This Earth on Turtle's Back, Breaking Silence,* which won an American Book Award, and *Returning the Gift.*

Bruchac is also revered as a storyteller, drawing on the traditional tales of the Adirondack region and of the Native people of the northeastern woodlands. His work as a storyteller has taken him all over the country and to Europe. He has been a featured performer at such prestigious events as the British Storytelling Festival and the National Storytelling Festival in Jonesboro, Tennessee. He also conducts storytelling programs in schools throughout the United States.

Bruchac's many awards include a Rockefeller Humanities fellowship, a National Endowment for the Arts Writing Fellowship for Poetry, the Cherokee Nation Prose Award, the Knickerbocker Award, the Hope S. Dean Award for Notable Achievement in Children's Literature, and both the 1998 Writer of the Year Award and the 1998 Storyteller of the Year Award from the Wordcraft Circle of Native Writers and Storytellers. In 1999, he received the Lifetime Achievement Award from the Native Writers Circle of the Americas. Joseph Bruchac and his wife still live in Bruchac's childhood home. They have two sons, both of whom work as writers and storytellers.

## Further Reading

Bodin, Madeline. "Keeping Tradition Alive," *Publishers Weekly* (December 14, 1993): 23.

Champagne, Duane, ed. *Native North American Almanac.* Detroit: Gale Research, 1994, pp. 1021–1022.

Grossmann, Mary Ann. "American Indian Author Stresses Authenticity," *St. Paul Pioneer Press-Dispatch,* October 22, 1989, p. D3.

## Bryant, William Cullen
(1794–1878) *poet, editor, journalist*

Considered a child prodigy, William Cullen Bryant published his first poem at age 10 and his first book at age 13. Influenced by the poems of William Wordsworth, Bryant found his subject in the New England landscape of his birth and eventually rose to international fame, writing poems based on the American landscape. Despite this recognition for his writing, Bryant never devoted himself completely to writing. He worked as a lawyer and justice of the peace, then later pursued a very successful career in magazine publishing, serving as an editor at the *New York Review* and *Atheneum* magazine and later as editor-in-chief at the *Evening Post.* His editorials for this newspaper helped to make it one of the most highly respected papers in the country.

William Cullen Bryant was born on November 3, 1794, at Cummington, Hampshire County, Massachusetts, to Peter Bryant, a physician, and Sarah (Snell) Bryant. Both sides of the family traced their ancestors to the *Mayflower.* Bryant's father was a literary man who had traveled extensively and who exposed his family to a rich cultural life, but the general atmosphere was one of strict order and discipline, as was customary in the 19th century.

As a young student, Bryant studied both Latin and Greek. His father's library was full of classics, which the young poet devoured. The frequent classical allusions in his poems testify his intense interest in these works. His father was quite influential in Bryant's education and career. He encouraged him to study law, but also critiqued his poems and assisted him in his efforts to publish.

When Bryant was 16, he entered Williams College in Williamstown, Massachusetts, where he studied for two years before withdrawing in 1812 to study law. He was admitted to the bar in 1815 and practiced with distinction at Plainfield and later at Great Barrington, but his heart was always with literature.

In 1818, while practicing as a lawyer, Bryant published "Thanatopsis," which became his most famous poem. "Thanatopsis" was composed when Bryant was just 17 and is a meditation on death (as the title indicates) as well as a meditation on nature. It recalls Wordsworth's *Lyrical Ballads* and anticipates the transcendentalists. When the poem was sent to the *North American Review,* Richard H. Dana, the editor, was so surprised at its excellence that he doubted that it had actually been written by an American. Bryant went on to publish several prose pieces with the review and to write a number of his most significant poems during this period, including "Green River," "The West

Wind," "Blessed Are They That Mourn," and "The Hymn to Death," which was written while his father was dying at age 54.

In 1820, Bryant married Frances Fairchild and published his first collection of poems. He was recognized as a writer of significance by this point in his career, but he continued to work as a lawyer and write poems in his spare time until 1825, when he left the law profession to work as an editor and write. He was appointed assistant editor of the *New York Review* and *Atheneum* magazine. When the review failed, Bryant moved on to the *Evening Post,* where he worked until his death. Bryant's international reputation as a poet was established with the 1932 publication of his collected poems, which was released in England (with a preface by WASHING-TON IRVING) and in the United States at about the same time.

Bryant took up traveling during the next few decades, leaving first in 1834 for a trip through France, Italy, and Germany. He returned to Europe in 1845 and again in 1849, when he expanded his itinerary to include Egypt and Syria. During these years, he also traveled throughout the United States and Cuba. He wrote many letters during his trips, and these were collected in *Letters of a Traveler* (1850). He subsequently published *Letters from Spain and Other Countries* and a new edition of his poems was printed in 1855. *Thirty Poems,* a collection of new work, was published in 1863, and his translations of the *Iliad* and the *Odyssey* came out in 1870 and 1871 respectively. These blank verse translations were considered the best English versions of these epic tales in print at that time. Bryant had begun working with Sydney Howard Gay on a history of the United States, but it was incomplete when he died.

Due to his wide popular appeal, Bryant often wrote public appreciations of other well-known Americans. He pronounced the funeral oration for artist and personal friend Thomas Cole in 1848. He was a significant influence on the Hudson Valley school of art, of which Thomas Cole was a member. He also delivered lectures on the life and work of JAMES FENIMORE COOPER in 1852 and on Washington Irving in 1860, spoke on the life of S. F. B. Morse in 1871, and on Shakespeare's work in 1872. He died in New York on June 12, 1878.

William Cullen Bryant's first book of poems was published when he was just 13 years old. *(Library of Congress, Prints and Photographs Division, [LC-USZ62-5526])*

**Further Reading**

Branch, Michael P. "William Cullen Bryant: The Nature Poet as Environmental Journalist." *The American-Transcendental-Quarterly (AQT),* Index 12, no. 3 (September 1998): 179.

Brown, Charles H. *William Cullen Bryant.* New York: Scribner, 1971.

McLean, Albert F. *William Cullen Bryant.* 2d ed. New York: Twayne, 1989.

## Buck, Pearl S.
### (Pearl Comfort Sydenstricker, John Sedges)
(1892–1973) *novelist, short story writer, memoirist, poet, translator, biographer*

The first American woman to win the Nobel Prize in literature, Pearl S. Buck is known for her novels and stories set in China, where she lived the first half of her life. She published more than 70 books in numerous genres and was active in American civil rights and women's rights activities after moving permanently to the United States in 1934.

Pearl Comfort Sydenstricker was born on June 26, 1892, in Hillsboro, West Virginia, to Absalom and Caroline Sydenstricker, who were southern Presbyterian missionaries temporarily on leave from their work abroad. When Pearl was just three months old, the family returned to China, where Pearl lived most of her first 40 years. Of her six siblings, all but two died before reaching adulthood.

Pearl's family lived in Chinkiang, in Kiangsu Province, a small city located where the Yangtze River met the Grand Canal. Her father traveled away from home for months at a time, searching for Christian converts, while her mother ran a clinic serving Chinese women. Pearl grew up speaking both Chinese and English and was educated by her mother and a Chinese tutor, Mr. Kung. She attended college in the United States, graduating from Randolph Macon Women's College in Lynchburg, Virginia, in 1914. She returned immediately to China and lived there permanently, with the exception of one year spent at New York's Cornell University, where she earned an M.A. degree in 1924.

In 1917, Pearl married John Lossing Buck, an agricultural economist and Cornell graduate. The couple moved to Nanhsuchou in Anhwei Province, an impoverished and extremely rural region that provided Pearl with the inspiration and material she later used in writing *The Good Earth* and other books.

In 1920, the Bucks moved to Nanking, where they both held teaching positions at Nanking University. Their daughter, Carol, was born in 1921. She suffered profound retardation as a result of phenylketonuria (PKU), a genetic disorder that prevents the normal use of protein food. In addition, a uterine tumor was discovered during the birth and Buck underwent a hysterectomy shortly thereafter. In 1925, the Bucks adopted a baby girl, Janice, but their marriage was reportedly an unhappy one.

In March 1927, the Bucks lived through the Nanking Incident, a period in which the Japanese military captured the city of Nanking and proceed-ed to kill and rape large numbers of Chinese citizens. After hiding for a day, in fear for their lives, the Bucks were rescued by U.S. gunboats and taken to Shanghai. They later moved to Unzen, Japan, but returned to Nanking a year later, though conditions remained quite unstable. During this period of instability, Buck began to publish her work. Her stories and essays appeared in such publications as *The Nation, The Chinese Recorder, Asia,* and *Atlantic Monthly.* Her first novel, *East Wind, West Wind,* was published in 1930 by the John Day Company. John Day's publisher, Richard Walsh, became Buck's second husband in 1935, after her divorce from her first husband.

In 1931, John Day published *The Good Earth,* Buck's second novel and the one that would bring her international fame. Set in rural China, the book is often praised for its unstereotypical portrayal of Chinese people and its positive influence on Westerners' perceptions of China. *The Good Earth* was the best-selling book of both 1931 and 1932, won the Pulitzer Prize and the Howells Medal in 1935, and was adapted as a major MGM Studios film in 1937. Following this success, Buck published numerous other novels and works of nonfiction. *Sons* (1932) and *A House Divided* (1935) followed *The Good Earth* to form a trilogy about the Wang family. In 1938, she won the Nobel Prize in literature, the first American woman to do so.

Her life changed dramatically in the midst of all this success when she chose to return to the United States to live. She wished to be closer to Richard Walsh and her daughter, Carol, who was living in an institution in New Jersey. Buck purchased Green Hills Farm in Bucks County, Pennsylvania, and went on to adopt six more children with her second husband. She also became quite active in civil rights and women's rights work. She published essays in *The Crisis,* the journal of the National Association for the Advancement of Colored People (NAACP), and *Opportunity,* the magazine of the Urban League. She served as a trustee of Howard University, and she and Richard Walsh founded the East and West Association in 1942, devoted to fostering cultural exchange and understanding between Asia and the West. In addition, she set up the first international, interracial adoption agency, Welcome House, and later

Pearl Buck was the first American woman to win the Nobel Prize in literature. *(Photo by Arnold Genthe. Library of Congress, Prints and Photographs Division [LC-USZ62-10297])*

established the Pearl S. Buck Foundation to provide sponsorship funding for the adoption of thousands of children across Asia.

Other notable works by Buck include *The First Wife and Other Stories* (1933); *All Men Are Brothers* (1933), a translation of the Chinese novel *Shui Hu Chuan; The Mother* (1934); and *This Proud Heart* (1938). She wrote biographies of both her mother and her father, *The Exile* and *Fighting Angel*, which were published in 1936 and later brought out together under the title of *The Spirit and the Flesh* (1944). *The Time Is Now*, a fictionalized account of the Bucks' emotional experiences, appeared in 1967, although it had been written many years earlier.

Pearl S. Buck died in March 1973, two months before her 81st birthday. She is buried at Green Hills Farm.

**Further Reading**

Liao, Kang. *Pearl S. Buck: A Cultural Bridge across the Pacific*. Westport, Conn.: Greenwood Press, 1997.

Lipscomb, Elizabeth, and Frances E. Webb, eds. *The Several Worlds of Pearl S. Buck: Essays Presented at a Centennial Symposium, Randolph Macon Women's College, March 26–28, 1982*. Westport, Conn.: Greenwood Press, 1994.

Shaffer, Robert. "Pearl S. Buck and the Politics of Food." *Proteus: A Journal of Ideas* 17, no. 1 (spring 2000) 9–14.

## Bukowski, Charles
(1920–1994) *poet, novelist, short story writer, memoirist, screenwriter*

Although Charles Bukowski was never actually associated with the bona fide beatniks of his time, such as ALLEN GINSBERG and JACK KEROUAC, he is generally considered a Beat writer, albeit underground and less prolific. He is most recognized for his poetry, and his writing style is distinctly informal and raw. Bukowski has referred to poetic "form" as "a paycheck for learning to turn the same screw that has held things together." Bukowski's favorite subjects concern life among the dirty, down-and-out souls of American society. His writing is marked by gritty descriptions and details. Many of his themes appear to be taken from his own life experiences and can be identified primarily through frequent main character and alter ego Henry Chinaski, considered to be Bukowski's autobiographical personality. Chinaski is a tough, hard-drinking womanizer who lives with the bums and criminals, while occasionally visiting high society. Introduced in the autobiographical *Confessions of a Man Insane Enough to Live with the Beats* (1965), Chinaski's adventures were further chronicled in the novels *Post Office* (1971), in which he survives the tyranny of paid labor; *Factotum* (1975); *Women* (1978); and *Ham on Rye* (1982).

Charles Bukowski was born on August 16, 1920, in Andernach, Germany. His mother was German and his father was an American soldier stationed in Germany. His family moved to the United States when Charles was just three years old. He spent most of his early years in Los

Angeles and was educated through his second year at Los Angeles City College, which he left in 1941. He published his first short story, "Aftermath of the Lengthy Rejection Slip," in 1944 at the age of 24 and began writing poetry when he was 35. During this time, Bukowski held various jobs to support his writing, including stints as a dishwasher, truck driver, mail carrier, guard, gas station attendant, stock boy, warehouse worker, parking lot attendant, Red Cross orderly, and elevator operator. As the story goes, after publishing his first short story, Bukowski gave up writing for a life among the destitute transients, drunks, and whores of the Los Angeles underworld, all of whom were primary themes in his writing. Although Bukowski dabbled in short stories, novels, and screenplays, he is predominantly known for his poetry. However, he has said that he does not consider himself a poet, but simply a writer. "To say I'm a poet puts me in the company of versifiers, neonasters, fools, clods, and scoundrels masquerading as wise men," he has said. Because Bukowski's early work was published in obscure literary journals, it is difficult to track and much of it is impossible to locate. Some of his most notable collections of poetry and stories include *The Roominghouse Madrigals: Early Selected Poems 1946–1966* (1989), *Betting on the Muse: Poems & Stories* (1996), and *Septuagenarian Stew* (2000).

Although Bukowski has denied it, his bibliography indicates that he continued to publish somewhat consistently throughout the next four decades following his initial publications. This was an era in which Bukowski roamed from odd job to odd roominghouse from the West Coast to the East Coast. His longest stint as an employee was that of a postal clerk and carrier for the U.S. Postal Service, from roughly 1960 to 1970. As depicted in the novel *Post Office*, this was a time of obeying orders and drinking to make it through the day. During this period, Bukowski is known to have confided in close friend John Martin of Black Sparrow Press, "If I don't get out of here, I'm going to die." After receiving a stipend through Martin, Bukowski finally abandoned the post office and dedicated himself entirely to writing. According to his own myth making, he returned to writing the very day

he quit the post office, and proceeded to produce *Post Office* in just three weeks.

In 1975, *Factotum* was published. This novel was a picaresque describing Bukowski (as Chinaski) during his drifting, drunken days, bouncing from job to job. Then came the movie *Barfly*, which was made in 1987 as an adaptation of both *Factotum* and Bukowski's life in general. With the screenplay written by Bukowski, the film was produced by Francis Ford Coppola and featured actors Mickey Rourke and Faye Dunaway. *Barfly* had the effect of making Bukowski a household name. Of the movie, Bukowski noted, "*Barfly* is not a great film, but it kicks along. I've seen it two or three times, and it always makes me thirsty." He published *Hollywood* in 1989 to describe his screenwriting experience. Some of his other books have been made into feature films as well—*Tales of Ordinary Madness*, for example, was based on a similarly titled Bukowski book published in 1973. Since 1985, Bukowski had been married to Linda Lee Beighle, a health food store proprietor 25 years his junior. They had met in 1976. Their relationship contributed to a more balanced period in his life. Toward the end of his days, Bukowski lived in a house with a swimming pool, drove a black BMW, and wrote on a computer. Bukowski died of leukemia on March 9, 1994, in Los Angeles.

### Further Reading

Cherkovski, Neeli. *Hank: The Life of Charles Bukowski.* New York: Random House, 1991.

Christy, Jim. *The Buk Book: Musings on Charles Bukowski.* Toronto: ECW Press, 1997.

Dorbin, Sanford. *A Bibliography of Charles Bukowski.* Los Angeles: Black Sparrow Press, 1969.

Sherman, Jory. *Bukowski: Friendship, Fame, and Bestial Myth.* Augusta, Ga.: Blue Horse Publications, 1981.

## Burroughs, Edgar Rice
(1875–1950) *novelist, adventure fiction writer, historical fantasy writer*

Edgar Rice Burroughs was best known as the creator of the famous character of Tarzan. He wrote nearly 70 books and was one of the most commercially successful writers of the adventure-romance story in 20th-century America. Sales of his books, which also included science fiction and crime novels, total more than 100 million copies. Burroughs was a formula writer who took the attributes of the epic tradition—violence, quest, and romance—and popularized them in fantastic stories written to entertain a reading public. He incorporated hideous creatures into his stories, which were set in locations strange or exotic to Americans, such as the jungles of Africa, or even Mars or a place beneath the Earth's crust. He painted fanciful landscapes and populated them with an entirely imaginary species of beings as background for his stories, which usually involved a hero faced with a multitude of challenges.

Edgar Rice Burroughs was born on September 1, 1875, in Chicago, Illinois, into a prosperous family. His father, George Tyler Burroughs, was a Civil War veteran. Burroughs attended several private schools, including the Michigan Military Academy. He served in the Seventh Cavalry in the Arizona Territory and in the Illinois Reserve Militia. In 1900, he married Emma Centennia Hulbert and they eventually had two sons and a daughter.

The family lived near poverty for a decade as Burroughs struggled to succeed in various occupations, including those of an office manager, a salesman, and a railroad policeman. It was not until age 35 that Burroughs tried his success at writing and submitted a science fiction story to *The All-Story Magazine*. The story was published in serial form in 1912 as "Under the Moons of Mars" and introduced popular invincible hero John Carter, who is transported to Mars following a battle with Apaches in Arizona. Burroughs followed this with his novel *Tarzan of the Apes* (1917). He eventually wrote two dozen more Tarzan books.

The protagonist in the Tarzan books is John Clayton, Lord Greystoke, whose aristocratic parents die after they are abandoned on the west coast of Africa by mutinous sailors. Tarzan is raised by an ape and becomes a leader of the hairy tribe because of his intelligence and fighting skills. In the jungle, Tarzan learns to read when he finds a book from the remnants of his parents' hut. Another party of whites is marooned in the area and Tarzan falls in love with Jane Porter, becomes a hero, and finds his aristocratic roots. Eventually Jane becomes Tarzan's

wife and they have a son. In several Tarzan books, the invincible hero is involved with lost races, hidden cultures, or even with an entire lost continent, but he never shows any inclination of taking more than his share of fortunes during his adventures.

Burroughs purchased a large ranch in California's San Fernando Valley in 1919 and later developed it into the suburb of Tarzana. He wrote an average of three novels a year. The first Tarzan film titled simply *Tarzan*, was produced in 1918. The films became wildly popular in the 1930s after Olympic swimming champion Johnny Weissmuller took the role as Tarzan.

In addition to the Tarzan series, Burroughs wrote other major adventure series: the Martian series, the Carson of Venus books, the Pellucidar tales, and the Land That Time Forgot trilogy. Burroughs's science fiction novels are full of a sense of adventure, taking the reader on a fantastic voyage to strange and unfamiliar lands, much as Homer did in his *Odyssey*. In the Martian series, John Carter, the major hero, eventually wins the hand of Princess Thoris. The Pellucidar series began with *At the Earth's Core* (1922), in which a group of scientists use their drilling machine to tunnel down into the hollow space at the center of the planet. *The Land That Time Forgot* (1924) was a Darwinist story set on a mysterious island near the South Pole, where dinosaurs and other primitive species have survived.

Burroughs's first marriage ended in divorce in 1934. He married Florence Dearholt in 1935 and they divorced in 1942. During World War II, the 66-year-old Burroughs served as a war correspondent in the South Pacific. Although he was a popular and commercially successful writer, he failed to win critical acclaim. He often said that he wrote merely and expressly to entertain and provide an escape to the problems of daily life. Burroughs died of a heart ailment on March 19, 1950.

## Further Reading

Holtsmark, Erling B. *Edgar Rice Burroughs*. Boston: Twayne Publishers, 1986.
———. *Tarzan and Tradition: Classical Myth in Popular Literature*. Westport, Conn.: Greenwood Press, 1981.
Lupoff, Richard. *Edgar Rice Burroughs: Master of Adventure*. New York: Canaveral Press, 1964.

## Burroughs, John
(1837–1921) *essayist, biographer, poet, nature writer*

Sometimes called the father of American nature writing, John Burroughs published more than 30 books and established the nature essay as a genre. An associate of naturalists, writers, and other luminaries such as Jay Gould, RALPH WALDO EMERSON, John Muir, WALT WHITMAN, and Theodore Roosevelt, Burroughs was a likeable man whose ideas about simple living and the importance of nature had broad appeal and made him an extremely popular writer during his day.

John Burroughs was born on April 3, 1837, in the Catskill Mountains, near the town of Roxbury, New York. His boyhood on his parents' farm exposed him to the natural world from an early age and became the environment that he would love and write about throughout his life.

Although he hated to write as a boy, by the time he was 20 years old, he was determined to write books, but it would take some time before his work would be published. After a short stint of teaching, Burroughs moved to Washington, D.C., with his wife, Ursula North, where he took a job as a clerk at the Treasury Department. He spent nine years living in Washington and honing his craft. He published articles in *The Bloomville Mirror, Saturday Press,* and the *New York Leader,* and his first book, *Notes on Walt Whitman as Poet and Person,* the first ever biography of Walt Whitman, appeared in 1867.

Four years after the biography appeared, *Wake-Robin* was published, and for the first time readers were given the writer's skillful essays on the natural world. It was the beginning of what would become a grand opus of nature writing, encompassing 23 collections of essays. Following the success of *Wake-Robin,* Burroughs returned to New York and settled on the west bank of the Hudson River, at West Park. He named his farm and home "Riverby" and built a rustic cabin called "Slabsides" on the property with his son in 1895. He lived there the rest of his life, keeping the orchards and writing books.

In 1911, Burroughs restored an old farmhouse on the family farm in the Catskills. He named the place "Woodchuck Lodge" and found much inspiration in the familiar environs of his childhood.

Father of the nature essay as a genre, John Burroughs also wrote the first biography of Walt Whitman, *Notes on Walt Whitman as Poet and Person* (1867). *(Library of Congress, Prints and Photographs Division [LC-USZ62-130730])*

The home became Burroughs's summer residence until his death. Burroughs wrote many books during his productive years in New York State. These include *Winter Sunshine* (1876), *Fresh Fields* (1885), *Signs and Seasons* (1886), *Riverby* (1894), *Whitman: A Study* (1896), *Literary Values and Other Papers* (1902), *Far and Near* (1904), and *Accepting the Universe* (1920). Many different editions of his collected essays exist, including a collection of all 23 books of essays, but the best known is probably the *Riverby Edition* (1904).

John Burroughs died on March 29, 1921, while returning from a winter trip to California. He was buried on his birthday, April 3, in a field on the family farm in Roxbury, as he had requested. His grave is a New York State Historic Site. Shortly after his death, the John Burroughs Association was established to foster the love of nature and to preserve the places associated with Burroughs's life. The foundation awards a medal each year to the author of a distinguished book of natural history. His name also lives on in the 11 schools that were named for him during his lifetime.

## Further Reading

Barrus, Clara. *The Life and Letters of John Burroughs.* Boston: Houghton Mifflin, 1925.

Kanze, Edward. *The World of John Burroughs.* New York: Harry N. Abrams, 1993.

Kelley, Elizabeth Burroughs. *John Burroughs, Naturalist: The Story of His Work and Family by His Granddaughters.* New York: Exposition Press, 1959.

Wadsworth, Ginger. *John Burroughs: The Sage of Slabsides.* New York: Clarion Books, 1997.

Westbrook, Perry. *John Burroughs.* New York: Twayne, 1974.

## Burroughs, William S.
### (William Seward Burroughs)
(1914–1997)  *novelist, short story writer, playwright, essayist*

The controversial Beat Generation writer William S. Burroughs may be best remembered for his experimental novel *Naked Lunch* (1960). Along with younger and slightly less reckless Beat writers like ALLEN GINSBERG and JACK KEROUAC (who were preoccupied with writing careers at a time when Burroughs still had not begun to write; he did not do so until his late 30s), Burroughs embodied his generation's experimentation with sex, drugs, and the written word. His frankness in describing personal experiences with drug addiction and homosexuality won him a following among writers of the Beat movement. Burroughs also became known for his "cut-up" writing technique, in which he composed novels from snippets and various texts. In addition to his other well-known books, such as *The Soft Machine* (1961), *The Yage Letters* (1963), and *The Wild Boys* (1971), Burroughs also wrote plays, film scripts, and essays. His infamously unconventional and—to some—offensive work has been banned throughout history. In the early 1990s

there was even a magazine devoted exclusively to disgust with what the editors viewed as Burroughs's gender-based offenses. Still, however, Burroughs remains a strong presence in all realms of contemporary artistic expression. He was inducted into the American Academy and Institute of Arts and Letters in 1983.

William Seward Burroughs was born on February 5, 1914, to a successful business family in St. Louis, Missouri. His grandfather was the inventor of the Burroughs adding machine and his mother was a direct descendent of Gen. Robert E. Lee. Burroughs's upper-class midwestern background did not suit his tastes. He was inclined instead toward breaking rules and experimenting with an entirely reckless lifestyle. After Burroughs graduated from Harvard, his parents continued to support him financially as he made his way through an array of locations and lifestyles.

In his early 30s, Burroughs traveled to New York to join the gangster world and to explore the city's infamous underground societies. There he became a heroin addict deliberately, and befriended Allen Ginsberg, Jack Kerouac, Lucien Carr, and his future common-law wife Joan Vollmer Adams. On August 13, 1944, Lucien Carr killed another one of Burroughs's friends, David Kammerer, in self-defense. Kerouac and Burroughs were arrested as material witnesses and later collaborated on a novel based on these events called *And the Hippos Were Boiled in Their Tanks,* which was never published. During this time, Kerouac introduced Adams to Benzedrine inhalers, which soon led to her addiction and to her and Burroughs's relocations to Texas, New Orleans, and Mexico City, all of which were areas were drugs were more easily obtainable. On July 21, 1947, Joan gave birth to a son, William Burroughs III, called Billy.

Then came the tragedy that would change Burroughs's life. On Thursday, September 6, 1951, while trying to show off his marksmanship to a couple of friends at a party, Burroughs announced that he was going to do his Wilhelm Tell act. Joan put a highball glass on her head, and missing his target, Burroughs killed her with a single shot. Following Joan's death, Burroughs's young son Billy was sent back to the United States to be cared for by his grandparents in Florida. In the meantime,

Burroughs continued to wander the globe, certain that he was locked in a lifelong battle with the "invader" that had possessed him at the time of Joan's death. Burroughs believed that his only option was to write his way out of life. Of this event he has said, "I'm forced to the appalling conclusion that I would never have become a writer but for Joan's death." He settled for a while in Tangiers, Morocco, where he continued to record his experiences with an even deeper addiction to heroin. During a visit in 1956 from Kerouac, Ginsberg, and Peter Orlovsky, Kerouac helped Burroughs organize the "routines" that would later become the novel *The Naked Lunch.*

In 1958 Burroughs relocated to Paris to stay with Ginsberg where he met Maurice Girodias of Olympia Press, who agreed to publish *Naked Lunch* in 1960. Burroughs then continued to write prolifically and live nomadically throughout the 1960s. He returned to New York in 1974, where he made the acquaintance of James Grauerholz, who become his life manager and helped him to organize and publish his writings. Burroughs's son Billy, sick with loneliness and drug addictions, died in a ditch on March 3, 1981.

Burroughs resettled in Lawrence, Kansas, where he became a writer in residence at the University of Kansas and devoted his spare time to a vegetable garden. During his last years, Burroughs was known to have an affinity for cats, handguns, and rifles. He died on August 2, 1997, of a heart attack, at age 83.

## Further Reading

Miles, Barry. *William Burroughs.* New York: Hyperion, 1993.

Morgan, Ted. *Literary Outlaw: The Life and Times of William S. Burroughs.* New York: Henry Holt, 1988.

Mottram, Eric. *William Burroughs: The Algebra of Need.* London: Marion Boyars, 1978.

Vernon, J. *The Garden and the Map.* Chicago: University of Illinois Press, 1973.

# C

## Caldwell, Erskine
(1903–1987) *novelist, short story writer*

Erskine Caldwell, known as the "master of rural ribaldry," was a prolific southern writer whose themes centered on poverty, class, ignorance, racism, and the tenant farming system. Caldwell was one of the most widely read authors of the 20th century; 80 million of his books were sold to readers in 43 different languages. He wrote 25 novels, 150 short stories, and 12 nonfiction books. Caldwell's most famous novels were *Tobacco Road* (1932) and *God's Little Acre* (1933). His stories combined social realism with sex and violence, making him one of the most censored writers of his time.

Erskine Caldwell was born on December 17, 1903, in White Oak, Georgia, the son of a Presbyterian minister who moved the family nearly every six months. It was during these years that Caldwell became well acquainted with the lives of the impoverished sharecroppers he often encountered. At age 18 he went on a gun-running boat to South America. Caldwell briefly attended Erskine College in South Carolina and the universities of Virginia and Pennsylvania. He held a variety of jobs, including working as a mill hand and cotton picker. He also worked briefly as a reporter on the *Atlanta Journal*. In the 1920s Caldwell moved to Maine to devote himself to writing. The story "Country Full of Swedes" was published in the *Yale Review* and won Caldwell a $1,000 award in 1933.

During his five years in Maine, Caldwell wrote *Tobacco Road* and *God's Little Acre*. The novels were criticized as obscene and were banned from many libraries. But Caldwell was also seen as a sociologist who painted a realistic picture of rural poverty. *Tobacco Road* was about a family of white sharecroppers driven to desperation by the oppression of a changing economic system. In 1998, the Modern Library named it one of the 100 best novels of the 20th century. *God's Little Acre* was censored by the Georgia Literary Commission and was banned in Boston. When the New York Society for the Prevention of Vice tried to ban *God's Little Acre*, Caldwell took the case to court. With testimony from H. L. MENCKEN and SHERWOOD ANDERSON, he won his case and it became a landmark in First Amendment litigation. The *Saturday Review of Literature* called the book "one of the finest studies of the southern poor white which has ever come into our literature."

In 1936, Caldwell met the photographer Margaret Bourke-White, with whom he traveled for the next six years. They collaborated on four books and produced a documentary account of poverty in the American South. A similar book combining photographs and text appeared just before the outbreak of World War II depicting Czechoslovakia. During World War II, Caldwell worked as a newspaper correspondent in the Soviet Union, witnessing the German invasion in 1941.

Caldwell worked as a scriptwriter in Hollywood for several years and was editor of *American Folkways*, a series of regional books. He was elected to the American Academy of Arts and Letters in 1984. WILLIAM FAULKNER thought

Caldwell was one of America's five greatest novelists, and as late as 1960, Caldwell was under consideration for the Nobel Prize. As one of the first authors to be published in mass-market paperback editions, he is a key figure in the history of American publishing. Sales of his books in Signet and Gold Medal editions established NAL (New American Library) as one of the dominant paperback houses in the world. Caldwell continued publishing novels into the 1970s, but they were often considered semipornographic. Caldwell was married four times; his first three marriages ended in divorce. He died of inoperable cancer in Paradise Valley, California, on April 11, 1987.

### Further Reading

Devlin, James E. *Erskine Caldwell.* Boston: Twayne, 1984.
Klevar, Harvey L. *Erskine Caldwell: A Biography.* Knoxville: University of Tennessee Press, 1993.
Miller, Dan B. *Erskine Caldwell: The Journey from Tobacco Road.* New York: Knopf, 1995.

## Capote, Truman
### (Truman Streckfus Persons)
(1924–1984) *novelist, nonfiction writer, screenwriter, journalist, playwright, poet*

Truman Capote was a Southern Gothic novelist, short story writer, playwright, journalist, and celebrated man-about-town. His early works include his novel of alienated youth, *Other Voices, Other Rooms* (1948); the gothic short story collection, *A Tree of Night* (1949); and the lighter novel *The Grass Harp* (1951). The novella *Breakfast at Tiffany's* (1958) introduced the charming, self-indulgent Holly Golightly as a heroine. Childhood reflections formed the basis for two short stories that were adapted for television: "A Christmas Memory" (1956) and "The Thanksgiving Visitor" (1968). Capote's "nonfiction novel" *In Cold Blood* (1966) was based on a six-year study of the murder of a rural Kansas family by two young drifters. Although the number of Capote's works is not extensive, the painstaking impeccability and patience with which he wrote are elements that solidly distinguish him as one of the greatest writers of the 20th century.

Truman Streckfus Persons was born on September 30, 1924, in New Orleans, Louisiana, the son of a salesman and a 16-year-old beauty queen. His father worked as a clerk for a steamboat company for a period of time but was unable to hold onto this and other jobs for very long. As a result, his father frequently left home in search of new opportunities. His parents' unhappy marriage gradually disintegrated and the two divorced when he was just four. The boy then moved to Monroeville, Alabama, where he was raised by his cousins and elderly aunts (one of whom became the model for the loving, elderly spinster in several of his novels, stories, and plays). As a child he lived a rather lonely existence and turned to writing for solace. Of his early days, Capote related, "I began writing really sort of seriously when I was about eleven. I say seriously in the sense that like other kids go home and practice the violin or the piano or whatever, I used to go home from school every day and I would write for about three hours. I was obsessed by it."

When his mother married again, this time to well-to-do businessman Joseph Garcia Capote, Truman moved to New York and adopted his stepfather's surname. While in New York, he attended the Trinity School and St. John's Academy, as well as the public schools of Greenwich, Connecticut. Then, at the age of 17, due to difficulty adjusting to his new life in the city, Capote dropped out of high school and began work as an office boy at the *New Yorker* until he was fired for angering ROBERT FROST at one of his readings. In 1945, Capote's stories began to appear in magazines, and were immediately well received by readers. Among his first books was *Other Voices, Other Rooms* (1948), a novel about an adolescent boy in a run-down southern mansion. The protagonist falls into a relationship with a decadent transvestite. *Other Voices, Other Rooms* gained wide public success, partly due to the controversy it created as a result of its treatment of homosexuality.

In 1949, Capote went to Europe, where he wrote both fiction and nonfiction. Among his major works was a profile of Marlon Brando that was published in the *New Yorker.* Capote's travels accompanying a tour of *Porgy and Bess* in the Soviet Union produced *The Muses Are Heard,* which subtly mocked the whole presentation of the play. His European years also marked the beginning of his work with theater and films. In 1949 *A Tree of Night* appeared, a compilation of short stories that had been published in *Harper's Bazaar*, *Mademoiselle*, and other magazines. In the 1950s, Capote wrote *The House of Flowers*, a musical set in a West Indies bordello. His lighter novel *The Grass Harp* (1951), the story of a young man and his cousin who rebel against the conventions and materialism of society, was adapted into a television movie in 1996, starring Piper Laurie, Sissy Spacek, and Walter Matthau. Capote's first important film work, though, was a collaboration with John Huston on *Beat the Devil* (1954).

Capote's literary success led to increasing social recognition. He was praised by high society and seen regularly at the best parties, clubs, and restaurants. His short novel, *Breakfast at Tiffany's* (1958), was heavily inspired by these experiences, and with the publication of the novel and the subsequent hit film (not written by Capote) starring Audrey Hepburn, his reputation among society's elite was assured. He soon developed a different ambition, though—to revolutionize the field of journalism. In 1959, Capote set about creating a new literary genre that he dubbed the nonfiction novel. *In Cold Blood* (1966), the book that most consider his masterpiece, is the story of the 1959 murder of the four members of a Kansas farming family, the Clutters. Capote stationed himself in Holcomb, Kansas, to delve into the small-town life and record the process by which the town coped with its loss. During his stay, the two murderers were caught, and Capote began an involved interview with both. For six years, he became enmeshed in the lives of both the killers and the townspeople, taking thousands of pages of notes. Of *In Cold Blood*, Capote said, "This book was an important event for me. While writing it, I realized I just might have found a solution to what had always been my greatest creative quandary. I wanted to produce a journalistic novel, something on a large scale that would have the credibility of fact, the immediacy of film, the depth and freedom of prose, and the precision of poetry." *In Cold Blood* sold out instantly and became one of the most talked-about books of its time.

After the publication of *In Cold Blood*, Capote planned to write a novel called *Answered Prayers*, but problems with drink and drugs, and disputes with other writers, such as Gore Vidal, exhausted Capote's creative energies, and he never completed the work. Capote died in Los Angeles, California, on August 26, 1984, of liver disease complicated by phlebitis and multiple drug intoxications. His other works include *The Dogs Bark: Public People and Private Places* (1973) and *Answered Prayers*, his unfinished novel, which was published posthumously in 1987.

**Further Reading**

Brinnin, J. M. *Sextet: T. S. Eliot and Truman Capote and Others*. New York: Delacorte Press, 1981.

Bryer, Jackson R., and Irving Malin, eds. *Truman Capote's "In Cold Blood": A Critical Handbook*. Belmont, Calif.: Wadsworth, 1968.

Clarke, Gerald. *Truman Capote: A Biography*. New York: Simon and Schuster, 1988.

Moates, Marianne M., and Jennings Faulk Carter. *Truman Capote's Southern Years*. Birmingham: University of Alabama Press, 1996.

Nance, William L. *The Worlds of Truman Capote*. New York: Stein and Day, 1970.

## Carver, Raymond
### (Raymond Carver, Jr.)
(1938–1988)  *short story writer, poet*

Frequently set in the Pacific Northwest of his birth and peopled by working-class characters, Raymond Carver's stories are known for their realist style. He was a significant force in the revitalization of the short story, and his work is often placed in the same tradition as that of STEPHEN CRANE and ERNEST HEMINGWAY. Carver's early death from cancer, just a decade after his recovery from alcoholism, cut short a career of outstanding literary achievement and left his readers mourning the loss of the stories Carver never had the chance to write.

Raymond Carver, Jr., was born on May 25, 1938, in Clatskanie, Oregon. His father, Clevie Raymond Carver, was a sawmill worker and a violent alcoholic. Carver's mother, Ella Beatrice Casey, sometimes worked as a waitress or retail clerk. The

Carver family moved to Yakima, Washington, shortly after Raymond's birth, and he attended school there until he graduated from high school in 1956. In 1957, the same year that Carver's father suffered a physical breakdown, the 19-year-old Carver married his high school sweetheart, 16-year-old Maryann Burk, who was pregnant. Their daughter, Christine LaRae, was born on December 2, 1957. That same year, Carver had also enrolled part time in a community college and worked at various low-paying jobs—as a janitor, a gas station attendant, and a deliveryman for a pharmacy. The couple had a second child, Vance Lindsay, by the time Maryann was 18. Following the birth of his son, Carver began taking creative writing classes at school, and it was in these classes that he found the inspiration to be a writer. He eventually transferred to Humboldt State College, where he graduated with a B.A. degree in 1963. It was during his time at Humboldt that Carver's work was first published.

From Humboldt, Carver moved to Iowa City, Iowa, to study at the Iowa Writers' Workshop. He received his M.F.A. degree in creative writing in 1966. In 1967, the Carvers filed for bankruptcy. That same year, Carver's father died. It was during these years of struggling to make ends meet, to write, and to raise children that Carver started to drink heavily. His work was gaining more recognition, but his personal life was beginning to spin out of control. In 1967, his story "Will You Please Be Quiet, Please?" was chosen for inclusion in *Best American Short Stories,* edited by Martha Foley. In 1968, his collection *Near Klamath* was published, and in 1970 *Winter Insomnia* was published.

In 1971, when Carver was 33, he was appointed a visiting lecturer in creative writing at the University of California at Santa Cruz. He held several other teaching positions during the early 1970s but was sometimes unable to fulfill his teaching responsibilities as a result of alcoholism. During these years, he was hospitalized four separate times for acute alcoholism. In 1973, he and JOHN CHEEVER were both visiting teachers in the Iowa Writers' Workshop. Carver's collection of short stories *Put Yourself in My Shoes* came out in 1974. It was followed two years later by *Will You Please Be Quiet, Please?,* the book that firmly established Carver's reputation as a writer of great significance. It was nominated for a National Book Award. By the mid-1970s, however, the Carvers' marriage was in a shambles and they had filed for a second bankruptcy.

The turning point came on June 2, 1977, when Carver stopped drinking with the help of Alcoholics Anonymous. His first marriage ended in 1977, although the couple did not legally divorce until 1980. Carver began to live with his longtime companion, poet Tess Gallagher, whom he had met years earlier at a writers' conference in Dallas. The couple moved around the country, taking teaching positions in different universities and working on poems and stories. Carver wrote and published much of his work during this productive period. Some of the works that appeared during these years are *Cathedral* (1983), which was nominated for the Pulitzer Prize; *Where Water Comes Together with Other Water* (1985); and *Where I'm Calling From* (1989).

Although he was probably best known for his stories, Carver's poems—narratives written in the vernacular tradition of WILLIAM CARLOS WILLIAMS— were quite accomplished as well. His last two collections of poetry, *Where Water Comes Together with Other Water* (1985) and *Ultramarine* (1986), won the 1985 Levinson Prize. His numerous other awards included a National Endowment for the Arts award in fiction (1980) and a Guggenheim fellowship (1979–80). In 1983, he was a recipient of the "Mildred and Harold Strauss Livings," an award conferred by a special panel of the American Academy and Institute of Arts and Letters. *Short Cuts,* a film by Robert Altman released in 1993, uses material from Carver's short stories in a postmodern indictment of contemporary life.

During their last years together, Carver and Gallagher traveled the globe, visiting South America, Ireland, Germany, England, Scotland, and Italy. It was shortly after returning from these travels that Carver's lung cancer was diagnosed, when he began to suffer pulmonary hemorrhages. Doctors removed two-thirds of his left lung at this time, and later he underwent radiation treatment when the cancer reappeared. The radiation was ultimately unsuccessful. Carver and Gallagher married in Reno, Nevada, on June 17, 1988; returned to Port Angeles, Washington; and bought a new house. Their final trip was to Alaska to fish. Carver died at home on August 2, 1988.

### Further Reading

Gentry, Marshall B., and William Stull, eds. *Conversations with Raymond Carver.* Jackson: University Press of Mississippi, 1990.

Hallett, Cynthia W. *Minimalism and the Short Story: Raymond Carver, Amy Hempel, and Mary Robison.* Lewiston, N.Y.: Edwin Mellen Press, 1999.

Halpert, Sam, ed. *. . . When We Talk about Raymond Carver.* Layton, Utah: Gibbs Smith, 1991.

Horn, Nicholas. "Seeing Double: The Two Lives of Raymond Carver." *A–B: Auto-Biography Studies* 13, no. 2 (fall 1998): 271–97.

Runyon, Randolph. *Reading Raymond Carver.* Syracuse, N.Y.: Syracuse University Press, 1992.

Stull, William L., and Maureen P. Carroll. *Remembering Ray: A Composite Biography of Raymond Carver.* Santa Barbara, Calif.: Capra, 1993.

## Cather, Willa
### (Wilella Sibert Cather)
(1873–1947)  *novelist, short story writer*

Willa Cather, best known for her depiction of pioneer life, brought American regions to life through her loving portrayals of individuals within local cultures. Drawing from her childhood in Nebraska, Cather brought to national consciousness the beauty and vastness of the western plains, a region she described as the "happiness and curse" of her life. She was able to evoke a strong sense of place for other regions as well, including the Southwest, Virginia, France, and Quebec. Devoted to values such as the importance of family and the need for human courage and dignity, she created strong female characters whose sort of strength and determination had previously been attributed only to men. Her novels express her deep love of the land and her distaste for the materialism and conformity of modern life. Of her 12 novels, *My Ántonia* (1918) and *Death Comes for the Archbishop* (1927) are considered among the finest. She won a Pulitzer Prize for *One of Ours* (1922), about a soldier during World War I.

Wilella Sibert Cather (she later answered to "Willa") was born on December 7, 1873, in Back Creek, Virginia, to James and Mary Virginia Cather. Ten years later she and her family moved to Catherton, Nebraska. In 1885 the family resettled in Red Cloud. Cather was captivated by the landscape of her new home, as well as the customs and languages of the diverse immigrant population of Webster County. She spent a great deal of time with the older immigrant women, visiting them and listening to their stories. Cather moved to Lincoln in 1890 to continue her education at the University of Nebraska, initially planning to pursue her childhood dream of becoming a physician. But her aspirations changed after a professor submitted an essay she wrote on the British writer Thomas Carlyle to the Lincoln newspaper for publication. Cather later recalled that seeing her name in print had a "hypnotic effect" on her and she decided to become a writer. She became managing editor of the school newspaper, the author of short stories, and a theater critic and columnist for the *Nebraska State Journal* as well as for the Lincoln *Courier*. She produced four columns per week while attending school full time. Cather's classmates remembered her as one of the most colorful personalities on campus: intelligent, outspoken, talented, and masculine in dress.

One year after graduation, in 1896, Cather accepted a job as managing editor for the *Home Monthly,* a women's magazine published in Pittsburgh. At the same time, she wrote theater reviews for the Pittsburgh *Leader* and the *Nebraska State Journal.* Cather met a fellow theater lover, Isabelle McClung, who became her closest friend. She encouraged Cather's creativity. Cather took a break from journalism between 1901 and 1906 to teach English in local high schools. During this time, she published *April Twilights* (1903), a book of verse, and *The Troll Garden* (1905), a collection of short stories. Her short stories caught the eye of S. S. McClure, editor of the famous muckraking journal *McClure's Magazine.* He arranged for the publication of *The Troll Garden* and then invited Cather to join his magazine staff. Cather enjoyed the prestige of editing the most widely circulated general monthly in the nation, but she remained unfulfilled. Her friend and mentor SARAH ORNE

JEWETT encouraged her to leave the hectic pace of the magazine to develop her craft. Just shy of her 38th birthday, Cather embarked on a full-time writing career in fiction.

Cather's first novel, *Alexander's Bridge* (1912), appeared serially in *McClure's* as *Alexander's Masquerade*. Later she dismissed the work as imitative of EDITH WHARTON and HENRY JAMES. The following year Cather took Jewett's advice and wrote about the land and people she knew best. She published *O Pioneers!*, the story that celebrates the immigrant farmers and their determination to cultivate the prairie. Reviewers were enthusiastic about the novel, recognizing a new voice in American letters. In her next book, *The Song of the Lark* (1915), Cather wrote about a young Swedish immigrant and her quest to develop her artistic talent. Her next achievement, *My Ántonia*, became her best-loved novel and received critical praise. Cather recognized it as the best work she had ever written. She placed her childhood friend Annie Pavelka at the center of the story, renaming her Ántonia. The story is told through the eyes of Jim, a young boy, but his experiences are taken from Cather's. When he leaves Nebraska, he leaves behind Ántonia, who was his Bohemian neighbor and playmate. She comes to represent the West as well as Jim's memories of his lost youth. Cather believed that the artist's material must come from impressions formed before adolescence.

Cather's next novel, *One of Ours* (1922), was a departure from her previous work. It was a World War I story based on the life of her cousin G. P. Cather. Although many critics panned it, it won the Pulitzer Prize. She received scores of letters from former soldiers who thanked her for capturing how they felt during the war. Cather published *My Mortal Enemy* (1926) before producing what critics hailed as an American classic, *Death Comes for the Archbishop*. In this novel, Cather depicted the beauty and the history of the southwestern United States while drawing from the life of Archbishop Lamy, a French Roman Catholic missionary to New Mexico in the 1850s. Cather's character, Bishop Latour, ministers to the Mexican, Navajo, Hopi, and American people of his diocese. The novel explores the spirituality of nature as compared to the trivia of modern life.

Willa Cather is often associated with the midwestern plains, the setting of many of her novels. *(Library of Congress, Prints and Photographs Division, Carl Van Vechten Collection [LC-USZ62-42538])*

The pace of Cather's writing slowed during the 1930s as World War II loomed and she struggled with problems with her right hand. Her last completed novel, *Sapphira and the Slave Girl* (1940), drew on her family history in Virginia. Cather's faithful portrayal of immigrant cultures has attracted readers outside the United States, and her work has been translated into several languages, including Japanese, German, Russian, French, Czech, Polish, and Swedish.

Cather fiercely guarded her personal life. She tried to destroy all of her letters before her death, but thousands that did escape destruction were protected from reproduction or quotation by Cather's will. The poet WALLACE STEVENS once said of her: "We have nothing better than she is. She takes so much pain to conceal her sophistication that it is easy to miss her quality." Cather's sexual orientation has been a matter of debate. She lived with her companion Edith Lewis, who was also from Nebraska, for 40 years until her death.

In addition to the Pulitzer Prize, Cather received the Howells Medal, the French Prix Femina Américain, and the gold medal for fiction from the National Institute of Arts and Letters in 1944, an honor that marked a decade of achievement. She received honorary degrees from Yale, Princeton, and Berkeley, in addition to the ones she had already received from the universities of Nebraska and Michigan. Cather was the first woman voted into the Nebraska Hall of Fame. She was also inducted into the Hall of Great Westerners and the National Women's Hall of Fame. She died of a brain hemorrhage in 1947 in New York City.

## Further Reading

Ambrose, Jamie. *Willa Cather: Writing at the Frontier.* New York: St. Martin's Press, 1988.

Gerber, Philip L. *Willa Cather.* Boston: Twayne Publishers, 1995.

Wagenknecht, Edward. *Willa Cather.* New York: Continuum, 1994.

Woodress, James L. *Willa Cather: A Literary Life.* Lincoln: University of Nebraska Press, 1987.

## Chandler, Raymond
### (Raymond Thornton Chandler)
(1888–1959) *novelist, short story writer, screenwriter, detective mystery writer*

An American writer of hard-edged detective novels, Raymond Chandler set the style for mainstream American detective fiction. His series hero, Philip Marlowe, is tough, loyal, and incorruptible in his dealings with people from the seedy side of American life and politics. Chandler wrote such original screenplays as *The Blue Dahlia* (1946) and cowrote *Double Indemnity* (1944) and *Strangers on a Train* (1951). Six of his novels were successfully adapted to film, including *The Big Sleep* (1939; film, 1946) with Humphrey Bogart as Marlowe; *Farewell, My Lovely* (1940; films, 1944 and 1975); and *The Long Goodbye* (1953; film, 1973), which won the 1954 Edgar Allan Poe Award.

Raymond Thornton Chandler was born on July 23, 1888, in Chicago, Illinois. His father, an alcoholic, was known to desert the family for extended absences, which ultimately resulted in the divorce of Chandler's parents. Following the divorce, young Raymond moved with his mother, Florence, to England. There they lived with Florence's mother and sister. The young Chandler was the beneficiary of a classical British education. He attended Dulwich College Preparatory School in London and studied international law in France and Germany. He worked as a substitute teacher at Dulwich College and published poems and essays in the *Academy, The Chamber's Journal,* and *Westminstern Gazette.* Before returning to the United States in 1912, Chandler had already published poetry and his first story, "The Rose-Leaf Romance."

In America, Chandler had a somewhat erratic employment history, which was partially due to his problems with alcohol, an addiction that he would struggle with for the rest of his life. Chandler's work included stints as a ranch hand, as a sporting goods representative, and as a bookkeeper in a creamery. During World War I, he served in the Canadian army (1917–18) and was later transferred to the Royal Air Force (1918–19). Chandler considered his experience in the Canadian army—the trench warfare and being a 20-year-old sergeant leading his platoon into direct machine-gun fire—to be a turning point in his development and the end of his innocence. Of this time, Chandler said, "Nothing is ever the same again." In 1924, he married Pearl Cecily "Cissy" Hurlburt, 18 years his senior, who had already been married and divorced twice.

After the war Chandler worked in a bank in San Francisco, wrote for the *Daily Express,* then became a bookkeeper and auditor for Dabney Oil Syndicate from 1922 to 1932. During the Great Depression, Chandler's drinking problem worsened. He often engaged in extended episodes of heavy drinking and erratic behavior, which eventually resulted in his 1932 termination for drunkenness and absenteeism. This event proved to be an awakening for Chandler and, as a result, he replaced his drinking habit with writing. At the age of 45, with the support of his wife, Chandler devoted himself entirely to his writing and prepared himself for his first submission by carefully studying other pulp fiction writers. "Pulps" were cheaply produced magazines full of mystery, romance, and adventure fiction. Chandler spent five months writing his first story, "Blackmailers Don't Shoot," which appeared in December 1933 in *Black Mask,* the foremost among magazines publishing in the "hard-boiled" school. He would go on to publish 10 more stories in *Black Mask* between 1934 and 1937. His rate of production, however, was not high enough to sustain a decent standard of living. Pulp writers were paid by the word, and not well paid at that. Chandler, ever the perfectionist, was unable to generate stories at the rate of his colleagues.

In addition to publishing his work in *Black Mask,* Chandler also published seven stories in *Dime Detective,* and one in *Detective Fiction Weekly* between 1934 and 1939. His fourth published story, "Killer in the Rain," was expanded upon in *The Big Sleep* (1939), Chandler's first novel. The story introduced Philip Marlowe, who would be the series hero throughout Chandler's subsequent novels. Marlowe is about 40, tall, with gray eyes and a hard jaw. He is a first-rate detective and a terrible businessman. He is regularly betrayed and swindled by lying clients, women, and even his friends. However, he is clever and tends to make up for his gullibility with a constant flow of wisecracks.

In 1954, Cissy, Chandler's wife of 30 years, passed away after a lengthy illness. Chandler plunged more deeply than ever into drink. His episodic bouts of drinking adversely affected his health, resulting in multiple extended hospitalizations, and damaged his professional and personal relationships. However, toward the end of his life, Chandler still managed to produce some of the English language's greatest crime fiction. In 1958, on a suggestion from British espionage author Ian Fleming, he traveled to Capri to interview deported Italian-American mafioso "Lucky" Luciano for the *London Sunday Times.* This interview was never published, however, for legal reasons. During the last year of his life Chandler was president of the Mystery Writers of America.

Chandler was hospitalized in 1959 for pneumonia. His system was weakened by heavy alcohol abuse, and he passed away at Scripps Clinic on March 26, 1959.

**Further Reading**

Bruccoli, Matthew J. *Raymond Chandler: A Descriptive Bibliography.* Pittsburgh: University of Pittsburgh Press, 1979.

Gardiner, Dorothy, et al., eds. *Raymond Chandler Speaking.* Los Angeles: University of California Press, 1997.

MacShane, Frank. *The Life of Raymond Chandler.* New York: Dutton, 1976.

Van Dover, J. K., ed. *The Critical Response to Raymond Chandler.* Westport, Conn.: Greenwood Press, 1995.

Ward, Elizabeth, and Alain Silver. *Raymond Chandler's Los Angeles.* Woodstock, N.Y.: Overlook Press, 1997.

## Chávez, Denise

(1948–   ) *novelist, short story writer, poet, playwright*

Born and raised in Las Cruces, New Mexico, Denise Chávez still lives in the same house where she grew up and writes in the room where she was born. Her work is drawn directly from her life experience on the Mexican-American border, and she is known for the bilingualism of her work and for her insightful explorations of her Chicana characters.

Chávez was born in Las Cruces on August 15, 1948, to Epifanio and Delfina Chávez. Her father was mostly absent during her childhood, so Chávez was raised in an all-female household with her mother, a schoolteacher, and her two sisters, as well as the Mexican women who worked in the house, cooking, cleaning, and helping to take care of the Chávez girls. In addition to the bilingual nature of her home, with Mexican women speaking Spanish and Chávez's family speaking mostly English, Chávez was exposed to the art of storytelling on a daily basis and has called herself a "performance writer" since oral storytelling has had such a huge influence on her writing.

When asked by an interviewer if her work is autobiographical, Chávez responded

There is a part of me that writes family stories, and stories of my background, but I write fiction, also. I feel that is the way it should be with writers. We should have many voices. With me, it all turns around family, culture, tradition, mercy, etc.

People ask if that isn't autobiography. I say that is the dreaded question for all writers. I think that we take what we have from our lives, and if you are an artist or a writer, art takes a leap and becomes something universal. It becomes the story of the world, bigger than me, Denise Chávez, bigger than Las Cruces, bigger than the world.

Chávez discovered theater while a student at Madonna High School in Mesilla, New Mexico. She took a drama class there and was awarded a drama scholarship to New Mexico State University, where she studied with Mark Medoff, author of the play *Children of a Lesser God*.

After she received her undergraduate degree in drama in 1974, she went on to study at Trinity University in San Antonio, Texas, where she received an M.F.A. degree in drama. Chávez then took a job working for the Dallas Theater Center, while she continued to study drama and writing. In 1984, she graduated from the University of New Mexico with another M.F.A. degree, this time in creative writing.

Chávez began writing and publishing plays in the early 1970s. Some of her better known works include *The Flying Tortilla Man* (1975), a play that has frequently been anthologized for young adult readers. Her first book of fiction did not appear until 1986, when *The Last of the Menu Girls*, a collection of stories, was published as a novel. This collection's title story has also been anthologized in *The Norton Anthology of American Literature* (1989) and was the recipient of the Puerto del Sol Fiction Award. Since its publication, she has written and published *The Woman Who Knew the Language of Animals* (1992), *Face of an Angel* (1994) and *Loving Pedro Infante* (2000). *Face of an Angel* won the 1995 American Book Award, the Premio Axtlan Award, given to an outstanding novel written by a Chicano/Chicana writer, and the 1995 Mesilla Valley Author of the Year Award. In addition, Chávez received the 1995 Governor's Award in Literature.

Although Chávez keeps busy with her writing she works as a professor of creative writing at New Mexico State University in Las Cruces and is involved in a number of community activities, including directing the Border Book Festival in Las Cruces. Chávez also performs her one-woman play, *Women in the State of Grace,* for audiences across the country and lectures and teaches a variety of workshops, including International Body Language, Multiethnic Drama, The Art of the Monologue, Work as Metaphor, The Essence of Latina/Latino Writers, Performance Writing, and The *Cuenista:* The Storyteller.

### Further Reading

Anderson, Douglas. "Displaced Abjection and States of Grace: Denise Chávez's *The Last of the Menu Girls.*" *American Women Short Story Writers.* New York: Garland, 1995, pp. 235–250.

Clark, William. "Denise Chávez: It's All One Language Here." *Publishers Weekly* 241, no. 33 (1994): 77.

Drabanski, Emily. "Sound and Spirit of Life in a New Mexico Town." *Los Angeles Times,* November 1994, E6.

Eysturoy, Annie O. "Denise Chávez." *This Is About Vision: Interviews with Southwestern Writers.* Albuquerque: University of New Mexico Press, 1990: 48.

## Cheever, John
(1912–1982) *novelist, short story writer*

John Cheever's short stories and novels explore the moral void of suburbia and the myth of the American dream as experienced by wealthy suburbanites. Cheever, who relied on deft use of parody and satire to weave stories of tangential happiness juxtaposing soul-wrenching despair, won numerous awards, including the National Medal for Literature. A collection of his short stories, *The Stories of John Cheever* (1978), won the Pulitzer Prize and the National Book Critics Circle Award. His first novel, *The Wapshot Chronicle* (1957), was a critical success and won the National Book Award, heralding a successful writing career that would span some 30 years.

John Cheever was born May 27, 1912, in Quincy, Massachusetts. The Cheevers were, for a time, a wealthy family. His father owned a successful shoe factory while his mother stayed home to raise him and his older brother, Fred. They lived in a grand clapboard house on Winthrop Avenue. In 1926, Cheever's father sold the shoe factory and placed his earnings in stocks, then watched helplessly as their value shrunk to nothing with the stock market crash of 1929.

Years of stifled anger between Cheever's parents followed their financial loss. Monetary strife would be a source of tension that endured for years. His mother opened a gift shop to make ends meet, but Cheever's father, a proud Yankee, could not reconcile himself to his wife's successful venture while his had so miserably failed. Eventually, Cheever's father began drinking alcohol and sank into depression. The years of his parents' silent anger left a mark on the young Cheever that would affect his future writing.

In 1927, Cheever attended the Thayer Academy, but had to leave due to his father's money troubles. Aided by his mother's gift shop income, he returned to Thayer in 1929, only to be expelled for smoking in 1930. His experience at Thayer became the basis of his first published story, "Expelled," which he sold to *The New Republic* at age 18.

Cheever moved to New York City in fall 1930. During that time, his parents lost their house to foreclosure and moved from house to house of friends and family for three years, before settling down in Quincy. In an alternative telling of why he left Thayer Academy, Cheever would say it was his parents' financial crisis that caused his departure. In any case, he left school and moved to New York City to pursue his writing career.

Profitable work in New York City was not easy to come by for the young Cheever. Though he managed to sell stories to *Harper's Bazaar, Collier's,* and *Story,* and worked for Metro-Goldwyn-Mayer (MGM) writing synopses at five dollars a book, he could not afford to live on his own without help from his brother, Fred, who sent 10 dollars a week to the boardinghouse where Cheever lived.

Poverty strengthened Cheever. He took pride in his struggles as a young writer in New York. Poverty may have forced him into lowly living conditions at first, but through his writing he managed to establish a network of well-connected literary friends who offered him the creature comforts he could not have otherwise afforded.

In 1930, eager to sell his stories, Cheever met with a young editor at *The New Republic,* Malcolm Cowley. Cowley bought "Expelled" and struck up a friendship with Cheever. Cowley took Cheever under his wing; he was older and more worldly and offered inspiration and editorial advice to the young writer. Through Cowley, Cheever was invited to literary parties in New York and was able to meet other writers and editors. He became friends with E. E. CUMMINGS, JAMES AGEE, and James T. Farrell. In 1935, Cheever published his first short story in the *New Yorker,* marking the beginning of a prolific relationship. Over the years, Cheever would publish 120 stories in the *New Yorker.* Cowley encouraged Cheever to experience the world and expand his artistic vision. In 1931, Cheever and his brother took a walking tour of Germany and Great Britain. Years later, with his family, Cheever would move to Italy for a year.

Cowley also introduced Cheever to Elizabeth Ames, the director of a writers' colony in Saratoga Springs, New York, called Yaddo. Yaddo was comprised of a lovely stone mansion, outbuildings, grand fountains, formal gardens, and woods. Yaddo's owner, the late Katrina Trask Peabody, had established an endowment for the use of Yaddo by talented writers, artists, and composers wishing to find a quiet place to create. In 1934, Cheever made his first of many trips to Yaddo to work on his short stories, as well as his novels. His fond affiliation with Yaddo would last his entire life. He went on to mentor young writers there, including PHILIP ROTH.

In 1938, Cheever met a young graduate of Sarah Lawrence College as both were heading toward the office of Maxim Leiber, a literary agent. Her name was Mary Winternitz. They married in March 1941 and had three children. Cheever's marriage seemed to take on the unhealthy characteristics of his parents' marriage, with silent anger and brooding commonplace over the years.

Cheever entered the army in 1942. He was stationed at Camp Gordon, in Augusta, Georgia. He found the military life to be dull and monotonous, always waiting, it seemed, for orders. Because of his writing skills, he was not sent overseas. Instead, he became a member of the Signal Corps. He met and befriended other writers in the military, including Irwin Shaw. Being a member of the Signal Corps allowed Cheever to live at home with his wife and children and report each day to the army.

In 1943, Cheever published his first book, *The Way Some People Live,* a collection of stories about his experiences as an army recruit and also about the suburban landscape of postwar New York. Cheever disliked his early work and called the stories, "embarrassingly immature." Critics, too, disliked them, saying they were "sometimes obtuse, almost always clumsy."

After the war, Cheever worked as a teacher and wrote television scripts for CBS. In 1951, he received a Guggenheim Fellowship, which allowed him to concentrate full time on his writing. Another collection of stories, *The Enormous Radio and Other Stories,* was published in 1953. Most of these stories had appeared in the *New Yorker.*

By 1951, the Cheevers had two children, Susan (born in 1943) and Ben (born in 1948). Cramped in an Upper East Side apartment, they wished to move. By chance, one of Cheever's friends, a staff writer at the *New Yorker,* described a rental property that he and his wife would soon leave. Located in Scarborough, New York, the rental was part of the imposing Beechwood Estate, owned by the prosperous Vanderlip family. Cheever and his family moved into the little white house on the estate, which once was a workshop. While there, he worked on an autobiographical novel, *The Wapshot Chronicle,* which was published in 1957 to rave reviews. The book won the National Book Award in 1958, but not without harsh feelings from the Vanderlip family, who felt betrayed by the writer as they saw many of the details within the book based upon their lives.

Alcohol was a constant presence in Cheever's life. In 1969, when his novel *Bullet Park* was published, critics who read it declared his writing career over, and Cheever turned to alcohol for solace. He hid bottles in the hedge outside his home and behind books on shelves, and kept a bottle inside his desk.

In the 1970s, Cheever taught a semester at the University of Iowa Writers Workshop. Though he enjoyed attending football games and walking through museums, he did not enjoy the work. In 1974, in need of money, Cheever accepted a job as a visiting professor at Boston University. While in Boston, he sank into a deep depression and began drinking heavily. Writer and friend John Irving once called on Cheever at the campus rooming house where he lived. A drunken Cheever greeted Irving at the door, unabashedly naked. Cheever's brother Fred picked Cheever up and drove him back to New York. He entered the Smithers Rehabilitation Center in New York City and stayed for one month. His experiences about rehabilitation inspired his novel *Falconer. Falconer* also touched upon homosexual love, an issue over which Cheever had struggled throughout his life. Published in 1977, *Falconer* brought Cheever back from the brink of obscurity. He was a success with his picture on a *Newsweek* cover and a number-one-selling book. Cheever had been shown a new direction in life. He embraced the ideals of Alcoholics Anonymous and never took another drink.

In 1978, an editor at Knopf suggested publishing a selection of Cheever's stories written from 1947 through 1978. Cheever was unsure of the venture; it seemed to rely on past triumphs. Eventually, he acquiesced to his editor and *The Stories of John Cheever* was published in 1978 to rave reviews. The book sold very well and became a Book-of-the-Month Club selection. In 1979, it won the Pulitzer Prize and the National Book Critics Circle Award.

During the last years of his life, Cheever finally made peace with his sexuality. He began a close relationship with a young writer, Russell Cheney, who cared about him. His relationship with his wife, Mary, which had taken on a coldness much like his parents' marriage, seemed to thaw. One evening at Yaddo, while taking a break from working on his novel *Oh What a Paradise It Seems,* Cheever suffered the first of two grand mal seizures. His physical strength slowly left him. In 1981,

Cheever was diagnosed with cancer of the kidney. He died at his home in Ossining, New York, on June 18, 1982.

**Further Reading**

Bosha, Francis J., ed. *The Critical Response to John Cheever*. Westport, Conn.: Greenwood Publishing Group, 1994.

Donaldson, Scott. *John Cheever: A Biography*. New York: Random House, 1988.

Dyer, John, "'The Sorrows of Gin' and the Consciousness of a child." Available online. URL: http://xroads. virginia.edu/MA95/dyer/sorrow.html. Downloaded September 10, 2003.

O'Hara, J. E. *John Cheever: A Study of the Short Fiction*. New York: Macmillan, 1989.

## Chesnutt, Charles Waddell

(1858–1932) *novelist, short story writer, essayist, biographer*

Often referred to as America's first great African-American novelist, Charles Waddell Chesnutt was considered one of the most important fiction writers of his day. His realist work contributed to the general deromanticizing of post–Civil War literature in the South. A stenographer by trade, he initially wrote essays and humorous pieces. His first short story appeared in the *Atlantic Monthly,* one of the most prestigious magazines of its day, when Chesnutt was 29.

Charles Waddell Chesnutt was born in Cleveland, Ohio, on June 20, 1858, to Andrew "Jack" Chesnutt and Ann Maria Chesnutt, free blacks who had emigrated north from Fayetteville, North Carolina. The first son born to the couple, Charles eventually had two brothers, Lewis and Andrew; a sister died in infancy. The Chesnutt family lived in Cleveland and then in Oberlin, Ohio, for eight years before returning to Fayetteville to run the family grocery store, which was owned by Jack's father. Charles attended Howard School, a Freedman's Bureau school in Fayetteville, and worked for his father in the grocery store, but the grocery business eventually failed and Charles was forced to seek other work. The family by this time had grown to include Jack's

second wife, Mary Ochilee, and a total of 12 children, including Charles.

In 1872, Charles began a teaching career in Charlotte, North Carolina. He returned to Fayetteville in 1877, married in 1878, and became principal of the Fayetteville State Normal School for Negroes in 1880. Although financial strain had forced Chesnutt to work full time, he kept up his studies during his private time, reading, learning foreign languages and music, and studying stenography. In 1883, with the hopes of becoming a writer, he moved his family to Cleveland, Ohio. After settling in, Chesnutt passed the state bar exam with the highest grade in his class, and started his own court reporting business, which became quite successful. His family was financially comfortable, and Chesnutt established himself as a prominent Clevelander.

During this time of business success, Chesnutt also began to publish his stories. "The Goophered Grapevine," a story written in dialect, was published in the August 1887 issue of the *Atlantic Monthly,* the first time a short story by a black writer had appeared in the magazine's pages. The story was notable for its insight into black folk culture and its use of rural southern dialect. Chesnutt continued to write similar stories and eventually published a collection of these, *The Conjure Woman,* which was published in 1899 by Houghton Mifflin. *The Wife of His Youth and Other Stories of the Color Line* also appeared in 1899 and contained stories about racial experience in both the South and the North. *The House Behind the Cedars,* Chesnutt's first novel, was published in 1900 by Houghton Mifflin and examined the dilemmas faced by people of mixed race in the South. These first books met with modest success, but when Chesnutt's second novel, *The Marrow of Tradition* (1901), based on the Wilmington (North Carolina) race riot of 1898, failed to sell well, he gave up his dream of supporting himself and his family with his writing. Critics, however, praised the book, which Chesnutt had hoped would be the *Uncle Tom's Cabin* of his generation. He published one more novel, *The Colonel's Dream,* in 1905.

Although he continued to write and publish fiction occasionally during in later life, his work failed to receive much attention. The Harlem

Renaissance writers of the 1920s attracted most of the attention from the public and critics alike, eclipsing the small amount of interest that remained for Chesnutt's work. He did receive the Spingarn Medal in 1928 from the National Association for the Advancement of Colored People (NAACP) for his "pioneer work as a literary artist depicting the life and struggles of Americans of Negro descent, and for his long and useful career as scholar, worker, and freeman," but it was not until well after his death that he began to be widely recognized as one of the great innovators in the rich tradition of African-American literature. Chesnutt lived with his family in Cleveland until he died in November 1932. The Fayetteville State University library is named for Chesnutt; a state highway historical marker marks where he taught in Fayetteville, North Carolina; and in Cleveland, Ohio, a street and a school are named in his honor.

### Further Reading

Chesnutt, Helen M. *Charles Waddell Chesnutt: Pioneer of the Color Line.* Chapel Hill: University of North Carolina Press, 1952.

Ellison, Curtis W., and E. W. Metcalf, Jr. *Charles W. Chesnutt: A Reference Guide.* Boston: G. K. Hall and Co., 1977.

Heermance, J. Noel. *Charles W. Chesnutt America's First Great Black Novelist.* Hamden Conn.: Archon Book, 1974.

McElrath, Joseph, Jr., Robert Lertz III, and Jesse Crisler. *Charles W. Chesnutt: Essays and Speeches.* Stanford, Calif.: Stanford University Press, 1999.

Render, Sylvia L. *The Short Fiction of Charles W. Chesnutt.* Washington, D.C.: Howard University Press, 1974.

## Chin, Marilyn
## (Mei Ling Chin)
## (1955–   ) *poet*

Marilyn Chin is a poet-activist pitted against the dominant culture in which she lives. Her cultural politics are clearly demonstrated in her poems, which skillfully articulate the interplay of and tension between the cultures in which she lives. Chin masterfully plays with language and is not afraid to mix tones and styles within the same poem. Her works often evoke radically variant moods and create strange juxtapositions with her differing literary voices. Chin's work could be said to embody a double consciousness because she mixes an ancestral Chinese past and cultural history with an American present.

In 1955, Mei Ling Chin was born in Hong Kong. Shortly after her birth, the family moved to the United States and settled in Portland, Oregon. Once in the states, Mei Ling's name was changed to Marilyn. One of her poems, *How I Got That Name,* describes how she was renamed Marilyn by her father, who was obsessed at the time with the American actress Marilyn Monroe. Chin earned her bachelor of arts degree in Chinese literature from the University of Massachusetts and an M.F.A. degree from the University of Iowa.

Chin's writings about the struggles of Asians trying to fit into U.S. society are artistically innova-

Poet Marilyn Chin's work is known for its political content. *(Photo by Niki Berg. Courtesy Milkweed.)*

tive. Her work discusses the many stereotypes of Asian Americans and how Asians learn to deal with them. Chin's poems symbolize her own struggles with assimilation. She mixed traditional Chinese culture with U.S. culture and describes the struggles both have in adapting to each other. Her abundant use of symbols and images make Chin's poetry much more powerful than if she were to have written the obvious—yet her works are not so obscure that the average reader would have difficulty understanding her meaning.

As an activist, Chin objects to the poetry of American authors based on her observation that it was self-satisfied and did not push the limits. She is quoted in an interview for the Duke University *Chronicle*, "I think there needs to be a dedication, both content-wise and form-wise. I just think that poetry is a vibrant art, vibrant and complicated. But I don't think American poets have taken advantage of the many possibilities that poetry can offer." It is Chin's central philosophy that poetry must be more than art for art's sake. It is a higher order that Chin refers to and is based on her belief that "what we write can change the world," Chin wants her poetry to stimulate change, to make a difference, or at the very least, to make something happen.

Chin has been praised for the intensity and clarity of her voice, as well as for her often bold and unshrinking articulation of her view from the boundaries of two cultures. Her two collections of poems, *Dwarf Bamboo* (1987), and *The Phoenix Gone, the Terrace Empty* (1994), illustrate her own challenges with cultural assimilation and demonstrate a passionate struggle with the pull between the country left behind and America—what she considers to be a troubled landscape that is now her home. Chin is interested in cultivating the consummate political poem. Chin's work is daring and ambitious, both technically and thematically. She both delicately and apocalyptically melds East and West.

Chin received the Mary Roberts Rinehart Award in 1983; grants from the National Endowment for the Arts in 1984–85; and fellowships from the MacDowell Colony, Djerassi Foundation, Centrum and Virginia Center for the Creative Arts, and the Stegner Fellowship at Stanford University in 1984–85.

As an instructor in the Master of Fine Arts program at San Diego State University, Chin wants to instill in students the need to read with a "global" mind—to pay attention to what they are reading and try to learn and relate to poetry as though it were literally another language. She is constantly looking for ways to expose students to poetry's many different forms and how those forms cross cultures and languages.

## Further Reading

Lee, James K. "Li-Young hee." *Words Matters: Conversations with Asian American Writers.* Edited by King K. Cheung. Honolulu: University of Hawaii Press, 2000.

Slowik, Mary. "Beyond Lot's Wife: The Immigration Poems of Marilyn Chin, Garrett Hongo, Li-Young hee, and David Mura." *MELUS* 25, no. 3–4 (fall-winter 2000): 221–42.

Want, L. Ling-chi, and Henry Yiheng Zhao. *Chinese American Poetry: An Anthology.* Seattle: University of Washington Press, 1991.

Wong, Shawn, and Ishmael Reed. *Asian-American Literature: A Brief Introduction and Anthology.* Boston: Addison-Wesley, 1997.

## Chopin, Kate
### (Katherine O'Flaherty)
(1851–1904) *short story writer, novelist*

Kate Chopin has been described as an artist who dared and defied, but in many ways she lived a typical life of gentility. Her realistic style brought to life memorable characters and themes in her early work, but turn-of-the-century America was not yet ready for her most serious and influential work, *The Awakening,* which explores gender and sexuality themes. This book, now considered her highest artistic achievement, effectively ended her career. For this reason, she undoubtedly influenced future generations of women more than the women of her own time.

Born in St. Louis, Missouri, on February 8, 1851, Katherine O'Flaherty was the third child of an immigrant Irish father and French-American mother. Her carefree childhood was shattered at age five by the sudden death of her father. This event forced her to reshape her concept of self and of her world, which had largely revolved around a father figure as the center of the household and family. After his death, the survival of Kate's family fell on the shoulders of her widowed mother, widowed grandmother, and widowed great-grandmother. The lack of male role models and men as central figures shaped her experience of life and had a profound influence on her writing.

Kate O'Flaherty graduated from St. Louis Academy of the Sacred Heart in 1868. As a young southern debutante, she was expected to comply with the societal limitations imposed on women of her time. However, her upbringing in a household of autonomous, authoritative women, and her education in a girls' school under the administration of nuns, dictated a different inclination. Undoubtedly, her upbringing and exposure to strong female figures contributed significantly to the characters in her stories.

Kate married Oscar Chopin in 1870 and moved to New Orleans where her husband worked as a cotton broker. During their marriage, Kate fulfilled the social responsibilities and obligations of the wife of a prominent businessman. The couple had six children and were said to have been happy. When Oscar died unexpectedly in 1882, Kate's world was once again transformed dramatically.

As a widow left to support her children, Chopin returned to St. Louis to be near her family, especially her mother, to whom she had always remained close. But when her mother died shortly after the move, Kate was devastated by yet another personal loss. Critics speculate that the number of abrupt losses in her life may have been a driving force behind the search for self-understanding and self-identification witnessed in her protagonists. Just as she was searching for self and purpose, so did her characters struggle to find their identity and place within society.

Whether driven by a need to support her children, the desire to resolve questions of identity, or simply encouragement from her many friends with literary interests, Kate Chopin began to write seriously in 1889. That year, she wrote *Wiser Than a God*, along with three more short stories. In 1889, Chopin also began her first novel, *At Fault*, which was published in 1890. She published a collection of short stories in 1894, *Bayou Folk*, which launched her acceptance as a writer of local-color fiction. These works, superficial and slightly more sentimental than her earlier stories, depicted her interest and receptivity to Creole, Cajun, black, and Indian cultures and focused primarily on popular motifs of the period. They were laced with richly flavored local dialect and insightful views into the heterogeneous culture of southern Louisiana. Characters emerge as self-reliant women, who shun post–Civil War racism, have sensual male/female relationships, and reject male chauvinism, thus setting the stage for her best-known character, Edna Pontellier, in *The Awakening*.

While rich in content, *The Awakening* was published at a time when the social conservatism of the 19th century had not yet caught up with the burgeoning openness of the 20th century. As explained by Emily Toth in her critical biography *Unveiling Kate Chopin*, "In discovering herself, [protagonist] Edna Pontellier is discovering her fate. In exploring Edna's regression, as she puts aside adult life, retracing her experience to its beginnings . . ., Chopin describes as well a journey inward, evoking all the prodigal richness of longing, fantasy, and memory. The novel is not a simulated case study, but an exploration of the solitary soul still enchanted by the primal, charged, and intimate encounter of naked sensation with the astonishing world." The book was scandalous. Its taboo themes and sexually aware and shocking protagonist propelled Chopin, and her career as a serious writer, into literary oblivion, It is ironic that her highest artistic achievement as a novelist effectively ended her literary career and placed her in obscurity for almost half a century. It was not until the women's rights movement of the early 1970s that she finally emerged from society's morally imposed obscurity to be recognized as one of the most important of U.S. women novelists. Now an American classic, *The Awakening* is often required reading for literature courses. It stands as a benchmark for the transition of American women writers from the themes of romance and contented domesticity to the exploration of the emotional and sexual needs of women.

The critical abuse and personal rejection that followed publication of *The Awakening* extinguished

Chopin's creativity. Obscure and bitter, she died from a brain hemorrhage in 1904.

## Further Reading
Caudle, David J., and Suzanne Disheroon Green. *Kate Chopin: An Annotated Bibliography of Critical Works.* Westport, Conn.: Greenwood Press, 1999.

Cutter, Martha J. *Unruly Tongue: Identity and Voice of American Women's Writing, 1850–1930.* Jackson: University Press of Mississippi, 1999.

McCullough, Kate. *Region of Identity: The Construction of America in Women's Fiction, 1885–1914.* Stanford, Calif.: Stanford University Press, 1999.

Toth, Emily. *Unveiling Kate Chopin.* Jackson: University Press of Mississippi, 1999.

## Cisneros, Sandra
(1954–   ) *short story writer, poet, novelist*

One of the most widely read Chicana writers in the United States, Sandra Cisneros is known for her lyrical prose. Her stories and poems draw on her childhood experiences as the daughter of a Mexican father and a Mexican-American mother, moving back and forth between Chicago and Mexico City. With characters that are often struggling to carve out a place for their own cultural heritage inside the larger American culture, Cisneros's work has been described as bridging the gap between Hispanic and Anglo.

Sandra Cisneros was born on December 20, 1954, in Chicago, Illinois, the only daughter among seven children. She has said that she felt like she had seven fathers, since her brothers often attempted to force her to assume a traditionally female role. The family moved frequently between Chicago and Mexico City due to her father's homesickness for Mexico and his devotion to his mother, who still lived there. As a result, Cisneros has said that she grew up feeling displaced, never settling into one place long enough to establish her own roots. Her way of coping was to retreat into books, which she began to do early in life.

Cisneros found great comfort in Lee Burton's *The Little House* for its depiction of one family living together in one house that was permanent and stable. She also read Lewis Carroll's *Alice's Adventures in Wonderland.* As a child and adolescent, she sometimes wrote poems and short stories but did not really think of herself as a writer until she took her first creative writing class in college in 1974, at Loyola University in Chicago. In the class, she tried to imitate the voices of those poets she was studying—such poets as Richard Hugo, THEODORE ROETHKE, and JAMES WRIGHT. It took some time for her to find her own voice and her own subject matter, but that eventually happened when she attended the University of Iowa Writers' Workshop in 1976, after graduating from Loyola with a B.A. degree that same year.

While writing in Iowa, Cisneros realized that her experiences as a Latina really were unique, and it was then that she found her subject and decided to write about the things she knew so well—the struggle of growing up in two places at once, always with divided cultural identities, always feeling alienated, and dealing with poverty on top of it all. Cisneros graduated from the Iowa workshop in 1978 and returned to Chicago, taking a job first teaching high school dropouts in the Chicano barrio, then moving on to a position as an administrative assistant at Loyola. In both of these jobs, she was exposed to the problems faced by young Latinas in Chicago, which inspired and informed her writing.

While working at these jobs in Chicago, Cisneros completed her first books—*Bad Boys*, a collection of poems that appeared in 1980 and *The House on Mango Street*, which was published in 1983 and received the Before Columbus American Book Award in 1985. *The House on Mango Street* has been widely taught in high school and college classrooms ever since. These first books were followed in 1987 by a collection of poems, *My Wicked Wicked Ways*. Other titles include *Woman Hollering Creek and Other Stories* (1991), *Loose Woman: Poems* (1994), and *Caramelo* (2002). Cisneros's other awards include two National Endowment for the Arts fellowships.

## Further Reading
Doyle, Jacqueline. "More Room of Her Own: Sandra Cisneros's *The House on Mango Street*." *The Journal of the Society for the Study of the Multi-Ethnic*

Literature of the United States (MELUS) 19, no. 4 (winter 1994): 5–35.

Lewis, L. M. "Ethnic and Gender Identity: Parallel Growth in Sandra Cisneros' *Woman Hollering Creek.*" *Short Story* 2, no. 2 (fall 1994): 69–78.

Rangil, Viviana. "Pro-Claiming a Space: The Poetry of Sandra Cisneros and Judith Ortiz Cofer." *Multicultural Review* 9, no. 3 (September 2000): 48–51, 54–55.

Yarbo-Bejarano, Yvonne. "Chicana Literature from a Chicana Feminist Perspective." *Chicana Creativity and Criticism: Charting New Frontiers in American Literature.* Houston, Tex.: Arte Publico Press, 1988, pp. 139–145.

## Clifton, Lucille
### (Thelma Louise Sayles)
(1936–    )  *poet, short story writer, children's writer*

Lucille Clifton draws on her African ancestry to write poetry with a historical resonance that praises African Americans and their resilience. Clifton gained national attention in 1969 with her first collection of poems, *Good Times*, which was published during the heyday of the Black Arts movement. The volume was praised for its craft and its evocation of the ordinary life of urban African Americans. Clifton said much of her voice was shaped in the company of writers JAMES BALDWIN, Sterling Brown, and Chloe Wofford, the author now known as TONI MORRISON. Clifton has published ten collections of poems, an autobiographical prose work, and 19 children's books. Her work has been included in more than 100 poetry anthologies. Although her early work is significant to the Black Arts movement, later volumes show that her poetry is broader. "The proper subject matter for poetry is life. I tell students all the time that there are people who would say, 'Well, how can I relate to your poetry? I am a white male.' But, I write about being human. If you have ever been human, I invite you to that place that we share, and I think you can then share it," Clifton once said. Clifton's books for young people reflect the same themes as her poetry and are intended to teach children self-reliance, self-acceptance, and responsibility.

Lucille Clifton was born Thelma Louise Sayles in Depew, New York, in 1936 to a working-class family. Her great-great-grandmother Caroline was taken to enslavement in America from Dahomey (present-day Benin), a former kingdom where women wielded considerable power. Caroline's daughter, Lucille, was the first black woman lynched in Virginia. Although neither of Thelma's parents was formally educated, they provided their large family with an appreciation for and an abundance of books, especially those by African Americans. Thelma's mother occasionally wrote poetry. In 1952, Thelma left home at age 16 to study theater at Howard University in Washington, D.C. She was the first person in her family to finish high school and to consider college. Her Howard associates included such intellectuals as Sterling A. Brown, A. B. Spellman, Chloe Wofford—who later edited her writings for Random House—and Fred Clifton, whom she married in 1958. At Howard, Lucille Clifton discovered that the divide between the haves and the havenots could be stark and brutal, even when everyone was the same race. "I learned that people aren't all the same, and that one could write and take it seriously and have it matter," she told *The Washington Post*.

After transferring to Fredonia State Teachers College in New York in 1955, Clifton worked as an actor and began to cultivate her poetry. "Like other prominent Black Aesthetic poets consciously breaking with Eurocentric conventions . . . Clifton developed such stylistic features as concise, untitled free verse lyrics of mostly iambic trimeter lines, occasional slant rhymes, anaphora and other forms of repetition, puns and allusions, lowercase letters, sparse punctuation, and a lean lexicon of rudimentary but evocative words," wrote Jocelyn K. Moody in the *Oxford Companion to African American Literature*. Poet Robert Hayden entered Clifton's poems into competition for the 1969 YW-YMHA Poetry Center Discovery Award. She won the award and with it the publication of her first volume of poems, *Good Times*. The *New York Times* called it one of the year's 10 best books.

Clifton was frequently inspired by her own family, especially her six young children. Her early poems are celebrations of African-American ancestry, heritage, and culture, and they praise

African Americans for their historic resistance to oppression and economic and political racism. She has been likened to GWENDOLYN BROOKS, WALT WHITMAN, and EMILY DICKINSON in her style. Her poems use simple language and reflect the commonplace. Spirituality shapes much of her poetry, which includes strong characters and historical and biblical figures. Her female characters represent known and unknown heroes who have taken responsibility and stands. Clifton draws on positive male role models, including her father, in creating black male characters who are strong and worthy of respect. Clifton attempts to keep historical memory alive through her poetry but is not trapped or defeated by it.

Clifton worked in state and federal government positions until 1971, when she became a writer in residence at Coppin State College in Baltimore, Maryland. Remaining at Coppin until 1974, she produced two more books of poetry, *Good News About the Earth* (1972) and *An Ordinary Woman* (1974). Clifton's later poetry collections include *Next: New Poems* (1987), *Quilting: Poems 1987–1990* (1991), and *The Terrible Stories* (1996). *Generations: A Memoir* (1976) is a prose piece celebrating her origins, and *Good Woman: Poems and a Memoir: 1969–1980* (1987) collects some of her previously published verse. Among Clifton's children's books was an award-winning series about Everett Anderson, a young black boy. These include *Some of the Days of Everett Anderson* (1970) and *Everett Anderson's Goodbye* (1983). The latter received the Coretta Scott King Award in 1984. Another of her children's books, *Sonora Beautiful* (1981), represents a thematic departure for Clifton in that it features a white girl as the main character.

In 1988, Clifton became the first author to have two books of poetry chosen as finalists for the Pulitzer Prize (*Good Woman: Poems and a Memoir* and *Next: New Poems*). She won the 2000 National Book Award for poetry for *Blessing the Boats: New and Selected Poems (1988–2000)*, a collection of 19 poems that confronts tragedy and loss. The poems examine pain and the transformation of life's "boats," which carry us from one point to another. Clifton had three times before been a finalist for the award. Other honors

include a Lannan Literary Award, two fellowships from the National Endowment for the Arts, and the Shelley Memorial Award. In 1999 Clifton was elected a chancellor of the Academy of American Poets. She has served as poet laureate for the state of Maryland and is currently Distinguished Professor of Humanities at St. Mary's College of Maryland.

**Further Reading**

Davis, Katie. "Poet Lucille Clifton Discusses Her Work and Her Life." National Public Radio: All Things Considered. October 24, 1993.

Evans, Mari, ed. *Black Women Writers 1950–1980: A Critical Evaluation.* New York: Knopf, 1984, pp. 137–161.

Harris, Trudier, and Thadious Davis, eds. *Dictionary of Literary Biography: Afro-American Poets Since 1955.* 1985, pp. 55–60.

Hine, Darlene Clark, Elsa Barkley Brown, and Rosalyn Terborg-Penn, eds. *Black Women in America: An Historical Encyclopedia.* Bloomington & Indianapolis: Indiana University Press, 1993, pp. 254–255.

## Cooper, James Fenimore
(1789–1851) *novelist*

America's first major novelist, James Fenimore Cooper wrote the famous Leather-Stocking Tales, which included *The Last of the Mohicans* (1826) and *The Deerslayer* (1840). Natty Bumppo, the central character of these novels, became the archetypal 18th-century frontiersman, living an unspoiled existence close to nature while civilization and all its ills creep up on him.

James Fenimore Cooper was born on September 15, 1789, in Burlington, New Jersey. His father, Judge William Cooper, was a landowner who had become quite wealthy by developing virgin land. He was also a representative of the Fourth and Sixth Congress. Cooper's mother was Elisabeth Fenimore Cooper. When Cooper was young, the family moved to Cooperstown, New York, a settlement founded by and named after Judge Cooper on the shores of Lake Otsego. Here Cooper enjoyed an idyllic childhood, roaming the family estate and the surrounding forests. The love of nature he developed during these years undoubtedly shaped his writing.

Cooper attended the village school, then studied from 1800 to 1802 in the house of the rector of St. Peter's Church in Cooperstown. Sent to study at Yale at age 13, Cooper was dismissed from school during his third year for his involvement in a series of pranks. At his father's urging, he joined the navy and served on a series of ships between 1807 and 1809. His experience on the *Sterling,* the *Vesuvius,* and the *Wasp* inspired his sea stories later in life. When his father died in 1809, the younger Cooper inherited the family's wealth and left the navy. In 1811, he married Susan Augusta DeLancey, a descendant of the early governors of the New York colony, and settled down to the comfortable life of a gentleman farmer. The Coopers lived first in Mamaroneck, New York, from 1811 to 1814, then in Cooperstown, and from 1817 to 1821 in Scarsdale, New York.

An avid reader, Cooper determined one day that he could write a better story than the one he had just finished reading. When his wife challenged him to the task, his writing career began. Although he did not get an early start as a writer, he met with success soon after he began publishing and proved himself a prolific writer. His first book, *Precaution,* which came out in 1820, did not sell well, but his second book, *The Spy,* published in 1821, was an immediate commercial success. *The Pioneers* was published in 1823 and introduced Cooper's famous character, Natty Bumppo, who was also called "Leather-Stocking." From this time on, Cooper was fascinated with the subject of frontier life. The so-called Leather-Stocking Tales were not written chronologically and include the novels *The Deerslayer, The Pathfinder, The Prairie,* and *The Last of the Mohicans,* which has several times been made into a major motion picture.

After Cooper began to publish his novels, he and his wife moved to New York City, where he participated in the cultural and political life of the city. In addition to working on the Leather-Stocking Tales, he also wrote a series of sea stories, beginning in 1827, which occupied his attention in part through the 1840s. In 1826, the Coopers moved to Europe, where they lived until 1833. Cooper served as the U.S. consul at Lyons, France,

and became friends with Sir Walter Scott and the marquis de Lafayette, among other notable thinkers of his time.

After returning to New York, Cooper continued to write, but his books no longer sold as well as they had at the beginning of his career. He blamed journalists for not giving him positive press and retaliated with libel suits, most of which he won. His rancorous spirit during this time sometimes made his life more difficult than it might otherwise have been. The books of his later career, including *Satanstoe* (1845), *The Chainbearer* (1845), and *The Red Skins* (1846), are more polemical than his early works and address his political and social concerns, which had become more conservative over the years.

Cooper died at Otsego Hall on September 14, 1851, and was buried in the Cooperstown cemetery.

### Further Reading

Fields, Wayne, ed. *James Fenimore Cooper, a Collection of Critical Essays.* Englewood Cliffs, N.J.: Prentice-Hall, 1979.

Franklin, Wayne. *The New World of James Fenimore Cooper.* Chicago: University of Chicago Press, 1982.

Long, Robert Emmet. *James Fenimore Cooper.* New York: Continuum, 1990.

Reuben, Paul P. "Chapter 3: Early Nineteenth Century—James Fenimore Cooper." PAL: Perspectives in American Literature—A Research and Reference Guide. Available online. URL: http://www. csustan.edu/english/reuben/pal/chap3/cooper.html. Posted January 5, 2003.

Ringe, Donald A. *James Fenimore Cooper.* Boston: Twayne, 1988.

## Crane, Hart
### (Harold Hart Crane)
### (1899–1932) *poet*

Hart Crane was a poet best known for his long and mystical poem *The Bridge,* published in 1930. In it, he used the Brooklyn Bridge as a symbol in his attempt to link the present with the past in an epic continuum. While his works showed the influence of the French symbolists and poets such as T. S. ELIOT, it differed through his emphasis on the positive, even to the point of the ecstatic.

Hart Crane, born on July 21, 1899, in Garrettsville, Ohio, was a highly anxious and volatile child. Crane's father was a candy manufacturer. Crane began writing verse in his early teen years and never completed his final year of high school. At age 17, Crane persuaded his recently divorced parents to let him move to New York City to prepare for college. Between 1917 and 1924, however, he drifted between Cleveland and New York, occasionally working as a cub reporter, but more often doing menial tasks in his father's candy store in Cleveland. During this time, he also worked as a copywriter for mail order catalogues and advertising agencies in New York City. His unsettled life made him sensitive to the problems of being uprooted, a theme that would later be prominent in his poetry.

While in New York, Crane befriended many important literary figures, including ALLEN TATE, KATHERINE ANNE PORTER, E. E. CUMMINGS, and JEAN TOOMER, but his heavy drinking and chronic instability frustrated any attempts at lasting friendships. Crane admired the style of T. S. Eliot and his poems combines the style of Eliot with the influences of European literature and traditional versification with a particularly American sensibility he derived from WALT WHITMAN.

Crane's first collection of poems, *White Buildings*, was published in 1926. It reflected his enthusiasm for city life and attracted considerable attention from critics. While compared to T. S. Eliot's style, Crane's work is much less pessimistic. Crane's first attempt to write a long poem resulted in his small series of poems entitled *Voyages*, which is included in *White Buildings*. It was an important precursor to *The Bridge*.

His major work, the book-length poem *The Bridge*, follows more in the tradition of Walt Whitman's writing. This is an epic poem in which Crane attempts to link a dreamlike perception of the past with modern industrial reality using the Brooklyn Bridge as the central symbol. Its 15 sections move the reader from New York to California, and it features historical figures as well as technological and natural wonders. Like Eliot, Crane used the landscape of the modern, industrial city to create a powerful new symbolic literature. This poem received critical acclaim and, on the strength of its reception, Crane was awarded a Guggenheim fellowship.

With the money from his fellowship, Crane traveled to Mexico with plans to begin another epic poem, this time around an Aztec theme. However, his dream of an Aztec epic resulted in less than a handful of poems. His only other serious work, written shortly before he left Mexico, was entitled *The Broken Tower* and was published in 1932. *The Broken Tower* was a love poem that tellingly betrayed his longing for a time in his past that was intensely energetic and that now seemed unattainably remote. Crane was an alcoholic and this was a vulnerable time in his life. His friends were scattered or dead, years of drinking had ravaged his physical condition and undermined his mental stability, and he was certain that tales of his drunken exploits in Mexico had preceded his return to New York. On a ship somewhere north of Havana, Cuba, in the Gulf of Mexico, on April 27, 1932, a passenger watched in horror as a man dressed only in pajamas and overcoat walked purposefully to the ship's stern, mounted the railing, slipped the coat from his shoulders, and then threw himself into the water. A cry went up and a life preserver was thrown out, but Hart Crane quickly vanished. *The Complete Poems and Selected Letters and Prose,* was published posthumously in 1966.

**Further Reading**

Fisher, Clive. *Hart Crane: A Biography*. New Haven: Yale University Press, 2002.

Bennett, Maria F. *Unfractioned Idiom: Hart Crane and Modernism*. New York: Peter Lang Publications, 1987.

Unterecker, John. *Voyager: A Life of Hart Crane*. New York: Farrar, Straus & Giroux, 1969.

Weber, Brom. "Introduction," in *The Complete Poems and Selected Letters and Prose of Hart Crane*. New York: Anchor Press, 1966, pp. 8–25.

## Crane, Stephen
(1871–1900) *novelist, poet, short story writer*

One of America's first naturalist writers, Stephen Crane described humanity with truth and objectivity. Through his best works, Crane demonstrated a rare ability to shape colorful settings, dramatic action, and perspective characterization into ironic explorations of human nature and destiny.

Born in Newark, New Jersey, on November 1, 1871, Stephen Crane was the youngest of 14 children born to a Methodist Church elder. Crane was restless as a child and enjoyed playing baseball, boxing, and hunting. He never cared for school, but loved writing and began writing stories when he was in grade school. During his childhood, Crane's family moved three times within the New York City area. Life taught him at an early age that change is inevitable, which was further reinforced by the death of his father when Crane was nine years old. After his father's death, Crane's mother took a job writing for the *Methodist Papers* and the *New York Tribune* to support her large family.

In 1883, Mrs. Crane moved her family to Asbury Park, New Jersey, where Stephen continued his education and his writing. In 1885, Crane wrote *Uncle Jack and the Bell-Handle*, which was never published during his lifetime. Also in 1885, he attended Pennington Seminary in Pennington, New Jersey, but withdrew in December 1887. In 1888, Crane attended Claverack College in Claverack, New York, where he published a short story, "Henry M. Stanley," in the school magazine.

After poor attendance at Lafayette College in 1890, Crane attended Syracuse University, where he continued to write and sell his short stories and sketches to the *Detroit Free Press*. For a time at Syracuse, Crane's most noteworthy accomplishments, however, were performed on the baseball field. Crane honed his powers as observer of psychological and social reality while alternating his surroundings living between the Bowery slums of New York City and a medical students' boardinghouse as he freelanced his way to a literary career. Crane's first novel, *Maggie: A Girl of the Streets* (1893), was about the people he saw there. Publishers were not interested in the book, so Crane borrowed money and printed it himself. He sold copies at newsstands for 50 cents a copy, but by the end of a year, had sold fewer than 100 copies.

War and other forms of physical and mental violence fascinated Crane. It was not until Crane published *The Red Badge of Courage* in 1895 that he gained international acclaim. Crane was 24.

Though he was born six years after the end of the Civil War, veterans praised him for his uncanny power to imagine and reproduce a sense of actual combat. Editors who had formerly turned down his works now hounded him for stories. Almost literally overnight, Crane, who had not had a permanent roof over his head for years, knew comparative security. Unfortunately, he spent what he earned as fast as the money came in.

In 1895, Crane embarked on a trip through the American West and Mexico, all the while writing special articles for the Bacheller-Johnson newspaper syndicate. He published a free verse volume titled *The Black Riders and Other Lines,* in 1895. Then in 1896, he published *George's Mother*, a revised version of *Maggie: A Girl of the Streets,* and his first short story collection, entitled *The Little Regiment and Other Episodes of the American Civil War.*

While traveling to Cuba in January 1897, Crane's ship, *The Commodore,* was shipwrecked off the Florida coast. His experiences on this voyage led him to write *The Open Boat,* which was published that same year. Crane became a reporter for the *New York Journal* and *Westminster Gazette* during the brief Greco-Turkish War, and during that time, also published *The Third Violet,* a story about his love for an Akron, Ohio, woman named Nellie Crouse.

Crane became a war correspondent for the *New York World* and the *New York Journal* during the Spanish-American war, working with Cora Taylor, a young woman he had met the previous fall. Taylor and Crane eventually married. During this era, Crane published several of his works: *The Open Boat and Other Tales of Adventure* (1898), *The Bride Comes to Yellow Sky* (1896), *The Monster and Other Stories* (1899), and *The Blue Hotel* (1896).

He and Cora rented an old English castle for a short period and settled in England, where he made friends with famous writers of the time, including H. G. Wells and HENRY JAMES. In 1899, Crane began writing a new novel, *The O'Ruddy,* which was his final book. Crane lived out his life as a penniless artist who eventually became well known as a poet, journalist, and realist. In 1900, after suffering several tuberculosis attacks, Crane died at age 28 in a sanatorium in Badenweiler, Germany. He is buried in Hillside, New Jersey. His book *Whilomville Stories* and his Cuban war stories, *Wounds in the Rain,* were published posthumously in 1905.

## Further Reading

Benfey, Christopher. *The Double Life of Stephen Crane.* New York: Alfred A. Knopf, 1992.

Berryman, John. *Stephen Crane.* New York: Cooper Square Press, 2001.

Gullason, Thomas A. *Stephen Crane's Career: Perspectives and Evaluations.* New York: New York University Press, 1972.

## Creeley, Robert

(1926–  )  *poet, novelist, short story writer*

Known as one of the Black Mountain poets, from his days with Charles Olson and other writers during the 1950s at Black Mountain College in North Carolina, Robert Creeley has had a prolific career as a poet. His poems often address love and the emotions of intimate relationships or the natural world. He has stated that he learned from jazz musicians to "write directly from that which he felt." Indeed, his minimalist style is distinctive for its lack of concrete description and characterization and its careful use of silence as a tool for developing meaning.

Robert Creeley was born in Arlington, Massachusetts, on May 21, 1926. His father, a prominent physician, died before Creeley was five years old. Creeley also lost his left eye before the age of five; both events altered Creeley's life considerably. After his father's death, Creeley moved with his mother and sister to live on a small farm in West Acton that had been the family's country home. His mother worked as a public health nurse to support her children.

Creeley attended Harvard University from 1943 to 1946, where he met Ann MacKinnon, whom he married in 1946. Creeley wrote and published his first poem, "Return," during the winter of 1945. In it, Creeley expresses relief at finally discovering a "door" on a seemingly "endless" street of feeling apart. It was also during the late 1940s, while Creeley was living in New Hampshire, that he initiated his lengthy correspondence with poet Charles Olson. The Creeley-Olson letters became especially important in strengthening Creeley's resolve to pursue a literary career.

With school and his job as a copy boy in Boston intolerably tedious for Creeley, he took an assignment to drive ambulances for the American Field Service in India and Burma. Upon his return from India, Creeley was reinstated at Harvard, where he became involved in the publication of *Wake* magazine, which at the time was an alternative to the Harvard *Advocate.* His friendship with the editors of *Wake* led to the publication of several of his early poems.

Two years later, Creeley left school and attempted to launch his own magazine, but the venture failed. In search of a cheaper way of life and less expensive publishing opportunities, Creeley and Ann moved to France in 1951, then to Majorca a year later. Creeley's first three books of poetry, *Le Fou, The Kind of Act of,* and *The Immoral Proposition,* were all published in 1953 while Creeley was in Europe. The couple's home in Majorca served as the setting for Creeley's only novel, *The Island,* which was published in 1963. The couple stayed in Majorca until their divorce in 1955. During their stay in Majorca, they established Divers Press, where Creeley printed *The Gold Diggers,* in 1954. Divers also printed books by Robert Duncan, Charles Olson, and other of Creeley's acquaintances.

While Creeley's poems were open in their uncertainties and elusiveness, the moral atmosphere of his work lacked the readiness and trustful momentum critics associated with writers in the Olson group. It was not until the publication of his poems in *Poetry* magazine during the 1950s that his work became available to a wider reading public, which ultimately paved the way for his academic acceptance.

Upon returning to the United States, and at the invitation of his friend Charles Olson, Creeley taught at Black Mountain College, an experimental arts college in North Carolina. He eventually joined the faculty and edited the *Black Mountain Review* from 1954 to 1957. Creeley published *All That Is Lovely in Men* in 1953 and *If You* in 1956, shortly after returning to America. In 1960, he received a master's degree from the University of New Mexico at Albuquerque.

Creeley's style has usually been called minimal, in that his work is sparse or barren compared to that of some of his contemporaries. His poems have few or no descriptions, characterizations, or incidents and build subtleties and resonances by juxtapositions of short, simple lines and phrases, manipulating syntax and rhythm using metaphor. Creeley derived much of his style from jazz musicians, whose experimentation with rhythm and silence showed Creeley how subtle and refined expression could be. In his preface to *All That Is Lovely in Men,* Creeley acknowledged his debt to jazz.

The 1968 book *Pieces,* which contained elliptical fragments presented as jottings in a continuing notebook or journal, moved his work more toward the open ethos of the time. *A Day Book* (1972) and *Hello* (1976) went even further in this direction. Some readers and critics found this trend more vital, as in *For My Mother,* which was considered one of Creeley's best achievements.

Aside from being a prolific writer, Creeley has been an active member of the literary community. He participated in many writers' workshops and poetry conferences; the Vancouver Poetry Festival (summer 1963) and the Berkeley Poetry Conference (summer 1965) were perhaps the most significant. Creeley has taught in a variety of places, including Guatemala, the University of New Mexico, the University of British Columbia, and the State University of New York at Buffalo. In April 1964, he read with Robert Duncan and DENISE LEVERTOV at the Guggenheim Museum in New York, and after that, read at virtually every major university in the United States and Britain.

Creeley has published more than 60 books of poetry in the United States and abroad, and more than a dozen books of prose, essays, and interviews. His honors include the Lannan Lifetime Achievement Award, the Frost Medal, the Shelley Memorial Award, a National Endowment for the Arts grant, a Rockefeller Foundation grant, and fellowships from the Guggenheim Foundation. He served as New York State Poet from 1989 to 1991 and was honored as the Samuel P. Capen Professor of poetry and humanities at the State University of New York at Buffalo. He was also elected a chancellor of the Academy of American Poets in 1999.

## Further Reading

Clark, Tom. *Robert Creeley and the Genius of the American Common Place: Together with the Poet's Own Autobiography.* New York: New Directions, 1993.

Faas, Ekbert, et al. *Irving Layton and Robert Creeley: The Complete Correspondence.* Montreal: McGill–Queen's University Press, 1990.

———. *Robert Creeley: A Biography.* Lebanon, N.H.: University Press of New England, 2001.

Wilson, John, ed. *Robert Creeley's Life and Work: A Sense of Increment.* Ann Arbor: University of Michigan Press, 1988.

## Cullen, Countee
### (Countee Porter, Countee P. Cullen)
(1903–1946) *poet, novelist, children's fiction writer, playwright*

One of the leading figures, along with LANGSTON HUGHES, in the Harlem Renaissance of the 1920s, Countee Cullen was considered conservative, poetically speaking, and became known for his use of the sonnet and other traditional forms. At a time when experimentation with form and provocative themes were in vogue, Cullen found inspiration in the English romantic poets, especially John Keats, and later in his career completely shunned the racial themes that had been so popular during the Harlem Renaissance.

Born in Louisville, Kentucky, on March 30, 1903, Countee Cullen was initially reared by a woman who was probably his paternal grandmother before being unofficially adopted by the Reverend A. F. Cullen and his wife, Carolyn, who lived in New York City. Apparently he went by the name of Countee Porter until 1918 but became Countee P. Cullen by 1921, and eventually just Countee Cullen. Cullen's adoption was never "official," and it is impossible to say if Cullen was ever legally an orphan at any stage in his childhood.

In any case, Reverend Cullen was a pioneer black activist minister of the Salem Methodist Episcopal Church, one of the largest congregations in Harlem, and it was there that Cullen grew up. An outstanding student, Cullen attended DeWitt Clinton High School in New York and began writing poetry at age 14. While still in high school, he won his first poetry contest, a citywide competition, with the poem "I Have a Rendezvous with Life," which was inspired by Alan Seeger's "I Have a Rendezvous with Death." In 1922, Cullen entered New York University, where he found a mentor in W. E. B. DUBOIS. Cullen's poems were published in *The Crisis*, the magazine of the National Association for the Advancement of Colored People (NAACP), and *Opportunity*—a magazine of the National Urban League. It did not take long before his poems began to appear in *Harper's, Century Magazine*, and *Poetry*.

Cullen graduated Phi Beta Kappa from New York University in 1925, then continued his studies at Harvard, where he completed a master's degree. While at Harvard, Cullen worked as an assistant editor for *Opportunity* and wrote a column called "The Dark Tower," which attracted lots of attention in the literary world. It was through his work on *Opportunity* that Cullen came to know the important figures in the Harlem Renaissance— ZORA NEALE HURSTON, JEAN TOOMER, ARNA BONTEMPS, and others.

Cullen's first collection of poems, *Color* (1925), was published to popular and critical acclaim before he finished college. Written in a careful, traditional style and addressing the themes of racism and black beauty, the book included Cullen's most famous poem, "Heritage." Cullen's subsequent collections of poems were not as popular as his first. *The Ballad of the Brown Girl*, which appeared in 1927, and *Copper Sun*, which also came out in 1927, failed to address the issue of race satisfactorily for his many black readers. Unlike other Harlem Renaissance writers, Cullen did not agree with the use of black art forms, such as blues and jazz, in poetry. He did not think the race of the poet should be a factor in the poem. Thus, as Cullen grew older, his writing veered further away from the subject of race. *The Black Christ and Other Poems*, his final collection of poems for adults, was published in 1929 but received little praise from critics.

Although his reputation as a poet had waned by the late 1920s, Cullen received a Guggenheim fellowship in 1928, which enabled him to travel abroad. He studied and wrote full time between 1928 and 1934, dividing his time between France

A leader in the Harlem Renaissance despite his poetic conservatism, Countee Cullen is shown here in Central Park. *(Library of Congress, Prints and Photographs Division [LC-USZ62-42529])*

and the United States. He also married in 1928, in a ceremony that symbolized, as one Cullen biographer has said, "the union of the grand black intellectual patriarch and the new breed of younger Negroes who were responsible for much of the excitement of the Renaissance." His wife was Nina Yolande DuBois, the daughter of W. E. B. DuBois, his mentor and the leading black intellectual of the Harlem Renaissance, but the marriage was unsuccessful and ended in divorce in 1930. Cullen married Ida Mae Robertson in 1940.

Cullen's only novel, *One Way to Heaven*, appeared in 1934. After that, he spent most of his time teaching and helping to promote the works of other black writers. Beginning in 1934, he taught

English, French, and creative writing at Frederick Douglass Junior High School in New York City. He also wrote several children's books during this time, including *The Lost Zoo* (1940), a collection of poems about the animals Noah did not take on the ark, and *My Lives and How I Lost Them* (1943), an autobiography of his cat. He also wrote numerous pieces for the theater, including a musical, *St. Louis Woman* (1946), which he cowrote with Arna Bontemps.

Cullen won more major literary prizes than any other black writer of the 1920s. His awards included first prize in the Witter Bynner poetry contest in 1925, *Poetry* magazine's John Reed Memorial Prize, the Amy Spingarn Award from *The Crisis,* second prize in *Opportunity* magazine's first poetry contest, and second prize in the poetry contest of *Palms.* In addition, he was the second African American to win a Guggenheim Fellowship.

Cullen died unexpectedly on January 9, 1946, from high blood pressure and uremic poisoning. For many years following his death, Cullen's work went unnoticed and fell out of print, but in the late 20th century, there was a resurgence of interest in Cullen's writing, and many of his books were reprinted.

**Further Reading**

Early, Gerald, ed. *My Soul's High Song: The Collected Writings of Countee Cullen, Voice of the Harlem Renaissance.* New York: Doubleday, 1991.

———. "About Countee Cullen's Life and Career." *Modern American Poetry.* Available online. URL: http://www.english.uiuc.edu/maps/poets/a_f/cullen/life.htm. Posted March 21, 2001.

Ferguson, Blanche E. *Countee Cullen and the Negro Renaissance.* New York: Dodd, Mead, 1966.

Perry, Margaret. *A Bio-Bibliography of Countee P. Cullen, 1903–1946.* Westport, Conn.: Greenwood Press, 1971.

Shucard, Alan R. *Countee Cullen.* Boston: Twayne, 1984.

## cummings, e. e.
### (edward estlin cummings)
(1894–1962) *poet, novelist*

e. e. cummings was known as a diverse American poet and painter who first attracted attention for his eccentric punctuation in his writing. He styled his name without capital letters. Despite typographical anarchism and his devotion to the avant-garde, cummings's works are in many respects quite traditional, addressing common personal struggles and the challenges involved in maintaining individuality despite the pressure of society. His unique writing style helped him to address these weighty themes with elements of lightness and satire. cummings was an artist in many regards: he was almost equally known for his still-life pictures and landscapes, which he painted to a professional level alongside his writing.

edward estlin cummings ("estlin") was born on October 14, 1894, in Cambridge, Massachusetts, to Edward and Rebecca Clarke Cummings. Estlin's father was an energetic, talented, and highly articulate professor of sociology and political science at Harvard University in the 1890s; in 1900 he was ordained as the minister of the South Congregational Church in Boston. Young cummings grew up attending public schools in Cambridge and vacationing in Maine and at the family summer home, Joy Farm, in Silver Lake, New Hampshire. In 1911, cummings entered Harvard, specializing in Greek and other foreign languages. It was during this time that he began to cultivate his poetry talent, contributing poems to Harvard periodicals and exposing himself to the work of EZRA POUND and other modernist writers and painters. In 1915, cummings graduated magna cum laude in classic literature and delivered his class's commencement address on the topic of "the New Art." One year later, cummings obtained his M.A. degree from Harvard and began cubist-style painting.

In 1917, cummings moved to New York City, but shortly thereafter he volunteered for Norton-Harjes Ambulance Corps and on April 28, 1917, he set sail for France and World War I. He drove an ambulance for U.S. troops stationed there. During his time abroad, cummings wrote letters back home criticizing the conduct of the war, and after just five weeks in Paris, nervous French censors had him arrested for espionage. cummings was sent to Dépôt de Triage, La Ferté-Macé, a detention center on the western front, where he remained for three months before being released and sent home. This experience formed the basis for his novel *The Enormous Room* (1922), regarded as one of the best American works to come out of World War I. Written as a journal of his prison stay, it is heightened by a hatred of a bureaucracy that could treat helpless and innocent civilians so cruelly. Upon his return from France, refusing his family's wish that he seek a commission, cummings was drafted into the army and stationed at Camp Devens, Massachusetts, until shortly after the Armistice in 1918. He depicts military life satirically in such poems as "i sing of Olaf glad and big" (1931). After the Armistice, cummings returned again to New York where he met Elaine Orr, whom he later married and with whom he had a daughter, Nancy, cummings's only child. Also during this time, cummings worked seriously at his painting and, upon his father's urging, began to write *The Enormous Room.*

In 1921, cummings went to Paris to study art, where he befriended fellow poets Ezra Pound, HART CRANE, and Archibald MacLeish. Upon his return to New York in 1924, he found himself to be a celebrity, both for *The Enormous Room* and for *Tulips and Chimneys* (1923), his first collection of poetry. Clearly influenced by GERTRUDE STEIN's syntactical and AMY LOWELL's imagistic experiments, cummings had nevertheless discovered an original way of describing sensuous experience. For the next six years, cummings wrote many pieces of work, including *&* (1925), *XLI Poems* (1925), and *Is 5* (1926). Also during that time, cummings's marriage ended in a rather complicated divorce. Love poems, satirical squibs, and descriptive nature poems became his best-loved forms. In 1926, a roving assignment from *Vanity Fair* allowed cummings to travel again, thus establishing his lifelong routine of painting in the afternoons and writing at night. In the same year, *Is 5* was published, cummings's father was killed, and his mother was seriously injured in a car accident. With his new love interest, Anne Barton, cummings discovered his father's death at a small party in New York. cummings and his sister, Elizabeth, immediately rushed to their mother's bedside. Although she was not expected to live through the week, Rebecca was inspired by her children to continue living and she miraculously

survived a fractured skull. Then on May 1, 1929, cummings married Anne Barton; this marriage also ended in a divorce, after less than three years.

In 1931, cummings traveled in the Soviet Union and recorded later his impressions in *Eimi* (1933), a version of Dante's *Descent into Hell,* in which he saw the Russians as "undead." He also published a collection of drawings and paintings that year, *CIOPW* (its title an acronym for the materials used: charcoal, ink, oil, pencil, watercolor), and over the next three decades had many individual shows in New York. He married his third wife, Marion Morehouse, a photographer, model, and actress, in 1932, with whom he remained until his death. (It is actually uncertain whether the two ever officially exchanged vows, although their role in each other's lives was undoubtedly that of husband and wife.) The two divided their time between 4 Patchin Place, in New York City, and his family's farm in New Hampshire. In 1933, the same year *Eimi* was published, cummings was awarded a Guggenheim fellowship.

Morehouse and cummings traveled the world, venturing to, among other places, Tunisia, Russia, Mexico, and France. Throughout these trips, cummings managed to publish eight works: *The Red Front* (1933), *Eimi* (1933), *No Thanks* (1935), *Tom* (1935), *Collected Poems* (1940), *1x1* (1944), and *Santa Claus* (1946). In Europe, cummings wrote many antiwar poems protesting U.S. involvement in Europe and the Pacific. He wrote the poem "plato told" as a continuation of the work his late father had done as the executive secretary of the World Peace Foundation. His work was then cut short for a brief period with the sudden deterioration of his mother's health. In January 1947, Rebecca Cummings suffered a stroke and fell into a coma. She died weeks later, never regaining consciousness.

From 1952 to 1953, cummings was a professor at Harvard. His series of lectures were published as *i: six nonlectures.* In 1957, he received a special citation from the National Book Award Committee for *Poems, 1923–1954,* and also won the Bollingen Prize for poetry. Then, 15 years after his mother's death, edward estlin cummings collapsed from a cerebral hemorrhage at his summer home, Joy Farm. cummings died leaving behind more than 25 books of prose, poetry, charcoal and pencil drawings, plays, and stories.

## Further Reading

Belouf, Robert L. *E. E. Cummings: The Prosodic Shape of His Poems.* Ann Arbor: University of Michigan Press, 1978.

Dumas, Bethany K. *E. E. Cummings: A Remembrance of Miracles.* London: Vision Press, 1974.

Friedman, Norman. *E. E. Cummings: The Art of His Poetry.* Baltimore: The Johns Hopkins Press, 1960.

Kostelanetz, Richard, and John Rocco, eds. *AnOther E. E. Cummings.* New York: Liveright, 1998.

Rotella, Guy. "Nature, Time and Transcendence in Cummings' Later Poems." *Critical Essays on E. E. Cummings.* Boston: G. K. Hall & Co., 1984.

# D

## Davies, Robertson
(1913–1995) *novelist, essayist, editor, playwright*

One of Canada's most important literary figures, Robertson Davies was initially an actor and playwright before settling into his career as a best-selling novelist. Davies had a lifelong interest in psychology and studied the works of both Freud and Jung in depth. His works often focused on moral conflicts and themes. His Deptford trilogy, which is comprised of *Fifth Business* (1970), *The Manticore* (1972), and *World of Wonders* (1975), draws heavily on his study of psychology and is considered to be some of his finest work.

Robertson Davies was born on August 28, 1913, in Thamesville, Ontario. His father was newspaper publisher and Liberal senator William Rupert Davies; his mother was Florence Sheppard McKay Davies. Both were theater lovers, so Davies grew up surrounded by theater life and involved himself in school productions from an early age. The youngest of three sons, Davies was educated at Upper Canada College, where he was very involved in school theatrical productions and was editor of the school newspaper. He went on to study at Queen's University in Kingston, where he was active in the Drama Guild, and to earn a degree in literature from Oxford University in 1938. His thesis, entitled "Shakespeare's Boy Actors," was published the following year.

Following graduation, Davies pursued work in the theater, joining the prestigious Old Vic Theatre Company in London. The stage manager, Brenda Matthews, became Davies's lifelong wife. He soon shifted to journalism. In 1940, Davies and his wife returned to Canada, where he became the literary editor of *Saturday Live*, a weekly review of the arts and politics. His first daughter was born in December 1940. Davies then became editor of the Peterborough *Examiner* in 1942, a paper owned by his father. During this time, Davies established himself as a witty and astute columnist, the pseudonymous Samuel Marchbanks, and also began writing plays and, later, novels. His columns for the paper were eventually published in three volumes between 1947 and 1967.

Davies became the publisher of the *Examiner* in 1955, a position he held until 1965, and his plays were being performed and published as well. His first play, *Eros at Breakfast*, won the Dominion Drama Festival Award in 1948 for best Canadian play. This play and *Fortune, My Foe* were both published in 1949. Another play, *At My Heart's Core*, appeared in 1950. The Salterton trilogy of novels, including *Tempest-Tost*, *Leaven of Malice*, and *A Mixture of Frailties*, was published during the 1950s. He is also remembered for his work during the 1950s to establish the Stratford Festival, a drama and music festival.

In 1961, Davies published a well-received collection of scholarly essays, *A Voice from the Attic*, which won the Lorne Pierce Medal. He then began his teaching career, working first as a visiting professor at Trinity College in the University of

Toronto before being appointed Master of Massey College, a position he held until his retirement in 1981. Davies also worked to establish the Graduate Centre for the Study of Drama with Clifford Leech. It was during his time as Master of Massey College that Davies wrote the novels that would bring him international recognition.

Davies published the Deptford trilogy in the 1970s, winning the Governor General's Award for *The Manticore,* the second novel in the series. His novels of the 1980s included *The Rebel Angels, The Cunning Man,* and *What's Bred in the Bone,* which was short-listed for the 1986 Booker Prize and awarded the 1986 Canadian Author's Association Literary Award for best fiction and the Medal of Honor for Literature by New York's National Arts Club in 1987.

In addition to the awards already mentioned, Davies received honorary degrees from more than 20 universities in the United States and Canada and was the first Canadian to become an honorary member of the American Academy and Institute of Arts and Letters. He also received an honorary doctorate from Oxford and was a Companion of the Order of Canada.

Davies died on December 2, 1995, from a heart attack. His death was quite unexpected. He had been working during the last year of his life on an opera, tributes to several friends, and a book about old age. Following his death, his widow and daughter published *The Merry Heart,* a selection of his writings from 1980 to 1995, as well as *Happy Alchemy,* a collection of his writings on theater. In 1999, the Toronto Opera Company produced his opera, *The Golden Asse,* to extremely favorable reviews. A selection of his letters, *For Your Eyes Alone: Robertson Davies' Letters 1976–1995,* appeared also in 1999 from his biographer Judith Skelton Grant.

## Further Reading

Davis, J. Madison. *Conversations with Robertson Davies.* Jackson: University Press of Mississippi, 1989.

Grant, Judith Skelton. *Robertson Davies: Man of Myth.* New York: Viking, 1994.

La Bossiere, Camille R., and Linda M. Morra. *Robertson Davies: A Mingling of Contrarieties.* Ottawa: University of Ottawa Press, 2001.

Stone-Blackburn, Susan. *Robertson Davies, Playwright: A Search for the Self on the Canadian Stage.* Vancouver: University of British Columbia Press, 1985.

## Davis, Rebecca Harding
### (Rebecca Blaine Harding)
(1831–1910) *novelist, short story writer, journalist*

A pioneer of American literary realism and a successful journalist, Rebecca Harding Davis in her fiction and nonfiction addressed the social ills of her time. She wrote from a very young age, and she wrote about what she saw growing up in Wheeling, West Virginia. Poverty, racism, political corruption, and the Civil War were just a few of her subjects. In all, during her 50-year career, she published more than 500 works, including nearly 300 stories and nine novels. Although her work was forgotten soon after her death, the 1972 reprinting of her novella *Life in the Iron Mills* inspired renewed interest in her life and writing.

Rebecca Blaine Harding was born on June 24, 1831, in Washington, Pennsylvania, but lived from the age of five in Wheeling, West Virginia, where her father became a successful businessman. Inspired by her mother's love of language and her father's storytelling, she developed her own love of books and writing. She often wiled away the hours reading in her backyard treehouse. She read many writers but named NATHANIEL HAWTHORNE as the most important influence on her choice of subjects as a writer. She studied at home, under the tutelage of her mother, until she was 14, at which time she enrolled in Washington Female Seminary in Pennsylvania. After graduating in 1848 as class valedictorian, she returned to Wheeling and lived with her family for the next 12 years. During this time, she helped raise her younger brothers and sisters and went to work for the Wheeling *Intelligencer,* where she began to develop her writing skills.

She began publishing reviews and stories in a local Wheeling newspaper in the late 1850s. In December 1860, she submitted her novella *Life in the Iron Mills* to the *Atlantic Monthly,* which accepted it immediately and published it in 1861, rocketing the unknown writer into the center of literary America.

One of the first examples of literary realism, the genre that dominated American literature in the last three decades of the 19th century, *Life in the Iron Mills* received both critical and popular acclaim. Harding had learned from living in Wheeling about the dangers faced by industrial workers, and she meant to educate those Americans who had not been exposed as she had. Following the success of her first publication, she met many East Coast writers and intellectuals. Her second book, the novel *Margaret Howth: A Story of Today,* appeared in 1862 and also was widely praised. In 1863, she married the journalist L. Clarke Davis and moved with him to Philadelphia. The couple had a daughter and two sons, one of whom, Richard Harding Davis, followed in his mother's footsteps to become a successful novelist, playwright, and war correspondent. By 1900, Rebecca Harding Davis had published eight more novels and gone to work as a reporter for the *New York Tribune.*

Throughout her career, Davis wrote with the deliberate intention of effecting social change. She also pioneered the realist and naturalistic fiction that such writers as STEPHEN CRANE, UPTON SINCLAIR, and William Dean Howells would practice several decades after she began publishing. Her impact was enormous, although it has taken some time for this to be widely recognized.

Rebecca Harding Davis died of heart failure in 1910 at the home of her son Richard in Mount Kisco, New York. Her funeral was held in her home in Philadelphia, and she was cremated and interred next to her husband at Leverington Cemetery in Roxborough, Pennsylvania, her husband's hometown.

## Further Reading

Harris, Sharon M. *Rebecca Harding Davis and American Realism.* Philadelphia: University of Pennsylvania Press, 1991.

Pfaelzer, Jean. *Parlor Radical: Rebecca Harding Davis and the Origins of American Social Realism.* Pittsburgh: University of Pittsburgh Press, 1996.

Rose, Jane Atteridge. *Rebecca Harding Davis.* New York: Twayne, 1993.

## DeLillo, Don

(1936–   ) *novelist, short story writer, essayist, playwright*

A master of the postmodern novel, Don DeLillo addresses the dark side of contemporary American culture, often looking obsessively at themes such as consumerism, conspiracy, and celebrity. His work has won him critical acclaim, as well as the devoted following of his readers who have founded the Don DeLillo Society for the study of his work.

Born on November 20, 1936, to Italian immigrants, Don DeLillo was raised in the Fordham section of the Bronx, New York. His father worked for the Metropolitan Life Insurance Company as an auditor. DeLillo's childhood was spent largely in the streets, playing all kinds of ball and shooting pool. He lived in the midst of a bustling Italian-American neighborhood, with food shops and restaurants, and constant activity on the street. DeLillo has cited his Catholic upbringing and the ritual elements of the religion for awakening in him an awareness of the feelings that art sometimes creates. He has also recalled working as a playground attendant when he was 18, and spending most of his time on the job reading the novels of WILLIAM FAULKNER, ERNEST HEMINGWAY, and James Joyce, learning for the first time the beauty and possibility in language.

DeLillo graduated from Cardinal Hayes High School and later Fordham University, where he majored in communication arts. DeLillo never liked school and found little inspiration there for being a writer. Instead, his early influences included New York City, paintings at the Museum of Modern Art, music at such clubs as the Jazz Gallery and the Village Vanguard, and European movies by Federico Fellini, Jean-Luc Godard, and others.

Following his graduation from college, DeLillo tried to get a job in publishing but failed and wound up working in advertising as a copywriter for about five years. After he finally quit, in 1964, he occasionally wrote short stories, but it was not until 1966 that he began his first novel, which took him some time to write because he was always interrupting the writing to find some work that would pay the bills. He had yet to develop a routine for his writing and a commitment to the process that would enable him to be productive. He was living at this time in the Murray Hill section of Manhattan in an apartment so small that there was no stove, and the refrigerator sat in the bathroom.

Following the writing of *Americana*, his first novel, DeLillo immersed himself in reading mathematics texts, wanting to get as far as possible from his own usual interests. He wanted a fresh view of the world, and he ended up writing a novel and a play about mathematicians. Drawn to the intricacy of mathematics and the unique language of science, DeLillo wrote *Great Jones Street* (1973) and *Ratner's Star* (1976).

In 1975, he married Barbara Bennett, who was a banker at the time. She has since become a landscape designer. The couple lived in Toronto for a year, where she was working at Citibank. Then, while writing *The Names* (1982), DeLillo lived in Greece and traveled throughout the Middle East and India, where the exposure to many foreign languages and different landscapes inspired the attention given to language in the novel. *White Noise* (1985), which won the National Book Award, was written following his return to America, when he was acutely aware of the constant bombardment of television and other media in U.S. culture.

DeLillo's novels since the mid-1980s include *Libra* (1988), *Mao II* (1991), and *The Body Artist* (2001). *Underworld*, which was released in 1997, is considered by many to be his masterpiece thus far. He has also written several plays and published essays and short fiction in *Epoch*, *Sports Illustrated*, *Rolling Stone*, *The New York Times Magazine*, the *New Yorker*, *Harper's*, and other publications. DeLillo's numerous honors include the 1999 Jerusalem Prize, awarded to an author "whose work expresses the theme of the freedom of the individual in society." He was the first American to receive the honor. He lives in New York with his wife.

## Further Reading

Civello, Paul. "Don DeLillo." *Dictionary of Literary Biography: American Novelists Since WWII*, Volume 173, 5th Series, edited by James R. Giles and Wanda H. Giles. Detroit: Gale Research, 1996.

Cowart, David. *Don DeLillo: The Physics of Language*. Athens: University of Georgia Press, 2002.

Duvall, John. *Don DeLillo's Underworld: A Reader's Guide*. New York and London: Continuum Publishing, 2002.

Keesey, Douglas. *Don DeLillo*. New York: Twayne, 1993.

Ruppersburg, Hugh, and Tim Engles, eds. *Critical Essays on Don DeLillo*. New York: G. K. Hall, 2000.

## Dickey, James
### (James Lafayette Dickey III)
### (1923–1997)  *poet, novelist, literary critic*

American poet, novelist, critic, athlete, and hunter, James Dickey may be best known for his novel *Deliverance* (1970), an adventure story of four businessmen canoeing down the Cahulawassee River in rural Georgia. The story evolved into a nightmare of survival against both natural and human threats. Dickey's dominant medium was poetry, though, and he maintained that poetry should be concerned with basic human emotions. He published more than 50 books of poetry, fiction, and criticism during his writing career and continues to be remembered for his portrayal of such realistic themes as birth, death, war, murder, sports, and nature. In addition to a host of literary awards and poetry recognition, Dickey also enjoyed the honor of reading at President Jimmy Carter's inauguration ceremony in 1977. His most notable publications include: *Into the Stone and Other Poems*, *Drowning with Others*, *Buckdancer's Choice*, *Deliverance*, and *Jericho: The South Beheld*.

James Lafayette Dickey III was born on February 2, 1923, to Maibelle and Eugene Dickey in Buckhead, a suburb of Atlanta, Georgia. His father was a lawyer and used to read young James famous speeches to the jury, which helped awaken his interest in poetry and writing. Dickey grew up in Atlanta, attending the Ed S. Cook Elementary School and North Fulton High School in Buckhead. An athletic boy, he ran track and played football in high school. Although Dickey planned for a promising career in football at the Clemson University, in South Carolina, his time there was cut short after just one semester due to the onset of World War II. That winter, in 1942, Dickey enlisted in the U.S. Army Air Corps and went through flight training school. He then served as radar observer and navigator for the air force. During the war, Dickey flew 39 missions in the 418th Night Fighter Squadron, which was based in the South Pacific. Dickey has attributed this experience to his initial foray into poetry. Between combat missions, Dickey read CONRAD AIKEN and Dylan Thomas. In addition, fearing that the girls back home would forget about him, he began to focus on writing creative letters from the Pacific. This hobby ultimately blossomed into a career for Dickey and, with little knowledge of formal writing technique, he began to cultivate his talent. His first book, *Into the Stone,* was published in 1960, when he was 37 years old. It was an exploration into death and primeval instincts, most likely a theme with origins tied to Dickey's experience during the war. His fourth collection of poems, *Buckdancer's Choice,* dealt with similar issues and was awarded the National Book Award in 1965 for its realistic portrayals of compassion and human suffering.

On November 4, 1948, Dickey married Maxine Webster Syerson in Nashville, Tennessee, where he had been attending Vanderbilt University on the G.I. Bill. There he received a B.A. degree in English with a minor in philosophy and graduated 14th in his class. He also received an M.A. degree in English and began teaching at Rice University in Houston, Texas. At Rice, Dickey was able to work extensively on his notebooks and fully document his development as a poet and critic. He became a full-time poet upon being awarded a *Sewanee Review* writer's fellowship, which enabled him to take his family to France and Italy in 1954 to live for a year. Upon his return from Europe, Dickey taught at the University of Florida until his reading of his poem "The Father's Body" to a local women's group stirred a controversy. At the center of the controversy was an attempt to censor his work; as a result, Dickey left teaching and began a career in advertising with McCann-Erickson Agency in New York, returning to Atlanta in 1956.

After years in advertising and "selling his soul to the devil in the daytime and buying it back at night," according to Dickey, in 1961, after the 1960 publication of *Into the Stone and Other Poems,* he received a Guggenheim fellowship that allowed him, his wife, and his two sons to return to Europe and spend another year in Italy during 1961–62.

Following this important hiatus, which ended Dickey's work in the commercial world and began his true life's work as a poet, Dickey returned to the United States to a series of poet-in-residence positions at Reed College, San Fernando Valley State College, and the University of Wisconsin. In 1966 and again in 1967, he was appointed Consultant in Poetry to the Library of Congress, the American equivalent of poet laureate at that time.

In August 1968, Dickey and his wife, Maxine, and their two sons, Christopher and Kevin, moved to Columbia, South Carolina, where Dickey had been appointed poet-in-residence and a chaired professor of English at the University of South Carolina. The publication of his most famous work, the novel *Deliverance,* in 1970 brought more accolades, including France's Prix Medicis, which is given for best foreign book of the year. Dickey went on to write the screenplay for the film, which enjoyed its own success, including an Academy Award nomination. He remained at the University of South Carolina as a distinguished poet and teacher until his death on January 19, 1997, following complications from lung disease.

### Further Reading

Baughman, Ronald. *Understanding James Dickey.* Columbia: University of South Carolina Press, 1985.

Bruccoli, Matthew J., and Judith Baughman. *James Dickey: A Descriptive Bibliography.* Pittsburgh: University of Pittsburgh Press, 1990.

Calhoun, Richard J., and Robert W. Hill. *James Dickey.* Boston: G. K. Hall, 1983.

Dickey, Christopher. *Summer of Deliverance: A Memoir of Father and Son.* New York: Simon and Schuster, 1998.

Kirschten, Robert, ed. *Critical Essays on James Dickey.* New York: G. K. Hall, 1994.

## Dickinson, Emily
### (Emily Elizabeth Dickinson)
(1830–1886) *poet, letter writer*

One of America's most revered and intelligent poets, Emily Dickinson's ability to seize a moment in time and describe on paper what it meant to be alive has earned her a place in the pantheon of artistic genius. By choice, she led a secluded life in the home of her father. She wrote tirelessly in poetic form her ideas about God, life, death, and eternity. Though only seven works of poetry were published during her lifetime, her death revealed 1,775 poems and hundreds of letters hidden in her bedroom. Her use of compressed verse and unconventional rhyming methods, derived from English hymnology, went unappreciated by the few literary men with whom she corresponded. Years would pass before her highly original style would emerge, unaltered by intrusive editors, and become an enduring hallmark of her artistic genius.

Emily Elizabeth Dickinson was born December 10, 1830, in Amherst, Massachusetts, to Edward and Emily Norcross Dickinson. With Austin, her older brother, and Lavinia (Vinnie), her younger

This portrait shows 19th-century poet Emily Dickinson, who wrote more than 1,000 poems. *(From* Letters of Emily Dickinson, *1894. Library of Congress, Prints and Photographs Division [LC-USZ62-90564])*

sister, Emily was born into a family of wealth and influence. Her ancestors, among the first white settlers of the Connecticut Valley in 1630, were homesteaders and farmers. The early Dickinsons were fruitful and multiplied. A family historian noted that the Dickinson family "threatened to choke out all other forms of vegetation" in the area of Amherst.

Her father, Edward, a graduate of Yale, was a successful lawyer and served as a member of the Massachusetts State Senate and the U.S. House of Representatives. Edward was a busy man who served on various committees and undertook varied functions in Amherst, including that of fire warden, justice of the peace, and town meeting moderator, to name a few. He was noted as being a remote, sober man who did not give in to happy whimsy. His life embraced a Puritan's sense of duty to God, family, and country. Toward his children he was an authoritative, but not unloving, father.

Emily's grandfather, Samuel Fowler Dickinson, graduated from Dartmouth. A driven man, he wished to establish a learning institution for the education of young religious men and became one of the founders of Amherst College. Edward, his son, later became the college's treasurer.

The Dickinson family inherited the traits of their Puritan ancestors as well as a New England frugality. A measure of this frugality was demonstrated by Emily's penchant for writing her poems on scraps of paper, such as on the back of shopping lists and invitations. When Emily Dickinson turned 16, she enrolled at Mount Holyoke Female Seminary in South Hadley, Massachusetts. Along with a rigorous academic schedule, the seminary paid considerable attention to the girls' religious enrichment. Dickinson, who enjoyed the teachers and her classwork, found herself nonetheless alienated.

At this time, revivalism was sweeping New England. At Mount Holyoke, students were asked regularly to submit to faith through conversion, which entailed a public confession of faith in Christ. At the beginning of the school year, students were placed in one of two groups according to who was chosen and who was not chosen for conversion. As the other girls at Mount Holyoke were choosing Christ as their savior and surrendering their lives to his will, Dickinson remained unconverted. Her inability to yield to moral convention left upon her a stigma that lasted her entire life. In a letter to her friend Abiah Root, Dickinson lamented, "I am one of the lingering bad ones, and so do I slink away, and pause and ponder, and ponder and pause, and do work without knowing why, not surely, for this brief world, and more sure it is not for heaven, and I ask what this message means that they ask for so very eagerly; you know of this depth and fullness, will you try to tell me about it?" Dickinson seemed unable to accept the strictures of her Puritan upbringing. This may explain her self-imposed seclusion. She was aware of the stultifying air which pervaded New England towns such as Amherst—the hypocrisy and self-righteous culture of the people who lived there. Seclusion was the price she paid for not bowing to the Puritan doctrines of faith that were part of her family and town life. To her friend Jane Humphrey, she wrote, "Christ is calling everyone here, all my companions have answered, even my darling Vinnie [her younger sister] believes she loves, and trusts him, and I am standing alone in rebellion. . . ."

Dickinson completed one year at Mount Holyoke. Suffering a severe bout of the flu, her anxious father called for her to return home in 1848. His decision, no doubt, brought relief to her mind. Home would be a place of comfort to Dickinson; in the years to come, she seldom left it.

The Dickinson family, except for the father, suffered eye ailments. Dickinson's vision was perhaps the most gravely affected. In 1855, she traveled to Philadelphia (one of only four trips she made in her lifetime) to seek treatment for her eye trouble. While there, she met the Reverend Charles Wadsworth, a 41-year-old charismatic Presbyterian preacher. She began a correspondence with Wadsworth that lasted until his death in 1882. Wadsworth became her spiritual "shepherd" and adviser.

Dickinson seldom left home and it was through correspondence with men like Wadsworth that she found her creative muse. She began writing seriously in her early twenties, and Wadsworth, it is believed, became the focal point of many of her love poems.

In 1862, responding to an article he wrote in the *Atlantic Monthly*, Dickinson sent a letter to a literary man named Thomas Wentworth Higginson. With the letter, she enclosed four of her poems and asked his advice about publishing them. Higginson responded, saying her work seemed unready for the public. He described her verse as "spasmodic." He did, however, value the originality of her work, though he did not understand it, and kept in contact as her "preceptor," as she called him. It was a friendship that endured until her death.

After Higginson's correspondence, Dickinson decided against seeking her poetry's publication. With Higginson as the sole judge of her artistic talent, she acquiesced to his suggestion and never again sought publication. It may be that she was not content with simply being a published poet. She envisioned something more heroic for her poetry. Perhaps she knew, in the time she lived, there would be little appreciation for her complex and innovative style. It may also be true that she wished to concentrate privately on her art, without the outside interference that a publishing career would inevitably bring. She once stated, "Publication—is the auction of the mind . . ."

Emily Dickinson's poetry centered on themes most important to her: nature, friendship, love, God, death, and eternity. As the years passed and many of her close friends and family died, her work became more obsessed with death.

In 1885, Dickinson began suffering from a terminal illness. A streptococcal infection had invaded her kidneys. She lingered for months, confined to her bed. On May 15, 1886 she died at the age of 56. Shortly thereafter, her unmarried sister, Vinnie, who had lived with Emily in their father's house all their lives, was putting Emily's room in order when she came across Emily's poems, some bound together with string to look like booklets.

Determined that the poems should be published, Vinnie asked and obtained the help of her brother Austin's mistress, Mabel Todd. Todd approached Higginson, who agreed to publish a series of Emily's poems in 1890, and a second series in 1891. Higginson never could reconcile his view that Emily's poems were not strong, and publishing them seemed to go against his critical fiber. It appears he never understood Dickinson's work, though he feigned understanding. He edited her grammar for publication, thereby changing the ideas that Emily had tried to convey.

Emily Dickinson lived most of her life in a seclusion that allowed her to focus upon her art. In the time after her death, attempts by well-meaning editors to standardize her poems stripped them of their fundamental meaning. For years, the result of her reworked poetry left readers to think she was an undisciplined and shallow poet; the subtleties of her poetry had been erased. Then, in 1955, Thomas Johnson published her poems as she had written and intended them, preserving for future generations her unique voice and securing her place in the history of American literature.

### Further Reading

Eberwein, Jane Donahue. *An Emily Dickinson Encyclopedia.* Westport, Conn.: Greenwood Press, 1998.

Guthrie, James R. *Emily Dickinson's Vision: Illness and Identity in Her Poetry.* St. Augustine: University Press of Florida, 1998.

Wolff, Cynthia Griffin. *Emily Dickinson.* Boston: Addison Wesley, 1986.

## Didion, Joan
(1934–  ) *novelist, essayist, screenwriter, journalist*

Joan Didion is known as one of the most astute commentators on American life in the latter half of the 20th century. Her widely anthologized essays have been required reading for two generations of college students. Didion's writing is noted for its intense, lean style that often evokes a sense of disconnection and cultural despair. A combination of old-fashioned investigative reporting teamed with the subjectivity of New Journalism became the trademark of her style, which she brought to bear on a variety of cultural phenomena. Her topics have ranged from her marriage, to the rock group The Doors, to U.S. foreign and domestic policy.

Joan Didion is a fifth-generation Californian. Born in Sacramento, California, on December 5, 1934, Didion grew up in the Great Central Plains area of California, a location that would later become the setting for many of her novels. She describes herself as being an "outsider" in high school, and in an interview, Didion admitted to having "spent her entire time in high school cutting class, reading novels, and smoking in the parking lot." She graduated in 1952.

After being denied admission to Stanford University, Didion attended the University of California at Berkley, where she majored in English. While at the university, she won an essay prize sponsored by *Vogue* magazine. After graduating in 1956, Didion was hired by *Vogue*. She moved to New York City, where she worked for the magazine for eight years, eventually taking the position of associate features editor. She also contributed to *Mademoiselle* and the *National Review* during that time, then left the magazine industry to work on her first novel.

Many of Didion's novels focused on her experiences growing up in California during the 1950s and her coming of age in the 1960s, a time when she grew more and more distant from her family and her roots. In her first and second novels, *Run River* (1963) and *Play It As It Lays* (1970), she discusses the people and places, as well as the times that were California in the 1950s and 1960s. Through her characters' delusions, Didion exposes her own concern about the disintegration of North American society—the political and psychological shortcomings of an American dream gone sour. Her books gave voice to the disillusionment and pessimism that was also the face of radicalism of the 1960s. Didion received critical acclaim for *River Run, Play It As It Lays* was nominated for a National Book Award and became a best-seller.

While Didion began her career as a novelist, she is perhaps best known for her essay collections *Slouching Toward Bethlehem* (1968) and *The White Album* (1979). *Slouching Toward Bethlehem,* which has become a modern classic, contains a collection of Didion's magazine pieces that focus on the drug culture in California. In this book, she captured the mood of 1960s America, especially the center of its counterculture, California. *The White Album* is another collection of essays that present a mosaic of the late 1960s and 1970s—an era of self-discovery in California. In *The White Album,* Didion discusses such personalities as the members of the Manson family and such events as a Black Panther Party press conference.

In addition to her work as a columnist, essayist, and fiction writer, Didion also focused her powers of observation in two documentary, book-length studies: *Salvador* (1983) and *Miami* (1987). In *Salvador,* Didion tells of the war in El Salvador, describing that country's particular brand of terrorism through a description of her travels from battlefields to body dumps and an interview with a "puppet" president. In *Miami,* Didion discusses the plight of Cuban exiles in Miami, Florida.

In 1996, she published another novel, *The Last Thing He Wanted.* In this book, Didion focused on U.S. cultural and political values by depicting individual Americans and their experiences in locations such as Southeast Asia or Central America during times of political strife.

U.S. foreign policy has always been a chief concern of Didion's, particularly as it pertained to Central America. It was not until 1988, however, when *The New York Review of Books* asked her to cover the presidential election, that she even considered addressing domestic politics in her writing. She was reluctant to take the assignment and kept postponing it. She was put off by the resistant, recondite, somewhat occult irreconcilability that she sensed existed in domestic politics. It was, however, exactly these qualities that she would later term "deeply silly" aspects of political life and, once she began her assignment, would become the primary subject matter of her essays.

In *Political Fictions* (2001), Didion gathered together eight essays she wrote for *The New York Review of Books.* Throughout the essays, she argues that the American political process is controlled by a professional class that includes, among others, politicians, journalists, and commentators. She looks at Washington politics from an outsider's perspective, explaining how those working in campaign politics—from candidates to journalists—are removed from the "real life" of the country. She discusses the "disconnect," which she describes as "the divergence between what the press thought and what the public thought," the disparity between political insiders and regular people.

In her cool, unexcitable style and mordant wit, Didion chronicled and dissected U.S. politics over the next 12 years in her series of essays recording the political strategies and manipulations of politics during those years. She is quoted as saying in an interview with Jonathan Schell of the *Washington Post* in September 2001, ". . . this period of American politics became the almost exclusive preserve of a permanent professional political class—a new self-created and self-referring class, a new kind of managerial elite, made up of that small but highly visible group of people who, day by day and through administration, relay Washington to the world." She includes in this class television and print reporters, columnists, pollsters, campaign advisers, fund raisers, and rich people and powerful organizations from whom the funds are raised. And while Didion noted that this new class is on the rise, she also cautioned that "voters are dropping out."

Didion is today considered a major contemporary American novelist and journalist. Her work has held popular appeal and has been widely studied from a variety of literary perspectives as well as for its philosophical, psychological, and political insights into contemporary times and topics. Her *Where I Was From,* a collection of new essays on California, was published in 2003 to admiring reviews. She and her husband have lived in California for more than 25 years and have also collaborated on several screenplays, including *Panic in Needle Park* (1971), which was a Cannes Film Festival prizewinner; *A Star Is Born* (1976); *Up Close and Personal* (1996).

## Further Reading

Felton, Sharon. *The Critical Response to Joan Didion.* Critical Responses in Arts and Letters. Westport, Conn.: Greenwood Publishing Group, 1994.

Freedman, Ellen, ed. *Joan Didion: Essays and Conversations.* New York: Persea Books, 1984.

Reinert, Thomas. "Joan Didion and Political Irony." *Raritan: A Quarterly Review* 15, no. 3 (winter 1996): 122–136.

Stout, Janis P. *Strategies of Reticence: Silence and Meaning in the Works of Jane Austin, Willa Carter, Katherine Anne Porter, and Joan Didion.* Charlottesville: University Press of Virginia, 1990.

## Dillard, Annie
### (Annie Doak Dillard)
(1945–  ) *poet, essayist, nonfiction writer, novelist, autobiographer, nature writer*

Author of the nonfiction book *Pilgrim at Tinker Creek*, which was written when she was 29 and won her the Pulitzer Prize, Annie Dillard is often called a "modern-day mystic" for her fascination with the spiritual, her inclination to be a wanderer, and her attentiveness to the natural world.

Annie Doak was born on April 4, 1945, in Pittsburgh, Pennsylvania, to affluent parents who encouraged her sense of creativity and exploration. Educated and involved in many different cultural activities, the Doaks provided Annie and her two younger sisters with many opportunities, including piano and dance lessons and field trips to collect bugs and rocks. They also exposed their daughters to religion. Annie attended a Presbyterian church as a child and spent several summers at a fundamentalist summer camp, but during a rebellious period in high school, she found much fault with organized religion and quit going to church. Her interest in the spiritual world stayed with her, though. Following college, she learned about various religions, including Buddhism, Sufism, and the religion of the Inuit. She began to incorporate ideas from all these religions into her own spiritual views. Later in life, when she was in her late 40s, she converted to Catholicism.

Although an excellent student, Annie rebelled against her "country-club" upbringing when she was in high school. She began to get in trouble at school and turned away from both her friends and family. It was during this period that she began to write poetry and to read the transcendentalist writers, such as RALPH WALDO EMERSON and HENRY DAVID THOREAU, who would have such an important impact on her own writing. She was always interested in the outdoor world. One of her favorite books from childhood, which she still rereads every year, is *The Field Book of Ponds & Streams*.

Annie went to Hollins College, near Roanoke, Virginia, where she studied English, theology, and creative writing. Her first husband, Richard Dillard, was her creative writing professor there, a man Dillard has said "taught her everything she knows" about writing. She graduated from Hollins in 1968 with a master's degree in English, having written her dissertation on Thoreau's *Walden*. *Pilgrim at Tinker Creek*, her first book of nonfiction, clearly reveals Thoreau's influence.

Following her graduation, Dillard spent a couple of years painting and writing, during which time she published several poems. She began writing *Pilgrim at Tinker Creek* after a serious bout with pneumonia convinced her that she needed to experience life more fully. She spent four seasons living at Tinker Creek in Virginia's Blue Ridge Mountains, exploring the forests and creeks and the extensive animal life in the area. Although she spent most of her time wandering outdoors, she also read lots of books. After she had been there for a year, she started to keep a journal of her experiences. Eventually, her journal grew to include 20 volumes, at which time Dillard thought about turning it into a book. She did this by transcribing her journal onto note cards, and then working with the note cards to shape the manuscript that became her best-selling first book. At the height of the process, she was spending 15 to 16 hours a day writing, completely absorbed in the book. She lived on caffeine, lost 30 pounds, and even let all her plants die.

The book was published in 1975 and won the Pulitzer Prize. She found the attention she received somewhat disarming and subsequently moved to the Puget Sound area of Washington State, before finally settling in Connecticut and beginning to teach at Wesleyan College.

In 1982, Dillard was invited to take part in a cultural delegation of scholars traveling to China. She did, and subsequently wrote *Encounters with Chinese Writers* (1984). Her other books include three collections of poems—*Tickets for a Prayer Wheel* (1974), *Holy the Firm* (1977), and *Mornings Like This: Found Poems* (1996)—a memoir, *An American Childhood* (1988); and two books of essays—*Living by Fiction* (1988) and *Teaching a Stone to Talk: Expeditions and Encounters* (1992). Her epic novel *The Living* appeared in 1993. In addition to her book publications, her work often appears in periodicals, including the *Atlantic*, *Harper's*, the *Christian Science Monitor*, and *Cosmopolitan*.

In addition to the Pulitzer Prize, Dillard has received several Guggenheim fellowships, a National Endowment for the Arts fellowship, the Governor's Award from both Washington State and Connecticut, and the New York Press Club Award. She has divorced and remarried several times. Her daughter was born in 1984. Since the early 1980s, Dillard has taught at Wesleyan University in Connecticut.

## Further Reading

Chenetier, Marc. "Tinkering, Extravagance: Thoreau, Melville, and Annie Dillard." *Critique* 31, no. 3 (spring 1990): 157–172.

Parrish, Nancy C. *Lee Smith, Annie Dillard, and the Hollins Group.* Baton Rouge: Louisiana State University Press, 1998.

Smith, Linda L. *Annie Dillard.* New York: Twayne, 1991.

## di Prima, Diane
(1934–   ) *poet, memoirist*

During the Beat movement of the 1950s and 1960s, Diane di Prima emerged as a strong female presence in the otherwise male-dominated cultural underground of New York City and San Francisco. A striking woman, with long, flowing dark hair and large brown eyes, she became an icon of the Beat Generation. Her early memoirs gave readers a glimpse into the bohemian lifestyle of a beatnik. Often excluded by her male counterparts, who included JACK KEROUAC and ALLEN GINSBERG, di Prima focused on work, which helped sustain her as others enjoyed the fame that eluded her. While her use of free verse and simplistic language has been criticized by some, there is no doubt di Prima contributed a powerful feminine voice to the group of writers who helped shape the Beat scene.

Diane di Prima was born on August 6, 1934, in New York City, a second-generation American of Italian descent. If her home life seemed less than ideal—both parents were emotionally distant—it did not stop her from writing. She knew at age 14 she would devote her life to poetry. An early influence was her Italian grandfather, Domenico, an anarchist and atheist. He took his granddaughter to meetings in which anarchistic ideas were

explored. She was entranced. Her parents worried about the effect such meetings might have upon their daughter and eventually forbade her to go. Even so, the die was cast; her grandfather, perhaps unknowingly, had instilled within her a taste for freedom from societal constraints.

Di Prima was academically gifted. In 1951, she enrolled at Swarthmore College in Pennsylvania and majored in physics. There she discovered the writings of EZRA POUND and E. E. CUMMINGS, both of whom influenced her later writing. Feeling stifled— "Swarthmore was not a place to write," she once said—di Prima left the college in 1953 to devote her time to writing.

She moved to Greenwich Village, which agreed with her artistic sensibility, and entered into the bohemian lifestyle that would direct her future work. She took both men and women as lovers and with her friends, "made art, smoked dope, dug the new jazz." Drawing upon her sensual awakening, she authored *Memoirs of a Beatnik* in 1969. Later in her life she would say *Memoirs* was all true, except for the parts about the sex.

Her first book of poetry, *This Kind of Bird Flies Backward*, was published in 1958 and was followed by a collection of short stories, *Dinners and Nightmares* (1961). It was difficult, in the early days of the Beats, to find acceptance through major publishing houses, which tended to reflect the conservative mainstream. Di Prima's work, along with that of other Beats, was controversial and viewed by some as pornographic. Most of her early works were published by small alternative presses whose distribution was limited.

In the first of several artistic collaborations with poet AMIRI BARAKA (Le Roi Jones), she cofounded with him the New York Poets Theatre in 1961. She also coedited with Baraka *The Floating Bear*, a literary newsletter, in which she, as well as Baraka and other notable Beat artists, placed her work.

Her relationship with Baraka deepened. She found in him artistic inspiration. In her book *Recollections of My Life As a Woman*, she wrote about her decision to give birth to their daughter. In an interview for metroactive.com, di Prima said of Baraka, "I had lovers before him, but I didn't fall in love until I met him, and after him I didn't fall in love for a long, long time."

Di Prima's ability to create forums for new writing talent included the establishment of a publishing press in 1964, The Poets Press, which featured the work of avant-garde poets. In 1965, di Prima moved to upstate New York and participated in Timothy Leary's psychedelic community at Millbrook. Leary, who taught psychology at Harvard, believed the use of LSD deepened spiritual connections; one of his lectures was titled, "Turn On, Tune In and Drop Out." Though Leary first experimented on prisoners, he also turned to his friends, including di Prima and Allen Ginsberg, as well as others, to experiment with hallucinogenic drugs.

Like other Beat writers, di Prima moved west to California. In 1968, she participated in the political activities of the Diggers, an anarchist group located in Northern California. In 1974, her interest in Buddhism led her to join with Chogyam Trungpa, Ginsberg, and others in establishing the Naropa Institute in Boulder, Colorado, a university of contemplative education.

Her work in the 1970s reflected her feminist leanings. She wrote the epic poem *Loba* in 1978. *Loba* was said to be the female counterpart to Ginsberg's successful book-length poem *Howl.* In California she continued upon a journey of self-discovery and spiritualism, studying Buddhism, Sanskrit, and alchemy. Her views of Eastern philosophy influenced many of her later poems.

From 1980 to 1986 she taught hermetic and esoteric traditions in poetry at the New College of California. Since 1986, di Prima has lived in San Francisco, where she is one of the cofounders and teachers of the San Francisco Institute of Magical and Healing Arts. She received an honorary doctor of literature degree from St. Lawrence University in 1999. She was master poet-in-residence at Columbia College, Chicago, in spring 2000. Her autobiography, *Recollections of My Life as a Woman: the New York Years,* was published by Viking in 2001. Critics have called it her best work of nonfiction to date.

**Further Reading**

Butterick, George F. "Diane di Prima," in *The Beats: Literary Bohemians in Postwar America,* edited by Ann Charters, *Dictionary of Literary Biography.* Vol. 16. Detroit: Gale Research, 1983, pp. 149–160.

Knight, Brenda, et al., ed. *Women of the Beat Generation: The Writers, Artists and Muses at the Heart of a Revolution.* York Beach, Maine: Conari Press, 1996.

McDarrah, Fred W., and Gloria S. McDarrah. *Beat Generation: Glory Days in Greenwich Village.* New York: Schirmer Books, 2000.

## Doctorow, E. L.
### (Edgar Laurence Doctorow)
(1931–   ) *novelist, historical fantasy writer*

E. L. Doctorow has been celebrated for his vivid evocations of 19th- and 20th-century life in America, particularly in and around New York City. His novels place historical figures in unusual, and sometimes bizarre, settings and are written in a subtle and diverse prose style. Doctorow has experimented with several different genres of novels, including westerns, science fiction, and crime. With *The Book of Daniel* (1971), Doctorow established himself as a major American writer. The story was inspired by the anticommunist fervor of the 1950s and focuses on a boy whose parents were executed. The novel was made into a film, as were two of Doctorow's subsequent novels, *Ragtime* (1975) and *Billy Bathgate* (1989). *Ragtime* was also made into a Broadway musical.

Edgar Lawrence Doctorow was born in New York City on January 6, 1931. He attended the Bronx High School of Science and graduated with honors in 1952 from Kenyon College, where he had studied philosophy and literature. He continued his studies with graduate work at Columbia University and was drafted into the army, serving in Germany from 1953–55. Doctorow served as senior editor for New American Library from 1959–64 and editor in chief of Dial Press from 1964 to 1969. Since 1969, Doctorow has devoted his time to writing and teaching at schools such as the University of California, Irvine; Sarah Lawrence College; Yale University Drama School; Princeton University; and New York University.

*Welcome to Hard Times* (1960), a western, was Doctorow's first book. He turned to science fiction for his second novel, *Big As Life* (1966). The story unfolds after people wake up one morning to find two giant human figures standing immobile in the

Hudson River. Doctorow's subsequent books, most of which are also set in and around New York City, have fixed New York at particular moments in history and sought to render it realistically. "We live in the past to an astonishing degree, the myths we live by, the presumptions we make," Doctorow once said in an interview. "Nobody can look in the mirror and not see his mother or father. So maybe there's not such a distinction to be made."

His novel *Ragtime* (1975) took the literary world by storm. Set in the decade prior to World War I, the novel includes historical figures such as Harry Houdini, William Howard Taft, J. P. Morgan, and Sigmund Freud. *Ragtime* received the National Book Critics Circle Award for fiction in 1976 as well as the Arts and Letters Award given by the American Academy and National Institute of Arts and Letters. Doctorow's memoir, *World's Fair* (1985), won the 1986 National Book Award. He followed it with *Billy Bathgate* (1989), a coming-of-age novel about a young man's apprenticeship to New York City's most glamorous 1920s gangster, Dutch Schultz. *The Book of Daniel* draws on the story of the Julius and Ethel Rosenberg, Americans who were convicted of spying for the Soviets and executed in 1951. It is set in the 1960s but ventures frequently back into the McCarthyite 1950s. In *City of God* (2000), Doctorow uses several literary forms and genres to present fragmented biographical sketches, Homeric verse poems, and prayers. The story's central issue is the mystery of the stolen cross.

Doctorow has won the F. Scott Fitzgerald Award, the National Book Critics Circle Award, and the PEN/Faulkner Award. He also received the William Dean Howells Medal of the American Academy of Arts and Letters, the National Book Award, and the National Book Critics Circle Award. Doctorow lives in New Rochelle, in Sag Harbor and, for periods of teaching, in New York City. He is married to Helen Henslee and the couple has three children. He is a Glucksman professor of English and American Letters at New York University.

**Further Reading**

DeMott, Benjamin. "Pilgrim Among the Culturati." *The New York Times Book Review,* November 11, 1984, p. 1.

Levine, Paul. *E. L. Doctorow.* New York: Methuen, 1985.

Morris, Christopher D. *Conversations with E. L. Doctorow.* Jackson: University Press of Mississippi, 1999.

Trenner, Richard, ed. *E. L. Doctorow: Essays and Conversations.* Princeton, N.J.: Ontario Review Press, 1983.

## Dorris, Michael
(1945–1997) *novelist, nonfiction writer, essayist, screenwriter, adventure fiction writer, children's fiction writer, memoirist*

Michael Dorris is best remembered for his nonfiction work, *The Broken Cord* (1989), in which he described the challenges and sorrow he experienced as the adoptive father of his son, Abel, who suffered from fetal alcohol syndrome (FAS). Winner of a National Book Critics Circle Award for nonfiction, *The Broken Cord* served not only to introduce readers to the struggles of children and families of children with FAS but also acted as an impetus for Congress to approve legislation to warn women of the dangers (which include irreparable brain damage) to their fetuses due to drinking while pregnant. In addition to this noteworthy accomplishment, Dorris's first novel, *A Yellow Raft in Blue Water* (1987), was considered to be among the finest literary debuts of the late 20th century. In 1972, Dorris founded the Native American Studies Program at Dartmouth College, where he taught off and on for more than 25 years. Dorris and his wife, writer LOUISE ERDRICH, author of *The Bingo Palace, Tracks,* and *Love Medicine,* among others, collaborated to produce *The Crown of Columbus* (1991), a modern romance, detective, adventure, and historical novel. Dorris often addressed Native American themes and anthropology in his writing.

Michael Dorris was born on January 30, 1945, in Louisville, Kentucky. His mother was of Irish and Swiss descent and his father of Modoc Indian, French, and English descent. Growing up, Dorris spent time with his father's family in Tacoma, Washington, and on various Indian reservations in the Pacific Northwest. Following his father's premature death (it has been said that Dorris's father committed suicide), Dorris was raised by his mother and an aunt. The first member of his family to attend college, he graduated from Georgetown University in 1967 with honors in English and classical studies. He then received his graduate degrees in anthropology and philosophy from Yale. In 1972, Dorris founded the Native American Studies Program at Dartmouth College, where he continued to teach until 1995. While at Dartmouth, Dorris made the acquaintance of his student Louise Erdrich, who was one of the first women to be accepted to Dartmouth in 1976. The pair was later reacquainted at one of Erdrich's poetry readings. They married in 1981 and, in addition to Dorris's three adopted children (two boys and a girl, all of whom suffered some degree of fetal alcohol effects), the couple bore three children together. Dorris and Erdrich were known to have had a very intense and cooperative relationship as two successful writers raising six children together. Professionally, the couple collaborated on numerous books, including works of romantic fiction, which they published under the name Milou North. They coauthored two other books—*The Crown of Columbus* and *Route Two,* a collection of travel essays. In addition, Dorris edited many of Erdrich's novels before they were handed over to her publisher.

The couple endured a good deal of difficulty with at least two of their adoptive children. After *The Broken Cord* was published, Dorris said the experience of writing the book was not ". . . cathartic. One of the problems with this book is that it does not have an ending . . . it keeps going on. It's like constantly opening doors into a dark room." Even as a young man, Dorris recalled, his son Abel had to be reminded to bathe, change clothes, and eat. Abel lived in a group home and died in 1991 after being hit by a car. The perpetrator fled the scene after hitting Abel and was never found.

After Abel's death, Dorris and Erdrich experienced trouble with their adopted son, Jeffrey. Jeffrey had spent time in mental institutions as a result of fetal alcohol effect (a milder form of FAS) and had done jail time. In 1995, after a series of court cases, Jeffrey was unsuccessfully prosecuted after he threatened Dorris and Erdrich with physical harm if they did not give him $15,000 and publish a manuscript he wrote. Fearful of the threats, Dorris and Erdrich left Dartmouth for Montana

and eventually settled in Minneapolis, where Erdrich still resides with her children.

The couple eventually separated in 1996, in part due to Dorris's depression that he was known to have had since the beginning of their marriage. Erdrich moved just six blocks away and the couple attempted to continue a cooperative professional and parental relationship. However, Dorris's mental state worsened in the last year of his life. He was supposed to have begun teaching as a visiting English professor at the University of Minnesota that spring, but canceled due to illness. The *New York Times* stated that publishing lawyer Charles Rembar said Dorris had been "uncharacteristically out of touch in recent weeks" but was not especially surprised in light of his book tour to promote his recent novel, *The Cloud Chamber.* Then came accusations that Dorris had been abusing one of his young daughters. Afraid that the investigation would set off a media "feeding frenzy" and destroy him and his family, Dorris took his life on April 10, 1997. In an interview with Cable News Network (CNN) a close friend said that Dorris "didn't know how to fight [the allegations] without making things worse. And he had a realistic idea that no matter how baseless the allegations were, they were going to have a strong negative effect on his family and his work."

### Further Reading

Bourne, Daniel. "A Conversation with Michael Dorris." *Artful Dodge.* Available online. URL: http://www.wooster.edu/artfuldodge/interviews/dorris.htm. Posted October 17, 1996.

Charles, Jim. "The Young Adult Novels of Michael Dorris." *The Alan Review* (spring 1998): 46–54.

Chavkin, Allan, and Nancy Feyl Chavkin, eds. *Conversations with Louise Erdrich and Michael Dorris.* Jackson: University Press of Mississippi, 1994.

## Dos Passos, John
### (1896–1970) *novelist*

John Dos Passos was a prolific writer who produced impressionistic novels that bitterly attacked what he saw as the hypocrisy and materialism of the United States between the two world wars. He made his greatest literary impression with the trilogy *U.S.A.* (1938), a deep, searing indictment of industrial society. Through *U.S.A.*, Dos Passos developed an experimental literary device using intersecting narratives that continued from one novel to the next. The trilogy also included what became known as "newsreels," which were impressionistic collections of slogans, popular song lyrics, newspaper headlines, and extracts from political speeches. Dos Passos was embroiled in the politics of his era, embracing liberalism and later a conservatism that would alienate him from his peers.

John Dos Passos was born in Chicago on January 14, 1896, to John Randolph Dos Passos and Lucy Addison Sprigg Madison. His father was a prominent corporate attorney and his mother was from an aristocratic Virginia family. Both of his parents were married to other people at the time Dos Passos was born. He spent the first 15 years of his life with his mother, living between Virginia and Europe. His father came to visit them occasionally, but it was not until his first wife died that he was able to marry Lucy Madison. As a teenager, Dos Passos initially had trouble adjusting to the preparatory school in Connecticut that he attended. He was teased for his foreign accent, acquired while living in Europe, and gawky frame. He eventually settled in, graduated, and went on to study at Harvard University.

After graduating from Harvard in 1916, Dos Passos moved to New York City. There he associated with other writers who were on the cutting edge of the literary scene, such as F. SCOTT FITZGERALD and E. E. CUMMINGS. And, like many of his peers, Dos Passos enlisted in the military during World War I. Like ERNEST HEMINGWAY, whom he had met in France, Dos Passos drew on his wartime experience as an ambulance driver in France as background for his first novel, *One Man's Initiation* (1920). He embraced the left-wing politics of many other writers of that era, rebelling against regulations from the far-off bureaucracies that he felt were responsible for the war. Both critical and popular recognition followed his next antiwar novel, *Three Soldiers* (1921). He wrote a few other novels before publishing the immensely successful *Manhattan Transfer* (1925), a panoramic view of life in New York City between 1890 and 1925. It con-

tained fragments of popular songs, news headlines, and stream-of-consciousness monologues from a horde of unrelated characters. Dos Passos felt that his novels should paint a picture of society as it was, to expose human difficulties by showing them realistically. Following the directions of an author he admired, WALT WHITMAN, Dos Passos sought to use a "moral microscope" upon humanity.

Dos Passos married Katharine Smith in 1929. His most widely known work was his trilogy *U.S.A.*, which expanded his panorama to encompass the entire nation. The trilogy, which consists of the novels *The 42nd Parallel* (1930), *1919* (1932), and *The Big Money* (1936), depicts the growth of American materialism from the 1890s to the Great Depression of the early 1930s through characters who live through a wide array of troubles in America and Europe. During the 1930s, Dos Passos began to change his political ideas from the left to the right. The views he formed about the Spanish Civil War changed his opinions about world events. He saw the war as one between fascists on one side and communists on the other, both of whom he found equally unappealing. At the same time his writing became less impassioned and his style more direct and simple. Throughout the 1940s and 1950s, he continued to produce a great deal of work, including several novels, books of personal observation, history, biography, and travel. The best-received was *Midcentury* (1961), a novel in which he returned to the kaleidoscopic technique of his earlier successes to depict a panoramic view of postwar America.

Dos Passos's shift to the political right alienated most of his close literary acquaintances for the rest of his life, including Hemingway. Further trouble came for Dos Passos when a car accident claimed the life of his wife and made him lose his right eye in 1947. He married Elizabeth Holdridge in 1949 and they had a daughter. Dos Passos lived out much the remainder of his life on the farmland that he had inherited from his father.

John Dos Passos was a member of the American Academy of Arts and Letters and a winner of the gold medal for fiction from the National Institute of Arts and Letters. He also won the Feltrinelli Prize for Fiction. Dos Passos died of heart failure on September 28, 1970, in Baltimore, Maryland. He was 74 years old.

## Further Reading

Carr, Virginia S. *Dos Passos: A Life.* New York: Doubleday, 1984.

Nanney, Lisa. *John Dos Passos.* Boston: Twayne Publishers, 1998.

Whittemore, Reed. *Six Literary Lives: The Shared Impiety of Adams, London, Sinclair, Williams, Dos Passos, and Tate.* St. Louis: University of Missouri Press, 1993.

## Dove, Rita
### (Rita Frances Dove)
(1952–  ) *poet, short story writer, novelist, playwright*

Rita Dove was the first African-American writer and youngest person ever to be appointed poet laureate of the United States, an appointment she held from 1993 to 1995. Much of her works focus on the beauty and significance of everyday events, showing how such events make up the history of ordinary individuals and add to the experiences that human beings share. By the time she published her first poetry collection in 1980, publications in magazines and anthologies had already won Dove national acclaim.

Born in Akron, Ohio, on August 28, 1952, Rita Frances Dove was the daughter of the first black research chemist at the Goodyear tire plant in Akron. Her mother was a homemaker. Rita was a passionate reader as a child and was encouraged by her parents to read anything that interested her. Rita graduated summa cum laude from Miami University of Ohio. She received a master of fine arts degree from the University of Iowa in 1977. While attending the University of Iowa, she met a German novelist and playwright, Fred Viebahn. The two writers married in 1979.

Dove has received numerous prestigious awards and has been honored with fellowships from the National Endowment of the Arts and the Guggenheim Foundation. Her first collection of poetry, *The Yellow House on the Corner,* was published in 1980. The poems in this book deal with such topics as adolescence, romantic encounters, and glimpses into slave history. This book was followed by the publications of *Museum* in 1983 and *Thomas and Beulah* in 1986. *Thomas and Beulah* is a collection of narrative poems that are loosely based on the life of Dove's grandparents. It gives their viewpoints regarding each other and life, covering topics that range from marriage to their experiences as African Americans. Her comprehensive biography quotes one critic as saying, "She speaks with a directness and a dramatic intensity that commands attention . . . Rita Dove fashions imaginative constructs that strike the reader as much by their 'rightness' as their originality." *Thomas and Beulah* earned Dove the Pulitzer Prize in 1987 and made her the second African-American poet ever to receive the prestigious award. (GWENDOLYN BROOKS was the first.)

Dove's fourth book, *Grace Notes,* was published in 1989. In this book of poems, Dove uses humor and irony to describe elements of her own life. The poems in *Mother Love* (1995) explore family life and motherhood within the framework of the Greek myth of Demeter and Persephone. In 1999, Dove published *On the Bus with Rosa Parks,* which looks at the wide range of human experiences and includes a poem about U.S. civil-rights activist Rosa Parks.

In 1994, Dove was invited to read her poem "Lady Freedom Among Us," at the ceremony commemorating the bicentennial of the U.S. Capitol and celebrating the restoration of the Freedom Statue on the Capitol's dome. Her poetry has earned her fellowships from the National Endowment for the Arts, the Guggenheim Foundation, and the National Humanities Center, among others. In 1993, she was named one of the 10 "Outstanding Women of the Year" by *Glamour* magazine, and the NAACP honored her with its "Great American Artist" award. Dove has received honorary doctorates from several universities and colleges, and she held residences at Tuskegee University, the National Humanities Center, and the Rockefeller Foundation's Villa Serbelloni in Italy. Among the many awards she has received are the Duke Ellington Award (2001) and the Levinson Prize from *Poetry* magazine (1998).

In addition to her many collections of poetry, Dove also wrote a collection of short stories, *Fifth*

Rita Dove was the first African-American poet laureate of the United States. *(Photo of Rita Dove © by Fred Viebahn)*

CNN, and was the subject of a *Bill Moyers Journal* special on PBS. In addition, in 1994 Dove produced, in collaboration with the Library of Virginia, *Shine Up Your Words: A Morning with Rita Dove,* a program that became a nationally televised one-hour program for elementary children about poetry.

Rita Dove holds the chair as Commonwealth Professor of English at the University of Virginia in Charlottesville, where she currently lives with her husband and their daughter, Aviva.

**Further Reading**

Oh, Ray. "Rita Dove." *Voices from the Gaps.* Available online. URL: http://voices.cla.umn.edu/authors/DOVErita.html. Downloaded June 6, 2003.

Pereira, Malin. *Rita Dove's Cosmopolitanism.* Champaign: University of Illinois Press, 2003.

Seffen, Therese. *Crossing Color: Transcultural Space and Place in Rita Dove's Poetry, Fiction, and Drama,* The W. E. B. DuBois Institute Series. New York: Oxford University Press, 2001.

## Dreiser, Theodore
## (Theodore Herman Albert Dreiser)
### (1871–1945) *novelist*

A pioneer of naturalism in American literature, Theodore Dreiser wrote novels reflecting his mechanistic view of life, a concept that held people victims of the ungovernable forces of economics, biology, society, and even chance. Dreiser tended to focus on the conflict between basic human needs and society's demand for material success and social recognition. In his works, conventional morality is unimportant; virtuous behavior has little to do with material success and happiness. Dreiser's novels were held to be amoral, and he battled throughout his career against censorship and popular taste, beginning with his first novel, *Sister Carrie* (1900). It was not until 1981 that this work was published in original form. Throughout the course of his writing career, Dreiser became known as a writer whose personal battles against censorship helped pave the way for literary freedom in America. As his career progressed, he became heavily involved in politics. He

*Sunday* (1985); a novel, *Through the Ivory Gate* (1992); a book of her laureate lectures entitled *The Poet's World* (1995); and a verse drama, *The Darker Face of the Earth* (1994, with a revised edition released in 1996).

Dove's declared intention is "to bring poetry into everyday discourse . . . to make it much more of a household word." She is doing exactly that with her involvement with young children and appearances on such television programs as *Sesame Street* and *The Today Show.* Her objective in these appearances is to draw people who have little prior interest to poetry. Dove has read her poetry at a White House state dinner, has been featured on gradually replaced fiction writing with a devotion to social activities. He fought for a fair trial for the Scottsboro "boys" (several young African-American men who had been accused of rape in Alabama), he spoke out against American imperialism abroad, he attacked the abuses of financial corporations, he went to Kentucky's Harlan Coal Mines to publicize the wrongs suffered by striking miners, and he became an advocate in America for aid to the victims of the Spanish Civil War. Dreiser's dedication to fixing America's social inequalities and what he considered to be its failings abroad will forever shape his reputation. He will be remembered as not only a writer but also as an activist who, until his last days, refused to stray from his philosophical path.

Theodore Herman Albert Dreiser was born in Terre Haute, Indiana, on August 27, 1871. He was the ninth of 10 children born to Sarah Schanab and Johann Dreiser. Johann had emigrated from Mayen, Germany, in 1844, and Sarah was from a devout Mennonite family that had come to Ohio from Pennsylvania. The couple had been forced to elope and eventually chose to settle in Terre Haute, where Johann became a moderately successful proprietor of a wool mill. However, following a fire in 1869, Johann suffered a debilitating injury, the wool mill was destroyed, and, in conjunction with the economic depression of the early 1870s, the family would never recover from their economic fall. Young Dreiser's birth coincided with his family's hardship and personal tension. His youth was emotionally unstable and he had few educational opportunities, which was especially difficult for such a bookish boy.

Dreiser never completed high school. Instead, he decided at age 16 to seek work in Chicago. Then in 1889 he was sent to Indiana University by a former teacher, Mildred Fielding, and studied there for one year before he landed a job as a reporter for the *Chicago Globe*. A few years later he abandoned journalism to work as a freelance writer for such national magazines as *Harper's Monthly* and *Success*. It was then that Dreiser began writing his first novel, *Sister Carrie*, a nonmoralizing account of a woman and the limitations of her life in late 19th-century America. The Doubleday Company published the novel in 1900 under protest. The

One of the founders of American naturalism, Theodore Dreiser played an important role in establishing the groundwork for literary freedom in America, as he fought censorship issues with his own writing throughout his life. *(Library of Congress, Prints and Photographs Division [LC-USZ62-42486])*

event became one of the most famous stories in U.S. publishing history, a symbol of literary freedom for an entire generation.

In 1901, Dreiser began a second novel, *Jennie Gerhardt*, but after writing 40 chapters in five months, he was overtaken by a severe bout of writer's block and was unable to complete the novel for 10 years. He later attributed this inability to write to the suppression of *Sister Carrie*. During this period, Dreiser sought work in editorial jobs with the *New York Daily News* and the magazine *Broadway*, and then accepted the position of editor in chief of the prestigious *Delineator*, which specialized in women's fashions. Dreiser returned to his writing desk full time in 1910 and finally completed *Jennie Gerhardt*, along with 14 other books, between 1911 and 1925. The last of these, *An American Tragedy,* is a powerful murder story about a weak-willed young man who destroys himself with a little help from the materialistic society in which he lives. The book explores the flipside of the American dream and remains one of Dreiser's most impressive works.

Dreiser's life changed dramatically during this period. He moved to Greenwich Village and began a lifelong practice of what he called "varietism," a term he used to describe his habit of being sexually involved with more than one woman at the same time. In addition, it was during this time that Dreiser's involvement with leftist political thinkers and anarchists began to take form. He befriended such radicals as Emma Goldman, Max Eastman, and Daniel DeLeon. He also began to write for leftist journals such as *The Masses* and *Seven Arts.*

Throughout his life as a writer, Dreiser struggled incessantly with the threat of censorship. Publishers often refused to print manuscripts as Dreiser wrote them. Editors substantially cut both fiction and nonfiction works before publication. Also, several of Dreiser's works were even removed from bookshelves. But Dreiser continued to write prolifically throughout his publishing turmoil. His books, however, which often suffered from inadequate publicity and support, tended to enjoy critical esteem rather than high sales, and by 1919, Dreiser was at a low point financially and mentally.

Then he met Helen Richardson, whose grandmother was the sister of Dreiser's mother. The couple endured a stormy 25-year relationship, marked by periods of estrangement, separation, and many romantic affairs on Dreiser's part. The two eventually married in 1944 and permanently settled in Los Angeles. Dreiser died of heart failure on December 28, 1945, before completing the last chapter in his last book, *The Stoic* (the book was later published with an appendix by Helen Dreiser that outlined the novelist's plans for the ending). Dreiser published 27 books in his lifetime, including poetry, plays, travel books, autobiographies, and philosophical essays. Although much of his writing has received scholarly attention, his novels remain the source of his reputation.

## Further Reading

Kazin, Alfred, and Charles Shapiro. *The Stature of Theodore Dreiser.* Bloomington: Indiana University Press, 1955.

Matthiessen, F. O. *Theodore Dreiser.* New York: William Sloane, 1951.

Moers, Ellen. *Two Dreisers.* New York: Viking, 1969.

Pizer, Donald. *The Novels of Theodore Dreiser: A Critical Study.* Minneapolis: University of Minnesota Press, 1976.

Salzman, Jack. *Theodore Dreiser: The Critical Reception.* New York: David Lewis, 1972.

Wilson, Kenneth E. "A New Historical Reading of Dreiser's Fiction: Money, Labor, and Ideals." *Dreiser Studies* 26, no. 1 (spring 1995): 11–19.

## DuBois, W. E. B.
### (William Edward Burghardt DuBois)
(1868–1963) *nonfiction writer, editor, literary critic, essayist*

W. E. B. DuBois was an often controversial writer and leader of African-American thought for more than half a century. As a sociologist, educator, and civil rights leader, the outspoken DuBois frequently disagreed not only with whites but also with African Americans. DuBois was the inspiration for the literary movement known as the Harlem Renaissance and was a founder of the Pan-African movement, the belief that all people of African descent had common interests and should work together for freedom. He was also one of the founders of the National Association for the Advancement of Colored People (NAACP) and was editor of its magazine, *The Crisis.* DuBois nurtured and promoted many young and talented African Americans and believed that true integration would occur when selected blacks—the so-called Talented Tenth—excelled in literature and the fine arts. DuBois went to the West African country of Ghana late in his life as director of the *Encyclopedia Africana,* which was sponsored by the Ghanaian government, and later became a Ghanaian citizen.

William Edward Burghardt DuBois was born in the provincial town of Great Barrington, Massachusetts, on February 23, 1868, to Mary Silvina and Alfred DuBois. In his autobiography,

W. E. B. DuBois is often credited with inspiring the Harlem Renaissance. *(Photo by C. M. Battey, 1918. Library of Congress, Prints and Photographs Division [LC-USZ62-16767])*

*Dusk of Dawn* (1940), DuBois wrote that he was born with "a flood of Negro blood, a strain of French, a bit of Dutch, but, thank God, no Anglo-Saxon." He became the local correspondent for the *New York Globe* at age 15 and graduated from high school early. While at Fisk University in Tennessee, DuBois spent two summers teaching at a county school to learn more about the South and African Americans. He studied for two years at the University of Berlin and received his doctoral degree from Harvard University. His dissertation, "The Suppression of the African Slave Trade to the United States of America, 1638–1870," was the first volume published in the Harvard Historical Studies series. The dissertation pioneered the study of the international slave trade and its international and domestic legal consequences.

DuBois was a professor of Greek and Latin at Wilberforce University, in Ohio, from 1894 to 1896. He married Nina Gomer, who would later bear him two children, Burghardt (who died at age three) and Yolande. (After Nina died, in 1950, DuBois married Shirley Graham, a writer.) DuBois went on to teach sociology at the University of Pennsylvania, and it was during this time that he conducted the research for his landmark work, *The Philadelphia Negro* (1899), a sociological study of African Americans in Philadelphia. DuBois believed that the race problem was one of ignorance and he was determined to discover as much knowledge as he could. DuBois disagreed with the doctrine of BOOKER T. WASHINGTON that African Americans should raise themselves up by their own bootstraps and strive for an education that was basically vocational. DuBois envisioned the education of a "talented tenth" that would lead a self-sufficient African-American society.

A prolific writer capable of expressing himself in many disciplines, DuBois also wrote historical books such as *John Brown* (1909) and *Black Reconstruction* (1935) and novels such as *Quest of the Silver Fleece* (1911). *Black Reconstruction* dealt with the socioeconomic development of the United States after the Civil War. It portrayed the contributions of African Americans to this period, whereas before, they were always portrayed as disorganized and chaotic. In *The Souls of Black Folk* (1903), DuBois tells of the death of his young son in Atlanta and expresses the rage, sadness, and frustration that he repressed in his less personal writing. But the book also provides an overview of African-American life following the Emancipation Proclamation, a memorable critique of Booker T. Washington, and a description of the "double consciousness" of black people, who struggled to be both American and "Negro."

DuBois served as professor of economics and history at Atlanta University from 1897 to 1910. He also began to carve out a role for himself as a scholar-activist. He helped organize meetings of the Pan-African Congress and the Universal Races Congress. In 1905, DuBois and a group of pioneering African-American scholars and leaders met to discuss the issue of civil rights. This group, known as the Niagara Movement, eventually led to the formation of the NAACP in 1910. As editor of *The Crisis*, DuBois encouraged the development of black literature and art and urged his readers to see "beauty in black."

Following his bitter departure from the NAACP in 1934, DuBois increasingly became involved with progressive socialist thinkers and activists who related the problems of African Americans in terms of capitalist oppression. He had became increasingly convinced that the basic policies and ideals of the NAACP, such as its mostly white board of directors, had to be discarded if he was to remain at the organization. He believed that his race should develop a separate "group economy" of producers' and consumers' cooperatives as a weapon for fighting economic discrimination and black poverty. In *Black Folk: Then and Now* (1939), DuBois proposed that the masses of the world proletariat were African and their uprising would elevate the peoples of the world. For the next 10 years, he taught at Atlanta again, only to resign in 1944 to return to the NAACP as director of research. Four years later, after another disagreement, he left the NAACP for good. In his later years, DuBois joined the U.S. Communist Party and traveled extensively in Communist China and the Soviet Union.

DuBois was reserved and somewhat formal, and always immaculately dressed. His few intimate friends found him warm and companionable, however. Martin Luther King, Jr., wrote that history could not forget DuBois because he was a tireless explorer and a gifted discoverer of social truths: "His singular greatness lay in his quest for truth about his own people. There were very few scholars who concerned themselves with honest study of the black man and he sought to fill this immense void."

DuBois was a life member and fellow of the American Association for the Advancement of Science. He received the Spingarn Medal from NAACP, the Lenin International Peace Prize, and a Grand International Prize from the World Peace Council. He was the first African American elected to the National Institute of Arts and Letters. He received degrees from Harvard University, Atlanta University, Fisk University, and Wilberforce University and honorary degrees from Morgan State College, the University of Berlin, and Charles University. DuBois died in Ghana on August 27, 1963, at the age of 95.

## Further Reading

Andrews, William L. *Critical Essays on W. E. B. DuBois.* New York: G. K. Hall, 1985.

DuBois, W. E. B. *Dusk of Dawn.* New York: Harcourt, Brace, 1940.

Lewis, David L. *W. E. B. DuBois: Biography of a Race, 1868–1919.* New York: Holt, 1993.

———. *W. E. B. DuBois: The Fight for Equality and the American Century, 1919–1963.* New York: Henry Holt, 2000.

Moore, Jack B. *W. E. B. DuBois.* Boston: Twayne, 1981.

Rudwick, Elliott M. *W. E. B. DuBois, Voice of the Black Protest Movement.* Champaign: University of Illinois Press, 1982.

## Eliot, T. S.
### (Thomas Stearns Eliot)
(1888–1965) *poet, playwright, literary critic*

One of the most distinguished literary figures of the 20th century, T. S. Eliot wrote poetry and critical works that helped shape modern literature. In 1948 he was awarded the Nobel Prize for literature. Eliot's first major poem, "The Love Song of J. Alfred Prufrock," revealed his early style of combining humor with pessimism. *The Waste Land* (1922) expressed his horror at the spiritual turmoil of modern Europe. Eliot's "Ash-Wednesday" (1930) is more traditional, with a religious emphasis, and more hopeful than his previous work. Eliot also wrote several plays, including *Murder in the Cathedral* (1935), *The Family Reunion* (1939), *The Cocktail Party* (1950), *The Confidential Clerk* (1954), and *The Elder Statesman* (1958).

Thomas Stearns Eliot was born on September 26, 1888, in St. Louis, Missouri. He was the son of Henry Ware Eliot, president of the Hydraulic-Press Brick Company, and Charlotte Champe Stearns, a former teacher and amateur poet. Eliot was the youngest of seven children, born when his parents were prosperous and secure in their mid-forties. Afflicted with a congenital double hernia, he was in the constant eye of his mother, five older sisters, and Annie Dunne, his Irish nurse. Eliot attended Miss Locke's Primary School and Smith Academy in St. Louis. His first poems and prose pieces appeared in the *Smith Academy Record* in 1905, the year of his graduation. He spent the 1905–06 academic year at Milton Academy, a private prep school in Massachusetts, and then entered Harvard University, where his courses were so eclectic that he soon wound up on academic probation. He recovered and persisted, obtaining a B.A. degree in an elective program best described as comparative literature in three years and an M.A. degree in English literature in the fourth.

Beginning in fall 1910, Eliot spent a year in Paris, reading, writing (his works then included "The Winter Evening Settles Down" and "The Boston Evening Transcript," although he would not publish again until 1915), soaking up atmosphere, and taking courses at the Sorbonne. Upon his return to America, Eliot returned to Harvard where he undertook graduate studies in philosophy and also served as a teaching assistant. Awarded a traveling fellowship for the 1914–15 academic year, he intended to study in Germany, but the outbreak of World War I in August 1914 forced him to leave the country after only several weeks.

He made his way to London, England, which would become his home for the remaining 50 years of his life. There, on September 22, 1914, through a Harvard classmate, he met EZRA POUND, who would exert a great influence over the development of his work and his literary career. In the spring of the following year, Eliot made the acquaintance of Vivien Haigh-Wood, a vivacious young woman, different from everything he was accustomed to, who intrigued him with her uniqueness and whom he married on June 26, 1915, after an acquaintance of only two months. At his parents' urging, Eliot finished his doctoral dissertation and submitted it to Harvard, but he never completed his degree or became a professor, most likely due to Vivien's insistence that the couple not travel overseas during wartime. In spring 1917, Eliot found steady employment; his knowledge of languages qualified him for a job in the foreign section of Lloyds Bank, where he evaluated a broad range of continental documents. The job gave him the security he needed to turn back to poetry, and in 1917 he received an enormous boost from the publication of his first book, *Prufrock and Other Observations,* printed by the *Egoist* with the silent financial support of Ezra and Dorothy Pound. "The Love Song of J. Alfred Prufrock," the book's central poem, stirred up the literary world who found its combination of elevated "poetic" language and modern urban imagery new and exciting. The work is noted for its defiance of poetic convention and its reliance on fragmentation as a unifying element.

The subsequent years of Eliot's literary career were marked by increasing family worries. Eliot's father died in January 1919, producing a fit of guilt in the son who had hoped he would have time to heal the bad feelings caused by his marriage and emigration. At the same time, Vivien's emotional and physical health deteriorated, and the financial and emotional strain of her condition took its toll on Eliot. After an extended visit in the summer of 1921 from his mother and sister Marion, Eliot suffered a nervous collapse and, on his physician's advice, took a three-month rest cure, first on the coast at Margate and then at a sanitarium in Lausanne, Switzerland. During his recuperation in Lausanne, he finished writing *The Waste Land,* a poem of more than 400 lines. It was published in 1922, after Eliot adopted Pound's recommendations, resulting in the omission of much extraneous material. This work immediately became the most famous and the most controversial example of new poetry of the time. Conservative critics denounced it as impenetrable and disjointed because of its rapid shifts of setting and speaker and because of its references and quotations in numerous languages. Other readers responded to the poem's depiction of a sordid society, empty of spiritual values, in the wake of World War I. Only gradually, as Eliot's life became more visible, did audiences come to fully appreciate his spiritual questing in the poem, and only after his death did it become clear how autobiographical its descriptions of marital tension were. Eliot finally separated from Vivien in 1933 and went to great lengths thereafter to avoid personal contact with her; she was subsequently institutionalized and died in a nursing home in 1947.

Following the publication of *The Waste Land,* in search of spiritual guidance and having long found his family's Unitarianism unsatisfying, Eliot turned to the Anglican Church (the Church of England). The seeds of his future faith can be found in "The Hollow Men," though the poem was thought to be a sequel to the philosophical despair of *The Waste Land* when it appeared in *Poems 1909–1925* (1925). In June 1927, few were prepared for Eliot's baptism into the Church of England. And so, within five years of his avant-garde success, Eliot provoked a second storm. The furor grew in November 1927 when Eliot took British citizenship and again in 1928 when he collected a group of politically conservative essays under the title of *For Lancelot Andrewes,* prefacing them with a declaration that he considered himself a "classicist in literature, royalist in politics, and Anglo-Catholic in religion." Some of these writings dismayed many of his admirers, especially when he expressed a cultural nostalgia for a society organized around the Christian church and suggested that such a society could afford only a limited number of "free-thinking Jews." Such comments, coupled with several even more blatant references in some of his earlier poems, demonstrate an undeniable and deplorable anti-Semitic element in Eliot's beliefs.

His last major work of nondramatic poetry was *Four Quartets* (1943), a volume of four previously published long poems. Philosophical in nature, *Four Quartets* concerned itself with issues of time and spiritual renewal. To some, it represented the apex of Eliot's skill; for others, it lacked the dynamic tension that had informed his earlier masterpieces. In any event, *Four Quartets* ultimately paved the way for Eliot's awards in 1948 of both the Order of Merit and the Nobel Prize for literature.

T. S. Eliot died on January 4, 1965, in London, and, according to his own instructions, his ashes were interred in the church of St.

Michael's in East Coker. A commemorative plaque on the church wall bears lines chosen from *Four Quartets*: "In my beginning is my end. In my end is my beginning."

## Further Reading

Ackroyd, Peter. *T. S. Eliot*. London: Hamilton Press, 1984.

Behr, Caroline. *T. S. Eliot: A Chronology of His Life and Works*. London: Macmillan, 1983.

Blalock, Susan E. *A Guide to the Secular Poetry of T. S. Eliot*. New York: G. K. Hall, 1996.

Bush, Ronald. *T. S. Eliot: A Study in Character and Style*. New York: Oxford University Press, 1984.

Chiari, Joseph. *T. S. Eliot. A Memoir*. London: Enitharmon Press, 1982.

Gordon, Lyndall. *Eliot's Early Years*. New York: Oxford University Press, 1977.

———. *Eliot's New Life*. New York: Farrar, Straus & Giroux, 1988.

Kirk, Russell. *Eliot and His Age: T. S. Eliot's Moral Imagination in the Twentieth Century*. Chicago: Sherwood Sugden & Company, 1971.

Riquelme, John Paul. *Harmony of Dissonances: T. S. Eliot, Romanticism and Imagination*. Baltimore: Johns Hopkins University Press, 1991.

## Ellison, Ralph
### (Ralph Waldo Ellison)
(1914–1994) *novelist, short story writer, essayist*

Internationally famous following the publication of his one and only completed novel, *Invisible Man*, Ralph Ellison published just two additional books— collections of essays—during the remainder of his career. Nevertheless, he has always been considered one of the great American writers of the 20th century.

Ralph Waldo Ellison was born the grandson of slaves in Oklahoma City on March 1, 1914. "I'm raising this boy to be a poet," said his father, Lewis Alfred Ellison, who named the boy after RALPH WALDO EMERSON. Lewis, a small businessman, died when Ellison was three, and his mother, Ida (Millsap) Ellison, worked as a domestic to support the family. She also recruited for the Socialist Party.

Despite growing up without his father, Ellison did not lack opportunity or positive role models. He attended a grammar school named for Frederick Douglass and later won a music scholarship to Tuskegee Institute, the college for blacks founded by BOOKER T. WASHINGTON.

Ellison's mother bought the boy a used coronet when he was eight years old, and from that time on he wanted to be a musician. To pay for his trumpet lessons, he found jobs cutting grass, and he worked for two years as an elevator operator, earning eight dollars a week, to save for his college tuition. When he was awarded the scholarship to Tuskegee, he caught rides on freight trains from Oklahoma to Alabama, since he did not have enough money to pay for a ticket. Ellison eventually earned his doctorate from Tuskegee in 1963.

When Ellison traveled to New York City in 1936, in an unsuccessful attempt to find work and earn enough money to pay his senior year tuition at Tuskegee, he met RICHARD WRIGHT, who encouraged him to try writing. Wright published Ellison's first piece, a book review, in *New Challenge*, the magazine he edited. From that time on, Ellison began to focus on writing. He continued to study music and always linked music and writing, applying what he had learned in his formal study of music to the practice of composing fiction. Critics have often cited the rhythmic qualities of Ellison's prose and likened it to jazz composition.

When Ellison's mother was dying of a sudden illness, in 1937, he moved to Cincinnati to be with her. Alone in a strange city, without friends, and distraught over his mother's sudden passing, Ellison began to write every day. He was befriended by one of the first black lawyers in Dayton, Ohio, during this time, who gave him the keys to his office, so that he could write there in the evenings, when the law firm was closed. Here, Ellison wrote his first short stories. He also published early writings in the *Negro Quarterly* and the left-wing journal *New Masses*.

Ellison enlisted in the U.S. Merchant Marine during World War II and managed to write and publish several short stories during this time. Following the war, he began work on what, after seven years, became *Invisible Man*. He also married Fanny McConnell in 1946. *Invisible Man* was published to immediate acclaim in 1952 and won the National Book Award in 1953. The book explores the dangers inherent in relying on the visual aspects of humanity as a means of understanding who we are. It chronicles the travels of its young, nameless, black narrator as he moves through the many levels of cultural blindness in America. But *Invisible Man* is a book about more than race; it is a book about the human struggle for identity. Ellison shows the reader that anyone can be an invisible man. Acclaim for the book persisted throughout the 20th century. In 1965, a survey of 200 prominent literary figures pronounced *Invisible Man* the greatest American novel since World War II.

The book's publication brought Ellison instant fame, but some blacks criticized what they saw as the novel's less-than-militant stance against racism. Indeed, Ellison was not a militant. In his essay "The World and the Jug," written in 1963, Ellison stated that he did not write from a belief that suffering and rage are the only outlets available to blacks, but from "an American Negro tradition which teaches one to deflect racial provocation and to master and contain pain. It is a tradition which abhors as obscene any trading on one's own anguish for gain and sympathy; which springs not from a desire to deny the harshness of existence but from a will to deal with it as men at their best have always done." Ellison was a humanist at a time when mere humanism was unfashionable.

He went on to publish two books of essays during his lifetime—*Shadow and Act* (1964) and *Going to the Territory* (1986). In 1970, he became Albert Schweitzer Professor of the Humanities at New York University, where he lectured extensively on black folk culture.

For many years, Ellison worked on a second novel, but when he died of pancreatic cancer, just six weeks after his 80th birthday on April 16, 1994, the novel remained unfinished. Nevertheless, a portion of Ellison's long-awaited second novel was published posthumously under the title *Juneteenth* in 1999. *Flying Home and Other Stories* was also published posthumously in 1996. Ellison and his wife lived for more than 40 years on Riverside Drive in Harlem in New York City. In May 2003, a monument to Ellison by African-American sculptor Elizabeth Catlett was erected in a park near Ellison's longtime home.

## Further Reading

Bloom, Harold. *Modern Critical Interpretations: Invisible Man*. New York: Chelsea House Publishers, 1999.

Busby, Mark. *Ralph Ellison*. Boston: Twayne Publishers, 1991.

Corliss, Richard. "Invincible Man: Ralph Ellison 1914–1994." *Time*, April 25, 1994, p. 90.

Jackson, Lawrence. *Ralph Ellison: Emergence of Genius*. New York: Wiley, 2002.

## Emerson, Ralph Waldo
(1803–1882) *poet, essayist, editor, nonfiction writer*

Ralph Waldo Emerson was the center of the American transcendental movement, whose followers believed in the importance of individuality, as well as in a deep connection to nature. Emerson set out most of his ideas and values in the book *Nature* (1836), which represented at least 10 years of intense study in philosophy, religion, and literature. His theories that the human imagination is shaped by nature helped spark an entirely new philosophical movement in New England. He called for the birth of American individualism inspired by nature. A great prose poet, Emerson influenced a long line of American poets, including WALT WHITMAN, EMILY DICKINSON, and ROBERT FROST. He is also credited with influencing the work of philosophers such as Friedrich Nietzsche.

Ralph Waldo Emerson was born in Boston, Massachusetts, on May 25, 1803, to a conservative Unitarian minister. Most of his ancestors were clergymen and his mother was quietly devout. Emerson was a middle son of whom relatively little was expected. His father died when he was eight, the first of many premature deaths that would shape Emerson's life. He was educated in Boston and at Harvard, like his father, and graduated in 1821. While at Harvard, he began keeping a journal, which became a source of his later lectures, essays, and books. In 1825, he began to study at the Harvard Divinity School and the next year he was licensed to preach by the Middlesex Association of Ministers.

Emerson married 17-year-old Ellen Louisa Tucker in 1829; she died two years later from tuberculosis. Emerson's first and only settlement was at the important Second Unitarian Church of Boston, where he became sole pastor in 1830. Three years later he had a crisis of faith, finding that he "was not interested" in the rite of Communion. Although many accused him of subverting Christianity, he explained that for him "to be a good minister, it was necessary to leave the church" and he resigned. The address he delivered in 1838 at his alma mater, the Harvard Divinity School, made him unwelcome at Harvard for 30 years. In it, Emerson accused the church of acting "as if God were dead" and of emphasizing dogma while stifling the spirit. He then traveled extensively in Europe. He met William Wordsworth, Samuel Taylor Coleridge, and Thomas Carlyle, with whom he corresponded for half a century.

When Emerson returned to the United States, he began a career of lecturing on natural history, biology, and history. In 1835, he married Lydia Jackson. They settled in Concord, Massachusetts, and had four children while Emerson settled into his life of conversations, reading and writing, and lecturing, which provided a comfortable income. The year after his marriage, his first book, *Nature*, a collection of essays, was published. In it, Emerson emphasized individualism and rejected traditional authority. He suggested that people should "enjoy an original relation to the universe" and emphasized "the infinitude of the private man." He believed that all creation was one and that people should try to live a simple life in harmony with nature and with others. He wrote in *Nature* that "the currents of the Universal Being circulate through me; I am part or particle of God." His lectures "The American Scholar" (1837) and "Address at Divinity College" (1838) challenged the Harvard intelligentsia and warned about a lifeless Christian tradition. Twentieth-century critics have paid particular attention to Emerson's acquaintance with Asian cultural beliefs and suggested links between Emerson's transcendentalism and Asian religions, especially Taoism. Emerson was ostracized by Harvard for many years, but his message attracted young disciples, who joined the informal Transcendental Club, organized in 1836 by the Unitarian clergyman F. H. Hedge.

In 1840, Emerson took part in starting a magazine, *The Dial*, which was edited by MARGARET FULLER. The magazine served as an open forum for new ideas on the reformation of society. He published a selection of his earlier lectures and writings under the title *Essays* in 1841. It was followed by *Essays: Second Series* (1844), a collection of lectures annexed to a reprint of *Nature*. In 1845, Emerson began extensive lecturing on "the uses of great men," a series that culminated with the 1850 publication of *Representative Men* (1850). In *Nature* and *Representative Men*, Emerson encouraged his readers to trust instinct, to use their potential talents for authentic self-discovery, and to perceive nature as

Ralph Waldo Emerson was the central figure in the American transcendental movement. *(Photogravure by A. W. Elson and Co., 1901. Library of Congress, Prints and Photographs Division [LC-USZ62-9034])*

a source of inspiration and great truths. By this time, Emerson was giving as many as 80 lectures a year and his books became a source of moderate income. His *English Traits,* a summary of English character and history, appeared in 1856. It drew on a trip he made to England in 1847. While there, he noticed in particular the industrialization and the divide between upper and lower classes.

In 1851, Emerson began a series of lectures which would become *The Conduct of Life* (1860). He was vigorous in middle age, traveling frequently, but was increasingly aware of his limits and failing energy. He had become quite famous, a major figure in the U.S. literary landscape, a celebrity who brought both adulation and satire. He had been a profound inspiration for many writers, especially HENRY DAVID THOREAU and Walt Whitman. Later Emerson became involved in the antislavery movement and worked for women's rights.

Through a career of 40 years, Emerson gave about 1,500 public lectures, traveling as far as California and Canada but generally staying in Massachusetts. His audiences were captivated by his speaking style. Many of his phrases have long since passed into common English usage, such as "a minority of one" and "the devil's attorney." His essays had a sermon-like quality, which was linked to his practice as a Unitarian minister. Emerson's aim was to encourage people to cultivate "self-trust," to become what they ought to be, and to be open to the intuitive world of experience.

Emerson's heath started to fail after the partial burning of his house in 1872. He made his last tour abroad that year and then withdrew more and more from public life. Emerson died of pneumonia on April 27, 1882, in Concord.

**Further Reading**

Jacobson, David. *Emerson's Pragmatic Vision: The Dance of the Eye.* University Park: Pennsylvania State University Press, 1993.

Levin, Jonathan. *The Poetics of Transition: Emerson, Pragmatism & American Literary Modernism.* Durham, N.C.: Duke University Press, 1999.

Richardson, Robert D., Jr. *Emerson: The Mind on Fire.* Berkeley: University of California Press, 1995.

Yannella, Donald. *Ralph Waldo Emerson.* Boston: Twayne Publishers, 1982.

## Erdrich, Louise
### (Karen Louise Erdrich)
(1954–    ) *novelist, short story writer, memoirist, adventure fiction writer, children's fiction writer*

One of only a handful of American Indian writers who are widely read, Louise Erdrich published her first two books—*Jacklight,* a collection of poems, and *Love Medicine,* a novel—at the age of 30. *Love Medicine* won immediate acclaim for its use of multiple narrators and its nonchronological storytelling and anchored the writer in what would become a series of interrelated novels, with recurring characters, places, and themes.

Karen Louise Erdrich was born on July 6, 1954, in Little Falls, Minnesota, but grew up in Wahpeton, North Dakota. The first child of seven born to her Chippewa Indian mother and German-American father, she was encouraged to write from an early age. Her parents were schoolteachers at the Bureau of Indian Affairs school, and her Chippewa grandfather had been the tribal chair of the nearby Turtle Mountain Reservation. Erdrich once told an interviewer that her father paid her a nickel for each story she wrote, and her mother designed covers for her first books. Throughout high school, Erdrich kept a journal.

When she entered Dartmouth College in 1972, a member of the first Dartmouth class to include women, her chosen major was English and creative writing. She also took courses in the newly established Native American studies program, founded by her future husband and literary collaborator, MICHAEL DORRIS. Erdrich graduated from Dartmouth in 1976 and went on to Johns Hopkins University to earn her M.A. degree in creative writing in 1979. Her master's thesis later became her first collection of poems, *Jacklight.* Following graduation, Erdrich moved to Boston, where she worked for the Boston Indian Council's newspaper, *The Circle.* When she returned to Dartmouth to read from her work, she met Dorris again, and the two began a lengthy correspondence while Dorris lived in New Zealand conducting field research. They wrote letters and sent work back and forth, laying the groundwork for the collaborative relationship that would serve them for many years.

In 1980, Dorris returned to Dartmouth and Erdrich was invited to be writer-in-residence in the Native American Studies program. They married in 1981 and began collaborating on short stories. "The World's Greatest Fisherman" won them $5,000 in the Nelson Algren Fiction Prize. The story, which appeared in Erdrich's name, eventually became the first chapter of her first novel, *Love Medicine*. For many years, Dorris and Erdrich read and edited each other's work, with both of them investing themselves fully in the process. Despite this process, only two works carry both Erdrich's and Dorris's names—*The Crown of Columbus* and *Route Two*, a collection of travel essays. Most of the time, the writer who had the original idea became the named author of the book, regardless of the other's input.

This collaboration spilled over into their personal lives as well. Dorris had adopted three children before marrying Erdrich. Erdrich adopted them as well, and later the couple had three children together.

Following *Love Medicine*, which received the National Book Critics Circle Award, Erdrich wrote five more novels involving many of the same characters and settings. These include *The Beet Queen* (1986), *Tracks* (1988), *The Bingo Palace* (1994), *Tales of Burning Love* (1996), and *The Last Report on the Miracles at Little No Horse* (2002). She also wrote *The Blue Jay's Dance* (1995), a memoir about her life as a mother; *Grandmother's Pigeon* (1996), a children's story; *Antelope Wife: A Novel* (1998); *The Range Eternal* (2002) and *The Birchbark House* (2002), both children's books. *The Crown of Columbus*, the novel she cowrote with Dorris, was released in 1991.

Erdrich has been the recipient of numerous prizes for her writing, including the Pushcart Prize in Poetry, the O. Henry Prize for short fiction, the Western Literary Association Award, and a Guggenheim fellowship. Her stories have appeared in *The Best American Short Stories* series, as well as in such periodicals as the *New Yorker*, *Harper's Magazine*, *Atlantic Monthly*, and *Paris Review*.

In 1996, after 15 years of marriage, Erdrich and Dorris separated, citing the strain from the death of their oldest son in a car accident in 1991 and other family pressures, including allegations that Dorris had abused one of his children, as the cause. In 1997, Dorris committed suicide. Erdrich later revealed that her husband had been depressed and suicidal during their marriage. Erdrich lives in Minneapolis, just a few hours away from her parents in North Dakota.

### Further Reading

Chaukin, Allan, ed. *The Chippewa Landscape of Louise Erdrich*. Tuscaloosa: University of Alabama Press, 1999.

Hafen, Jane P. "Louise Erdrich," *Concise Dictionary of Literary Biography, Supplement: Modern Writers 1900–1998*, edited by Tracy S. Bitonti. Detroit: Bruccoli, Clark, Layman Inc., 1998.

Jones, Daniel, and John D. Jorgenson, eds. *Contemporary Authors*. New Revision Series, Vol. 62. Detroit: Gale Research Inc., 1998.

Moritz, Charles, ed. *Current Biography Yearbook*. New York: H. W. Wilson, 1989.

Pearlman, Mickey. *American Women Writing Fiction: Memory, Identity, Family, Space*. Louisville: University Press of Kentucky, 1989.

# F

## Faulkner, William
## (William Falkner)
(1897–1962) *novelist, short story writer, poet, screenwriter*

One of the great American writers of the 20th century, William Faulkner concentrated in his writing on his own region, the Deep South. Most of his novels are set in Yoknapatawpha County, an imaginary area in Mississippi with a colorful history and a richly varied population. The county is a microcosm of the South as a whole, and Faulkner's novels examine the effects of the dissolution of traditional values and authority on all levels of southern society. His themes centered on racism, class divisions, and family. He described the South through families who often reappeared from novel to novel. These reappearing characters usually grow older and cannot cope with social change. The reclusive Faulkner won the Nobel Prize and the Pulitzer Prize and was best known for his novels *The Sound and the Fury* (1929), *Light in August* (1932), and *Absalom, Absalom!* (1936). He also published several volumes of short stories, collections of essays, and poems.

William Faulkner was born on September 25, 1897, in New Albany, Mississippi, to Murray Falkner (William Faulkner added the "u" to his last name) and Maud (Butler) Falkner. His great-grandfather was a plantation owner, a colonel in the Confederate army, a railroad builder, and an author. William Faulkner's father moved from job to job before becoming the business manager of the

The famous southern writer William Faulkner created the imaginary Yoknapatawpha County, Mississippi, as the setting for most of his novels. *(Library of Congress, Prints and Photographs Division, Carl Van Vechten Collection [LC-USZ62-117954])*

University of Mississippi in Oxford. Faulkner began to write poetry as a teenager and dropped out of school in the 10th grade. During World War I, he was rejected by the U.S. Air Force because he was too short, so he enlisted in the Canadian air force. He did not see combat. Faulkner was accepted to the University of Mississippi and wrote stories and poems as well as drew cartoons for school publications. He quickly earned a reputation as an eccentric. His swanky dress and inability to hold down a job earned him the nickname "Count No 'count." His first book of poetry, *The Marble Faun* (1924), was critically panned and sold poorly.

Faulkner left the university in 1920 without a degree and moved to New York City, where he worked as a clerk in a bookstore. Then he returned to Oxford, where he supported himself as a postmaster at the university. He was fired for reading on the job. Faulkner drifted to New Orleans, where he intended on boarding a ship for Europe. Instead, he met novelist and short story writer SHERWOOD ANDERSON, who encouraged Faulkner to write fiction rather than poetry. Faulkner stayed in New Orleans and finished his first novel, *Soldier's Pay* (1926), in six weeks. It was critically accepted but sold few copies. Faulkner eventually did travel to Europe, visiting Italy, Switzerland, France, and England, but quickly returned to Oxford to write. In 1929, Faulkner married Estelle Oldham Franklin, his childhood sweetheart. They had one daughter, Jill. He also purchased a traditional southern pillared house in Oxford, which he named Rowan Oak, and gained a reputation as a reclusive curmudgeon. None of his next four novels, *Mosquitoes* (1927), *Sartoris* (1929), *The Sound and the Fury*, and *As I Lay Dying* (1930), sold well. After *Sanctuary* (1931), a scandalously lurid potboiler, was published, Faulkner's work began to sell, and even magazines that had rejected his stories in the past clamored to publish them.

One of Faulkner's primary themes was the abuse of blacks by southern whites and his novels are peppered with violent and sordid events. His writing diverged from that of his realistic contemporaries such as ERNEST HEMINGWAY. Faulkner mastered a rhetorical, highly symbolic style and frequently used convoluted time sequences and stream of consciousness. He often forced the reader to piece together events from a seemingly random and fragmentary series of impressions experienced by a variety of narrators. His narrative

style varies from traditional storytelling (*Light in August*) to a series of snapshots (*As I Lay Dying*) or collage (*The Sound and the Fury*). The distortion of time through the use of the inner monologue is used particularly successfully in *The Sound and the Fury*; the downfall of the Compson family is seen through the minds of several characters. Faulkner's strength at stream-of-consciousness writing has been especially noted in this book's first chapter, which displays the point of view of a mentally challenged narrator. The novel *Sanctuary* is about the degeneration of Temple Drake, a young girl from a distinguished southern family. Its sequel, *Requiem for a Nun* (1951), written partly as a drama, centered on the courtroom trial of an African-American woman who had once been a party to Temple Drake's debauchery. In *Light in August*, prejudice is shown to be most destructive when it is internalized. The theme of racial prejudice is brought up again in *Absalom, Absalom!*, which is generally considered to be Faulkner's masterpiece. It records a range of voices in a story about a young man who is rejected by his father and brother because of his mixed racial heritage. Faulkner's most outspoken moral evaluation of the relationship and the problems between blacks and whites is to be found in *Intruder in the Dust* (1948). *The Reivers* (1962), a nostalgic comedy of boyhood, was his last novel and had many similarities to MARK TWAIN's *Huckleberry Finn*.

By 1945, when Faulkner's novels were out of print, he moved to Hollywood to write, under contract, movie scripts. Faulkner cowrote screenplays to earn money, including *To Have and Have Not* (1944), based on Ernest Hemingway's novel, and *The Big Sleep* (1946), based on RAYMOND CHANDLER's novel. "Sometimes I think if I do one more treatment or screenplay, I'll lose whatever power I have as a writer," he once said. Faulkner's second period of success started in 1946 with the publication of *The Portable Faulkner*, which rescued him from near oblivion. However, his health was seriously debilitated by hard drinking, and his wife's drug addiction and declining health further shadowed his life. "I will always believe that my first responsibility is to the artist, the work," he wrote in a letter. "It is terrible that my wife does not realize or at least accept that." Faulkner had a series of affairs over the years, including one with Meta Dougherty Carpenter, which lasted for 15 years. Faulkner did not become famous until he was awarded the Nobel Prize in literature in 1949. After this award, Faulkner became a public figure and he accepted an invitation by the U.S. State Department to go on goodwill tours throughout the world.

He won the Pulitzer Prize in 1954 for *A Fable*, the National Book Award for fiction, and the Gold Medal for fiction from the National Institute of Arts and Letters. In the latter part of the 1950s, he spent some time away from Oxford, including spending a year as a writer-in-residence at the University of Virginia. He returned to Oxford in 1962 and, after his third fall from a horse in as many years, died of a heart attack on July 6, 1962. He was 64 years old.

**Further Reading**

Baker, Charles. *William Faulkner's Postcolonial South*. New York: Peter Lang, 2000.

Brooks, Cleanth. *William Faulkner: First Encounters*. New Haven: Yale University Press, 1983.

Chabrier, Gwendolyn. *Faulkner's Families: A Southern Saga*. New York: Gordian Press, 1993.

Fowler, Doreen. *Faulkner: The Return of the Repressed*. Charlottesville: University Press of Virginia, 1997.

Watson, James G. *William Faulkner: Self-Presentation and Performance*. Austin: University of Texas Press, 2000.

# Ferlinghetti, Lawrence
(1919– ) *poet*

Lawrence Ferlinghetti was known as a poet and a businessman who supported the work of poets in San Francisco during the years of the Beat scene. As the owner of City Lights Bookstore, he created a forum for himself and other struggling writers and was a central figure in nurturing the cultural renaissance of San Francisco. His poetry was written to be accessible and often reflected social and political issues of importance to him. While several of his poems contained the "outsider" view of society espoused by the Beats, they also reflected hope for a better future.

Lawrence Ferlinghetti was born on March 24, 1919, in Yonkers, New York. He spent his first years of life in France, living with relatives after his mother had been committed to an insane asylum shortly after his birth. He returned to the United States at age five and attended boarding school. After completing high school, he enrolled at University of North Carolina at Chapel Hill where he was influenced by the works of ERNEST HEMINGWAY, WILLIAM FAULKNER, and THOMAS WOLFE.

During World War II, Ferlinghetti was a lieutenant commander in the navy. He took part in the invasion of Normandy. He was called to Nagasaki six weeks after the atom bomb was dropped and witnessed firsthand the carnage and devastation. His time in Japan would influence his pacifist leanings in later years. He left the military and, with help from the G.I. Bill, earned a master's degree from Columbia University in 1947. He returned to France, enrolled at the Sorbonne, and received his Ph.D.

In 1951, he married Selden Kirby-Smith. The couple eventually had two children, Julie and Lorenzo. He and his family settled in San Francisco, where Ferlinghetti met Peter Martin, and together they published *City Lights*, a magazine committed to publishing the works of cutting-edge writers examining social and political issues. As a side venture, the men decided to open City Lights Bookstore, the only bookstore specializing in paperbacks in 1953. The City Lights Bookstore became a haven for the city's avant-garde poets and writers, and brought to the city a cultural élan. The famous Beat poetry readings, which launched the careers of ALLEN GINSBERG, WILLIAM S. BURROUGHS, and, indirectly, JACK KEROUAC, were performed at City Lights.

During the 1950s, Ferlinghetti published the Pocket Poets series, small volumes of poetry meant to introduce readers to a wider world of ideas. He ran into legal trouble after publishing Allen Ginsberg's long poem *Howl*, and was ordered to trial on obscenity charges. Prominent novelists, critics, and other literary types supported his innocence and he was eventually acquitted. The verdict marked a victory over those who would deny the protection of the First Amendment to the boundary-pushing Beats.

Ferlinghetti authored more than 30 books of poetry, including *A Coney Island of the Mind* (1958) and *The Secret Meaning of Things* (1969).

His poetic themes centered around his political ideals as well as the Beat Generation's view of being on the outside, looking in upon a conformist society. He stood against literary elitism and his poems employed commonplace words, making them accessible to most readers.

In 1998, Ferlinghetti was named the first poet laureate of San Francisco. During this time, he suggested the development of a newspaper column devoted to news in poetry, and shortly after, began writing the "Poetry as News" column for the *San Francisco Chronicle*. His concern that technology would turn people inward, away from a community of ideas, prompted him to develop the City Lights Foundation, a nonprofit organization that funded programs supporting the literary arts and its diversity of voices.

In 2000, he became the recipient of a lifetime achievement award from the National Book Critics Circle. He has remained politically active in San Francisco, speaking out about the city's gentrification and daring its people to retain the free-minded cultural atmosphere that made San Francisco special. Although divorced from his wife of 20 years, Ferlinghetti still lives near City Lights, which continues to operate as a bookstore.

### Further Reading

Cherkovski, Neeli. *Ferlinghetti: A Biography*. New York: Doubleday, 1979.

Infante, Victor. "The Beat Goes On: Lawrence Ferlinghetti Is Still a Rebel." About.com. Available online. URL: http://poetry.about.com/library/weekly/aa060600a.htm. Downloaded June 6, 2003.

Silesky, Barry. *Ferlinghetti, the Artist in His Time*. New York: Warner Books, 1990.

Smith, Larry. *Lawrence Ferlinghetti, Poet-at-Large*. Carbondale: Southern Illinois University Press, 1983.

## Fitzgerald, F. Scott
### (Francis Scott Key Fitzgerald)
(1896–1940) *novelist, short story writer, essayist, screenwriter*

F. Scott Fitzgerald became as famous for his personal life as he eventually did for his novels. He and his wife, Zelda Sayre, came to epitomize the boom of the 1920s and the depression of the 1930s as Fitzgerald descended into alcoholism and Zelda into madness. Among Fitzgerald's constant themes were youth, nostalgia, and aspiration. Although he considered himself to be a failure toward the end of his short life, *The Great Gatsby* (1925) came to define the classic American novel. Fitzgerald nurtured a cult of doomed youth, whereby to be young, rich, and beautiful was to be most fully alive, and to be old was nothing. He conveyed, as the critic H. L. MENCKEN put it, something of the "inexplicable tragedy of being alive."

Francis Scott Key Fitzgerald was born in Saint Paul, Minnesota, on September 24, 1896, to Edward and Mary (Mollie) McQuillan. Fitzgerald was the namesake and second cousin three times removed of Francis Scott Key, the author of the U.S. national anthem. His father was from Maryland, with an allegiance to the old South and its values. Fitzgerald's mother was the daughter of an Irish immigrant who became wealthy as a wholesale grocer in Saint Paul. Edward Fitzgerald failed as a manufacturer of wicker furniture in Saint Paul, and he became a salesman for Procter and Gamble in upstate New York. After he was dismissed, the family returned to Saint Paul and lived comfortably on Mollie Fitzgerald's inheritance. Fitzgerald began writing stories while attending the Saint Paul Academy. He later attended a Catholic preparatory school and was accepted at Princeton University. While he was there, Fitzgerald's literary apprenticeship took precedence over his studies. He wrote scripts and lyrics for the Princeton Triangle Club musicals and was a contributor to the *Princeton Tiger* humor magazine and the *Nassau Literary Magazine*. He quit Princeton to join the army in 1917 and was commissioned a second lieutenant in the infantry. Convinced that he would die in the war, he rapidly wrote a novel, *The Romantic Egoist*. Publisher Charles Scribner's Sons rejected the novel but praised its originality and asked for a revision. That was rejected as well.

While stationed near Montgomery, Alabama, Fitzgerald fell in love with a vivacious and sometimes reckless belle, 18-year-old Zelda Sayre, the youngest daughter of an Alabama judge. The war ended just before Fitzgerald was to be sent overseas. He went to New York City in 1919 to seek his fortune in the advertising business so he could marry Zelda, but she broke off their engagement because she was unwilling to wait for his success and unwilling to live on his small salary.

Fitzgerald's first novel, revised and renamed as *This Side of Paradise* (1920), was finally accepted by Scribners. Zelda agreed to marry Fitzgerald a week later. Set mainly at Princeton, the novel deals with the post–World War I generation and their disillusioned lives. *This Side of Paradise* made the 24-year-old Fitzgerald famous almost overnight. He then began writing stories for mass-circulation magazines, mainly to earn money. *The Saturday Evening Post* became Fitzgerald's best story market, and he was regarded as a *"Post* writer." His early commercial stories about young love introduced a fresh

F. Scott Fitzgerald wrote several American classics, including *The Great Gatsby,* before his early death at the age of 44. *(Library of Congress, Prints and Photographs Division [LC-USZ62-88103])*

character: the independent, determined young American woman who appeared in "The Offshore Pirate" and "Bernice Bobs Her Hair." Fitzgerald's more ambitious stories, such as "May Day" and "The Diamond As Big As the Ritz," were published in *The Smart Set,* which had a small circulation.

Meanwhile, the Fitzgeralds embarked on an extravagant life as young celebrities and he felt as though "life would never be so sweet again." Fitzgerald's playboy image impeded his effort to establish a serious literary reputation. The couple took an apartment in New York City and Fitzgerald wrote his second novel, *The Beautiful and Damned* (1922), a naturalistic chronicle of the dissipation of Anthony and Gloria Patch. Zelda gave birth to their only child, Frances (Scottie), and the family settled in Great Neck, on New York's Long Island. Fitzgerald expected his play *The Vegetable* to be an enormous success. The political satire, which was subtitled "From President to Postman," failed at its tryout in 1923. Fitzgerald's drinking increased. Although he was an alcoholic he wrote when he was sober. Zelda regularly drank, but she was not an alcoholic. Their frequent arguments, though, were usually triggered by alcohol.

The Fitzgeralds spent the next several years in Europe. The marriage became damaged by Zelda's involvement with a French naval aviator. In the meantime, Fitzgerald wrote *The Great Gatsby,* which marked a striking advance in his technique, utilizing a complex structure and a controlled narrative point of view. Fitzgerald's achievement received critical praise, but sales of *Gatsby* were disappointing. Stage and movie rights, however, brought additional income. In Paris, Fitzgerald formed a friendship with GERTRUDE STEIN and ERNEST HEMINGWAY, whom he admired greatly. Above all, Fitzgerald envied Hemingway's vigorous worldliness, his swagger and adventurousness. But the relationship later soured as Hemingway's star rose and Fitzgerald's began to dim. Hemingway also insulted Fitzgerald in private by referring to him as "poor old Scott" and mocking his drinking and reliance on Zelda. The Fitzgeralds remained in France until the end of 1926, alternating between Paris and the Riviera. During these years Zelda's unconventional behavior became increasingly eccentric.

The Fitzgeralds returned to the United States and after a short, unsuccessful stint of screenwriting in Hollywood, they moved into a mansion near Wilmington, Delaware. Zelda commenced ballet training, intending to become a professional dancer. The Fitzgeralds returned to France in 1929, where Zelda's intense ballet work damaged her health and estranged them. The next year she suffered her first breakdown and was treated at Prangins clinic in Switzerland. Fitzgerald lived in Swiss hotels and worked on short stories to pay for his wife's psychiatric treatment. They returned to America and rented a house in Montgomery, Alabama. Zelda suffered a relapse in 1932 and entered Johns Hopkins Hospital in Baltimore. While there, she rapidly wrote *Save Me the Waltz,* an autobiographical novel that generated considerable bitterness between the couple. Fitzgerald regarded it as preempting the material that he was using in his novel-in-progress, *Tender Is the Night* (1934). Although it was his most ambitious novel, it was a commercial failure and its merits were matters of critical dispute. Set in France during the 1920s, *Tender Is the Night* examines the deterioration of Dick Diver, a brilliant American psychiatrist, during the course of his marriage to a wealthy mental patient. For several years Fitzgerald lived near Baltimore and made several failed efforts to write. Zelda remained in and out of mental hospitals.

Ill, drunk, in debt, and unable to write commercial stories, Fitzgerald lived in hotels in the region near Asheville, North Carolina, where in 1936 Zelda entered Highland Hospital. After Baltimore, Fitzgerald did not maintain a home for Scottie. When she was 14, she went to boarding school. Nonetheless, Fitzgerald functioned as a concerned father by mail, attempting to supervise Scottie's education and to shape her social values. Fitzgerald went to Hollywood alone in the summer of 1937 with a six-month Metro-Goldwyn-Mayer (MGM) contract. Although he paid off most of his debts, he was unable to save. His trips east to visit Zelda were disastrous. In California, Fitzgerald fell in love with a movie columnist, Sheilah Graham. In 1939, he began his Hollywood novel, *The Love of the Last Tycoon* (which was published posthumously and incomplete as *The Last Tycoon* in 1941) and had written more than half of a working draft when he died of a heart attack in Graham's apartment on December 21, 1940; he was 44. Zelda Fitzgerald perished in a fire at Highland Hospital in 1948.

**Further Reading**

Berman, Ronald. *The Great Gatsby and Modern Times.* Champaign: University of Illinois Press, 1994.

Bruccoli, Matthew J. *A Brief Life of Fitzgerald.* Charles Scribner's Sons. Originally appeared in *F. Scott Fitzgerald: A Life in Letters.* New York: Scribners, 1994.

———. *Some Sort of Epic Grandeur: The Life of F. Scott Fitzgerald.* New York: Carroll & Graf Publishers, 1993.

Bruccoli, Matthew J., Scottie Fitzgerald Smith, and Joan P. Kerr. *The Romantic Egoists: Scott and Zelda Fitzgerald.* New York: Charles Scribner's Sons, 1974.

Prigozy, Ruth. *F. Scott Fitzgerald. An Overlook Press Illustrated Life.* New York: Overlook Press, 2002.

## Ford, Richard
(1944–   ) *novelist, short story writer*

Best known for his two award-winning novels that feature Frank Bascombe, *The Sportswriter* and *Independence Day,* Richard Ford was originally lauded for his short stories. *Independence Day* was the first novel ever to win both the Pulitzer Prize and the PEN/Faulkner Award and stirred critics to deem Ford a master, even a genius. For his part, Ford takes a practical approach to his chosen career. Once in an interview, he said, "Writing is the only thing I've ever done with persistence, except for being married."

The son of a salesman and a homemaker, Richard Ford was born in Jackson, Mississippi, on February 16, 1944. He remembers his mother pointing out EUDORA WELTY, who also lived in Jackson, and knew from his mother's tone of voice that being a writer was something quite worthy. As a child with dyslexia, however, Ford struggled to learn to read. He had to sound out each word, one by one, an intense process which, he has mused, may have helped him learn to create stories one word at a time. He graduated with a B.A. degree from Michigan State University in 1966, then enrolled in law school for a short time before turning his attention to writing. He received his M.F.A. degree from the University of California at Irvine in 1970.

Ford's work first began to draw attention in the late 1970s, when he was primarily writing short fiction. He became labeled as one of the New Minimalists, along with writers Tobias Wolff, RAYMOND CARVER, and Ann Beattie. He was also referred to as a regional writer after publication of his first novel, *A Piece of My Heart,* which was set in the South of his upbringing. Ford has never liked either of these labels, always insisting that his region is America, and his body of work has proven both of them inadequate.

He has published five novels and three short story collections, including *A Piece of My Heart* (1976); *The Ultimate Good Luck* (1981); *Wildlife* (1990); *The Sportswriter* (1986); and *Independence Day* (1996). Frank Bascombe, the protagonist of *The Sportswriter* and *Independence Day,* has been praised by critics as a modern-day mythic American Everyman. Ford's short fiction collections include *Rock Springs* (1987), *Women with Men* (1997), and *A Multitude of Sins: Stories* (2002). He has also written two plays, *American Tropical* and *Bright Angel,* and a work of nonfiction, *My Mother in Memory* (1987).

Ford and his wife of more than 30 years, Kristina, have lived in more than a dozen different states. In the early part of his career, Ford taught writing at such places as Princeton University, Williams College, and the University of Michigan. Since retiring from teaching in 1981, he has moved even more frequently. Much has been said by critics and readers of Ford's propensity for travel, for not becoming too rooted in any one place. Ford, himself, believes that people make too much out of his tendency to move often. Ford's wife works in city planning and her career has often initiated their moves. Nevertheless, Ford readily admits that he enjoys the stimulus of new places. In 2000, the places he declared he enjoyed living most, and indeed they are the places where he owned houses at the time, were Montana, the Mississippi Delta, and Paris.

Ford's numerous awards include a Guggenheim fellowship (1977–78), two National Endowment for the Arts fellowships (1979–80, 1985–86), an American Academy of Arts and Letters Award for Literature, and the 1994 Rea Award, which is given annually to a writer who has made a contribution to the short story as an art form. In August 2001, Ford became the literary executor of Eudora Welty's estate.

## Further Reading

Guagliardo, Huey, ed. *Conversations with Richard Ford.* Jackson: University Press of Mississippi, 2001.

———. *Perspectives on Richard Ford.* Jackson: University Press of Mississippi, 2000.

Lee, Don. "About Richard Ford: A Profile," *Ploughshares* 22 (fall 1996): 226–235.

Walker, Elinor Ann. *Richard Ford.* New York: Twayne, 2000.

## Freeman, Mary Wilkins
## (Mary E. Wilkins, Mary Eleanor Wilkins Freeman)
(1852–1930) *short story writer, novelist, children's fiction writer, poet, playwright*

Mary Eleanor Wilkins Freeman is considered an early feminist writer. She became known for her short stories, which describe New England village life during the late 19th century. Her work reflects her Puritan religious background and often deals with matters of conscience. The central character in several of Freeman's stories is an older woman in conflict with her family, village society, or a suitor. Freeman's best stories were published in the two collections *A Humble Romance* (1887) and *A New England Nun* (1891). In addition to short stories, Freeman wrote children's stories, a play, poems, and 12 novels. Her novels were not as well received as her short stories.

Mary Eleanor Wilkins was born in Randolph, Massachusetts, on October 31, 1852, to Warren Wilkins and Eleanor Lothrop Wilkins. Her father was a Civil War veteran who struggled with depression and whose work as a carpenter barely supported the family. Increasing poverty forced the family to move to Brattleboro, Vermont, in 1867, where Wilkins attended high school. After only a year at Mount Holyoke, she returned to Brattleboro in 1870, where she briefly taught school, but she generally was not able to help the family's financial state. She also painted to help support the family. The years of poverty stuck with Wilkins and for the rest of her life she would cherish the security of a financially stable home. In the early 1880s, she began earning money by writing stories for children's magazines.

By the time she was 30, Wilkins's sister, mother, and father had died. She moved back to Randolph and moved in with a childhood friend, Mary Wales. The security helped her become a more productive writer. In the 1880s her stories were well received and brought her acclaim as a realist whose style was admired for its simplicity, directness, and forcefulness. Her relationship to her Randolph neighbors was sometimes strained, however, as they saw themselves reflected in some of the unfavorable characterizations of Wilkins's stories. She has often been categorized as a regional writer, a view that has tended to minimize her work. Although she offered a vivid sense of life in New England, her most important contribution is considered to be the focus she offered on the psychology of women's conflicts at the turn of the 20th century. One of her most popular early stories was "The Revolt of Mother." But Wilkins said the story lacked realism, telling the *Saturday Evening Post* in 1917, long after the story had been published: "There never was in New England a woman like Mother. If there had been she certainly would have lacked the nerve. She would also have lacked the imagination."

Wilkins had begun to write novels in the 1890s, and while these did not meet with the same success as her stories, she continued to be praised for her insightful depiction of New England characters and settings. Her novels included *Jane Field* (1892) and *Pembroke* (1894). Wilkins did not marry until she was almost 50 years old. In 1902, she married Dr. Charles Freeman after a 10-year, and on her part often reluctant, romance. They moved to a home they had built in Metuchen, New Jersey. But Freeman's marriage brought her little happiness. Charles Freeman became addicted to alcohol and drugs, and in 1920 Freeman had him committed to a state hospital. She was legally separated from him by 1922 and he died the next year. Freeman returned to Randolph and in 1925 won

the William Dean Howells Medal for outstanding fiction. She died of heart failure on March 13, 1930.

**Further Reading**
Foster, Edward. *Mary E. Wilkins Freeman.* New York: Hendricks House, 1956.
Glasser, Leah Blatt. *In a Closet Hidden: The Life and Work of Mary E. Wilkins Freeman.* Amherst: University of Massachusetts Press, 1996.
Marchalonis, Shirley, ed. *Critical essays on Mary Wilkins Freeman.* New York: G. K. Hall, 1991.
Westbrook, Perry D. *Mary Wilkins Freeman.* Boston: Twayne Publishers, 1988.

## Freneau, Philip
### (Philip Morin Fresneau)
(1752–1832) *poet, essayist, journalist*

A leading poet of the American Revolution and one of the key figures in 18th-century literary naturalism, Philip Freneau is widely regarded as the father of American poetry. He was the first poet to employ themes from American nature and throughout his life, he struggled to satisfy the romantic poet within, as well as the part of him that was called to public service. In addition to his work as a poet, Freneau was also a successful journalist and editor, a government official, trader, and farmer.

Philip Morin Freneau was born on January 2, 1752, in New York City to parents of French Huguenot and Scottish descent. His father, Pierre Fresneau (former spelling) was a wine merchant. The younger Freneau studied the classics with tutor William Tennent, then entered Princeton in 1768. The year before Freneau entered Princeton, his father had suffered huge financial losses and died. Freneau's mother supported her son's education despite the financial hardships it created. She hoped Freneau would study theology and join the clergy. Freneau was a serious student of theology for a time, but he was passionate about literature and soon became known at Princeton for his wit and skill with words. Freneau's years at Princeton preceded the Revolutionary War and were a time of intense political concern. Although he had written several notable poems before coming to Princeton, he soon found himself drawn to public writing. He and his friends, including James Madison, William Bradford, Jr., and Hugh Henry Brackenridge, founded the American Whig Society. Members of the society often debated the more conservative members of the Cliosophic Society at Princeton, providing ample opportunity for Freneau and others to hone their skills in prose and poetic satire. *Father Bombo's Pilgrimage to Mecca in Arabia,* a narrative written by Freneau and Brackenridge, is a comic tale of life in 18th-century America and considered by some to be the first piece of prose fiction written in America. Freneau and Brackenridge later collaborated on an epic patriotic poem, "The Rising Glory of America," which came to symbolize the vision and energy of the young revolutionary generation.

Following Princeton, Freneau tried his hand at teaching but did not like it. He studied theology again but gave it up, feeling pulled toward a career of public service. Despite this, he also had a desire to escape the turmoil of politics and war. In 1776, Freneau sailed to the West Indies, where he spent two years writing and learning to sail. In 1778, he returned to New Jersey, joined the militia, and became the captain of a ship. During his time as a sailor, he spent six weeks on a British prison ship, which again gave him the time and inspiration to write. The trading voyages of this time also made possible his naval ballads, which some critics believe are his most original work.

Freneau had published two collections of poetry by the time he was 38 and developed a reputation as a committed supporter of Thomas Jefferson's Republican ideals and as a skilled sea captain. Freneau decided to settle down. He married Eleanor Forman and took a position as an assistant editor in New York, but it was not long before Jefferson and Madison called on him to set up his own newspaper in Philadelphia in opposition to the newspaper run by John Fenno, who was an avid supporter of Alexander Hamilton. Freneau founded the *National Gazette,* which took upon itself the mission of upholding Jefferson's principles. The paper even criticized George Washington's foreign policy. Freneau remained active in public life throughout the 1790s but retired once again into his private writing once Jefferson was elected in

1801. During the last 30 years of Freneau's life, he lived on a farm, worked on his poems, and wrote political essays. In order to earn an adequate income, he sold small pieces of land when needed. Despite the greater attention he was able to give to his writing, the poems of this period did not rival the poems he had written in the midst of the political fervor of the 1780s, poems such as "The Indian Burying Ground" and "The Wild Honey Suckle," which are considered his finest works. Freneau died near Freehold, New Jersey, in 1832.

## Further Reading

Austin, Mary S. *Philip Freneau, the Poet of the Revolution: A History of His Life and Times.* Detroit: Gale Research Co., 1968.

Axelrad, Jacob. *Philip Freneau, Champion of Democracy.* Austin: University of Texas Press, 1967.

Bowden, Mary W. *Philip Freneau.* Boston: Twayne, 1976.

"Philip Freneau." Bartleby.com. Available online. URL: http://www.bartleby.com/225/0918.html. Posted January 2000.

Vitzthum, Richard C. *Land and Sea: The Lyric Poetry of Philip Freneau.* Minneapolis: University of Minnesota Press, 1978.

## Frost, Robert
## (Robert Lee Frost)
### (1874–1963) *poet*

Robert Frost is generally thought of as the New England master of traditional verse forms. A rather conservative man, Frost maintained a guarded distance from the literary fashions of his time, but he was nevertheless a thoroughly modern poet in his use of everyday language and irony. The four-time winner of the Pulitzer Prize also became one of the most widely read and anthologized poets of 20th-century America.

Born in San Francisco on March 26, 1874, Robert Frost was the son of a journalist and local politician who died when Frost was just 11. Frost's mother, the former Isabelle Moody, a woman of Scottish descent, moved her family to Lawrence, Massachusetts, to live with Frost's paternal grandfather. She resumed her career as a schoolteacher in order to support her son and daughter, Jeanie, who was two years younger than Frost. Frost entered Lawrence High School in 1888, published his first poem, "La Noche Triste," in 1890, and graduated from high school in 1892, sharing the valedictorian honors with Elinor Miriam White, his future wife. In fall 1892, Frost enrolled in Dartmouth College but dropped out before the end of the term. Over the next 10 years, he taught in the local schools, worked as a bobbin boy in a textile mill, and held a position as a reporter for the *Lawrence Sentinel.* In 1894, he published his poem "My Butterfly" in the *New York Independent.*

Frost married Elinor White on December 19, 1895, in Lawrence. The couple's first child, Elliott, was born the following September. One year later, Frost entered Harvard University, where he studied for two years, before leaving in March 1899. Frost's second child, daughter Lesley, was born one month later. The following year proved difficult. Frost's firstborn child died in the summer of 1900 and his mother died of cancer later that year. In October 1900, the family moved to a farm in Derry, New Hampshire, where they remained for the next decade. Frost worked there as a cobbler, farmer, and teacher at Pinkerton Academy and at the state normal school in Plymouth. The Frosts had four more children during their years in Derry—son Carol in 1902; daughter Irma in 1903; daughter Marjorie in 1905; and daughter Elinor Bettina in 1907. All survived into adulthood except the youngest daughter, who died within days of her birth.

In 1911, the Frosts sold the farm in Derry, and one year later they sailed for England. Frost's first book of poetry, *A Boy's Will,* was published shortly after their arrival in England, when Frost was 39 years old. It was followed in 1914 by *North Boston,* a book that gained an international following and contained some of Frost's most widely read poems, including "Mending Wall," "After Apple-Picking," and "The Wood-Pile."

The Frosts remained in England until 1915, and then returned to New Hampshire, where they purchased another farm, this one in Franconia. Frost taught at Amherst College, in Amherst, Massachusetts, from 1916 through 1938. His third collection of poems, *Mountain Interval,* appeared in 1916, the same year that he was inducted into the National Institute of Arts and Letters. "The Road

Not Taken," and "Birches" stand out as some of the most notable poems in this collection.

Frost and his family remained in New England for the rest of their lives, with Frost purchasing several additional farms, including the Stone House in Shaftsbury, Vermont, near Middlebury College. At Middlebury, Frost founded the Bread Loaf School and Conference of English. Although his work was widely read and praised, the latter years of Frost's life were filled with difficulty and sadness. In 1938, Elinor died of a heart attack while in Florida. Two of Frost's daughters suffered mental breakdowns, and his son Carol committed suicide just two years after Elinor's death. Frost himself suffered from depression throughout his life.

Following his wife's death, Frost hired Kay Morrison to be his secretary and adviser. He was deeply attracted to her and composed one of his finest love poems, "A Witness Tree," in her honor. From the 1950s until his death in 1963, Frost did quite a bit of traveling for a man who was most comfortable at home. In 1957, he and his future biographer, Lawrance Thompson, traveled to England; in 1961, the pair went to Israel and Greece together. Frost recited two of his poems at President John F. Kennedy's inauguration in 1961, and in 1962 he journeyed to the Soviet Union as a member of a goodwill group.

Frost published more than 30 books during his lifetime, including several plays and collections of essays and letters, but most of his publications were poetry. Of these, some of the other most widely known titles are *Collected Poems of Robert Frost* (1930, 1939), *From Snow to Snow* (1936), *Steeple Bush* (1947), *Aforesaid* (1954), *You Come Too* (1959), *In the Clearing* (1962), and *The Poetry of Robert Frost,* published posthumously in 1969.

Frost received countless honors and awards during his lifetime. Included among these were tributes from the U.S. Senate in 1950, the American Academy of Poets in 1953, New York University in 1956, and the Huntington Hartford Foundation in 1958. He received the Congressional Gold Medal and the Edward MacDowell Medal, both in 1962. He was also appointed Simpson Lecturer for Life by Amherst College in 1949, and in 1958 he was named poetry consultant for the Library of Congress.

Robert Frost died in Boston on January 29, 1963. He is buried in the family plot in Bennington, Vermont.

### Further Reading

Cox, Sidney. *A Swinger of Birches; A Portrait of Robert Frost.* New York: New York University Press, 1969.

Fleissner, Robert F. *Frost's Road Taken.* New York: Peter Lang, 1996.

Francis, Robert. *Frost: A Time to Talk; Conversations & Indiscretions.* Amherst: University of Massachusetts Press, 1972.

Greiner, Donald J. *Robert Frost.* Chicago: American Library Association, 1974.

Meyers, Jeffrey. *Robert Frost: A Biography.* Boston: Houghton Mifflin, 1996.

Oster, Judith. *Toward Robert Frost: The Reader and the Poet.* Athens: University of Georgia Press, 1991.

Parini, Jay. *Robert Frost: A Life.* New York: Henry Holt, 1999.

## Fuller, Margaret
## (Sarah Margaret Fuller, Margaret Fuller Ossoli)
(1810–1850) *nonfiction writer, journalist, editor, essayist, literary critic*

The first female foreign correspondent and the first book review editor in the United States, Margaret Fuller was a transcendentalist and cofounder of the literary magazine *The Dial*, with RALPH WALDO EMERSON. Her classic work, *Woman in the Nineteenth Century*, became a key text in the early feminist movement and has remained an important piece of literature for feminists in more than 150 years since it was first published.

Sarah Margaret Fuller was born on May 23, 1810, in Cambridgeport (now part of Cambridge), Massachusetts, to Timothy Fuller and Margaret Crane Fuller. Her father was a lawyer who later served in the Senate. She was educated at home by her father, who believed that his daughter should receive the most rigorous and broad education possible. She was a precocious student and suffered from nightmares and severe headaches that plagued her all her life. At the age of six, she was reading Virgil and reciting it at night for her father.

After Virgil, she went on to Plutarch and Shakespeare. Fuller attended a finishing school in Groton, Massachusetts, where she learned several modern languages and began to read the literature of other cultures.

When Fuller was in her mid-20s, she began her career as a teacher at the progressive Temple School, having been hired by Bronson Alcott, the father of LOUISA MAY ALCOTT. After one year, she moved to Providence, Rhode Island, and became the principal teacher at the Green Street School. She returned to Boston in 1839, where she became a member of the Transcendental Club, whose other members included Ralph Waldo Emerson, HENRY DAVID THOREAU, Elizabeth Palmer Peabody, and Bronson Alcott, among other intellectuals. She also began hosting "conversations" in

Among other achievements, Margaret Fuller became the first U.S. female foreign corespondent before her death in a shipwreck at the age of 40. *(Library of Congress, Prints and Photographs Division [LC-USZ62-47039])*

her home. These were gatherings of people to listen to a chosen speaker and then discuss the ideas.

Along with Emerson and the critic and reformer, George Ripley, she cofounded *The Dial* magazine and served as its editor from 1840 to 1842. She also frequently wrote art reviews and other articles for the quarterly publication. In 1843, her essay calling for equal rights for women, "The Great Lawsuit: Man versus Men, Woman versus Women," was published in *The Dial.*

In 1841, Brook Farm was created by George and Sophia Dana Ripley as an experiment in communal living near West Roxbury, Massachusetts. Both Fuller and Emerson decided not to join the community but were frequent visitors, participating in the community's rich intellectual life.

Her first book, *Summer on the Lakes,* was a travel memoir published in 1844. She was invited to join the staff of the *New York Tribune* as a book review editor shortly after her first book appeared. Fuller took it upon herself in her role as a reviewer to expose U.S. readers to American literature. Prior to this time, most Americans looked to British writers for literature. Her book *Woman in the Nineteenth Century,* published in 1845, became a classic feminist text and was instrumental in inspiring the Seneca Falls Women's Convention in 1849.

Fuller became a foreign correspondent for the *New York Tribune* in 1846 and traveled to Europe, where she wrote on a variety of subjects. Her articles were collected in the book *At Home and Abroad,* which was published in 1856. Shortly after arriving in Europe, Fuller was visiting Rome and met Marchese Giovanni Angelo d'Ossoli, a nobleman involved in revolutionary activities. The couple had a son named Angelo in 1847 and married the following year. During the Revolution of 1848 and the siege of Rome by the French forces, Fuller took the job of managing one of the hospitals of the city, while her husband took part in the fighting. When the city fell in 1850, Fuller and her family were forced to flee. They sailed to America in May 1850, and had almost reached the coast of New York, when a storm developed and their ship ran aground and was wrecked near Fire Island on July 19, 1850. Many of Fuller's friends searched for her body, including Thoreau, but it was never found. Her two-year-old son's body was recovered. A Margaret Fuller memorial was established in Pyrola Path in Cambridge, Massachusetts.

## Further Reading

Blanchard, Paula. *Margaret Fuller from Transcendentalism to Revolution.* New York: Dell, 1978.

Cole, Phyllis. "The Nineteenth-Century Women's Rights Movement and the Canonization of Margaret Fuller." *ESQ* 44, nos. 1–2 (1998): 1–35.

Fleischmann, Fritz, ed. *Margaret Fuller's Cultural Critique: Her Age and Legacy.* New York: Peter Lang, 2000.

Kornfeld, Eve. *Margaret Fuller: A Brief Biography with Documents.* Boston: Bedford Books, 1997.

Slater, Abby. *In Search of Margaret Fuller: A Biography.* New York: Delacorte Press, 1978.

# Gibbons, Kaye
## (Bertha Kaye Batts)
(1960–  ) *novelist, short story writer, memoirist*

The author of numerous critically acclaimed novels, Kaye Gibbons is known for her resilient female southern narrators, whose voices are both lyrical and strong. As one interviewer put it, "Her characters not only look life square in the face, but can, if necessary, stare it down." Ellen Foster, the titular narrator of her first and most famous novel, has often been called "a southern Holden Caulfield." Gibbons is also known for her frank exploration, in both fiction and nonfiction, of her experience with manic-depression, an illness that has plagued her since she was a young adult.

Kaye Gibbons was born Bertha Kaye Batts in 1960 in Rocky Mount, North Carolina, a small town of tobacco and cotton farmers at the edge of North Carolina's coastal plain. Her mother committed suicide when Kaye was 10, and her alcoholic, abusive father died shortly thereafter. From then on, Gibbons was passed among numerous incapable family members until she finally landed in the caring home of her foster mother.

Gibbons was an excellent student and graduated from Rocky Mount Senior High School in 1978. She enrolled at North Carolina State University after receiving a last-minute scholarship. She supported herself in college by working part time as a waitress and tutor and became interested in literature. She was hospitalized for her first serious depression in 1980, married soon after, and had her first daughter, Mary, in 1984. When Mary developed chronic ear infections, Gibbons dropped out of college to care for her full time. But she did eventually work her way into a class taught by the legendary professor of writing and literature, Louis Rubin, at the nearby University of North Carolina. It was while reading *Huckleberry Finn* that she realized her own voice might be able to carry a story. She wrote what was to be the beginning of *Ellen Foster* and showed it to Rubin, who told her simply to finish it. When she did, he accepted it immediately for publication at Algonquin Press, and Gibbons's autobiographical first novel was soon released. It was 1987, and Gibbons was 27. *Ellen Foster* won the Sue Kaufman Prize from the American Academy and Institute of Arts and Letters and received generous praise from literary greats such as EUDORA WELTY and WALKER PERCY. It was an overnight success and has never been out of print.

Since that time, Gibbons has written and published a novel just about every two years, had two more daughters, divorced, and married again. Her second husband, Frank Ward, is a Raleigh attorney. The two met when he was president of the North Carolina State University Friends of the Library, a position that found him introducing Gibbons when she gave public readings. The couple married in 1993 and are known for having forged an extremely warm and affectionate marriage.

Although none of Gibbons's subsequent novels has received the critical and popular acclaim of

*Ellen Foster*, all have been well received. Her fourth book, *Charms for the Easy Life*, was on the *New York Times* bestseller list, as was *Sights Unseen*, her fifth novel, which successfully explores the effects of a mother's manic-depression on her three daughters, borrowing generously again from Gibbons's life. *On the Occasion of My Last Afternoon*, her sixth novel, was published in 1997.

In addition to numerous awards for her writing, including a special citation from the Ernest Hemingway Foundation for *Ellen Foster*, a National Endowment for the Arts fellowship, a PEN/Revson Award, and the *Chicago Tribune*'s Heartland Prize, two of Gibbons's books—*Ellen Foster* and *A Virtuous Woman*—were chosen for Oprah's Book Club. Each book sold more than 800,000 copies after being selected. A made-for-television film of *Ellen Foster* was released in 1998. In 1996, she was awarded the Chevalier de L'Ordre des Arts et des Lettres, a French knighthood recognizing her contribution to literature. She was the youngest writer ever to receive this award. Gibbons has continued to live with her family and write in Raleigh, North Carolina.

## Further Reading

Groover, Kristina K. *The Wilderness Within: American Women Writers and Spiritual Quest*. Fayetteville: University of Arkansas Press, 1998.

Guinn, Matthew. *After Southern Modernism: Fiction of the Contemporary South*. Jackson: University Press of Mississippi, 1999.

Makowsky, Veronica A. "'The Only Hard Part Was the Food': Recipes for Self-Nurture in Kaye Gibbons' Novels." *Southern Quarterly* 30 (1992): 43–52.

## Gilchrist, Ellen

(1935–   ) *novelist, short story writer, poet*

A writer of poems, short stories, novels, and nonfiction commentaries, Ellen Gilchrist is a diverse writer whom critics have praised repeatedly for her subtle perceptions, unique characters, and innovative plotlines set in her native Mississippi. As Sabine Durrant commented in the *London Times*, her writing "swings between the familiar and the shocking, the everyday and the traumatic. . . . She writes about ordinary happenings in out of the way places, of meetings between recognizable characters from her other fiction and strangers, above all of domestic routine disrupted by violence." The world of her fiction is crooked; the surprise endings that are characteristic of her works often shock readers. "It is disorienting stuff," noted Durrant, "but controlled always by Gilchrist's wry tone and gentle insight."

Ellen Gilchrist was born February 20, 1935, in Vicksburg, Mississippi. She was the only daughter in the family, having an older brother named Dooley. Of being the sister in her family, Gilchrist has said, "My mother liked him best and my father liked him best and my maternal grandparents liked him best." Gilchrist spent most of her childhood being brought up by her maternal grandparents on a plantation in Issaquena County, Mississippi. At age 14, she wrote a column called "Chit and Chat About This and That" for a local Franklin, Kentucky, paper. She attended Vanderbilt University, in Nashville, Tennessee, and then earned her B.A. degree from Millsaps College in Jackson, Mississippi. Gilchrist eloped at age 19, marrying Marshall Walker, an engineering student, with whom she had three children. When she divorced Walker (she subsequently remarried and divorced two more times), she enrolled in a creative writing course at Millsaps College, where she was taught by EUDORA WELTY. She also studied creative writing at the University of Arkansas in Fayetteville.

Gilchrist worked as an author and journalist, as a contributing editor for the *Vieux Carré Courier* from 1976 to 1979, and as a commentator on National Public Radio's (NPR) *Morning Edition* from 1984 to 1985. Her commentaries for NPR have been published in her book *Falling Through Space* (1987, 2000).

Gilchrist's first book was a book of poetry, *The Land Surveyor's Daughter* (1979). A few years later, she followed it up with *Riding Out the Tropical Depression: Selected Poems, 1975–1985* (1986). But it is as a fiction writer that she has garnered the most attention. She attracted critical and popular accolades upon the publication of her book of short fiction, *In the Land of Dreamy Dreams*, in 1981. In its first 10 months in print, the volume sold more than 10,000 copies in the Southwest alone, a feat particularly impressive given that the book was published by a university press and thus lacked the aggressive marketing of larger, commercial publishers. Critics shared the public's opinion of the book. In a review for the *Washington Post Book World*, Susan Wood wrote, "Gilchrist may serve as prime evidence for the optimists among us who continue to believe that few truly gifted writers remain unknown forever. And Gilchrist is the real thing all right. In fact, it's difficult to review a first book as good as this without resorting to every known superlative cliché—there are, after all, just so many ways to say 'auspicious debut.'" Gilchrist followed up with her first novel, *The Anunciation*, in 1983, and the following year, a second collection of stories, *Victory over Japan*, which won the 1984 American Book Award for fiction. Like her earlier collection, it was received warmly by critics. Beverly Lowry in the *New York Times Book Review* wrote, "Those who loved *In the Land of Dreamy Dreams* will not be disappointed. Many of the same characters reappear. . . . Often new characters show up with old names. . . . These crossovers are neither distracting nor accidental. . . . Ellen Gilchrist is only changing costumes, and she can 'do wonderful tricks with her voice.'"

As of 2003, Gilchrist has more than 17 published books to her credit. She has received numerous awards, including the Mississippi Arts Festival Poetry Award, the New York Quarterly Craft in Poetry Award, the National Endowment for the Arts Grant in fiction, and the Mississippi Academy of Arts and Science Award for fiction. In addition, she has received the Mississippi Institute of Arts and Letters Literature Award three times, for *In the Land of Dreamy Dreams*, *Victory Over Japan*, and *I Cannot Get You Close Enough*, respectively. The last-named collection of three novellas was published in 1990.

Gilchrist has continued to publish fiction, alternating between short story collections and novels. Although some critics have found her more recent work to be uneven, most concede that such unevenness is only in relation to the tremendous achievement of her earliest work. In 2000, Gilchrist published *Collected Stories*, which featured 34 stories from seven different collections spanning her

career, and in 2002 another collection, *I, Rhoda Manning, Go Hunting with My Daddy: And Other Stories* was published.

**Further Reading**

Abbot, Dorothy. *Mississippi Authors: An Anthology.* Jackson: University Press of Mississippi, 1991.

Gilchrist, Ellen. *Falling Through Space: The Journals of Ellen Gilchrist.* Jackson: University Press of Mississippi, 2000.

McCay, Mary A. *Ellen Gilchrist.* Boston: Twayne, 1997.

## Gilman, Charlotte Perkins (Charlotte Anna Perkins, Charlotte Perkins Stetson)
(1860–1935) *novelist, nonfiction writer, short story writer, editor*

American writer, economist, lecturer, and early theorist of the feminist movement, Charlotte Perkins Gilman wrote more than 200 short stories and more than 10 novels during her prolific career. Gilman refused to call herself a feminist, but instead referred to her work and goals as those of a "humanist," which included campaigning for the cause of women's suffrage as well as working and living in opposition to the traditional and domestic roles of women. Gilman viewed the domestic environment as an institution that oppressed women. Her famous story, "The Yellow Wall-Paper" (1892), depicted a depressed woman who slowly descended into madness in her room while her well-meaning husband was often away working at his hospital.

Charlotte Anna Perkins was born in Hartford, Connecticut, on July 3, 1860, the daughter of Frederick Beecher Perkins, a librarian and writer, and Mary Westcott Perkins. As a result of being abandoned by her husband following the death of one of their children in 1866, Mary was forced to care for her children while living on the brink of poverty and often drifting among boardinghouses and various relatives' homes. Perkins would often spend time with her great-aunts, Catherine Beecher, advocate of "domestic feminism"; Isabella Beecher Hooker, an ardent suffragist; and HARRIET BEECHER STOWE, author of *Uncle Tom's Cabin*. Although she was a voracious reader and largely self-educated, Perkins studied two years at Rhode Island School of Design (1878–80) and then earned her living designing greeting cards. In 1884, she married Charles Walter Stetson, an aspiring artist. After the birth of their daughter Katharine, she was beset by depression. She eventually entered a sanitarium in Philadelphia in 1886 and, under the orders of Dr. Silas Weir Mitchell, underwent a "rest cure," then a popular (but sometimes controversial) treatment for "nervous prostration," which forbade any type of physical activity or intellectual stimulation. His recommendations, "Live as domestic a life as possible" and "Never touch a pen, brush or pencil as long as you live," she later satirized in her autobiography and in her most renowned short story, "The Yellow Wall-Paper," which first appeared in *New England Magazine* (1892). The narrator is a young mother suffering from a nervous depression. Her husband, John, a physician, does not believe in such things. He has ordered her to rest in the bedroom of their rented house. The patterns of the room's hideous yellow wallpaper start to haunt her. She sees a woman creeping through it, as if she wants to get out.

After a month of hospitalization, the writer returned to her husband and daughter and subsequently suffered a nervous breakdown. In 1888, she left Stetson and moved with Katherine to California, where her recovery was swift.

In the early 1890s, she began writing and lecturing. She followed "The Yellow Wall-Paper" with *In This Our World* (1893), a volume of satiric poems with feminist themes. In 1898, she published her most famous book, *Women and Economics*, in which she attacked the old division of social roles. She believed that male aggressiveness and maternal roles of women are artificial and not necessary for survival anymore: "There is no female mind. The brain is not an organ of sex. As well speak of a female liver." Only economic independence could bring true freedom for women and make them equal partners to their husbands, she asserted. In *Concerning Children* (1900), Perkins advocated professional child care.

She married her cousin George Gilman, a New York lawyer, in 1902. During the next two decades she gained fame with her lectures on women's issues, ethics, labor, and social concerns. Gilman

founded, edited, and wrote her own monthly journal, *Forerunner,* from 1909 to 1916. Several of her novels appeared first in the paper. Then in 1922, annoyed with life in a multiracial metropolis, she moved with her husband from New York to Norwich, Connecticut, and wrote *His Religion and Hers,* in which she planned a religion freed from the dictates of oppressive patriarchal instincts. In 1932, she was diagnosed with breast cancer. After her husband died in 1934, she returned to California to live near her daughter. Gilman died on August 17, 1935, in Pasadena, California; she ended her own life by taking an overdose of chloroform. Her autobiography, *The Living of Charlotte Perkins Gilman* (1935), appeared posthumously. Gilman's mystery novel, *Unpunished,* was not published during her lifetime, but appeared in 1997 by The Feminist Press. Gilman and her work were mostly forgotten for two decades until the feminist movement of the 1960s revived public interest in her.

### Further Reading

Karpinski, Joanne B. *Critical Essays on Charlotte Perkins Gilman.* New York: G. K. Hall & Company, 1992.

Lane, Ann J. *To Herland and Beyond: The Life of Charlotte Perkins Gilman.* New York: Pantheon Books, 1980.

Weinstock, Jeffrey Andrew. *The Pedagogical Wallpaper: Teaching Charlotte Perkins Gilman's "The Yellow Wall-Paper."* New York: Peter Lang Publishing, 2003.

Wynn-Allen, Polly. *Building Domestic Liberty: Charlotte Perkins Gilman's Architectural Feminism.* Boston: University of Massachusetts Press, 1988.

## Ginsberg, Allen
(1926–1997) *poet*

As a core member of what became known as the Beat writers, whose members included JACK KEROUAC and WILLIAM S. BURROUGHS, Allen Ginsberg wrote poetry that voiced his alienation from a materialistic postwar American society. Using his own life as poetic material, Ginsberg wrote long, rambling poems that echoed his natural speaking cadence. His controversial poem *Howl,* in which he wrote about his homosexuality and drug use, brought to his friend and publisher, LAWRENCE FERLINGHETTI, obscenity charges. His first reading of *Howl* at San Francisco's Six Gallery in October 1955 heralded the poetry renaissance in that city. In what is considered Ginsberg's greatest work, *Kaddish,* he wrote about the mental illness and death of his mother. He was a political and social activist, speaking out against the Vietnam War, homosexual intolerance, and the environmental degradation by corporations. He was awarded the National Book Award for a poetry collection, *The Fall of America.* In later years, he became a member of the prestigious American Academy and Institute of Arts and Letters.

Allen Ginsberg was born in Newark, New Jersey, on June 3, 1926. He and his older brother Eugene lived with their father, Louis, a poet and high school English teacher, and their mother, Naomi. Ginsberg's mother suffered from severe mental illness. She endured frightening episodes of paranoid psychosis in which she believed mind-draining wires protruded from her head. While he was a junior in high school, Ginsberg's mother begged him to take her to a therapist at a nearby nursing home for treatment. She would spend the rest of her life in psychiatric institutions, undergoing electric shock therapy and a lobotomy before dying at Pilgrim State Hospital in 1956.

Naomi Ginsberg's illness would have a profound effect on her younger son. In later years, Ginsberg's poetry would try to encompass all that his mother's life and illness had meant to him. Her mental illness brought complex feelings to a boy who already felt outcast for being homosexual. After graduating from East Side High School, he entered Columbia University on a scholarship in 1943. He intended to study law to please his father, but his plans changed when he started to hang around campus with a motley group of friends.

The group of men with whom Ginsberg met included Lucien Carr, William S. Burroughs, Jack Kerouac, John Clellon Holmes, a drug addict from Times Square named Herbert Huncke, and a drifter from Denver named Neal Cassady. Together, they formed the core of what became known as the Beat writers. The term *beat* came about when Jack Kerouac used it to describe their feeling of spiritual depletion and alienation from a society they viewed as hypocritical, materialistic, and spiritually bankrupt. It was not long before Ginsberg fell in love with the charismatic Neal Cassady and a relationship followed. Cassady continued to pursue heterosexual affairs at the same time. Kerouac wrote about the couple's intense relationship in his book *On the Road.*

Influenced by the work of WALT WHITMAN and William Blake, Ginsberg felt confined by the traditional poetry he had been studying at Columbia. During his senior year at Columbia, he began to experiment with drugs, hoping to achieve an altered state of being by which he could create poetry that bore a visionary meaning beyond rhythm and meter and pretty words and images.

In 1949, Ginsberg was arrested for allowing Huncke to store stolen goods in his apartment. Instead of doing jail time, with the help of his professors, Ginsberg was placed in the Columbia Psychiatric Institute for eight months. During that time, he met and befriended a young writer named Carl Solomon, who was being treated for depression.

After traveling to Mexico in 1953 to work at a Yucatán archeological site, Ginsberg moved to San Francisco where he met and fell in love with Peter Orlovsky. Ginsberg settled down to a marketing research job and thought about enrolling in a graduate program at the University of California at Berkeley.

In 1955, Ginsberg wrote an epic poem dedicated to Carl Solomon, called *Howl for Carl Solomon.* Inspiration for the style of *Howl* came after Ginsberg read a poem by Jack Kerouac entitled "Mexico City Blues." In October, at a gathering of poets and friends at the Six Gallery in San Francisco, Ginsberg read the first part of *Howl.* With Kerouac passing around jugs of wine to the audience, and slapping the side of a bottle while chanting, "Go!" Ginsberg loosened up and let the energy of the moment carry himself and his work. When he had finished his reading, the crowd reacted with thunderous applause. Everyone agreed that something wonderful and defining had happened that night. It was, they thought, a cultural renaissance.

Through Lawrence Ferlinghetti, owner of the City Lights Bookstore and City Lights publishing, *Howl* was published as number four in the City Lights Pocket Poets series. After *Howl's* publication, the pocket booklets were quickly confiscated by U.S.

Customs and the San Francisco police. Ferlinghetti and his City Lights store manager were arrested and charged with publishing and selling obscene material.

With support from members of the mainstream literary community behind them and the American Civil Liberties Union defending them, Ferlinghetti and his store manager were found not guilty in a highly publicized trial in October 1957. The judge ruled *Howl* had social importance. Ginsberg left California after the trial. With Orlovsky, he traveled to Paris to escape the furor created over *Howl.*

The couple returned to New York City in 1958. Ginsberg was a member of Timothy Leary's psychedelic community at Millbrook in upstate New York and continued to experiment with different drugs. He tried to make sense of his mother's suffering and death and his relationship with her. He felt remorse and guilt for not being there when she died in 1956. While ingesting various drugs, Ginsberg wrote *Kaddish for Naomi Ginsberg. Kaddish* was published in 1961 and was an overwhelming success.

In 1962, while traveling in India, Ginsberg met with holy men whom he asked for help in meditating. He was introduced to Buddhism and other Eastern philosophies. He realized, during a train journey through Japan, that meditation was the key to enlightenment, not drugs. He returned to the United States in 1963, having written a poem about his experience called "The Change."

During the Democratic National Convention of 1968, held in Chicago, Ginsberg created a sensation when he mounted a makeshift stage and chanted "om" while a clash between protesters and police played out before him at Chicago's Grant Park. He became the elder spokesman for the next generation of antiestablishment-minded youngsters—the hippies.

In 1971, Ginsberg, along with poet Anne Waldman, created a writing program at the Naropa Institute in Boulder, Colorado, which they named the Jack Kerouac School of Disembodied Poetics. Naropa was the first Buddhist accredited university in North America. During the summer, Ginsberg taught poetry classes at Naropa, and then headed east to lecture at Brooklyn College during the academic school year.

Ginsberg continued to speak out against the government's drug policies, for the rights of gays and lesbians, and the need for environmental protection. Though suffering from the effects of diabetes and a stroke, he continued to travel extensively and to publish. In April 1997, at the age of 70, he died of liver cancer at his home in the East Village, in New York City.

### Further Reading

Caveney, Graham. *Screaming with Joy: The Life of Allen Ginsberg.* New York: Broadway Books, 1999.

Ginsberg, Allen, et al. *Spontaneous Mind: Selected Interviews.* New York: HarperCollins, 2001.

Miles, Barry. *Ginsberg: A Biography.* New York: HarperCollins, 1990.

## Giovanni, Nikki
### (Yolande Cornelia Giovanni, Jr.)
(1943–  ) *poet*

Long known as the "Princess of Black Poetry," Nikki Giovanni has honed her poetic voice into a strikingly honest and passionate one that clearly transcends racial confines. She is the author of 13 books of poetry, including *Love Poems,* for which she received a National Association for the Advancement of Colored People (NAACP) Image Award, as well as *Truth Is on Its Way,* her 1971 record album for which she was awarded the National Association of Radio and Television Announcers Award (NARTAA) for the Best Spoken Word Album. Giovanni also holds the Langston Hughes Medal for Outstanding Poetry and has been named Woman of the Year by *Mademoiselle, Ladies' Home Journal,* and *Essence.* Her poetry was also the subject of the 1987 Public Broadcasting System (PBS) film *Spirit to Spirit: The Poetry of Nikki Giovanni.* Giovanni has taught English and creative writing at Queens College, Rutgers University, and Ohio State University. In 1987, under the Commonwealth Visiting Professor Program, she began teaching writing, poetry, and literature at Virginia Polytechnic Institute and State University (Virginia Tech) and has since accepted a permanent position as a professor of English.

Born Yolande Cornelia Giovanni, Jr., on June 7, 1943, in Knoxville, Tennessee, she was raised in the Lincoln Heights area of Cincinnati, Ohio, and attended the all-black Fisk University. It was at Fisk that her first political and artistic contributions to the black community began to take form. Giovanni was an active member of both the Writers' Workshop and the Student Non-Violent Coordinating Committee (SNCC). Upon her graduation, she became a member of the Black Arts movement, a group of black intellectuals armed with politically charged radical poetry intended to open black awareness to the injustices of the time. In 1967, Giovanni entered the University of Pennsylvania's School of Social Work with a Ford Foundation fellowship, then received a grant from the National Foundation of the Arts to attend Columbia University's School of Fine Arts in 1968. That year Giovanni published her first book of poetry, *Black Feeling, Black Talk,* followed with *Black Judgment,* in 1969. An advocate of the Black Aesthetic, Giovanni believed a poet must use her craft toward social revolution and must inspire her audience with her language.

On August 31, 1969, Giovanni gave birth to her son, Thomas Watson Giovanni. At the time she was teaching at Queens College and at Rutgers University. With the birth of Thomas, Giovanni's tone began to change—from a younger, more militant one to a softer, more maternal one. It was during this period in her life that challenges as a single mother began to influence her writing style. *Spin a Soft Black Song* (1971), *Ego-Tripping* (1973), and *Vacation Time* (1980) were all collections of poetry created for children. Her writing was infused with emotions of loneliness, family affection, and disappointment. The release of her 1971 album *Truth Is On Its Way,* for which she was awarded the NAR-TAA for the Best Spoken Word Album and *Mademoiselle*'s Highest Achievement Award, was a compilation of lyrics resounding with expectation and rebirth. Then in 1974, Giovanni published *Gemini: An Extended Autobiographical Statement on My First Twenty-Five Years of Being a Black Poet,* her first journey into prose. It was not until 1983 and her publication of *Those Who Ride the Night Winds* that Giovanni really returned to a political agenda in her writing.

Nikki Giovanni accepted a permanent position as professor of English at Virginia Tech in 1989, where she still continues to teach. In August 1999, she became a University Distinguished Professor. She received honorary doctorates of humane letters from Indiana University and from Otterbein College in Westerville, Ohio, in 1991 and 1992, respectively. Her numerous awards include the SHero Award for Lifetime Achievement (2001) and the Rosa Parks Women of Courage Award, of which she was the first recipient in 2001. In 2002, she published *Quilting the Black-Eyed Pea: Poems and Not Quite Poems.* Giovanni has been a critical leader within the Black Arts movement throughout her career and continues to inspire and educate people of all ages and ethnicities with her strong spoken word.

## Further Reading

Fowler, Virginia C. *Nikki Giovanni.* New York: Twayne Publishing, 1992.

Gergoudaki, Ekaterini. "Nikki Giovanni: The Poet as Explorer of Outer and Inner Space." *Women, Creators of Culture.* Thessaloniki: Aristotle Press, 1997.

Gibson, Donald B., ed. *Modern Black Poets: A Collection of Critical Essays.* Englewood Cliffs, N.J.: Prentice-Hall, 1973.

Pinkerton, Josephson Judith. *Nikki Giovanni: Poet of the People.* Berkeley Heights, N.J.: Enslow Publishers, 2000.

Roberts, Crystal Kimpson. "Poet Laureate Shows Her Views on Carving Out a Successful Career." *The Black Collegian* 30 (February 2000): 155.

## Glasgow, Ellen
### (Ellen Anderson Gholson Glasgow)
(1873–1945) *novelist, short story writer, poet*

Ellen Glasgow was an intensely private woman who pioneered a poetic realism that influenced a generation of southern writers. Despite her importance to literature and the autobiographical intensity of her work, however, Glasgow never received the attention accorded to writers such as EDITH WHARTON and WILLA CATHER, the novelists she was most often compared with, during her lifetime. She published her first novel, *The Descendant* (1897), when she was 24 years old. Glasgow's literary career included 20 novels, one collection of poems, one of stories, and a book of literary criticism. A recurring theme in her literature was the idea of a woman trying to live up to a man's ideal. She won the Pulitzer Prize for her last published novel, *In This Our Life* (1941). Her autobiography, *A Woman Within*, was published posthumously in 1954.

Born in Richmond, Virginia, on April 22, 1873, Ellen Anderson Gholson Glasgow grew up in an aristocratic family. She developed her education by reading philosophy, social and political theory, and European literature. Although she lived most of her life in Richmond, Glasgow was never comfortable with the role that southern culture assigned to its women and was seen by her neighbors as a colorful eccentric. Self-educated, she was an early suffragist and bitterly critical of the romanticism through which the South viewed the history of the Confederacy. Yet her own attitudes towards race were often confused and naive. Glasgow survived a sickly childhood, the premature deaths of her mother and favorite sister, and the suicides of a brother and brother-in-law. She also struggled with deafness, which afflicted her from her early 20s. She traveled widely to Europe and the Middle East, meeting other writers, including Thomas Hardy, Joseph Conrad, and Arnold Bennett. She was engaged to lawyer Henry Anderson for many years, but never married, and was involved with a married man she identified only as Gerald B.

From the beginning of her creative life, Glasgow rejected the Victorian definitions of femininity that dominated the social attitudes of her day. She produced seven novels of enduring literary merit. *The Deliverance* (1904), among the best of her early novels, offers a naturalistic treatment of the class conflicts emerging after the Civil War. In her women's trilogy, *Virginia* (1913), *Life and Gabriella* (1916), and *Barren Ground* (1925), "Glasgow assigns each of her Virginia heroines a fate determined by her response to the patriarchal code of feminine behavior that had formed her, a code that, as Glasgow shows so well in *Barren Ground*, always pitted women against their own biological natures," wrote Tonette Bond Inge in the *Encyclopedia of Southern Culture*. Glasgow then produced three comedies of manners, *The Romantic Comedians* (1926), *They Stooped to Folly* (1929),

and *The Sheltered Life* (1932). According to Inge, "In these novels of urban Virginian life depicting the clash of generations, she again shows her women characters reacting to patriarchal stereotypes limiting their individuality and growth, while at the same time exposing either with comic or with satiric irony the limitations these views of women place on the male characters who hold them."

In her novels, Glasgow said, she was seeking the "living pulse" of experience. A popular writer, she was on the best-seller lists five times. Glasgow's artistic recognition had reached its height in 1931 when, as the acknowledged doyenne of southern letters, she presided over the Southern Writers Conference at the University of Virginia. She suffered from heart disease for many years and died in her sleep at home in Richmond on November 21, 1945, at age 72.

## Further Reading

Auchincloss, Louis. *Ellen Glasgow*. Minneapolis: University of Minnesota Press, 1964.

Godbold, E. Stanly, Jr. *Ellen Glasgow and the Woman Within*. Baton Rouge: Louisiana State University Press, 1972.

Raper, Julius R. *From the Sunken Garden: The Fiction of Ellen Glasgow, 1916–1945*. Baton Rouge: Louisiana State University Press, 1980.

Scura, Dorothy M. *Ellen Glasgow: New Perspectives*. Nashville: University of Tennessee Press, 1995.

Wagner, Linda W. *Ellen Glasgow: Beyond Convention*. Austin: University of Texas Press, 1982.

## Glück, Louise
### (Louise Elisabeth Glück, Louise Glueck)
(1943– ) *poet, literary critic*

Known as a master of the contemporary lyric, Louise Glück explores in her poems the mythic, the spiritual, and the archetypal, addressing the themes of rejection, loss, and isolation in deceptively simple language. In her work, the reader encounters grand voices that speak with the most ordinary words. The author of nine collections of poetry and one collection of essays on poetry, Glück has established herself as one of the leading poets writing at the beginning of the 21st century.

Louise Elisabeth Glück (pronounced "Glick") was born April 22, 1943, in New York City. She grew up in Long Island and graduated from Hewlett High School in 1961. She attended Sarah Lawrence College and Columbia University, before beginning her teaching career at Goddard College in Vermont.

Glück's first collection of poems, *Firstborn*, appeared in 1968 and won the Academy of American Poets Prize. Although many critics found it disturbing, often citing the angry tone of the first-person narrators encountered in the book, they nevertheless praised its exacting language and inventive use of rhyme. *The House on Marshland*, which was published in 1975, introduced Glück's fascination with mythic and historical characters. Her poems, which have continued throughout her career to delve into myth and the mystical, have been praised for the way they tell tales with the simplest words coming from a voice of "spiritual prophecy," as the critic Helen Vendler has called it. This "hierarchic and unearthly tone" and the use of little, everyday words are perhaps the most memorable features of her work. About her use of simple language, Glück wrote in an essay in *Proofs & Theories*:

> From the time, at four or five or six, I first started reading poems, first thought of the poets I read as my companions, my predecessors—from the beginning I preferred the simplest vocabulary. What fascinated me were the possibilities of context. What I responded to, on the page, was the way a poem could liberate, by means of a word's setting, through subtleties of timing, of pacing, that word's full and surprising range of meaning. It seemed to me that simple language best suited this enterprise; such language, in being generic, is likely to contain the greatest and most dramatic variety of meaning within individual words.

*Descending Figure* (1980) was Glück's third collection and was followed by *Triumph of Achilles* (1985), the winner of the National Book Critics Circle Award for Poetry that year. *Ararat* was published in

1990 to significant critical acclaim as well, and then Glück won the Pulitzer Prize for her collection *The Wild Iris* (1992). Her other books include *The First Five Books of Poems* (1997), *Vita Nova* (1999), and *The Seven Ages* (2001). Glück has also published a highly regarded book of essays, *Proofs & Theories* (1994), which won the PEN/Martha Albrand Nonfiction Award. She also edited *The Best American Poetry 1993*.

In addition to the awards already mentioned, Glück has been the recipient of several Guggenheim fellowships and the Rebekah Johnson Bobbitt National Prize for Poetry, is a member of the American Academy of Arts and Letters, and was the recipient of an Honorary Phi Beta Kappa from Harvard. In 1999, she was also named a special consultant to the Library of Congress poet laureate, Robert Pinsky, along with former poet laureate RITA DOVE.

Louise Glück has worked for some time at Williams College in Williamstown, Massachusetts, where she is the Preston S. Parish Third Century Lecturer in English. She lives in Cambridge, Massachusetts, has one son, and is divorced.

**Further Reading**

Dodd, Elizabeth. *The Veiled Mirror and the Woman Poet: H.D., Louise Bogan, Elizabeth Bishop, and Louise Glück.* Columbia: University of Missouri Press, 1992.

Frost, Elisabeth. "Disharmonies of Desire." *The Women's Review of Books* 14, no. 2 (November 1996): 24.

Gordon, Emily. "Above an Abyss." *The Nation*, April 29, 1996, pp. 28–29.

Longenbach, James. "Poetry in Review." *The Yale Review* 84, no. 4 (September 1996): 158–162.

# Green, Paul
## (Paul Eliot Green)
(1894–1981) *playwright, novelist, short story writer, poet*

Paul Green, dramatist, teacher and author, was one of North Carolina's most revered writers and one of America's most distinguished. His outlooks on challenging issues—equal rights, desegregation, war, and nuclear arms—were all prevalent themes in his writing. In the 1920s, his plays about black life were among the early attempts in American literature to take seriously the experience of African Americans in the American South. One of his plays, *In Abraham's Bosom*, won a Pulitzer Prize in 1927. *Hymn to the Rising Son* (1935) is a powerful work that furthered the movement to abolish chain gangs in the South. In *Johnny Johnson* (1936), with his collaborator, the composer Kurt Weill, Green created a poignant musical drama on the urgency of world peace. Of Green's numerous plays, 11 had Broadway or other professional productions.

Paul Eliot Green was born on March 17, 1894, in Harnett County, North Carolina. He was the son of William Archibald and Betty Lorine Byrd Green. He grew up on his father's farm, engaging in the labors and pleasures of rural life, the latter of which included minor-league baseball and music. At a young age, Green taught himself to play the violin and later composed music for his plays. After earning enough money for tuition, Green enrolled in the University of North Carolina in 1916 and began his career in writing, producing poems that were published in *The Carolina Magazine* and a play that was produced by his senior class during their commencement ceremony.

In April 1917, before finishing his first year at the university, Green enlisted in the U.S. Army for service in World War I. Before leaving for France, he published, at his own expense, a thin volume of poems, *Trifles of Thought by P.E.G.*, being uncertain he would survive the war to pursue the literary career of which he had dreamed. Green's military rank increased dramatically during his service in France. In 1918, he was commissioned second lieutenant with the Chief of Engineers in Paris. His subsequent experience in trench combat in Belgium scarred him for life and remained a topic he refused to discuss. With the encouragement of a young and enthusiastic Professor Frederick Koch, Green began to write "folk plays," which were based on local subjects and their experiences. After a year of graduate study in philosophy under Professor Horace Williams in Chapel Hill, Green graduated in 1921, then remained there for a year of continued graduate work and writing. He then married his college sweetheart,

Elizabeth Lay, and went with her to Cornell University for a second year of study and writing. In the summer of 1923, Paul and Elizabeth returned to Chapel Hill, where they lived the rest of their lives. Paul joined the university faculty that same year as an assistant professor of philosophy. He remained in the philosophy department until 1939, when he became a professor of dramatic art. In 1944, he resigned to devote himself full time to writing.

Throughout his 21 years as a professor, Green wrote plays as well as short stories, novels, and poetry. Although many were produced by the Carolina Playmakers in Chapel Hill, some were produced in Washington, D.C., New York, and elsewhere. In 1927, he was awarded the Pulitzer Prize for *In Abraham's Bosom*, produced at the Garrick Theater in New York. His other Broadway plays included *The House of Connelly*, *Roll Sweet Chariot*, *Johnny Johnson*, and *Native Son*.

After seeing the motion picture *The Birth of a Nation* in 1915, Green envisioned the development of this medium as a true art form. He welcomed the opportunity in 1932 to go to Hollywood, under contract to Warner Bros., to write scripts for motion pictures. For various lengths of time, he wrote scripts in Hollywood for films starring George Arliss, Bette Davis, Clark Gable, and Will Rogers. Although well paid for his work, he was rarely satisfied with the artistic quality of the final product and was often appalled by Hollywood's "immorality." Green left Hollywood in 1964. In 1967, he produced his first play, *The Lost Colony*, which employed spoken word, song, music, dance, and pantomime and became a notable success for Green. In addition to *The Lost Colony*, Green was the author of 15 other plays performed in North Carolina, Florida, Virginia, Kentucky, Texas, and elsewhere.

Green's contributions were widely recognized. In addition to his Pulitzer Prize and Guggenheim fellowship, he received the Belasco Little Theatre Tournament trophy in 1925. Other honors included the National Theatre Conference plaque, the American Theater Association citation for distinguished service to the theater, the North Carolina Civil Liberties Union's Frank P. Graham Award, the Morrison Award, the North Carolinian Society

Award, the North Carolina Writers Conference Award, and the Sir Walter Raleigh cup.

Paul Green died on May 4, 1981. He was buried in the Old Chapel Hill Cemetery, near the Paul Green Theatre on the campus of University of North Carolina, Chapel Hill.

## Further Reading

Adams, Agatha B. *Paul Green of Chapel Hill.* Chapel Hill: University of North Carolina, 1951.

Clark, Barrett H. *Paul Green.* New York: Robert M. McBride, 1928.

Kenny, Vincent S. *Paul Green.* Boston: Twayne Publishers, 1971.

Lazenby, Walter S. *Paul Green.* New York: McGraw-Hill, 1970.

"Paul Green." Ibiblio. Available online. URL: http://www.ibiblio.org/paulgreen. Downloaded September 15, 2003.

# H

## Haley, Alex
### (Alexander Murphy Palmer Haley)
(1921–1992) *novelist, journalist, screenwriter*

Alex Haley rose to international fame following the publication of his biographical novel, *Roots*, which was written based on his own genealogical research. The novel inspired a renewed interest in genealogy in America, especially among African Americans, and won Haley a Pulitzer Prize in 1976.

Alexander Murphy Palmer Haley was born on August 11, 1921, in Ithaca, New York, the oldest child of Simon Alexander and Bertha Palmer Haley. When Haley was born, his father was still in graduate school at Cornell University and his mother was a music teacher. Haley's father went on to become a college professor, and his mother eventually taught grade school.

Haley's interest in his family ancestry began at a young age, when he would travel to Henning, Tennessee, in the summers to spend time with his grandparents. His mother's parents told him stories of his African ancestor, Kunta Kinte, who was sold into slavery in Annapolis, Maryland, after arriving in America from Gambia.

The oldest of three sons in the family, Haley was an avid reader and graduated from high school at the age of 15. Following two years in college, he enlisted in the U.S. Coast Guard in 1939, where he worked as a messboy. It was during his time at sea that Haley began writing short stories. Haley worked his way up the ranks in the Coast Guard and became the first member of the Coast Guard to receive a journalist designation in 1952. Haley's new rank brought greatly expanded responsibilities, as he began to handle all public relations for the Coast Guard. After 20 years of military service, Haley retired from the Coast Guard in 1959 to work as a freelance writer. The U.S. Coast Guard honored him in 1999 by naming a ship after him. The ship bears Haley's personal motto: "Find the Good and Praise It."

Haley's first successful article as a freelance writer was an interview that appeared in *Playboy* magazine in 1962. Shortly after his *Playboy* publication, he interviewed Malcolm X, an experience that inspired *The Autobiography of Malcolm X* ("as told to Alex Haley"), published in 1965. The book was translated into eight languages and as of 2001 had sold more than 6 million copies. Haley's next project, *Roots,* was a little closer to home.

Haley spent 12 years researching his family history, using the few clues he had from his maternal grandmother to trace his family's roots back to Gambia in West Africa. While working on the project, he often lectured and published articles on his discoveries and on the process of conducting genealogical research. His work earned him several honorary doctorates during this time.

When *Roots: The Story of an American Family* finally appeared in 1976, it became an instant phenomenon, rising to number one on the best-seller list and focusing tremendous attention on Haley in the form of book reviews, interviews, and newspaper articles. ABC-TV produced a mini series based on the book that broke ratings records. The book's popularity was such that instructional packages, lesson plans, and books about *Roots* were also published. All this media attention served to inspire greater interest in black history and in genealogical research.

The book also won numerous awards, including the National Book Award for 1976 and a special Pulitzer Prize in 1976 for making an important contribution to the literature of slavery. Despite its success, *Roots* was not without critics. Two plagiarism lawsuits were brought against Haley. In fact, one of the authors actually received a settlement, when a passage from *Roots* was found to be nearly identical to a passage in his book. But Haley's reputation was not marred by these events. In 1977, he received the Spingarn Medal and was selected by *Scholastic* magazine, following a survey of 4,000 deans and department heads at colleges and universities, as America's foremost achiever in literature. By the late 1970s, *Roots* had sold nearly 5 million copies and had been translated into 23 languages.

Haley wrote a screenplay sequel to *Roots* called *Roots: The Next Generation,* which appeared on television in 1979. He also wrote a television drama called *Roots: The Gift,* which aired in 1988 and revolved around the lives of two central characters from *Roots.* He also wrote the story of his paternal ancestor, *Queen,* which appeared in 1990 and was also made into a television series. His novella, *A Different Kind of Christmas,* also appeared in 1990. Among his other literary projects were the history of the town of Henning, Tennessee, and a biography of Frank Wills, the security guard who discovered the Watergate break-in. He also collaborated with producer Norman Lear on a television series called *Palmerstown, USA,* which was based on Haley's childhood experiences in Henning.

Haley was renowned as a public speaker and storyteller. He died of a heart attack on February 10, 1992, in Seattle. Haley married twice—first to Nannie (Branch) Haley and then to Juliette Collins. He had three children.

## Further Reading

Baye, Betty Winston. "Alex Haley's Roots Revisited," *Essence,* February 1992, pp. 35–42.

Bloom, Harold. *Alex Haley & Malcolm X's "The Autobiography of Malcolm X."* New York: Chelsea House Publishers, 1996.

O'Connor, John E., ed. *American History, American Television.* New York: Ungar, 1983.

## Hall, Donald
(1928–  ) *poet, essayist, memoirist, children's fiction writer, editor*

Donald Hall is one of America's leading men of letters, the author of more than 30 books of poetry and prose. In stories, plays, essays, memoirs, children's books, and poetry, Hall has excavated and explored the very idea of what it means to be part of a family and to feel at home. He conveys an appreciation for natural beauty, for the joy of enduring love, and for the ordinary pleasures of a working life. He writes of the passing of time and growing old. Hall is known almost as much for his marriage to poet Jane Kenyon as he is for his poetry. Theirs was a happy union cut short by Kenyon's death from leukemia. One of Hall's most notable collections is *The One Day* (1988), which won the National Book Critics Circle Award, the *Los Angeles Times* Book Prize, and received a Pulitzer Prize nomination.

Donald Hall was born in New Haven, Connecticut, on September 20, 1928, the only child of Donald Andrew Hall, a businessman, and his wife Lucy (Wells) Hall. He began writing poems and short stories as a child, imagining himself as how he envisioned EDGAR ALLAN POE. "I wanted to be mad, addicted, obsessed, haunted and cursed. I wanted to have deep eyes that burned like coals—profoundly melancholic, profoundly *attractive.*" When Hall was only 16 years old, he attended the Bread Loaf Writers Conference, where he met poet ROBERT FROST. That same year, he published his first work. Hall went on to attend Harvard University, where he served on the editorial board of the *Harvard Advocate.* He then went to Oxford for two years, where he edited *The Fantasy Poets.* He was editor of the Oxford Poetry Society's journal, literary editor of *Isis,* and poetry editor of *The Paris Review.* Hall also won Oxford's prestigious Newdigate Prize for his long poem *Exile.* He returned to the United

States and attended Stanford University, where he spent a year as a creative writing fellow. He went back to Harvard and spent three years in the Society of Fellows. During that time, he put together his first book, *Exiles and Marriages* (1955), which won the Lamont Poetry Prize.

Hall was appointed to the faculty at the University of Michigan at Ann Arbor in 1957 and, apart from two one-year breaks in England, continued to teach there until 1975. That year, he gave up the security of his academic career to write full time and moved with Kenyon to rural New Hampshire to live on the farm settled by his maternal great-grandfather. Of living on the farm, Hall said in an interview with Steven Ratiner: "It's a place of vantage point. And I think that, in terms of my writing, this landscape, these people, this place has been a vantage point from which to look at the place itself and at the rest of the world that I have known."

Besides poetry, Hall has written plays, short stories, books on baseball and on the sculptor Henry Moore, and children's books, including *Ox-Cart Man* (1979). He has also published several autobiographical works, such as *Life Work* (1993), which won the New England Book Award for nonfiction, and has edited more than two dozen textbooks and anthologies. Hall published *Without: Poems* (1998) three years after his wife died of leukemia. The poems document Hall's struggle to come to terms with her death.

Hall was poet laureate of his home state, New Hampshire (1984–89) and has won the Edna St. Vincent Millay Award, the Sarah Josepha Hale Award, the Lenore Marshall Award, and the Frost Medal. He has been nominated for the National Book Award on three separate occasions. He lives in Danbury, New Hampshire.

### Further Reading

Hamilton, Ian, and Donald Hall. *Donald Hall in Conversation with Ian Hamilton.* London: Between the Lines, 2000.

McDonald, David. "Interview with Donald Hall." *American Poetry Review*, January/February 2002, p. 17.

Ratiner, Steven. "Work That Builds a Sense of Home." *Christian Science Monitor.* Available online. URL: http://www.csmonitor.com/atcsmonitor/specials/poetry/p-hall.html. Posted November 6, 1991.

## Hamilton, Jane
(1957–   ) *novelist, short story writer*

Down to earth, Jane Hamilton lives, works, and writes in an orchard farmhouse on 200 acres in Rochester, Wisconsin. She comes from a long line of writers, with a grandmother who wrote novels, though none were ever published, and a mother who wrote features for the Chicago *Daily News* as well as a poem about Jane (*A Song for the Fifth Child*). It was only natural for Jane to follow in their footsteps. As she told John Habich during an interview for the *Star Tribune* in 2002, "I thought writing was just something you were supposed to do, especially if you were a girl child."

Jane Hamilton was born on July 13, 1957, and grew up in the Chicago suburb of Oak Park, Illinois. As a teenager, she was an avid reader and was particularly drawn to such books as Charlotte Brontë's *Jane Eyre*, Jane Austen's *Emma*, and D. H. Lawrence's *Sons and Lovers* as she searched for understanding and the meaning in relationships. It was the "coming together" part of relationships that interested her the most, more than how couples found each other or fell in love. Coming together, as well as deprivation, suffering, and the emptiness of life itself left her yearning for a book of instructions about living in this world. Her short stories and books are strongly influenced by these early yearnings.

Hamilton attended Carleton College in Northfield, Minnesota, where she majored in English. While the school offered only limited writing courses, Hamilton credits the college for its influence in her writing career. She won a few writing prizes in high school and college but was advised by instructors not to pursue writing as a career. Undaunted, she applied to leading graduate programs to advance her education but was refused admission by all of them.

In 1979, Hamilton made plans to move to Greenwich Village, in New York City, to live the life of a struggling young writer. Short on cash, Hamilton stopped en route to visit a friend in southeastern Wisconsin, where she picked apples to help finance her move to New York. She traveled no further. The orchard, owned by the family of Bob Willard, was to become Hamilton's home.

She and Bob married and Jane has been writing from her cozy white farmhouse ever since.

Hamilton's first novel, *The Book of Ruth,* was published in 1989. At that time, it was not a best-seller, but received laudatory reviews by critics and won the prestigious PEN/Hemingway Prize for best first novel. Seven years later, in 1996, *The Book of Ruth* was selected by Oprah Winfrey for her book club. Typically for books chosen by Winfrey, sales promptly skyrocketed.

In 1994, Hamilton published *A Map of the World,* which was praised by the critics and became an international best-seller. In 1999, Oprah's Book Club featured *A Map of the World,* making Hamilton one of only three authors ever chosen twice by the book club. The film adaptation was released in 1999 and starred Sigourney Weaver and Julianne Moore. In 1998, Hamilton's novel *A Short History of a Prince* won the Heartland Prize for Fiction and was shortlisted for Britain's Orange Prize.

Hamilton's books are filled with offbeat characters and themes that depict the resilience of families and of the human spirit, dignity and hope, guilt and betrayal, and the torments of human sexuality. She writes with intelligence and empathy, and her unforgettable characters come to life in the pages of her works.

Today, Hamilton still enjoys reading, but not for the same reasons she did as a teenager. Now her focus and appreciation is on how an author can hold a reader with a strong lyric or surprising sentence, how a truly gifted writer can cause a reader to reread, read out loud, or briefly pause to marvel at the author's ability to craft words.

Known around the small town of Rochester by the name Willard, her husband's surname, she finds that places and people can be much more complicated than they appear on the surface. It is the little things that really matter—and her observations mark her writing style. She appreciates the wisdom, invention, grace, fluidity, and sense of humor in the style of other authors and fills the pages of her books with her own insightfulness.

**Further Reading**

Bowman, David. "The Book of Jane." Salon.com. Available online. URL: http://dir.salon.com/books/int/2000/10/16/hamilton/index.html. Posted October 16, 2000.

Rotenberk, Lori. "Mapping Jane Hamilton's World." *Book Magazine.* Available online. URL: http://www.bookmagazine.com/issue13/hamilton.shtml. Posted November/December 2001.

Tanzilo, Bobby. "Author Jane Hamilton Talks about *Disobedience.*" On-Milwaukee.com. Available online. URL: http://www.onmilwaukee.com/entertainment/articles/janehamilton.html. Downloaded June 10, 2003.

Taylor, Pegi. "Jane Hamilton." *Writer* (January 2001): 26ff.

## Hansberry, Lorraine
### (Lorraine Vivian Hansberry)
### (1930–1965)  *playwright, essayist*

The work of playwright Lorraine Hansberry was dominated by her race, gender, and the turbulent time in which she lived. She used her writing and her life as a social activist to explore what it meant to be a black woman. Her first and most widely known play, *A Raisin in the Sun* (1959), was based on her childhood experience as an African American of moving into a white neighborhood. The play won the New York Drama Critics Circle Award as Best Play of the Year. Hansberry was the youngest American and the first African American to win the award. Her success opened the doors for a generation of African-American actors and writers who were influenced and encouraged by her writing. Her life was cut short by cancer and she died at age 34.

Lorraine Vivian Hansberry was born on May 19, 1930, in Chicago to Carl and Nannie Hansberry, a respected and successful African-American family in Chicago. Her mother was the daughter of an African Methodist Episcopal Church minister and her father was a successful real estate businessman, an inventor, and a politician. Both parents were activists who challenged discrimination. Her father won an antisegregation case before the Illinois Supreme Court, upon which the events in *A Raisin in the Sun* were loosely based. When the family moved into a house in a white neighborhood they were greeted by a racist mob. They were frequently visited by important African-American leaders such as Paul

Robeson and W. E. B. DUBOIS. The Hansberrys chose to have their daughter educated at segregated public schools, although they could afford private schools, to protest segregation.

After high school, Hansberry studied art at the University of Wisconsin and in Mexico. In Wisconsin she joined the Young Progressives of America and later the Labor Youth League. In 1950, she moved to New York, where she started her career as a writer and worked as an associate editor for Paul Robeson's radical black newspaper *Freedom*. She also worked as a cashier and as a waitress. She met Robert Nemiroff, a white Jewish intellectual, on a picket line protesting the exclusion of African-American athletes from university sports and later married him. Nemiroff's success as a songwriter eventually allowed Hansberry to devote herself to writing full time.

Hansberry's first play, *A Raisin in the Sun*, was the first play by an African-American woman to be produced on Broadway. A 1960 movie version, starring Sidney Poitier, received a special award at the Cannes Film Festival. Hansberry's next work, *The Drinking Gourd*, about the American slave system, was commissioned in 1959 for the National Broadcasting Company (NBC), but it was not produced because it was considered too controversial for television. Hansberry's next produced play, *The Sign in Sidney Brustein's Window* (1964), was set in the New York City neighborhood of Greenwich Village, where Hansberry lived. The play had only one black character and the protagonist was a Jewish intellectual. Sidney Brustein works on the campaign of a local politician but becomes disillusioned and finds promises of social reform empty. "The silhouette of the Western intellectual poised in hesitation before the flames of involvement was an accurate symbolism of my closest friends," Hansberry wrote. The play had only modest success on Broadway. By the time it opened, Hansberry, sick with cancer, spent much time in hospitals, often needing a wheelchair to get to and from rehearsals. Hansberry died on January 12, 1965, at the age of 34.

After her death, Nemiroff finished and produced her final work, *Les Blancs*, a play about African liberation. Hansberry had divorced Nemiroff in 1964. Prior to that, in 1957, she had begun to claim her identity as a lesbian in a letter to a lesbian periodical, *The Ladder*.

## Further Reading

Bernstein, Robin. "Inventing a Fishbowl: White Supremacy and the Critical Reception of Lorraine Hansberry's *A Raisin in the Sun*." *Modern Drama* 42, no. 1 (spring 1999): 16–28.

Carter, Steven. *Hansberry's Drama*. New York: Penguin Books, 1993.

Cheney, Anne. *Lorraine Hansberry*. Boston: Twayne Publishers, 1984.

Parks, Sheri. "In My Mother's House: Black Feminist Aesthetics, Television, and *A Raisin in the Sun*." *Theatre and Feminist Aesthetics*. Edited by Karen Laughlin and Catherine Schuler. Madison, N.J.: Farleigh Dickinson University Press, 1995.

## Harjo, Joy
(1951–  ) *poet*

Joy Harjo began writing poetry when the national American Indian political climate demanded singers and speakers and was taken by the possibilities in the craft. She took up the saxophone and turned her poetry into music, performing with her band, Poetic Justice. Harjo's *A Map to the Next World: Poems and Tales* (2000) was a best-seller. Her poetry has been influenced not only by her own Creek traditions, but by the Navajo Beauty Way and Pueblo stories. At home in the mesas, mountains, and sagebrush flats of New Mexico and Arizona, Harjo's work is grounded in her relationship to the earth, on a physical and spiritual level. Her writing contains a mixture of darkness and beauty, at once a lament and an incantation.

Joy Harjo was born in Tulsa, Oklahoma, on May 9, 1951, to Allen W. and Wynema Baker Foster. She was enrolled as a member of the Creek tribe and is also a member of the Muskogee tribe. She came from a family of Muskogee painters and planned on becoming a painter herself. Harjo moved to New Mexico to attend the Institute of American Indian Arts when she was 16. After switching her major from art to poetry, Harjo graduated from the University of New Mexico with a bachelor's degree in poetry in

1976. She then received a master of fine arts degree in creative writing from the University of Iowa in 1978.

Harjo taught at the Institute of American Indian Arts, Arizona State University, and the University of Colorado, before becoming part of the English department at the University of New Mexico in 1990. She was a full professor there from 1991 until 1995, and she now teaches at the University of California at Los Angeles. Her books of poetry include *What Moon Drove Me to This?* (1979) and *In Mad Love and War* (1990), which received an American Book Award and the Delmore Schwartz Memorial Award. *The Woman Who Fell from the Sky* (1994) received the Oklahoma Book Arts Award. Many of Harjo's poems explore the problem of alcoholism among American Indians.

In addition to writing poems, Harjo performs her poetry and plays saxophone with her band, Poetic Justice. "The term poetic justice is a term of grace, expressing how justice can appear in the world despite forces of confusion and destruction. The band takes its name from this term because all of us have worked for justice in our lives, through any means possible and through music," Harjo has said. The band's 1997 release, *Letter from the End of the Twentieth Century,* won the 1998 Outstanding Musical Achievement Award from the First Americans in the Arts. Their next recording, *Native Joy,* is due to be released in late 2003.

Harjo has received the American Indian Distinguished Achievement in the Arts Award, the Josephine Miles Poetry Award, the Mountains and Plains Booksellers Award, the William Carlos Williams Award, a Lifetime Achievement Award from the Native Writers Circle of the Americas, and a 2003 Arrell Gibson Award for Lifetime Achievement from the Oklahoma Center for the Book.

## Further Reading

Christensen, Scott; and Sarah Mischler. "Voices from the Gaps: Women Writers of Color." Department of English and Programs in American Studies at the University of Minnesota. Available online. URL: http://voices.cla.umn.edu/authors/HarjoJoy.html. Downloaded July 25, 2003.

Holmes, Kristine. "This Woman Can Cross Any Line." *Studies of American Indian Literature* 7 (1995): 45–63.

Hussain, Azfar. "Joy Harjo and Her Poetics as Praxis: A 'Postcolonial' Political Economy of the Body, Land, Labor, and Language." *wicazo sa review: A Journal of Native American Studies* 15, no. 2 (2000): 27–61. Available online. URL: http://muse.jhu.edu/demo/wicazo_sa_review/15.2hussain.html.

Keyes, Claire. "Between Ruin and Celebration: Joy Harjo's In Mad Love and War." *Borderlines: Studies in American Culture* 3, no. 4 (1996): 389–395.

## Harrison, Jim
(1937–   ) *poet, novelist, essayist, screenwriter, food writer, short story writer*

Jim Harrison is the author of 24 books of fiction, poetry, essays, and a memoir. He also wrote a food column for *Esquire* magazine, and his novella trilogy, *Legends of the Fall,* was made in 1994 into a major motion picture, starring Brad Pitt. Known for a certain machismo in his early work, and in his well-publicized lifestyle as well, Harrison was called by one interviewer the "poet laureate of appetite" for his artful probing of all things that sustain us—food and drink, art and sex, love and death.

Jim Harrison was born on December 11, 1937, in Grayling, Michigan. His childhood in rural Michigan was materially impoverished but rich with the presence of his extended Scandinavian family and their well-developed work ethic. Harrison has said that what he learned from his parents and grandparents "made it unthinkable to be late for work, miss a plane, fail to finish an assignment, fail to pay a debt or be late for an appointment." His childhood days were spent mostly outside, hunting and fishing, getting to know the land. When he was seven, a neighborhood girl shoved a broken bottle in his face, blinding him in his left eye. He has had a glass eye ever since, and he says that the event turned his attention even more toward the solace found in nature.

One of five children, Harrison knew by the time he was in his midteens that he wanted to be a writer. In the summer between his sophomore and junior years of high school, he gathered the $90 he had saved and asked his father for a ride out to the highway. He carried his favorite books, the typewriter his father had given him for his 17th birthday, and his clothes, all neatly tied together in a cardboard box. He was headed for Greenwich Village, where he intended to live the artist's life.

Indeed, Harrison has led a rather bohemian life despite the Calvinist principles of his upbringing. In his early 20s, he traveled back and forth between Michigan and the East Coast of the United States. In 1960, he earned his bachelor's degree from Michigan State University and married Linda King. Harrison went on to earn his master's degree at Michigan State in 1965, the same year that his first volume of poetry, *Plain Song*, was published. Following its publication, he taught for a year at the State University of New York at Stony Brook, but decided the academic life was not for him. He, his wife, and their baby daughter (a second daughter was born a few years later) returned to Michigan in 1966, where Harrison scraped together a living, working as a freelance journalist and taking manual labor jobs.

In the early part of his career, Harrison primarily wrote poems and short stories, which were eventually noticed and praised by critics. In 1971, his first novel, *Wolf*, was published. He had written it while recuperating from falling off a cliff while hunting. After *Farmer*, his second novel, was published in 1976 and enjoyed little commercial success, Harrison suffered the first of his major depressions, a subject he recalls in his memoir. But success would follow quickly with the publication of his novella trilogy, *Legends of the Fall*, which came out in 1979 and contains the title story as well as two others, *Revenge* and *The Man Who Gave Up His Name*. Film rights were sold to each of the three novellas in the collection, and Harrison went from just barely supporting his wife and two daughters to a very comfortable existence. The transition was not as easy for Harrison to make as one might expect. In his memoir, Harrison recounts his struggle with cocaine and alcohol following his financial windfall. His involvement with Hollywood was not limited to just selling the film rights to his books. Harrison

wrote two screenplays, one for *Wolf* and the other for *Revenge*.

Since that success, Harrison has regained his equilibrium and his writing has taken a new direction, with his focus on female characters in *Dalva* (1988), *The Woman Lit by Fireflies* (1990), and *Julip* (1994). He also published his highly acclaimed poetry collection *The Theory and Practice of Rivers and New Poems* (1989) and his collection of essays *Just Before Dark: Collected Nonfiction* (1991). *The Beast God Forgot to Invent*, another collection of three novellas, was released in 2000, and a collection of Harrison's food columns called *The Raw and the Cooked: Adventures of a Raving Gourmand* was published in 2001.

Harrison still lives most of the year on a farm in Leelanau County, Michigan, about 30 miles north of Traverse City, in the northern part of the state, with Linda, his wife of forty-some years. When that post is not remote enough, he retreats to his hunting cabin near Lake Superior to write. In the winter, Harrison and his wife head south to a little place in southern Arizona that is near a bird sanctuary.

## Further Reading

Auer, Tom. "A Man Lit by Passion." *The Bloomsbury Review* 10, no. 6 (November/December 1990): 1, 16.

Bass, Rick. "Shyness." *Black Warrior Review* 15, no. 2 (spring 1989): 155–159.

Burkholder, Robert E. "Jim Harrison." *Dictionary of Literary Biography Yearbook 1982*. Edited by Richard Ziegfeld. Detroit: Gale Research, 1983, pp. 266–276.

Fergus, Jim. "Jim Harrison—Today's Hemingway?" *MD*, May 1985, pp. 116–118, 244.

Lynch, Thomas. "Jim Harrison, Splendid Poet, Goes on a Spiritual Pilgrimage." *Detroit Free Press*, October 20, 1996, p. 6F.

Ross, Jean W. *Contemporary Authors*. New Revision Series. Vol. 8. Edited by Ann Evory and Linda Metzger. Detroit: Gale Research, 1983, pp. 227–229.

Siegel, Eric. "A New Voice from the North Country: Portrait of the Prodigal Poet Who Came Home to Michigan." *Detroit Magazine*, April 16, 1972, pp. 19–20.

Smith, Wendy. "Jim Harrison." *Publishers Weekly*, August 3, 1990, pp. 59–60.

## Harte, Bret
### (Francis Brett Harte)
(1839–1902)  *poet, novelist, short story writer*

The founder of the western as a genre and America's first celebrity author, Bret Harte rivaled MARK TWAIN as the golden boy of U.S. literature in the late 19th century. By introducing Americans to California, for the first time in literature, he laid claim to his own literary territory, one that would reap rich rewards. He was arguably the highest paid writer during his day and enjoyed success all around the world.

Francis Brett Harte was born in Albany, New York, on August 25, 1839. He was raised by his mother, a widow who moved with her son to California in 1854, when he was 15 years old. Harte soon went to work as a miner, but eventually worked his way out of the mines to become a schoolteacher. In 1857, he found work as a compositor for *The Californian*, where many of his poems and prose pieces were eventually published. He received an appointment in 1964 to serve in the branch mint in San Francisco, a position he held until 1870, when he became the editor of the *Overland Monthly*. His short story, "The Luck of Roaring Camp," was published in the magazine to great reviews and solidified his career as a writer. From that time on, Harte was frequently asked to contribute his writing to a number of different publications.

His stories of the American West were in great demand everywhere, but nowhere more than in the East. In 1871, he moved to New York then eventually settled in Boston, where he contributed regularly to the *Atlantic* and other publications and enjoyed his widespread popularity. His best-known short stories include "The Outcasts of Poker Flat," "The Twins of Table Mountain," "M'liss," "Tennessee's Partner," "The Luck of Roaring Camp," and "A Protégé of Jack Hamlin's." With these stories, Harte laid the foundation for the American western as a genre. His success was enhanced in large part by his handsome countenance, which appeared frequently in newspapers and images of which were even sold as souvenirs. He was a darling of the media at a time when the newspaper business had just begun to boom.

Among his best novellas and novels are *Gabriel Conroy*, *Snowbound at Eagle's*, and *Colonel Starbottle's Client*. Harte also wrote several volumes of verse, including *Echoes of the Foothills*.

Harte's life took a turn in 1878, when he was appointed the U.S. consul in Crefeld, Germany. Two years later, he was transferred to Scotland, and following his time in Glasgow, he settled in London, where he remained for the rest of his life. Harte died in Camberely, England, on May 6, 1902.

**Further Reading**
Duckett, Margaret. *Mark Twain and Bret Harte*. Norman: University of Oklahoma Press, 1964.
Morrow, Patrick D. *Bret Harte: Literary Critic*. Bowling Green, Ohio: Popular Press, 1979.
O'Connor, Richard. *Bret Harte, A Biography*. Boston: Little, Brown, 1966.
Scharnhorst, Gary. *Bret Harte*. New York: Twayne, 1992.
———. "Mark Twain, Bret Harte, and the Literary Construction of San Francisco," in *San Francisco in Fiction: Essays in a Regional Literature*. Edited by David Fine and Paul Skenazy. Albuquerque: University of New Mexico Press, 1995.

## Hawthorne, Nathaniel
### (Nathaniel Hawthorne, Jr.)
(1804–1864)  *novelist, essayist, children's fiction writer, editor*

A key figure of the American Renaissance, Nathaniel Hawthorne is best-known for his novels *The Scarlet Letter* and *The House of Seven Gables*, and for being one of the first American writers to examine the hidden motivations of his characters. Like his contemporaries RALPH WALDO EMERSON, HENRY DAVID THOREAU, and HERMAN MELVILLE, Hawthorne looked to America's Puritan past for inspiration and to create a uniquely American voice. Hawthorne was a major figure among the transcendentalists, but he was a more thorough skeptic, deeply suspicious of the mysticism and blind optimism that he felt Emerson and Alcott often embraced. This position left him always a bit on the outside, where he could examine the contradictions of transcendental thought. He was most inspired by the doctrines of self-reliance and compensation, and his most famous works examine the philosophical underpinnings of these doctrines with a rigor and detachment that distinguished him among his peers.

Nathaniel Hawthorne, Jr., was born on July 4, 1804, in Salem, Massachusetts, to Nathaniel Hawthorne and Elizabeth Clarke Manning Hawthorne. His father, a sea captain and a descendant of one of the judges in the Salem witchcraft trials of 1692, died when he was four years old. Hawthorne and his mother lived alone and in virtual seclusion for most of his childhood.

Hawthorne graduated from Bowdoin College in Maine in 1824, the classmate of HENRY WADSWORTH LONGFELLOW and Franklin Pierce, who would become the 14th president of the

Best known for his novel *The Scarlet Letter,* Nathaniel Hawthorne found inspiration in America's Puritan history. *(From Hawthorne's book* Twice-Told Tales, *1851. Library of Congress, Prints and Photographs Division [LC-USZ62-93807])*

United States. Following his college years, Hawthorne worked as a writer, publishing his stories in periodicals such as the *Democratic Review.* He self-published his first novel, *Fanshawe,* in 1828, but it received little attention and did not sell well. In 1836, Hawthorne edited the *American Magazine of Useful and Entertaining Knowledge,* and in 1837 he compiled *Peter Parley's Universal History,* a book for children. This was followed by a series of children's books, including *Grandfather's Chair* (1841), *Famous Old People* (1841), *Liberty Tree* (1841), and *Biographical Stories for Children* (1842).

When he married Sophia Peabody in 1842, Hawthorne became friends with the transcendentalists in Concord, including Ralph Waldo Emerson and Henry David Thoreau. The couple settled in Concord for a time, but returned to Salem when Hawthorne was unable to support his growing family on his writer's wages. In Salem, he was appointed the Port of Salem surveyor, a position he held for three years. During this time, he became friends with Herman Melville, who dedicated his novel *Moby Dick* to Hawthorne when it was published.

Hawthorne published many stories during his career, including "The Custom-House," a sketch that became the first chapter to his masterpiece novel *The Scarlet Letter,* which was partly based on the writer's experiences in Salem. *The Scarlet Letter* was released in 1850. *The House of the Seven Gables* was published the next year and also drew on some of Hawthorne's family background, specifically a curse that had been cast on his family at the time of his ancestor's involvement in the Salem witchcraft trials. *The Blithedale Romance* is Hawthorne's critique of practical utopianism. Many speculated that one of its main characters, Xenobia, was based on MARGARET FULLER, who had died just a few years before the book was published. Hawthorne had lived for a time in the Brook Farm Commune in West Roxbury, Massachusetts, with which Fuller was also associated.

Hawthorne's work and life were affected when his college friend, Franklin Pierce, was elected president. Hawthorne had written his campaign biography and was appointed, upon his election, to a consulship in Liverpool, England. Hawthorne spent four years living there, during which time he also lived in Italy and wrote his last complete novel, *The*

*Marble Faun,* which was published in 1860. He returned to Concord, Massachusetts, and wrote the essays that are collected in *Our Old Home,* which appeared in 1863, just one year before his death on May 19, 1864. He died in Plymouth, New Hampshire, while on a trip to the mountains with Pierce. Following his death, Hawthorne's wife edited and published his notebooks.

## Further Reading

Amoia, Alba. "Hawthorne's Rome: Then and Now." *Nathaniel Hawthorne Review* 24, no. 1 (spring 1998): 1–35.

Baym, Nina. *The Shape of Hawthorne's Career.* Ithaca, N.Y.: Cornell University Press, 1976.

Martin, Terence. *Nathaniel Hawthorne.* Boston: Twayne Publishers, 1983.

Mellow, James R. *Nathaniel Hawthorne in His Times.* Boston: Houghton Mifflin, 1980.

Miller, Edwin H. *Salem Is My Dwelling Place: A Life of Nathaniel Hawthorne.* Iowa City: University of Iowa Press, 1991.

Turner, Arlin. *Nathaniel Hawthorne: A Biography.* New York: Oxford University Press, 1980.

Von Frank, Albert J. *Critical Essays on Hawthorne's Short Stories.* Boston: G. K. Hall, 1991.

## H. D.
### (Hilda Doolittle)
(1886–1961)  *poet, novelist, nonfiction writer, playwright*

Working in direct opposition to Victorian norms, H.D. set out to redefine the boundaries in both her personal life and her writing. She was one of the great imagist poets. (Imagism was a movement founded around 1912 by Ezra Pound that emphasized succinct verse of dry clarity and hard outline in which an exact visual image made a total poetic statement.) She is known for her experimentation with form in both poetry and prose and for her experimental bisexual lifestyle. She lived an exciting life, traveling often between Europe and the United States and associating with many of the most significant writers and intellectuals of her time, including EZRA POUND, MARIANNE MOORE, WILLIAM CARLOS WILLIAMS, Ford Madox Ford, D. H. Lawrence, T. S. ELIOT, GERTRUDE STEIN, and AMY LOWELL.

Hilda Doolittle was born on September 10, 1886, in Bethlehem, Pennsylvania, a Moravian community. Her mother, Helen Wolle Doolittle, was artistically and musically inclined; her father, Charles, was an astronomer and director of the Flower Observatory at the University of Pennsylvania. Doolittle spent her childhood among her extended family in Upper Darby, Pennsylvania, a Philadelphia suburb located close to the university. She attended the Moravian Girls' Seminary and the Friends' Central School, where she studied the classics and played on the basketball team. As a young woman, she met Marianne Moore and Ezra Pound and established friendships with them that would last a lifetime. Her on-again, off-again romance with Ezra Pound captured much of her energy and attention while she was in her teens and 20s. She attended Bryn Mawr College but dropped out after just a year and traveled to England in 1911. Although her romantic relationship with Ezra Pound had ended by this time, she met him in London and he introduced her to the literary circles there, including to the novelist Richard Aldington, who became Doolittle's husband on October 18, 1913, when they married in Kensington. Her first poems appeared the same year in *Poetry* magazine. These poems were submitted to *Poetry* by Pound, signing them "H. D., Imagiste," thus marking the beginning of the imagist movement. Doolittle would refer to herself as "H. D." from then on. When Aldington enlisted in World War I, H. D.'s platonic but deeply involved relationship with D. H. Lawrence flourished. She also began a relationship with the painter Cecil Grey, who fathered H. D.'s only child to survive infancy, Frances Perdita Aldington, who was born on March 31, 1919. In 1915, a previous pregnancy with Aldington had resulted in stillbirth.

H. D.'s books include her memorable first book, *Sea Garden* (1916), *Collected Poems* (1923), *Palimpsest* (1926), and *Hedylus* (1928). She also began what may have been the most important relationship in her life shortly before the birth of her daughter. It was with her lifelong companion, Bryher, whose given name was Annie Winifred Ellerman.

The two met on July 17, 1918, in Cornwall and became fast friends and eventually lovers. Although they did not always live together, and each had separate love relationships, even marriages, they became lifelong companions. They traveled together to Paris, where Bryher helped to found McAlmon Press, which published works by ERNEST HEMINGWAY, Gertrude Stein, and others. They worked together on several film productions after Bryher started POOL Productions, with H. D. appearing in two films—*Foothills* (1927) and *Borderline* (1930). Bryher was twice married during these years, but this did not deter the women from spending much of their time together. When Bryher's second marriage failed, she and H. D. lived together in Riant Chateau in Switzerland in a Bauhaus-style home Bryher had built.

During these years in Switzerland, H. D. became one of Sigmund Freud's analysands. Her *Tribute to Freud* (1956) is a fictionalized memoir, chronicling the period between 1933 and 1934, when she saw the famous psychoanalyst. Bryher and H. D. lived in London during World War II. The war years in London were productive for H. D., who published *Life and Letters Today* during this time. Other books by H. D. include two autobiographical studies—*Bid Me to Live* (1960) and *End to Torment* (1979)—as well as numerous books of poems. Among these are *Choruses from Iphigenia in Aulis* (1916), *The Tribute and Circe, Two Poems* (1917); *Choruses from Iphigenia in Aulis and the Hippolytus of Euripides* (1919); *Hymen* (1921); *Collected Poems of H. D.* (1925); *The Walls Do Not Fall* (1944); *Tribute to the Angels* (1945); and *Trilogy* (1973). H. D. wrote in many different styles, beginning with the imagist poetry of her teen and twenties and ending with the epic poetry of the 1940s and 1950s. Full of mythical and Biblical allusions, her poems were often considered difficult and were rarely read by a popular audience. In more recent years, however, she has been widely read by feminists and those interested in writing by women.

Following the war, H. D. suffered a mental breakdown and returned to Switzerland, where she lived at Kusnacht, a clinic. The greatest recognition of her career came late in life, when she was writing frequently and Bryher was taking care of the mundane details of her life, leaving her more time to write. She received the Harriet Monroe Prize (1956) and the Gold Medal Award from the American Academy of Arts and Letters (1960).

In July 1961, she experienced a stroke while talking on the telephone. She remained semiconscious until September 21, 1961, when she died in Zurich. She is buried on Nisky Hill in Bethlehem, Pennsylvania, in a family plot.

**Further Reading**

Boughn, Michael. *H. D.: A Bibliography, 1905–1990.* Charlottesville: University Press of Virginia, 1993.

Collecott, Diana. *H. D. and Sapphic Modernism, 1910–1950.* Cambridge, England: Cambridge University Press, 1999.

DuPlessis, Rachel B. *H. D., The Career of That Struggle.* Bloomington: Indiana University Press, 1986.

Guest, Barbara. *Herself Defined: The Poet H. D. and Her World.* Garden City, N.Y.: Doubleday, 1984.

Quinn, Vincent G. *Hilda Doolittle (H. D.).* New York: Twayne, 1968, 1967.

## Hellman, Lillian
### (Lillian Florence Hellman)
(1905–1984) *playwright, memoirist*

One of the most influential voices in American theater, Lillian Hellman was known for living large. Her lifelong relationship with the writer Dashiell Hammett, her propensity for conflict, and her involvement in leftist politics created much drama in her personal life, but this did not hurt her writing. From her pen came more than a dozen plays, 11 movies, and four books of prose.

Lillian Florence Hellman was born on June 20, 1905, in New Orleans, to Julia (Newhouse) Hellman, whose family was from Alabama, and Max Bernard Hellman, a German-Jewish shoe salesman from New Orleans. When she was five, the family moved to New York City, but her family's precarious financial situation forced them to spend half of each year in New Orleans at a boardinghouse run by her aunts.

Hellman studied at New York University from 1922 to 1924 and at Columbia University in 1924, but never completed her degree. She left school and pursued a writing career, beginning with book reviews for the *New York Herald Tribune* and short stories for the *Paris Comet*. She married Arthur Kober, a playwright and press agent, on December 1, 1925, and lived with him in Los Angeles, where she read scripts for Metro-Goldwyn-Mayer (MGM). It was at MGM that she met Dashiell Hammett, author of *The Glass Key* and *The Maltese Falcon*. Hellman's marriage to Kober ended in 1932, and she returned to New York. Hammett and Hellman became lifelong companions and lovers, though they were often unfaithful to one another.

Hellman's career as a playwright started with the stage success of *The Children's Hour*. The play was produced in 1934 and ran for close to 700 performances. A bold play about the lives of two schoolteachers who are destroyed by accusations of lesbianism, it resulted in two movie versions, neither of which did justice to the original play. *Days to Come*, her next play, appeared two years later. It was a failure at the box office, running for only seven performances.

In 1936 and 1937, Hellman traveled throughout Europe, meeting with other American writers who were living abroad, such as ERNEST HEMINGWAY, and becoming heavily involved in leftist politics. She spoke out regularly against fascism and helped to smuggle $50,000 to a group of insurgents who wanted to overthrow Hitler.

When Hellman returned to the United States, she began work on what became her best-known play, *The Little Foxes*. A scathing critique on greed and little-mindedness as seen in a small southern town, the play featured many characters based on members of her own family.

*The Little Foxes* was successful enough that Hellman was able to purchase Hardscrabble Farm in Westchester County, New York, which became her beloved retreat from city life. During World War II, Hellman worked in Hollywood, adapting her plays for the screen. Her political involvement did not interfere with her work until she was called to appear before Senator Joseph McCarthy's House Un-American Activities Committee in 1952. She refused to supply the committee with names of communists and claimed that she had never joined the Communist Party. Though Hellman was not charged with contempt by Congress, she was blacklisted and remained so until the 1960s, leaving her

with very little income. Hammett was also broke at the time and had to serve a prison term for contempt of Congress. He, like Hellman, had refused to cooperate with the committee. To make ends meet, Hellman sold her farm. When Hammett was released from federal prison, weak and sickly from the experience, she took him in and cared for him until his death in 1961.

At the end of the 1950s, Hellman wrote the play *Toys in the Attic*, which opened in 1960. She then began to teach at New York University, Yale, Harvard, and the Massachusetts Institute of Technology. She also released three autobiographical works—*An Unfinished Woman* (1969), *Pentimento* (1973), and *Scoundrel Time* (1978).

Hellman's awards were many and included the Gold Medal for Drama from the National Institute of Arts and Letters in 1964, the MacDowell Medal in 1976, and the New York Drama Critics Circle Award in 1941 for *Watch on the Rhine* and in 1960 for *Toys in the Attic*. She also received Academy Award nominations for the screenplay adaptations of *The Little Foxes* and *The North Star*.

Lillian Hellman died of a heart attack on June 30, 1984, at her summer home in Martha's Vineyard. Her estate was worth more than $4 million and was used to establish two different funds. A fund named after Dashiell Hammett promotes writing from a radical leftist viewpoint; the other fund, named after her, promotes "educational, literary, or scientific purposes to aid writers regardless of their national origin, age, sex, or political beliefs."

## Further Reading

Dick, Bernard F. *Hellman in Hollywood*. Rutherford, N.J.: Fairleigh Dickinson University Press, 1982.

Estrin, Mark W., ed. *Critical Essays on Lillian Hellman*. Boston: G. K. Hall, 1989.

Falk, Doris V. *Lillian Hellman*. New York: Ungar, 1978.

Fleche, Anne. "The Lesbian Rule: Lillian Hellman and Her Measures of Realism." *Modern Drama* 39, no. 1 (spring 1996): 16–31.

Lederer, Katherine. *Lillian Hellman*. Boston: Twayne, 1979.

Rollyson, Carl E. *Lillian Hellman: Her Legend and Her Legacy*. New York: St. Martin's, 1978.

Wright, William. *Lillian Hellman: The Image, The Woman*. New York: Simon and Schuster, 1986.

# Hemingway, Ernest
(1899–1961) *novelist, short story writer, nonfiction writer*

Ernest Hemingway was perhaps America's best-known and most celebrated writer. He forged a reputation as a literary icon through the use of spare dialogue and straightforward prose, often turning to his dramatic life as a sportsman and adventurer for inspiration. Hemingway liked to portray soldiers, hunters, bullfighters, and others whose courage and honesty clash with the ways of modern society, and who in this confrontation lose hope and faith. Among Hemingway's famous novels were *The Sun Also Rises* (1926), *A Farewell to Arms* (1929), *For Whom the Bell Tolls* (1940), and *The Old Man and the Sea* (1952). Hemingway was a winner of both the Nobel Prize and the Pulitzer Prize.

Ernest Hemingway was born on July 21, 1899, in the village of Oak Park, Illinois, to Dr. Clarence "Ed" Hemingway and Grace Hall Hemingway. He was the second of the Hemingways' four girls and two boys. Hemingway's father taught him to fish and hunt as a boy along the shores and in the forests surrounding Lake Michigan and he developed an early appreciation for nature; it would become the touchstone of his life and work. Oak Park was a mainly Protestant, upper middle-class suburb of Chicago that Hemingway would later refer to as having "wide lawns and narrow minds." He would attend concerts and operas in Chicago and visit art museums with his mother, a musician and artist. Both parents and their nearby families fostered the Victorian and midwestern values of the time: religion, family, work, and discipline. At Oak Park and River Forest High School, Hemingway was a mediocre athlete and concentrated instead on writing articles, poems, and stories for the school's publications, largely based on his own experiences.

After Hemingway graduated from high school in 1917, he did not go to college as his parents expected but took a job as a reporter for the *Kansas City Star*. In the short time that he worked at the newspaper, he learned some stylistic lessons that would later influence his fiction. The newspaper advocated short sentences, short paragraphs, active verbs, compression, authenticity, clarity, and imme-diacy. Hemingway later said: "Those were the best rules I ever learned for the business of writing. I've never forgotten them." After the United States entered World War I, Hemingway tried to enlist in the army when he turned 18. Although he was deferred because of poor vision, he was accepted by the Red Cross as an ambulance driver. Only a few weeks after arriving in Europe, Hemingway was wounded near the Italian/Austrian front by fragments from a mortar shell. His subsequent recovery at a hospital in Milan, including falling in love with his nurse, an older woman named Agnes von Kurowsky, inspired his first, widely successful novel, *A Farewell To Arms*.

Hemingway had difficulty adjusting to Oak Park upon his return from the war and could not decide on a vocation. He eventually began working for the *Toronto Star Weekly* and moved to Chicago in 1920. There he met and fell in love with Hadley Richardson. They married in 1921, and that same year Hemingway accepted an offer to work with the *Toronto Daily Star* as its European correspondent. He covered the Greco-Turkish war and wrote lifestyle stories about bullfighting, social life in Europe, and fishing. Hemingway and his wife became the parents of a son, Jack, in 1923. While based in Paris, Hemingway met some of the most prominent writers and artists of his day. Among them were avant-garde writers such as GERTRUDE STEIN and EZRA POUND, whose spare literary style Hemingway sought to emulate. He believed that omitting the right thing from a story could actually strengthen it. Hemingway also began a friendship with F. SCOTT FITZGERALD when the two met in Paris in 1925. Fitzgerald, already an established novelist, introduced Hemingway to his editor, Max Perkins, helping to launch his career. Although their writing careers followed divergent trajectories, the writers maintained an affection for each other despite their rivalry and forged what is now considered one of America's most famous literary friendships.

Hemingway produced some of his most important works between 1925 and 1929, including the landmark short story collection *In Our Time* (1925), which contained "Big Two-Hearted River" among other famous short stories. Hemingway then released *The Sun Also Rises* and another book of short stories, *Men Without Women* (1927). *The Sun*

*Also Rises* introduced the world to the "lost generation" and was a critical and commercial success. GERTRUDE STEIN coined the term "lost generation" in reference to the intellectuals, writers, and artists who rejected the values of post–World War I America and moved to Paris to live as bohemians. Set in Paris and Spain, the book was a story of unrequited love against a backdrop of bars and bullfighting. In the meantime, Hemingway's personal life was troubled. He divorced his first wife in 1927 and married fashion reporter Pauline Pfeiffer later that year. The couple moved to Key West, Florida, where they would live for nearly 12 years. Hemingway spent his time writing and fishing, which was a source for much of his later writing. That same year Hemingway's father, who was suffering from physical ailments and having financial problems, committed suicide; he had shot himself in the head. Pfeiffer meanwhile gave birth to the first of their two sons. *A Farewell to Arms* was published in 1929 to a level of critical acclaim that Hemingway would not see again until 1940, with the publication of his Spanish Civil War novel *For Whom the Bell Tolls*. *A Farewell to Arms*, which is considered one of the best novels to emerge from World War I, was about a U.S. ambulance officer's disillusionment in war, his role as a deserter, and the romance between him and his nurse. Hemingway went from being an unknown writer to being the most important writer of his generation in just four years.

Hemingway then entered an experimental phase that confounded critics but still, to some extent, satisfied his audience. Among the works he published in this phase were his 1932 Spanish nonfiction bullfighting dissertation, *Death in the Afternoon*. After growing success with his groundbreaking style, Hemingway turned to writing for causes, including democracy as he knew it during the Spanish Civil War and World War II. The Hemingways traveled to Africa for a big game safari in 1933. Hemingway spent three months testing his hunting skills against some of the biggest and most dangerous animals on Earth. In 1935 he published *Green Hills of Africa*, a pseudo-nonfiction account of his safari in which he harshly criticized his supposed friends while portraying himself as courageous and skillful.

From the same safari, Hemingway gathered the material for two of his finest short stories, "The Snows of Kilimanjaro" and "The Short Happy Life of Francis Macomber." In "The Snows of Kilimanjaro," a dying writer laments the talent he wasted through drink, women, and laziness. Hemingway seemed to allow the more negative details of his life to show up in his fiction, whereas he portrayed himself as heroic in his nonfiction.

Hemingway traveled to Spain in 1937 to cover the Spanish Civil War for the North American Newspaper Alliance and worked alongside a young writer named Martha Gellhorn. They had met in Key West and had an affair for almost four years before Hemingway divorced his wife and married Gellhorn. They moved to Havana, Cuba. Hemingway's reportorial experiences covering the Spanish Civil War were used to write the novel *For Whom the Bell Tolls* (1940). The book was a huge success, both critically and commercially. Though unanimously voted the best novel of the year by the Pulitzer Prize committee, it was vetoed for political reasons by the conservative president of Columbia University; no prize was awarded that year.

Hemingway then covered World War II in Europe, where he met another woman, Mary Welsh. He divorced Gellhorn to marry Welsh in 1941. In the years following World War II, many critics said Hemingway's best writing was over. But he surprised them all by publishing a novella, *The Old Man and the Sea* (1952), a critical and commercially successful story about a poor Cuban fisherman's struggle to land a great fish. The novella won him the Pulitzer Prize in 1952. Two years later he received the Nobel Prize.

Physical ailments, caused in part by two small plane crashes in Africa, as well as alcohol abuse, took their toll on Hemingway. Despite his difficulties he continued work on his memoirs, which would be published in 1964 as *A Moveable Feast*. Hemingway would not live to see the success of this book, which critics praised for its tenderness and beauty and for its rare look at the expatriate lifestyle of Paris in the 1920s. There was a control in his writing that had not been evident in a long time. Hemingway and his wife had moved to Ketchum, Idaho. But he was suffering from severe depression that eventually led to electroshock therapy. One of the side effects of shock therapy is memory loss, and without his memory Hemingway could no longer recall the facts and images he required to write. The memory loss exacerbated the effects of his lifelong depressions, illnesses, and accidents. He was gripped by paranoia and threatened suicide on many occasions. On July 2, 1961, he shot himself, ending his life in Ketchum. He was 61 years old. His novel *True at First Light* was edited by his son Patrick and published posthumously in 1999.

## Further Reading

Dardis, Tom. *The Thirsty Muse: Alcohol and American Writer.* Boston: Ticknor & Fields, 1989.

Eby, Carl P. *Hemingway's Fetishism, Psychoanalysis and the Mirror of Manhood.* Albany: State University of New York Press, 1999.

Hemingway, Mary Welsh. *How It Was.* New York: Knopf, 1976.

Mellow, James R. *Hemingway: A Life Without Consequences.* New York: Houghton Mifflin, 1992.

Meyers, Jeffrey. *Hemingway, A Biography.* New York: Harper & Row, 1985.

## Henry, O.
### (William Sydney Porter)
(1862–1910)  *short story writer*

O. Henry was a prolific short story writer and a master of surprise endings who wrote about the life of ordinary people in New York City and other regions. O. Henry typically used humor and a twist of plot that turned on an ironic or coincidental circumstance. The public loved his work, although some critics were not so enthusiastic. He wrote some 600 short stories in a life cut short by alcoholism.

William Sydney Porter was born in Greensboro, North Carolina, on September 11, 1862. His father, Algernon Porter, was a physician. When William was three, his mother died, and he was raised by a relative. He left school at the age of 15 but was an avid reader. He went to Texas in 1882, worked at various jobs and started a humorous weekly, *The Rolling Stone.* He married Athol Estes in 1887 and she gave birth to a daughter in 1889. When the weekly failed, Porter joined the *Houston Daily Post* as a reporter and columnist. He also held various odd jobs during this time including one as a teller in an Austin bank. He was summoned from Houston to Austin to stand trial for embezzlement after a shortage was discovered in his accounts at the bank. It is presumed he would have been pardoned, because the shortage discovered was likely due to bad bookkeeping rather than criminal intent. However, while making a train connection from Houston to Austin for the trial, he decided to board a train heading in the other direction. Leaving his wife and child in Houston, he made his way to New Orleans, where he unloaded banana boats. He eventually ended up in Honduras and later South America, reportedly consorting with famous criminals. These two years on the run provided the initial fuel for his stories.

In 1897, after learning of his wife's declining health, Porter returned to Austin knowing that it meant a prison term. His wife died of tuberculosis that year, and in 1898 he was sentenced to five years in the federal penitentiary in Columbus, Ohio. His jobs as the prison's night druggist and as secretary to the steward allowed him time to write, and he was able to earn money to help support his daughter, Margaret. Porter's first published work from prison was "Whistling Dick's Christmas Stocking" (1899), which appeared in *McClure's Magazine.* The stories of adventure in the U.S. Southwest and in Central America were immediately successful among readers. He used several pseudonyms, but upon his early release for good behavior, he chose to write as O. Henry. According to some sources, he acquired the pseudonym from a warder called Orrin Henry. It also could be an abbreviation of the name of a French pharmacist, Eteinne-Ossian Henry, found in the *U.S. Dispensatory,* a reference work Porter used when he was in the prison pharmacy.

O. Henry moved to New York City in 1902. He wrote a story a week for the New York *World* and wrote for magazines as well. O. Henry's personal life was marred by alcohol abuse, and editors often waited out his bouts of drinking to receive their copy. O. Henry's first collection, *Cabbages and Kings,* appeared in 1904. He wrote 65 short stories in 1904 alone, and 50 the next year, including his most famous story "The Gift of the Magi." His accomplishments were that much more remarkable considering that he consumed an average of two quarts of whisky a day. His second collection, *The Four Million* (1906), included "The Gift of the Magi" and "The Furnished Room." O. Henry's other best-known work is perhaps the much anthologized "The Ransom of Red Chief," which was published in the collection *Whirligigs* in 1910. The story is about two men who kidnap the young son of a prominent man. After discovering the child to be a nuisance they agree to pay the boy's father to take him back.

O. Henry's stories follow a standard formula, dealing with commonplace events in the lives of ordinary people and arriving at a surprise ending through coincidence. His two favorite themes were the situation of the imposter and fate as the one unavoidable reality of life. Although his stories have been criticized for sentimentality and for their surprise endings, they remain popular to this day for those very reasons, and because of their author's unmistakable affection for the foibles of human nature.

O. Henry's final years were shadowed by alcoholism, ill health, and financial problems. He remarried in 1907, to Sara Lindsay, but died of tuberculosis, complicated by alcoholism and diabetes, on June 5, 1910. The O. Henry Memorial Awards were established in 1918 to be given annually to the writers of the best magazine stories.

## Further Reading

Lowry, Raymond. "An Exile in Paradise." *Coconut Telegraph.* Available online. URL: http://www.bayislands.com/cocotel/feature.htm. Downloaded June 10, 2003.

O'Quinn, Trueman E. *Time to Write: How William Sidney Porter Became O. Henry.* Austin, Tex.: Eakin Press, 1986.

Stuart, David. *O. Henry: A Biography.* Lanham, Md.: Scarborough House, 1990.

## Hijuelos, Oscar

(1951–  ) *novelist*

The first Hispanic-American novelist to win the Pulitzer Prize, Oscar Hijuelos is known as a quintessential New York writer. Most of his novels are set on the Upper West Side of Manhattan, overlooking the Hudson River, in the neighborhood where he was raised. His novels are driven largely by geography, he has said.

Oscar Hijuelos was born in New York City on August 24, 1951, to Cuban immigrants, Jose Hijuelos and Magdalena Torrens. His father was a hotel worker, and his mother was a homemaker. As a child, Hijuelos attended public schools in New York. He went to college at the City University of New York, where he graduated with a B.A. degree in 1975 and then studied with DONALD BARTHELME and others to earn his master's degree in English and writing in 1976.

Following his graduation, Hijuelos went to work at Transportation Display, Inc., as an advertising media traffic manager. He held this position from 1977 to 1984, working during the day and spending much of his free time writing short stories. Hijuelo's career as a writer received a big boost when several of his stories were published in the *Best of Pushcart Press III* anthology in 1978. One of these works, "Columbus Discovering America," received an outstanding writer award from Pushcart Press, which helped him to win an Oscar Cintas fiction-writing grant and then a Bread Loaf Writer's Conference Scholarship the following year. Hijuelos also received support early in his career from the Creative Artists Programs Service and the Ingram Merrill Foundation. Each of these awards bought Hijuelos a little more time for his writing and led to the publication of his first novel, *Our House in the Last World* (1983).

This novel about Cuban family life drew heavily on Hijuelos's own family and received significant praise from critics. He was awarded a National Endowment for the Arts creative writing fellowship in 1985. In 1989, Hijuelos published his second novel, *The Mambo Kings Play Songs of Love.* Again, the work received heaps of praise from critics. It was also nominated for a National Book Critics Circle Award and the National Book Award in 1989. In 1990, it won the Pulitzer Prize for fiction. It also sparked a landmark lawsuit, when Gloria Parker, the leader of an all-women rumba band that was portrayed in the novel, brought a $15 million libel suit against Hijuelos, claiming the novel had defamed her. The lawsuit was considered a test case because it involved a work of fiction instead of nonfiction, but the lawsuit was dismissed in a New York federal district court in 1991. The book was adapted for the screen as *The Mambo Kings* (1992). Starring Antonio Banderas and Armand Assante, the film was nearly as successful with movie fans as the novel had been with readers.

Hijuelos's third novel appeared in 1993 to mixed reviews. *The Fourteen Sisters of Emilio Montez O'Brien* was primarily criticized for weak characterization, a result of the novel trying to juggle all 14 sisters alluded to in the title. Overall, the novel was still well received.

Hijuelos's next project was a musical one, a CD collaboration entitled *Stranger Than Fiction* with other writers, including Dave Barry, Molly Ivins, STEPHEN KING, AMY TAN, and others. It is a collection of various writers making music; some of them are together, and some are not. Hijuelos performed lead vocal and guitar on some of the tracks for the CD, the proceeds of which are donated to the PEN Writers Special Fund and other charities.

*Empress of the Splendid Season,* Hijuelos's fourth novel, came out in 1999. A smaller, more modest effort than his other books, this novel solidified Hijuelos's reputation as a talented portrayer of New York City's immigrant neighborhoods and the working poor who inhabit them.

Hijuelos married Lori Carlson in December 1998. The two share an apartment on Riverside Drive in Manhattan.

**Further Reading**

Kanellos, Nicolas, ed. *Hispanic-American Almanac.* Detroit: Gale, 1993.

Ryan, Bryan. *Hispanic Writers.* Detroit: Gale, 1991.

Turner, Allan. "Hijuelos Sings Fresh Tune." Houston Chronicle.com. Available online. URL: http://www.chron.com/cs/CDA/story.hts/ae/books/reviews/1463621. Posted June 21, 2002.

## Hughes, Langston
(1902–1967) *poet, novelist*

Langston Hughes was considered one of the leading voices in the Harlem Renaissance of the 1920s.

Influenced by the Bible, W. E. B. DUBOIS, and WALT WHITMAN, Hughes realistically depicted the ordinary lives of African Americans and became one of the foremost interpreters of racial relationships in the United States. He wrote about southern violence, Harlem street life, poverty, prejudice, hunger, and hopelessness. Hughes had a reputation for an unrivaled command of the nuances of African-American urban culture, and worked hard to contrast a character's struggle for good against oppressive circumstances. He published more than 35 books. Many of his poems, written in rhythmic language, have been set to music.

Langston Hughes was born February 1, 1902, in Joplin, Missouri. His parents separated when he was young and his mother moved from city to city in search of work. In his rootless childhood, Hughes lived in Kansas, Colorado, Indiana, and New York. Hughes read books to escape his loneliness. As an adolescent in Cleveland, he participated in the Karamu Players and published his first play, *The Golden Piece,* in 1921. After graduating from a high school in Cleveland, he spent a year in Mexico with his father. Hughes gathered new impressions and new insights about race, class, and ethnicity in Mexico, where his ability to speak Spanish and his appearance often allowed him to blend in. Even white Americans who would not have spoken to him in the United States would talk to him as a "Mexican" on the train.

By the time Hughes entered Columbia University he had already launched his literary career with his poem "The Negro Speaks of Rivers" in the *Crisis,* edited by DuBois. He committed himself to writing mainly about African Americans. He abandoned his studies in 1922 and participated in more entertaining jazz and blues activities in nearby Harlem. Hughes held a series of menial jobs and enlisted as a steward on a freighter bound for West Africa. He traveled to Paris, worked as a doorman of a nightclub, and continued on to Italy. He returned to the United States late in 1924. By this time, he was well known in African-American literary circles as a gifted young poet.

His poetry earned him a scholarship to Lincoln University in Pennsylvania and he received his B.A. degree there in 1929. His poems appeared in the anthology *The New Negro* (1925). CARL SANDBURG, whom Hughes later called "my guiding star," was instrumental in leading Hughes toward free verse. Hughes became one of the celebrated young talents of the Harlem Renaissance, but not all African Americans appreciated his use of dialect, his interpretation of blues and jazz, or the way he portrayed African-American workers. Some said Hughes was no poet laureate, but rather the "poet low-rate" of Harlem. His devotion to blues and jazz inspired him to fuse them with traditional verse in his first two books, *The Weary Blues* (1926) and *Fine Clothes to the Jew* (1927). His emphasis on lower-class African-American life led to harsh attacks on him in the black press. In 1926, in the *Nation,* Hughes provided the Harlem Renaissance with a manifesto when he skillfully argued the need for both race pride and artistic independence in his most memorable essay, "The Negro Artist and the Racial Mountain."

Langston Hughes was a prominent voice of the Harlem Renaissance. *(Library of Congress, Prints and Photographs Division, FSA/OWI Collection [LC-USW3-033841-C])*

Hughes's patron, Charlotte Mason, generously supported him in the late 1920s and supervised the writing of his first novel, *Not Without Laughter* (1930), which received a cordial reception. It was about a sensitive black boy from the Midwest and his struggling family. At about the time the novel appeared, Hughes separated from Mason's control and financial support and eventually became one of the first black authors who could support himself by his writings. In the 1930s, he traveled in the Soviet Union, Haiti, and Japan. During his visit in the Soviet Union he wrote the poem "Goodbye, Christ," which was attacked by a right-wing religious group in the 1940s. Although Hughes decided to repudiate the poem publicly, he also embraced radical leftist politics, publishing a collection of satiric short stories, *The Ways of White Folks* (1943). Hughes emphasized the importance of African culture and shared DuBois's belief that renewal could only come from an understanding of African roots.

Hughes's play *The Mulatto* (1935), revised without his knowledge with the insertion of a rape into the play, opened on Broadway in 1935. The same year, Hughes won a Guggenheim Fellowship. He wrote other plays, including comedies such as *Little Ham* (1936) and a historical drama, *Emperor of Haiti* (1936), which were only moderate successes. He also collaborated with ZORA NEALE HURSTON in 1931 on a play called *Mule Bone.* The collaboration became famous due to the two writers' many disagreements, which kept the play from being performed during their lifetimes. In the Spanish Civil War, Hughes worked as a correspondent for the *Baltimore Afro-American* and became friends with ERNEST HEMINGWAY. In 1942, Hughes made Harlem his permanent home and began lecturing at universities around the country. He founded black theater groups in Harlem, Chicago, and Los Angeles.

With the onset of World War II, Hughes moved away from the left and toward the center politically. His first volume of autobiography, *The Big Sea* (1940), written in an episodic, lightly comic manner, made virtually no mention of his leftist sympathies. In his books of verse *Shakespeare in Harlem* (1942) and *Jim Crow's Last Stand* (1943), Hughes strongly attacked racial segregation. He began writing a column for the *Chicago Defender* in

1942 and continued to do so for the next 20 years. He often depicted conversations on race and racism between an offbeat Harlem character called Jesse B. Semple, or Simple, and a staid narrator in a neighborhood bar. Simple became Hughes's most celebrated and beloved fictional creation, and the subject of five collections edited by Hughes, starting in 1950 with *Simple Speaks His Mind*.

In *Montage of a Dream Deferred* (1951), Hughes broke new ground with verse accented by the discordant nature of the new bebop jazz that reflected a growing desperation in the black urban communities of the North. During the same period, he was constantly harassed by conservatives about his leftist ties. Senator Joseph McCarthy forced him to testify about his political beliefs in 1953, and Hughes denied that he had ever been a member of the Communist Party. He conceded, however, that some of his radical verse had been ill-advised. Eventually Hughes wrote at length about his years in the Soviet Union in *I Wonder as I Wander* (1956), his much-admired second volume of autobiography.

The Simple books inspired a musical show, *Simply Heavenly* (1957), that had some success. However, Hughes's *Tambourines to Glory* (1963), a gospel musical play satirizing corruption in a black storefront church, failed badly, with some critics accusing him of creating caricatures of African-American life. Nevertheless, his love of gospel music led to other acclaimed stage efforts, including *Black Nativity* (1961) and *Jericho—Jim Crow* (1964), which mixed words, music, and dance in an atmosphere of improvisation. Hughes also wrote more than a dozen children's books, including *Popo and Fifina* (1932), a tale set in Haiti and written with ARNA BONTEMPS. His children's books covered subjects such as jazz, Africa, and the West Indies. He also wrote a commissioned history of the National Association for the Advancement of Colored People (NAACP) and the text of the much praised *A Pictorial History of the Negro in America* (1956).

Hughes was inducted into the National Institute of Arts and Letters in 1961, the year he published his innovative book of poems to be read with jazz accompaniment, *Ask Your Mama: 12 Moods for Jazz*. He published an ambitious book-length poem called *Ask Your Mama* in 1962, which

was filled with allusions to black culture and music. However, the reviews were dismissive. Although Hughes was hailed in 1966 as a historic artistic figure at the First World Festival of Negro Arts in Dakar, Senegal, he also found himself increasingly rejected by young African-American militants at home as the Civil Rights movement moved toward Black Power.

Hughes's last book was posthumously published volume of verse, *The Panther and the Lash* (1967), which was mainly about civil rights. He died May 22, 1967, in New York City, following prostate surgery.

**Further Reading**

Dace, Tish. ed. Langston Hughes: *The Contemporary Reviews*. New York: Cambridge University Press, 1997.

Haskins, James. *Always Movin' On: The Life of Langston Hughes*. Trenton, N.J.: Africa World Press, 1993.

McClaren, Joseph. *Langston Hughes: Folk Dramatist in the Protest Tradition, 1921–1943*. Westport, Conn.: Greenwood Press, 1997.

Meltzer, Milton. *Langston Hughes: A Biography*. New York: Crowell, 1968.

Rampersad, Arnold. *The Life of Langston Hughes*. 2 vols. New York: Oxford University Press, 1986–1988.

Walker, Alice. *Langston Hughes, American Poet*. New York: Crowell, 1974.

## Hurston, Zora Neale

(1891–1960) *novelist, short story writer, nonfiction writer, folklorist*

A central figure in the Harlem Renaissance, Zora Neale Hurston was both a writer and anthropologist, whose peers considered her an authority on black culture. Hurston's aim was to combine the two disciplines in order to more fully discover black culture and affirm its worth.

Zora Neale Hurston's birthdate is difficult to pin down, but most sources give it as January 7, 1891. The place has been definitely identified as Notasulga, Alabama. Hurston's father was a Baptist preacher, tenant farmer, and carpenter. Her mother was a homemaker. When Hurston was three years old, the family moved to Eatonville, Florida, which was the first incorporated black community in America. Her father eventually became the town's mayor. Eatonville would appear over the years in Hurston's writing as a black utopian society, immune to the prejudices of white society.

She graduated from Morgan Academy in 1918, then went on to Howard University in Washington, D.C. She eventually graduated from Barnard College, Columbia University, in 1928 with a degree in anthropology. At Barnard, she was a favorite student of noted anthropologist Franz Boas. After several years of anthropological research, which took her to the Florida Everglades, Georgia's sea islands, New Orleans, and Haiti, Hurston published her first novel, *Jonah's Gourd Vine*, in 1934 to critical success. In 1935, her book *Mules and Men*, which investigated voodoo practices in black communities in Florida and New Orleans, also won praise. *Their Eyes Were Watching God*, considered Hurston's greatest achievement, was published in 1937. The novel was widely acclaimed but criticized by many blacks because of her refusal to portray blacks as "victims of the myth of inferiority." Nevertheless, this story of a woman who defines her life in opposition to the expectations of her small southern town influenced later generations of black women writers and helped to shape the Harlem Renaissance.

*Their Eyes Were Watching God* was followed by *Tell My Horse* (1938), her travelogue and study of Caribbean voodoo, which received mixed reviews. *Moses, Man of the Mountain*, appeared in 1939, also to little praise. Her final two books were released in 1942 and 1948. *Dust Tracks on a Road*, her autobiography, was a commercial success, but the last book, a novel called *Seraph on the Suwanee*, found no support among critics.

In addition to writing, she worked at various other jobs throughout her life. She worked for a time as a writer for Warner Bros., the film studio; taught at North Carolina State University; and was on the staff of the Library of Congress, but financial stability eluded her. Her writing fell out of favor during the civil rights era, in large part due to the fact that she never addressed racism in her books. This was exacerbated when she publicly criticized the Civil Rights movement, choosing instead to support ultra-conservative politicians. She spent the last years of her life in poverty in Florida, and

Writer Zora Neale Hurston used her skills as an anthropologist to explore African-American culture in the early 20th century. *(Library of Congress, Prints and Photographs Division [LC-USZ62-126945])*

her work was forgotten and out of print until the 1970s, when the novelist ALICE WALKER led the effort to revitalize interest in Hurston's work. Many of her books have been reprinted since that time, and some previously unpublished work has been collected and published. She died on January 28, 1960, in Fort Pierce, Florida.

## Further Reading

Bloom, Harold. *Zora Neale Hurston*. New York: Chelsea House, 1986.

Gates, Henry Louis, and K. A. Appiah, eds. *Zora Neale Hurston: Critical Perspectives Past and Present*. New York: Amistad, 1993.

Glassman, Steve, and Kathryn Lee Seidel. *Zora in Florida*. Orlando: University of Central Florida Press, 1991.

Howard, Lillie P. *Alice Walker and Zora Neale Hurston: The Common Bond*. Westport, Conn.: Greenwood Press, 1993.

# Hwang, David Henry
(1957– ) *playwright, screenwriter*

Hailed by drama critic William A. Henry III, writing in *Time*, as having the potential "to become the first important dramatist of American public life since Arthur Miller, and maybe the best of them all," David Henry Hwang, at a very young age, has taken center stage as a playwright and screenwriter. His numerous award-winning plays include *F.O.B.*, which stands for "fresh off the boat"; *Golden Child*; *Bondage*; and *M. Butterfly*. His screenplays include *M. Butterfly*, *Golden Gate*, and an early adaptation of *Seven Years in Tibet*. His work often deals with the struggle of Asian immigrants as they try simultaneously to fit in with the dominant culture, while preserving their own unique heritage, but his work should not be pigeonholed as strictly Asian American. As Hwang himself said, "I've found that the more culturally specific you are, the more universal the work is. There's no conflict between wanting to reach a large audience and being particular and culturally accurate."

David Henry Hwang was born on August 11, 1957, in Los Angeles, California. He is the eldest of three children, and the only son born to parents of Chinese heritage. His father, Henry Yuan Hwang, arrived in California in the late 1940s, after leaving his native Shanghai around the time of the communist takeover. He studied business at the University of Southern California (USC) and eventually became a banker. His mother, Dorothy Huang Hwang, was born in China and raised in the Philippines; she studied music at USC and taught piano at the Coburn School of the Arts.

David Henry Hwang attended public schools and then graduated from Stanford University in 1979 with a B.A. degree in English literature. He actually wrote his first play, *F.O.B.*, before graduating from Stanford, where it was originally produced. With financial support from his father, *F.O.B.* was later produced at the National Playwrights Conference in 1979. The following year, it won an Obie Award for the best new Off Broadway play of the season, when it was produced at the New York Shakespeare Festival's Public

Theater. Hwang taught high school for a year after graduating from college and then enrolled in the famous Yale School of Drama, where he studied for two years, from 1980 to 1982.

During this time, Hwang wrote two more influential plays—*The Dance and the Railroad* and *Family Devotions*, both of which appeared in 1981 and treated the subject of immigrants' lives. In 1985, Hwang married the artist Ophelia Y. M. Chong, but the marriage ended in divorce four years later. Hwang subsequently married Kathryn Lang, an actress, and they have a son named Noah. By the late 1980s, Hwang's work was moving away from his early focus on the immigrant experience to a broader treatment of race, gender, and culture. This movement culminated in Hwang's creation of *M. Butterfly*, the play that established him as a major U.S. playwright. Hwang's career took off in 1988 when the play became a spectacular Broadway hit. He received a Tony Award for best Broadway play that year—becoming the first Asian American to ever win a Tony—and a Pulitzer Prize in 1989, as well as a Drama Desk Award and an Outer Critics Circle Award. *M. Butterfly* weaves a complex story of mistaken sexual identity and espionage that appeals to a broad audience. Hwang adapted and executive produced the screen version of *M. Butterfly*, which came out in 1993, but the film achieved only a small portion of the success the play enjoyed. It did, however, commence a career in film and television for Hwang, who has gone on to write several other screenplays and to produce a television miniseries called *The Monkey King*, which aired on NBC in 2001.

Hwang's other plays include *Sound and the Beauty* (1983), *Rich Relations* (1986), *Face Value* (1993), and the critically acclaimed *Golden Child*, which opened on Broadway in 1998. He has also written the libretti for a number of works, including *Aida* for Elton John and Tim Rice, *1000 Airplanes on the Roof* and *The Voyage* for Philip Glass, and *The Silver River*, with music by Bright Sheng, which premiered at the Spoleto USA Festival 2000.

The recipient of numerous awards, Hwang has been supported by grants from the Guggenheim and Rockefeller Foundations, the National Endowment for the Arts, and the PEW/TCG

National Artist Residency Fellowship. He has served on the council of the Dramatists Guild and as vice president of Theatre Communication Group. President Bill Clinton appointed Hwang to the President's Committee on the Arts and Humanities in 1994.

## Further Reading

Kerkhoff, Ingrid. "David Henry Hwang." Contemporary Theatre and Drama in the U.S. (since 1980). Available online. URL: http://www.fb10.uni-bremen.de/anglistik/kerkhoff/ContempDrama/Hwang.htm. Downloaded June 10, 2003.

Lui, Mary Ting Li. "'Sheer Elegance': The Intersection of Woman and 'the Orient.'" *Privileging Positions: The Sites of Asian American Studies.* Edited by Gary Okihiro, Marilyn Alquizola, et al. Pullman: Washington State University Press, 1995, pp. 57–65.

Moyi, James S. *Marginal Sights: Staging the Chinese in America.* Iowa City: University of Iowa Press, 1993.

Skloot, Robert. "Breaking the Butterfly: The Politics of David Henry Hwang." *Modern Drama,* March 1990, pp. 59–66.

Street, Douglas. *David Henry Hwang.* Boise, Idaho: Boise State University Press, 1989.

# I

## Inge, William
(1913–1973) *playwright*

A midwestern playwright, William Inge made his mark with four plays that were all adopted into popular Hollywood films. *Picnic* (1953) won a Pulitzer Prize. His work is praised for its sensitive portrayal of the complexities of small-town American families.

William Inge was born in Independence, Kansas, on May 3, 1913, the second son and the youngest of five children of Luther Clay Inge and Maude Sarah Gibson-Inge. His father, a traveling salesman, was away a great deal and his mother sometimes took in boarders to help support herself and her family. Inge's fascination with the theater began at a young age. In the 1920s, Independence was a notably wealthy community and offered many top artists and shows as stopovers between performances in Kansas City, Missouri, and Tulsa, Oklahoma. Although Inge was not from a well-to-do family, he did get to see many shows because he was a member of the town's local Boy Scout troop. The small town of Independence had a profound influence on the young Inge, and he would later attribute his understanding of human behavior to growing up in this environment. "I've often wondered how people raised in our great cities ever develop any knowledge of humankind. People who grow up in small towns get to know each other so much more closely than they do in cities." In his late plays, Inge's characters tended to exude this knowledge of humankind and many of his themes revolved around the small-town atmosphere with which he was so familiar.

Inge was educated at the University of Kansas at Lawrence where he graduated with a B.A. degree in speech and drama in 1935. There he participated in student productions and performed in touring tent shows during the summer months. Then, an emotional breakdown delayed his completion of an M.A. degree in Tennessee and, when he found himself unable to brave the uncertainties of professional acting, he took a job as a small-town English teacher. He first taught high school in Kansas, then college for five years at Stephens College in Missouri. He eventually returned to his graduate work and earned an M.A. degree from the George Peabody College for Teachers in 1943.

In 1943 Inge left his teaching position to become the art, music, book, and drama critic for the *St. Louis Star-Times*. Late in 1944 he sought an interview with emerging young playwright TEN-NESSEE WILLIAMS, who was visiting his parents in St. Louis while his play *The Glass Menagerie* was being prepared for its pre-Broadway tryout in Chicago. Inge told Williams that he wanted to write plays, and Williams encouraged him to do so. Later, Williams arranged for Dallas theater pioneer Margo Jones to read Inge's first play, *Farther Off from Heaven*, and she produced it in Dallas in 1947. Consequently, four more Inge plays became Broadway hits in the next decade—*Come Back Little Sheba* (1950), *Picnic* (1953), *Bus Stop* (1955), and *The Dark at the Top of the Stairs* (1957). All four were subsequently made into successful films. *The*

*Dark at the Top of the Stairs,* a reworking of his first play, premiered on Broadway. This somewhat autobiographical drama would come to be considered Inge's finest play. He would later describe it as his "first cautious attempt to look at the past, with an effort to find order and meaning in experiences that were once too close to be seen clearly." *The Dark at the Top of the Stairs* was released as a film starring Dorothy McGuire, Robert Preston, Shirley Knight, Eve Arden, and Angela Lansbury in 1960. Shortly thereafter, two Inge collections were published, *Four Plays* (1958) and *Summer Brave and Eleven Short Plays* (1962). Inge won a Pulitzer Prize for *Picnic.*

In 1959, *A Loss of Roses* opened to poor reviews and closed after a three-week run. Inge was devastated by the criticism. In 1960 he announced plans to teach at the University of Kansas in Lawrence, although his plans never came to fruition. In 1960, Inge wrote his first screenplay, *Splendor in the Grass,* which was set in New York. It starred Natalie Wood, Pat Hingle, and newcomer Warren Beatty. It also featured the only screen appearance of Inge himself, who played the part of Reverend Whitman. He was shown giving part of a sermon and bidding farewell to his parishioners as they leave the church. *Splendor in the Grass* was a triumph for Inge and won him an Academy Award for Best Screenplay.

However, after being almost universally deemed "the next Williams," Inge's success had begun to slow down dramatically. In fact, following the success of *Splendor in the Grass,* Inge enjoyed only minor successes in the public eye. The products of his remaining years were two novels: *Good Luck, Miss Wyckoff* (1970) and *My Son Is a Splendid Driver* (1971), a largely autobiographical account of Inge's boyhood years. Convinced that he could no longer write, Inge committed suicide on June 10, 1973, at his home in Hollywood, where he lived with his sister, Helene. He was 60 years old. He was buried in the Mt. Hope Cemetery in his hometown of Independence, Kansas. His headstone reads simply, "Playwright."

## Further Reading

Finkle, David. "Requiem for William." TheaterMania.com. Available online. URL: http://www.theatermania. com/content/news.cfm?int_news_id=3147. Posted February 18, 2003.

McClure, Arthur F. *Memories of Splendor: The Midwestern World of William Inge.* Topeka: Kansas State Historical Society, 1989.

McClure, Arthur F., and C. David Rice, ed. *A Bibliographical Guide to the Works of William Inge.* Lewiston, N.Y.: Edwin Mellen Press, 1991.

Voss, Ralph. *A Life of William Inge: The Strains of Triumph.* Lawrence: University Press of Kansas, 1990.

## Irving, Washington
### (Diedrich Knickerbocker, Geoffrey Crayon)
(1783–1859) *novelist, biographer, travel writer, journalist, poet, short story writer*

Essayist, poet, travel book writer, biographer, and columnist, Irving has been called the father of the American short story. He is best known for his stories "The Legend of Sleepy Hollow," in which the schoolmaster Ichabod Crane meets a headless horseman, and "Rip Van Winkle," about a man who falls asleep for 20 years. Irving's career was exceptionally prolific and diverse. In addition to his famous written works, he also spent significant periods of his life employed as a successful businessman and merchant, as the U.S. ambassador to Spain, as the president of the Library of New York, as a lawyer, and as a military aide to New York governor Daniel D. Tompkins.

Washington Irving was born in New York City (near present-day Wall Street) at the end of the Revolutionary War, on April 3, 1783, and was the youngest of 11 children. His father was a wealthy merchant, and his mother, an Englishwoman, was the granddaughter of a clergyman. His parents were great admirers of General George Washington, and named their son after their hero. Young Irving had many interests, including writing, architecture, landscape design, traveling, and diplomacy. He enjoyed visiting different places and a large part of his life was spent in Europe, particularly England, France, Germany, and Spain. He often wrote about the places he visited. For example, his novel *Bracebridge Hall* (1822) is a view of life in England and *The Life and Voyages of Christopher Columbus* (1828) was a carefully written historical account of

Columbus's life and travels throughout Europe and the Americas.

Irving's career as a writer commenced with journals and newspapers. He contributed to *Morning Chronicle* (1802–03), which was edited by his brother Peter, and published *Salmagundi* (1807–08), a collection of satirical literary essays written in collaboration with his brother William and James Kirke Paulding. From 1812 to 1814 he was an editor of *Analetic* magazine in Philadelphia and New York. In 1809, Irving suffered a severe personal tragedy when his fiancée, Matilda Hoffmann, died at the young age of 17. Later he wrote, "For years I could not talk on the subject of this hopeless regret; I could not even mention her name; but her image was continually before me, and I dreamt of her incessantly."

Initially, Irving wrote under pen names, one of which was "Diedrich Knickerbocker." In 1809, using this pen name, Irving wrote *A History of New York,* which describes and pokes fun at the lives of the early Dutch settlers in Manhattan. Eventually, this pen name came to mean a person from New York and is where the New York Knickerbockers (Knicks) basketball team got its name. Irving's success continued with *The Sketch Book of Geoffrey Crayon, Gent.* (1819–20), which was a collection of stories that allowed him to become the first person known in American history to make a living solely on writing.

After the death of his mother, Irving decided to relocate to Europe, where he remained for 17 years from 1815 to 1832. He lived in Dresden, London, and Paris. After a romantic liaison with Mary Shelley he settled in Spain, where he worked for the U.S. Embassy in Madrid from 1826 to 1829. In 1829–32 he was a secretary to the American Legation under Martin Van Buren. During his stay in Spain, he wrote *Columbus* (1828), *Conquest of Granada* (1829), and *The Companions of Columbus* (1831), all of which were based on careful historical research. In 1829 he moved to London and published *Alhambra* (1832), which concerned the history and legends of Moorish Spain. Among his literary friends were Shelley and HENRY WADSWORTH LONGFELLOW.

Feeling a desire to be among fellow Americans and his family, Irving returned in 1832 from Europe

Washington Irving is sometimes called the father of the American short story. *(Photo by M. B. Brady. Library of Congress, Prints and Photographs Division [LC-USZ62-4238])*

to Tarrytown, New York, where he established his home, Sunnyside, which he designed and built. Irving never married or had children. Rather, for the next 25 years he shared Sunnyside with his brother Ebenezer and Ebenezer's five daughters. Upon his return to the states, Irving found that he had become a household name, both in America and internationally. The Spanish were so pleased with Irving's writing that in 1828, they elected him to the Real Academia de la Historia. In 1830, Irving received a gold medal in history from the Royal Society of Literature in London and also received honorary degrees from Oxford, Columbia, and Harvard.

Irving died in Tarrytown on November 28, 1859. Just before retiring for the night, the author had said, "Well, I must arrange my pillows for another weary night . . . if this could only end!" He was buried in the Sleepy Hollow Cemetery at the Old Dutch Church in Sleepy Hollow, New York. Irving's major works were published in 1860–61 in 21 volumes.

## Further Reading

Adams, Charles, and Washington Irving. *Memoir of Washington Irving.* Freeport, N.Y.: Books for Libraries Press, 1971.

Aderman, Ralph M. *Washington Irving Reconsidered: A Symposium.* Hartford, Conn.: Transcendental Books, 1969.

Bowden, Mary Weatherspoon. *Washington Irving.* Boston: Twayne Publishers, 1981.

Curtis, George William. *Washington Irving: A Sketch.* Folcroft, Penn.: Folcroft Library Editions, 1976.

Hedges, William L. *Washington Irving: An American Study, 1802–1832.* Westport, Conn.: Greenwood Press, 1980.

Neider, Charles, ed. *The Complete Tales of Washington Irving.* Cambridge, Mass.: Da Capo Press, 1998.

# J

## Jackson, Laura Riding
### (Laura Riding, Laura Reichenthal, Laura Riding Gottschalk, Madeleine Vara)
(1901–1991) *poet, short story writer, novelist, essayist, literary critic*

Ironically, the poet Laura Riding Jackson achieved her greatest fame when she renounced poetry midway through her career. Poems written in the early part of her career have been praised as among the best from the early 20th century, but it was literary criticism and nonfiction that occupied much of her writing life. She was the author of more than a dozen books of poetry, several collections of short stories, numerous books of essays, a novel, and several philological works.

Laura Riding Jackson was born Laura Reichenthal on January 16, 1901, in New York City, the daughter of Nathaniel Reichenthal and Sadie Edersheim Reichenthal. She had a half-sister, Isabel, who was the daughter of her father's first wife, Laura Lorber.

Reichenthal attended Cornell University from 1918 to 1921. In 1920, she married Louis Gottschalk, a professor of history at Cornell. In 1923, Reichenthal, who went by the name Laura Riding Gottschalk at the time, published her first poem in *The Fugitive*, the magazine edited by JOHN CROWE RANSOM, ALLEN TATE, and ROBERT PENN WARREN, among others. In 1924, she received the Nashville Prize for poetry from *The Fugitive* and was invited to join the group. The Fugitives were originally a group of southern writers and critics concerned with the artistic and intellectual ideas of modernism. Over time, however, they evolved into defendants of the traditional agrarian South, which they felt stood as the last hope for humanity in an age of industrialization and materialism. The following year, in 1925, she officially accepted the offer to be a member of the Fugitives, divorced her husband, and moved to New York City, where she became friends with HART CRANE and other writers.

Her reputation grew quickly, and by 1925 Robert Graves had invited Reichenthal to collaborate on a book with him. She lived in England and Majorca, Spain, from 1926 to 1939. Her first book of poems, *The Close Chaplet*, was published by Leonard and Virginia Woolf's Hogarth Press in England and by Adelphi in the United States in 1926.

In 1927, she officially changed her name to Laura Riding. That same year, she and Graves established Seizin Press, and she served as managing partner of the press until 1938. The pair also cowrote *A Survey of Modernist Poetry*, which was published in 1927, and they coedited the literary journal *Epilogue* from 1935 to 1938. The essays and reviews published in the journal helped to influence the development of New Criticism. The term *New Criticism* took its name from a book of essays by noted critic John Crowe Ransom and refers to a critical approach, promoted by Ransom, in which the critic studies and relies on the actual texts of poems instead of the biographies of the poets and the specific details surrounding the poems' composition. Other works published by Riding during her years abroad include her most important works of criticism, all published in 1928—*Contemporaries and Snobs; Anarchism Is Not Enough;* and *A Pamphlet Against Anthologies,* which was cowritten with Graves.

In 1929, Riding attempted suicide, an event that resulted in her move with Graves to Majorca, where they relocated the Seizin Press. During her years in Majorca, Riding published several volumes of poetry, including *Experts Are Puzzled* (1930), *Twenty Poems Less* (1930), *Four Unposted Letters to Catherine* (1930), and her *Collected Poems,* which came out in 1938, just one year before her return to the United States. Her return was prompted by the advent of the Spanish Civil War. *Lives of Wives,* a historical novel, was published in 1939 and was her most successful book.

In 1941, shortly after Riding returned to the United States, she married Schuyler Brinckerhoff Jackson, who was a poet, critic, and former poetry editor of *Time* magazine. The couple moved to Wabasso, Florida, in 1943, where they owned a citrus farm. Riding and Jackson worked together to complete *A Dictionary of Related Meanings,* which Riding had begun in the 1930s. They also collaborated on *Rational Meaning: A New Foundation for the Definition of Words,* which Riding completed in 1974, six years after Schuyler Jackson's death on July 4, 1968.

In 1955, Riding began publishing under the name Laura Riding Jackson for the first time. This was also the first appearance in print of her renunciation of writing poetry, a stance for which she would be long remembered. Despite this, Jackson continued to publish collections of short stories and essays under several different forms of her name, as well as under the pseudonym Madeleine Vara. Over the course of her career, she published more than a dozen books of poetry and several books of nonfiction, including *The Telling* (1973) and *How a Poem Comes to Be* (1980).

Jackson received numerous honors late in her career. She was given the Mark Rothko Appreciation Award in 1971, a Guggenheim fellowship in 1973, a National Endowment for the Arts fellowship in 1979, and, in 1991, Yale University's Bollingen Prize for her lifetime contribution to poetry. During these years, many of her early books were reissued, as well. Laura Riding Jackson died in Sebastian, Florida, on September 2, 1991.

## Further Reading

Baker, Deborah. *In Extremis: The Life of Laura Riding.* New York: Grove Press, 1993.

Friedmann, Elizabeth. *A Mannered Grace: The Life of Laura (Riding) Jackson.* New York: Persea Books, 2004.

Benzel, Kathyrn. "Laura [Riding] Jackson, 1901–1991." *Modern American Poetry.* Available online. URL: http://www.english.uiuc.edu/maps/poets/g_1/jackson/jackson.htm. Downloaded March 8, 2003.

## Jackson, Shirley
(1919–1965)  *short story writer, novelist*

Shirley Jackson is best remembered as the author of the classic short story "The Lottery," a dark and unforgettable tale of a murderous custom in a small New England town. Initially rejected as immoral and twisted, the short story now appears in many English texts and school anthologies. Jackson is also the author of several American gothic novels, such as *We Have Always Lived in the Castle* and *The Haunting of Hill House.* Primarily published in *The New Yorker, Redbook, The Saturday Evening Post,* and *Harper's Bazaar,* Jackson's stories subtly explore themes of psychological turmoil, isolation, and the inequity of fate.

Shirley Jackson was born on December 14, 1919, in San Francisco, California, to Leslie and Geraldine Jackson. Her father was an employee of a lithography company and her mother was a housewife. Early on, Jackson's family relocated to Burlingame, California, where she enjoyed a childhood pursuing her interests in sports and writing. From a young age, Jackson was an exceptionally talented writer; she won a poetry prize at age 12 and in high school began keeping a diary to record her writing progress. She enrolled in the liberal arts program at the University of Rochester in 1934, but due to bouts of depression and mental illness, was forced to withdraw from school. Jackson recovered her health over the next few years by living quietly at home and writing, conscientiously turning out 1,000 words of prose a day. She made a strong effort to cultivate her skills as a professional writer and developed very rigorous work habits, which she maintained for the rest of her life. In 1937, she enrolled at Syracuse University and over the next two years published 15 pieces in various campus magazines and became the fiction editor of *The Syracusan,* the college humor magazine. When her position was eliminated, she and classmate Stanley Edgar Hyman began to plan a literary magazine. In 1939 the first edition of *The Spectre* was published. The magazine was quite popular but fell into disfavor with its sponsors in the English department because of its biting editorials and critical essays. Despite the English department's disapproval, a modern literature professor, Leonard Brown, supported the students and the publication. Jackson always referred to Brown as her mentor, and in 1959, she dedicated *The Haunting of Hill House* to him.

After their graduation from college, Jackson and Hyman married and settled in the small college town of North Bennington, Vermont, where Hyman taught literature. They had four children while continuing to live active literary careers. Jackson's first national publication was a humorous story written after a job at a department store during the Christmas rush: "My Life with R. H. Macy" appeared in *The New Republic* in 1941. Her first child was born the next year, but she continued to write every day on a disciplined schedule, selling her stories to magazines and publishing novels. It was during this time that Jackson published her first novel, *The Road Through the Wall,* and her best-known work, "The Lottery," a story about a small village's annual practice of choosing one of its citizens to stone to death. It was inspired by the frosty relationship Shirley endured with the townsfolk in North Bennington. When "The Lottery" was first published, in the *New Yorker* in 1948, it prompted a widespread cry of outrage. Hundreds of canceled *New Yorker* subscriptions and thousands of letters came from incensed people who described Jackson as "un-American," "perverted," and "modern," or believed the story was based on fact and wanted to know which town practiced this lottery. The next year, "The Lottery" was republished in a collection of short stories. By that time, critics had decided

Jackson was a writer of an unusual scope and vision. Despite the fact that she was a full-time housewife and a mother of four, she always found time to dedicate to her writing. She was known to bolt to the typewriter whenever an idea entered her head.

In 1949, Jackson and her family moved to Westport, Connecticut. Throughout the late 1940s and 1950s, Jackson was an extremely prolific writer, publishing at least 44 short stories, six articles, two collections of family memoirs, one nonfiction children's book, and four novels. Six of her stories were published in various prominent magazines, including *The New Mexico Quarterly Review, Collier's,* and *The Reader's Digest. The Haunting of Hill House* (1959) was particularly successful. Adapted for the screen several different times, the tale of subtle psychological terror also contained an undercurrent of lesbianism. Her works during these years reflect the emotional distress she was fighting. She suffered from severe bouts of anxiety and depression, which worsened as the years progressed. She also had gained a great deal of weight, which some critics have interpreted as a rebellion against a society to which she never felt she belonged and against her debutante mother who used to send her corsets in the mail as "gentle suggestion" about her weight. On top of her anxiety attacks and weight problems, Jackson also suffered from asthma and arthritis, which developed in the ends of her fingers. Despite all these hardships, she never stopped writing. In 1965, after years of self-therapy at the typewriter and two years of professional psychiatric sessions, Jackson was finally reaching a level of mental stability. Then, in the afternoon of August 8, 1965, Shirley Jackson went upstairs to take a nap and died in her sleep. Owing to her courage to step out in a genre still undeveloped and unfamiliar to most Americans, Jackson will always be remembered as one of the most influential gothic writers in American history.

## Further Reading

Friedman, Lenemaja. *Shirley Jackson.* Boston: Twayne Publishers, 1975.

Lethen, Jonathan. "Monstrous Acts and Little Murders," Salon.com. Available online. URL: http://www.salon.com/jan97/jackson970106.html. Posted January 1997.

Oppenheimer, Judy. *Private Demons: The Life of Shirley Jackson.* New York: G. P. Putnam's Sons, 1988.

Wylie-Hall, Joan. *Shirley Jackson: A Study of the Short Fiction.* Boston: Twayne Publishers, 1993.

## James, Henry

(1843–1916) *novelist, short story writer, playwright*

Henry James was the master of the psychological novel and one of the most distinctive prose stylists in English of his time. Perhaps more than any previous writer, James refined the technique of narrating a novel from the point of view of a character, thereby laying the foundations of modern stream-of-consciousness fiction. He also introduced the concept of the unreliable narrator, which greatly influenced the modernists and post modernists who followed him. Although James was American-born, he spent much of his life in Europe and eventually became a British citizen. Characteristic of many of the 20 novels that James wrote were sensitively drawn female characters. His main themes were the innocence of the New World in conflict with the corruption and wisdom of the Old. Among his best works were *Daisy Miller* (1879), and *The Portrait of a Lady* (1881). James also wrote more than 100 short stories and novellas, as well as literary criticism, plays, travelogues, and reviews.

Henry James was born on April 15, 1843, in New York City to Henry James, Sr., and Mary Walsh Robertson. James, Jr., had three brothers and a sister. One of his brothers, William, became a philosopher and psychologist and helped found the American Society for Psychical Research. James, Sr., the son of an Irish immigrant, was one of 13 children, born in Albany, New York, and was one of the best-known intellectuals in mid-19th-century America. He devoted his time to the study of theology, philosophy, and mysticism, rejecting his own father's Presbyterian Church to follow the teachings of Swedish Christian mystic Emanuel Swedenborg. The James children were educated in a variety of often unorthodox circumstances: sometimes at schools, sometimes with private tutors, but always with access to books and new experiences. MARGARET FULLER and WASHINGTON IRVING were among the visitors to the James home. In 1855, the James family embarked on a three-year-long trip to Geneva, London, and Paris. The experience influenced James, Jr.'s decision, as an adult, to live and write in Europe rather than his native America.

Upon their return from Europe, the family continued contact with prominent writers and thinkers, including RALPH WALDO EMERSON and HENRY DAVID THOREAU. James was a voracious reader and divided his teenage years between the United States and Europe. He studied for a time in Newport, Rhode Island, with painter William Morris Hunt, but his brother William was a more adept artist and James turned to writing. James briefly attended Harvard Law School, but was more interested in literature. He published his first story, "A Tragedy of Error," in

Known for his sensitively written female characters, Henry James wrote 20 novels, including *The Portrait of a Lady* and *Daisy Miller. (Photo by Alice Boughton. Library of Congress, Prints and Photographs Division [LC-B7901-66])*

the *Continental Monthly* in 1864 when he was 20. He also wrote critical articles and reviews for the *Atlantic Monthly*, a periodical in which several of his novels later appeared in serial form. James made several trips to Europe, and while there he became associated with such notable literary figures as Gustave Flaubert. In 1876 he settled permanently in London. "I could come back to America to die—but never, never to live," James wrote in a 1913 letter to Mrs. William James. The outbreak of World War I was a shock for James and in 1915 he became a British citizen as a show of loyalty to his adopted country and in protest against the early refusal of the United States to enter the war.

James devoted himself to literature and travel. From an early age he had read the classics of English, American, French, German and Russian (in translation) literature. His first novel, *Watch and Ward* (1871), was written while he was traveling through Venice and Paris. It tells a story of a bachelor who adopts a 12-year-old girl and plans to marry her. After living in Paris, where James was contributor to the *New York Tribune*, he moved to England, living first in London and then in Rye, Sussex. In his early novels, including *Roderick Hudson* (1876), *The American* (1877), *Daisy Miller*, and *The Portrait of a Lady*, as well as some of his later work, James contrasts the sophisticated, though somewhat staid, Europeans with the innocent, eager, though often brash, Americans. In the novels of his middle period, *The Bostonians* (1886), *The Princess Casamassima* (1886), and *The Tragic Muse* (1890), he turned his attention from the international theme to reformers, revolutionaries, and political aspirants. "A novel is in its broadest sense a personal, a direct impression of life: that, to begin with, constitutes its value, which is greater or less according to the intensity of the impression," James was quoted as saying in *The Art of Fiction* (1885).

During and after an unsuccessful six-year attempt (1889–95) to win recognition as a playwright, James wrote a series of short, powerful novels, including *The Aspern Papers* (1888), *What Maisie Knew* (1897), *The Spoils of Poynton* (1897), *The Turn of the Screw* (1898), and *The Sacred Fount* (1901). His last novels, *The Wings of the Dove* (1902), *The Ambassadors* (1903), and *The Golden Bowl* (1904), returned to the international theme. "James reached his highest development in the portrayal of the intricate subtleties of character and in the use of a complex, convoluted style to express delicate nuances of thought," according to one critic. James considered *The Ambassadors* to be his best work of art.

*The Turn of the Screw* became the most widely read of all James's works of fiction. The subject matter stems from a 19th-century fascination with ghosts. James was familiar with the topic in part because his family had exposed him to it. James, Sr., had been praised by the Society for Psychical Research for his observations of spirit phenomena. James's brother William was president of the society from 1894 to 1896 and devoted time to the research of spiritual phenomena. James's notebooks record a visit in 1895 to his friend, Edward White Benson, Archbishop of Canterbury, who told him a tale of young children corrupted by the ghosts of servants, and another friend, Edward Gurney, published an account of a woman and child living in a house haunted by two wicked servants. The novel is written mostly in the form of a journal kept by a governess, who works on a lonely estate in England. She tries to save her two young charges from the demonic influence of the apparitions of two former servants in the household. In his treatment of subject matter, James felt that no aspect of life should be excluded. He said that "the province of art is all life, all feeling, all observation, all vision . . . it is all experience. That is a sufficient answer to those who maintain that it must not touch the sad things of life. . . ."

James never married. Although there is no evidence, some critics theorize that he was homosexual, pointing to what they perceive as homoeroticism in relationships in some of his stories and citing James's facility with female voices in his writing. Others suggest his cousin Mary "Minny" Temple was the object of his affection and that her death from tuberculosis at the age of 24 in 1870 prompted his celibacy. James based several of his heroines, including Daisy Miller and Isabel Archer of *Portrait of a Lady*, on her. Biographer Lyndall Gordon calls attention to a 14-year relationship that James had with Constance Woolson. Her death, caused by a fall from a Venice bedroom window, might have been suicide. James suffered a stroke in December

1915. He expected to die and reportedly exclaimed: "So this is it at last, the distinguished thing!" He died in Rye on February 28, 1916, at the age of 73.

## Further Reading

Berland, Alwyn. *Culture and Conduct in the Novels of Henry James.* New York: Cambridge University Press, 1981.

Bradley, John R., ed. *Henry James and Homo-Erotic Desire.* New York: St. Martin's Press, 1998.

Hutchinson, Stuart. *Henry James, an American, as Modernist.* New York: Barnes & Noble Books, 1983.

White, Allon. *The Uses of Obscurity: The Fiction of Early Modernism.* London: Routledge & Kegan Paul, 1981.

## Jarrell, Randall

(1914–1965) *poet, children's fiction writer, editor, literary critic, novelist*

Randall Jarrell, a man who loved teaching as much as writing, attempted to compose poems that would speak to a wide audience. He used a plain voice and had an ability to identify with the heartbreak, loneliness, and dreams of everyday life. Jarrell wrote nine books of poetry, four books of literary criticism, four children's books, five anthologies, and a best-selling academic novel. His collections include *Little Friend, Little Friend* (1945), *The Woman at the Washington Zoo* (1960), and *The Lost World* (1965). *The Woman at the Washington Zoo* received the National Book Award for poetry in 1961.

Randall Jarrell was born on May 6, 1914, in Nashville, Tennessee, to Anna (Campbell) and Owen Jarrell. When Jarrell was one year old, his parents moved to Long Beach, California, where his father was employed as a photographer's assistant. His parents divorced and Randall and his younger brother, Charles, moved back to Nashville with their mother. Randall also lived for a time with his grandparents in California. In high school, Jarrell developed his tennis skills and was involved in dramatics and journalism. After graduating in 1931, he attended Vanderbilt University, where he edited the *Masquerader,* won a varsity letter as captain of the tennis team, made Phi Beta Kappa, and graduated magna cum laude. Jarrell studied psy-

chology as an undergraduate and then stayed on to pursue a graduate degree in literature. He studied under ROBERT PENN WARREN, who first published his criticism. Jarrell went on to teach at Kenyon College and while there he met future fiction writer Peter Taylor and the future poet ROBERT LOWELL. The two writers would remain Jarrell's friends for life. Jarrell's first published poems appeared in the May 1934 issue of *The American Review.*

Jarrell moved on to teach at the University of Texas, where he met and married Mackie Langham, a colleague. His first book of poetry, *Blood for a Stranger,* was published in 1942. He enlisted in the army during World War II and served as a technical sergeant, teaching celestial navigation until the war ended. Then he spent a year in New York teaching at Sarah Lawrence College and working as acting literary editor of *The Nation.* Jarrell returned to the South to teach at Woman's College of the University of North Carolina (University of North Carolina at Greensboro) and remained there, except for leaves of absence, for the rest of his life. His leaves of absence included a two-year appointment as poetry consultant (later designated poet laureate) at the Library of Congress. Jarrell loved teaching and has been quoted often as saying that if he were a rich man, he would pay money to teach. His courses were always filled, and he was revered by his students, a number of whom went on to successful careers as writers. "To Randall's friends there was always the feeling that he was their teacher. To Randall's students there was always the feeling that he was their friend. And with good reason for both," Peter Taylor said of Jarrell.

Jarrell's reputation as a poet was established in 1945, while he was still serving in the army, with the publication of his second book, *Little Friend, Little Friend.* His poems documented, with empathy and sensitivity, the intense fears and moral struggles of young soldiers. In addition to receiving praise for his poetry, Jarrell was highly regarded as a literary essayist, and was considered the most astute, and sometimes most feared, poetry critic of his generation.

Jarrell's fourth book of poetry, *The Seven-League Crutches,* appeared in 1951. By that time, Jarrell and his wife Mackie Langham had separated.

Jarrell then met Mary von Schrader, who had two young daughters, in California and they married in 1952. Jarrell drew attention on the college campuses where he worked. He was devoted to his cats and he had a passion for tennis and sports cars. These and his other interests, including ballet, science fiction, zoos, and French impressionism, made their way into his poetry and prose. Jarrell's only novel, *Pictures from an Institution,* a satire about a progressive woman's college, was published in 1954.

Jarrell won the National Book Award for Poetry for *The Woman at the Washington Zoo.* Among his other honors were Guggenheim and National Arts and Letters grants, Chancellor of the American Poetry Society, election to the National Institute of Arts and Letters Committee for the Bollingen Award, and the American University Women Award for Juvenile Literature. Jarrell was also awarded the O. Max Gardner Award from the University of North Carolina. Jarrell was struck by an automobile on a dark road in Chapel Hill at the age of 50 on the evening of October 14, 1965; he died instantly.

## Further Reading

Bryant, J. A., Jr. *Understanding Randall Jarrell.* Columbia: University of South Carolina Press, 1986.

Ferguson, Suzanne, ed. *Jarrell, Bishop, Lowell, & Co.* Knoxville: University of Tennessee Press, 2003.

Flynn, Richard. *Randall Jarrell and the Lost World of Childhood.* Athens: University of Georgia Press, 1990.

Jarrell, Mary, ed. *Randall Jarrell's Letters: An Autobiographical and Literary Selection.* Boston, Mass.: Houghton Mifflin, 1985.

Prichard, William H. *Randall Jarrell: A Literary Life.* New York: Farrar, Straus and Giroux, 1990.

Quinn, Bernetta. *Randall Jarrell.* Boston: Twayne, 1981.

## Jeffers, Robinson
## (John Robinson Jeffers)
## (1887–1962) *poet*

Robinson Jeffers wrote poetry using themes combined from ancient tragedies, the Old Testament, and the natural beauty surrounding his coastal California home. Jeffers called for a poetry of "dangerous images" that would "reclaim substance and sense, and psychological reality." He brought enormous learning in literature, religion, philosophy, languages, myth, and sciences to his poetry. One of his favorite themes was the intense, rugged beauty of the landscape in opposition to the "inhumanism" he described as the condition of modern life. With few exceptions, his poetry praises beauty and emphasizes his belief that such splendor demands tragedy.

John Robinson Jeffers was born in Pittsburgh, Pennsylvania, on January 10, 1887. He was the son of the Reverend Dr. William Hamilton Jeffers and Annie Robinson Tuttle. Jeffers's father was a Presbyterian minister and a professor of Old Testament literature and biblical history at Western Theology Seminary in Pittsburgh. A reserved and reclusive man, he supervised his son's education, and Jeffers began to study Greek at the age of five. The family traveled frequently to Europe, where Jeffers attended boarding schools in Leipzig, Vevey, Lausanne, Geneva, and Zurich. Jeffers entered the University of Western Pennsylvania (now the University of Pittsburgh) in 1902 as a sophomore, with a mastery of French, German, Greek, and Latin. When the family moved to Lost Angeles the next year, Jeffers matriculated as a junior at Occidental College. After graduating in 1905, he immediately entered graduate school as a student of literature at the University of Southern California (USC). He returned to Switzerland in 1906 to study philosophy and literature at the University of Zurich. He returned to USC the next year and was admitted to the medical school. He did not complete the program and in 1910 he entered the University of Washington to study forestry for a year. As an undergraduate and graduate student Jeffers had regularly contributed poems to various student publications.

Jeffers met Una Call Kuster in 1906. She was married to a prominent Los Angeles attorney but divorced him and married Jeffers in 1913. She and Jeffers stimulated each other emotionally and intellectually. The couple moved to Carmel, California, and in 1916 they became the parents of twin sons. Jeffers built a stone cottage for his family that included a 40-foot stone tower. The house and tower were called "Tor House." Both the home and

Jeffers was influenced by philosopher Friedrich Nietzsche's concept of individualism and believed that human beings had developed a destructive, self-centered view of the world. He believed that people must learn to respect the rest of creation. Jeffers used themes that involved what he later identified as "inhumanism." The metaphors of incest in "Tamar" and other works symbolized humankind's inability to "uncenter" itself. The 1920s and early 1930s were productive for Jeffers, and his reputation was secure. In *Cawdor and Other Poems* (1928); *Dear Judas and Other Poems* (1929); *Descent to the Dead, Poems Written in Ireland and Great Britain* (1931); *Thurso's Landing* (1932); and *Give Your Heart to the Hawks* (1933), Jeffers continued to explore the questions of how human beings could become less egocentric. Jeffers's adaptation of Euripedes' play *Medea* (1946) was a great success when it was produced in New York in 1947. But many of Jeffers's references to current events and political figures highlighted his isolationism and raised questions about his patriotism. *The Double Axe and Other Poems* (1948) appeared with a disclaimer from the publisher.

Jeffers's wife, Una, died of cancer in 1950. Among the many roles she played for him was as observer to the social world he shunned. Jeffers's last volume, *Hungerfield and Other Poems* (1954), contains a eulogy to Una. Jeffers died at home on January 20, 1962. He was 74 years old.

### Further Reading

Bennett, Melba Berry. *The Stone Mason of Tor House: The Life and Times of Robinson Jeffers*. Los Angeles: Ward Ritchie Press, 1966.

Karman, James. *Robinson Jeffers: Poet of California*. Ashland, Oreg.: Story Line Press, 1995.

Milosz, Czeslaw. *Visions from San Francisco Bay*, translated by Richard Lourie. New York: Farrar, Straus & Giroux, 1982.

Robinson Jeffers's poetry focused on the contrast between natural beauty and human imperfection. *(Library of Congress, Prints and Photographs Division [LC-USZ62-117928])*

its location on the coast figure strongly in Jeffers's life and poetry. His verse celebrates the sweeping tides, the cliffs, clouds, and mountains. After inheriting enough money, Jeffers was able to devote himself to writing poetry. His first book, *Flagons and Apples* (1912), was a collection of simple love poems that were written to Kuster and other women. It was followed by *Californians* (1916), which described the coastal region and its people. Jeffers's breakthrough collection was *Tamar and Other Poems* (1924), which was praised by T. S. ELIOT and established his reputation. The intensity of the long narratives contrasted with his earlier work and the work of other poets as well. The subject of the narrative title poem was incest. It drew loosely on the biblical story of King David's daughter and exhibited Jeffers's preoccupation with the theme of self-obsession.

## Jewett, Sarah Orne
### (Theodora Sarah Orne Jewett, A. D. Eliot, Alice Eliot, Sarah C. Sweet)
### (1849–1909) *short story writer, novelist*

Sarah Orne Jewett was a New England regional writer whose stories featured strong women characters. Jewett's work features the people she was most familiar with, namely the inhabitants of the villages and coastal towns of Maine. Jewett's works include several children's stories, novels, and short stories, including *A Country Doctor* (1884) and "A White Heron" (1886). *The Country of the Pointed Firs* (1896) was her most popular novel. It included a series of short sketches linked by a narrator, a woman writer, during her stay in a Maine seacoast village and illustrates her growing involvement in the quiet lives of its people.

Theodora Sarah Orne Jewett was born on September 3, 1849, in South Berwick, Maine, to Theodore Herman Jewett and Caroline Frances Jewett. Her father was a country doctor, and she often accompanied him on his horse-and-buggy rounds among sick people on the local farms. She later said that she got her real education from these trips rather than from her classes at Miss Rayne's School and the Berwick Academy. She had a fine ear for local speech and idiom, which she used to good effect in her stories. The Jewetts were an old New England family, part of Maine's provincial elite. They had an extended family of merchants, sea captains, doctors, and editors. Jewett was raised around books. Impressed as a girl by the sympathetic depiction of local color in the fiction of HARRIET BEECHER STOWE, Jewett began to write stories herself, publishing her earliest one, "Jenny Garrow's Lovers," in a Boston weekly when she was 18 years old.

Jewett's work was accepted by the *Atlantic Monthly* by William Dean Howells when she was 20 and her career was launched. With Howells's encouragement, Jewett continued to craft tales about the rural inhabitants of Deephaven, a fictional town based on the bygone days of South Berwick. Jewett published her first collection of stories, *Deephaven,* in 1877. Also during this time, one of her early works for children, "The Baby-House Famine" (a poem), was accepted for *Our Young Folks.* Throughout her career Jewett would continue to find an outlet for her children's writing, from the outset fostering an important connection with Horace Scudder, then editor of the *Riverside Magazine for Young People,* as well as appearing regularly throughout the 1870s on the children's page of the *Independent* and in *Merry's Museum.*

Although she was a confident writer, Jewett also suffered from occasional insecurity. She was demoralized when she was unable to convince *The Atlantic* to accept another story following the publication of "Mr. Bruce." She wrote the editors and asked if she should give up writing. Howells told her not to give up, saying it was "eminently worthwhile" for her to continue her efforts. He did, however, discourage her from writing poetry, which had been her first love.

Jewett published a story collection in 1878 called *Old Friends and New,* followed by several more collections and novels. She also published work under the pen names A. D. Eliot, Alice Eliot, and Sarah C. Sweet. Jewett traveled extensively throughout her life. On various European trips, she met other writers such as MARK TWAIN, Rudyard Kipling, and Christina Rosetti. Jewett read the work of Gustave Flaubert, Emile Zola, Leo Tolstoy, and HENRY JAMES. Jewett took her favorite motto from Flaubert: "One should write of ordinary life as if one were writing history." Her masterpiece, *The Country of the Pointed Firs* (1896), was told from the point of view of a worldly, anonymous writer who hopes to find peace and solitude in the Maine fishing village where she has gone to spend the summer. The community's power and complexity are slowly revealed as she gains the acceptance and trust of the people of the village. The sketches portray the difficulty and loneliness of rural life but also show the dignity and strength displayed by the inhabitants, particularly mothers, daughters, and friends. Jewett's work has been criticized as having too little plot and not much worthy of critical study, a slight directed at many women writers, that because their stories dealt with relationships and the domestic lives of women, their work was viewed as inferior. More recently, however, Jewett has received renewed critical interest from feminist scholars.

Just as Nan Prince in *A Country Doctor* chooses her career over her personal life, Jewett never married. Her early life was very much like the one she sketches in her novel, in that she and Prince shared the characteristics of an independent childhood followed by an unconventional womanhood. Like WILLA CATHER, Jewett had a long relationship with another woman, Annie Fields, the widow of famous publisher James T. Fields. The two women shared what is commonly called a "Boston marriage." While Jewett felt strong attachments to women, there is no evidence to decide her sexual orientation, one way or the other. Fields was Jewett's closest companion from 1881 until her death.

In 1902 Jewett was in a carriage accident and suffered serious head and back injuries. This accident effectively ended Jewett's writing career. She had pain, dizzy spells, memory loss, and lost the ability to concentrate until she died of unrelated causes on June 24, 1909.

## Further Reading

Blanchard, Paula. *Sarah Orne Jewett: Her World and Her Work.* Boston: Addison-Wesley Pub. Co., 1994.

Campbell, Donna M. *Resisting Regionalism: Gender and Naturalism in American Fiction, 1885–1915.* Athens: Ohio University Press, 1997.

Donovan, Josephine. *Sarah Orne Jewett.* New York: F. Ungar Pub. Co., 1980.

Nagel, Gwen L. *Critical Essays on Sarah Orne Jewett.* Boston: G. K. Hall, 1984.

Westbrook, Perry D. *Acres of Flint: Sarah Orne Jewett and Her Contemporaries.* Lanham, Md.: Scarecrow Press, 1981.

## Jin, Ha
## (Xuefei)
## (1956–  ) *novelist, short story writer, poet*

A Chinese dissident and veteran of the People's Liberation Army, Ha Jin (a pen name chosen when his first poem was published in *The Paris Review*) is known as the first Chinese Communist to make fictional use of life under the Party. His stories of life during the Cultural Revolution have garnered praise for their simple style and subtle beauty. In the brief time that he has been writing in English— little more than a decade—he has won the PEN/Hemingway Award, the Flannery O'Connor Award for Short Fiction, the National Book Award, and the PEN/Faulkner Award.

Born on February 21, 1956, in mainland China, Ha Jin grew up in a small rural town in Liaoning Province. His parents were both army doctors, and Jin has said that it was because his father was an officer in the army that his family received certain privileges. Joining the army at the age of 14 (instead of the standard 16) was one of the privileges Jin enjoyed. He was eager to leave home. The schools were closed and there was nothing to do but wait in fear of a Russian air raid. He volunteered in the army for five and a half years, serving on the unsettled northeastern border between Chinese-governed Manchuria and Soviet Siberia.

Although Jin's education had been minimal before joining the army, he became interested in learning English. "I wanted to read," Jin said. "In the beginning, I was basically illiterate. I couldn't read. Then in the second year the border calmed down. We knew there would be no war, we would live in peace, and I began to think of education. I wanted to go to college, to be a learned person, well-read."

Following his service, Jin worked as a telegrapher at a railroad company for three years in Jiamusi, a remote northeastern frontier city. During these years, he began to follow the English learner's program on the radio, hoping that someday he could read Friedrich Engels's *The Condition of the Working Class in England in 1844* in the original English.

When colleges reopened in 1977, Jin passed the entrance exams and went to Heilongjiang University in Harbin where he was assigned to study English, even though it was his last choice for a major. He received a B.A. degree in English in 1981. He then studied American literature at Shandong University, where he received an M.A. degree in 1984. The following year he came to the United States to do graduate work at Brandeis University, in Waltham, Massachusetts, from which he earned a Ph.D. in English in 1993. His dissertation was on modernist poets T. S. ELIOT, EZRA POUND, W. H. AUDEN, and W. B. Yeats. About his work at Brandeis, Jin said, "Those four have poems which are related to Chinese texts and poems that reference the culture. My dissertation was aimed at a Chinese job market. I planned to return to China." But he was working on more than his dissertation during this time. Jin was also studying fiction writing at Boston University with the novelists Leslie Epstein and Aharon Appelfeld.

Although Jin had married his wife, Lisha Bian, before coming to the United States and had a son, Wen, born in 1983, his family remained in China during most of his time in graduate school and Jin intended to return to China after graduating. The Tiananmen Square Massacre of 1989, in which the Chinese Army attacked nonviolent student protesters in Beijing, changed all that. Jin knew he could not return to serve a government who would take up arms against its own people. His son, who was six years old in 1989, was quickly granted a visa and flew by himself to San Francisco, where his parents met him. Lisha Bian was already in Boston with Jin at the time of the massacre.

Once Jin had chosen to immigrate, his decision to write in English came easily. He had no audience in China. "For the initial years it was like having a blood transfusion, like you are changing your blood," says Jin, who still speaks with a thick accent. After several years of taking odd jobs as a night watchman and busboy while trying to find a teaching job, Jin was hired by Emory University, in Atlanta, Georgia, as an associate professor of poetry. The University of Chicago Press published his first book, *Between Silences*, a volume of poetry, in 1990. *Facing Shadows*, another poetry volume, came next in 1996 from Hanging Loose Press and was quickly followed by two books of short fiction, *Ocean of Words: Army Stories* (Zoland Books, 1996), which received the PEN/Hemingway Award, and *Under the Red Flag* (University of Georgia Press, 1997), which received the Flannery O'Connor Award for Short Fiction and was a finalist for the Kiriyama Pacific Rim Book Award.

Jin's short stories have won him high praise. The *New York Times* described the stories in *Ocean of Words* as "achingly human" and went on to comment that the characters in his stories "form a group portrait that suggests how an entire people struggles to keep its basic humanity within the stiff, unnatural confines of Maoist ideology."

Since the publication of his two highly acclaimed story collections, Jin has published several more books, including the humorous novella *In the Pond*, published by Zoland Books in 1998, which was selected as a best fiction book of 1998 by the *Chicago Tribune*; *The Bridegroom: Stories*, which was released by Pantheon Books in 2000; *Waiting*, his first novel and winner of the 1999 National Book Award; and *Wreckage*, his most recent book of poetry, published by Hanging Loose Press in 2001.

Although few Chinese authors have enjoyed much success with readers in the United States, Jin's first novel, *Waiting*, has rocketed him into literary stardom. The story of an army doctor in 1960s Communist China, *Waiting* has been praised, by an online review on Chinanow website, for the way it "depicts this corner of China without romanticism, exoticism or Orientalist stereotypes [and the way it] manages to do so in a book that is highly compelling (though not pandering) to an English-language readership."

It is tempting to see autobiographical elements in this novel. After all, Jin's parents were army doctors in China and Jin's childhood spanned the 1960s, but Jin denies that his work is autobiographical. "When you construct a piece of work, a novel or a story, you need a lot of drama and a message," the author has explained in an interview with *Emory Magazine* in the spring of 1998. "But when you write an autobiographical piece, you cannot create a happening. If this has not happened, you cannot say it happened. It is not faithful to reality, and so that is the limitation. In addition to that, I want to make my work better than myself."

Jin became a U.S. citizen in 1997, but to date his writing has been set almost solely in China. In 1998, however, Jin said in an interview, "I want to write about the feeling of being a first-generation immigrant. I think very often it is the children or grandchildren who write about their parents, but how did the parents feel when they were here? There hasn't been a lot written about that, and I think maybe I can write a little bit about that." In 2001, Jin left his position at Emory University to write full time.

## Further Reading

Chinanow.com. "Ha Jin, Waiting." Available online. URL: http://www.chinanow.com/english/kunming/city/books/waiting.html. Downloaded February 5, 2003.

Kennedy, X. J., and Dana Gioia. *Introduction to Fiction.* New York: Longman, 2002.

PBS Online NewsHour. "National Book Awards." Available online. URL: http://www.pbs.org/newshour/bb/

entertainment/july-dec99/ha-jin_nba_11-30.html. Downloaded February 5, 2003.

Sweet Briar College World Writers. "Ha Jin Links." Available online. URL: http://worldwriters.english. sbc.edu/links.html#jin2. Downloaded February 5, 2003.

## Johnson, Charles
### (Charles Richard Johnson)
(1948– ) *novelist, short story writer, essayist, screenwriter*

Charles Johnson has published three highly acclaimed novels, 20 screenplays, and dozens of essays and reviews. His 1990 novel, *Middle Passage,* won the National Book Award for fiction, and he has received, among other awards, a prestigious MacArthur fellowship from the John D. and Catherine T. MacArthur Foundation. He is perhaps best known for his keen awareness of and interest in the connection between philosophy and fiction. His outspoken views on the direction of black literature, as explored in his critical essays, have elicited much attention as well.

Charles Richard Johnson was born on April 23, 1948, Evanston, Illinois. He began his career while still a teenager, pursuing his love for drawing by working as a cartoonist. Under the tutelage of cartoonist Lawrence Lariar, he saw his work published by the time he was 17 years old. His two collections of cartoons—*Black Humor* (1970) and *Half-Past Nation Time* (1972)—were acclaimed for their subtle but pointed satire of race relations. The success of his two book collections led to the creation of "Charlie's Pad," a 1971 series on public television that Johnson created, coproduced, and hosted. In 1992, Johnson also produced the KCTS-PBS (Seattle) series *Words with Writers.*

Johnson attended Southern Illinois State University, where he had the good fortune to study with the famous novelist and literary theorist John Gardner. Johnson was greatly influenced by Gardner's conception of "moral fiction," which he understood as demanding an absolute commitment to technique, imagination, and ethics. Largely as a result of Gardner's influence, Johnson set out, early in his career as a writer of fiction, to write philo-sophical novels, citing the void in philosophical fiction by black writers. Johnson published his first novel, *Faith and the Good Thing,* in 1974, while he was still a Ph.D. student at the State University of New York at Stony Brook, studying phenomenology and literary aesthetics.

Since that time, Johnson has published several additional novels, including *Oxherding Tale* in 1982, *Middle Passage* in 1990, and *Dreamer: A Novel,* a fictionalized account of the last year of Martin Luther King, Jr.'s life that came out in 1998. He has also published *Still I Rise: A Cartoon History of African Americans* with Rowen Owen Laird in 1997; a collection of short stories called *The Sorcerer's Apprentice* (1986); and an anthology called *Black Men Speaking* (1997). *Being and Race: Black Writing since 1970* is a collection of Johnson's essays that was published in 1988 and his second collection of essays on aesthetics and cultural criticism, *I Call Myself an Artist: Writings By and About Charles Johnson* was released in 1999. *Turning the Wheel: Essays on Buddhism and Writing* was published in 2003. Johnson's books have been translated into seven languages.

His numerous screenplays include *Charlie Smith and the Fritter Tree* (1978)—the story of the oldest living African American cowboy—and *Booker* (1984)—a program on Booker T. Washington—both of which appeared on PBS and have also been broadcast on the Disney Channel. In 1993, Johnson completed a screenplay for his novel *Middle Passage.*

In addition to the National Book Award for *Middle Passage,* Johnson has twice received the Washington State Governor's Award for Literature, in 1983 and 1989. His book of short stories, *Sorcerer's Apprentice,* was a finalist for the 1987 PEN/Faulkner Award, and his short stories have been anthologized in the *Best American Short Stories of the Eighties, Best American Short Stories* (1992), and *O. Henry Prize Stories* (1993). He has received a National Endowment for the Arts grant (1979) and a Guggenheim fellowship (1986). Johnson is also the recipient of two honorary doctorates from universities in his home state. Northwestern University awarded him an honorary doctor of arts degree in 1994, and in 1995 he received an honorary doctorate in humane letters from Southern Illinois University. Johnson's screenplay *Booker* won the international

Prix Jeunesse Award, a 1985 Writers Guild Award for "outstanding script in the television category of children's shows," and was released for home video in 1996 by Bonneville Worldwide Entertainment.

Johnson was formerly the director of the creative writing program at the University of Washington, where he has taught since 1976 when he came to the university as an assistant professor. He now holds an endowed chair, the Pollock Professorship for Excellence in English, and teaches fiction. He has served as the fiction editor of *The Seattle Review* since 1978. In addition to teaching, he has lectured in seven countries for the U.S. Information Agency and has delivered more than 180 readings and lectures on campuses around the United States.

Johnson is an active supporter of young writers. He sponsors the Marie Clair Davis Award in Creative Writing, given to a secondary student at Evanston Township (Illinois) High School, and the University Prep Award for Excellence in Writing at University Preparatory Academy in Seattle. Southern Illinois University has administered since 1994 the Charles Johnson Award for Fiction and Poetry, a nationwide competition for college students.

### Further Reading

Fagel, Brian. "Passages from the Middle: Coloniality and Postcoloniality in Charles Johnson's *Middle Passage.*" *African American Review* 30, no. 4 (winter 1996): 633.

Little, Jonathan. *Charles Johnson's Spiritual Imagination.* St. Louis: University of Missouri Press, 1997.

Nash, William R. *Charles Johnson's Fiction.* Carbondale: University of Illinois Press, 2002.

Parrish, Timothy L. "Imagining Slavery: Toni Morrison and Charles Johnson," *Studies in American Fiction* 25, no. 1 (spring 1997): 81–99.

## Johnson, James Weldon
### (James William Johnson)
(1871–1938) *poet, novelist, journalist, literary critic, autobiographer*

One of the primary figures of the Harlem Renaissance, James Weldon Johnson was a man of many talents, whose work in literature, diplomacy, and political activism gave him a powerful voice in the first half of the 20th century. Often compared to W. E. B. DUBOIS for his wide-ranging influence, Johnson was a field secretary for the National Association for the Advancement of Colored People (NAACP), a U.S. diplomat in Venezuela, and the first black man admitted to the Florida bar since the end of Reconstruction, in addition to being a well-known poet and novelist.

James Weldon Johnson was born James William Johnson on June 17, 1871, in Jacksonville, Florida. (He changed his middle name to "Weldon" in 1913.) His father, James Johnson, was a headwaiter at the St. James Hotel in Jacksonville. His mother, Helen Louise Dillet, was the first female black public school teacher in Florida. Both parents traced their family lineage to Nassau, Bahamas. Johnson's maternal grandfather served in the House of Assembly in the Bahamas for 30 years. Johnson was the middle of three children, and his parents encouraged his interests in reading and music. He was first educated at home by his mother, then later attended the Stanton School. Following his graduation at the age of 16, Johnson spent time in the Bahamas and then in New York before attending Atlanta University, where he studied English literature and classical music.

Johnson graduated in 1894 and returned to the Stanton School to serve as its principal. One year later, he founded the *Daily American*, a newspaper for the black community in Jacksonville. He could only keep the paper afloat for one year before it folded due to lack of funds, but Johnson later said that the experiment with the paper was not a total failure because it made both W. E. B. DUBOIS and BOOKER T. WASHINGTON aware of his presence, which eventually led to other opportunities.

Johnson then studied law with Thomas A. Ledwith, a young white lawyer. He quickly built up a successful law practice but grew tired of the work. Johnson and his brother began collaborating on musical compositions about this time, with Johnson supplying the lyrics to his brother's songs. The pair made their way to New York in the first decade of the 20th century, where they worked together writing songs. The most famous composition for which they are still known, "Lift Every Voice and Sing," was written for a celebration of Abraham Lincoln's birthday at the Stanton School. It was eventually adopted by the NAACP as the "Negro National Anthem."

Johnson began to study literature formally, at Columbia University, around 1904. This endeavor, which was meant to give him more time for his writing, actually coincided with his decision to become U.S. consul to Venezuela in 1906. Johnson's life was always a mixture of art and politics, and throughout his life, the desire to work in both worlds fueled his decisions.

Johnson completed his only novel, *The Autobiography of an Ex-Colored Man*, during his three years in Venezuela. It was published anonymously in 1912. Although Johnson declared some years later, in 1927, that the book was fiction, the public persisted in reading it as nonfiction. This compelled Johnson to write his actual autobiography, *Along This Way*, in 1933.

In 1920, Johnson became the national organizer for the NAACP, a position he held until the early 1930s. He had become, by the 1920s, a leading voice in the Harlem Renaissance, and his life was quite full with all his literary work. He edited *The Book of American Negro Poetry* (1922), *The Book of American Negro Spirituals* (1925), *The Second Book of American Negro Spirituals* (1926), and wrote *Black Manhattan* (1930). He had published poems in *Century Magazine* and *The Independent* while serving as a diplomat, but it was not until 1927 that he published his first collection of poems, *God's Trombones, Seven Negro Sermons in Verse*.

Johnson retired from the NAACP and became professor of creative literature and writing at Fisk University. During his last years, he lectured often on the topic of civil rights and wrote *Negro Americans, What Now?* (1934), as well as his final collection of poems, *Saint Peter Relates an Incident: Selected Poems* (1934). Johnson died tragically on June 26, 1938, when the car he was driving was hit by a train while he was on the way to his vacation home in Maine.

### Further Reading

Bergevin, Gerald W. "Theorizing through an Ethnic Lens." *Modern Language Studies* 24, no. 4 (1996): 13–26.

Fleming, Robert E. *James Weldon Johnson*. Boston: Twayne, 1987.

Kinnamon, Kenneth. "Three Black Writers and the Anthologized Canon," in Scharnhorst, Gary, ed. *American Realism and the Canon*. Newark: University of Delaware Press, 1994.

Levy, Eugene. *James Weldon Johnson: Black Leader, Black Voice*. Chicago: University of Chicago Press, 1973.

Wilson, Sondra Kathryn, ed. *The Selected Writings of James Weldon Johnson*. 2 vols. New York: Oxford University Press, 1995.

James Weldon Johnson was an influential diplomat and political activist, as well as an accomplished writer. *(Library of Congress, Prints and Photographs Division, Carl Van Vechten Collection [LC-USZ62-42498])*

## Jong, Erica
### (Erica Mann)
(1942–   ) *poet, novelist, essayist, memoirist*

The author of numerous best-selling books and a cultural icon of the 1960s, Erica Jong is best known for her explicit treatment of women's sexuality in her best-selling novel *Fear of Flying*. Written when she was a promising young poet, the book catapulted her into international stardom and secured her place in U.S. literary history.

Erica Mann was born on March 26, 1942, to a Jewish intellectual family on Manhattan's Upper East Side. Her childhood was rich with opportunity and exposure to the arts. Her father, Seymour Mann, was a musician, and her mother, Eda Mirsky, followed in her father's footsteps as a successful portrait painter and commercial artist. The arts surrounded Mann, and she has often told of painting alongside her grandfather in the rambling Manhattan apartment where her parents and grandparents lived until the birth of her younger sister. Both of Mann's parents worked in the arts when they were first married. Her mother also designed clothing and fabric. Her father worked on Broadway and performed on stage in Cole Porter's *Jubilee*, before quitting the theater when his wife became pregnant with their first child. He subsequently worked as a salesman.

From the time she was quite young, Mann wrote stories and poems and kept journals. She took piano and skating lessons and attended summer camps and art schools. She has described her childhood as "smothered" with opportunity. She graduated from the High School of Music and Art and went on to Barnard College, where she studied English literature and received her B.A. degree in 1963, graduating Phi Beta Kappa and magna cum laude. While at Barnard, she edited the literary magazine and produced radio programs on poetry for the campus station. Mann did her graduate work at Columbia University, where she received her M.A. degree in 18th-century English literature, but she left before finishing her Ph.D. in order to devote more time to her writing.

Mann had married fellow graduate student Michael Werthman during this time, but the union ended in divorce in 1966, and Jong then married Allan Jong, a Chinese-American psychiatrist in the U.S. military. She followed her husband to Germany when the military stationed him there, and spent her time writing and teaching at the University of Maryland Overseas Division. Her first book of poems, *Fruits and Vegetables*, came out in

1971 and won critical acclaim as well as numerous prizes for the young author. She was given an Academy of American Poets award, the Bess Hokin Prize from *Poetry* magazine, the Borestone Mountain Award in poetry, the Madeline Sadin Award from *New York Quarterly*, and the Alice Faye di Castagnolia Award from the Poetry Society of America.

*Half-Lives*, her second book of poems, and *Fear of Flying* her first novel, were both published in 1973. The book of poems was well received but the novel caused quite a stir among critics and readers alike and received high praise from such well-known writers as JOHN UPDIKE and HENRY MILLER. The public debate it created has persisted in the decades since its publication. As of 2002, *Fear of Flying* had sold more than 12.5 million copies and had been translated into 27 languages.

Jong's body of work has grown quite large over the years. She has published six collections of poetry and eight works of fiction. She is also the author of a memoir about Henry Miller, *The Devil at Large*, and a memoir of her own life, *Fear of Fifty*. Her latest book, *Sappho's Leap: A Novel*, was published in 2003.

In addition to the University of Maryland's Overseas Division, Erica Jong has taught at the City University of New York; the 92nd Street Y in Manhattan; the Bread Loaf Writers Conference, in Middlebury, Vermont; the Salzburg Seminar, in Salzburg, Austria; Ben-Gurion University, in Beersheba, Israel; and Bennington College, in Vermont. Erica Jong lives in New York City and Weston, Connecticut.

## Further Reading

"Erica Jong." Now with Bill Moyers. PBS. Available online. URL: http://www.pbs.org/now/arts/jong.html. Posted June 27, 2003.

Luzzi, Michael. "Jong Sees Reversal in Divorce." The New York Times on the Web. Available online. URL: http://www.NYtimes.com/1984/October/21.

Templin, Charlotte. *Feminism and the Politics of Literary Reputation: The Example of Erica Jong*. Lawrence: University Press of Kansas, 2000.

Templin, Charlotte A., and Erica Jong, eds. *Conversations with Erica Jong*. Jackson: University Press of Mississippi, 2002.

## Kerouac, Jack
### (Jean-Louis Lebris de Kerouac)
### (1922–1969) *novelist*

Arguably the most talented among a small group of friends who later became known as the Beat writers, Jack Kerouac stood as an enduring symbol of the Beats' quest for spiritual enlightenment and artistic freedom. His pivotal work, *On the Road*, helped usher him toward the long-awaited fame that eventually became his undoing.

Jack Kerouac was born Jean-Louis Lebris de Kerouac, of French-Canadian descent, on March 12, 1922, in Lowell, Massachusetts. The youngest of three children, Kerouac lived with his parents, Leo and Gabrielle, who immigrated to the United States from Quebec. Kerouac's family moved from house to house within the city of Lowell. By the time he entered high school, the Kerouacs had changed residences nine times. His restless wanderings, of which Kerouac wrote in great depth, appear to have as their source the constant shuffling of his familial home when he was a youngster.

Another profound influence on his writing was the death of his older brother, Gerard, who succumbed to rheumatic fever at age nine. Death and eternity were recurring ideas in Kerouac's writing and he wrote poignantly of Gerard in his novel *Visions of Gerard* (1963).

A gifted athlete, Kerouac received a football scholarship to Columbia University. Hoping to aid his financially strapped father, he planned to graduate and enter the insurance business. At Columbia, however, his plan backfired when he broke his leg during a game. When he returned in the fall, he argued with his coach over his place on the team. The coach refused to let him play. Disillusioned, Kerouac left Columbia in his sophomore year. He turned his sights toward becoming "an adventurer, a lonesome traveler," so that he might realize his dream of one day becoming a notable American writer, following in the footsteps of writers he admired, including JACK LONDON, ERNEST HEMINGWAY, and THOMAS WOLFE. During World War II, Kerouac was a seaman with the U.S. Merchant Marine. When he was not sailing around the world, he worked on a novel, *The Sea Is My Brother*, which he completed in 1943. It was also during this time that Kerouac met a group of people around the Columbia campus, in upper Manhattan, who became his friends. They formed the core of what became known as the Beat Generation.

Kerouac first used the term *beat* to describe himself and his friends in a conversation he had with friend and novelist John Clellon Holmes. It was meant to convey defeat and disillusionment. Yet, he also meant the name to reflect a religious outlook, as in beatific, meaning spiritually pure. Kerouac and his friends found themselves disillusioned with the status quo. They searched for a new way of living and thinking. "Flopping" in shabby apartments and shacks, using drugs as a way to enhance their artistic vision, hitchhiking across the country, they became self-imposed hobos and outcasts. It was only through turning their backs on conventional society that they saw a means to finding the essential truth about life, which they could write about. Kerouac later defended his lifestyle, saying he was not "beat," but a "strange solitary crazy Catholic mystic." His parents did not approve of his new friends, including ALLEN GINSBERG, Lucien Carr, WILLIAM S. BURROUGHS, and Neal Cassady. Throughout his life, Kerouac would find it impossible to bridge the chasm between being a member of a straitlaced Catholic family and also being part of a free-minded, drug-experimenting crowd at Columbia.

Drawing on his double life—a conventional home, wild friends—he wrote a novel, *The Town and City*, which Allen Ginsberg, through his professors at Columbia, helped to get published in 1950. It would be Kerouac's most traditional novel. It gave him a modicum of esteem, but it did not bring him fame.

In 1951, Kerouac began experimenting with a freer, more spontaneous writing style in which he did not fictionalize or rationalize. He called his new method of writing "spontaneous prose." With his new approach to writing, it took a mere three weeks for Kerouac to complete the first draft of *On the Road* in April 1951. To write without losing momentum, he taped together sheets of tracing paper and typed the novel onto one unbroken 120-foot scroll. Six years of rejection and myriad changes would follow before the novel was published in September 1957.

*On the Road* was an autobiographical novel—"creative nonfiction," in today's parlance—of Kerouac's cross-country travels with his friend and creative muse, Neal Cassady. In an introduction to the novel, published by Penguin Classics in 1991, a Kerouac biographer, Ann Charters, wrote, "*On the Road* can be read as an American classic along with MARK TWAIN's *Huckleberry Finn* and F. SCOTT FITZGERALD's *The Great Gatsby* as a novel that explores the theme of personal freedom and challenges the promise of the 'American dream.'" Praised by the *New York Times* and the *Village Voice*, *On the Road* also generated controversy. Some critics thought it incoherent, while others found its portrait of ill-mannered characters offensive. Though controversial, his novel became a popular success.

In the 1950s, Kerouac moved to the San Francisco Bay Area of California and befriended a Zen poet named GARY SNYDER. Snyder introduced Kerouac to Buddhism. With his psyche attuned to meditation and prayer, Kerouac's works became filled with religious musings. He published *The Dharma Bums* in 1955, followed by *Big Sur* in 1960. While these novels further explored themes most important to Kerouac—universal kindness and the simplicity of truth—they never matched *On the Road* in popularity.

Something happened to Kerouac after *On the Road* was published. Having endured years of rejection, he became an overnight success. No one, it seemed, was interested in his work and what he was trying to accomplish so much as finding out what it meant to be a Beat writer, or learning about the lifestyle he had lived on the road. Though to all appearances he was a bastion of the Beat wave, Kerouac was actually drowning in it. To make matters worse, Kerouac's work was not taken seriously by critics who viewed the Beats as a fad. He began to drink heavily. Though he wrote and appeared publicly after he became famous, Kerouac's artistic vision had been shattered.

In the 1960s, Kerouac left California and returned to the East Coast, where he lived with his mother for the rest of his life. During his life, he married three times. His third wife, Stella Sampas, was a childhood friend from Lowell. With Stella to help his aging mother, they moved from Northport, Long Island, New York, to Saint Petersburg, Florida.

On October 21, 1969, his body wracked by years of drug use and heavy drinking, Kerouac suffered an abdominal hemorrhage and died at home. He was 47 years old.

## Further Reading

Charters, Ann, ed. *The Beats: Literary Bohemians in Postwar America.* Detroit: Gale, 1983.

French, Warren G. *Jack Kerouac.* Boston: Twayne Publishers, 1986.

Robertson, David. "Real Matter, Spiritual Mountain: Gary Snyder and Jack Kerouac on Mt. Tamalpais," in *Western American Literature* 27, no. 3 (fall 1992): 209–226.

Turner, Steve. *Jack Kerouac: Angelheaded Hipster.* New York: Viking, 1996.

## Kesey, Ken
(1935–2001)  *novelist*

Author of the critically acclaimed novel *One Flew over the Cuckoo's Nest*, Ken Kesey transformed the social climate of the 1960s with his wild parties and outrageous lifestyle. As a cultural icon as well as a celebrated novelist, Kesey and his band of friends, the Merry Pranksters, brought a psychedelic era to the young generation of the 1960s. Infamous for his use of mind-altering hallucinogenic drugs, Kesey hoped to reconfigure society by breaking through conventional thoughts. Though his subsequent novels, including *Sometimes a Great Notion*, did not garner the commercial success of *Cuckoo's Nest*, Kesey was not only a novelist but an important figure in creating the hippie culture of San Francisco in late 1960s.

Born September 17, 1935, in La Junta, Colorado, Ken Kesey grew up there and in the Pacific Northwest. In 1946, his family moved to Springfield, Oregon, where they owned a farm. Kesey's family was religious, and he absorbed the Christian ideals and ethics which were a part of his home life.

A charismatic boy, Kesey was voted "most likely to succeed" his senior year at high school. He was a champion wrestler and set numerous records both at high school and college. After graduating from high school, Kesey eloped with Faye Haxby, his young sweetheart. He attended the University of Oregon and majored in speech and communications. After graduation, he received a fellowship to enroll in the creative writing program at Stanford.

At Stanford, Kesey became part of a government research study in the psychology department to earn extra money. He ingested psychedelic chemicals, including mescaline and LSD. This experience had a profound influence on him. While working as an orderly in a psychiatric ward at Menlo Park Veterans Hospital, Kesey hallucinated about an Indian sweeping the floors. This image became the basis of his most famous novel, *One Flew over the Cuckoo's Nest* (1962), which he wrote as a student at Stanford.

*One Flew over the Cuckoo's Nest* was an instant hit, both commercially and critically. The book dealt with the effects of a cold, unfeeling society as portrayed by Nurse Ratched, and an unlikely con man savior, McMurphy, who tries to rescue the patients from a living death. The story was adapted to the stage, and made into an Academy Award–winning film in 1975.

At Stanford, Kesey was known for throwing outrageous parties and living a bohemian lifestyle. He attracted a following of like-minded students. When it came time to write his second novel, he moved his family and his party friends to La Honda, a town located in the mountains outside San Francisco. His second novel, *Sometimes a Great Notion,* was published in 1964, but did not attain critical success. A story about a family of loggers, it detailed the clash between rugged individualism and intellectualism.

At La Honda, Kesey and his friends threw parties, serving a variety of drugs, including LSD. Sometimes the partygoers consumed LSD without their knowledge. He believed a person's demons should be confronted under the influence of hallucinogenics. Kesey called these parties "acid tests."

After he published his second novel, Kesey and his friends, who called themselves the Merry Pranksters, bought a large 1939 school bus, which they named "Further," and painted it with day-glo colors. They asked Neal Cassady, a member of the Beat Generation, to drive the bus. With their stash of marijuana and LSD, they worked their way across the country to New York to promote the book and to see the 1964 World's Fair. Along the way, they made stops in various towns, hopping on top of the bus to conduct free-wheeling speeches or to play their discordant brand of music.

Kesey filmed the journey of the Merry Pranksters and wrote a screenplay to go with the images called *The Further Inquiry.* Once the group arrived in New York, they met with ALLEN GINSBERG, who was immediately taken by the Pranksters and offered to introduce them to another psychedelic pioneer, Timothy Leary, at his compound in Millbrook, New York. The introduction did not go very well. Leary came outside, said hello, then returned to his room. After one day at Millbrook, Further sped back down the dirt road and out of sight.

The Merry Pranksters helped usher in the psychedelic era of the 1960s and epitomized the image of California hippies. When LSD became illegal, Kesey faked his suicide and fled to Mexico to escape imprisonment. He was eventually caught and taken to jail in San Mateo. He renounced LSD, saying it could offer the user nothing but delusions.

When he was released from jail, Kesey and his family moved to a farm in Oregon. He published his third novel, *Sailor Song*, in 1992. Through the years, Kesey had written shorter pieces and compilations. Kesey died on November 10, 2001, after surgery to remove cancer on his liver.

**Further Reading**

Gatto, John Taylor. *Ken Kesey's One Flew over the Cuckoo's Nest: A Critical Commentary.* Grass Lake, Mich.: Monarch Press, 1975.

McClanahan, Ed. *Spit in the Ocean: All About Ken Kesey.* New York: Penguin, 2003.

Tanner, Stephen L. *Ken Kesey.* Boston: Twayne Publishers, 1983.

Wissen, Thomas. *Classic Cult Fiction: A Companion to Popular Cult Literature.* Westport, Conn.: Greenwood Press, 1992.

# Kincaid, Jamaica
## (Elaine Potter Richardson)
(1949–  ) *novelist, short story writer, memoirist, essayist*

Arguably the most important West Indian woman writing at the beginning of the 21st century, Jamaica Kincaid has addressed themes of racism, colonialism, and grief in prose that is sharp, yet lyrical. Her work in all genres has been praised for its searing emotional honesty, although some critics have been troubled by the anger in her voice. She is perhaps best known for her exploration in both fiction and nonfiction of the mother-daughter bond.

Jamaica Kincaid was born Elaine Potter Richardson in St. John's, Antigua, on May 25, 1949. For nine years, she was the only child in the family, but then her three younger brothers were born, and Kincaid began to grow isolated from her mother and her environment. She has traced these troubles to the time when her brothers were born and when the resources, both emotional and finan-

cial, available to her dwindled considerably. In her writing Kincaid has always been significantly concerned with the bitterness of this period in her childhood, by the loss she felt when her relationship with her mother changed.

Kincaid attended government schools, which were quite rigid and authoritarian. Although she was considered bright, she was somewhat rebellious. As a teenager, she retreated into books, stealing them or the money to buy them, if necessary. When she was 17, she left Antigua and moved to New York City to work as an au pair. After three years of caring for other women's children all day and taking night classes at a community college, she won a full scholarship to Franconia College, in New Hampshire. After one year, she dropped out and moved back to New York, feeling too old for school. She took a job writing interviews for a teenage girls' magazine and eventually began to publish in *The Village Voice* and *Ingenue*. When William Shawn, longtime editor of the *New Yorker*, read some of her work, he contacted her and hired her in 1976 as a staff writer. This was the turning point in Kincaid's career. Shawn believed in her writing, which in turn helped Kincaid understand the importance of her work. She became a featured columnist for the "Talk of the Town" section of the magazine, a position she held for nine years.

In 1978, her first piece of published fiction appeared in the *New Yorker*. This story later became part of *At the Bottom of the River*, Kincaid's first book, which came out in 1983. Praised for its mesmerizing prose and captivating, repetitive rhythms, *At the Bottom of the River* was nominated for the PEN/Faulkner Award and won the Morton Darwen Zabel Award of the American Academy of Arts and Letters. The stories in the collection drew largely on Kincaid's childhood for inspiration and addressed the complexity of the mother-daughter relationship, as did her novel *Annie John*, which appeared in 1985. Kincaid was selected as one of three finalists for the 1985 international Ritz Paris Hemingway Award for her work on *Annie John*. She has also been the recipient of the Anisfield-Wolf Book Award and the Lila Wallace–Reader's Digest Fund Award.

Kincaid's other major works include *My Brother* (1987), a nonfiction account of Kincaid's relationship with her youngest brother during his losing battle with AIDS; *A Small Place* (1988); *Lucy* (1990); *The Autobiography of My Mother* (1996); *My Garden* (1999); *Talk Stories* (2000); *Seed Gathering atop the World* (2002); and *Mr. Potter* (2002).

Kincaid lives in Bennington, Vermont, with her husband, Allen Shawn, a composer and son of William Shawn, Kincaid's editor and mentor from the *New Yorker*. The couple have two children. She has taught creative writing at numerous universities around the country, including Bennington College and Harvard University.

## Further Reading

Ferguson, Moira. *Jamaica Kincaid: Where the Land Meets the Body*. Charlottesville: University Press of Virginia, 1994.

Lindfors, Bernth, and Reinhard Sander, eds. *Twentieth-Century Caribbean and Black African Writers, Third Series*. Detroit: Gale Research, 1996.

Nelson, Emmanuel S., ed. *Contemporary African American Novelists: A Bio-Bibliographical Critical Sourcebook*. Westport, Conn.: Greenwood Press, 1999.

Parvisini-Gebert, Lizabeth. *Jamaica Kincaid: A Critical Companion*. Westport, Conn.: Greenwood Press, 1999.

Simmons, Diane. *Jamaica Kincaid*. New York: Twayne, 1994.

## King, Stephen
### (Richard Bachman, Stephen Edwin King)
(1947–   ) *novelist, short story writer, essayist, screenwriter, horror fiction writer*

One of the best-selling and most prolific authors in the world, Stephen King has published more than 50 books, most of them horror stories written in the 19th-century Gothic tradition of writers such as EDGAR ALLAN POE. His novels are known for their cinematic style, and many have been made into successful movies, some with screenplays written by King himself. His books have been translated into 33 different languages and published in more than 35 different countries. King is also known for his experimentation with innovative publishing techniques, including serialization of novels and electronic publishing through his official web site.

Stephen Edwin King was born on September 21, 1947, at the Maine General Hospital in Portland, Maine, to Donald Edwin King and Ruth Pillsbury King. His brother, David, had been adopted at birth two years earlier. King's father was a merchant seaman who deserted the family when King was about three years old. King, his mother, and his older brother traveled throughout several states after Donald King's departure before finally settling back in Durham, Maine, in 1958, where King spent the rest of his childhood.

King's writing career was launched in 1959, when he and his brother published their own local newspaper, *Dave's Rag*, printed with a mimeograph machine David had purchased and sold for five cents an issue. His next writing adventure came in 1963, while attending Lisbon High School in Lisbon, Maine. King and his best friend, Chris Chesley, published a collection of 18 short stories called *People, Places, and Things—Volume I*. One year later, the amateur press established by the two buddies published King's two-part book, *The Star Invaders*. In 1965, King's story "I Was a Teenage Grave Robber" appeared in the magazine *Comics Review*. King graduated from high school in 1966. By his own account, his high school career was "totally undistinguished."

Nevertheless, writing was already a regular part of King's life. He began his first novel the summer after graduation. His first completed novel, *The Long Walk*, was written during his first year of college. King submitted it to Random House, which rejected it, and King subsequently stashed the book away. He did manage to earn his first paycheck from writing while still in college, when he sold his short story "The Glass Floor" for publication. King graduated from the University of Maine in 1970 with a B.S. degree in English and a high school teaching certificate.

Following college, King took a job pumping gas and began working on the Dark Tower saga but was unable to finish the work due to his lack of income. He did begin earning a little money around this time for short stories he submitted to men's magazines. On January 2, 1971, King married Tabitha

Jane Spruce, his college sweetheart. In the fall following their marriage, he took a teaching job at Hampden Academy, and the couple moved to Hermon, a town near Bangor, Maine. The couple's first child was born in 1971, and King began work on what would become the novel *Carrie*, his first published book. Although at one point he threw the story in the trash, believing it to be worthless, his wife rescued it and encouraged him to finish the story. King sold *Carrie*, a horror story about a high school girl who uses her telekinetic powers to get revenge on a town that ostracized her, to Doubleday in January 1973, and in May of that year, Doubleday sold the paperback rights, which netted King $200,000. He quit his teaching job and went to work full time as a writer.

King's next novels were *'Salem's Lot* (1975), *The Shining* (1975), and *The Stand* (1978). In the late 1970s, he began to publish paperbacks under the name Richard Bachman. These novels included *The Long Walk* (1979), *Roadwork* (1981), *The Running Man* (1982), *Thinner* (1984), and *The Regulators* (1996). Arnold Schwarzenegger starred in the movie version of *The Running Man*, which was filmed in 1989, and a television miniseries was made from *Thinner*.

By the early 1980s, King had become a household name and developed his highly loyal following of readers. King published his first book of nonfiction, *Danse Macabre*, in 1981 which some critics have praised as one of his finest works. It was the result of a class he taught at the University of Maine titled "Themes in Supernatural Literature." He collected his thoughts on horror writing following the course and wrote the essays in the book, which cover everything from folktales and literature to radio and junk movies. *On Writing*, another book of essays, appeared in 2000. He has also written several highly successful books outside the horror genre. *The Body*, a novella, was made into the major motion picture *Stand by Me* (1986), directed by Rob Reiner. Another novella by King, *Rita Hayworth and Shawshank Redemption*, became the highly successful and critically praised film *The Shawshank Redemption* (1994), starring Tim Robbins.

Other notable novels by King include *Christine* (1983), *Misery* (1987), *Needful Things* (1991), *Dolores Claiborne* (1992), and *Insomnia* (1994).

King's Dark Tower series moves into the realm of science fiction/fantasy and includes the following titles: *The Gunslinger* (1982), *The Drawing of the Three* (1987), *The Waste Lands* (1991), and *Wizard and Glass* (1997). He has also published several collections of short fiction, including *Night Shift* (1978), *Skeleton Crew* (1985), and *Nightmares and Dreamscapes* (1994).

In addition to his career as a best-selling novelist, many of King's books have been made into successful major motion pictures. Some of these films include *Carrie, The Shining* (1980), *The Dead Zone* (1983), and *Misery* (1990). In addition to writing some of the screenplays for his filmed novels, King sometimes plays small roles in the films. He even tried his hand at directing in 1986, when *Maximum Overdrive* was filmed. He also directed the first five episodes of the television series *Stephen King's The Golden Years* (1991). King's other work for television includes the miniseries and movies *It* (1990), *Sometimes They Come Back* (1991), *The Tommyknockers* (1993), *The Stand* (1994), and *The Langoliers* (1995).

King has also experimented with different types of publishing, including serializing his novel *The Green Mile* (1996), which appeared in six paperback installments. He also published his novella *Riding the Bullet* (2000) as an electronic book to be read on a computer. The first chapters of *The Plant* (2000) were electronically self-published on King's official web site before the project was halted.

In June 1999, King suffered extensive injuries, including broken ribs, a broken leg, a severely fractured hip, and injuries to his lung, when he was struck by a van. He endured three weeks of operations at the Central Maine Medical Center before being released to go home, where he subsequently spent many months confined to his bed and undergoing intensive rehabilitation so that he could learn to walk again. King still lives in Maine with his wife of more than 30 years, Tabitha. They have three children, Naomi Rachel, Joe Hill, and Owen Phillip.

**Further Reading**

Beahm, G. W. *Stephen King from A to Z: An Encyclopedia of His Life and Work.* Kansas City, Mo.: Andrews McMeel Publishing, 1998.

O'Hehir, Andrew. "Up Close and Personal with Stephen King." Salon. Available online. URL: http://www.cnn.com/books/news/9809/24/king.interview.salon. Downloaded June 11, 2003.

Spignesi, S. J. *The Essential Stephen King.* Franklin Lakes, N.J.: New Page Books, 2001.

Wiater, S., et al. *The Stephen King Universe: A Guide to the Worlds of the King of Horror.* New York: St. Martin's Press, 2001.

## Kingsolver, Barbara
(1955–   ) *novelist, short story writer, essayist, journalist*

A born storyteller, Kingsolver is known for her fiction, rich with the imagery and language of her native Kentucky, but she has also worked as a freelance journalist and a science writer, publishing articles in *The Nation, The New York Times,* and *Smithsonian,* among other publications. She is widely praised for her ability to integrate social and political concerns into her fiction.

Barbara Kingsolver was born on April 8, 1955, in Annapolis, Maryland, to Dr. Wendell R. Kingsolver and Virginia Lee Henry Kingsolver, both of whom were originally from Lexington, Kentucky. Shortly following Barbara's birth, the family returned to Kentucky, this time settling in the small town of Carlisle, where her parents opened a medical practice and worked. Kingsolver and her siblings were raised in Carlisle. Her older brother, Robert, became a professor of biology at Kentucky Wesleyan College, and her younger sister, Ann, became a professor of anthropology at the University of California, Santa Cruz. Although the family lived in a rural area, they gained exposure to the larger world when their father chose to practice medicine in the Congo (now Democratic Republic of the Congo) and in St. Lucia in the Caribbean.

Kingsolver graduated from Nicholas County High School then went on to DePauw University in Indiana on a music scholarship. She graduated magna cum laude in 1977 with a double major in biology and English, having already traveled to Athens and Paris. She then moved to Tucson to pursue graduate studies in the University of Arizona's Department of Ecology and Evolutionary Biology. She graduated in 1981 with a master's degree in animal behavior.

Kingsolver's first job following graduate school was with the Arid Lands Institute, where she worked as a science writer. This led her to writing feature articles for newspapers and periodicals. Kingsolver has credited her science writing and journalism with teaching her a writer's discipline and broadening her "fictional possibilities." Her work over the years has appeared in a variety of publications, including *The New York Times* and *National Geographic.* In 1986, she won an Arizona Press Club award for outstanding feature writing. Kingsolver worked as a freelance journalist from 1985 through 1987. She married a chemist in 1985 and became pregnant the following year. It was during this pregnancy that she began work on her first novel, *The Bean Trees,* which was published in 1988. The story of a Kentucky woman who moves out west, *The Bean Trees* was praised by critics and ordinary readers alike.

Kingsolver's other works include *Homeland and Other Stories* (1989); the novels *Animal Dreams* (1990), *Pigs in Heaven* (1993), *The Poisonwood Bible* (1999), and *Prodigal Summer* (2000); the bestselling *High Tide in Tucson: Essays from Now and Never* (1995); and *Small Wonder* (2002), a collection of essays that got its start when Kingsolver was asked to write a response to the September 11, 2001, attacks on the United States. Most notable of these works, *The Poisonwood Bible* (1999), an Oprah Book Club selection and nominee for the Pulitzer Prize, is about an evangelical Baptist minister's family pursuing missionary work in the Belgian Congo. The novel spans 30 years, during which time the family's fate becomes inextricably entwined with the fate of the Congo. Kingsolver has also published a collection of poetry, *Another America: Otra America* (1992), and a nonfiction book, *Holding the Line: Women in the Great Arizona Mine Strike of 1983* (1989). Kingsolver's work has won numerous awards, including the American Booksellers Book of the Year Award, the Los Angeles Time Fiction Prize, the Edward Abbey Award for Ecofiction, several New York Times Notable Book awards, nominations for the Pulitzer Prize, the Orange Prize, the PEN/Faulkner Award, and a Writers Digest 100 Best Writers of the 20th Century Award.

Kingsolver has made her home in Tucson throughout her adult life. She and her first husband divorced and she remarried Steven Hopp, a guitarist. The couple lives with Camille, Kingsolver's daughter from her first marriage, and Lily, who was born in 1996.

### Further Reading

Gussow, Joan. "Calling across the Fence." *The Green Guide* 93 (November–December 2002): 4.

Meadows, Bonnie J. "Serendipity and the Southwest: A Conversation with Barbara Kingsolver." *Bloomsbury Review* (November–December 1990): 3.

Nolan, Kate. "Kingsolver: Author for Our Place and Time," *Arizona Republic* (March 30, 2002): V3.

## Kingston, Maxine Hong
(1940–  ) *novelist, short story writer, memoirist*

One of the most outspoken contemporary feminist writers, Maxine Hong Kingston is known as a "word warrior," whose books take direct aim at social and racial injustice. One of the most widely read Chinese-American writers, Kingston is often praised for interweaving autobiography with legend and traditional stories to create her own unique and powerful style.

Maxine Hong Kingston was born on October 27, 1940, in Stockton, California, to Tom and Ying Lan Hong. The first of six children born to her parents in America (the two oldest children were born in China but died before their parents came to the United States), Maxine was named after a lucky blond gambler who often visited the gambling house where her father worked in Stockton. Her father had been raised in China to be a classical scholar, and he taught school in Sun Woi, near Canton, before leaving China. When he arrived in America, he washed windows and worked in a laundry before becoming the manager of an illegal gambling house, where part of his job was to get arrested and never reveal his real name. Kingston's mother, whose name means "Brave Orchid," was a doctor and midwife in China and remained there for 15 years after her husband left for the United States.

A gifted student, Maxine grew up speaking Say Yup, a dialect of Cantonese, as her first language, but by the age of nine, she was writing poems in English. Like her mother, she was a gifted storyteller and had been surrounded by the stories of her own family and other immigrants from the time she was born. Maxine, though, preferred writing to oral storytelling. She attended the University of California at Berkeley, supported by 11 scholarships. Although her first declared major was engineering, she soon switched to English literature and received her B.A. degree in 1962, the same year she married the actor Earl Kingston. After getting her teaching certificate at Berkeley in 1965, Kingston taught school in Hayward, California, for a couple of years before moving with her husband to Hawaii in 1967. The couple had been heavily involved in antiwar activities at Berkeley and had become concerned about the increasing violence and heavy drug use that surrounded the movement. They decided to move to Japan but stopped on the way in Hawaii, where they stayed for 17 years. Kingston and her husband both taught school in Hawaii, and their son, Joseph, was born there.

Kingston's first book, *The Woman Warrior: Memoirs of a Girlhood Among Ghosts*, was published in 1976 while she was teaching creative writing at the Mid-Pacific Institute. Critics generally loved the book for its fresh use of multiple narrators and the Chinese rhythms of the prose. The book became an immediate best-seller and remained on the trade paperback best-sellers list for more than a decade. It won the National Book Critics Circle Award in nonfiction in 1976 and was rated as one of the top 10 nonfiction books of the decade. In 1977, Kingston became a visiting professor at the University of Hawaii at Honolulu. Kingston's second book, *China Men*, which she has called the male companion to *The Woman Warrior*, came out in 1980 and received mixed reviews but also won a National Book Award. Kingston's first two books have been widely taught in literature, history, and sociology classes.

*Hawaii One Summer*, a collection of 12 prose pieces, was published in 1987. By this time, Kingston had given up teaching in order to write full time, but she continued to teach as a visiting professor in Hawaii, California, and Michigan. Her next book, *Tripmaster Monkey: His Fake Book,* was also published in 1987. In 1992, Kingston became a member of the Academy of Arts and Sciences.

Although Kingston's harshest critics have often been Asian Americans, who fault her for what they feel is her inaccurate representation of traditional Chinese myths and stories, most critics have seen her work as important pieces of postmodernism.

Kingston's other books include *Conversations with Maxine Hong Kingston* (1998), *To Be the Poet* (2002), and *The Fifth Book of Peace* (2003). She edited *The Literature of California: Native American Beginnings to 1945.* (Volume 1, 2000). Kingston teaches at the University of California at Berkeley.

## Further Reading

Brownmiller, Susan. "Susan Brownmiller Talks with Maxine Hong Kingston." *Mademoiselle,* March 1977, pp. 148–216.

Janette, Michele. "The Angle We're Joined At: A Conversation with Maxine Hong Kingston." *Transition* 71 (spring 1997): 142–157.

Lesniak, James, and Susan Trosky, eds. "Maxine Hong Kingston," in *Contemporary Authors, New Revision Series.* Detroit: Gale Research, 1993, pp. 206–210.

Moritz, Charles, ed. "Maxine Hong Kingston," in *Current Biography Yearbook.* New York: H. W. Wilson, 1990, pp. 359–363.

Yalom, Marilyn. *Women Writers of the West Coast: Speaking of Their Lives and Careers.* Santa Barbara, Calif.: Capra Press, 1983.

## Kinsella, W. P.
### (William Patrick Kinsella)
(1932–   ) *novelist, short story writer*

Canadian author W. P. Kinsella has published 17 books and more than 200 short stories. He is best known for his award-winning novel *Shoeless Joe,* which was made into the highly praised film *Field of Dreams* (1989). A reviewer for the *New York Times* said that his work "defines a world in which magic and reality combine to make us laugh and think about the perceptions we take for granted." His life, like his fiction, seems to have an element of magic to it. Many of Kinsella's works focus on baseball, the game he loves and grew up watching. Some of his popular "baseball works" include *The Thrill of the Grass* (1985), *The Iowa Baseball Confederacy* (1996), and *Magic Time* (2001). He also incorporates Native American themes and characters in much of his writing, which may be seen in novels such as *The Moccasin Telegraph* (1985) and *The Fencepost Chronicles* (1987).

William Patrick Kinsella was born on May 25, 1935, in Edmonton, Alberta. He grew up on a farm as an only child in a relatively isolated town in northern Alberta. He did not attend school until fifth grade, studying instead at home by correspondence. Since he had no playmates, he made up fictional friends and wrote about them as a young boy. Although he began writing at the age of 17, he did not pursue it as a career until much later in life. In his 20s, he worked at a series of jobs—including stints as a clerk, insurance investigator, and restaurateur—until he eventually went back to school and received a B.A. degree in creative writing at the age of 39. Kinsella was educated both at the University of Victoria, in British Columbia, and at the University of Iowa. He then taught writing at the University of Calgary from 1978 to 1983.

Kinsella's first published story collection, *Dance Me Outside* (1977), is about the rich fictional world of narrator Simon Ermineskin of the Ermineskin Indian Band. Kinsella's first story about baseball was *Shoeless Joe Jackson Comes to Iowa* (1980). The title story of this collection was also expanded into a novel, *Shoeless Joe* (1982), a light-hearted and magical fantasy about a long-gone baseball team that comes back to life for one more game. *Shoeless Joe* won both the Houghton Mifflin Literary Fellowship in 1982 and the Books in Canada Award for First Novel in 1983. It was then adapted for film as *Field of Dreams* in 1989. Kinsella's second novel was *The Iowa Baseball Confederacy* (1985). He also won the Stephen Leacock Award for Humor for *The Fencepost Chronicles* (1986). In 1988, Kinsella staged *The Thrill of the Grass,* which comprising three one-act plays based on baseball stories.

W. P. Kinsella currently resides in White Rock, British Columbia, most of the year, although he spends time at his Palm Springs, Florida, apartment too. He is still generating well-loved fiction. His most recent book, *Japanese Baseball and Other Stories* (2000), marks his return to the baseball quick read. The stories in the collection run from wry to melancholy. Of Kinsella's evolving tone, *The Backlight Review* has said "Kinsella's voice has matured somewhat from the comparatively youthful exuberance of his earlier work, which in many ways could be compared with Garrison Keillor: folksy, anecdotal and gently humorous."

**Further Reading**

Aitken, Brian. "Baseball as Sacred Doorway in the Writing of W. P. Kinsella," *Aethlon* 8, no. 1 (fall 1990): 61–75.

Candelaria, Cordelia. *Seeking the Perfect Game: Baseball in American Literature.* New York: Greenwood Press, 1989.

Peterson, Richard. "Only Fairy Tales: The Baseball Short Story from Lardner to Kinsella," *Aethlon* 14, no. 2 (spring 1997): 63–70.

## Koch, Kenneth
### (Jay Kenneth Koch)
(1925–2002) *poet, playwright, novelist*

Kenneth Koch is widely remembered for his association with the New York School of Poetry, a cosmopolitan movement influenced by French surrealism and European avant-gardism. In addition to his many books of poetry, including *One Train* (1994) and *On the Great Atlantic Rainway: Selected Poems, 1950–1988* (1994), which together won the Bollingen Prize for poetry in 1995, and *New Addresses* (2000), a finalist for the National Book Award, Koch wrote plays, a novel, a libretto, and criticism. He is also known for his influential books on teaching creative writing to children, including *Wishes, Lies, and Dreams* (1970) and *Rose, Where Did You Get That Red?* (1973). Koch lived in New York City, where he was professor of English at Columbia University.

Jay Kenneth Koch was born in Cincinnati, Ohio, on February 27, 1925. As a young man, Koch could not wait to grow up. "The whole idea of writing poetry has a lot to do with escaping," Koch liked to say, and Cincinnati (and provincialism in general) was what he struggled to escape. Drafted into

the U.S. Army, Koch was sent to the Philippines to fight in World War II. He wrote movingly about the experience in "To World War Two." The importance of this poem lies in the attention it gives to the concept of war, which is an abstract and often elusive topic.

After being discharged from the army, Koch attended Harvard University on the GI Bill. He graduated with honors in 1948. While at Harvard, he befriended fellow poet and lifelong friend JOHN ASHBERY. Their social circle, which eventually moved to New York City and expanded to include such notables as FRANK O'HARA and James Schuyler, as well as painters Larry Rivers, Jane Freilicher, and Fairfield Porter, formed the core of the New York school of poets. The New York school derived much of its inspiration from the works of "action painters" such as Jackson Pollock, Willem de Kooning, and Larry Rivers, whom the poets met in the 1950s after settling in New York City. The poetry of the New York school represented a shift away from the popular and widespread confessional poetry, which was defined largely by an element of intense personal exposure, which was in opposition to the free-flowing cosmopolitan spirit of the New York school's writing.

Unlike Ashbery and O'Hara, who earned their livings as professional art critics, Koch chose to pursue an academic career. On a Fulbright fellowship, he traveled to Aix-en-Provence, France, where he enjoyed the sound of spoken French and the experience of not having full command of the language, which enabled him to interpret the language using all of his senses. He tried, he later remarked, to inject the "same incomprehensible excitement" into his own work. Koch then studied briefly at University of California at Berkeley, where he met his first wife, Janice. The two honeymooned in France and Italy, and followed that trip with several subsequent fellowship trips to Europe. In Rome, in 1956, their daughter Katherine was born; soon after, the Kochs returned to the United States, where at Columbia University Kenneth earned both a master's degree and a Ph.D.

Koch's continued association with the New York school and his writing style in general grew in popularity throughout the decades. Many critics found his early work obscure, such as *Poems* (1953), and the epic *Ko, or A Season on Earth* (1959), yet remarked upon his subsequent writing for its clarity, lyricism, and humor, such as in *The Art of Love* (1975), which was praised as a graceful, humorous book. His other collections of poetry include *One Train* (1994) and *On the Great Atlantic Rainway, Selected Poems 1950–1988* (1994), which together earned him the Bollingen Prize in 1995, *Straits* (1998), and *New Addresses* (2000), winner of the Phi Beta Kappa Poetry Award and a finalist for the National Book Award.

Koch's short plays, many of them produced Off- and "off-off" Broadway, are collected in *The Gold Standard: A Book of Plays.* He has also published *Making Your Own Days: The Pleasures of Reading and Writing Poetry* (1998), the novel *The Red Robins* (1975), *Hotel Lambosa and Other Stories* (1993), and several books on teaching children to write poetry. Koch also wrote the libretto for composer Marcello Panni's *The Banquet*, which premiered in Bremen, Germany, in June 1998. In addition, his collaborations with painters have been the subject of exhibitions at the Ipswich Museum in England and the De Nagy Gallery in New York. Koch's numerous honors include the Rebekah Johnson Bobbitt National Prize for Poetry, awarded by the Library of Congress in 1996, as well as awards from the American Academy of Arts and Letters and the Fulbright, Guggenheim, and Ingram-Merrill foundations. In 1996 he was inducted as a member of the American Academy of Arts and Letters. Kenneth Koch lived in New York City, where he remained a professor of English at Columbia University until his death, on July 6, 2002, from leukemia.

Through his teaching and his books on teaching, Koch has probably influenced as many readers as has any U.S. poet of his generation. His second wife, Karen Koch (Janice died in 1981), recalled, "I had never heard anybody make such sensible statements about how to write poetry and certainly how to teach it." Though he won many awards for his poetry and attracted many devoted and accomplished disciples, Koch struggled with the possibility that his teaching might overshadow his writing. Today, not long after his death, his poetic genius

continues to grow in popularity as a new generation of ambitious readers discovers the poets of the New York school.

## Further Reading

"Kenneth Koch's Seasons on Earth." Columbia College Today. Available online. URL: http://www.college.columbia.edu/cct/nov02/nov02_cover_koch.php. Posted November 2002.

"Online NewsHour: Poet Kenneth Koch." Available online. URL: http://www.pbs.org/newshour/bb/entertainment/november96/koch_11-28.html. Posted November 28, 1996.

Tranter, John. "Very Rapid Acceleration: An Interview with Kenneth Koch." Jacket 5. Available online. URL: http://jacketmagazine.com/05/Koch89.html. Posted October 1998.

## Kunitz, Stanley
(1905–  ) *poet, essayist, translator*

In 2000, at the age of 95, Stanley Kunitz became America's 10th poet laureate. His lengthy career spanned most of the 20th century and has included work as a poet, teacher, translator, and editor. Known for poems written in a conversational style that belies the complexity of his themes, he has written often about loss, specifically the loss of a father, and about gardening, a hobby about which he is passionate.

Stanley Kunitz was born in Worcester, Massachusetts, in 1905. Just a few weeks before his birth, his father committed suicide in a public park after his successful dress-manufacturing business went bankrupt. Kunitz's mother, a Lithuanian immigrant, opened a dry goods business to support her family. She refused to talk about her late husband and married again, to Mark Dine. Dine's death when Kunitz was 14 and the death of Kunitz's sister at an early age, on top of the loss of his biological father, have haunted Kunitz throughout his life.

As a student at Worcester Classical High School, Kunitz began to read the poetry of British masters Robert Herrick, John Keats, William Wordsworth, and William Blake. Kunitz was an excellent student and won a scholarship to study at Harvard, where he graduated summa cum laude in

1926. His hopes to teach in the English department at Harvard were dashed when he was subtly informed that due to his Jewish background there would be no position for him at Harvard.

Kunitz left the university to work as reporter and editor before trying his hand as a farmer during the Great Depression. He also traveled to Europe, where he served from abroad as editor of the Wilson Library Bulletin. He began to publish his poems during these years in *Poetry* magazine, *The Dial, The Nation, The New Republic,* and *Commonweal. Intellectual Things,* his first collection, appeared in 1930. Published at a time when modernism generally dominated poetic style, Kunitz's metaphysical explorations of the mind were not particularly well received. He did not publish another book of poems for 14 years but continued, instead, to work as an editor.

His next book, *Passport to the War* (1940) also struck its own very unique chord and failed to find much support among critics. Kunitz was a conscientious objector during World War II, but he served three years in the army, most of which was spent in North Carolina. When he was discharged in 1945, with the rank of sergeant, he spent a year in Santa Fe, New Mexico, on a Guggenheim grant, before returning to the northeast to begin his teaching career at Bennington College in Vermont. Twice divorced during the early part of his life, he married the painter Elise Asher in 1958. The two lived in Greenwich Village, New York City, and Provincetown, Massachusetts, during most of their life together.

His 1958 collection, *Selected Poems, 1928–1958,* won a Pulitzer Prize and solidified his career as a poet and creative writing teacher. Since that time, he has published many books, including *The Poems of Stanley Kunitz, 1928–1978* (1978), which won the Lenore Marshall Poetry Prize; *Next-to-Last Things: New Poems and Essays* (1985); *Passing Through: The Later Poems, New and Selected* (1995), which won the National Book Award; and *The Collected Poems of Stanley Kunitz* (2000). Inspired by a trip to the Soviet Union in 1967, Kunitz cotranslated several volumes of poetry, including *Poems of Akhmatova* (1973), *Story Under Full Sail* (1974) by Andrei Voznesensky, and *Orchard Lamps* (1978) by Ivan Drach. He also edited *The Essential Blake* (1987), *Poems of John Keats* (1964), and various works in The Yale Series of Younger Poets from 1969 to 1977.

In addition to his prolific writing career, Kunitz is renowned for his teaching. He held positions at Yale, Princeton, Rutgers, the New School for Social Research, and Columbia University, among other places. He also founded the Provincetown Fine Arts Work Center in Provincetown, Massachusetts, in 1967.

Kunitz is the recipient of many literary awards, including the Bollingen Prize, a National Endowment for the Arts Senior Fellowship, a Harriet Monroe Award, and a Ford Foundation Award. He received the National Medal of the Arts in 1993 and an "In Celebration of Winters" award from *Poets & Writers* magazine in 1999. A member of the American Academy of Arts and Letters, he has also served as consultant in poetry at the Library of Congress and as state poet of New York.

## Further Reading

Henault, Marie. *Stanley Kunitz.* Boston: Twayne, 1980.

Kunitz, Stanley. *Interviews and Encounters with Stanley Kunitz.* Hanover, N.H.: Sheep Meadow Press, 1990.

Moss, Stanley, ed. *To Stanley Kunitz with Love: From Poet Friends for His 96th Birthday.* Hanover, N.H.: Sheep Meadow Press, 2001.

Orr, Gregory. *Stanley Kunitz: An Introduction to the Poetry.* New York: Columbia University Press, 1985.

Vinson, James, ed. *Contemporary Poets.* Detroit: St. James Press, 1975.

# L

## Lee, Chang-rae
(1965– ) *novelist*

Although he has published only two novels, Chang-rae Lee has won the highest praise of critics and readers alike. He won the PEN/Hemingway Foundation Award for his debut novel *Native Speaker* and was also deemed one of the 20 best American writers under 40 by the *New Yorker*, just a few years after being named a finalist for a similar list compiled by *Granta* magazine.

Chang-rae Lee was born on July 29, 1965, in Seoul, Korea. He immigrated with his family to the United States when he was three years old. The Lees lived briefly in Pittsburgh, Pennsylvania, and then moved to New York's Upper West Side before settling in the suburbs of Westchester County, New York, where Lee was raised. Lee's father, a physician, learned English quickly and became a psychiatrist, which Lee has described as inspiring, simply because of his father's courage in taking up a profession so dependent on mastery of the language. Lee thought about changing his name when he was a young boy, considering such all-American sounding names as Chuck and Tom, but ultimately decided to stick with Chang-rae. He attended the prestigious Phillips Exeter Academy, then went on to study at Yale University, where he received his B.A. degree in English literature. He continued his education at the University of Oregon, graduating with a master's degree in creative writing.

Lee then worked for a year on Wall Street as an equities analyst before quitting to devote himself entirely to writing. In an interview, he said about this decision, "I didn't leave Wall Street because the work was against my nature—I do have a pretty good head for numbers. I left because I had this love for writing."

Lee's first novel, *Native Speaker*, appeared in 1995, when he was 29 and won the PEN/Hemingway Foundation Award, the American Book Award, Quality Paperback Book Club's New Voices Award, the Barnes & Noble Discover Great New Writers Award, and the Oregon Book Award. It was also an American Library Association Notable Book of the Year and a finalist for a PEN West Award. *Native Speaker* is the story of a Korean-American man involved in espionage, but on a more universal scale, it is a story of cultural alienation and even personal alienation.

His follow-up novel *A Gesture Life* (1999) follows the life of an elderly medic who treated Korean "comfort women" during World War II. It won the Anisfeld-Wolf Prize in Fiction and the Asian-American Literary Award for Fiction. *A Gesture Life* was also chosen as the fifth book in Seattle's annual reading event, "If All of Seattle Read the Same Book." Both of Lee's first two novels are set in Westchester County, New York and both explore themes of identity, belonging, and assimilation. He has said in an interview about his subject matter, "I'm interested in people who find themselves in places, either of their choosing or not, and who are forced to decide how best to live there. That feeling of both citizenship and exile, of always being an expatriate—with all the attendant

Korean-American writer Chang-rae Lee won the Hemingway Foundation/PEN Award for his first novel, *Native Speaker*. *(Courtesy Princeton University, Office of Communications)*

**Further Reading**

"Chang-rae Lee." *Granta.* Available online. URL: http://www.granta.com/authors/53. Downloaded June 10, 2003.

Engles, Tim. "'Visions of Me in the Whitest Raw Light': Assimilation and Doxic Whiteness in Chang-rae Lee's *Native Speaker.*" *Hitting Critical Mass: A Journal of Asian American Cultural Studies* 4, no. 2 (summer 1997): 27–48.

Lee, Jin Ah. "Award-Winning Novelist Discusses the Art of Writing and Reading." *Yale Bulletin: Calender* 28, no. 28. Available online. URL: http://www.yale.edu/opa/V28.N28/story10.html. Posted April 14, 2000.

# Le Guin, Ursula
## (Ursula Kroeber)
(1929–    ) *novelist, children's fiction writer, science fiction writer*

U.S. author of fantasy and science fiction works, poetry, and essays Ursula Le Guin is widely regarded as one of the best science fiction authors known. She has published more than 100 short stories, two collections of essays, 13 books for children, five volumes of poetry, and 19 novels. She is noted for her exploration of Taoist, anarchist, feminist, psychological, and sociological themes and for her exemplary and cutting-edge writing style.

Ursula Kroeber was born October 21, 1929, in Berkeley, California. Her father, Alfred Kroeber, was an anthropologist, and her mother, Theodora, was a noted anthropologist and writer who collected Native American folktales and who published a biographical work about a primitive individual plunged into the modern world. Theodora also wrote children's books. The Kroebers had one son together and two sons by Theodora's first marriage, in addition to Ursula. Ursula was influenced from an early age by her frequent exposure to anthropological ideas and theories. She became acquainted with many important anthropologists in her parents' professional circles. Part of her childhood reading included Sir James Frazier's mythology collection *The Golden Bough.* She was significantly influenced by Norse mythology and the pulp science fiction of the 1940. She later discovered the work

problems and complications and delight." In addition to his two novels, he has published stories and articles in *The New Yorker, The New York Times,* and *Granta* magazine, and his work has been anthologized in *The Best American Essays* and numerous other collections.

Lee taught at Hunter College in New York and directed its creative writing program for several years before accepting a position at Princeton University as a professor in the Council of the Humanities and the Program in Creative Writing. He lives with his wife and two-year-old daughter in Bergen County, New Jersey, just a few miles northwest of Manhattan. His forthcoming book, not yet titled, concerns the lives of Americans in Korea during the Korean War.

of Lord Dunsany, an English writer of fantasy stories in the first half of the 20th century, which provided her first recognition that "people were still creating myths." Le Guin spent her college years at Radcliffe, where she received her B.A. degree in 1951, and at Columbia University where she earned her M.A. degree in French and Italian Renaissance literature in 1952. Kroeber then began working on a Ph.D., but during her studies in France in 1953, a result of being awarded a Fulbright fellowship, she made the acquaintance of her future husband, Charles A. Le Guin; the two married the following December and Charles's career eventually led the two to settle in Oregon, where he taught at Portland State University.

Le Guin had begun writing as a child, and since 1951 had been submitting stories, poems, and novels for publication, with little success (although some of them resurfaced in altered form years later in *Orsinian Tales* and *Malafrena*). These early writings were nonfantastic stories of imaginary countries, which, at the time, fit no known genre. Then in 1960, two life-altering events occurred: Her father died, and she rediscovered science fiction, which finally provided her with a path to publication. Her first sale was a short story that appeared in *Fantastic*. In 1964, she published the first stories set in the fantasy world of Earthsea, and in 1966 published the first of her *Hainish* novels. The years between 1966 and 1979 were Le Guin's most creative and productive period. During this time she wrote 10 novels, along with numerous short stories, poems, and essays, including much of her most highly regarded work. She was asked in 1967 to write "a book for older children," which was published in 1968 as *A Wizard of Earthsea* and was widely hailed as her first great work. Of *A Wizard of Earthsea*, Le Guin has noted, "Fantasy is the medium best suited to a description of that journey (i.e., the journey 'into the self'), its perils and rewards. The events of a voyage into the unconscious are not describable in the language of rational daily life; only the symbolic language of the deeper psyche will fit them without trivializing them."

*A Wizard of Earthsea* won the 1969 Boston Globe–Horn Book Award. The following year, Le Guin published *The Left Hand of Darkness*, which won the Nebula and the Hugo Awards for best

Science Fiction Novel of the Year. Her second *Earthsea* novel, *The Tombs of Atuan*, was published in 1971 and received a Newbery Honor citation. *The Farthest Shore* won the National Book Award for children's literature in 1972. In 1974, Le Guin became the first writer to twice receive both awards for best novel when she won Nebula and Hugo for *The Dispossessed*. In addition to her novels and writing career, Le Guin has worked as a visiting lecturer and writer at many institutions, including Mercer University in Georgia, and the University of Idaho. She currently resides in Portland, Oregon, with her husband. She has continued to publish volumes in the Earthsea series, the most recent being *Tales from Earthsea* (2001). Her translation of the *Tao Te Ching: A Book about the Way and the Paves of the Way*, completed with Jerome P. Seaton, was published in 1997.

## Further Reading

Bittner, James W. *Approaches to the Fiction of Ursula K. Le Guin.* Ann Arbor, Mich.: UMI Research Press, 1984.

Bloom, Harold, ed. *Ursula K. Le Guin.* New York: Chelsea House, 1986.

Cummins. Elizabeth. *Understanding Ursula K. Le Guin.* Columbia: University of South Carolina Press, 1990.

DeBolt, Joe, ed. *Ursula K. Le Guin: Voyager to Inner Lands and to Outer Space.* Port Washington, N.Y.: Kennikat Press, 1979.

Justice, Faith L. "Ursula K. Le Guin." Salon.com Available online. URL: http://archive.salon.com/people/bc/2001/01/23/le_guin/print.html. Posted January 23, 2001.

## Levertov, Denise
(1923–1997) *poet, essayist*

A member of the Black Mountain group of writers, which included fellow poet ROBERT CREELEY, Denise Levertov was one of the most influential and prolific poets of her generation. She published 23 volumes of poetry, as well as several collections of essays and translations during her lengthy career. Her poems are known for their unique blend of spirituality and political awareness. In addition to her writing career, Levertov was a prominent feminist and antiwar activist in the 1960s and 1970s.

Denise Levertov was born October 24, 1923, in Ilford, Essex, England. Her father, raised a Hasidic Jew, had converted to Christianity while attending university in Germany. By the time Denise was born he had settled in England and had become an Anglican parson. Her mother, who was Welsh, read the works of such authors as WILLA CATHER, Joseph Conrad, Charles Dickens, and Leo Tolstoy aloud to the family. Levertov was educated entirely at home, and claimed to have decided to become a writer at the age of five. At age 12, Levertov sent some of her poetry to T. S. ELIOT, who responded to the aspiring writer with advice that further encouraged her to continue cultivating her skill. *Poetry Quarterly* published her first works when she was 17. As a young woman, Levertov felt college did not agree with her, so she decided instead to train as a nurse and spent three years in London rehabilitating war veterans during World War II. Every night after her shift, she would return home to write. Her first book, *The Double Image*, published in 1946, brought her recognition as one of a group of poets dubbed the "New Romantics." Jean Gould, author of *Modern American Women Poets,* wrote of this book, "The young poet possessed a strong social consciousness and showed indications of the militant pacifist she was to become."

In 1948, Levertov married Mitchell Goodman, an American writer. The newlyweds soon relocated to New York City, where Levertov completed her second book of poetry, *Here and Now,* which showed her fresh, decidedly American voice. Her next book, *With Eyes at the Back of Our Heads,* established her as one of the great American poets, and her British origins were soon forgotten. Through her husband's friendship with poet Robert Creeley, she became associated with the Black Mountain group of poets, particularly Creeley, Charles Olson, and Robert Duncan, who had formed a short-lived but groundbreaking school in 1933 in North Carolina. The Black Mountain poets emphasized the phrasing of poetry in accordance with the spontaneity of the breath pause in speech. Some of her work was published in the 1950s in the *Black Mountain Review.* Levertov acknowledged these influences, but disclaimed membership in any poetic school. She was poetry editor of *The Nation* magazine in 1961 and from 1963 to 1965. During the 1960s and the Vietnam War, activism and feminism became prominent in her poetry. After hearing ALLEN GINSBERG's epic poem *Howl,* Levertov traveled to San Francisco in pursuit of more direct political activism. There she caught up with the popular antiwar movement; her involvement in protests eventually landed her in jail. Critics soon began to shun her political poetry, demanding a separation in her work. Levertov refused, saying poetry cannot be "divided from the rest of life necessary to it. Both life and poetry fade, wilt, shrink, when they are divorced." During this period she produced one of her most memorable works of rage and sadness, *The Sorrow Dance* (1967), which encompassed her feelings toward the war and the death of her older sister. From 1975 to 1978, she was poetry editor of *Mother Jones* magazine.

Levertov went on to publish more than 20 volumes of poetry, including *Freeing the Dust* (1975), which won the Lenore Marshall Poetry Prize. She was also the author of four books of prose, most recently *Tesserae* (1995), and translator of three volumes of poetry, among them Jean Joubert's *Black Iris* (1989). From 1982 to 1993, she taught at Stanford University. She spent the last decade of her life in Seattle, Washington, during which time she published *Poems 1968–1972* (1987), *Breathing the Water* (1987), *A Door in the Hive* (1989), *Evening Train* (1992), and *The Sands of the Well* (1996). On December 20, 1997, Denise Levertov died at the age of 74 from complications of lymphoma.

### Further Reading

Bodo Murray. "Denise Levertov: A Memoir and Appreciation." *Image 27* (summer 2000): 82–93.

Brooker, Jewel S. *Conversations with Denise Levertov.* Jackson: University Press of Mississippi, 1998.

Marten, Harry. *Understanding Denise Levertov.* Columbia: University of South Carolina Press, 1988.

Packard, William, ed. *The Craft of Poetry.* Garden City, N.J.: Doubleday, 1974.

Rodgers, Audrey T. *Denise Levertov: The Poetry of Engagement.* Rutherford, N.J.: Fairleigh Dickinson University Press, 1993.

## Levine, Philip
(1928–  ) *poet*

Philip Levine has been a leading contemporary U.S. poet whose style is characterized by a haunting lyricism that pays tribute to ethnic and working-class issues. Much of his writing deals with his youth in the industrial city of Detroit, especially his work in various factories there. His poetry collection *The Simple Truth* (1994) won the Pulitzer Prize. He won the National Book Award for his 1991 volume *What Work Is*. He is the author of at least 16 books of poetry.

Philip Levine was born on January 10, 1928, in Detroit, Michigan, to Russian Jewish immigrant parents. He was educated in local schools and began writing poetry while going to night school at Wayne State University. His earliest poems were relatively formal in character. He was employed in a succession of industrial jobs, including working in one of Detroit's auto manufacturing plants. "In that intersection of two different kinds of labor, Levine discovered that few of the fundamental experiences of working class life had rarely, if ever, found expression in the realms of contemporary American poetry," Fred Marchant wrote. "The epiphany that launched Levine was his sense that the clang of industrial labor—and all the human spirit that was swallowed up in it—could be a source of a poetry that probed the many forms of alienation found in and among those people he knew best, those who had to work hard for a living."

Levine left Detroit for good in 1954 and lived in various parts of the United States before settling in Fresno, California. He has published collections at regular intervals since *On the Edge* appeared in 1963. His second book, *Not This Pig* (1968), broke with formality and marked the emergence of Levine's style which is known for its everyday, blue-collar language and settings and its often elegiac narrative form. The poetry in *On the Edge* and *Not This Pig* focuses on those who suddenly realize they are trapped in some murderous processes not of their own making.

Levine has periodically lived in Spain, and its people, landscape, and history are a strong presence in his poems. His elegy for a Republican soldier, "To P.L., 1916–1937," appeared in *They Feed They Lion* (1972), which is considered one of Levine's strongest collections. The title poem of *They Feed They Lion* (1972), written following the aftermath of the 1967 Detroit riots, forms the refrain of a chant that conjures the fury of the thwarted and dispossessed in the context of the American dream. In his collection *1933* (1974), which was Levine's most explicitly autobiographical work, family members and the physical geography of Detroit are uniquely invoked in poems such as "Letters for the Dead," "Uncle," and "1933." More poems were set in Detroit in Levine's next volume, *The Names of the Lost* (1976). "Belle Isle, 1949," describes a young couple who baptize themselves in the polluted Detroit River.

Though he has written about Spain and Detroit, Levine has lived much of his adult life in northern California, and a number of his poems reflect the dry dust and hot climate of Fresno Valley. Some consider Levine a religious poet because of his use of spirituality to evoke the sense of a landscape or a particular mental state. Some of his most explicitly religious poems are included in *Ashes* (1979). Many of the poems collected here explore Levine's Jewish roots. *Ashes* was the recipient of the National Book Critics Circle Award for poetry and the first book to receive the American Book Award for poetry.

Among Levine's other works are: *The Names of the Lost* (1975), which won the Lenore Marshall Poetry Prize; *7 Years From Somewhere* (1979), which won the National Book Critics Circle Award; and *New Selected Poems* (1991). He has also edited *The Essential Keats* (1987) and published a collection of essays, *The Bread of Time: Toward an Autobiography* (1994). The Pulitzer Prize–winning collection *The Simple Truth* (1994) is written in a voice that moves between elegy and prayer. It contains 33 poems whose aim is to weave a complex tapestry of myth, history (both public and private), family, memory, and invention in a search for elusive basic and universal truths.

Levine has received the Ruth Lilly Poetry Prize, the Harriet Monroe Memorial Prize, the Frank O'Hara Prize, and two Guggenheim Foundation fellowships. He served for two years as chairman of the literature panel of the National

Endowment for the Arts, and he was elected a chancellor of the Academy of American Poets in 2000. Levine lives in New York City and Fresno, California, He has taught at New York University and California State University.

## Further Reading

Buckley, Christopher, ed. *On the Poetry of Philip Levine*. Ann Arbor: University of Michigan Press, 1991.

Marchant, Fred, and Jay Parini. "About Philip Levine." *Modern American Poetry*. Available online. URL: http://www.english.uiuc.edu/maps/poets/g_l/levine/life.htm. Downloaded September 15, 2003.

Mariani, Paul. "A Conversation with Philip Levine." *Image* 14 (summer 1996): 61–76.

Suarez, Ernest. "Philip Levine." *Five Points* 3, no. 2 (winter 1999): 20–38.

## Levis, Larry
### (Lawrence Patrick Levis)
(1946–1996)  *poet, short story writer, literary critic*

The author of five books of poetry and a volume of short stories, Larry Levis is remembered and admired for his narrative poems made of long lines and peopled with ordinary folks and for the generous spirit and sardonic humor found within those poems. Levis was the recipient of numerous awards, including the United States Award of the International Poetry Forum and the Lamont Poetry Prize, among others.

Born on September 30, 1946, in Fresno, California, Larry Levis grew up on his parents' farm, a place that occupied much of his imagination when he began to write poems. He earned his undergraduate degree at Fresno State College, now called California State University, in 1968. From there, Levis moved to Syracuse, New York, where he earned his master's degree in 1970 at Syracuse University. In 1974, he earned his Ph.D. from the University of Iowa. The poet PHILIP LEVINE, with whom Levis studied, recalled that Levis was "the most gifted and determined young poet I have ever had the good fortune to have in one of my classes."

Levis taught English at the University of Missouri from 1974 until 1980. During this period

he married Marsha Southwick and the couple had a son, Nicholas, who was born in 1977. Levis went on to teach as an associate professor and director of the creative writing program at the University of Utah from 1980 to 1992, and from 1992 until his death, he was a professor of English at Virginia Commonwealth University in Richmond. He also taught for shorter periods at the University of Iowa and in the Warren Wilson Creative Writing Program.

*Wrecking Crew*, Levis's first book of poems, appeared in 1972 and won the United States Award from the International Poetry Forum. Two years later, his second book, *The Afterlife*, was the Lamont Poetry Selection of the American Academy of Poets. In 1981, *The Dollmaker's Ghost* was a winner of the Open Competition of the National Poetry Series. His other books include *Winter Stars* (1985), *The Widening Spell of the Leaves* (1991), and *Elegy* (1997), which was edited by Philip Levine and published posthumously. In 2000, the University of Pittsburgh Press published *The Selected Levis: Poems 1972–1992*, and in 2001, the University of Michigan Press's Poets on Poetry series issued *The Gazer Within*, edited by Randy Marshall, Andrew Miller, and John Venable. Levis also published one collection of short stories, *Black Freckles*, in 1992.

Among his other honors were a YM-YWHA Discovery Award, three fellowships in poetry from the National Endowment for the Arts, a Fulbright fellowship, a Guggenheim fellowship, and an individual artist's grant from the Virginia Commission for the Arts. In 1989, he was a senior Fulbright fellow in Yugoslavia. His work, including poems, essays, short stories, and reviews appeared in *American Poetry Review, The Southern Review, Field*, and the *New Yorker*, as well as many other magazines.

Larry Levis died suddenly of a heart attack in Richmond, Virginia, on May 8, 1996. Several awards were established in his honor following his death, including the Larry Levis Editors' Prize at the *Missouri Review*.

## Further Reading

Hoagland, Tony. "Let's Get Lost: The Image as Escape in the Poems of Larry Levis." *Marlboro Review*.

Available online. URL: http://www.marlboro review.com/hoagland.html. Posted 1997.

"Levis, Larry," in *Contemporary Authors*, New Revision Series 80 (1999): 235–237.

Wilson, Steven M. "Larry Levis." *Dictionary of Literary Biography*, 3rd ser. 120 (1992): 189–195.

## Lewis, Sinclair
### (Harry Lewis, Tom Graham)
(1885–1951) *novelist, playwright*

The first American ever to win the Nobel Prize for literature, Sinclair Lewis is remembered as the greatest satirist of his age. He is best known for his stinging critiques of American materialism, as represented by his most famous novel, *Babbitt*. A prolific writer, he published 22 novels and three plays.

Sinclair Lewis was born in the small village of Sauk Center, Minnesota, the third son of a country doctor. His mother, who was the daughter of a Canadian physician, died of tuberculosis when Lewis was six years old. One year later his father married Isabel Warner, whom Lewis thought of as his mother. She read to him and he had access to the 300 or 400 volumes, exclusive of medical books, in his father's library. Later Lewis characterized Sauk Center as "narrow-minded and socially provincial"; books offered him an escape. His life was also made miserable by teasing—he was strange-looking with his red hair and very bad skin. At the age of 13, Lewis ran away from home to become a drummer boy in the Spanish-American War, but his father caught up with him at the railroad station, and brought the boy home. Lewis started to write and kept a diary early in his youth; he produced romantic poetry, and stories about knights and fair ladies.

In 1902, Lewis entered Oberlin Academy. He later moved to Yale University, where he contributed to the *Yale Literary Magazine*. He also met JACK LONDON while at Yale and later sold the older writer short story plots. A lifelong wanderer, Lewis spent one summer vacation in England, working on a cattle boat, and in another year, went to Panama in search of a job on the canal. He also worked as a janitor in 1906–07 at UPTON SINCLAIR's ill-fated socialist commune, Helicon Hall.

Following his graduation from Yale with an M.A. degree in 1908, Lewis worked for various publishing houses and magazines in Iowa, California, Washington, D.C., and New York City. In Greenwich Village he associated occasionally with such radicals as John Reed and Floyd Dell and was briefly a member of the Socialist Party.

Lewis's first two published books were *Hike and the Aeroplane* (1912), which he published under the pseudonym Tom Graham, and *Our Mr. Wrenn* (1914). He once described how his early novels were written on the Long Island Rail Road trains that he rode into New York City each day to his job at a publishing company. In 1913, Lewis began publishing a syndicated book page, which helped him to gain favorable reviews from other writers. In 1914, he married Grace Livingston Hegger, an editor at *Vogue* magazine. The couple had one son, Wells, who was killed overseas in 1944 during World War II. Lewis kept his job as an editor and advertising manager at the book publishing company George H. Doran until 1916, when he quit and traveled around the country with his wife.

From this time on, Lewis devoted himself full time to writing. He became famous with the publication of *Main Street* in 1920, a novel focused on the tension between idealism and reality in a small, provincial town. The Pulitzer Prize jury voted for *Main Street* that year, but they were overruled by the Columbia University trustees in favor of EDITH WHARTON's *The Age of Innocence*. The publication of *Babbitt* in 1922, however, firmly secured Lewis's position as an important literary figure. Considered by many literary critics to be his most significant work, *Babbitt*, the satirical story of an unhappy businessman who tries to satisfy his restlessness by conforming to social standards, treats the themes of materialism and conformity that captivated Lewis for most of his writing career. These successful novels were followed by another satirical novel, *Arrowsmith*, in 1925, on which Lewis collaborated with Dr. Paul de Kruif. A satire on the medical profession, *Arrowsmith* was awarded the Pulitzer Prize, but Lewis refused to accept it. In a 1926 letter, Lewis wrote, "Every compulsion is put upon writers to become safe, polite, obedient, and sterile. In protest, I declined election to the National Institute of Arts and Letters some years ago, and now I must decline the Pulitzer Prize." A film version of *Arrowsmith* was produced by Samuel Goldwyn in 1931.

In 1925 Lewis divorced his first wife. Three years later, in 1928, he married Dorothy Thompson, a newspaper foreign correspondent, with whom he traveled to London, Berlin, Vienna, and Moscow. Despite Lewis's increasing problems as a result of alcoholism, the couple remained married until 1942 and had one son, Michael.

Lewis's subsequent novels included *Elmer Gantry* (1927); *Dodsworth* (1929), which was adapted to the stage by Lewis and Sidney Howard in 1934; *Ann Vickers* (1933); *It Can't Happen Here* (1935); *Cass Timberlane* (1945); *Kingsblood Royal* (1947); and *World So Wide* (1951). In *Elmer Gantry*, the title character is a traveling salesman turned evangelist in this biting portrait of the business of religion, set in the Depression-era Midwest.

Lewis traveled often in his later years. He loved beautiful surroundings and enjoyed residences in several different locales. He had a stately old house in Williamstown, Massachusetts, and a grand, ostentatious villa in Florence, Italy. When he traveled, he always stayed in the very best hotels. After Lewis and Thompson divorced in 1942, he spent much of his time with a young actress, Marcella Powers, but she later married someone else. Lewis spent his final years in Europe, suffering from failing health after a life of heavy drinking and a serious skin disease that irritated his already short temper. During his final years, he hired secretaries to play chess with him and keep him company. He was alone when he died in Rome from complications of advanced alcoholism on January 10, 1951.

### Further Reading
Bloom, Harold, ed. *Sinclair Lewis*. New York: Chelsea, 1987.

Grebstein, Sheldon N. *Sinclair Lewis*. New York: Twayne Publishers, 1962.

Hutchisson, James M. *The Rise of Sinclair Lewis, 1920–1930*. University Park: Pennsylvania State University Press, 1996.

Lundquist, James. *Sinclair Lewis*. New York: Ungar, 1972, 1973.

Schorer, Mark. *Sinclair Lewis: An American Life*. New York: McGraw-Hill, 1961.

———. *Sinclair Lewis*. Minneapolis: University of Minnesota Press, 1963.

Sheean, Vincent. *Dorothy and Red*. Boston: Houghton Mifflin, 1963.

Sinclair Lewis was the first American to win the Nobel Prize in literature. *(Photo by Arnold Genthe. Library of Congress, Prints and Photographs Division [LC-USZ62-94694])*

### Lindsay, Vachel
### (Nicholas Vachel Lindsay)
(1879–1931)  *poet, nonfiction book writer*

A poet who became known during the early part of the 20th century as a modern-day troubadour, Vachel Lindsay traveled the United States and Europe, selling his poems and drawings. Lindsay gained quite a bit of popularity when Harriet Monroe, the editor of the newly founded *Poetry* in

Chicago, published his "General William Booth Enters into Heaven" as the lead poem in her fourth edition of the magazine. His true fame, however, derived from the recitations of his poems, which combined theater and oratory in an attempt to captivate the masses.

Nicholas Vachel Lindsay was born in Springfield, Illinois, on November 10, 1879, to physician Vachel Thomas Lindsay and Esther Catherine Frazee. Lindsay's parents were devout Campbellites, followers of a church founded in 1830 by Alexander Campbell, a Scotch-Irish clergyman who emphasized "individual spirituality, the missionary role of American democracy, and the hope for a nondenominational Christian church." These principles undoubtedly had a significant effect on Lindsay's choice to be a performing poet. When he was seven, Lindsay began keeping a diary, a practice he continued throughout his life. Each diary was inscribed with a dedication at the beginning that read "This book belongs to Christ" and with his diaries, Lindsay devoted himself to the redemptive process of art.

Lindsay attended Hiram College in Ohio, a Campbellite school, from 1897 to 1899, but never finished his degree. In 1901, he enrolled at the Art Institute of Chicago, where he studied until 1903. Although Lindsay never distinguished himself as an art student, his belief in the power of art and its importance never waned. He drew many illustrations of his poems during these years that were imitative of William Blake and the pre-Raphaelites. From Chicago, Lindsay moved to New York, where he studied for a year at the New York School of Art, spent lots of time admiring the Egyptian exhibits at the Metropolitan Museum of Art, and tried unsuccessfully to publish his poems.

Lindsay began to experience visions in the summer of 1904. His visions inspired his mystical poems, as well as drawings such as "Map of the Universe," which was reproduced as the frontispiece for his *Collected Poems*. In 1905, Lindsay began printing copies of his poems to sell on the streets of New York, thus establishing a pattern that would stick with him the rest of his life. His first journey as a wandering poet began in 1906, when he walked from Jacksonville, Florida, through Georgia, the Carolinas, Kentucky, and back to

Springfield, Illinois. Lindsay supported himself along the way by giving poetry recitals and lectures and selling copies of his poems. Following his return home to Springfield, Lindsay traveled with his family to Europe. Lindsay wrote another mystical poem following his return home to Springfield from Europe. "I Heard Immanuel Singing" was inspired by a vision Lindsay had of Christ the night his ship docked in New York.

In spring 1907, Lindsay began traveling again. Over the next few years, he lectured against racism and alcohol. During the summer and fall of 1909 he published his five *War Bulletins*, in which he attacked the evils of racial prejudice, greed, and urbanization. At this time, he also published his collection of poems *The Tramp's Excuse*.

Lindsay lived in Springfield from 1909 to 1912, during which time he published one issue of *The Village Magazine*, which consisted largely of editorials but drew attention from Hamlin Garland, a well-known Chicago novelist, who invited Lindsay to address the Cliff Dwellers, a club in Chicago for writers, artists, and professional men.

Lindsay embarked on his longest journey in the spring of 1912, when he set out from Springfield and headed for Los Angeles. His intention was to make a full loop, traveling up the coast to Seattle, before heading back east. Lindsay got as far as New Mexico before he gave up walking and took a train the rest of the way to Los Angeles. While there, he spent one month writing "General William Booth Enters into Heaven," a tribute to the founder of the Salvation Army. When Harriet Monroe published the poem in the fourth edition of *Poetry*, Lindsay's name became instantly known among the literary elite. Critics and other poets such as William Dean Howells and William Butler Yeats praised the poem, and Monroe became a devoted follower of Lindsay's work, introducing him to EDGAR LEE MASTERS and CARL SANDBURG and ensuring that Lindsay received a $100 prize for his poem.

Lindsay's first book, *General William Booth Enters into Heaven and Other Poems*, was published in the fall of 1913 by Mitchell Kennerley. The title poem of this first book and several other poems, including "The Congo," "The Chinese Nightingale," and "The Santa Fe Trail," were often recited by

Lindsay with his embellished combination of song and speech. He called these poems that were written for recitation "the Higher Vaudeville" and they became the mainstay of his career. Lindsay struggled the rest of his life to balance the demand for these performances with his pleasure in giving them and his knowledge that they took time away from his work by keeping him always on the road, traveling from one performance to the next.

Although Lindsay readily formed romantic attachments to women, they were almost always one-sided and unrealistic. In February 1914, he met the poet SARA TEASDALE, following a period in which they had been writing one another letters. He and Teasdale traveled together to New York, where Lindsay met many other writers, including Stephen Vincent Benet, THEODORE DREISER, and UPTON SINCLAIR. Lindsay's second book, *The Congo and Other Poems,* was published later that year by Macmillan. Mitchell Kennerley also published a book by Lindsay, *Adventures While Preaching the Gospel of Beauty,* which recounted his travels as a wandering poet. In November 1914, Lindsay learned that Teasdale had become engaged to a shoe manufacturer whom she married the very next month, news that left him confused and depressed.

Lindsay's fame continued to grow. In February 1915 he recited his work before President Woodrow Wilson's cabinet and received the Levinson Prize from *Poetry* magazine for his poem "The Chinese Nightingale." Lindsay's book on the motion picture revolution, called *The Art of the Moving Picture,* was published by Macmillan in 1915. Lindsay continued to travel throughout the United States and England, where he was always well received and was called by the *Observer* (London) "easily the most important living American poet." But Lindsay's reputation in the United States began to fail with the publication of *The Golden Book of Springfield,* a utopian prose work that was published in 1920.

Although he went on to publish other books, including *The Daniel Jazz and Other Poems* (1920), *The Candle in the Cabin: A Weaving Together of Script and Singing* (1926), *Going-to-the-Stars* (1926), *Johnny Appleseed* (1928), *Every Soul Is a Circus* (1929), *The Litany of Washington Street* (1929), and *Selected Poems* (1931), Lindsay's reputation contin-

ued its decline. He had also reached a point in his life where he no longer wanted to travel, but his financial success depended on it. As his work fell out of favor with critics, there was even greater need for Lindsay to continue his public recitations, which were as popular as ever. In January 1923, Lindsay traveled to Mississippi to deliver a recital at the Gulfport Junior College for Girls but collapsed and was forced to cancel the rest of his tour. It was during his period of recovery in Gulfport that Lindsay began to suffer paranoid delusions that would be with him the rest of his life.

Lindsay was diagnosed as epileptic in June 1924 at the Mayo Clinic in Rochester, Minnesota. He moved to Spokane, Washington, in July 1924, where he met and married Elizabeth Conner, a high school teacher. The couple had two children. By 1930, the delusions had begun to severely interfere with Lindsay's life. His literary reputation continued to decline, and his family life was also problematic, as he had unfounded delusions of his wife's infidelity. In 1930, he was made Doctor Honoris Causa by Hiram College, one of several honorary doctorates Lindsay received, but this was not enough to stop his mental decline. He had begun to threaten his wife and children with violence. On December 5, 1931, Lindsay committed suicide at home by drinking Lysol. His doctor reported the cause of death as heart failure. Vachel Lindsay's *Collected Poems* was published posthumously in 1933. This book has since been superseded by *The Poetry of Vachel Lindsay* (1984). *The Prose of Vachel Lindsay* (1988) collected in two volumes Lindsay's published prose, along with his drawings.

**Further Reading**

Engler, Balz. *Poetry and Community.* Tubingen, Germany: Stauffenburg, 1990.

Kronick, Joseph G. "Vachel Lindsay's Life." *Modern American Poetry.* Available online. URL: http://www.english.uiuc.edu/maps/poets/gl/lindsay/lindsaylife.htm. Posted March 18, 2001.

Massa, Ann. *Vachel Lindsay: Fieldworker for the American Dream.* Indianapolis: Indiana University Press, 1970.

Masters, Edgar Lee. *Vachel Lindsay, a Poet in America.* Frankfurt, Germany: Biblo-Moser, 1969.

## London, Jack
## (John Griffith London)
(1876–1916)  *novelist, short story writer*

Jack London fought his way up out of life among greasy factories and waterfront dives to become the most popular novelist and short story writer of his time. He wrote passionately and prolifically about the great questions of life and death, about the struggle to survive with dignity and integrity, and he did so by drawing from his own personal experiences—at sea off the Pacific coast, in Alaska during the Klondike gold rush, and even back to his days exhausting himself in factories for 10 cents an hour just to get by. Today, London's writing still appeals worldwide to the masses, for he addressed circumstances, trials, and emotions that everyone, regardless of social stature or location, has had to face. His adventure novels remain popular for their environmental and animal rights messages.

He was born on January 12, 1876, in San Francisco, California, to astrologer William Henry Chaney and music teacher and spiritualist Flora Wellman. At a young age London was abandoned by his father. Following his mother's second marriage, to John London, whose surname he took, London began a life of utter poverty, in which his family was forced to move frequently in search of subsistence. The era of an economy sustained by agriculture and farming was being rapidly replaced by one of industry and technology. London's family, along with countless others, were casualties of this American transition and thus, at a very young age, London set out as a "work beast," enduring 14-hour days, six and seven days a week for 10 cents an hour to augment his family's income. As a result of this struggle, London became engaged in the extreme left-wing liberal movements that were taking the country by storm. He adopted socialistic views as "a member of the protest armies of unemployed." He left school at the age of 14 and began living as a vagabond—riding freight trains, working as a seaman, and taking on other odd jobs to make ends meet. These transient years made London determined to better himself financially and intellectually; they also provided him with material that he would later infuse into such works as *The Sea-Wolf* (1904), which was partly based on his horrific

experiences as a sailor and *The Road* (1907), a collection of short stories that strongly inspired and influenced such later writers as JOHN STEINBECK and JACK KEROUAC.

Lacking much formal education, London educated himself in public libraries and gained, at age 19, admittance to the University of California at Berkeley. However, London abandoned his studies before he had completed his first year at Berkeley in search of instant wealth. He traveled north to Alaska where he took part in the Klondike gold rush of 1897. Sadly, London's attempt to strike gold never came to fruition and he spent that winter in Dawson City, British Columbia, suffering from scurvy before he returned the following spring to San Francisco. For the remainder of that year, London attempted to earn his living exclusively by writing. His early stories appeared in the *Overland Monthly* and *Atlantic Monthly*. In 1900 he married Elisabeth (Bess) Maddern, but (following his father's example) left her and their two young daughters three years later for Charmian Kittredge, whom he married on November 19, 1905.

In 1901, London ran unsuccessfully on the Socialist Party ticket for mayor of Oakland, California. He had also begun to steadily produce novels, nonfiction, and short stories, which quickly made him one of the most popular authors of his day. London's first novel, *The Son of the Wolf*, appeared in 1900 and gained a wide audience, as did his Alaska stories—*The Call of the Wild* (1903), in which a giant dog, Buck, finds his survival instincts in Yukon; *White Fang* (1906), in which White Fang, half wolf and half dog, is born to a starving pack of wolves, raised by an uncaring Indian, sold to an abusive man who forces him to fight other dogs, and then finally saved by another man who takes White Fang to California, where he mates with a collie and lives out the rest of his life in quiet domestic splendor; and *Burning Daylight* (1910).

In 1902, he went to England, where he studied the living conditions in the East End and other working-class areas of London, the capital city. His report about the economic degradation of the poor, *The People of the Abyss* (1903), was a surprise success in the United States, though it was heavily criticized in England. In the middle of his bitter marital separation in 1904, London traveled to Korea as a correspondent for William Randolph Hearst's newspapers to cover the war between Russia and Japan (1904–05). The following year he published his first collection of nonfiction pieces, *The War of the Classes*, which included his lectures on socialism. In 1907 London and his new wife, Charmian Kittredge, started aboard the *Snark*, embarking on a sailing trip around the world that was to last seven years. However, as a result of London's health, the couple was forced to shorten their journey, departing from Australia back to the United States after 26 months of sailing.

In 1910, London purchased a large tract of land near Glen Ellen in Sonoma County, California, where he devoted his energy, time, and money to expanding his property, on which his Beauty Ranch sat. In 1913, after having spent more than $80,000 on its reconstruction and when finishing touches were just being made, London watched in the middle of the night as his ranch burned to the ground, most likely the result of arson. During this time, London was told by his doctor that his kidneys were failing. The two tragedies drove London into a deep depression. Not only had his dreams of a brilliant new home been shattered, but he also found himself again suddenly penniless and desperate for work to make ends meet.

Debts, alcoholism, illness, and fear of losing his creativity darkened London's final years. He died on November 22, 1916, officially of gastrointestinal uremia. There have been speculations that London committed suicide with morphine, although evidence points otherwise. Two vials of morphine were found at London's bedside, but they did not contain the dose required for suicide. London was buried on Beauty Ranch.

### Further Reading

Auerbach, Johnathan. *Male Call: Becoming Jack London.* Durham, N.C.: Duke University Press, 1996.

Calder-Marshall, Arthur. *Lone Wolf: The Story of Jack London.* New York: Duell, Sloan and Pearce, 1962.

Hedrick, Joan D. *Solitary Comrade, Jack London and His Work.* Chapel Hill: University of North Carolina Press, 1982.

Kershaw, Alex. *Jack London: A Life.* New York: St. Martin's, 1997.

McClintock, James I. *White Logic: Jack London's Short Stories.* Grand Rapids, Mich.: Wolf House Books, 1975.

Perry, John. *Jack London, an American Myth.* Chicago: Nelson-Hall, 1981.

Watson, Charles N. *The Novels of Jack London: A Reappraisal.* Madison: University of Wisconsin Press, 1983.

## Longfellow, Henry Wadsworth
(1807–1882) *poet*

Henry Wadsworth Longfellow has long been one of the best-loved American poets around the world. The popularity and significance of his poetry is largely due to the ease of his rhyme. He wrote poetry with a natural grace and melody. Also, Longfellow wrote about themes that appeal to all kinds of people; his poems are easily understood. Above all, there is joyousness in them, a spirit of optimism and faith in the goodness of life; his writing evokes immediate responses in the emotions of his readers. Longfellow was also the first writer to address native themes in his poetry. He wrote about the American landscape and about Native American traditions. His most well-known works include *Song of Hiawatha* (1855), *The Courtship of Miles Standish* (1858), *Tales of a Wayside Inn* (1863), a translation of Dante's *The Divine Comedy* (1865–67), and *Christus: A Mystery* (1872).

Henry Wadsworth Longfellow was born in Portland, Maine (a district of Massachusetts at the time), on February 27, 1807. The second son of seven siblings, Henry was named after his uncle, Henry Wadsworth, who served in the navy aboard the fireship *Intrepid* and who heroically died aboard the ship in 1804. When he was just three years old, Longfellow attended school with his older brother Stephen. By age six he knew Latin grammar and could read, spell, and multiply. He then continued his education at the Portland Academy, where he remained until he enrolled in college. At the Portland Academy he studied algebra, Latin, and Greek, and his family hired a private tutor to teach him French. Longfellow's mother encouraged her children to participate in music, and as a result, Longfellow learned to play the piano and flute, which resulted in a lifelong love of music.

Longfellow started college at Bowdoin when he was only 14 years old. At age 19, ranking fourth in a class of 38 students, he delivered one of the commencement speeches during his graduation ceremony of 1825. After graduating, Longfellow was asked to become the first professor of modern languages at Bowdoin. He accepted the position with the provision that the college allow him to travel to Europe for study. Bowdoin initially offered him a salary of $1,000, but while Longfellow was in Europe, the college decided he was too young for the position of professor and offered him a tutorial position for less money. Furious, Longfellow declined the position. Bowdoin then reconsidered and offered Longfellow the professorship, provided he become the school librarian as well. Longfellow accepted the offer, with salaries of $800 as professor and $100 as librarian. After three years spent traveling throughout England, France, Germany, Holland, Italy, and Spain, Longfellow returned home in 1829 to teach at Bowdoin, where he remained for six years before taking a professorship at Harvard University in 1834. At Harvard, Longfellow served as Smith Professor of Modern Languages from 1836 to 1854.

Accompanied by his new wife, Mary Storer Potter, he returned in the early 1830s to Europe for a year to study German. Between appointments and meetings (he had letters of introduction to influential people), the two toured Denmark, England, Germany, Holland, Sweden, and Switzerland. Tragedy occurred in 1835 when Mary died of a miscarriage while the couple was in Rotterdam. Longfellow returned to Cambridge and, in 1839, published his first book of poems, *Voices of the Night.* He resigned from Harvard in 1854, believing that teaching interfered with his writing. In June of that year he started writing "The Song of Hiawatha" the classic epic poem about the relationship between a white man and a Native American. The rhyming poem is one of the first works of American literature to incorporate Native themes.

Eight months after Mary's death, while still in Europe, Longfellow met Frances Appleton (nick-

named Fanny), the daughter of prominent Boston merchant Nathan Appleton. Seven years after he returned to Cambridge, the two were reacquainted and, following a long courtship, they married on July 13, 1843. By this time, Nathan Appleton had purchased Boston's Craigie House (the former dwelling of George Washington) and later gave the home to Longfellow and his bride as a wedding gift. Their home became a meeting place for students as well as literary and philosophical figures such as RALPH WALDO EMERSON, NATHANIEL HAWTHORNE, Julia Ward Howe, and Charles Sumner. During their happy marriage, the couple had six children (two boys and four girls). Fanny became the first obstetric recipient of ether in the United States on April 7, 1847, during her third pregnancy. Her daughter, also named Fanny, died one year later. Longfellow based the heroine in "Hyperion," written in 1839, on his wife's experience. His children also heavily influenced his writing, as seen in his poem "The Children's Hour." Starting in 1857 with the first issue, *The Atlantic Monthly* magazine published more than 50 of Longfellow's poems. In 1858, Longfellow published *The Courtship of Miles Standish,* which sold more than 15,000 copies during the first week of publication.

Tragedy struck again on July 9, 1861, when Fanny and two of their daughters died in a house fire. While melting wax to seal envelopes containing cuttings of her children's hair, Fanny dropped a match onto her dress. Fanny was only 44 years old; their two youngest daughters were five and seven. Longfellow had tried to rescue Fanny by smothering the flames with a rug. As a result, he received terrible burns on his hands and face, and, since shaving became difficult due to scars from the fire, Longfellow grew a beard. Deeply depressed, he immersed himself in translating Dante into English and returned to Europe.

In 1868, Longfellow traveled one last time with his children to Europe where he received honorary degrees at Oxford and Cambridge in England. He was selected as a member of the Russian Academy of Sciences and of the Spanish Academy. He also immortalized the Wayside Inn in Sudbury, Massachusetts, with his *Tales of a Wayside Inn* in 1863. When the chestnut tree featured in his poem "A Village Blacksmith" ("Under a spreading chestnut tree") was cut down, the children of Cambridge collected pennies to have a chair made for Longfellow from the chestnut tree's wood for his 72nd birthday.

Longfellow published more than 20 books during his career. "The Bells of San Blas" (his last poem) was written close to March 24, 1882, the date he died at age 75 of peritonitis, which claimed his life within five days. Henry Wadsworth Longfellow is buried in Mount Auburn Cemetery in Cambridge, Massachusetts. Two years after his death, he was the first American poet whose bust was placed in the Poet's Corner in Westminster Abbey.

## Further Reading

Arvin, Newton. *Longfellow, His Life and Work.* Westport Conn.: Greenwood Publishing Group, 1977.

Hatfield, James. *New Light on Longfellow: With Special Reference to His Relations with Germany.* New York: Gordian Press, 1970.

Lukes, Bonnie L. *Henry Wadsworth Longfellow: America's Beloved Poet.* Greensboro, N.C.: Morgan Reynolds, 2002.

## Lopez, Barry
### (Barry Holstun Lopez)

(1945– ) *essayist, nonfiction writer, short story writer, novelist, nature writer*

Hailed by many critics as one of contemporary America's greatest nature writers, Barry Lopez explores the relationship between landscape and human culture. The author of more than a dozen books, including eight book-length collections of fiction, a novella-length fable, and six works of nonfiction, Lopez is a recipient of a National Book Award, the Literature Award from the American Academy of Arts and Letters, and the John Burroughs Medal, among others. His work has been widely translated and appears in many anthologies.

Barry Holstun Lopez was born in Port Chester, New York, in 1945 and grew up exploring the desert in an agricultural part of Southern California until the age of 11, when his mother remarried and he was transplanted to New York City. He has described how that first desert landscape of his childhood still plays a part in the way he perceives

the world. Lopez attended a Jesuit high school and then went on to study at Notre Dame University, where he earned an undergraduate degree in 1966 and then a graduate degree two years later. Lopez married his wife, Sandra, in 1967 and then went on to do further graduate study from 1969 to 1970 at the University of Oregon.

Lopez considered becoming a Trappist monk when he was a young man but decided that life would be too easy for him and determined to become a writer instead. Although he does accept occasional invitations to lecture or teach, he has worked almost soley at his writing since about 1970. His first book, *Desert Notes: Reflections in the Eye of a Raven* (1976), was the first of what eventually became a trilogy, including *River Notes: The Dance of Herons* (1979) and *Field Notes: The Grace Note of the Canyon Wren* (1994).

Lopez has long had a fascination with the history of Native people in the Northwest, and his second book was a collection of Indian legends titled *Giving Birth to Thunder, Sleeping with His Daughter* (1977). His third book, a nonfiction study called *Of Wolves and Men,* appeared in 1978 and remains one of his best-selling books. Lopez's first collection of short stories, *Winter Count,* was published in 1981 and also discusses American Indian history and culture as its subject.

In 1986, *Arctic Dreams: Imagination and Desire in a Northern Landscape,* another nonfiction study, catapulted Lopez into the literary spotlight when it won the National Book Award. Lopez has published frequently in national magazines and journals, such as *Harper's* and *The Paris Review,* and these essays and articles were collected in a book entitled *Crossing Open Ground* in 1988. Another collection of magazine pieces came out in 1991 entitled *The Rediscovery of America. Crow and Weasel,* a novella-length fable for children, was published in 1990 and includes his own illustrations. *About This Life* (1998) is a collection of essays that reveal the nature of the author, covering such diverse landscapes as the Arctic setting of his famous early book *Arctic Dreams* and the magical, organic process of pottery firing on the coast of Oregon. In *Light Action in the Caribbean* (2000), a collection of stories, Lopez does his best to prove that he can do more than nature writing. The title piece tells the story of a yuppie couple on a Caribbean vacation, but other of the book's tales more closely resemble his usual subject and style.

Lopez has been the Distinguished Visiting Writer at Eastern Washington University, a Beam Visiting Professor at the University of Iowa, the Welch Professor of American Studies at the University of Notre Dame, and a fiction teacher at the Bread Loaf Writers Conference. He has delivered memorial lectures at the University of Utah, the University of Kentucky, Bates College, the University of Missouri, and elsewhere.

In addition to traveling frequently to conduct research for his writing, Lopez is active in numerous collaborative projects with other artists. He has collaborated with composer John Luther Adams on several concert and theater productions and spoken at openings for sculptor Michael Singer and photographer Robert Adams. He has also written about painter Alan Magee, mask maker Lillian Pitt, and potter Richard Rowland. He collaborated with playwright Jim Leonard, Jr., on a theater production of "Crow and Weasel," which opened at the Children's Theatre in Minneapolis, and he worked with music producer Manfred Eicher at ECM Records in Munich. Currently he is working with Alan Magee on a fine press limited edition book and on a city monument in Portland, Oregon, with architect William Tripp. In 1997 he developed a fine press limited edition of his essay "Apologia" with artist Robin Eschner, designer Charles Hobson, and Sandy Tilcock at Lone Goose press. Lopez is also on the advisory board of Theater Grottesco in Santa Fe, and he has recently collaborated with writer E. O. Wilson in the design of a university curriculum that will combine the sciences and humanities in a new undergraduate major.

Lopez's other awards and honors include Guggenheim and Lannan fellowships, the John Hay Award for 2001, a Governor's Award, and Pushcart Prizes in fiction and nonfiction. He lives in rural western Oregon.

**Further Reading**

"An Interview with Barry Lopez." Capitola Book Café. Available online. URL: http://www.capitolabookcafe.com/andrea/lopez.html. Downloaded March 3, 2003.

Paul, Sherman. *Hewing to Experience: Essays and Reviews on Recent American Poetry and Poetics, Nature and Culture.* Iowa City: University of Iowa Press, 2003.

Richards, Linda. "An Interview with Barry Lopez." January Magazine. Available online. URL: http://www.januarymagazine.com/profiles/blopez.html. Downloaded March 3, 2003.

## Lorde, Audre
**(Adise Gamba, Audre Geraldine Lorde)**
(1934–1992)  *poet, essayist, memoirist*

Audre Lorde was an intensely passionate American poet and activist. Her provocative writing reflects her deeply held convictions regarding love, anger, civil rights, politics, and sexuality. During her life, Lorde's voice offered hope and leadership to a generation struggling to define itself in the face of social turmoil and transition. She became a role model specifically for black woman, but she inspired all those who believed, as she did, that "liberation is not the private province of any one particular group."

Audre Geraldine Lorde was born to a middle-class West Indian immigrant parents in New York City. She grew up in Manhattan attending Roman Catholic schools. Lorde attended the National University of Mexico in 1954; Hunter College in New York City, where she earned her B.A. degree in 1959; and Columbia University in 1961, where she earned her master's degree in library science. As a young girl, Lorde was inarticulate and assumed mute until the age of five. Although she became passionately interested in reading at a young age and even began writing poetry at age 12, she was discouraged from doing so by her parents. Lorde published her first poem at the age of 15. She had written of her first love affair, with a boy in Hunter High School, but her teacher told her it was too romantic. On her own, Lorde sent the poem to *Seventeen* magazine because the school would not print it, and thus commenced her career in poetry. She proceeded to publish more than a dozen books on poetry and six books of prose.

Lorde worked as a librarian while refining her talents as a writer. In 1968, amid escalating racial tensions, she accepted an invitation to become the poet in residence at Tougaloo College, a small black college in Jackson, Mississippi, where the violence that greeted the Civil Rights movement was constantly close at hand. "It changed my life," Lorde recalled. "I had a chance to work with young black poets in what was essentially a crisis situation. White townspeople were shooting up the edges of Tougaloo at night. Many of the students had been arrested. I realized I could take my art in the realest way and make it do what I wanted. I began bringing together my poetry and my deepest held convictions."

Lorde's first volume of poetry, *The First Cities,* was also published in 1968. Her second volume, *Cables to Rage* (1970), first published abroad, focused on themes of birth, love, and betrayal. In 1972 Lorde received a Creative Artists Public Service grant, and a year later she published her third book of poetry, *From a Land Where Other People Live.* Nominated for a National Book Award, this volume addressed issues of global injustice and oppression as well as personal themes concerning motherhood. *New York Head Shot and Museum,* probably her most political and rhetorical work, was published in 1974. Written from the perspective of a city dweller, the poems express Lorde's vision of life in New York City, focusing specifically on what it is like to be a woman, a mother, and black. The first of Lorde's books to be accepted by a major publisher was *Coal,* which came out in 1976. A compilation of her first two books, *Coal* attracted a wider audience to her work. Her seventh book of poetry, *The Black Unicorn* (1978), is considered to be her most personal work and is thought to reveal Lorde at the height of her poetic vision. Poet and critic ADRIENNE RICH said of *The Black Unicorn,* "refusing to be circumscribed by any simple identity, Audre Lorde writes as a Black woman, a mother, a daughter, a Lesbian, a feminist, a visionary; poems of elemental wildness and healing, nightmare and lucidity."

Lorde went on to provide avenues of expression to future generations of writers by cofounding Kitchen Table: Women of Color Press. She was at the center of the movement to preserve and celebrate African-American culture at a time when the destruction of these institutions was on the rise. Her dedication extended beyond international boundaries when she formed the Sisterhood in Support of Sisters in South Africa. She was also one of the featured speakers at the First National March for Gay and Lesbian Liberation in Washington, D.C. in 1979. In 1989, she helped organize disaster relief efforts for St. Croix, U.S. Virgin Islands, in the wake of Hurricane Hugo.

A 14-year struggle with cancer led Lorde to publish her first prose collection, *The Cancer Journals,* which won the American Library Association Gay Caucus Book of the Year for 1981. In the autobiographical account of her struggle with the breast cancer that ultimately claimed her life, Lorde explores the feeling of hopelessness and despair as she faces death. She felt that this book gave her strength and power to explore her experience with cancer and to share it with other women. Lorde continued her prose writing with *Zami: A New Spelling of My Name* (1982), a "biomythography" about the difficult relationship between a mother and her daughter; *Sister Outsider: Essays and Speeches* (1984); and *A Burst of Light* (1988). Her final poetry collections included *Chosen Poems Old and New* (1982) and *Our Dead behind Us* (1986). Audre Lorde died of cancer in St. Croix on November 17, 1992.

**Further Reading**

"Audre Lorde: A Special Section." *Callaloo* 14, no. 1 (winter 1991): 39–95.

Burr, Zofia. *Of Women, Poetry, and Power.* Urbana: University of Illinois Press, 2002.

Hall, Lynda. "Passion(ate) Plays 'Whenever We Found Space': Lorde and Gomez Queer(y)ing Boundaries and Acting In." *Callaloo* 23, no. 1 (winter 2000): 394–421.

Keating, Analouise. *Women Reading Women Writing: Self-Invention in Paula Gunn Allen, Gloria Anzaldúa, and Audre Lorde.* Philadelphia: Temple University Press, 1996.

## Lowell, Amy
### (Amy Lawrence Lowell)
### (1874–1925) *poet, biographer*

Amy Lowell may best be remembered for popularizing the imagist movement of writing in America.

Her own work, full of lush imagery but slim on excess verbiage, was similar to that of H. D. (Hilda Doolittle) and EZRA POUND. Lowell, a fan of such writing, traveled to England to research the movement and ended up bringing back volumes of poetry to fully introduce imagist work to the United States. Lowell dedicated her life to poetry, promoting and teaching aspiring American poets and often acting as their patron. She also wrote many essays, translated the works of others, and wrote literary biographies. Her two-volume biography of Keats was well received in the United States, though it was rejected in England as presumptuous. Her most well-known poetic works include *A Dome of Many-Colored Glass* (1912), *Sword Blades and Poppy Seed* (1914), *Men, Women and Ghosts* (1916), and *What's a Clock* (1925), for which she won the Pulitzer Prize.

Amy Lawrence Lowell was born on February 9, 1874, to Augustus Lowell and Katherine Bigelow Lawrence Lowell. Her family was Episcopalian, of old New England stock, and at the top of Boston society. Lowell was the youngest of five children. Her elder brother Abbott Lawrence, a freshman at Harvard at the time of her birth, went on to become president of Harvard College. Raised on a 10-acre estate named Sevenels, Lowell first received tutoring at home by governesses before she attended private schools in Boston until the age of 17, when she secluded herself in the 7,000-book library at Sevenels to study literature. Lowell was encouraged to write from an early age. In 1887 she, with her mother and sister, wrote *Dream Drops or Stories from Fairy Land by a Dreamer,* printed privately by the Boston firm Cupples and Hurd. Her poem "Fixed Idea" was published in 1910 by the *Atlantic Monthly,* after which Lowell published individual poems in various journals. In October 1912, Houghton Mifflin published her first collection, *A Dome of Many-Colored Glass.*

Actress Ada Russell became the love of Lowell's life. The two met in 1909 and they remained together until Amy's death in 1925. Amy wrote many poems about Ada. In the beginning, as with her previous poems about women, she wrote in such a way that only those who knew the inspiration for a poem would recognize its lesbian content. But as time went on, she censored her work less and less. By the time she wrote *Pictures of the Floating World* (1919) her poems about Ada were much more blatantly erotic. The series "Planes of Personality: Two Speak Together" chronicles their relationship, including the intensely erotic poem "A Decade" that celebrates their 10th anniversary.

Lowell, a vivacious and outspoken businesswoman, tended to excite controversy. She was deeply interested in and influenced by the imagist movement, led by Ezra Pound. The primary imagists were Pound, Ford Madox Ford, H. D. (Hilda Doolittle), and Richard Aldington. This Anglo-American movement believed, in Lowell's words, that "concentration is of the very essence of poetry" and strove to "produce poetry that is hard and clear, never blurred nor indefinite." Lowell campaigned for the success of imagist poetry in America and embraced its principles in her own work. She acted as a publicity agent for the movement, editing and contributing to an anthology of imagist poets in 1915. Her enthusiastic involvement and influence contributed to Pound's separation from the movement. (Pound felt Lowell overexploited the format, making the style seem too technically neat. He stated that Lowell had altered the style, shifting it to "Lowellism.") As Lowell continued to explore the imagist style, she pioneered the use of "polyphonic prose" in English, mixing formal and free verse. Later she was drawn to and influenced by Chinese and Japanese poetry. This interest led her to collaborate with translator Florence Ayscough on *Fir-Flower Tablets* in 1921. Lowell had a lifelong love for the British poet John Keats, whose letters she collected and whose influence can be seen in her poems. She believed him to be the forbearer of imagism. Her biography of Keats was published in 1925, the same year she won the Pulitzer Prize for her collection *What's a Clock.* Other works by Lowell include two books of criticism—*Six French Poets,* (1915) featuring symbolist poets who were not well-known in America, and *Tendencies in Modern American Poetry* (1917).

Afflicted by chronic hernia problems since 1916, Lowell underwent numerous corrective operations, but she never let her illness interfere with her poetry. Then, on May 10, 1925, she canceled a lecture tour after suffering from her most serious hernia attack. Two days later, Lowell died on her Brookline estate of a cerebral hemorrhage.

## Further Reading

Galvin, Mary. *Queer Poetics: Five Modernist Women Writers.* Westport, Conn.: Greenwood Press, 1999.

Hughes, Glenn. *Imagism and the Imagists: A Study in Modern Poetry.* New York: Biblo and Tannen, 1972.

MacNair, Harley Farnsworth. *Florence Ayscough and Amy Lowell: Correspondence of a Friendship.* Chicago: University of Chicago Press, 1945.

## Lowell, Robert
### (Robert Traill Spence Lowell IV)
(1917–1977) *poet*

Robert Lowell was an American poet noted for his complex poetry and turbulent life, which was entangled with the social, political, and ideological movements in the United States during the post–World War II decades. Lowell was named the father of the confessional poets, a term used to describe, among others, SYLVIA PLATH, ANNE SEXTON, and JOHN BERRYMAN. Confessional poetry has been called a "poetry of pain." It was distinguished by its introspective focus on the dark side of life and its often autobiographical sources. It revolutionized poetry by breaking all taboos about appropriate topics. For the Confessional poets, no topic was too sensitive or sacred to be dissected in a poem. Alcoholism, suicide attempts, mental breakdowns, and marriage troubles were all fair game. During his career Lowell was twice awarded the Pulitzer Prize, as well as the Bollingen Poetry Award and the National Book Award.

Robert Traill Spence Lowell IV was born on March 1, 1917, in Boston, Massachusetts to Robert Traill Spence Lowell III, a naval officer, and Charlotte (Winslow) Lowell. He was a member of one of Boston's oldest and most intellectually distinguished families, whose members included the poet and critic James Russell Lowell and the poet AMY LOWELL. Lowell began writing at St. Mark's School in Boston, where his teacher was the poet Richard Eberhart. He then attended Harvard College for two years before, in response to his family's forbiddance of his marriage proposal to short

story writer and novelist Jean Stafford, he transferred to Kenyon College, where he earned his B.A. degree in 1940. That same year, Lowell married Stafford and, also against his family wishes, converted to Roman Catholicism as a repudiation of his ancestors' New England Protestantism. Lowell and Stafford soon moved to Louisiana, where he took graduate courses at the state university and studied with ROBERT PENN WARREN and Cleanth Brooks.

In the beginning of World War II, Lowell attempted to enlist in the armed forces, but was rejected due to poor eyesight. In 1943, though, he received a conscription notice. However, shocked and dismayed by the Allied firebombing of civilians in German cities such as Dresden, Lowell had declared himself a conscientious objector. As a result he served five months in prison, an experience that formed the basis of "Memories of West Street and Lepke." During these months, he finished and published his first book, *Land of Unlikeness.* The following year, he revised the book and published the new version as *Lord Weary's Castle* in 1946, for which he received a Pulitzer Prize at the age of 30. During the late 1940s, Lowell's personal life was full of marital and psychological turmoil. He suffered from severe episodes of manic-depression, for which he was repeatedly hospitalized. He and Stafford divorced in 1948 and in 1949 Lowell married the novelist and critic Elizabeth Hardwick.

During the next several years, Lowell and Hardwick traveled abroad, spending a large amount of time in Italy. While overseas Lowell suffered a number of mental breakdowns, which resulted from the manic-depression that plagued him throughout his life. After his mother's death in 1954 (his father died in 1950), Lowell was hospitalized at McLean Hospital in Massachusetts.

After being absent from the literary scene for a period of time, Lowell's publication of *Life Studies* in 1959 renewed his reputation; the book received the National Book Award in 1960. Though some readers intensely disliked the new poems, finding them both technically slack and personally embarrassing, many readers viewed the book as nothing short of a shift in the American poetic landscape. It was *Life Studies,* more than any other book, that inaugurated what eventually became the Confessional school and secured a place for Lowell as its leader. During the early 1960s, Lowell was energetically involved in both poetry and politics. He befriended Jacqueline Kennedy and her brother-in-law Robert Kennedy, as well as Senator Eugene McCarthy. He addressed, in such poems as "For the Union Dead," the dreadful possibility of the nuclear annihilation of humanity and condemned the popular culture that endorsed this possibility. During this period Lowell also published *Imitations*, a collection of loose translations of poems by Rainer Maria Rilke, Arthur Rimbaud, and others, which won the Bollingen Poetry Translation Prize in 1962.

In 1972 Lowell divorced Elizabeth Hardwick. During the 1970s he lived in England, where he was a visiting fellow at All Souls College, Oxford, and a visiting lecturer at the University of Essex and the University of Kent. In 1973 Lowell published three collections of poetry: *History* recreated a host of historical figures from biblical times to the present. In *For Lizzie and Harriet* he talked about Hardwick and his daughter. *The Dolphin* dealt with Lowell's move to England as he left one wife for another. For *The Dolphin*, Lowell was awarded another Pulitzer Prize.

Robert Lowell died of heart failure at the age of 60, on September 12, 1977, in New York. His last collection, *Day by Day*, a record of his painful domestic history, received posthumously in 1978 the National Book Critics Circle Award. In this work Lowell abandoned the sonnet form for an irregular free verse.

**Further Reading**

Axelrod, S. G. *Robert Lowell: Life and Art.* Princeton, N.J.: Princeton University Press, 1978.

Fein, R. J. *Robert Lowell.* Boston: Twayne Publishers, 1979.

Hamilton, Ian. *Robert Lowell.* New York: Random House, 1982.

Mariani, P. *Lost Puritan: A Life of Robert Lowell.* New York: W. W. Norton, 1994.

Meuers, J. *Robert Lowell: Interview and Memoirs.* Ann Arbor: University of Michigan Press, 1988.

Stuart, Sarah Payne. *My First Cousin Once Removed.* New York: HarperCollins, 1998.

# M

## Mailer, Norman
### (Norman Kingsley Mailer)
(1923–   ) *novelist*

Norman Mailer gained notoriety for developing a form of writing that combined actual events, autobiography, and political commentary with fictional detail and character building. One of the most controversial and best-known writers of the latter half of the 20th century, Mailer has written more than 30 books. *The Armies of the Night* (1968), a narrative about the 1967 peace march on Washington, D.C., won the National Book Award and the Pulitzer Prize for nonfiction. *The Executioner's Song* (1980), his "true-life novel" that chronicled the life and death of convict Gary Gilmore, won the Pulitzer Prize in fiction. Mailer has generated controversy for his free-form journalistic style, as well as for his views on women and aspects of American life.

Norman Kingsley Mailer was born in Long Branch, New Jersey, on January 31, 1923. He was the first child of Fanny Schneider, an adoring mother, and Isaac Barnett Mailer, a South African Jewish bookkeeper. In 1927 his family moved to Eastern Parkway in Brooklyn, New York, where Mailer attended Boys High School. He grew up working class. At age nine he wrote a 250-page story called "Invasion from Mars." He graduated from high school in 1939 and at age 16 entered Harvard University. A short story, "The Greatest Thing in the World," which he wrote for the Harvard *Advocate*, won *Story* magazine's college fiction

Norman Mailer became controversial for blurring the boundaries between fact and fiction in his writing. Despite this, his works have won him some of the highest honors in American letters, including two Pulitzer Prizes and a National Book Award. *(Library of Congress, Prints and Photographs Division [LC-USZ62-42506])*

prize. Mailer graduated from Harvard in 1943 with a degree in aeronautical engineering.

When he was inducted into the army in 1944, Mailer wanted to go to Europe and be in the first wave of U.S. invasion troops. Instead, he was sent to the South Pacific where he worked as a surveyor, an intelligence clerk, and a rifleman with a reconnaissance platoon in the Philippine mountains. A fellow soldier later remembered that Mailer "had more combat with his supervisors than he did with the enemy." After he was discharged in 1946, Mailer enrolled at the Sorbonne in Paris. He used his experiences in World War II as the basis for a novel, *The Naked and the Dead* (1948). The book is praised for its skillful portrayal of both the gritty reality of ground combat and the complex intrigue of ideological conflicts at the strategic level. It was a critical and commercial success and brought Mailer, then age 25, immediate recognition as one of America's most promising writers. "Its success ripped away my former identity," Mailer has said.

He worked as a scriptwriter in Hollywood in the late 1940s and then moved to Greenwich Village in New York City. His next novels, *Barbary Shore* (1951) and *The Deer Park* (1955), did not receive acclaim that matched *The Naked and the Dead*. Mailer then turned his literary energies to journalism. Sex, drugs, and politics were Mailer's favorite themes throughout the 1950s. He helped found *The Village Voice* in 1954 and was editor of *Dissent* from 1952 until 1963.

Mailer in the mid-1950s began to gain fame as an anti-establishment essayist. In his essay "The White Negro: Superficial Reflections on the Hipster," Mailer defined the hipster as a philosophical psychopath and urban adventurer who had adopted elements from black culture and could be called "a White Negro." The essay was reprinted in Mailer's *Advertisements for Myself* (1959), a collection of essays, letters, and other writing from himself and others on his favorite themes of sex, drugs, and politics. Mailer received considerable attention for the work because it contained autobiographical passages of the pressures of success, money, liquor, and the literary marketplace on the serious American writer. Mailer had married artist Adele Morales in 1954. Their union was chaotic, and in

1960 Mailer stabbed her at the end of an all-night party in Manhattan with "a dirty three-inch penknife." Mailer had been planning to run for mayor. He was given a suspended sentence because Morales refused to press charges. She published a memoir, *The Last Party*, in 1997.

In the 1960s Mailer was listed among the New Journalists, who applied the techniques of novel writing to depict real events and people. Mailer was nominated for a National Book Award for *Why Are We in Vietnam?* (1967). He was jailed the year it was published for his role in demonstrations against the Vietnam War. *The Armies of the Night*, released in 1968, won both the Pulitzer Prize and the National Book Award, and brought Mailer both popular and critical acclaim. In *The Armies of the Night*, Mailer used the techniques of a novel to explore the 1967 antiwar march in Washington, D.C., during which he was arrested. His next book, *Miami and the Siege of Chicago* (1968), won a National Book Award for nonfiction. He also wrote *Of a Fire on the Moon* (1970), about the Apollo II moon landing.

Mailer's *The Prisoner of Sex* (1971) triggered the anger of many feminists. In the book, he proposed that gender might determine the way a person perceives and orders reality. He wrote *Marilyn* (1973), a biography of the life and career of Marilyn Monroe (with whom he had had a romantic relationship), and *The Fight* (1975), an account of the legendary bout between Muhammad Ali and George Foreman in Zaire.

Mailer returned to a book of the same epic proportions as *The Naked and the Dead* with *The Executioner's Song* (1980), a novel on the life and execution of real-life convicted murderer Gary Gilmore. *The Executioner's Song* won Mailer his second Pulitzer Prize and it also was nominated for the American Book Award and National Book Critics Circle Award. "A really great novel does not have something to say. It has the ability to stimulate the mind and spirit of the people who come in contact with it," Mailer has said. He wrote a 1,300-page novel about the Central Intelligence Agency titled *Harlot's Ghost* (1992), which he considered one of his best books. While gathering material for it, Mailer also found previously unknown Russian documents for *Oswald's Tale* (1995), his exhaustive biography of Lee Harvey Oswald.

Mailer has said that writing is similar to boxing, his favorite sport. Carolyn T. Hughes quoted him in *Poets & Writers* as saying,

There's one way in which they're very much alike, and that's the loneliness. A boxer is one of the loneliest people on earth about the time he gets in that ring. Even two days before the fight he can't get to sleep, thinking about the prowess of his opponent. It's that kind of immense inner fear of humiliation. Those lonely fears are analogous, although they're much more intense than the writer's fears, but I tell you, there's something terribly lonely about that blank page you face day after day, year after year.

In addition to his books, Mailer also has written, produced, directed, and acted in several films. The film *Tough Guys Don't Dance*, based on his 1984 novel, was well received at the 1987 Cannes Film Festival. Mailer also wrote the script for the film version of *The Executioner's Song* and received an Emmy nomination for best adaptation. He has been married six times and has nine children.

## Further Reading

Leigh, Nigel. *Radical Fictions and the Novels of Norman Mailer.* New York: St. Martin's Press, 1990.

Lennon, J. Michael, ed. *Conversations with Norman Mailer.* Jackson: University Press of Mississippi, 1988.

Mills, Hilary. *Mailer: A Biography.* New York: McGraw-Hill, 1984.

Poirier, Richard. *Norman Mailer.* New York: Viking, 1972.

Whalen-Bridge, John. "Norman Mailer." *Dictionary of Literary Biography.* Detroit: Gale, 1995: pp. 217–232.

## Malamud, Bernard

(1914–1986) *novelist, short story writer*

Bernard Malamud highlighted the struggles of ordinary men in his novels and short stories, many of which drew on his Jewish tradition. The theme of moral wisdom gained through suffering permeated his work. His parables out of Jewish immigrant life relied upon myth, legend, and magic. Malamud once described himself as a chronicler of "simple people struggling to make their lives better in a world of bad luck." He won the National Book Award and the Pulitzer Prize for *The Fixer* (1966), which was inspired by the story of a Jew who was tried for the ritual murder of a Christian in czarist Russia. Malamud's first collection of short stories, *The Magic Barrel,* won the National Book Award in 1959.

Bernard Malamud was born in Brooklyn, New York, on April 26, 1914. He was the elder of two sons of Russian Jewish immigrants, Max Malamud and Bertha Fidelman. His father ran a small grocery store, working 16 hours a day. Malamud later recalled that there were no books in his home and that he found cultural nourishment only on Sundays, when he would listen to someone else's piano through the living-room window. He attended Erasmus Hall High School in Brooklyn, and received his Bachelor of Arts degree from the City College of New York in 1936.

After graduation, Malamud wrote in his spare time while working in a factory, in various stores, and as a clerk in the Census Bureau in Washington, D.C. World War II and the Holocaust convinced Malamud that he had something to say as a writer. The war made him think much deeper about what it meant to be Jewish and compelled him to learn more about Jewish tradition and history. He got a job teaching at Erasmus Hall High School in 1940 and continued teaching in New York City high schools at night until 1949. While he was teaching, he earned a master's degree at Columbia University. He married Ann de Chiara in 1945 and they soon had a son, Paul.

Malamud got a job teaching English at Oregon State University in 1949, becoming an associate professor. His first novel, *The Natural* (1952), was a fable about the rise and fall of a baseball hero who is gifted with miraculous powers. It is different from most of his work in that there are no Jewish characters. Many critics consider his second novel, *The Assistant* (1957), to be his best. It tells of the relationship between a Jewish grocery-store owner, based on Malamud's father, and his Italian assistant during the Great Depression. Malamud's first collection of short stories, *The Magic Barrel,* won the National Book Award in 1959. In 1961, Malamud began teaching at Bennington College, in Vermont, where he taught for more than 20 years, with the exception of two years he spent as a visiting lecturer at Harvard from 1966 to 1968. His prize-winning novel *The Fixer* (1966) was inspired by the ordeal of Mendel Beiliss, a Jew tried and acquitted of ritual murder in Kiev in czarist Russia in 1913.

Critics had begun to think of Malamud as a primarily Jewish writer, along with SAUL BELLOW and PHILIP ROTH. Malamud, however, said that the three writers shared fewer similarities than differences, and that, in his case, Jewishness was more a spiritual than a cultural or a religious quality. After *The Natural* was made into a movie starring Robert Redford in 1984, Malamud said in an interview that he was grateful for the film because it allowed him "to be recognized once more as an American writer," as opposed to solely as a Jewish writer.

Malamud's other novels are: *A New Life* (1961), *The Tenants* (1971), *Dubin's Lives* (1979), and *God's Grace* (1982). His later works received mixed reviews, Although some critics saw growth in these novels, many critics cited a growing bleakness in his work. They said that his argument with God took on the feel of a seminar. Malamud acknowledged that sadness was one of his prime topics. "People say I write so much about misery," he said, but added, "you write about what you write best." He described the essential Malamud character as "someone who fears his fate, is caught up in it, yet manages to outrun it; he's the subject and object of laughter and pity."

Some critics believe Malamud's greatest talent was most apparent in his short stories. They were told in a spare, compressed prose that reflected the terse speech of their immigrant characters. In the stories, magical events often occur in grim city neighborhoods. In "The Jewbird," a Yiddish-accented vagabond enters an urban Jewish household in the form of a crow; in "Idiots First," the Angel of Death pursues a desperate Jew trying to scrape together enough money to send his idiot son to California on the midnight train. In addition to *The Magic Barrel,* Malamud's other short-story col-

lections include *Idiots First* (1963), *Pictures of Fidelman* (1969), and *Rembrandt's Hat* (1973).

Malamud was a firm believer that a story should tell a story. "With me, it's story, story, story," he once said. "Writers who can't invent stories often pursue other strategies, even substituting style for narrative. I feel that story is the basic element of fiction, though that ideal is not popular with disciples of the 'new novel.' They remind me of the painter who couldn't paint people, so he painted chairs."

In addition to the Pulitzer Prize and the National Book Awards, Malamud won the Rosenthal Award of the National Institute of Arts and Letters, Vermont's 1979 Governor's Award for Excellence in the Arts, and the 1981 Brandeis Creative Arts Award. He was a member of the American Academy and Institute of Arts and Letters, which in 1983 presented him its Gold Medal in Fiction. From 1979 to 1981 he was president of the PEN American Center. Malamud died on March 18, 1986, in Manhattan, at age 71. He was married with two children.

### Further Reading

Giroux, Robert. "Introduction" in *The Complete Stories.* Farrar, Straus & Giroux, 1997, pp. ix–xv.

———. "Introduction" in *The People and Uncollected Stories.* New York: Farrar, Straus & Giroux, 1989, pp. vii–xvi.

Lasher, Lawrence M., ed. *Conversations with Bernard Malamud.* Jackson: University Press of Mississippi, 1991.

## Mamet, David
### (David Alan Mamet)
(1947– ) *playwright, screenwriter*

David Mamet is one of a handful of American playwrights whose work has found almost as much success on the screen as it has on the stage. He is recognized for his strong male characters and the low-key, yet highly charged, verbal confrontations between them. He often portrays the plight of small-time drifters, salesmen, and hoods and the con games they play. Although reminiscent of such playwrights as HAROLD PINTER and SAMUEL BECKETT,

Mamet's clipped, gritty dialogue has become known as "Mametspeak." His plays often deal with the decline of morality in a world that has become an emotional and spiritual wasteland. He won the Pulitzer Prize for his play *Glengarry Glen Ross* (1984), which depicted competition among men at a Chicago real-estate office and was a scathing representation of American business practices. Mamet has also gained respect as a director and screenwriter.

David Alan Mamet was born in Chicago on November 30, 1947, and grew up in a small Jewish neighborhood on the south side of Chicago. His mother, Lenore Mamet, left her husband, a labor lawyer, and David and his sister lived with her and their stepfather until Mamet moved in with his father. Mamet studied at Goddard College in Vermont and at the Neighborhood Playhouse School of Theater in New York. He returned to his hometown of Chicago to found the St. Nicholas Theatre Company and also worked for a time as the artistic director of the famed Goodman Theatre.

Mamet began his career as an actor and director before achieving acclaim for three Off-Off Broadway plays: *Sexual Perversity in Chicago* (1974) was a bitingly humorous look at how modern society makes fulfilling relationships hard to come by. It was followed by *The Duck Variations* (1976), another comedy. *American Buffalo* (1976), which won the New York Drama Critics Circle Award in 1977, was a tragedy built around the American Dream.

His next plays *The Woods* (1977) and *Edmond* (1982) were followed by two enormously successful works, the Pulitzer Prize–winning *Glengarry Glen Ross* (1984) and *Speed-the-Plow* (1987). *Speed-the-Plow* exposed the dirty underside of the show business industry. *Glengarry Glen Ross* was later made into a film version in 1992 using Mamet's own script.

Beginning in the late 1970s, Mamet turned to writing for film, starting with *The Postman Always Rings Twice* (1981), adapted from the novel by James M. Cain. He then wrote screenplays for *The Verdict* (1982), with Paul Newman as a washed-up Boston lawyer, and *The Untouchables* (1987), a blockbuster update of the television series. Mamet made his film directorial debut with *House of Games* (1987), which he also wrote. It was a slick, engrossing study of confidence trickery.

Perhaps Mamet's most controversial play was *Oleanna* (1992), a two-character drama involving charges of sexual harassment between a male professor and one of his female students. He also wrote and directed the screen version of the play. Mamet has been criticized by feminists for his portrayal of women.

Mamet's plays often concern the everyday dramas of urban, working-class people—the small-time con artist, the cutthroat salesman, the ingenious factory worker. Mamet is most often credited with his unique sense of dialogue, which often includes cursing and other offensive language. He attributes his ear for dialogue to listening to his father talk and to several years of piano lessons, which gave him a feel for the musicality in speech. "Mamet deserves recognition for his careful, gorgeous, loving sense of language," wrote the *Village Voice*. "He has the most acute ear for dialogue of any American writer since J. D. Salinger."

"It's all very flattering, but it's also natural," Mamet has said of praise for his work. "Someone like me, who's been writing for a long time, naturally people coming up will look and say that's a good idea. Just like I would look at the works of Harold Pinter or Samuel Beckett and say that's good idea. The old phrase is 'Talent borrows, genius robs.' I don't mind if somebody wants to write like me. The only thing that disturbs me is if they do it better."

The autobiographical book *The Cabin: Reminiscence and Diversions* was published in 1992. Mamet has written poetry, two novels, a few children's books, and many essays. His 1997 acting handbook, *True and False*, received mixed reactions from the theatrical establishment. After writing the fairly unsuccessful *The Edge* (1997), an adventure drama starring Anthony Hopkins and Alec Baldwin, Mamet returned to the screen in 1999 with *The Winslow Boy*. It was a radical change in material for Mamet—an Edwardian courtroom drama originally written by famed British playwright Terence Rattigan—quite different from the raw, foul-mouthed work to which Mamet owed his fame. *The Winslow Boy* received critical acclaim and stood as a sizable testament to the playwright's versatility. His other screenplays include *The Spanish Prisoner* (1998) and *State and Main* (2000). He wrote and directed both films.

Mamet has taught at Goddard College, the Yale Drama School, and New York University. His awards include the Joseph Jefferson Award (1974); Obie Award (1976, 1983); New York Drama Critics Circle Award (1977, 1984); Outer Circle Award (1978); Society of West End Theatre Award (1983); Pulitzer Prize (1984); Dramatists Guild Hall-Warriner Award (1984); American Academy Award (1986); and Tony Award (1987).

Mamet regularly lectures at the Atlantic Theater Company, of which he is a founding member. Mamet's first wife was actress Lindsay Crouse. They have two daughters. He is currently married to actress Rebecca Pidgeon, who has appeared in many of his films. They have one daughter.

### Further Reading

Carroll, Dennis. *David Mamet*. New York: Macmillan, 1987.

Dean, Anne. *David Mamet: Language as Dramatic Action.* Teaneck, N.J.: Fairleigh Dickinson University Press, 1990.

Kane, Leslie, ed. *David Mamet: A Casebook.* New York: Garland, 1992.

## Masters, Edgar Lee
(1869–1950)  *poet, editor*

Although Edgar Lee Masters wrote prolifically throughout his life, many people consider him a "one-hit wonder." His *Spoon River Anthology* (1915)—a collection of fictitious epitaphs in free verse revealing the secret lives of dead citizens—was acclaimed for its treatment of small-town American life and gained him popularity and admiration, but it also became the standard by which all his other works were measured. Masters published numerous essays, poems, and stories, but nothing he produced was ever considered equal to his first masterpiece. Thus, despite a prolific career, Masters's position in literary history remains dubious.

Edgar Lee Masters was born on August 23, 1869, in Garnett, Kansas, to Hardin and Emma Masters. In 1880 his family settled at Lewistown,

Illinois, near Spoon River, where his family lived on Edgar's grandfather's farm. Edgar's experiences in the Midwest, namely the people he met and places he visited, inspired his writing. Following his father's example, Masters's first profession was law. He attended Knox College for one year, and then turned to private study. He was admitted to the bar in 1891, then moved to Chicago, where he practiced law for almost 30 years. In 1898, Masters married Helen M. Jenkins, the daughter of a prominent Chicago lawyer. The two had three children: Hardin, Marcia Lee, and Madeline.

Writing political pamphlets and essays was Masters's first creative work. He also produced *A Book of Verses* (1898) and several plays. *Spoon River Anthology*, his most famous work, was serialized in *Reedy's Mirror* between 1914 and 1915. The collection consisted of more than 200 free verse poems, which tell the story of Spoon River's long-dead residents. In the poetry, various townspeople speak from the grave, commenting on their lives in the small midwestern town. The realism and irony of these poems contrasted greatly with the literary romanticism that prevailed at the time of its publication. Masters received much critical acclaim, although many conservatives found the work unpatriotic. The sequel, *The New Spoon River* (1924), was for less successful than its predecessor. Masters persevered despite the loss of support for his work. He wrote more poetry, but he also delved into many other genres, including fiction and biography. His most memorable works deal with his childhood in Illinois. During the 1930s and 1940s, he published several such volumes: *Poems of People* (1936), *More People* (1939), *Illinois Poems* (1941), and *Along the Illinois* (1942).

In 1921, after a long period of marital strife, Masters requested a divorce from Helen, and upon being denied the divorce, left his family and fled to Europe. Later, as the height of the Chicago renaissance passed, Masters began to abandon his dream of returning to his midwestern hometown. Thus, he moved to New York and, after his divorce from Helen was finally settled, Masters remarried. His second wife, Ellen Coyne, was much younger than he. Her father was an immigrant from Ireland who had joined the U.S. Cavalry and patrolled Wyoming and Montana in the 1880s. As Edgar's wife, Ellen Masters pursued her own career as a teacher while her husband retired to the Chelsea Hotel to write. The hotel has also attracted such writers as THOMAS WOLFE, ARTHUR MILLER, MARK TWAIN, O. HENRY, and ALLEN GINSBERG.

Retired and in poor health, Masters eventually moved with his wife to her teaching positions in North Carolina and Pennsylvania. Throughout the 1940s he received several literary awards (including the Poetry Society of America medal, Shelley Memorial Award, and the Academy of American Poets fellowship). Masters died in Melrose, Pennsylvania, on March 5, 1950. He is buried in Oakland Cemetery in Petersburg, Illinois.

## Further Reading

Primeau, Ronald. *Beyond Spoon River: The Legacy of Edgar Lee Masters.* Austin: University of Texas Press, 1981.

Robinson, Frank K. *Edgar Lee Masters: An Exhibition in Commemoration of the Centenary of His Birth.* Austin, Tex.: Harry Ransom Humanities, 1970.

Russel, Herbert K. *Edgar Lee Masters: A Biography.* Chicago: University of Illinois Press, 2001.

## Mather, Cotton
(1663–1728) *nonfiction writer*

Cotton Mather was a congregational minister and author who became one of the strongest clerical figures of early New England Puritan society. As was customary for his time, he strongly believed in the existence of witchcraft, but he also had a modern scientific interest. Mather's medical and science journals were some of the first American studies in the sciences, and his theological writings had great influence. However, in modern times, Mather has been thought of as the archetypal intolerant, narrow Puritan. He took part in the Salem witch trials in 1692 and, although he did not approve of all the trials, he had helped to stir up the wave of hysterical fear by his *Memorable Providences Relating to Witchcraft and Possessions* (1689). Later he further pursued his inquiries into satanic possession with *Wonders of the Invisible World* (1693).

Cotton Mather was born on February 12, 1663, in Boston, Massachusetts Bay Colony, the son of Increase Mather. He spent his childhood studying Latin, Greek, and Hebrew. He entered Harvard University at age 12 and devoted himself to study and prayer. He increasingly studied the sciences and medicine as his stammer eroded his childhood aspirations of becoming a minister. But Mather was able to overcome his speech impediment with the help of his teacher and friend, Elijah Corlet. At 18 he received his master's degree from the hands of his father, who was president of Harvard. Mather preached his first sermon in his father's church in 1680. He was formally ordained in 1685 and became his father's colleague.

Mather devoted his life to praying, preaching, writing, and publishing. His book, *Bonifacius*, or *Essays to Do Good* (1710), instructed others in humanitarian acts. Some of Mather's ideas were ahead of his time. He suggested that schoolmasters reward instead of punish students and that the physician study the state of mind of patients as a probable cause of illness. Mather remained preoccupied with the idea of unity among all denominations of Christendom and his publications addressed international and interdenominational audiences. Although Mather had a keen interest in the sciences, his greatest body of work had more of a theological and historical focus. One of his most well-known works was *Magnalia Christi Americana (The Great Achievement of Christ in America)* (1702), an ecclesiastical history of America from the founding of New England to Mather's own time.

Mather also heavily involved himself in political issues in the Massachusetts Bay Colony. Although he took part in the Salem witch trials, he wrote about and spoke against making accusations of diabolical assistance. He believed that many of the reported demonic possessions were legitimate but, along with his father, also warned against relying on spectral evidence such as strange markings on the body.

Mather's scientific interest incurred popular disapproval as he led the fight for smallpox inoculation in 1721 during a severe epidemic. A bomb was thrown through his window when he inoculated his son, who almost died. Other members of his family became ill and some died. Mather became the first native-born American to become a fellow of the Royal Society of London, and his account of the inoculation episode was published in the society's transactions. He corresponded extensively with notable scientists such as Robert Boyle. His *Christian Philosopher* (1721) recognized God in the wonders of the Earth and the universe beyond. It was both philosophical and scientific and, ironically, anticipated 18th-century deism, even though Mather clung to the old order.

Mather wrote and published more than 400 works. His *Manuductio ad Ministerium* (1726) was a handbook of advice for young graduates to the ministry. Mather helped to advance learning and education and to make New England a cultural center. He was disappointed in his hopes of being president of Harvard but was one of the moving spirits in the founding of Yale. He died on February 13, 1728, in Boston. He had been married three times.

## Further Reading

Levin, David. *Cotton Mather: The Young Life of the Lord's Remembrance.* Cambridge, Mass.: Harvard University Press, 1978.

Marvin, Rev. Abijah P. *The Life and Times of Cotton Mather, D.D., F.R.S.* Boston: Congregational Sunday School and Publishing Co., 1892. Reprint, London: Haskell House Publishing, 1972.

Stout, Harry S. *The New England Soul.* New York: Oxford University Press, 1986.

Williams, Andrew P. "Shifting Signs: Increase Mather and the Comets of 1680 and 1682." *Early Modern Literary Studies* 1, no. 3 (1995): 4.1–34.

## McCarthy, Cormac
### (Charles McCarthy, C. J. McCarthy, Jr.)
(1933– )  *novelist*

The author of southern gothic novels often compared to those of WILLIAM FAULKNER and western novels that have reinvented the tired cowboy genre, Cormac McCarthy is known as a self-imposed outcast from the literary world, whose male-dominated stories of outdoor adventure and the harsh physical world have won him numerous elite literary prizes. The publication of his novel *All the Pretty Horses* won him many fans among readers and critics alike, as well as a spot on the *New York Times* best-seller list. His awards

include a MacArthur Foundation "genius" grant, a Rockefeller Foundation grant, and a Guggenheim Fellowship.

Cormac McCarthy was born Charles McCarthy on July 20, 1933, in Rhode Island, the third child and oldest son of Charles Joseph McCarthy and Gladys Christina McGrail McCarthy. Sources disagree as to who was responsible for the renaming, but his name was officially changed to Cormac, meaning "son of Charles" in Gaelic. When Cormac was four, the family moved to Knoxville, Tennessee, where his father became a lawyer for the Tennessee Valley Authority, a position he held until 1967. At that time, Cormac's parents moved to Washington, D.C., where his father worked as the principal attorney in a private law firm until his retirement.

Cormac McCarthy is the author of the best-selling novel *All the Pretty Horses.* (Photo by Marion Ettlinger. Courtesy Alfred A. Knopf)

Raised in a Roman Catholic family, Cormac and his siblings attended Catholic High School. He then went on the University of Tennessee in 1951, where his major was liberal arts. In 1953, McCarthy dropped out of college and joined the air force. He spent four years in the service, two of them stationed in Alaska, where he hosted a radio show.

When McCarthy returned to the University of Tennessee in 1957, he concentrated on his writing and published two short stories under the name C. J. McCarthy, Jr., in the student literary magazine, *The Phoenix.* In 1959, while still in school, McCarthy won an Ingram-Merrill Award for creative writing. He married a fellow student and writer, Lee Holleman, in 1961, and they had a son, Cullen, born in 1962. McCarthy left school again, still without his degree, and headed to Chicago with his new family. There, he began writing his first novel and supported himself and his family by working part time in an auto parts warehouse. The family returned to Tennessee within a few years, and the marriage ended.

McCarthy won a traveling fellowship from the American Academy of Arts and Letters in the early 1960s. Following the publication of *The Orchard Keeper* in 1965, McCarthy used his fellowship money to travel to Ireland. He left on the *Sylvania,* an American liner, intending to visit the home of his Irish ancestors, but on the ship he met Anne DeLisle, a young English singer and dancer, and they were married in England in 1966. McCarthy received another grant that same year from the Rockefeller Foundation, and he and Anne used the money to travel throughout Europe, visiting France, Switzerland, Italy, and Spain, before settling on the Mediterranean island of Ibiza, which was an artist's colony of sorts at the time. While on the island, McCarthy completed his revisions of the novel *Outer Dark,* which was published in 1968, shortly after the couple had returned to Tennessee to live. They then settled in Rockford, a town near Knoxville, and rented a house on a pig farm for $50 a month.

When McCarthy won a Guggenheim fellowship for creative writing in 1969, he and Anne moved into a barn near Louisville, Tennessee, which McCarthy renovated himself. According to Anne, he gathered stones and used them to build an addition to the barn. He also collected bricks from JAMES AGEE's boyhood home, which was being demolished to make way for urban renewal in Knoxville.

McCarthy's novel *Child of God* appeared in 1973 to more mixed reviews than his first two books had received. McCarthy then worked on a screenplay for a PBS film called *The Gardener's Son,* which premiered in 1977 and was eventually published in a revised edition by Ecco Press in 1994 called *The Stonemason.*

McCarthy separated from Anne DeLisle in 1976 and moved to El Paso, Texas, where he has lived ever since. He and DeLisle divorced a few years after the separation.

*Suttree,* a novel McCarthy had worked on for most of his writing life, was finally completed and published in 1979. Some critics have hailed *Suttree* as McCarthy's finest accomplishment as a writer. Its publication was followed by McCarthy receiving a MacArthur fellowship, which provided him with money to live on while he completed his next novel, a western set in Texas and Mexico. Now considered a major turning point in McCarthy's writing, *Blood Meridian* received little attention when it was published in 1985 but is now considered among his finest novels. Based on actual events, as many of his books are, the writing of *Blood Meridian* required extensive research on McCarthy's part, including learning to speak Spanish.

McCarthy's next book, *All the Pretty Horses* (1992) was the first in his Border Trilogy and the first of his books to make the *New York Times* bestseller list. A publishing sensation that was made into a major motion picture, *All the Pretty Horses* earned McCarthy the wide readership that had previously eluded him. He granted the one interview he has ever given to the *New York Times* following this book's publication, and according to him, he used the money from the book to buy a new pick-up truck and just kept on writing. The other two books of the Border Trilogy are *The Crossing* (1994) and *Cities of the Plain* (1998). The trilogy chronicles the lives of two young men coming of age in the Southwest and Mexico in the years prior to World War II. It has been praised for its portrayal of the American frontier and its haunting, poetic language. *All the Pretty Horses* won the National Book Award in 1992 as well as the Book Critics Circle Award.

## Further Reading

Bell, Vereen M. *The Achievement of Cormac McCarthy.* Baton Rouge: Louisiana State University Press, 1988.

Folks, Jeffrey J., and James A. Perkins, eds. *Southern Writers at Century's End.* Lexington: University Press of Kentucky, 1997.

"General Fiction Book Reviews, R.D." *Texas Monthly* (December 1944): 53.

Hall, Wade, and Rick Wallach, eds. *Sacred Violence: A Reader's Companion to Cormac McCarthy.* El Paso: Texas Western University Press, 1995.

Jarrett, Robert L. *Cormac McCarthy.* New York: Twayne, 1997.

Jones, Malcolm, "Brightening Western Star." *Newsweek* (June 13, 1994): 54.

Zoglin, Richard. "A Real Tape Turner." *Time* (August 29, 1994): 73.

## McCullers, Carson
### (Lula Carson Smith)
(1917–1967) *novelist, short story writer*

Carson McCullers was a southern gothic writer who examined the lives of lonely and isolated people. She wrote both of her best-known novels, *The Heart Is a Lonely Hunter* (1940) and *Reflections in a Golden Eye* (1942), before age 25. In the grotesque worlds that she created through her fiction, eccentric characters suffered from a loneliness that McCullers interpreted with unsentimental compassion.

Carson McCullers was born Lula Carson Smith on February 19, 1917, in Columbus, Georgia, the first child of Lamar Smith and Marguerite Waters Smith. As the daughter of a well-to-do watchmaker and jeweler, she was able to take piano lessons as a child. She received a typewriter from her father when she was 15 and soon began writing plays and short stories. Her first attempt to sell a short story, titled "Sucker," was unsuccessful. McCullers traveled to New York City at the age of 17 and worked in menial jobs as she devoted herself to writing. She studied creative writing at Columbia University and New York University and published the semiautobiographical "Wunderkind," which told of a musical prodigy's failure and adolescent insecurity, in *Story* magazine in 1936.

She married Reeves McCullers, an unsuccessful author, in 1937. They moved to North Carolina, and during the two years they lived there, Carson wrote *The Heart Is a Lonely Hunter,* a story that examines loneliness and affliction through the characters in a small mill town in Georgia in the 1930s. The town's most alienated people find themselves drawn to the story's deaf-mute protagonist. McCullers's next book, *Reflections in a Golden Eye,* was a sordid, scandalous tale about a bizarre group of people living on an army base. They included a latent homosexual major and his domineering, lustful wife. The U.S. Army tried in vain to ban the novel from U.S. bookstores. The story was turned into a movie in 1967, directed by John Huston and starring Marlon Brando and Elizabeth Taylor. *The Heart Is a Lonely Hunter* was produced for film in 1968.

In 1940, McCullers attended the Bread Loaf Writers' Conference in Middlebury, Vermont. The next year, she began divorce proceedings. Both McCullers and her husband had engaged in homosexual relationships. McCullers's health began to deteriorate early in her life. She was stricken with impaired vision, stabbing head pains, and partial paralysis. After World War II, McCullers lived mostly in Paris. Her close friends during these years included TRUMAN CAPOTE and TENNESSEE WILLIAMS. In 1945, McCullers reunited with Reeves McCullers. Over a period of five years she had worked on *The Member of the Wedding,* which was published in 1946. It is the story of an adolescent girl who, in her desperate attempt to be a part of something, becomes fixated on her brother's upcoming wedding.

Suffering from depression, McCullers attempted suicide in 1948. She published *The Ballad of the Sad Café* in 1951, returning to characters who struggle with physical and psychological defects, including a hunchbacked midget, an ex-convict, and a strapping woman. Shortly after its publication, Carson and Reeves reportedly fell for the same man, a composer. Their marital problems worsened and Reeves attempted suicide and tried to convince McCullers to do the same. He succeeded in a Paris hotel in 1953 with an overdose of sleeping pills. McCullers's play *The Square Root of Wonderful* (1958) was an attempt to examine this traumatic period of her life.

McCullers gained a reputation for becoming obsessed with particular friends or love interests, both men and women. She fell in love with fellow writer KATHERINE ANNE PORTER, who lived in the same artists' colony as McCullers while she was writing *The Member of the Wedding*. But Porter did not return McCullers's affections. McCullers received mixed reviews of her work from her colleagues. ARTHUR MILLER dismissed her as a "minor author," but Gore Vidal praised her work as "one of the few satisfying achievements of our second-rate culture." Of her craft, McCullers had said: "Writing, for me, is a search for God."

McCullers suffered throughout her life from several illnesses, including having contracted rheumatic fever at the age of 15. A longtime smoker and alcoholic, she suffered a series of strokes that left much of her body partially paralyzed for the better part of her adult years. She died in New York on September 29, 1967, after a stroke.

### Further Reading

Bloom, Harold, ed. *Carson McCullers*. Broomall, Pa.: Chelsea House Publishers, 1986.

Carr, Virginia Spencer. *The Lonely Hunter*. New York: Carroll and Graf, 1985.

Clark, Beverly Lyon, and Friedman, Melvin, eds. *Critical Essays on Carson McCullers*. New York: Hall, 1996.

## McMurtry, Larry
(1936–  ) *novelist, detective/mystery writer*

Larry McMurtry typically writes novels about the American Southwest, particularly Texas. Although he is perhaps best known for his epic novel *Lonesome Dove*, only seven of more than 25 books McMurtry has written in the last 40 years deal exclusively with the frontier. And in contrast to other typical westerns, McMurtry's writing maintains a sense of depth and historical accuracy.

Larry McMurtry was born on June 3, 1936, in Wichita Falls, Texas, to a cattle-ranching family. Growing up on a ranch in the Southwest, McMurtry became familiar with western folklore at a very young age and gained a sense of place that was solidly rooted in the harsh landscape of West Texas. About that land, McMurtry has said, "It's still such a strong landscape for me . . . I can't escape it in my fiction." Even his education did little to wean him from his attachment to his homeland. He enrolled at Rice University in Houston in 1954, but (as the story goes, intimidated by Rice's math requirements) transferred to North Texas State University in Denton, Texas, where he earned a bachelor's degree. McMurtry then returned to Rice for graduate work and was awarded a master's degree in English in 1960. He subsequently taught English at Rice until he left, in 1972, to devote himself full time to writing.

McMurtry has always been a book person; he has read voraciously throughout his life and has, in past years, acted as a "book scout," checking booksellers' stocks for unsuspected treasures. This was an avocation for which McMurtry had a gift; he even financed his college education, to a significant extent, by selling copies of collectible books that he had bought over the years. When he began writing, several things became obvious to McMurtry. First of all, he was decidedly a western writer. To some extent, this revealed itself in negative terms as he wrote about the disintegration of the western myths and the disappearance of the world that had long been recognized as "western." The other awareness that became apparent to McMurtry as he delved deeper into his writing was that he had a knack for portraying what was popular to the masses in America. For example, four of his first six books were made into successful feature films, including such classic films as *Hud* (1963) (from *Horseman, Pass By*), *The Last Picture Show* (1971), and *Terms of Endearment* (1975), which won the Academy Award for Best Picture in 1983. Having already written books that lent themselves to film, McMurtry found it an easy and logical progression to then write the respective screenplays. He has been successful at both and has also written volumes of essays and a biography.

*Lonesome Dove* (1985), for which McMurtry received the Pulitzer Prize, was a step back in time to the era that had spawned the cowboy myth in the first place. McMurtry believed he was constructing what would finally be a realistic correction to rampant cowboy romanticism. What he created clearly surpassed this expectation. When the novel was published, the *New York Times* referred to it as the "the *War and Peace* of cattle drive novels." *Lonesome Dove* was pieced together intricately and composed in an epic fashion, and its characters solidly displayed the heroism that was demanded of them. The vitality of the lengthy book, both in print and on screen, was obvious as producers, publishers, and readers clamored for more of the *Lonesome Dove* saga.

Then, following a heart attack in 1991, McMurtry had quadruple-bypass surgery and subsequently suffered from severe depression for more than a year. "I faded out of my life. Suddenly I found myself becoming an outline, and then what was within that outline vanished," McMurtry recalls. During this period he wrote *Streets of Laredo* (1993), a dark sequel to *Lonesome Dove*. McMurtry's companion, Diana Ossana, helped McMurtry pull himself out of his depression by pushing him to continue writing. He agreed to do so only if she would collaborate. The result was *Pretty Boy Floyd* (1994) and *Zeke and Ned* (1997), both of which received mixed reviews. With his more recent works, including *Duane's Depressed* (1999) and *Walter Benjamin at the Dairy Queen* (1999), McMurtry has returned to solo composition. He currently resides in Archer City, Texas, where he operates Booked Up, a bookstore specializing in used and rare volumes with an inventory of more than 300,000 books.

**Further Reading**

Busby, Mark. *Larry McMurtry and the West: An Ambivalent Relationship*. Dallas: University of North Texas Press, 1995.

Isle, Ray. "Three Days in McMurtryville." *Stanford Magazine* (November/December 1999): 52–55. Available online. URL: http://www.stanfordalumni.org/news/magazine/1999/novdec/articles/mcmurtry.html.

Reilly, John M. *Larry McMurtry: A Critical Companion*. Westport, Conn.: Greenwood Publishing Group, 2000.

## McNally, Terrence
(1939– ) *playwright*

The recipient of four Tony Awards, including Best Play for *Master Class* and for *Love! Valour! Compassion!,* as well as Best Book of a Musical awards for *Kiss of the Spider Woman* and *Ragtime,* Terrence McNally is one of America's most celebrated playwrights. Respected by some and branded blasphemous by others, McNally's plays are known for their socially relevant, though often controversial, subject matter. Despite his contentious reputation, his talent is unmistakable; his honors include a Pulitzer Prize, two Guggenheim fellowships, a Rockefeller grant, the Lucille Hortel Award, the Hull-Warriner Award, and a citation from the American Academy of Arts and letters.

Born on November 3, 1939, in St. Petersburg, Florida, Terrence McNally produced his first play in 1964 at the age of 25. Some of his early comedies, such as *Next* (1969) and *The Ritz* (1975), received quite a bit of praise, but it was not until later in his career that McNally achieved commercial success with works such as *Frankie and Johnny in the Claire de Lune* (1987), for which he also wrote the screen adaptation that starred Al Pacino and Michelle Pfeiffer.

In 1990, McNally won an Emmy Award for Best Writing in a Miniseries or Special for *Andre's Mother.* A year later, *Lips Together, Teeth Apart* (1991), a study of the irrational fears that many people harbor towards homosexuals and victims of AIDS, returned McNally to the stage. The play takes place over a Fourth of July weekend at a summerhouse on Fire Island, where two married couples are vacationing. The house has been willed to one of the women by her brother who has just died of AIDS, and it soon becomes evident that both couples are afraid to get in the pool, fearful that they might somehow contract AIDS. In *Kiss of the Spider Woman* (1992), McNally collaborated with John Kander (composer) and Fred Ebb (lyricist) on a script that explores the complex relationship between two men who are cellmates in a Latin American prison. *Kiss of the Spider Woman* earned McNally the 1993 Tony Award for Best Book of a Musical. McNally again collaborated with Kander and Ebb on *The Rink* which examines the past, present, and future of a tenuous mother-daughter relationship during the late 1970s in an eastern seaside town. He collaborated with Stephen Flaherty and Lynn Ahrens on *Ragtime* (1997), a musical adaptation of the novel by E. L. DOCTOROW, which tells the story of Coalhouse Walker, Jr., a spirited black piano man whose Model T is destroyed by a mob of white troublemakers.

In 1997, McNally created an international controversy with *Corpus Christi* (1997), a modern day retelling of the story of Jesus's birth, ministry, and death, in which he and all his disciples are gay. The play was initially cancelled because of death threats against the board members of the Manhattan Theatre Club, which was scheduled to produce the play. When several influential playwrights such as Tony Kushner threatened to withdraw their plays if *Corpus Christi* was not produced, the board finally relented and the play opened, with 2,000 protesters in attendance. When *Corpus Christi* opened in London, a British Muslim group called the Defenders of the Messenger Jesus issued a fatwa, or death sentence, on McNally.

McNally's other plays include *Love! Valour! Compassion!* (1994), which examines the relationships of eight gay men who abandon city life for three relaxing weeks in a country lake home, and *Master Class* (1995), a character study of legendary opera soprano Maria Callas, which won the 1996 Tony Award for Best Play. McNally also wrote about Callas in *The Lisbon Traviata* (1989). He has been a member of the Dramatists Guild Council since 1970 and has served as vice president since 1981. He is considered one of the leading U.S. dramatists writing today.

**Further Reading**

Terrence McNally: Librettist. "And Then One Night: The Making of *Dead Man Walking*." PBS. Available online. URL: http://www.pbs.org/kgod/onenight/creativeprocess/players/mcnally.html. Downloaded June 21, 2003.

Zinman, Toby Silverman. *Terrence McNally: A Casebook (Casebooks on Modern Dramatists)*. New York: Garland Publishing, 1997.

## Melville, Herman
### (Herman Melvill)
### (1819–1891) *novelist, short story writer, poet*

Most widely regarded for his sea adventure novel *Moby-Dick,* Herman Melville's work gained more success following his death than during his lifetime. Although he is now considered to be one of the most ingenious novelists of the 20th century, during his lifetime, his intentions and voice were widely misunderstood by readers and his career was infamously marked with financial and creative frustration.

Herman Melvill was born on August 1, 1819, in New York City into an established and socially well-connected merchant family. He was the third of eight children born to Allan and Maria Gansevoort Melvill. According to his socialite parents, young Herman did not meet their expectations of growing up to be a refined, noble, and God-fearing young man. After the collapse of the family's import business in 1830, Allan Melvill went bankrupt, became deranged, and died in 1832. His mother, Maria Gansevoort Melvill, was left alone to raise eight children with some occasional financial help from her wealthy relatives. Herman's oldest brother, Gansevoort, then took over his father's business and assumed responsibility for his family's financial health. After two years as a bank clerk and some months working on his uncle's farm, Herman joined his brother in the business. Also at about this time, Herman's branch of the family altered the spelling of their name to Melville.

Melville attended the Albany (New York) Classical School in 1835, but shortly thereafter abandoned school for self-education, devouring Shakespeare and historical, anthropological, and highly technical works. Then, in search of adventures, he shipped out as a cabin boy on the *St. Lawrence*, a merchant ship that departed New York in June 1839 en route to Liverpool, England. Melville later joined the U.S. Navy and commenced the first of his many yearlong voyages on ships. Hoping to assist his family in their financial struggles, he briefly returned home in search of more gainful employment, but unable to find a satisfying job, returned east in January 1841, sailing on the whaler *Acushnet* on a voyage to the South Seas. In June 1842 Melville's ship anchored in the Marquesas Islands in present-day French Polynesia. His adventures there, albeit somewhat romanticized, became the subject of his first novel, *Typee* (1846). One month after the ship was anchored, Melville and a companion jumped ship and, according to the novel, spent about four months as guest-captives of the reputedly cannibalistic Typee people. *Omoo* (1847), the sequel to *Typee*, also was based on Melville's experiences on the Polynesian Islands. Both *Typee* and *Omoo* were first published in England, where he enjoyed considerable more success and following. His older brother Gansevoort held a government position in London and helped to launch his career there. Following the publication of his third book, *Mardi and a Voyage Thither* (1849), Melville began to experience the unpredictable turns of popular acclaim.

In 1847 Melville married Elisabeth Shaw, daughter of the chief justice of Massachusetts, with whom he had four children. After three years of living back in New York, the couple bought a farm, Arrowhead, which was located near NATHANIEL HAWTHORNE's home in Pittsfield, Massachusetts. Melville and Hawthorne soon became friends and professional confidants. As Melville worked to complete *Moby-Dick,* Hawthorne encouraged him to change it from a story full of details about whaling into an allegorical novel. Inspired by Hawthorne's achievements, Melville took his advice and completed *Moby-Dick* in 1851. He worked at his desk all day, eating nothing until late in the afternoon; bursting with energy, he was known to have shouted, "Give me Vesuvius' crater for an inkstand!" Although now heralded as a landmark work in American literature, *Moby-Dick* received little acclaim upon its release. Selling only about 3,000 copies during Melville's lifetime, it was misunderstood both by those who read it and by those who reviewed it. The book can be read as a thrilling sea story or an examination of the conflict between man and nature. The battle between

Herman Melville, author of the classic novel *Moby-Dick,* died without ever achieving fame or economic success from his writing. *(From Melville's book* Journal Up the Straits, *1860. Library of Congress, Prints and Photographs Division [LC-USZ62-39759])*

Ahab and the whale is open to many interpretations. Some have viewed *Moby-Dick* as a pioneer novel about a journey on the sea; some believe it to be an allegory on the gold rush, the gold being a whale. Whatever Melville's motivation, the widespread confusion and misinterpretation resulted in limited success for the novel, thereby causing a blow to his self-esteem, one from which he never fully recovered.

Melville followed *Moby-Dick* with *Pierre* (1852), a novel that drew from his experiences as a youth (a financial and professional disaster), and *Israel Potter* (1855), for which he enjoyed modest success. Melville also wrote some great short fiction during those years, including "Bartleby the Scrivener: A Story of Wall Street" (1853), considered one of the first important works of fiction to treat the subject of dehumanization in the modern industrial society. In 1856 Melville journeyed to Europe for leisurely travel and one year later published the final novel of his lifetime, *The Confidence Man* (1857). He then retired from writing fiction and devoted himself instead to poetry. He published some of his poetry in his remaining years, but these works were of little note. In 1861, with two sons and daughters to support, Melville sought a consular post, but did not receive the appointment. When the Civil War broke out, he volunteered for the navy but was rejected. He then got some relief from an inheritance upon his father-in-law's death, and by the end of 1863 was living again in New York City. The war was much on Melville's mind and provided the subject for his first volume of verse, *Battle-Pieces and Aspects of the War* (1866). Four months after its publication, an appointment as a customs inspector on the New York docks finally brought Melville a secure income.

Melville's final years were marked by poor health and personal tragedy. His son Malcolm shot himself in 1867, and another son, Stanwix, died after a long and debilitating illness in 1886. During Melville's final years he returned to writing prose and completed the novel *Billy Budd*. This novel was not published until 1924, several decades after his death on September 28, 1891. In the 20th century, critics argued that Melville must have experienced homosexual relationships throughout his life, basing their allegations on allusions to homosexuality in both *Pierre* and *Billy Budd*. There has also been much written about the likelihood that he physically abused his wife and that he was mentally ill, with most experts seeing a tendency toward manic-depressive behavior. Despite these allegations of personal struggles, some of which began while the writer was still living, by the end of the 1840s Melville was among the most celebrated of American writers. Ironically, his death evoked but a single obituary notice. However, after years of neglect, critics in the 1920s revived interest in his work and once again secured his reputation as one of the greatest American writers of his time.

## Further Reading

Bloom, Harold. *Herman Melville's Moby-Dick*. New York: Chelsea House, 1996.

Bryant, John. *A Companion to Melville Studies*. Westport, Conn.: Greenwood Press, 1986.

Davis, Clark. *After the Whale*. Tuscaloosa: University of Alabama Press, 1995.

Dimock, Wai-chee. *Empire for Liberty: Melville and the Poetics of Individualism*. Athens: University of Georgia Press, 1991.

Lee, A. Robert. *Herman Melville*. Totowa, N.J.: Barnes & Noble, 1984.

Levine, Robert S. *The Cambridge Companion to Herman Melville*. Cambridge: Cambridge University Press, 1998.

Parker, Hershel. *Herman Melville: A Biography: 1819–1851*. Baltimore, Md.: Johns Hopkins University Press, 1996.

Samson, John. *White Lies*. Ithaca. N.Y.: Cornell University Press, 1989.

## Mencken, H. L.
### (Henry Louis Mencken)
(1880–1956) *literary critic, journalist, essayist, memoirist*

The most prominent newspaperman, literary critic, and political commentator of his day, H. L. Mencken was a writer of enormous influence. He became, by the time of his death, the leading authority on American usage of the English language and was one of the most imposing intellectuals of the 20th century. He is remembered for his scathing social commentary, the great diversity of his writings, and his critical support of emerging writers.

Henry Louis Mencken was born on September 12, 1880, in Baltimore, Maryland, the only city he would ever call home. As a boy, he attended F. Knapp's Institute and later the Polytechnic Institute of Baltimore. His ancestors were German American, and his paternal grandfather was a cigar maker who settled in Baltimore in 1848. Mencken's father started a tobacco business, the Mencken Cigar Company, which was quite successful and provided the family with a comfortable income. The eldest of three sons and a daughter, H. L. Mencken held his first real job in his father's company but left soon after his father's death to pursue a career as a reporter. Throughout his life, however,

Mencken was rarely seen without a cigar close at hand.

At the age of eight, Mencken received a boy's printing press as a Christmas present, an event that forever shaped his life. Already an avid reader who immersed himself in literature and frequented the local public library, Mencken was now smitten with the whole printing process. At age 18, just a few days following his father's death, he left the family cigar business to take a job as a city reporter at the *Baltimore Morning Herald*. The paper soon promoted him to daily columnist and then to editor-at-large when he was just 23 years old.

In 1905, Mencken's first book, a critique of the plays of George Bernard Shaw, appeared. The following year, the *Herald* went out of business, and Mencken joined the *Baltimore Sun,* where he would remain for the rest of his career. There he wrote a column called "The Free Lance," which appeared in the *Evening Sun.* In 1917, Mencken gave up his desk responsibilities at the paper, which freed him to work on his own book projects, as well as on the magazines he edited.

Mencken published his major contribution to the field of philology, *The American Language,* in 1919. This scholarly study, which analyzes words, phrases, expressions, idioms, and unusual pronunciations and spellings that are unique to the United States, remains a classic. Over a period of 30 years, the book was brought out in numerous editions that grew in size with each reissue, and in 1945 and 1948 he published substantial supplements.

A newspaperman, critic, and political commentator, H. L. Mencken wielded great influence over the development of American letters in the 20th century. *(Library of Congress, Prints and Photographs Division [LC-USZ62-42489])*

Mencken's influence as a literary critic was greatly strengthened by his work as an editor on several literary magazines. From 1914 to 1923, Mencken and George Jean Nathan edited the *Smart Set*, which was one of the most influential magazines of American literature at the time. The pair founded the *American Mercury* in 1924, which Mencken edited until 1933. In these publications, Mencken had the opportunity to lambaste writers he thought unworthy and lavishly praise those who were deserving. His reviews and essays were collected in a six-volume work entitled *Prejudices*, which came out in 1927. Among those writers whose careers received support from Mencken's positive reviews were THEODORE DREISER, SINCLAIR LEWIS, SHERWOOD ANDERSON, F. SCOTT FITZGERALD, and Joseph Conrad.

Among Mencken's other books—he wrote a total of 30—are his first published volume, *Ventures into Verse: The Philosophy of Friedrich Nietzsche* (1908); *Men Versus the Man* with Robert Rives La Monte (1910); *A Book of Burlesques* (1916); *A Little Book in C Major* (1916); *A Book of Prefaces* (1917); *In Defense of Women* (1918); his trilogy of memoirs focused on the newspaper business—*Happy Days* (1940), *Newspaper Days* (1941), and *Heathen Days* (1943)—and *My Life as Author and Editor*, which was published in 1993, after having been sealed, at Mencken's request, for 35 years following his death. During his industrious career, he wrote book reviews for 12 different publications and articles for 20 or more publications.

In 1930, at the age of 50, Mencken married Sara Haardt, despite his longstanding antipathy toward the institution of marriage. Haardt died abruptly in 1935 at the age of 37, and Mencken never remarried.

Mencken continued to write and edit for the *Baltimore Sun*, while also spending increasing amounts of time on his memoirs and autobiography. His influence as a writer declined in his last years. In 1948, he suffered a stroke that left him unable to write and virtually unable to read. He died on January 29, 1956, at the age of 76.

## Further Reading

Angoff, Charles. *H. L. Mencken, A Portrait from Memory.* New York: T. Yoseloff, 1956.

Bode, Carl. *Mencken.* Carbondale: Southern Illinois University Press, 1969.

Fitzpatrick, Vincent. *H. L. Mencken.* New York: Continuum, 1989.

Hobson, Fred C. *Serpent in Eden: H. L. Mencken and the South.* Chapel Hill: University of North Carolina Press, 1974.

Mayfield, Sara. *The Constant Circle; H. L. Mencken and His Friends.* New York: Delacorte Press, 1968.

Martin, Edward A., ed. *In Defense of Marion Bloom: The Love of Marion Bloom and H. L. Mencken.* Athens: University of Georgia Press, 1996.

Williams, W. H. A. *H. L. Mencken Revisited.* New York: Twayne, 1998.

# Merrill, James
## (James Ingram Merrill)
### (1926–1995)  *poet, novelist, memoirist*

Most widely known as the "Ouija poet" for his highly praised narrative poems about the Ouija sessions he and a friend conducted with "spirits from another world," James Merrill is considered one of the leading lyric poets of his generation. His urbane voice and keen visual perceptiveness distinguished his poems and won him many accolades during his long career, including the Pulitzer Prize.

James Merrill was born in New York City on March 3, 1926, the son of Charles Merrill, cofounder of the brokerage firm Merrill Lynch, and his second wife, Hellen Ingram Merrill, who published a small newspaper. Merrill grew up in Manhattan and Southampton, New York, in an atmosphere of wealth and privilege, which continued even after his parents divorced in 1939. By the time he was eight years old, he had already begun to write poems. A governess taught him both French and German, and he developed a passion for music from an early age. He was especially fond of opera, to which he was introduced at the age of 11. When he was 16 and a student at Lawrenceville School in New Jersey, Merrill's father had a book of his juvenile poems privately printed under the title of *Jim's Book*.

When Merrill graduated from high school in 1943, he entered Amherst College but took a leave of absence the following year to serve in the U.S. Army until the end of World War II in 1945.

Despite the interruption of the war, Merrill excelled in his studies. He majored in English literature and wrote a thesis on French writer Marcel Proust, who became a major inspiration for his work. He graduated summa cum laude with a Phi Beta Kappa key in 1947.

Merrill's career as a poet began while he was at Amherst. By the time of his graduation, his verse had already appeared in *Poetry* and the *Kenyon Review,* and he had published his first book of poems, *The Black Swan* (1946). Following his graduation from Amherst, Merrill taught at Bard College for a year before leaving to travel in Europe and Asia for more than two years, a time when he apparently reflected on his life and family and came to terms with his homosexuality. He eventually settled in the small town of Stonington, Connecticut, with David Jackson, who became his longtime companion. During the 1960s, Merrill bought a house in Athens, Greece, and subsequently another residence in Key West, Florida, and divided his time among the three homes.

Merrill's first collection of verse following his college years was published as *First Poems* in 1951 and received mixed reviews, with critics generally praising its elegance but finding the work ultimately dull. Merrill concentrated next on prose, including two plays: *The Bait* (1953), about a brother-sister relationship, and *The Immortal Husband* (1955), a retelling of the Greek myth of Tithonus. Both plays were produced in New York and received mildly favorable reviews. *The Immortal Husband* appeared in *Playbook* in 1955. In 1956, Merrill used a portion of his inheritance to establish the Ingram Merrill Foundation in New York City, which has awarded grants to hundreds of artists and writers.

In 1957, Merrill published his first novel, *The Seraglio,* the story of an aging businessman and his predatory female admirers. The book received mixed reviews and Merrill turned back to poetry. He had published a volume of poems called *Short Stories* in 1954, but it received little attention. When *The Country of a Thousand Years of Peace* appeared in 1959, Merrill finally found the approval he had been seeking. *Water Street,* another well received collection of poems, was published in 1962. He wrote one more novel, *The (Diblos)*

*Notebook,* which was published in 1965 and was a finalist for the National Book Award for Fiction.

*Nights and Days* (1966) received the National Book Award for poetry in 1967. *The Fire Screen* (1969) was also well received and secured Merrill's place in American letters as an important poet. In 1971, Merrill was elected to the National Institute of Arts and Letters. *Braving the Elements* appeared in 1973 and won the coveted Bollingen Prize in 1973.

Merrill's work received even greater praise in the final decades of his life. He published *Divine Comedies* in 1976, which won the Pulitzer Prize for poetry. This book began a series of so-called Ouija poems published by Merrill in two subsequent volumes—*Mirabell: Books of Number* (1978), and *Scripts for the Pageant* (1980). The Ouija poems related messages that Merrill and Jackson had supposedly received via a Ouija board from deceased family members and others. Although many critics expressed skepticism, the series of poems was ultimately praised. All of the Ouija poems were published together as one epic poem in a revised version called *The Changing Light at Sandover* (1982).

Merrill's final collections of poems included *Late Settings* (1985) and *The Inner Room* (1988). A posthumous collection called *A Scattering of Salts* was published in 1995. Merrill also wrote a collection of short prose pieces called *Recitative* (1986) and a memoir, *A Different Person* (1994).

Merrill's other awards included a second National Book Award for *Mirabell: Books of Number,* the National Book Critics Circle Award for the epic poem *The Changing Light at Sandover* (1982), and the first Bobbitt National Prize for Poetry, awarded by the Library of Congress, for *The Inner Room* (1988). Merrill also served as chancellor of the Academy of American Poets from 1979 until his death. He died suddenly on February 6, 1995, of a heart attack while vacationing in Tucson, Arizona. He was 68 years old.

## Further Reading

Bloom, Harold, ed. *James Merrill.* New York: Chelsea, 1985.

Buckley, C. A. "Exploring the Changing Light at Sandover: An Interview with James Merrill."

*Twentieth Century Literature* 38, no. 4 (winter 1992): 415–435.

Labrie, Ross. *James Merrill.* Boston: Twayne, 1982.

Lurie, Alison. *Familiar Spirits: A Memoir of James Merrill and David Jackson.* New York: Viking, 2001.

Meyer, Steven, et al. "James Merrill: A Life in Writing." *Southwest Review* 80, no. 2–3 (spring–summer 1995): 159–185.

Simon, John. "Robed in Images: The Memoirs of James Merrill." *New Criterion* 12, no. 1 (September 1993): 75–80.

Yenser, Stephen. *The Consuming Myth: The Work of James Merrill.* Cambridge, Mass.: Harvard University Press, 1987.

## Michener, James
(1907–1997) *novelist*

James Michener was best known for his long and detailed novels, many of which were born in his workshop with assistants and researchers. He wrote his first book, *Tales of the South Pacific* (1947), at the age of 39 and immediately won a Pulitzer Prize. He evaluated American history through analysis of racism, imperialism, and corruption, presenting the reader with a narrative of the country through its good and bad times. Michener was an idealist whose beliefs were rooted in his Quaker upbringing and given breadth by his extensive travels. He believed that literature should be looked at from the "point of view of utility" because he could not conceive of "literature without purpose." Michener wrote some 40 books, which sold about 75 million copies. Many of his works have been adapted for film and television.

James Michener was born in New York City in 1907. His exact birthdate is unknown because he was an orphan. He was taken to Doylestown, Pennsylvania, and raised by a Quaker widow, Mabel Michener. He attended Doylestown High School and worked as a sportswriter and later as an editor at the school's newspaper. After graduation he attended Swarthmore College and studied English and history. During his teenage and college years Michener hitchhiked all over the United States, beginning a life of travel. He received a Lippincott traveling grant and attended St. Andrew's

University in Scotland, and studied Italian art in Sienna and at the British Museum in London. He also collected folk songs in the Hebrides and visited Spain while a crew member on a freighter. In 1935, Michener graduated from the University of Northern Colorado and married Patti Koon. He became an associate professor at the Colorado State College of Education until 1940 and was a visiting lecturer at Harvard and president of the Pennsylvania Electoral College.

Although as a Quaker Michener was exempt from military service, he enlisted in the navy when World War II broke out. From 1944 to 1946, he served as a naval historian in the South Pacific and traveled widely in the area. It was during this time that Michener began collecting material for his first book, *Tales of the South Pacific.* Michener divorced his first wife in 1948 and married Vange Nord. In 1949 he moved to Hawaii and completed his novel, which combined history and fiction. The story started from the geological beginnings of the islands to the migrations of the Polynesians and the arrival of the Europeans. The story was the basis for the famous Richard Rodgers–Oscar Hammerstein musical, *South Pacific* with such songs as "I'm Gonna Wash That Man Right Out of My Hair" and "Bali Ha'i." Critics classified Michener's book as fiction. The author considered it a novel because of the unified setting and the recurrence of several characters throughout the book. The stories depicted navy officers and enlisted men, marines, Seabees, and nurses as well as the inhabitants of the islands during the war.

Michener traveled extensively for the rest of his life, including reporting on the Korean War, operating behind Russian lines during the Hungarian Revolution in 1956, and visiting China with President Richard Nixon in 1972. Michener's book *The Bridges at Toko-Ri* (1953) depicted a self-sacrificing jet pilot during the Korean War. In *Sayonara* (1954), Michener wrote of an ill-fated romance between a U.S. officer and a Japanese woman. Shortly after the novel's publication Michener married his third wife, Mari Yoriko Sabusawa, a Japanese American. His subsequent large novels included the blockbuster *Hawaii* (1959), *Centennial* (1974), *Poland* (1983), *Texas* (1985), *Alaska* (1988), and *Mexico* (1992). He also wrote nonfiction, including *Kent State* (1971), a study of the events in 1970 that led to the killing of four students by the Ohio National Guard during a Vietnam War protest. *Legacy* (1987) was a short essay-like novel that criticized U.S. tendency to criticize the world, and *The Novel* (1991) was a story of the settlement of Pennsylvania by the Dutch.

Encountering serious health problems in the mid 1980s, Michener underwent quintuple bypass surgery. He wrote that his failing health sparked one of the most industrious periods of his life. Between 1986 and 1991, he wrote 11 books, a dramatic contrast to the three years he usually spent writing a single novel. He called himself a "working resident of the world," someone "who has labored to describe it with understanding and affection and share it with others. With my pen I have engraved warrants of citizenship in the most remote corners, for truly the world has been my home."

In addition to winning the Pulitzer Prize in 1948 for *Tales of the South Pacific*, Michener also won the Overseas Press Club Award, the Einstein Award, the Medal of Freedom, the Franklin Award for Distinguished Service, and the Badge of Order of Merit. In 1992, at the age of 85, Michener published his autobiography, *The World Is My Home*. He died on October 16, 1997, after his decision to stop treatment for renal disease.

## Further Reading

Kings, J. *In Search of Centennial.* New York: Random House, 1978.

Michener, James. *Literary Reflections.* Austin, Tex.: State House Press, 1993.

———. *The World Is My Home.* New York: Fawcett Books, 1992.

Severson, Marilyn S. *James A. Michener: A Critical Companion.* Westport, Conn.: Greenwood Press, 1996.

## Millay, Edna St. Vincent
### (Nancy Boyd)
(1892–1950) *poet, playwright*

Edna St. Vincent Millay was a powerful figure in the 1920s, enjoying extraordinary popularity for

heralding in verse the liberation of women. Millay was admired as much for the bohemian freedom of her youthful lifestyle as for her writing, asserting a woman's right to speak as openly as men of erotic love. In 1923, Millay became the first woman to receive a Pulitzer Prize for poetry, for *The Harp-Weaver and Other Poems.* Her verse is known for its easy and lively manner, and she is noted for her mastery of the sonnet form. Although Millay was renowned for unconventional living, her writing was infused with conventional forms. Among the themes she drew on were those of bittersweet love, sorrow, the inevitability of change, and ever-abiding nature.

Edna St. Vincent Millay was born in the small town of Rockland, Maine, on February 22, 1892. She was the daughter of Henry Tollman Millay, a schoolteacher, and Cora Buzzelle. In 1900 Cora Millay divorced her husband for financial irresponsibility and soon thereafter moved to Camden, Maine, with her three daughters. She supported them by nursing and encouraged her daughters to be independent, to read, and to appreciate music. Millay attended public high school, where she wrote for and edited the school magazine. She also published several pieces in *St. Nicholas Magazine.* In 1912, Millay won fourth place in a poetry contest for "Renascence," a mystical poem about spiritual interment and resurrection through the cycles of nature. It was published in the anthology *The Lyric Year*, bringing Millay immediate acclaim and a scholarship to Vassar, after a semester at Barnard College, in 1913. At Vassar, Millay continued to write poetry and became involved in the theater. She also developed intimate relationships with several women while in school, including the English actress Wynne Matthison.

The year she graduated, in 1917, Millay published her first book, *Renascence and Other Poems.* At the request of Vassar's drama department, she also wrote her first verse play, *The Lamp and the Bell* (1921), about love between women. Millay, whose friends called her "Vincent," then moved to New York's Greenwich Village, where she led a notoriously bohemian life and had numerous affairs. She lived in a nine-foot-wide attic and lived a "very, very poor and very, very merry" life along with the other writers of Greenwich Village. She joined the

Provincetown Players theater group in their early days. She published short stories and poems in *Ainslee's* magazine under the pseudonym Nancy Boyd. In 1919 she wrote and directed *Aria da Capo*, a one-act, antiwar verse play with a fairytale motif, for the Provincetown Players. Millay won a $100 prize from *Poetry: A Magazine of Verse* for "The Bean-Stalk" in 1920. Her second book of verse, *A Few Figs from Thistles* (1920), drew much attention for its controversial descriptions of female sexuality and feminism.

Millay traveled in Europe from 1920 to 1923. She had an agreement to write for *Vanity Fair*, but she was also recovering from a nervous breakdown. In 1921, she published two more plays and a collection of poetry, *Second April*. In 1923, Millay was honored as the first woman to be awarded the Pulitzer Prize for poetry for *The Harp-Weaver and Other Poems*. After a brief courtship, she married the 43-year-old widower Eugen Jan Boissevain. He was a burly American importer of Dutch-Irish extraction who was profeminist, considerate, and intelligent. The couple sailed around the world in 1924 as Millay went on reading tours. Boissevain gave up his own pursuits to manage Millay's literary career. She recounted that the couple remained "sexually open" throughout their 26-year marriage. The couple bought Steepletop, their permanent home, on 700 acres of farmland near Austerlitz, New York, in 1925. Shortly thereafter Millay wrote the libretto for the American grand opera *The King's Henchman* (1927).

Millay was actively engaged with public issues of the time, despite poor health and intermittent hospitalization. She became involved in the case of Nicola Sacco and Bartolomeo Vanzetti, Italian-born anarchists and labor agitators, who were convicted and executed for the 1920 murder of two payroll guards. Millay and other intellectuals felt that the men were persecuted for their political activism. Her protest, which landed her in jail for a short time, found expression in several poems, such as in "The Buck in the Snow" (1928). The impending war in Europe and the rise of totalitarianism preoccupied her increasingly in the late 1930s. She devoted her talent to propaganda for the democratic cause, writing newspaper verse, radio plays, and speeches. In *Huntsman, What Quarry?* (1939),

Millay had included stirring poems against fascism, Nazism, and imperialism. Much of her poetry of World War II was collected in *Make Bright the Arrows: 1940 Notebook* (1940). Her socially conscious later poetry was generally considered inferior to her early work.

Loss of friends and poor health plagued Millay during her last years. Boissevain lost his income after the Nazi invasion of Holland, and in 1944 Millay was hospitalized for several months due to a nervous breakdown and was unable to write for two years.

Millay was elected to the National Institute of Arts and Letters (1929) and the American Academy of Arts and Letters (1940).

Millay, who with her husband had drunk to excess since the 1930s, evidently grew more dependent on alcohol after her husband died in 1949. She died a year later on October 19, 1950, sitting at the foot of her staircase, alone, at Steepletop.

**Further Reading**

Dash, Joan. "Edna St. Vincent Millay," in *A Life of One's Own*. New York: Harper and Row, 1973, pp. 116–227.

Gray, James. *Edna St. Vincent Millay*. Minneapolis: University of Minnesota Press, 1967.

Milford, Nancy. *Savage Beauty: The Life of Edna St. Vincent Millay*. New York: Random House, 2001.

Walker, Cheryl. "Women on the Market: Edna St. Vincent Millay's Body Language," in *Masks Outrageous and Austere*. Bloomington: University of Indiana Press, 1991, pp. 135–164.

Wilson, Edmund. "Epilogue 1952: Edna St. Vincent Millay," in *The Shores of Light*. New York: Farrar, Straus, and Young, 1952, pp. 744–793.

# Miller, Arthur
## (Arthur Aster Miller)
(1915–   ) *playwright*

Arthur Miller has been a leading figure in postwar American theater, combining in his plays social awareness with deep insights into the personal weaknesses of his characters. His characters struggle with power conflicts, personal and social responsibility, their pasts, as well as guilt and hope. Much of Miller's best work centers on the ethical responsibility of the individual in conflict with the community. His plays continued a tradition of realism that began in the United States between the two world wars. Miller is best known for the play *Death of a Salesman* (1949), a character study of a failed traveling salesman that won Miller a Pulitzer Prize and a Tony Award. He has written more than 30 plays.

Arthur Aster Miller was born in New York City on October 17, 1915. His father was a ladieswear manufacturer and shopkeeper who was ruined in the depression. The family moved to a small house in Brooklyn, which is said to be the model for the Brooklyn home in *Death of a Salesman*. Miller spent his boyhood playing football and baseball and reading adventure stories. He graduated from Abraham Lincoln High School in 1932 and made money for college by working in an automotive warehouse, singing on a local radio station, and truck driving. He was the only Jew employed in the automotive warehouse and it was there that he had his first experiences of American anti-Semitism. Miller entered the University of Michigan in 1934 to study journalism. He was a reporter and night editor on the student paper, *The Michigan Daily*. He won awards for playwriting, alongside TENNESSEE WILLIAMS, and changed his major to English. After graduation in 1938, Miller returned to New York, where he wrote radio scripts and plays for the Federal Theatre Project.

Because of a football injury, Miller was exempt from the draft. In 1940, he married his first wife, Mary Slattery, and they had two children. Miller's first play to appear on Broadway was *The Man Who Had All the Luck* (1944), which closed after four performances. The following year, he published *Focus*, a novel that was his first major success. The book was adapted for the screen in 2001 in a film by the same name, starring William H. Macy and Laura Dern. In 1947 Miller gained acclaim for the play *All My Sons*, a powerful drama about a son who learns that his father cheated on the manufacturing of war matériel, causing the death of several U.S. pilots during World War I. The play dealt with the issues of guilt and dishonesty that Miller would revisit and expand upon in some of his more mem-

orable plays. *All My Sons* won the New York Drama Critics Circle Award. In 1944 Miller toured army camps to collect background material for the screenplay *The Story of GI Joe* (1945).

Miller then wrote *Death of a Salesman*, which is considered his masterwork and brought Miller international fame. The play won numerous awards, including the Pulitzer Prize. It relates the tragic story of a salesman named Willy Loman, whose past and present are mingled in expressionistic scenes. Loman is not the great success that he claims to be to his family and friends. Some critics criticized Miller for infusing the play with a deep sense of pity for the commonplace salesman, insisting that he was a "little man" and not worthy of the pathos reserved for such tragic heroes as Oedipus and Medea. Miller, however, argued that the tragic feeling is invoked whenever we are in the presence of any character who is ready to sacrifice his life, if need be, to secure his sense of personal dignity. "The American Dream is the largely unacknowledged screen in front of which all American writing plays itself out," Miller has said.

In the 1950s Miller was subjected to scrutiny by a committee of the U.S. Congress investigating communist influence in the arts. His 1953 award-winning play *The Crucible* was widely perceived to be an attack on the House Committee on Un-American Activities and Senator Joseph McCarthy. The play depicted the 17th-century Salem witch trials, during which one could be hanged because of "the inflamed human imagination, the poetry of suggestion." Miller was denied a passport to attend the Brussels premiere of *The Crucible*. When he refused to cooperate with the committee, he was cited for contempt of Congress, a conviction that was overturned on appeal. In the play he expressed his faith in the ability of an individual to resist conformist pressures. *The Crucible* became one of Miller's most-produced plays, although its first Broadway production flopped.

Miller continued to write popular successes like *A View from the Bridge* (1955), which was actually two short plays under a collective title. The drama was about incestuous love, jealousy, and betrayal. He further made headlines with his 1956 marriage to actress Marilyn Monroe. During his marriage to Monroe, Miller wrote *The Misfits*

(1961). Directed by John Huston and starring Monroe, Montgomery Clift, and Clark Gable, the offbeat western was not well received. He and Monroe were divorced the same year. A year later, Miller married Swedish photographer Inge Morath, with whom he collaborated on a number of books.

Miller returned to the stage in 1964 after a nine-year absence with the play *After the Fall,* a strongly autobiographical work. Many critics consider that Maggie, the self-destructive central character in the play, was modeled on Monroe, although Miller denied this. His reworking of the Book of Genesis, *The Creation of the World and Other Business* (1972) failed and marked the last new Miller play on Broadway for more than two decades. His subsequent plays have divided critics and audiences. Although many of Miller's plays have been filmed, only *The Crucible* had a screenplay credited to the author. In 1985, Dustin Hoffman reprised his stage portrayal of Willy Loman in *Death of a Salesman* for television with a script by Miller. In 1994, Miller returned to Broadway with *Broken Glass,* a drama that examined a troubled marriage and a wife's identification with Jewish oppression under the Nazis.

A modern tragedian, Miller has said he gets inspiration from the Greeks, particularly Sophocles. "I think the tragic feeling is evoked in us when we are in the presence of a character who is ready to lay down his life, if need be, to secure one thing—his sense of personal dignity," Miller wrote. "From Orestes to Hamlet, Medea to Macbeth, the underlying struggle is that of the individual attempting to gain his 'rightful' position in his society." Miller has considered the common man "as apt a subject for tragedy in its highest sense as kings were."

In 1965, he was elected president of PEN. Miller's writing has earned him a lifetime of honors, including the Pulitzer Prize, seven Tony Awards, two Drama Critics Circle Awards, an Obie, an Olivier, the John F. Kennedy Lifetime Achievement Award, and the Dorothy and Lillian Gish prize. He holds honorary doctorates from Oxford University and Harvard University. Miller's wife died in 2002. Their daughter, Rebecca, is an actor, writer, and director.

## Further Reading

Griffin, Alice. *Understanding Arthur Miller.* Columbia: University of South Carolina Press, 1996.

Hayman, Ronald. *Arthur Miller.* New York: Ungar, 1972.

Martin, Robert A. *Arthur Miller: New Perspectives.* New York: Prentice-Hall, 1982.

## Miller, Henry
### (Henry Valentine Miller)
### (1891–1980) *novelist*

Henry Miller wrote autobiographical novels that had a liberating influence on mid-20th-century literature. Miller's major novels were banned in several countries because of their frank portrayals of sexuality. In the 1960s Miller became one of the most widely read American authors. He had a long and lucrative career as a writer and published more than 36 creative and analytical works. His most famous works were the autobiographical *Tropic of Cancer* (1934) and *Tropic of Capricorn* (1939). Miller created a myth out of his own life, writing about his time spent between New York and Paris, often broke, and having numerous affairs. Miller influenced the Beat movement writers and became recognized for breaking down the barriers of censorship and for opening up the possibilities of modern fiction.

Henry Valentine Miller was born December 26, 1891, in New York City. He was the son of Heinrich Miller, a tailor, and Louise (Nieting) Miller. Henry went to school where his family lived in Brooklyn and was a good student. In 1909, Miller graduated from high school and entered City College of New York, which he attended for only two months. He then worked at a cement company and held jobs as a cab driver and a librarian. He traveled throughout the Southwest and Alaska with money that was supposed to finance him through Cornell University. In 1913, he went to work at his father's tailor shop.

In 1917, Miller married his first wife, Beatrice Sylvas Wickens, an amateur pianist, with whom he had one child. Miller worked at the Western Union Telegraph Company from 1920 to 1924, and it was there that his first endeavor into writing took place. His boss suggested that someone should write a book about messengers. Miller wrote "Clipped Wings," a story of 12 messengers, many of whom had gentle natures and suffered violence and

1929. Miller spent much of his time roaming the streets; his literary ideals were beginning to change but he was still producing very little publishable material. Tensions grew between Miller and Mansfield as she realized that she was the focus of his writing; she attempted to control her own literary portraits but Miller resented her input. Finally, Mansfield raised enough money for Miller to travel to Paris again in 1930. She followed but her stay was brief.

Once in Paris, Miller resumed his old habits of roaming the streets in search of inspiration and financial support. He began working on his "Paris book," which became *Tropic of Cancer*. The book was sexually explicit and was banned in English-speaking countries. Miller followed up with *Tropic of Capricorn*. Both books chronicle Miller's bohemian life and his loves in New York and as an expatriate in Paris. When the works were brought to the United States, they spawned a 30-year censorship debate that Miller eventually won. The first U.S. edition of *Tropic of Cancer* did not come out until 1961. Miller made numerous friends in Paris, many of whom were often called upon for financial support. Most significant among these was writer ANAÏS NIN. Miller, Nin, and Mansfield became embroiled in a complicated romantic triangle. Nin, who was married, was sexually involved with both Miller and Mansfield. Mansfield left Paris in 1932 and returned later that year. She left a short time later and she and Miller divorced. The long friendship between Miller and Nin was documented by Nin in a series of diaries and made famous in the 1992 feature film *Henry and June*.

Miller left Paris in 1939 and spent six months in Greece, which inspired him to write what many critics believe to be his finest work, *The Colossus of Maroussi* (1941). The time was filled with constant celebration until the outbreak of World War II, which prompted Miller's return to the United States. He traveled throughout the United States and wrote another travel book, *The Air-Conditioned Nightmare* (1945). He believed that the American way of life had "created a spiritual and cultural wasteland." He settled in Big Sur, California, in 1944 and lived there until 1963. His books began to sell and Miller became a sort of bohemian folk hero. His works became famous and were soon

Henry Miller is known for his frank treatment of sexuality in novels such as *Tropic of Cancer* and *Tropic of Capricorn,* which were banned in several countries. *(Library of Congress, Prints and Photographs Division, Carl Van Vechten Collection [LC-USZ62-42523])*

despair. Miller realized that the work was a failure because he knew nothing of writing, and he resolved to learn about it.

In the early 1920s, Miller left his family and moved in with June Mansfield, a Broadway dancer, who supported Miller so that he could pursue his writing. Miller was intrigued with Mansfield's creative and carefree personality. After a tumultuous courtship, they were married 1924. In 1928, Mansfield had saved enough money for the two of them to travel to Europe. They spent nine months overseas, seeing much of Europe by bicycle and train. There was little improvement in their financial situation upon their return to New York City in best-sellers. *Tropic of Cancer* sold more than 2.5 million copies in the first two years of publication in the United States, thus enabling Miller to live in comfort, something he had not known as a beggar in the streets of Paris. "I've known it all," Miller once said. "Every humiliation, degradation, poverty, starvation."

By the late 1950s Miller was finding himself increasingly honored by the literary establishment. In 1957, he was elected to the National Institute of Arts and Letters. He also began to receive some recognition as a watercolorist. When Miller moved to Big Sur he helped establish the area as an artists' colony with himself being the "leading prophet," aside from poet Robinson Jeffers. With an audience, Miller's writing went through a transformation. He became more "literary," which was a word and concept he disliked intensely. His writing formerly had been a stream-of-consciousness type of documentation.

While living in Big Sur, Miller married Janina Martha Lepska, with whom he had two children. After Miller and Lepska divorced, Miller married Eve McClure. He wrote *Big Sur and the Oranges of Hieronymus Bosch* (1957), a rambling memoir of life in Big Sur. He retired to Pacific Palisades, in southern California, and although he still wrote and published occasionally, writing was no longer the driving force in his life. In 1967, Miller married a young Japanese cabaret singer, Hiroko "Hoki" Tokuda. They divorced in 1977.

Miller spent the last 20 years of his life in Pacific Palisades. Of writing he had said: "It's a curse. Yes, it's a flame. It owns you. It has possession over you. You are not the master of yourself. You are consumed by this thing. And the books you write. They're not you. They're not me sitting here, this Henry Miller. They belong to someone else. It's terrible. You can never rest. People used to envy me my inspiration. I hate inspiration. It takes you over completely. I could never wait until it passed and I got rid of it." Miller died in Pacific Palisades on June 7, 1980. He was married five times.

## Further Reading
Balliet, Gay-Louise. *Henry Miller and Surrealist Metaphor: 'Riding the Ovarian Trilogy.'* New York: Peter Lang, 1996.

Kersnowski, Frank L., and Alice Hughes. *Conversations with Henry Miller.* Jackson: University Press of Mississippi, 1994.

Kraft, Barbara. "The Last Days of Henry Miller." *The Hudson Review* 46, no. 3 (autumn 1993): 477–490.

Moore, Thomas H., ed. *Henry Miller on Writing.* New York: New Directions, 1964.

Stuhlmann, Gunther, ed. *Henry Miller, Letters to Anaïs Nin.* New York: Putnam, 1965.

## Momaday, N. Scott
### (Navarre Scott Momaday, Tsoai-talee)
(1934–   ) *poet, novelist, short story writer, essayist*

The first Native American author to win a Pulitzer Prize in fiction, N. Scott Momaday is recognized as one of the most distinguished contemporary writers of American literature. His novels, short stories, poems, and essays often draw on the oral stories of his Kiowa ancestors. Known for work that draws on his rich multicultural heritage, N. Scott Momaday has published numerous award-winning books of poetry, fiction, essays, and stories. In 1969, he won the Pulitzer Prize for his first novel, *House Made of Dawn,* and was also elected into the Gourd Dance Society, the ancient fraternal organization of the Kiowa Indians. In addition to having a significant impact on the development of Native American literature, his career has helped bring attention to other gifted Native American writers, such as JAMES WELCH and LESLIE MARMON SILKO.

Born on February 27, 1934, in a Kiowa Indian hospital in Lawton, Oklahoma, Navarre Scott Momaday was the only child of Alfred Morris Momaday, a Kiowa artist, and Mayme Natachee Scott Momaday, a teacher. Mayme was a descendant of early American pioneers, and her middle name was handed down from her Cherokee great-grandmother. His father's inherited name, Momaday, was shortened from Mammedaty, the name his grandfather and great-grandfather carried as their only name before Christian missionaries arrived in Oklahoma and encouraged the adoption of Christian first names.

Momaday spent his first year on the Kiowa reservation, living in his grandparents' house, before leaving with his parents to live in the Southwest. One of the most notable events of his life occurred when he was just six months old and he accompanied his parents on a trip to Devil's Tower, in the Black Hills of Wyoming. Devil's Tower (Tsoai) became the source of Momaday's Kiowa name, Tsoai-talee, which was given to him by a Kiowa elder named Pohd-lohk (Old Wolf).

His mother loved books and English literature and passed along this love to Momaday, encouraging him to learn English as his first language. Momaday's creative imagination was fostered, he believes, by being an only child and living in remote, wild places, where the landscapes were full of mystery and life.

When he completed his high school degree at a Virginia military academy, Momaday considered attending West Point but eventually enrolled in the University of New Mexico in 1952, where he earned a bachelor's degree in political science in 1958 and became known for his talent as a public speaker and creative writer. Momaday took a year off from his studies to teach school on the Jicarilla Apache reservation before enrolling at Stanford University, where he had received the John Hay Whitney Fellowship in creative poetry writing and the Stanford Wilson Dissertation Fellowship. Momaday completed his master's degree in 1960 and his Ph.D. in 1963. He also became close friends with Yvor Winters, who had a significant influence on his early writing and on his decision to study the writing of naturalist Frederick Goddard Tuckerman, who became the subject of his first book. *The Complete Poems of Frederick Goddard Tuckerman* was based on Momaday's doctoral dissertation and published in 1965.

In 1963, Momaday was hired as an assistant professor of English at the University of California at Santa Barbara. He studied as a Guggenheim Fellow at Harvard University in 1966–67, then was named professor of English at the University of California, Berkeley, where he taught creative writing and designed a new curriculum focused on American Indian literature and mythology. *House Made of Dawn*, his groundbreaking first novel, appeared in 1968 to tremendous critical praise. The following year Momaday became the first Native American to receive the Pulitzer Prize for fiction.

His subsequent novel, *The Way to Rainy Mountain*, was published in 1969 and combined several Kiowa myths and legends with actual history of the tribe to tell the story of its migration from the Yellowstone region to the central plains. The book was illustrated by Momaday's father and, like its predecessor, received high praise from critics and general readers alike.

Momaday's other publications from the 1970s include *Colorado: Summer, Fall, Winter, Spring* (1973); *Angle of Geese and Other Poems* (1974); *The Gourd Dancer* (1976); and *The Names: A Memoir* (1976). *The Ancient Child* was his only book publication in the 1980s, appearing in 1989. Momaday published *In the Presence of the Sun*, a collection of poems and short stories, in 1991, and in 1993, *Circle of Wonder*, a poetic Christmas story that combines Native American and Christian traditions. Momaday also supplied the text for *The Native Americans: Indian Country*, a photobook that accompanied a national art exhibit that had toured across the country.

Momaday left Berkeley for Stanford in 1973. Since 1982, he has lived in Tucson and taught classes on oral tradition at the University of Arizona, giving occasional lectures at other schools including Princeton and Columbia. He is the father of four daughters.

## Further Reading

Commire, Anne, ed. *Something About the Author.* Vol. 48. Detroit: Gale, 1987, pp. 158–162.

Meredith, Howard. "N. Scott Momaday: A Man of Words." *World Literature Today* 64, no. 3 (1990): 405–408.

———. "N. Scott Momaday: Keeper of the Flame." PBS: New Perspectives on the West. Available online. URL: http://www.pbs.org./weta/thewest/program/producers/momaday.htm. Downloaded June 10, 2003.

Sadler, Geoff, ed. *Twentieth Century Western Writers*, second edition. Chicago: St. James Press, 1991, pp. 470–471.

Shubnell, Matthias. *N. Scott Momaday: The Cultural and Literary Background.* Norman: University of Oklahoma Press, 1985.

Woodward, Charles. *Ancestral Voice: Conversations with N. Scott Momaday.* Lincoln: University of Nebraska Press, 1989.

## Moore, Marianne
(1887–1972) *poet*

A Pulitzer Prize winner highly esteemed by her colleagues, American poet Marianne Moore has always been widely appreciated for the cryptic zigzag logic of her writing as well as for her eccentric rhythms and ironic wit. Her best-known poems feature animals and are written in precise, clear language. Moore was a friend to many of the greatest artists and writers of the 20th century, such as T. S. ELIOT, EZRA POUND, E. E. CUMMINGS, and ALLEN GINSBERG. Like many of her counterparts at the time, Moore was interested in the creative process and the relationship between expression and real things. Her poetry, marked by an unconventional but disciplined use of metrics and swift imagery transitions, has been compared to Picasso's cubist portraits. Her use of language is always extraordinarily condensed and precise, capable of suggesting a variety of ideas and associations within a single, compact image.

Marianne Moore was born on November 15, 1887, in Kirkwood, a suburb of St. Louis, Missouri. She was the daughter of John Milton Moore and Mary (Warner) Moore. At a young age, Marianne's father, an engineer, suffered a nervous breakdown after his plans to manufacture a smokeless furnace failed. As a result, he returned to his parents' home in Portsmouth, Ohio, and Mary Moore moved the family to the home of her own father, the Reverend John Riddle Warner, pastor of the Kirkwood Presbyterian Church. In 1894, following Reverend Warner's death, Moore's mother relocated again, this time to Carlisle, Pennsylvania, where she worked as a schoolteacher at the Metzger Institute. Moore entered Bryn Mawr College in 1905. Although she was not an outstanding student, she was popular, very active in the school's social life, and contributed to its student literary magazine, the *Tipyn O'Bob* or *Tip.* During her college years, Moore primarily considered herself a writer of

prose, as she had already explored odes and sonnets starting at age seven.

Moore graduated in 1909 with a degree in biology and histology. She taught typing and bookkeeping for four years at the U.S. Industrial Indian School in Carlisle. In 1911, she spent a summer in England and France. Her first poems appeared in the *Egoist,* an English periodical, and in Alfred Kreymborg's *Others* in 1915. Later that same year, Moore moved with her mother to Chatham, New Jersey, to keep house for her brother John, who was assigned there as a Presbyterian minister. After her brother joined the navy as chaplain, Moore and her mother moved to an apartment in New York City's Greenwich Village where she held brief employment as a secretary in a girl's school and as a private tutor. This era marked the beginning of her friendships with poets of Kreymbourg's *Others* group, including WILLIAM CARLOS WILLIAMS, WALLACE STEVENS, Kenneth Burke, and CONRAD AIKEN. From 1919 on, Moore devoted herself to her writing, but also worked as a secretary, private tutor, and library assistant at the Hudson Park branch of the New York Public Library.

Moore's first book, *Poems,* appeared in London in 1921, when she was 34. It was published without her knowledge by two of her friends, H. D. and Robert McAlmon. *Poems* was followed by *Marriage* (1923) and *Observations* (1924), which won the *Dial* Award for "distinguished service to American letters." T. S. Eliot noted her work early and wrote in 1923, "I can only think of five contemporary poets—English, Irish, French and German—whose works excite me as much or more than Miss Moore's." These works contain some of her best-known poems, including "To Steam Roller," "The Fish," "When I Buy Pictures," "Peter," "The Labors of Hercules," and "Poetry." In *Observations,* Moore brought to her verse the rhythm of prose; she also avoided the use of rhyme in about half of its poems.

In 1925, Moore became acting editor of *The Dial,* an influential American journal of literature and arts, where she worked until the journal was discontinued in 1929 for financial reasons. During these years she published texts from such writers as Paul Valery, T. S. Eliot, HART CRANE, Ezra Pound, and José Ortega y Gasset. The closing down of *Dial* was a severe blow to Moore's career as a critic, although she continued to publish essays on diverse subjects. Moore's *Selected Poems* (1935) was highly praised by Eliot, who wrote in the introduction, "My conviction, for what it is worth, had remained unchanged for the last fourteen years: that Miss Moore's poems form part of the small body of durable poetry written in our time."

In 1929, Moore and her mother moved to Brooklyn, where Moore remained until 1966, when she returned to Greenwich Village. Her subsequent books of poetry included *The Pangolin and Other Verse* (1936), *What Are Years* (1941), *Nevertheless* (1944), *Collected Poems* (1951) (which she dedicated to her late mother), *Like a Bulwark* (1956), *O To Be a Dragon* (1959), *The Arctic Ox* (1964), and *Complete Poems* (1967). Moore also translated La Fontaine's *Fables* (1954). She received many honors during her lifetime, including the election to the National Institute of Arts and Letters, the Bollingen Prize, a National Book Award, a Pulitzer Prize, and the Gold Medal for Poetry from the National Institute. Marianne Moore died on February 5, 1972; she was 84 years old.

## Further Reading

Diehl, Joanne Feit. *Elizabeth Bishop and Marianne Moore.* Princeton, N.J.: Princeton University Press, 1993.

Hall, Donald. *Marianne Moore: The Cage and the Animal.* New York: Pegasus, 1970.

Molesworth, Charles. *Marianne Moore: A Literary Life.* New York: Atheneum, 1990.

Stamy, Cynthia. *Marianne Moore and China: Orientalism and a Writing of America.* Oxford, England: Oxford University Press, 2000.

White, Pamela. *Marianne Moore: Poet of Affection.* Syracuse, N.Y.: Syracuse University Press, 1977.

## Morrison, Toni
### (Chloe Anthony Wofford)
(1931–  ) *novelist, essayist*

Toni Morrison is known for her deep exploration of the black experience in a racist American culture. Recipient of the 1993 Nobel Prize for literature, she has been a member of both the National Council on the Arts and the American Academy and Institute of Arts and Letters. Morrison has actively used her influence to defend the role of the artist and encouraged the publication of other black writers.

Chloe Anthony Wofford was born on February 18, 1931, in Lorain, Ohio. She was the second of four children born to George Wofford, a shipyard welder, and Ramah Willis Wofford. In an attempt to escape racism and find better opportunities in the North, Wofford's parents had relocated to Ohio from the Deep South before she was born. Growing up in Ohio allowed Wofford an opportunity to grow up relatively unscarred by racial discrimination. Her father was a hardworking and dignified man. While the children were growing up, he simultaneously worked three jobs for almost 17 years. Wofford's mother was very religious and was a devoted member of her church choir. Known to have been very proud of their heritage, Wofford's parents spent a good deal of time telling their children folktales and singing songs of southern black communities, thereby transferring their African-American legacies to a new generation.

Lorain was a small industrial town populated with immigrant Europeans, Mexicans, and southern blacks—all living together in relatively close vicinity. Growing up, Wofford attended an integrated school. In her first-grade class, she was the only black student and the only one who could read. She was friends with many of her white schoolmates and did not encounter discrimination until she reached adolescence and began dating. She was also a voracious reader, her early favorites being Russian writers Leo Tolstoy and Feodor Dostoyevski, French author Gustave Flaubert, and English novelist Jane Austen. An excellent student, she graduated with honors from Lorain High School in 1949.

Wofford then attended the prestigious Howard University in Washington, D.C., America's most distinguished black college, where she majored in English and minored in classics. Since many people could not pronounce her first name correctly, she changed it to Toni, a shortened version of her middle name. At Howard, she joined the repertory company, the Howard University Players, with which she made several trips to the South. Wofford continued her studies at Cornell University, in Ithaca, New York. She wrote her thesis on suicide in the works of WILLIAM FAULKNER and Virginia Woolf and received her M.A. degree from Cornell in 1955.

Between 1955 and 1957, Wofford was an instructor in introductory English at Texas Southern University, in Houston, Texas. Unlike Howard University, where she felt that black culture was neglected or minimized, at Texas Southern Wofford discovered a mindset that embraced and celebrated black ethnicity. Texas Southern "always had Negro history week" and introduced Wofford to the idea of black culture as a discipline rather than just personal family reminiscences. In 1957, she returned to Howard University to teach in the English department. This was a time in which the Civil Rights movement was becoming increasingly visible in U.S. society. Heavily invested in the struggle for black equality, Wofford met several people who were later active in the movement. She met the playwright and poet AMIRI BARAKA and Andrew Young (who later worked with Dr. Martin Luther King and later still became a mayor of Atlanta, Georgia). One of her students was Stokely Carmichael, who later became a leader of the Student Nonviolent Coordinating Committee (SNCC). Another of her students, Claude Brown, wrote *Manchild in the Promised Land,* published in 1965, which became a classic of African-American literature.

While at Howard, Wofford met and fell in love with a young Jamaican architect, Harold Morrison. They married in 1958 and their first son, Harold Ford, was born in 1961. Their marriage soon deteriorated, however, and while pregnant with their second child, Toni Morrison left her husband and her job at the university for a trip abroad with young Harold. She later divorced and returned to her parents' house in Lorain with her two sons.

In fall 1964 Morrison moved to Syracuse, New York, where she had obtained a position as a textbook editor. She was transferred after 18 months to the New York headquarters of Random House, where she edited books by prominent black Americans like Muhammad Ali, Andrew Young, Angela Davis, and TONI CADE BAMBARA. At this time Morrison was also busy sending her own novel to various publishers. *The Bluest Eye* (1970) is a story set in the black community of a small

midwestern town. The book was partly based on a story she wrote for a writers' group in 1966, which she joined when her marriage was suffering as a means of reprieve and emotional expression. The novel is about Pecola Breedlove, a black girl who believes that everything would be all right if only she had beautiful blue eyes. Published soon after was *Sula* (1973), a story depicting two black women and the relationship they have with their community in Medallion, Ohio. *Sula* won the National Book Critics Award and became an alternate selection of the Book-of-the-Month Club. Excerpts were published in *Redbook* magazine and it was nominated for the 1975 National Book Award in fiction.

In 1983 Morrison left her position at Random House, having worked there for almost 20 years. In 1984 she was named the Albert Schweitzer Professor of the Humanities at the State University of New York in Albany. While living in Albany, she started writing her first play, *Dreaming Emmett.* It was based on the true story of Emmett Till, a black teenager killed by racist whites in 1955 after being accused of whistling at a white woman. The play premiered on January 4, 1986, at the Marketplace Theater in Albany. Morrison's next novel, *Beloved,* was influenced by a published story about a Kentucky slave, Margaret Garner, who in 1851 escaped with her children to Ohio. When she was about to be recaptured, she tried to kill her children rather than return them to lives of slavery. One of the children died and Margaret was imprisoned for her deed. She refused to show remorse, saying she was "unwilling to have her children suffer as she had done." *Beloved* was published in 1987 and quickly became a best-seller. In 1988 it won the Pulitzer Prize for fiction. The film version of *Beloved* was released in 1999.

In 1987, Toni Morrison was named the Robert F. Goheen Professor in the Council of Humanities at Princeton University. She became the first black woman writer to hold a named chair at an Ivy League university. While accepting, Morrison said, "I take teaching as seriously as I do my writing." She taught creative writing and also took part in the African-American studies, American studies, and women's studies programs. She also started her next novel, *Jazz* (1992), a story about life in the

1920s. *Playing in the Dark: Whiteness and the Literary Imagination* (1992) is a collection of critical essays based on a series of lectures Morrison gave at Harvard University. *Paradise* (1997), her most recent novel, is a complex, multilayered tale of Ruby, Oklahoma, an all-black town established in 1949 by black families fleeing whites and other blacks. The novel spans the years from the town's founding to the 1970s, when some of the town's leaders decide to eliminate a group of women living in a convent just outside the town's borders. The novel unfolds, revealing the struggle between the men of Ruby and the five women of the convent. In 1993 Toni Morrison received the Nobel Prize in literature. She was the eighth woman and the first black woman to be so honored. Morrison currently divides her time between her homes in Rockland County, New York, and New York City.

### Further Reading

Donahue, Deirdre. "The Lyrical World of Toni Morrison" *USA Today.* September 28, 1987.

Italie, Hillel. "Toni Morrison's Paradise," *SouthCoast Today,* February 1, 1998.

Jaffrey, Zia. "The Salon Interview: Toni Morrison." Salon.com. Available online. URL: http://www.salonmagazine.com/books/int/1998/02/cov_si_02int.html. Posted February 1998.

The Toni Morrison Society Web Site. Available online. URL: http://www.gsu.edu/~wwwtms. Downloaded on April 20, 2003.

## Mowat, Farley
(1921– ) *nonfiction writer, novelist, essayist, biographer, children's fiction writer*

Known around the world for his stories about the Far North, Farley Mowat has published more than 30 books, including wilderness adventures, chronicles of the lives of indigenous people, and novels for children, which have been translated into 24 languages. His work has sometimes been controversial for its seamless blending of fact and fiction; some critics have even gone so far as to challenge the authenticity of Mowat's nonfiction work. Mowat remains, however, an extremely popular writer. He has said of himself, "I am a Northern Man . . . I like

to think I am a reincarnation of the Norse saga men and, like them, my chief concern is with the tales of men, and other animals, living under conditions of natural adversity."

Farley Mowat was born in Belleville, Ontario, on May 12, 1921, the only child of Angus and Helen Mowat. His father was a librarian, and the family moved often during the depression years for his father's job. After Belleville, they lived in Trenton, Windsor, Saskatoon, Toronto, and Richmond Hill. Despite all these moves, Mowat frequently lived in places where he was able to keep lots of animals. His dog, Mutt, was his constant companion and became the hero of his book *The Dog Who Wouldn't Be.* Mowat also had a pet rattlesnake, a squirrel, an owl, an alligator, several cats, and large collections of insects. He and some of his childhood friends started the Beaver Club of Amateur Naturalists for people interested in nature conservation. The club formed a museum in the Mowat family's basement, where it displayed such things as the joined skull of a two-headed calf, stuffed birds, and other things of note to young naturalists. By the time he was 13 years old, Mowat had started a magazine called *Nature Lore* and had begun to write a weekly nature column for the Saskatoon *Star-Phoenix.*

Around this time, in 1935, Mowat's uncle, an ornithologist, took him on a trip to the Arctic, which shaped his early love of nature. During World War II, Mowat served in the Canadian army, entering as a private and emerging as a captain. He attended the University of Toronto, where he went on a field trip as a student biologist and observed the Inuit people. Mowat became outraged at what he saw as the exploitation of their culture. His observations led to his first book, *People of the Deer,* which was published in 1952 and made Mowat an instant celebrity. The book, however, sparked much controversy about the veracity of the story. Many critics argued that Mowat was stretching the definition of "non fiction" too far.

Mowat worked as a government biologist in northern Canada following college. His assignment was to study the wolf population and, specifically, to look for proof that they were responsible for the dwindling caribou population. Mowat instead found that the wolves only killed the oldest or sickest caribou and were thus actually helping to strengthen the herd. He drew on this experience observing the wolves in *Never Cry Wolf,* which was published in 1963 and became one of his most widely read books, changing people's views on wolves. After the Russian edition was published, for example, the Soviet Union banned the killing of wolves.

Many of Mowat's books are at least partially autobiographical. *The Dog Who Wouldn't Be* (1957) and *Owls in the Family* (1961) are humorous reflections on his youth; *The Regiment* (1961) and *And No Birds Sang* (1979) address his World War II experiences. Three books focus on the eight years he lived in Burgeo, Newfoundland—*The Rock within the Sea* (1968), *The Boat Who Wouldn't Float* (1969), and *A Whale for the Killing* (1972). *Sea of Slaughter* (1984) chronicles the destruction of various species in the North Atlantic. As a result of his frequent criticisms of the government of both Canada and the United States, Mowat's name was placed in the American "lookout book" for undesirables, and he was refused entry into the United States in 1985. *My Discovery of America* (1985) offers his ironic speculation on the reasons for this. *Virunga: The Passion of Dian Fossey* (1987) is a biography of the well-known primatologist. His most recent books include *Rescue the Earth: Conversations,* (1990) which advocated his position on various ecological issues. He published two volumes of autobiography in the 1990s—*My Father's Son* (1993) and *Born Naked* (1995). *The Farfarers,* a tale of speculative history, was published in 1998.

Mowat has also published several novels for children, including *Lost in the Barrens,* which won the Governor General's Award when it was published in 1956. *The Dog Who Wouldn't Be* and *Owls in the Family* are two of his other most popular books for children.

Mowat lives in Port Hope, Ontario, with his second wife, Claire. He has one son, Sandy. For his body of work, he was awarded an honorary doctorate from McMaster University in 1994.

**Further Reading**

Burgess, Steve. "Northern Exposure," Salon. Available online. URL: http://www.salon.com/people/bc/1999/05/11/mowat. Posted May 11, 1999.

King, James, *Farley: The Life of Farley Mowat.* South Royalton, Vt.: Steerforth Press, 2003.

Shopstone, Joe. "Farley Mowat: On Writing Fiction, Non-fiction and Autobiography." *CM Archive.* Vol. 20, no. 6. (November 1992). Available online. URL: http://www.umanitoba.ca/cm/vol3/no1/farleymowat.html.

## Mukherjee, Bharati
(1940– ) *novelist, short story writer*

Called by one reviewer the "Grand Dame of diasporic Indian literature," Bharati Mukherjee writes novels and short stories that reflect her pride in both her Bengali heritage and the American life she chose when she became a permanent resident of the United States in 1980. She is the author of four novels, two short-story collections, and two works of nonfiction coauthored with her husband, Clark Blaise. Her fiction is often described as focused on the immigrant experience, but it also is focused on telling the tale of America's changing landscape. Her short story collection, *The Middleman and Other Stories,* won the National Book Critics' Circle Award for fiction in 1988.

Bharati Mukherjee was born on July 27, 1940, to an upper-middle class Brahmin family in Calcutta, India. The second of three daughters of Sudhir Lal, a chemist, and Bina Banerjee Mukherjee, she grew up with 40 or 50 relatives living in the same house until she was eight years old. Her favorite pastime as a child was listening to her grandmother tell Indian folktales. When her father was given a job in England in 1947, the family moved there and stayed until 1951, which provided Mukherjee the chance to perfect her English-language skills and to live apart from her relatives for the first time. By this time, Mukherjee had already read numerous classics of Indian and Russian literature, including works by Leo Tolstoy and Feodor Dostoevsky. At age nine, while living in England, she wrote her first novel, about a child detective.

When Mukherjee returned to Calcutta, she received the best English education available, attending Loretto House, a missionary school. When she graduated from there, she enrolled at the University of Calcutta, where she earned a B.A. degree with honors in 1959. Her family then moved to Baroda, India, where she earned her master's degree in English and ancient Indian culture in 1961. Since the age of three, according to Mukherjee, she has known that she wanted to be a writer, and in 1961, she left India to attend the Iowa Writers' Workshop at the University of Iowa in Iowa City. Although she had planned to return after two years and marry a man of her father's choosing, Mukherjee's plans changed forever on September 19, 1963, when she married her boyfriend of two weeks, Canadian writer Clark Blaise, in a lunchtime ceremony in a lawyer's office. Mukherjee went on to complete her M.F.A. degree in 1963 and then her Ph.D. in comparative literature in 1969.

After her education, Mukherjee moved with her husband to Canada, where they lived for 14 years. She has often spoken of what she felt was Canada's hostile attitude toward immigrants. Despite the difficulties she encountered living there, Mukherjee wrote her first two novels while teaching at McGill University, in Montreal. *The Tiger's Daughter* appeared in 1971, and *Wife* was published in 1975. *Darkness* (1985) her first collection of short stories, was not published until after she had moved to the United States, but it is reflective of the cultural separation that Mukherjee felt during her years in Canada. Her next two books were cowritten with her husband. *Days and Nights in Calcutta* (1986), her first book of nonfiction, tells the story of the couple's first trip back to India after their marriage. *The Sorrow and the Terror: The Haunting Legacy of the Air India Tragedy* came out in 1987. *The Middleman and Other Stories* (1988) is regarded as Mukherjee's most successful exploration of her chosen theme—the clash of cultures that immigrants experience and that changes not only the newcomer but also the country in which he or she settles. Mukherjee was the first naturalized American citizen to win the National Book Critics Circle Award, which she was given in 1988 for this memorable collection of stories. *Jasmine,* her most popular novel, was published in 1989 to mixed reviews. She has faced a considerable amount of criticism, specifically from East Indian scholars and critics, for presenting India as a land

without hope or a future and for failing to address the barriers of caste, education, gender, race, and history in the development of her characters' lives. Mukherjee's more recent novels include *The Holder of the World* (1992) and *Leave It to Me* (1997).

In addition to the National Book Critics Circle Award, Mukherjee has been the recipient of a National Endowment for the Arts fellowship, a Guggenheim fellowship, and numerous other awards. She lives in Berkeley, California, and shares what she calls a "literary marriage" with Blaise, who teaches at the University of Iowa. The couple have two sons.

**Further Reading**

Alam, Fakrul. *Bharati Mukherjee.* New York: Twayne, 1996.

Bahri, Deepika. "Always Becoming: Narratives of Nation and Self in Bharati Mukherjee's *Jasmine,*" in *Women, America, and Movement: Narratives of Relocation,* edited by Susan L. Roberson. Columbia: University of Missouri Press, 1998.

Bonnie, Fred. "An Interview with Bharati Mukherjee." *AWP Chronicle* 28, no. 2 (1995): 47.

Carb, Alison B. "An Interview with Bharati Mukherjee." *The Massachusetts Review* 29, no. 4 (1988): 645–654.

Connell, Michael, Jessie Grearson, and Tom Grimes. "An Interview with Bharati Mukherjee." *Iowa Review* 20, no. 3 (1990): 7–32.

Nelson, Emmanuel S., ed. *Bharati Mukherjee: Critical Perspectives.* New York: Garland, 1993.

Zia, Helen, and Susan B. Gall. *Notable Asian Americans.* Detroit: Gale Research, 1995.

## Munro, Alice

(1931– )   *short story writer, novelist*

One of Canada's most important contemporary authors, Alice Munro is best known as a brilliant short story writer whose exploration of human complexities is featured in what appear to be effortless anecdotes of everyday life. In one novel and eight collections of stories, Munro has established herself as a major voice among fiction writers. She has been awarded the Governor General's Award for *Dance of the Happy Shades* (1968) and for *Who*

*Do You Think You Are?* (1978), which was also runner-up for the Booker Prize. She is also the recipient of the Canadian Booksellers Association International Book Year Award for *Lives of Girls and Women* (1971), The Canada-Australia Literary Prize (1977), and the first winner of the Marian Engel Award (1986). Her themes have often related to the dilemmas of adolescent girls coming to terms with their families and small towns. Her more recent work has also addressed the problems of middle age, of women alone, and of the elderly.

Alice Laidlaw was born on July 10, 1931, in Wingham, Ontario. Her childhood years were spent in rural western Ontario, where, as a young girl, she had already begun to write. Munro's life experiences of growing up in a relatively poor provincial town during the depression and of exhibiting the rebelliousness and idealism typical in teenage life—discovering sex, leaving home, and then making an independent life for herself as an adult—all inform the fiction she writes. She has explained in various interviews that her stories are not autobiographical, but she does claim an "emotional reality" for her characters that is drawn from her own life. She graduated from Wingham and District High School in 1949. Following her graduation, she attended the University of Western Ontario from 1949 to 1951. She majored in English and began to take her writing seriously during this time. She was primarily influenced by such writers as EUDORA WELTY, CARSON McCULLERS, KATHERINE ANNE PORTER, and JAMES AGEE.

In 1950 she published her first short story, "The Dimensions of a Shadow." She soon met fellow writer James Munro, and after two years of college life, she married him. The newlyweds moved to Vancouver, British Columbia, where they began raising a family. The Munros had three daughters: Sheila, Jenny, and Sarah. In 1963 the family moved to Victoria and started their business, Munro's Books, which still operates on Vancouver Island. Munro turned to short stories as a logical response to the time constraints of motherhood. She once told a *New York Times* reporter that she never intended to be a short story writer. She started writing short stories because raising three children was so demanding that she did not have time to write anything else. In 1968, Munro published her first collection of short stories, entitled *Dance of the Happy Shades,* for which she won the Governor General's Literary Award, Canada's highest literary prize.

Munro's initial success was followed with the publication of *Lives of Girls and Women* (1971), a collection of linked stories that was published as a novel and won the Canadian Booksellers Association International Book Year Award. Although well received, *Lives of Girls and Women* also led many critics to deem her writing to be nearer autobiography than fiction. In the collection Munro has a character, Del Jordon, explain what she hopes to achieve in writing a work of fiction about small-town life in Ontario. Del works hard to portray not only what is actually "real" about the town, but also what is meaningfully "true," and in order to do so she must capture the dull, ordinary simplicity of her neighbors' daily lives. Del's description of her efforts has often been used by critics to describe Munro's own intentions as a writer. In response to her criticisms, Munro describes her writing as "autobiographical in form but not in fact."

Many commentators compare Munro's interest in small-town settings to the use that American regional writers make of the rural South. Her characters, like WILLIAM FAULKNER's or FLANNERY O'CONNOR's, often find themselves confronting entrenched customs and traditions, but their behavior is usually less overtly desperate and violently intense than that of their southern counterparts. To be sure, there are drunks, suicides, molesters, lunatics, and bizarre eccentrics in Munro's stories, but Faulkner's Emily Grierson and Abner Snopes or O'Connor's Misfit represent more extreme character types than the more ordinary men and women who populate Munro's fictions.

In 1972 Munro divorced James, who was then writer-in-residence at the University of Western Ontario. She then returned to southwestern Ontario and four years later was remarried, this time to Gerald Fremlin, a geographer. The Fremlins moved to a farm outside Clinton, Ontario (not far from Munro's hometown of Wingham), where they still reside today. The couple divides their time between their farm and Comox, British Columbia.

Between 1977 and 1998, Munro published 34 stories in *The New Yorker,* in addition to her many award-winning collections of short stories. Her most recent book, *The Love of a Good Woman,* has won an impressive collection of accolades: the Giller Prize (MARGARET ATWOOD was a member of the jury); the Canadian Booksellers Association People's Choice Award; Fiction Book of the Year and Author of the Year Awards; and the American National Book Critics Circle 1999 fiction prize. In 1995, *Open Secrets* received the W. H. Smith Award for the best book published in Britain throughout the previous year. Stories by Alice Munro have also been among the most popular ever published in prestigious periodicals like *The New Yorker, The Paris Review,* and *Atlantic Monthly.*

### Further Reading

Blodgett, E. D. *Alice Munro.* Boston: Twayne, 1988.

Lecker, Robert. *The Rest of the Story: Critical Essays on Alice Munro.* Toronto: ECW Press, 1999.

Thacker, Robert. *Reflections: Autobiography and Canadian Literature.* Ottawa: University of Ottawa Press, 1988.

Weaver, John. *Patterns of the Past: Interpreting Ontario's History.* Toronto: Dundurn, 1988.

# N

## Nabokov, Vladimir
### (Vladimir Vladimirovich Sirin)
(1899–1977) *novelist, short story writer, poet, translator*

Best known as the author of *Lolita*, one of the most controversial novels of the 20th century, Vladimir Nabokov wrote dozens of novels, as well as several collections of poetry, that were highly praised for their eloquence and stylistic innovations. Revered as the preeminent postmodern writer, his work influenced the development of postmodernism in American literature. Postmodernism in literature generally refers to a repetition of boundaries between high and low art forms and between genres, an emphasis on parody, irony, and playfulness, and a preference for reflexivity, fragmentation, and ambiguity. Although many of these characteristics are associated with modernism as well, it is the different attitude toward these trends that separates the two movements: Modernism lamented the loss of distinction between genres and a sense of wholeness and meaning in art; postmodernism embraces these trends.

Vladimir Nabokov was born in St. Petersburg, Russia, on (or about) April 23, 1899, into a prominent and well-to-do, educated family. He was the oldest of five children born to his father, a distinguished jurist and member of Kerensky's government, and his mother, Elena Ivanovna, a wealthy member of the Russian nobility whose family was noted for its artistic achievements. He is said to have inherited his sensitive and artistic nature from his mother and his work ethic and love of butterflies from his father.

Nabokov's family routinely spoke French, Russian, and English around the house, which had a great effect on the development of Nabokov's linguistic talents. The tutors who assisted with his education at home instructed him and his siblings in all three languages. In 1911, he began attending the highly respected Tenishev School.

Nabokov's childhood was shattered by the Bolshevik revolution, when the Nabokov children and their mother left St. Petersburg for Yalta, in the Crimea, where a friend had an estate. Nabokov's father remained in St. Petersburg and accepted a position in the provisional government following Czar Nicholas II's abdication, but after his imprisonment by the Bolsheviks, the senior Nabokov fled to Crimea, as well, where the family remained for approximately 18 months, at which time they went into exile in Europe.

Nabokov went to school in England, attending Trinity College, Cambridge, from 1919 to 1922. He originally studied zoology but eventually switched to Romance and Slavic languages. He wrote two volumes of poetry in Russian during these years, which were published in 1923. In 1922, he moved to Berlin, Germany, where his family now resided. That same year, his father was accidentally shot and killed. Nabokov married Vera Slonim in 1925 and lived in Berlin with her and their son, Dimitri, who was born in 1934, until 1937, writing for the Russian newspaper his father had founded under the pseudonym of Vladimir Sirin. He also coached tennis and boxing and composed chess problems and crosswords. Many of his early Russian novels were published during these years in Berlin. They include *Mashen'ka* (1926; *Mary*, 1970), *Korol', dama, valet* (1928; *King, Queen, Knave*, 1968), *Zashchita* (1930; *The Defense*, 1964), *Podvig* (1933; *Glory*, 1972), and *Camera obscura* (1933; revised and translated as *Laughter in the Dark*, 1938). Other Russian works were *Otchayaniye* (1936; *Despair*, 1937), *Dar* (1937; *The Gift*, 1963), and *Priglashenie na kazn* (1938; *Invitation to a Beheading*, 1959).

With the Nazi regime's rise to power, Nabokov became disgusted with Germany and fearful due to his wife's Jewish heritage. The family moved to Paris, where Nabokov met the Irish writer James Joyce, wrote several books in French, and wrote his first novel in English, *The Real Life of Sebastian Knight*, which was published in 1941. Nabokov decided at around this time that English was the language in which he should write in order to have the best prospects in publishing, but when he was unable to secure a position teaching in an English university, the Nabokov family moved once again, this time to the United States.

Nabokov settled with his family in 1940 in Boston and worked as a professor of English literature at Wellesley College from 1941 to 1948. In 1948, he took a position as a professor of Russian literature at Cornell University, where he remained until 1959, and became a research fellow in entomology at Harvard, pursuing his lifelong interest in butterflies. In all, Nabokov wrote 18 papers on entomology, some of which deal with his discovery and description of new species.

In 1945, Nabokov became a U.S. citizen. His novel, *Bend Sinister*, was published in 1947, and many of his short stories and poems appeared in the *New Yorker* during this period. His next novel, the infamous *Lolita*, was originally denied publication in the United States and Britain and so was first published in Paris in 1955. When the American publication appeared in 1958, it brought Nabokov instant fame and wealth. A film version (the first of two) was made of *Lolita* in 1962, directed by Stanley Kubrick. Within a few years, Nabokov gave up his teaching position at Cornell to focus entirely on his writing. He moved to Montreux, Switzerland, and lived the rest of his life at the Montreux Palace Hotel. *Lolita* was controversial for its explicit portrayal of a sexual relationship between a pathetic middle-aged professor and his 12-year-old stepdaughter. It became a classic postmodern novel because it expertly weaves numerous well-known literary devices in creating a parody of the romance novel. Critics have generally read the book as a satire, though Nabokov himself rejected the label.

Nabokov's other novels written in English include *Pnin* (1957), *Pale Fire* (1962), *Ada, or Ardor: A Family Chronicle* (1969), *Transparent Things* (1972), and *Look at the Harlequins* (1974). His books of short stories include *Nabokov's Dozen* (1958), *Tyrants Destroyed* (1975), and *The Stories of Vladimir Nabokov* (1995), a posthumous collection that includes 13 previously unpublished stories. In addition to the two books of poetry he published in Russian, Nabokov wrote one book of poems in English, entitled simply *Poems*. It appeared in 1959. He also wrote several scholarly works of nonfiction—*Nikolai Gogol* (1944), a critical study of the 19th-century Russian writer; *Strong Opinions* (1973), a collection of essays; *Lectures on Literature* (1980); and *Lectures on Russian Literature* (1981). He translated the novel *Eugene Onegin* by Alexander Pushkin and published the four-volume work with commentaries in 1964. He also wrote two autobiographical works. *Speak, Memory* (1966) is a compelling account of his childhood in Russia. It originally appeared under the title *Conclusive Evidence* in a shorter form in 1951.

Nabokov received the American National Medal for Literature in 1977, but enjoyed few other awards during his lifetime. He declined election to the National Institute of Arts and Letters, preferring a quiet life of writing and studying butterflies. Vladimir Nabokov died on July 2, 1977, in Montreux of a mysterious lung ailment.

**Further Reading**

Alexandrov, Vladimir. *Nabokov's Otherworld*. Princeton, N.J.: Princeton University Press, 1991.

Boyd, Brian. *Vladimir Nabokov: The American Years*. Princeton, N.J.: Princeton University Press, 1999.

———. *Vladimir Nabokov: The Russian Years*. Princeton, N.J.: Princeton University Press, 1993.

Connolly, Julian W. *Nabokov and His Fiction: New Perspectives*. Cambridge, England: Cambridge University Press, 1999.

————. *Nabokov's Early Fiction: Patterns of Self and Other.* Cambridge, England: Cambridge University Press, 1992.

Hyde, G. M. *Vladimir Nabokov: America's Russian Novelist.* London: Marion Boyars, 1977.

Rampton, David. *Vladimir Nabokov.* New York: St. Martin's, 1993.

Rivers, Julius Edwin, and Charles Nicol, eds. *Nabokov's Fifth Arc: Nabokov and Others on His Life's Work.* Austin: University of Texas Press, 1982.

## Nin, Anaïs
### (Anaïs Antolina Nin)
(1903–1977) *novelist, short story writer, memoirist, diarist/journal writer*

Best known for her series of intensely personal journals, published as *The Diary of Anaïs Nin* (10 volumes, 1966–83), Anaïs Nin is considered to be one of the most provocative and controversial female writers in the world. She is also well known for her many lovers, including HENRY MILLER, Edmund Wilson, Gore Vidal, and Otto Rank. She was married to Hugh Guiler, who tolerated her extramarital affairs, as well as a second, bigamous marriage to Rupert Cole in California. Nin's ideas about "masculine" and "feminine" natures have influenced a part of the feminist movement known as "difference feminism." She disassociated herself late in her life from the more political forms of feminism, believing instead that self-knowledge through journal writing was the source of personal liberation. She also wrote novels, short stories, and erotica, all clearly drawing on the contents of her journals.

Anaïs Antolina Nin was born on February 21, 1903, in Neuilly-sur-Seine, a suburb of Paris, France. Her parents were the Cuban-born Dutch opera singer Rosa Culmell and the infamous Spanish composer and pianist Joaquin Nin. As a child, she accompanied her parents on their musical tours throughout Europe, thereby gaining an early exposure to a diversity of cultures and life throughout the continent. After her parents separated at age 11, Anaïs's mother moved with her children from Spain to New York City. It was during this voyage to her new home that Anaïs began keeping a diary, initially intended as a letter to the father that she felt had abandoned her. She attended school in New York until she was 16, at which time she quit to help her mother run a boardinghouse. She continued to improve her English, however, by reading books from the New York Public Library. Nin also had a short-lived modeling career, an attempt to see her struggling family through their financial hardship. This period was also marked by religious turmoil as she began to reject the Catholicism that had always served as the primary structure in her life.

Nin first met Hugh Guiler in New York in 1921; sporadic visits and letters during Guiler's many trips established their relationship. But in 1922, while preparing to sacrifice herself to a marriage with a wealthy man for her family's benefit, Nin left New York for Cuba to stay with a wealthy aunt. However, this goal was thwarted when Guiler arrived in Havana in February 1923. The couple married on March 3, 1923, then returned to New York for a short time before relocating to Paris.

The move to Paris was occasioned by a number of factors, including Hugh's transfer, Nin's mother's debts, and her brother's ambition to become a pianist. Nin was both intrigued by the prospect of returning to France and frightened by the prospect of reuniting with her father. The next few years were marked by prosperity as Hugh advanced in his position at the bank. During this time, while frustrated with her life and duties as a banker's wife, Nin dabbled in different arts and desperately sought her own form of creative expression. The stock market crash in 1929 then forced the Guilers to move from Paris; they relocated to Louveciennes, a small village near the Paris suburb of St.-Cloud, where they rented an old house with a view of the city. Here, the feeling of isolation and the relentless self-analysis that had come to dominate Nin's life deepened.

On November 31, 1931, Nin met her lawyer friend Richard Osborn to discuss the copyright on her first book. At this meeting, she was introduced to the U.S. expatriate writer Henry Miller. This momentous meeting was to alter the personal and private lives of both writers. Miller lived in a world different from anything Nin had ever known. His companions were the gangsters, prostitutes, and drug addicts of Paris. He and his often-absent wife, June Mansfield, lived a life of extremes and were appealing to Nin in their opposition to everything she had known. Nin's friendship with Miller flourished over the next month, in which she listened to him talk obsessively about June, who was then in New York. Nin met June personally on December 30, 1931, and was immediately transfixed. Miller's jealousy grew as the two women courted for four weeks before June's departure from Paris. As Nin and Miller spent subsequent months analyzing and writing about June, their own relationship intensified and eventually grew into a love affair that lasted several years. Nin's professional career soon began to flourish and she published her first book, *D. H. Lawrence: An Unprofessional Study*, in 1932 and began the novella *House of Incest*, which focused on her affection for June.

To resolve her inner conflicts surrounding her marriage to Hugh, Nin entered therapy with the prominent Parisian psychoanalyst Rene Allendy and, later, with Otto Rank. Eventually, Nin studied under Rank at his practice in New York City. While in New York, she was engaged in the complicated process of keeping her numerous lovers, including Miller and her husband Hugh, separate and happy. In 1935, she returned to Paris to live with her husband. Hugh was transferred to London in 1937; the couple was still married but had decided to go their separate ways. They later reunited when Hugh moved to New York. Nin became friends with the writer Lawrence Durrell and continued to write, publishing *Winter of Artifice* in 1939. The threat of war at the end of the 1930s scattered her Paris circle, and even Miller left Paris and returned to New York. Nin, too, soon departed for New York, although she and Miller were never again to resume the same intense relationship that had marked the last decade.

At the end of 1939, back in New York with her husband, Nin became immersed in the New York literary scene. In 1940, she established her own printing press out of frustration from being rejected by publishers. The press published both Nin's works and the writing of others. However, her hard work earned little financial reward. This financial stress was relieved to some extent by financial aid from Miller, with whom she still corresponded.

In spring 1947, Nin met Rupert Pole, a man 20 years her junior, and soon moved to the West Coast with him. From this point onward, she divided her life between the two coasts, with Hugh in New York and Rupert in California, maintaining relationships with both men. In 1950, her book *The Four-Chambered Heart* was published. However, despite this success, her primary literary work remained hidden. She had been debating what to do with the *Diary*, a publishable form of her personal journals; it would be her major work, but she did not want to risk the exposure that publishing it entailed. Thus, she continued to publish fiction and forged an alliance with publisher Alan Swallow, who began the process of publishing and reissuing her works. This exposure prompted a turn in the critical tide and her popularity increased dramatically.

In 1964, Nin published another fictional work, *Collages*, and began editing the diary for publication, despite a general discouragement by close friends such as Miller, Rank, and Allendy, who felt that she was obsessed with diary writing. The first diary volume was published in 1966 and was met with favorable reviews and substantial critical acclaim. Following publication of subsequent volumes, Nin became a controversial figure in the feminist movement. She was simultaneously praised for her unflinching examination of the female psyche and vilified as someone who upheld archaic feminine stereotypes. Nevertheless, Nin remained in great demand as a lecturer at universities and traveled extensively to promote her publications. Her legacy was firmly entrenched by the time of her death from cancer on January 14, 1977, and subsequent years have served only to increase recognition of her literary contributions.

## Further Reading

Bair, Deirdre. *Anaïs Nin: A Biography.* New York: Putnam, 1995.

Evans, Oliver Wendell. *Anaïs Nin.* Carbondale: Southern Illinois University Press, 1968.

Fitch, Noel Riley. *Anaïs: The Erotic Life of Anaïs Nin.* Boston: Little Brown, 1993.

Nalbantian, Suzanne. *Anaïs Nin: Literary Perspectives.* New York: St. Martin's Press, 1997.

Richard-Allerdyce, Diane. *Anaïs Nin and the Remaking of Self: Gender, Modernism, and Narrative Identity.* DeKalb: Northern Illinois University Press, 1998.

## Oates, Joyce Carol
### (Rosamond Smith)
(1938–   ) *novelist, short story writer, detective/mystery writer, essayist*

Twice nominated for the Nobel Prize in literature, Joyce Carol Oates is one of America's most prolific and accomplished writers. She is the author of a number of distinguished books in several genres, all published within the past 25 years. In addition to numerous novels and short story collections, she has published several volumes of poetry, several books of plays, five books of literary criticism, and the book-length essay *On Boxing* (1987), a collection of profiles of nine boxing trainers. Her writing has earned her much praise and many awards, including the PEN/Malamud Award for Excellence in short fiction, the Rosenthal Award from the American Academy-Institute of Arts and Letters, a Guggenheim Fellowship, and the O. Henry Prize for Continued Achievement in the Short Story. Oates has produced some of the most controversial, and enduring fiction of the twentieth century. She won the National Book Award in 1970 for her novel *Them,* which is set amidst a backdrop of racial strife in 1960s Detroit. *Because It Is Bitter, and Because It Is My Heart* (1990) focused on an interracial teenage romance. *Black Water* (1992), a narrative based on the Kennedy-Chappaquiddick scandal, garnered a Pulitzer Prize nomination, and her national bestseller *Blonde* (2000), an epic work on American icon Marilyn Monroe, became a National Book Award finalist. Although Joyce

Carol Oates has called herself, "a serious writer, as distinct from entertainers or propagandists," her novels are known for captivating a wide audience; *We Were the Mulvaneys* (1996) earned the number-one spot on the *New York Times* best-seller list.

Joyce Carol Oates was born on June 16, 1938, in upstate New York to Frederic and Caroline Oates. She grew up in the small community of Lockport during a time when the nation was desperately struggling to climb out of a decade-old economic depression. Oates was a self-proclaimed serious child; she spent her elementary years attending a one-room schoolhouse where she had little in common with her classmates. Her parents saw early on that their daughter was exceptionally gifted, hardworking, and a perfectionist at all of her endeavors. As a young girl, Oates told stories by drawing and painting before she learned to write. After receiving a typewriter at age 14, she began consciously training herself, "writing novel after novel" throughout high school and college years.

Success came early for Oates. While attending Syracuse University on scholarship, she won the coveted *Mademoiselle* fiction contest. After graduating as valedictorian, she earned an M.A. degree in English at the University of Wisconsin, where she met and married Raymond J. Smith after a three-month courtship. The newlyweds soon moved to Texas, where she successfully wrote her first book of stories, then resettled in Detroit, Michigan, in 1962. Detroit's increasingly volatile social tensions, seen as a representation of the larger U.S. society, inspired Oates's early writing themes. The greatest impact this city would have on her involved the race riots of 1967. From this experience Oates wrote her National Book Award winner *Them*. "Detroit, my 'great' subject," she has written, "made me the person I am, consequently the writer I am—for better or worse." During this time Oates had begun to write about the new society that was erupting everywhere around her—strip malls, suburbia, and the chaos of city living. This was a time in her life when she began to write a string of novels depicting society as a whole. A couple of these novels included *Do with Me What You Will* (1973) and *The Assassins* (1975). Oates wrote the short story "Where Are You Going, Where Have You Been?" in early 1966. Dedicated to Bob Dylan, it was sparked by an idea that came to her while listening to a Dylan album; it is one of her most famous works and one of the most frequently anthologized short stories ever.

Between 1968 and 1978, Oates taught at the University of Windsor in Ontario, just across the Detroit River. During this immensely productive decade, she published new books at the rate of two or three per year, all the while maintaining a full-time academic career. Though still in her 30s, Oates had become one of the most respected and honored writers in the United States. Asked repeatedly how she managed to produce so much excellent work in a wide variety of genres, she gave variations of the same basic answer, telling the *New York Times* in 1975 that "I have always lived a very conventional life of moderation, absolutely regular hours, nothing exotic, no need, even, to organize my time." When a reporter labeled her a "workaholic," she replied, "I am not conscious of working especially hard, or of 'working' at all. Writing and teaching have always been, for me, so richly rewarding that I don't think of them as work in the usual sense of the word."

In 1978 Oates moved to Princeton, New Jersey, where she is currently the Roger S. Berlind Distinguished Professor of Humanities at Princeton University, and where she continues to teach in the creative writing program. She and her husband also operate a small press and publish a literary magazine, *The Ontario Review*. As a writer, critic, and professor, Oates dedicates her life to "promoting and exploring literature . . . I am not conscious of being in any particular literary tradition, though I share with my contemporaries an intense interest

in the formal aspects of writing; each of my books is an experiment of a kind, an investigation of the relationship between a certain consciousness and its formal aesthetic expression." Shortly after arriving in Princeton, Oates began writing *Bellefleur* (1980), the first in a series of ambitious gothic novels that simultaneously challenged and reworked established literary genres and reinterpreted large periods of American history. Published in the early 1980s, these novels marked a departure from the psychological realism of her earlier work.

Oates eventually returned to her powerful realistic mode with family chronicles such as *You Must Remember This* (1987) and with novels of female experience, *Solstice* (1984) and *Marya: A Life* (1986). Her most recent novels include *Middle Age: A Romance* (2001), *Big Mouth and Ugly Girl* (2002), *I'll Take You There* (2002), *Freaky Green Eyes* (2003), *The Tattooed Girl* (2003), and *Where Is Little Reynard* (2003). Her best-known novels remain those that were written with a deliberate and sophisticated awareness of genre and historical period. Oates has been the recipient of numerous prizes and awards. These include the PEN/Malamud Award for Excellence in short fiction, the Rosenthal Award from the American Academy Institute of Arts and Letters, a Guggenheim Fellowship, the O. Henry Prize, and the National Book Award. She has twice been nominated for the Nobel Prize in literature.

**Further Reading**

Johnson, Greg. *Invisible Writer: A Biography of Joyce Carol Oates*. New York: Dutton, 1998.

Lercangee, Francine. *Joyce Carol Oates: An Annotated Bibliography*. New York: Garland Press, 1986.

Milazzo, Lee. *Conversations with Joyce Carol Oates*. Jackson: University of Mississippi Press, 1989.

Wagner-Martin, Linda. *Critical Essays on Joyce Carol Oates*. Boston: G. K. Hall, 1979.

# O'Brien, Tim
## (William Timothy O'Brien)
(1946–  ) *novelist, short story writer, essayist, memoirist*

Known for gripping tales of the Vietnam War, both fiction and nonfiction, Tim O'Brien has been hailed as one of the most renowned writers of his generation. His first book, *If I Die in a Combat Zone, Box Me Up and Send Me Home,* a memoir of his experience during the Vietnam War, was named Outstanding Book of 1973 by the *New York Times,* and he won the National Book Award for *Going After Cacciato* in 1979.

Born in Austin, Minnesota, on October 1, 1946, Tim O'Brien grew up in the small town of Worthington, Minnesota. His father, William, was an insurance salesman, and his mother, Eva, was an elementary school teacher. As a child, O'Brien was a dreamer who loved entertaining himself by practicing magic tricks. As a teenager, he discovered several articles that his father had written about Iwo Jima and Okinawa when he was a soldier during World War II and decided that he wanted to be a writer.

When O'Brien graduated from high school, he entered Macalester College, where his chosen major was political science and his career ambition was to join the State Department. In 1968, following his graduation summa cum laude with a B.A. degree in political science, O'Brien was drafted. Although he opposed the war in Vietnam and had protested frequently during his college years, O'Brien reported for duty, all the time repressing the reality that he was being prepared to fight an actual war. He once wrote about this time in his life, "I couldn't believe any of it was happening to me, someone who hated Boy Scouts and bugs and rifles." O'Brien dutifully deferred his admission to Harvard, where he planned to pursue a graduate degree in government, and headed to boot camp. He was classified as a foot infantryman and assigned to the Third Platoon, A Company, Fifth Battalion, 46th Infantry. His platoon was stationed in My Lai in 1968, immediately following the My Lai Massacre, in which a village was destroyed and its civilian inhabitants were massacred.

While serving in Vietnam, O'Brien was awarded a Purple Heart and promoted to the rank of sergeant. He also wrote numerous personal reports of the war, which were published in newspapers back in Minnesota. He returned to the United States in 1970, having decided to pursue a doctoral degree in government at the Harvard School of Government. While at Harvard, O'Brien accepted an internship with the *Washington Post,* a fateful decision that led to his leaving Harvard and pursuing a career as a writer.

In 1973, the same year that he married a magazine production manager, his first book, and only book of nonfiction, was published. O'Brien's memoir of the war, *If I Die in a Combat Zone, Box Me Up and Ship Me Home,* was published about the same time that he was hired as a national affairs reporter for the *Washington Post.* He kept the reporting job for about a year before quitting to devote himself full time to writing books. The novel *Northern Lights* appeared in 1975, and *Going after Cacciato,* another novel, was published in 1978 and won the National Book Award in 1979. *The Nuclear Age* was released in 1985 and followed by *The Things They Carried* in 1990, which won France's Prix du Meilleur Livre Etranger and was a finalist for the National Book Critics Circle Award and the Pulitzer Prize. *In the Lake of the Woods* appeared in 1994 and according to O'Brien, this novel about a soldier coming to terms with his role in the My Lai massacre took everything out of him and left him feeling like he had nothing left to write for a while. "I feel like I've gone to the bottom of the well with this book," O'Brien said, when he finally finished the novel after working on it for six years.

The book received the James Fenimore Cooper Prize from the Society of American Historians and was named best novel of the year by *Time* magazine. *Tomcat in Love* (1998) and *July, July* (2002) are O'Brien's big departures from the Vietnam War. These novels look at the battle of the sexes and explore the lengths that men and women go to in pursuit of love.

O'Brien has also published his short fiction in numerous magazines including *Esquire, Harper's,* the *Atlantic,* and the *New Yorker.* His stories have also appeared in several editions of *The Best American Short Stories* and *The O. Henry Prize Stories.* His short story "The Things They Carried" received the National Magazine Award in 1987 and in 1999 was selected for inclusion in *The Best American Short Stories of the Century,* edited by JOHN UPDIKE.

In addition to the awards already mentioned, he has received fellowships from the American Academy of Arts and Letters, the Guggenheim

Foundation, and the National Endowment for the Arts. He holds a chair in creative writing at Southwest Texas State University.

## Further Reading

Campbell, Christopher D. "Conversation across a Century: The War Stories of Ambrose Bierce and Tim O'Brien." *War, Literature, and the Arts* 10, no. 2 (fall–winter 1998): 267–288.

Herzog, Tobey C. *Tim O'Brien.* New York: Twayne, 1997.

Kaplan, Steven. "An Interview with Tim O'Brien." *Missouri Review* 14, no. 3 (1991): 95–108.

McNerney, Brian C. "Responsibly Inventing History: An Interview with Tim O'Brien." *War, Literature, and the Arts* 6, no. 2 (fall–winter 1994): 1–26.

Timmerman, John H. "Tim O'Brien and the Art of the True War Story: 'Night March' and 'Speaking of Courage.'" *Twentieth Century Literature* 46, no. 1 (spring 2000): 100–114.

## O'Connor, Flannery
### (Mary Flannery O'Connor)
(1925–1964) *novelist, short story writer*

Flannery O'Connor, one of the most acclaimed writers of the 20th century, was particularly recognized for her combination of the comic with the tragic. Along with authors such as CARSON McCULLERS and EUDORA WELTY, O'Connor belonged to the southern gothic tradition that focused on the decaying South and its people. O'Connor broke down the conventional world of her subjects, offering them a clear view of reality, through the use of grotesque characters and shocking acts. She had a deep understanding of religious belief and the human condition. O'Connor's body of work was small, consisting of only 32 stories, two novels, and some speeches and letters. She died of lupus at the age of 39.

Mary Flannery O'Connor was born in Savannah, Georgia, on March 25, 1925, to Edward O'Connor and Regina (Cline) O'Connor. She was known throughout childhood as "Mary Flannery" but decided that it did not sound literary enough and went by "Flannery" when she got older. She began writing at a young age. O'Connor's father worked in real estate and later for a construction

company. Her mother came from a prominent Georgia family. When O'Connor was 12, the family moved from Savannah to Milledgeville, where O'Connor's grandfather was mayor. Three years later, O'Connor's father died of lupus. O'Connor attended the Peabody High School and enrolled in the Georgia State College for Women, where she edited the college magazine. After graduating in 1945, she continued her studies at the University of Iowa, pursuing a master of fine arts degree in literature. When she was 21, her first short story, "The Geranium," was published in *Accent.* But she often stated that her first claim to fame occurred when she was only five years old. A New York cameraman came to visit her after learning that she had taught a chicken to walk backwards. She also made clothes for her chickens.

O'Connor was invited to continue her writing at Yaddo, an artists' colony in upstate New York. She made great strides with her writing and read such thinkers as Pierre Teilhard de Chardin, George Santayana, and Hannah Arendt. She met a number of literary people with whom she formed lifelong friendships. Among those were her future editor, Robert Giroux, and the poet Robert Fitzgerald and his wife. She lived with the Fitzgerald family for two years in the Connecticut countryside and referred to them as her "adopted kin." She also met Caroline Gordon, on whom she relied throughout her life for literary criticism. O'Connor established herself as a writer with the publishing of four chapters of *Wise Blood* in *Mademoiselle,* the *Sewanee Review,* and *Partisan Review* in 1948 and 1949. The complete novel appeared in 1952. The story examines the bizarre relationship between a licentious young girl, a conniving widow, and a young man who deliberately blinds himself after failing to establish a church without Christ. O'Connor called it a "comic novel" and said it was therefore "very serious, for all comic novels that are any good must be about matters of life and death."

O'Connor found southern evangelicalism, with its Protestant emphasis on immediate conversion, worthy exploration. She came from a staunch Roman Catholic family in the region known as the Bible Belt of the southern states. Roman Catholics were a small religious minority in the South and even as a child in parochial school, O'Connor was aware of being regarded as somehow different. In her mature years as a writer, many of her artistic contemporaries regarded any kind of orthodoxy as odd, but O'Connor never lost her vital connection to her faith.

The writer developed lupus in 1950 at the age of 26. She believed she only had three years left to live. By the age of 30 she was using crutches but continued writing and produced a second novel, *The Violent Bear It Away* (1960). It tells of three generations of men obsessed by guilt and driven to violence. After killing his uncle's son, the protagonist sets fire to his own woods to clean himself, and like his great-uncle, a mad prophet, he becomes a prophet and a madman as well. In spite of her illness, O'Connor continued to write and occasionally lectured about creative writing in colleges. "She understands her country and its people so well that in her hands they become all humanity," according to the *New York Herald Tribune*.

O'Connor's short stories have been considered her finest work. With *A Good Man Is Hard to Find, and Other Stories* (1955) she was regarded as a master of the form. The book is a collection of tales about healing preachers, godless spectators, Civil War veterans, and a Bible salesman who steals a girl's wooden leg. In the title story of the collection, a white southern family, led by their religious grandmother, turns down a side road looking for an old southern mansion. They encounter some escaped convicts whom the matriarch preaches to about how hard it is to find a good man. The criminals casually wipe out the family when the grandmother recognizes one of them from a "Wanted" poster.

O'Connor's literary career was a race against time. Her lupus progressed with occasional remissions, but the medication that restrained it damaged her bone structure. Aware of the fragility of her existence, she wrote and revised with tireless intensity. She led a private and rather uneventful life that was focused almost exclusively on her vocation as a writer. O'Connor was an advocate of New Criticism, which held that a writer's life had no bearing on his or her work. She engaged in no known love affairs and lived quietly with friends or family. She held no jobs, subsisting solely on grants, fellowships, occasional teaching, and royalties from her writing. Her last years were spent at Andalusia, the family dairy farm near Milledgeville, under the care of her mother. She loved birds and often when she mailed a letter, she drew a peacock on it. She raised the birds as well and they became her trademark. O'Connor's second collection of short stories, *Everything That Rises Must Converge*, was published posthumously in 1965. *The Complete Short Stories* (1971) contained imaginative occasional prose and several stories that had not previously appeared in book form. O'Connor's letters, published as *The Habit of Being* (1979), reveal her conscious craftsmanship in writing and the role of Roman Catholicism in her life.

O'Connor received a National Institute of Arts and Letters grant in literature, won first prize in the O. Henry Memorial Awards three times, won a Henry H. Bellaman Foundation special award, the National Book Award, and the Board Award from the National Critics Circle. O'Connor died on August 3, 1964, at the age of 39.

**Further Reading**

Cash, Jean W. *Flannery O'Connor: A Life*. Nashville: University of Tennessee Press, 2002.

Magee, Rosemary M. *Conversations with Flannery O'Connor*. Literary Conversations Series. Jackson: University Press of Mississippi, 1987.

Martin, Regis. *Unmasking the Devil: Dramas of Sin and Grace in the World of Flannery O'Connor*. Ypsilanti, Mich.: Sapientia Press, 2002.

## Odets, Clifford
(1906–1963) *playwright*

America's leading playwright in the theater of social protest in the 1930s, Clifford Odets also wrote numerous screenplays and directed the films *None but the Lonely Heart* and *The Story on Page One*. At the beginning of his career, he helped to found the Group Theatre in New York City, which went on to have a significant impact on the American stage. His body of work remains one of the most distinctive contributions to American theater.

The son of Jewish immigrants, Clifford Odets was born in Philadelphia on July 18, 1906, but grew up in New York City. Determined to become an actor, Odets left school at age 17 and landed a series of small parts in the theater and on radio. He also helped to form the Group Theatre, whose members were committed to left-wing politics and to producing plays that would contribute important social commentary. The Group Theatre produced most of Odets's early plays.

Odets joined the American Communist Party in 1934 and had his first play, *Waiting for Lefty*, produced in 1935. An immediate success, the play dealt with trade union corruption and established as Odets's subject matter the lives of the urban underprivileged. His next two plays, *Awake and Sing!* (1935) and *Till the Day I Die* (1935) addressed similar themes. Following the production of his play *Paradise Lost* in 1935, Odets accepted an offer to become a screenwriter for films. He moved to Hollywood and married the Austrian actress Luise Rainer in 1936. Although his new work was financially very rewarding, Odets continued writing plays and enjoyed his greatest commercial success with *Golden Boy*, which premiered in 1937. His next productions were *Rocket to the Moon* (1938), *Night Music* (1940), *Clash by Night* (1941), *The Big Knife* (1949), *The Country Girl* (1950), and *Wild in the Country* (1961). These plays failed, for the most part, to live up to the promise of Odets's earlier work. They were poorly received by critics, which tormented Odets. His screenplay for the film *Sweet Smell of Success* (1957) was one of his most acclaimed later works. In 1953, Odets was investigated by Joseph McCarthy and the House Un-American Activities Committee. Odets successfully argued that while his work expressed his deep sympathy for the working classes, he had never been under the influence of the American Communist Party. Unlike many other actors and writers in Hollywood, Odets was never blacklisted and continued to work. In 1961, he became the story editor for the television series *The Richard Boone Show*, and in 1964, the year following his death, a musical was made based on *Golden Boy*. Clifford Odets died on August 18, 1963, in Los Angeles from complications of cancer.

Playwright Clifford Odets was an instrumental figure in the left-wing theater of the 1930s in New York City. *(Library of Congress, Prints and Photographs Division, Carl Van Vechten Collection [LCPP005A-52489])*

In addition to writing and working on films, Odets collected art and painted. During the years when he was investigated for communist activity, Odets painted often, creating a body of work that has since been exhibited with quotations from his journals, photographs, and other memorabilia. Odets owned art by Chagall, Picasso, Soutine, and Klee, among others. At one point, he owned more than 60 works by Klee, the largest collection in private hands in the United States.

## Further Reading

Brenman-Gibson, Margaret. *Clifford Odets, American Playwright: The Years from 1906 to 1940.* New York: Atheneum, 1981.

Cantor, Harold. *Clifford Odets, Playwright-Poet.* Metuchen, N.J.: Scarecrow Press, 1978.

Mendelsohn, Michael J. *Clifford Odets, Humane Dramatist.* Deland, Fla.: Everett/Edwards, 1969.

Miller, Gabriel. *Clifford Odets.* New York: Continuum, 1989.

Rubin, Mann. "Confessing with Clifford." *Written By.* June/July 2000. Available online. URL: http://www.wga.org/WrittenBy/0600/odets.html. Downloaded June 14, 2003.

Shuman, R. Baird. *Clifford Odets.* New York: Twayne Publishers, 1962.

Weales, Gerald. *Clifford Odets, Playwright.* New York: Pegasus, 1971.

## O'Hara, Frank
### (Francis Russell O'Hara)
(1926–1966) *poet*

Frank O'Hara's naturalistic style of autobiographical writing made him one of his generation's best-known poets. O'Hara led a movement known as the New York school of poetry, which also included fellow poets KENNETH KOCH, James Schuyler, and JOHN ASHBERY. O'Hara's poetry was different than that of his contemporaries. He became known as a cosmopolitan poet with a unique style that incorporated the different aspects of his life: a love for the city, the arts, homosexuality, and socializing. Although all of the poets from the New York school displayed an active sense of humor and a tendency for short, modern-day poems, none of them were as strongly autobiographical as O'Hara.

Francis Russell O'Hara was born on June 27, 1926, in Baltimore, Maryland. He grew up in Massachusetts and studied piano at the New England Conservatory in Boston from 1941 to 1944. O'Hara then served in the South Pacific and in Japan as a sonarman on the destroyer USS *Nicholas* during World War II. Following the war, O'Hara studied music at Harvard University. Although he also wrote poetry, he was more influenced by contemporary music—his first love—and art. While at Harvard, O'Hara met John Ashbery and soon began publishing poems in the *Harvard Advocate.* Despite his love for music, he changed his major and, in 1950, earned his bachelor's degree in English. He then attended graduate school at the University of Michigan, Ann Arbor, and received his M.A. degree in 1951. That same year he moved to New York City, where he took a job working at the front desk of the Museum of Modern Art. It was during this time that O'Hara began to write seriously.

O'Hara's early work was considered intensely provocative. In 1952, his first volume of poetry, *A City in Winter,* attracted favorable attention; his essays on painting and sculpture and his reviews for *ArtNews* were considered brilliant. O'Hara became one of the most distinguished members of the New York school of poets. In addition, O'Hara's association with painters such as Larry Rivers, Jackson Pollock, and Jasper Johns also became a source of inspiration for his highly original poetry. He attempted to produce with words the effects these artists had created on canvas. In certain instances, he collaborated with the painters to make "poem-paintings," which were paintings combined with text on canvas.

O'Hara would continue working at the Museum of Modern Art throughout his life, curating exhibitions and writing introductions and catalogs for exhibits and tours. In 1966, while vacationing on Fire Island, he was killed in a sand buggy accident. He was 40 years old.

O'Hara wrote poetry almost every day of his adult life. He would stop wherever he was to write a poem off the top of his head. Some of his most famous poems were written while he was on his lunch break or on his way to someplace. He said that many of his poems worked as unmade phone calls. They were all about his life and thoughts and feelings and were usually meant to convey ideas to his friends. Although he had several collections of poetry published during his lifetime, a large amount of his work was not seen until after his death. He was never very interested in having most of it released and would often only submit poems for publication if asked personally by an editor. Often, the act of writing the poem was more important to him than keeping the finished work for prosperity.

Some of his finest work was composed in the late 1950s, including "The Day Lady Died," "Steps," "A True Account of Talking to the Sun at Fire Island," and others. He was at the height of his powers in these poems, which bristle with immediacy and spontaneity, overflowing with the mundane details of life—place-names, names of friends, bits of telephone conversations, and music.

## Further Reading

Berkson, Bill, and Joe LeSueur, eds. *Homage to Frank O'Hara*. Berkeley, Calif.: Creative Arts Book Company, 1980.

Feldman, Alan. *Frank O'Hara*. Boston: Twayne Publishers, 1979.

Ferguson, Ellen A. "Tapinosis in the Poetry of Frank O'Hara and Philip Levine." *DAI* 58, no. 1 (July 1997): 38–52.

Myers, John Bernard. *The Poets of the New York School*. Philadelphia: University of Pennsylvania Press, 1969.

Perloff, Marjorie. *Frank O'Hara: Poet Among Painters*. New York: George Braziller, 1977.

Smith, Alexander. *Frank O'Hara: A Comprehensive Bibliography*. New York: Garland, 1979.

## Oliver, Mary

(1935–  ) *poet, essayist*

The author of more than 10 volumes of poetry and prose, Mary Oliver is known for poems that richly call forth the tradition of romantic nature poetry with a voice that is wholly of its time. She has won the Pulitzer Prize for poetry and the National Book Award for poetry, in addition to numerous other awards. Although she has lived and worked in quite a few different places and maintained her privacy by rarely granting interviews or talking about herself, she has a large and devoted popular following as well as many admirers among literary critics.

Mary Oliver was born on September 10, 1935, in Maple Heights, Ohio, just outside Cleveland, to Edward William Oliver, a teacher, and Helen M. V. Oliver. Following graduation from high school, she attended Ohio State University for one year before transferring to Vassar College, where she also spent just one year. Early in her writing life, Oliver was heavily influenced by the work of poet EDNA ST. VINCENT MILLAY. She published her first book of poems, *No Voyage and Other Poems*, in 1963. Other early books include *The River Styx, Ohio, and Other Poems* (1972) and *Twelve Moons* (1979).

Oliver lived in Provincetown, Massachusetts, during these years, where she became affiliated with the Fine Arts Workshop, a writer's and artist's workshop and retreat. In 1972, she was appointed chair of the workshop's writing department. That same year, she received a National Endowment for the Arts fellowship. More support came her way in 1980 when she was awarded the Mather Visiting Professorship at Case Western Reserve University in Ohio, which she held for two years, and a Guggenheim Fellowship for the 1980–81 academic year.

In 1983, Oliver published *American Primitive*, which won the Pulitzer Prize for poetry the following year and brought lots of new readers and public attention her way. Critics praised the poems in *American Primitive* for their muscular language, their keen observations of the natural world, and their celebratory but unromanticized spirit. Indeed, Oliver's poems vibrate with the movements of the plant and animal worlds. She writes about mushrooms, wild geese and humpback whales, merging with the nonhuman world in a celebration of the self's ability to identify with nature.

Oliver moved again in 1986, this time to Bucknell University, where she became the poet-in-residence. *Dream Work* appeared in 1986 and *House of Light* came out in 1990, winning the Christopher Award and the L. L. Winship/PEN New England Award. Then in 1991, Oliver accepted a position as the Margaret Bannister Writer-in-Residence at Sweet Briar College in Amherst, Virginia. *New and Selected Poems*, which won the National Book Award for poetry, was published in 1992.

Oliver's first book of nonfiction, *A Poetry Handbook*, appeared in 1994 and was followed in 1995 by *Blue Pastures*, a collection of prose writing on nature, and in 1998 by *Rules for the Dance: A Handbook for Writing and Reading Metrical Verse*. Her other collections of poetry include *White Pine* (1994); *Winter Hours: Prose, Prose Poems, and Poems* (1999); *The Leaf and the Cloud* (2000), a book-length poem that was a *Boston Globe* and a Book Sense best-seller; and *What Do We Know: Poems* (2002). Her other accolades include the Lannan Literary Award, the New England Book Award for Literary Excellence from the New England

Booksellers Association, the Poetry Society of America's Shelley Memorial Prize, and the Alice Fay di Castagnola Award. Mary Oliver holds the Catharine Osgood Foster Chair for Distinguished Teaching at Bennington College, and lives in Provincetown, Massachusetts, and Bennington, Vermont.

## Further Reading

Cox, Debbie. "The Mary Oliver Web Index Page." North Harris Montgomery Community College. Available online. URL: http://www.mclibrary.nhmccd.edu/lit/oliver.html. Posted on May 20, 2002.

De Mott, Robert. "Recent Poetry: 'The Night Traveler.'" *Western Humanities Review* 33, no. 2 (1979): 42–48.

Long, Mark C. "Mary Oliver, *The Leaf and the Cloud*." *ISLE: Interdisciplinary Studies in Literature and Environment* 8, no. 2 (summer 2001): 277–278.

Oates, Joyce Carol. "Poetry: The Night Traveler." *The New Republic* 179, no. 24 (December 9, 1978): 28–33.

## Olsen, Tillie
### (Tillie Lerner)
(1912 or 1913–   ) *short story writer, nonfiction writer, essayist*

Tillie Olsen has used her writing to highlight the plights of those of her gender and of the underprivileged class. Although she has published little in her lifetime, her work has left an enduring mark. She has been considered both a radical and a modernist because of her socialist upbringing, empathy for the powerless, and innovative use of language. Although Olsen published several widely admired pieces in periodicals during the 1930s, she did not achieve full national prominence until the 1960s with the appearance of her first book, *Tell Me a Riddle* (1961), a collection of stories about working-class America. Olsen also wrote *Silences* (1978), which was considered a benchmark of feminist criticism. It gives an account of the forces that have silenced the voices of women and writers throughout history. Olsen wrote one novel, *Yonnondio* (1974), over a period of 40 years.

Tillie Lerner was born in 1912 or 1913 (Olsen is unsure of the year) in Omaha, Nebraska, to Samuel and Ida Lerner. They were Jewish political refugees from Russia who had participated in the abortive 1905 Russian Revolution. Samuel Lerner held various jobs as a laborer and became state secretary of the Nebraska Socialist Party. Ida Lerner was illiterate until her 20s. The second oldest of six children, Tillie often had to care for her younger siblings. It was only because she was often sick that she had any opportunity to read, although her parents could not afford to buy books. Tillie had access to the Little Blue Books, which were designed to fit into a worker's shirt pocket. The five-cent books introduced her to modern poetry and to writers such as Thomas Hardy, who became a lifelong favorite. She also read "old revolutionary pamphlets" and journals she found around the house. She became politically active in her midteens as a writer of skits and musicals for the Young Socialist League. In 1931, she joined the Young Communist League.

Tillie Lerner attended Omaha Central High School but left school early to help support the family. Throughout the depression she worked as a tie presser, a meat trimmer, a domestic worker, and a waitress. Lerner never went to college. She has said that public libraries were her universities. At age 19, she began her only novel, *Yonnondio*. The title is taken from a WALT WHITMAN poem and means "a lament for the lost." Lerner has said that *Yonnondio* was heavily influenced by an unsigned novella published in an 1861 issue of *The Atlantic Monthly* titled "Life in the Iron Mills." She believed it was a rare piece of literature that focused on the lives of the proletariat and the struggles of labor as a subject for literature. It was not until the 1950s that Olsen would discover that the novella was written by REBECCA HARDING DAVIS.

In 1932, Lerner moved to Faribault, Minnesota. In 1934, she was jailed for her efforts to unionize packinghouse workers. She wrote two essays about the experience—"Thousand-Dollar Vagrant" and "The Strike"—for *The Nation* and *Partisan Review*. Lerner became pregnant and bore a daughter, Karla, at 19. The pregnancy was unplanned. She lived sporadically with the baby's father.

In 1934, Lerner published part of the first chapter of *Yonnondio* in *Partisan Review* as a short story called "The Iron Throat." Publishers attempted to track her down in order to publish more work. In the meantime, in 1936, she met fellow political activist Jack Olsen, whom she later married. Random House eventually succeeded in finding her and she signed a contract to produce a chapter a month in return for a stipend. She left her newborn daughter with relatives and moved to Los Angeles to complete the work. Unhappy at being separated from "her own kind of people," Tillie Olsen occasionally traveled to several California towns to help organize farmworkers. The separation from her daughter affected her most of all. In 1936, although she "felt like a terrible failure" for not having finished the novel, Olsen forfeited her contract, moved back to San Francisco, and brought her daughter home.

Three more daughters were born and Olsen devoted most of the next 20 years to raising them, working low-wage jobs, and participating in political activities. She copied passages from books that she could not afford to buy and tacked them on the wall by the kitchen sink for inspiration. She seized every moment she could. "Time on the bus, even when I had to stand, was enough; the stolen moments at work, enough; the deep night hours for as long as I could stay awake, after the kids were in bed, after the household tasks were done, sometimes during. It is no accident that the first work I considered publishable began: 'I stand here ironing, and what you asked me moves tormented back and forth with the iron.'"

Olsen did not return to writing until 1953 when her youngest child entered school. At age 41 she enrolled in a creative writing course at San Francisco State University. The instructor recommended that Olsen try a more advanced course. Olsen won a Stegner Fellowship at Stanford University for 1955 and 1956. During these years, she began work on the four short stories collected in *Tell Me a Riddle*. It contains the much-anthologized stories "Tell Me a Riddle" and "I Stand Here Ironing." "Tell Me a Riddle," a story of the death of a Russian Jewish immigrant and revolutionary, won the O. Henry Award for best short story of the year in 1961. *Time* included *Tell Me a Riddle* on its list of best 10 books in 1962.

Olsen used some of her popularity to urge the republication of *Life in the Iron Mills* in 1972. During the early 1970s, Jack Olsen discovered *Yonnondio* among Olsen's old papers and manuscripts. The novel was written on continuous sheets of paper as well as scrawled pages, envelopes, and discarded trash. Olsen pieced the novel together and then published it in 1974. She then published *Silences*, a collection of essays examining the circumstances that block people, especially women, from literary creation. MARGARET ATWOOD has said that other women writers should regard Olsen not simply with "respect" but "reverence."

Despite Olsen's lack of formal education, she has received more than a dozen honorary degrees, as well as several awards, grants, and fellowships. She lives in Berkeley, California, where she is an active lecturer, writer, and activist.

**Further Reading**

Faulkner, Mara. *Protest and Possibility in the Writing of Tillie Olsen.* Charlottesville: University Press of Virginia, 1993.

———. "Tillie Olsen and the Erotic Connection: A First Response." *Frontiers* 18, no. 3 (1997): 150–154.

Hoyle Nelson, Kay, and Nancy Huse, eds. *The Critical Response to Tillie Olsen.* Westport, Conn.: Greenwood Press, 1994.

Orr, Elaine Neil. *Tillie Olsen and a Feminist Spiritual Vision.* Jackson: University Press of Mississippi, 1987.

Pearlman, Mickey. *Tillie Olsen.* Boston: Twayne Publishers, 1991.

## Ondaatje, Michael
(1943–   ) *novelist, poet, playwright*

Michael Ondaatje was the first Canadian winner of the Booker Prize. He is most well known for the novel that won him that prize, *The English Patient* (1992), a fictional World War II romantic narrative that was later made into an Academy Award–winning film. Ondaatje has used a combination of the real and imagined, poetry and prose. His biographical account of life in his native Ceylon, *Running in the Family* (1982), revealed the eccentric and unconventional lives of members of the Ondaatje family during Ceylon's colonial period.

Michael Ondaatje was born on September 12, 1943, in Colombo, Ceylon (now Sri Lanka). He was the son of Mervyn Ondaatje and Doris Gratiaen, prominent members of Ceylon's colonial society. Mervyn Ondaatje was a tea and rubber-plantation superintendent who was afflicted with alcoholism. Doris Gratiaen performed part time as a radical dancer, inspired by Isadora Duncan. As a result of his father's alcoholism, Ondaatje's parents eventually separated in 1954 and he moved to England with his mother.

Ondaatje was educated initially at St. Thomas College in Colombo, Ceylon. After moving with his mother to England, he continued his education at Dulwich College in London. He also attended Bishop's University in Lennoxville, Quebec, and the University of Toronto. He received his M.A. degree at Queen's University, in Kingston, Ontario, in 1967. Ondaatje began his teaching career at the University of Western Ontario, London, and moved on in 1971 to become a member of the Department of English at Glendon College, York University, in Toronto, Ontario.

Ondaatje's first published work was a collection of poetry, *The Dainty Monsters* (1967), which he followed up with *The Man with Seven Toes* (1969) and *Rat Jelly* (1973). He won his first literary award in 1970 at age 27, when he won the Canadian Governor General's Award for his collection of poetry, *The Collected Works of Billy the Kid* (1970), written about the legendary outlaw. Ondaatje received a second Governor General's Award in 1979 for an earlier collection of poetry, *There's a Trick with a Knife I'm Learning to Do* (1963). His critical work on poet and songwriter Leonard Cohen was also well received.

Ondaatje's work is characterized by a bleakly evocative narrative and minimalist dialogue, blending documentary and fictional accounts of real characters, such as his novels *Coming through Slaughter* (1976), about the life of 1930s jazz musician Buddy Bolden, and *In the Skin of a Lion* (1988), a story about 1930s Canadian immigrants. Jazz and cinema have been recurring themes in Ondaatje's work; he has written a number of screenplays. His screen credits include *The Clinton Special, Sons of Captain Poetry,* and *Carry On Crime and Punishment.* Ondaatje's imagery is characterized by its preoccupation with romantic exoticism and multiculturalism. Secret codes of violence in personal and political life pepper his work. His work is also notable for its cinematic qualities in its frequent use of montage techniques and spare dramatic dialogue.

Ondaatje's most famous work, *The English Patient* (1992), takes place toward the end of World War II in a damaged villa north of Florence, Italy. The story revolves around the four occupants of the villa: Hana, a fatigued and dispassionate young nurse; Carvaggio, a former spy and thief who was caught by the enemy and physically maimed; Kip, the young Indian bomb disposal expert; and the English patient, a nameless man who was severely burned in the war and attempting to reconstruct his mysterious past. As the story unfolds, Ondaatje asserts the notion that we are all creatures of the past and try to define future events accordingly. He also probes the perception of "home" through the transience of the characters. His later works include *Handwriting: Poems* (1998) and *Anil's Ghost* (2001).

Ondaatje has received numerous awards and honors. He was awarded the Ralph Gustafson Award (1965), the Epstein Award (1966), and the President's Medal from the University of Ontario in (1967). Ondaatje currently resides in Toronto, where he has been editing *Literary Magazine* with his wife, novelist and editor Linda Spalding.

## Further Reading

Huggan, Graham. "Exoticism and Ethnicity in Michael Ondaatje's *Running in the Family.*" *Essays in Canadian Writing* 57 (1995): 116–127.

Friedman, Thomas B. "Michael Ondaatje: Bibliography of Primary Works." Thomas B. Friedman Home Page. Available online. URL: http://www.cariboo.bc.ca/ae/engml/friedman/ondaatjebiblio.htm. Downloaded March 5, 2003.

Kamiya, Gary. "An Interview with Michael Ondaatje." Salon.com. Available online. URL: http://archive.salon.com/nov96/ondaatje961118.htm. Posted November 18, 1996.

## O'Neill, Eugene
### (1888–1953) *playwright*

Eugene O'Neill is regarded as the first great American dramatist and one of the greatest dramatists of all time. He was the first American playwright to regard the stage as a literary medium and the only American playwright ever to receive the Nobel Prize for literature (1936). O'Neill also won the Pulitzer Prize for four of his plays: *Beyond the Horizon* (1920); *Anna Christie* (1922); *Strange Interlude* (1928); and *Long Day's Journey into Night* (1957). High drama and the struggle with God and religion distinguish many of O'Neill's plays.

Eugene O'Neill was born on October 16, 1888, in New York City, the son of popular American actor James O'Neill. His mother, Ella, accompanied her husband back and forth across the country, settling

The only American playwright to receive the Nobel Prize for literature, Eugene O'Neill wrote plays that have been performed around the world. *(Library of Congress, Prints and Photographs Division, Carl Van Vechten Collection [LC-USZ62-116607])*

down only briefly for the birth of her two sons. She became addicted to drugs—one of several dramatic threads that ran through young O'Neill's life and profoundly affected his art. The first seven years of O'Neill's life were spent in hotel rooms, on trains, and backstage as he traveled the country with his father. He spent six years in a Catholic boarding school and three years in the Betts Academy at Stamford, Connecticut. He attended Princeton for a short time, but when he was suspended at the end of his freshman year, he decided not to return and to begin what he later regarded as his real education, that of "life experience."

The next six years nearly ended his life. In 1909, O'Neill shipped to sea; lived a derelict's existence on the waterfronts of Buenos Aires, Liverpool, and New York City; lost himself in alcohol; and attempted suicide. Recovering briefly at age 24, he held a job for a few months as a reporter and contributor to the poetry column of the *New London Telegraph* but soon came down with tuberculosis. Confined to a sanitarium for six months, O'Neill began to read the classic dramatists, as well as others, including Swedish dramatist and novelist August Strindberg. O'Neill soon turned out 11 one-act plays and two full-length plays, as well as some poetry. He later defined this period as his "rebirth." A theater critic persuaded O'Neill's father to send him to Harvard to study with George Pierce Baker in his famous playwriting course, which helped set O'Neill firmly on the path to writing for the theater.

In 1916, O'Neill met the group that became the Provincetown Players in Provincetown, Massachusetts. Shortly thereafter, the group produced O'Neill's one-act play "Bound East for Cardiff." Other short pieces followed at the group's playhouse in Greenwich Village in New York and soon his plays became the mainstay of the experimental theatrical group. O'Neill crafted characters that were new to the American stage. He drew on his travel experiences, populating the stage with sailors, dockworkers, and outcasts. With the Broadway production of *Beyond the Horizon* in 1920, O'Neill began a steady rise to fame. The play impressed the critics with its tragic realism and O'Neill was awarded his first Pulitzer Prize in drama. He received countless productions both in

Eugene O'Neill, one of America's greatest playwrights, lived an itinerant life as a boy and spent his early adulthood wandering the waterfronts of the world's great cities and battling alcoholism. *(Photograph by Alice Boughton. Library of Congress, Prints and Photographs Division [LC-B7901-36])*

the United States and abroad, and when the Provincetown group finally collapsed, he became the Theater Guild's leading playwright. Other important O'Neill plays of the 1920s were *The Emperor Jones, Anna Christie, Desire under the Elms, Strange Interlude, Mourning Becomes Electra,* and *Moon for the Misbegotten.* These plays often employed radical devices and themes that made them emblems of modernism.

But by the time he received the Nobel Prize in 1936, O'Neill's popularity had begun to wane. The new generation of critics began to subject him to a closer scrutiny than their predecessors who had been satisfied simply to find an American play-wright of international stature. O'Neill's obscurity deepened more and more, but, ironically, it was during O'Neill's darker, more isolated years that his real development began. Maturing in silence and motivated only by his obsessive urge to write, he developed a profound artistic honesty that would result in several masterpieces of the modern theater. These included *The Iceman Cometh* (1939) and *A Long Day's Journey into Night* (1957).

*The Iceman Cometh,* perhaps the most complex of O'Neill's tragedies, did not appear on Broadway until 1946. Laced with subtle religious symbolism, the play is a study of man's need to cling to his hope for a better life, even if he must delude himself to do so. The posthumous production of *Long Day's Journey into Night* brought to light an autobiographical play that is considered one of O'Neill's greatest. It depicted the agonized relations between a father, mother, and two sons over the course of one day. The play stripped away each character's layers, revealing the mother as a defeated drug addict and the father as a failure who is frustrated in his career. The older son bitterly suffers from alcoholism, while the younger son struggles with tuberculosis and has only a slim chance for physical and spiritual survival.

Tragedy followed O'Neill well into adulthood and his life with his three wives and three children. His elder son, Eugene O'Neill, Jr. (by his first wife, Kathleen Jenkins), committed suicide at 40. His younger son, Shane (by his second wife, Agnes Boulton), was emotionally unstable. His daughter, Oona (also by Agnes Boulton), was cut out of his life when, at 18, she infuriated him by marrying actor and director Charlie Chaplin, who was O'Neill's age.

O'Neill continued to write until 1944 when he was stricken with Parkinson's disease. Unable to work, he longed for his death and sat waiting for it in a Boston hotel, seeing no one except his doctor, a nurse, and his third wife, Carlotta Monterey. He died on November 27, 1953.

## Further Reading

Black, Stephen A. *Eugene O'Neill: Beyond Mourning and Tragedy.* New Haven: Yale University Press, 1999.

Dubost, Thierry. *Struggle, Defeat or Rebirth: Eugene O'Neill's Vision of Humanity.* Asheville, N.C.: McFarland & Company, 1997.

Hinden, Michael. *Long Day's Journey into Night: Native Eloquence.* Boston: Twayne Publishers, 1990.

## Ortiz, Simon
(1941–  )  *poet, short story writer, essayist*

Recognized by scholars of Native American literature as one of the most significant voices to come out of the Native American renaissance of the 1960s and 1970s, Simon Ortiz is the author of several collections of short stories and essays, but he is primarily known as a poet. Interested in preserving the oral tradition of his Acoma ancestors, Ortiz strives to blend traditional forms and themes with an acknowledgment of the contemporary world. His work is celebrated for this effort, and he has received numerous awards, including a lifetime Achievement Award from the Western States Arts Federation in 1999.

Simon Ortiz was born in Albuquerque, New Mexico, on May 27, 1941. Raised in the Acoma village of McCartys, Ortiz attended a Bureau of Indian Affairs school through sixth grade, then transferred to St. Catherine's Indian School in Santa Fe, New Mexico, and then to the Albuquerque Indian boarding schools. After high school, Ortiz went to work in the uranium mining industry in Grants, New Mexico, but decided to go to college after a year to pursue a career as a chemist. Once in college, he discovered that he was more interested in writing than in chemistry. He attended Fort Lewis College from 1962 to 1963 but dropped out to join the army. He also spent some time in a veterans hospital in Fort Lyons, Colorado, due to alcoholism. In 1966, he decided to return to college and enrolled at the University of New Mexico, where he graduated in 1968. He then attended the University of Iowa's creative writing program from 1968 through 1969, when he received his master's degree.

Ortiz spent much of the following decade moving from one teaching job to another. He taught at San Diego State University, the Institute of American Indian Arts, the Navajo Community College, the College of Marin, the University of New Mexico, and Sinte Gleska College in South Dakota.

Ortiz's books of poetry include *Naked in the Wind* (1971), *A Good Journey* (1976), *From Sand Creek: Rising in This Heart Which Is Our America* (1981), and *Telling and Showing Her: The Earth, The Land* (1995). His works of fiction include *Many Farm Notes* (1975); *Fightin': New and Collected Short Stories* (1983); and *Men on the Moon: Collected Short Stories* (1999). He has also published several works of nonfiction and contributed to numerous anthologies.

Simon Ortiz is the father of three daughters: Raho Nez, Rainy Dawn, and Sara Marie. He is divorced from his wife, Marlene. In addition to teaching, he has worked as a journalist, a public relations director, editor of a community newspaper, and consulting editor of the Pueblo of Acoma Press. He also served as lieutenant governor of the pueblo.

His awards include a Discovery Award from the National Endowment for the Arts in 1969, a National Endowment for the Arts fellowship in 1981, the Pushcart Prize for Poetry in 1981 for his collection of poems *From Sand Creek*, and the Lifetime Achievement Award from the Native Writer's Circle of the Americas in 1993.

**Further Reading**
Maddox, Lucy. "Native American Poetry," in *The Columbia History of American Poetry*, edited by Jay Parini and Brett Miller. New York: Columbia University Press, 1993, pp. 728–749.
Roemer, Kenneth M. "Bear and Elk: The Nature(s) of Contemporary American Indian Poetry," *Studies in American Indian Literature*, edited by Paula Gunn Allen. New York: The Modern Language Association of America, 1983, pp. 69–79.
Scarberry-Garcia, Susan. "Simon J. Ortiz," *Dictionary of Literary Biography*, edited by Kenneth M. Romer. Detroit: Gale Research, 1997, pp. 208–221.
Wiget, Andrew. "Sending a Voice: The Emergence of Contemporary Native American Poetry." *College English* 46 (October 1984): 598–609.

## Ozick, Cynthia
(1928–  )  *novelist, short story writer, essayist*

Cynthia Ozick has been known as primarily a Jewish writer and for her precise, clever, and witty style. She ponders questions about the nature, purpose, and possibility of art, as well as questions of morality and idolatry. Her main areas of focus concern Jewish history, the Holocaust, HENRY JAMES, and the relation between an artist's life and work. Ozick is primarily a poet but has also written short stories, essays, novels, and plays. Three of her stories have won first prize in the O. Henry competition, and five of her stories were chosen for republication in the yearly *Best American Short Stories* anthologies.

Cynthia Ozick was born in New York City on April 17, 1928, the second of two children and grew up in the Bronx with her parents, Celia (Regelson) and William Ozick, who owned a pharmacy in the Pelham Bay section. Her parents had come to America from the severe northwest region of Russia. They came from the Lithuanian Jewish tradition of that region, which embodies skepticism, rationalism, and anti-mysticism. Ozick entered *heder,* the Yiddish-Hebrew "room" for religious instruction, and also attended public school in the Bronx where she excelled in grammar, spelling, reading, and writing. Ozick has described Pelham Bay as a lovely place, but she also encountered anti-Semitism and had stones thrown at her.

Ozick attended Hunter College High School in Manhattan, where academic excellence set students apart. The idea of becoming a writer grew stronger while she attended New York University. She earned a master's degree in English literature from Ohio State University. She has said that she was influenced by Henry James to become a worshiper of literature, one who, having to choose between ordinary human entanglement—real life—and exclusive devotion to art, chooses art. She chose art over life, she says, to her eternal regret. At age 24, in 1952, she married Bernard Hallote and they moved to New York.

After her marriage, over the next 13 years Ozick devoted herself exclusively to what she called "high art," working on a philosophical novel, *Mercy, Pity, Peace, and Love,* which she eventually abandoned. She also spent more than six years on another novel, *Trust* (1966). Ozick had begun to master the Jewish textual tradition, but she wrestled with the term "Jewish writer." She published several poems on Jewish themes in *Judaism* and produced *The Pagan Rabbi and Other Stories* (1971). She also wrote *Bloodshed and Three Novellas* (1976) and *Levitation: Five Fictions* (1982). "She is as authentic a voice of New York as was EDITH WHARTON before her, but Ozick's New York is an affair of battered suburbs, of cavernous municipal buildings, of ancient Hebrew teachers living above Cuban grocery stores, of public libraries, wily lovers and miraculous if inconvenient apparitions," wrote Anita Brookner in *The Spectator* (1999).

Ozick returned to writing novels after the settlement of a threatened lawsuit by a Jewish day school headmaster who believed that Ozick's 1980 short story "The Laughter of Akiva" was partly based on him. That story, enlarged and completely rewritten, became the novel *The Cannibal Galaxy* (1983). In 1980, Ozick published, in *The New Yorker,* "The Shawl," an impressionistic piece about the Holocaust that has remained her most noted work. In 1983, again in *The New Yorker,* Ozick published a sequel to "The Shawl," expanding it into "Rosa," a novella which prompted her publisher to issue *The Shawl* (1989) as a separate volume, consisting of the story and the novella. The novel *The Messiah of Stockholm* (1987) is sandwiched between two volumes of essays, *Art and Ardor* (1983) and *Metaphor and Memory* (1989). A third volume of essays, *Fame and Folly,* containing pieces on T. S. ELIOT, among others, was published in 1996. *Portrait of the Artist as a Bad Character and Other Essays on Writing* was published in 1994.

Ozick has received numerous literary awards, among them a Guggenheim Fellowship and a Mildred and Harold Straus Living Award from the American Academy and National Institute of Arts and Letters.

## Further Reading

Bolick, Katie. "The Many Faces of Cynthia Ozick." Atlantic Unbound. Available online. URL: http://www.theatlantic.com/unbound/factfict/ozick. htm. Posted: May 15, 1997.

Currier, Susan, and Daniel J. Cahill. "A Bibliography of the Writings of Cynthia Ozick." *Texas Studies in Literature and Language* 25, no. 2 (summer 1983): 313–321.

Moyers, Bill. "Heritage Conversation with Cynthia Ozick." Transcript, WNET-TV, New York, April 3, 1986.

Teicholz, Tom. "Interview with Cynthia Ozick." *Paris Review* 102 (spring 1987): 154–190.

# P

## Paley, Grace
## (Grace Goodside)
(1922–   ) *short story writer, poet*

Grace Paley—writer, feminist, and antiwar activist—is the author of three highly acclaimed collections of short stories—*The Little Disturbances of Man* (1959), *Enormous Changes at the Last Minute* (1974), and *Later the Same Day* (1985)—as well as three collections of poetry, including *Leaning Forward* (1985). Paley has taught at Columbia and Syracuse universities, and is presently writer-in-residence at City College of New York, and a professor of creative writing and literature at Sarah Lawrence College, where she has taught for 18 years. In 1989 Paley was the first recipient of the Edith Wharton Citation of Merit. She also received a Guggenheim fellowship in 1961, a grant from the National Endowment for the Arts in 1966, and an award from the National Institute of Arts and Letters in 1970. In three volumes of short stories, Paley has chronicled the lives of a wide array of characters—mostly women and often leftists, Jewish, and living in New York City—as they struggle with marriages, motherhood, friendships, and political beliefs. Paley's style is unmatched, combining political and personal realms into fiction celebrated for clarity, precision, and optimism. Paley divides her time between New York and Vermont, where she lives with her husband, landscape architect and writer Robert Nichols.

Grace Goodside was born on December 11, 1922, in the Bronx, New York. Her parents were Russian Jewish immigrants who had a radical anti-czar political history (although they were only 21 years old when they came to the United States). Paley studied at Hunter College and New York University before dropping out in 1942 to get married. She then settled with her first husband, Jess Paley, and their two children in Greenwich Village and commenced her dual career of writing and political activism. She published her first book of short stories, *The Little Disturbances of Man*, in 1959 while teaching creative writing at Sarah Lawrence College. This collection established her reputation as a writer with a remarkably graceful gift for language. When the book went out of print in 1965, its reputation survived and was strengthened by the occasional appearances of her stories in magazines such as *The Atlantic Monthly, Esquire*, the *Noble Savage, Genesis West*, the *New American Review, Ararat*, and *Fiction*.

While Paley's acclaim as a writer grew steadily, she remained staunchly politically active. In 1961 she helped found the Greenwich Village Peace Center, which became a nexus of draft resistance during the Vietnam War. At the height of the war, in 1969, Paley was a member of a delegation to North Vietnam to bring back three pilots who had been shot down. With regard to her antiwar activities (for which she spent a period of time in jail), Paley defined herself as a "somewhat combative pacifist and cooperative anarchist." During the World Peace Congress in Moscow in 1973, she condemned the Soviet Union for silencing political dissidents. In addition, Paley has long been a feminist and active in the antinuclear movement. She worked to oppose nuclear weapons in the Clamshell Alliance and in the War Resisters League. In 1980 she helped organize the Women's Pentagon Action and was active in the antinuclear campaigns at Seneca Falls, New York.

In 1974, Paley published *Enormous Changes at the Last Minute: Stories.* Her *Collected Stories* came out in 1994. *Just As I Thought* (1998) gathers her short essays, memoirs, and narratives in one collection that documents her life and career. Pieces included in the book treat topics such as the Vietnam War, the Persian Gulf War, and women's rights.

Paley has taught for more than 20 years at Sarah Lawrence College in New York and for semesters or quarters at City College, Columbia, Stanford, Johns Hopkins, and Dartmouth. She now resides in New York City with Robert Nichols. She has three grandchildren, Laura, Zamir, and Sienn.

## Further Reading

Bach, Gerhard. *Conversations with Grace Paley.* Jackson: University Press of Mississippi, 1997.

Eckhaus, Phyllis. "Every Action Was Essential: An Interview with Grace Paley," *Nonviolent Activist.* March/April 2000. Available online. URL: http://www.warresisters.org/nva0300-4.htm. Downloaded June 16, 2003.

*New York Times.* "Featured Author: Grace Paley." The New York Times on the Web. Available online. URL: http://www.nytimes.com/books/98/04/19/specials/paley.html. Downloaded March 8, 2003.

Taylor, Jacqueline. *Grace Paley: Illuminating the Dark Lives.* Austin: University of Texas Press, 1990.

## Parker, Dorothy
### (Dorothy Rothschild)
(1893–1967) *poet, short story writer, literary critic, screenwriter*

Brilliant, unrelenting, and fiercely witty, Dorothy Parker is still remembered as one of the most influential and frank writers of the 20th century. Parker's poetry overtly resonates with heartache and disenchantment and reflects her personal obsessions: incessant alcohol consumption, spoiled romance, social injustice, and the follies of the rich.

Her most acclaimed story "Big Blonde" won the O. Henry Prize in 1929. It depicts the drunken loneliness, dependence on men, and increasing desperation of an aging "kept woman." Like many of Parker's stories, "Big Blonde" intensely and intimately highlights the lack of possibilities that so many women of her generation faced. Other stories have been collected in *Laments for the Living* (1930), *After Such Pleasures* (1933), and *Here Lies* (1939). Parker also produced a great deal of literary criticism, published over many decades in the *New Yorker* (under the title "Constant Reader") and, from 1958 to 1963, in *Esquire.*

The youngest of three siblings by many years, Dorothy Rothschild was born on August 22, 1893, to a Jewish father, J. Henry Rothschild, and a Scottish mother, Eliza (Marston) Rothschild. Eliza Rothschild died when Dorothy was five years old, an event that devastated the young child. Soon thereafter, her father, who had made a small fortune in the garment industry, married a strict Roman Catholic woman whom Dorothy bitterly disliked. She was educated in private schools in New Jersey and New York City. Dorothy suffered two more remarkable tragedies as a young woman. Her brother Henry died aboard the *Titanic,* and a year later her father passed away, leaving her an orphan. During her father's illness (he was once again a widower at the time) she abruptly left school at the age of 14 to care for him. When he died in 1913, Rothschild, then 20 years old, moved into a boardinghouse and made a living playing piano at a Manhattan dance school.

In 1917 Rothschild married Edwin Pond Parker II, a stockbroker from Hartford, Connecticut. Although the marriage was brief, she was, from then on, known as Dorothy Parker. She soon began submitting her writing to various magazines and papers and that same year, she became a staff writer at *Vanity Fair* magazine and quickly distinguished herself there with her cutting and clever humor. In 1918, at age 25 and with little tolerance for the popular theater (although she would later write four plays herself), Parker succeeded P. G. Wodehouse as *Vanity Fair*'s drama critic. It was an unprecedented position for a woman of any age at that time. Parker was an immediate success: notoriously vicious and funny. "If you don't knit, bring a book," she moaned in one review. In the spring of 1919, Parker was invited to the Algonquin Hotel because of her connections at *Vanity Fair* and her reputation as a drama critic. This was the beginning of the famous Algonquin Round Table, a renowned intellectual literary circle. Parker was the only female founding member. It brought together such writers as Robert Benchley, Robert Sherwood, JAMES THURBER, George Kaufman, and many others. When Parker lost her job in 1920, after her famously tart reviews began to offend the theater elite, Robert Benchley, her close friend and fellow *Vanity Fair* writer, resigned in protest. It was, Parker said, "the greatest act of friendship I'd known."

Parker soon found another job at the magazine *Ainslee's* where she could be as sarcastic and witty as she pleased. Other noted *Ainslee's* writers include MARK TWAIN, STEPHEN CRANE, and O. HENRY. In 1922, Parker wrote her first short story "Such a Pretty Little Picture," marking the beginning of her own independent literary career. Despite her successful start, she became deeply dissatisfied with freelance magazine writing. She had serious money problems and was involved in a succession of painfully brief love affairs with men who cared little for her. All these troubles led to two failed suicide attempts, in 1923 (following an abortion) and 1925. Her marriage to the morphine-and-alcohol-addicted Edwin Parker finally ended in 1924. Parker moved into the Algonquin Hotel to focus on writing plays, her first being "Close Harmony." She also began writing reviews and poetry for the first several issues of the *New Yorker,* which was published for the first time in February 1925. Then at the suggestion of a friend, she collected a volume of her poetry in 1926 to pay for an overseas trip, although she felt her verse was not good enough for a book. To her great surprise, *Enough Rope* became an instant best-seller, rare for a book of poems. In Paris, Parker befriended ERNEST HEMINGWAY, a surprising friendship given his infamously chauvinistic attitudes. It is believed that the odd friendship flourished due to the pair's shared wit and intellects. Upon Parker's return to New York the following year, she became involved in the Sacco and Vanzetti trial. She traveled to Boston to join the protests against what she saw as the execution of two innocent men and when she was arrest-

ed, she refused to travel in the paddy wagon, insisting instead on walking to jail. She was a committed socialist from this day forward.

In 1929, Parker's short story "Big Blonde" was published and she won the prestigious O. Henry Award for the Best Short Story of the Year. That same year Parker began screenwriting in Hollywood and soon signed a contract with MGM. She wrote many screenplays over the next decade. In 1933, once again in Europe, Parker met her second husband, Alan Campbell. He was also of Scottish-Jewish descent, a rumored bisexual, and 11 years her junior. They became screenwriting partners and signed a contract with Paramount Pictures in 1935. In 1937, Parker won an Academy Award for her joint screenplay of *A Star Is Born.* Throughout the 1940s Parker continued writing prose and short stories along with her screenplays. She was widely published in many magazines and Viking released an anthology of her short stories and prose. In 1949, she divorced Alan Campbell (although she later remarried him).

During the McCarthy era of the 1950s, Parker, along with countless other American intellectuals and artists, was called before the House Un-American Activities Committee to provide the names of other people involved in "communist activities." Parker pleaded the First Amendment. Her support for radical political causes, her membership in the Communist Party in 1934, and her reportage of the Loyalist cause in Spain for *New Masses* in 1937 caused her to be blacklisted from the movie industry in 1949. Her career in screenwriting was over.

Parker then turned to writing book reviews for *Esquire* magazine. In 1959, she was inducted into the American Academy of Arts and Letters. She was a distinguished Visiting Professor of English at California State College in Los Angeles. In 1964, she published her final magazine piece in the November issue of *Esquire.* She died on June 7, 1967, of a heart attack in her room at Hotel Volney in New York City. She bequeathed her entire literary estate to the NAACP.

## Further Reading

Calhoun, Randall. *Dorothy Parker.* Westport, Conn.: Greenwood Publishing Group, 1992.

Frewin, Leslie. *The Late Mrs. Dorothy Parker*. New York: Macmillan, 1986.

Kinney, Arthur F. *Dorothy Parker, Revised*. Boston: Twayne Publishers, 1998.

Meade, Marion. *Dorothy Parker: What Fresh Hell Is This?* New York: Villard Books, 1987.

Melzer, Sondra. *The Rhetoric of Rage*. New York: Peter Lang, 1997.

Perelman, S. J. *The Last Laugh*. New York: Simon & Schuster, 1981.

## Percy, Walker
### (Walker Alexander Percey)
### (1916–1990) *novelist, essayist, literary critic*

Known for his southern roots and for the philosophical nature of his writing, Walker Percy has often been compared to such writers and thinkers as RALPH WALDO EMERSON and Soren Kierkegaard. The author of six novels, including *The Moviegoer, Love in the Ruins,* and *The Second Coming,* and three nonfiction works, many of which explore his fascination with language, Percy wrote for more than 30 years, producing a body of work that won him much acclaim as well as many dedicated readers.

Born in Birmingham, Alabama, to Leroy and Martha Percy on May 28, 1916, Walker Percy had a difficult childhood. His father, a successful Birmingham lawyer, took his own life with a shotgun in the attic of their home when Percy was 13. Two years later, his mother drove her car off a country bridge, an event that was deemed an accident, but Percy always suspected that she had taken her own life as well. He and his two younger brothers, Phin and Roy, were sent to Greenville, Mississippi, to live with their father's cousin, William Alexander Percy. A writer himself, William Percy provided a home full of books, works of art, and music. Uncle Will, as the boys called him, was an important and positive influence on his nephew. Another supportive relationship developed when Percy met future Civil War historian and novelist Shelby Foote, who also grew up in Greenville and soon became a lifelong friend. The two corresponded regularly for many years. Their letters were later published in a collection called *Conversations between Percy and Foote.*

When Percy graduated from high school in Greenville, he went on to the University of North Carolina in Chapel Hill, where he studied chemistry. Following his undergraduate studies, he entered Columbia University's medical school, the College of Physicians and Surgeons. He graduated with honors in 1941 and began an internship as a pathologist at Bellevue Hospital but was unable to complete it when he contracted tuberculosis. His illness forced him to resign from the internship. Although he returned to Columbia to teach for a time, a relapse of the tuberculosis eventually required that he retire from medicine permanently. While convalescing, Percy spent time reading French and Russian literature, philosophy, and psychology.

Percy married Mary Bernice Townsend, a medical technician, on November 7, 1946, and the couple moved back to the South, first to New Orleans, and later to Covington, Louisiana, where they raised their two daughters, Ann Boyd and Mary Pratt. From the very beginning of his writing career, Percy's chosen genres were the novel and the philosophical essay. Each of Percy's novels explores the conflict between his desire to express his own religious and moral beliefs and his essential commitment to the freedom of art—the play of many different voices in his stories. His first novel, *The Moviegoer,* was published to great acclaim in 1961 and won the National Book Award in 1962. Considered one of the great existentialist novels of the postwar era, *The Moviegoer* chronicles the life of Binx Bolling, a cinemaphile and investment banker who is searching for redemption in a world that has come to seem meaningless. Percy's portrayal of the South, especially in *The Moviegoer* and *The Last Gentleman,* explores the loss of antebellum Southern culture and the creation of a culture of survival in response. *The Last Gentleman* came out in 1966, followed by *Love in the Ruins: The Adventures of a Bad Catholic at a Time near the End of the World* (1971), *Lancelot* (1977), *The Second Coming* (1980), and *The Thanatos Syndrome* (1987). While Percy's first two novels are wholly realistic, his third novel, *Love in the Ruins,* begins his transition away from realism and into the realm of ideas. The last three novels maintain just enough detail and documentation to keep the human story plausible. Although he continued to treat the same moral and theological themes, the writing itself grew more philosophical in his later years.

Percy's first work of nonfiction, *The Message in the Bottle: How Queer Man Is, How Queer Language Is, and What One Has to Do with the Other*, appeared in 1975. *Lost in the Cosmos: The Last Self-Help Book* was published in 1983, and *Signposts in a Strange Land*, a collection of unpublished essays, was published posthumously in 1991. There were numerous other limited edition publications, and contributions to other books, as well as collections of interviews and the aforementioned collection of letters between Percy and Foote.

Percy's most widely praised books were without a doubt his novels. Following the first novel's National Book Award, *Love in the Ruins* won the National Catholic Book Award in 1972 and *The Second Coming* received the *Los Angeles Times* Book Prize, a National Book Critics Circle citation, an American Book Award nomination, a Notable Book citation from the American Library Association, and a PEN/Faulkner Award. *Lost in the Cosmos: The Last Self-Help Book* received the St. Louis Literary Award in 1986.

Walker Percy died of cancer on May 10, 1990, but since his death the substantial body of scholarship on his work has grown significantly. The Walker Percy Project a website, attests to this growing popularity. The center offers students, scholars, and readers from around the world access to information, resources, and people related to Walker Percy.

**Further Reading**

Lawson, Lewis. "Walker Percy," in *The History of Southern Literature*, edited by Louis D. Rubin, Jr., et al. Baton Rouge: Louisiana State University Press, 1990, pp. 505–509.

Samway, Patrick H. *Walker Percy: A Life*. New York: Farrar, Straus & Giroux, 1997.

Tolson, Jay. *Pilgrim in the Ruins: A Life of Walker Percy*. New York: Simon & Schuster, 1992.

"The Walker Percy Project: An Internet Literary Center." ibiblio. Available online. URL: http://www.ibiblio.org/wpercy/library.html. Downloaded on January 13, 2003.

# Plath, Sylvia
(1932–1962) *poet, memoirist, novelist*

A poet associated with the confessional school that came to prominence under ROBERT LOWELL's guidance in the 1960s, Sylvia Plath had a very brief but remarkable career, publishing just two books before her suicide at age 30. Poems published posthumously in four separate volumes brought her fame and attest to the boldness and originality of her talent. In 1982, she won the Pulitzer Prize for her *Collected Poems*, which was edited by her husband, Ted Hughes.

Born on October 27, 1932, in Jamaica Plain, a suburb of Boston, Massachusetts, Sylvia Plath was raised in a comfortable middle-class home. Her father, a college professor and expert on bees, was sick for many years, suffering from undiagnosed diabetes. He died when his daughter was eight, the same year that she published her first poem. Aside from the loss of her father, her childhood was characterized by great academic success and achievement in all her activities. She was, on the surface, a model child. By the time she graduated from high school, Plath had already accumulated an impressive list of publications. At Smith College, where she studied on a scholarship beginning in 1950, she wrote more than 400 poems. It was not until the end of her junior year at Smith that some of the underlying turmoil in Plath's life began to express itself.

Plath spent the summer following her junior year working as a student "guest editor" at *Mademoiselle* magazine in New York. When she returned home to Boston, somewhat distraught over a clash of personalities she experienced with an editor at the magazine, she learned that she had not been accepted into Frank O'Connor's writing class at Harvard, something she had been counting on. Both of these events put together proved more than she could handle, and she attempted to kill herself by overdosing on sleeping pills. She nearly succeeded and was hospitalized for several months at McLean Hospital, where she received insulin therapy, electroshock treatments, and psychotherapy. She later wrote about this experience in her semiautobiographical novel *The Bell Jar*, published in 1963.

Despite the trauma of this breakdown, Plath returned to Smith and successfully completed her senior year. She graduated summa cum laude and won a Fulbright scholarship to study at Newnham College in Cambridge, England. There, after a series of bad blind dates, Plath met the poet Ted Hughes, whom she married on June 16, 1956, in London.

Hughes and Plath lived in Boston for a time following their marriage, while Plath taught English at Smith College, before returning to England, where their daughter Frieda was born on April 1, 1960. *The Colossus*, Plath's first book of poems, was published later that same year. An accomplished first book, it attests to the dedication with which she had honed her craft, but it only hints at the groundbreaking work yet to come. In 1961, Plath and Hughes settled in a country village in Devon. In early February 1961, Plath was pregnant again but miscarried, an experience she wrote about in the poem "Parliament Hill Fields." Later that month, she underwent an appendectomy. She was soon pregnant again with her son, Nicolas, who was born on January 17, 1962.

In summer 1962, Plath learned that Hughes was having an affair. The couple took a trip to Ireland to repair their marriage but Hughes returned home ahead of Plath and moved in with his mistress. Plath spent the fall and winter of 1962–63 living in a flat in London that had once been home to W. B. Yeats. It was one of the coldest winters on record in London. Both her children came down with the flu, and Plath was severely depressed. The difficulty of her life, however, spurred in her the need to write. She wrote furiously during her last months, often working between four and eight in the morning, before the children woke. On February 11, 1963, she stuffed towels around the doorframe of the room where her children slept, placed her head in the oven, and killed herself with cooking gas. Two years later, in 1965, a collection of many of the last poems she wrote was published under the title *Ariel*. These poems were hailed for their ironic wit and emotional power, reined in expertly by technical perfection. Among the most famous of the poems in *Ariel* are "Lady Lazarus" and "Daddy." These poems exhibit Plath's incredible ear for music, as well as her ability to instill moments of despair and anger and near-madness with absolute clarity of vision. In "Daddy," the poet rages against her father for dying when she was 20. "Lady Lazarus," a reaction to the oppressive patriarchy of the early 1960s, is a chilling autobiographical account of Plath's suicide attempts. In the poem, Plath explores themes of confinement and repression as a woman artist trying to create in a male-dominated society. *Crossing the Water* and *Winter Trees* both came out in 1971. Her *Collected Poems*, edited by Ted Hughes, was published in 1981.

Sylvia Plath was buried in Heptonstall, West Yorkshire, England. Her fans frequently visit her grave.

**Further Reading**

Axelrod, Steven G. *Sylvia Plath: The Wound and the Cure of Words*. Baltimore: Johns Hopkins University Press, 1992.

Malcolm, Janet. "Annals of Biography: The Silent Woman." *The New Yorker*, August 23, 1993, 84ff.

Pollard, Emily. PlathOnline.com. Available online. URL: http://www.plathonline.com/. Downloaded January 4, 2003.

Stevenson, Anne. *Bitter Fame: A Life of Sylvia Plath*. Boston: Houghton Mifflin, 1989.

# Poe, Edgar Allan
(1809–1849) *poet, short story writer*

Edgar Allan Poe has had a tremendous influence on American literary history. Although he is often credited with inventing the modern detective story, his tales and poems extend far beyond the confines of a single genre. He deliberately sought great variety in his tales. A review of his more than 70 pieces of published fiction, which include explorations into mystery and science fiction, testifies to this range.

Edgar Allan Poe was born in poverty on January 19, 1809, in Boston, Massachusetts. Poe's family life was extremely difficult. His father, David Poe, Jr., whose first career was law, soon abandoned his family to pursue an acting career and therefore had little influence on young Poe. Elizabeth Arnold, often called Eliza, had married her first husband, actor Charles Hopkins, when she was just 15. Hopkins died at the age of 20, leaving Eliza alone yet again at the age of 18. In 1806 Eliza had met David Poe, Jr., and married him that same year. In the summer of 1811 she became very ill and by the following November, had become a charity case. Eliza finally died in 1811, leaving behind her three beloved children. She had written a message for her youngest son, Edgar, which read, "For my little son Edgar, who should ever love Boston the place of his birth, and where his mother found her best and most sympathetic friends." Elizabeth Poe was buried in the graveyard of St. John's Church. The cause of her death was tuberculosis. Edgar's two siblings, William Henry Leonard and Rosaline Poe, were taken in by separate families, which resulted in Poe having very little contact and distant relationships with them.

Following his mother's death, Poe moved in with John and Fanny Allan in Richmond, Virginia (although the Allans never formally adopted him). Mr. Allan had promised Poe's family that he would give him a good education, and Fanny, an orphan herself at a young age, took pity on the young boy. Thus, despite an often tenuous relationship, the Allans attempted to provide Poe with security and care. Fanny was a very organized housekeeper, but not well educated. John worked in a tobacco plant, which by 1817 was worth more than $300,000. The Allan's extended family never really accepted Poe, although this was not known to have deeply affected him. During their five-year stay in England, Fanny became very ill. Most blamed it on homesickness. They returned to New York immediately following the collapse of John's business, where the relationship between Poe and John grew increasingly worse. In 1827, Poe moved out, and two years later, Fanny Allan died. She asked to see Poe on the night before she died, but was unable to, as John had not relayed Fanny's wishes. Eventually Poe's and his adoptive father's relationship became significantly better, although not to a degree that warranted Poe's return home. John gave him a sum of money and not much else was said between the two for many years.

Meanwhile, Poe had met Sarah Elmira Royster in the Allan's neighborhood and had fallen hopelessly in love with her. The two were engaged with-

in a month, although Sarah's father disapproved of the marriage because Poe was just 16 and Sarah 15. Poe relocated to Charlottesville, from where he wrote to her often. Sarah's father intercepted all the letters, though, and when Poe returned to Richmond, he was devastated to find that Sarah had moved on. Twenty years later Poe found Sarah widowed with three children, but as beautiful as ever. She and Poe once again talked of marriage, although it never came to fruition.

The second most notable love of Poe's life was his cousin, Virginia Clemm. Poe met Virginia in 1831 while living in Baltimore with his aunt and her mother, Maria Clemm. Poe wrote of this difficult period in his letters to John, in which he indicated a fear of imprisonment for debt and mentioned that he was perishing for want of aid.

Edgar Allan Poe's work, including the famous poem "The Raven," has often been anthologized in collections of American literature. *(Photo by W. S. Hartshorn, 1848. Library of Congress, Prints and Photographs Division [LC-USZ62-10610])*

During this period, Poe was writing tales and selling them to journals in Baltimore and Philadelphia. Poe and Virginia eventually married and returned to Philadelphia, where for the first two years, they kept separate bedrooms. Virginia's health slowly deteriorated and she died of tuberculosis in 1847, leaving Poe alone once again. "The Raven" (1845), Poe's best-known poem, is thought to have been written after Virginia's death in portrayal of the tragedy that existed for the two lovers. Recalling Poe's unyielding hardships, it is not difficult to understand the bouts of rage and depression that haunted his life. After the death of his beloved Virginia and all the failed attempts at working, Poe's drug and alcohol addictions worsened. Although unproven, it is believed that Poe struggled desperately with opium addiction.

Poe died as mysteriously as some of the victims in his stories. On October 3, 1849, he was sent by carriage to the Washington College Hospital. The only written document as to why Poe died was handwritten by his doctor, John J. Moran. Poe had apparently been taken to a room where drunks were placed to avoid disturbing other patients. Poe was soon found to be completely sober; it was thought that perhaps he had been mugged, as his clothes were soiled and torn, although the truth was never fully discovered. In his four-day stay at Washington, he drifted in and out of consciousness and refused the brandy that was offered to him as a stimulant. Also during his stay, Poe was asked about his friends and was quoted as saying, "My best friend would be the man who gave me a pistol that I might blow out my brains." A week before he was admitted to the hospital he had been diagnosed with a weak heart and brain lesions. The cause stated on his official death certificate is "congestion of the brain."

Edgar Allan Poe's career in writing remained for the whole of his life no more than an exercise in survival. He never profited more than a few cents from any of his works, though he wielded tremendous influence over the short story as an art form and the development of the detective story as a genre. His greatest works include *Tamerlane and Other Poems* (1827); *The Narrative of Arthur Gordon Pym of Nantucket* (1838); *The Raven and Other Poems* (1845); and "The Fall of the House of

Usher," which was published in Poe's 1840 collection *Tales of the Grotesque and Arabesque*. A psychological thriller of sorts, Poe's famous horror story, "The Fall of the House of Usher," has been interpreted as an account of derangement and mental dissipation. The story delves into the inner workings of the imagination with frightening revelations about the dangers that lie therein. "The Cask of Amontillado," another often-anthologized short story by Poe, explores similar themes with haunting results.

"The Raven," a poem in 18 six-line stanzas, is told by a narrator from his bedroom on a dreary December night. The first-person account of the narrator waking to the sound of something tapping on his window explores the speaker's sadness and feelings of loss over the death of his lover, Lenore. The poem became so famous that Poe was referred to as "the raven." Poe may be forever remembered as an orphaned soul who endured relentless tragedy in his life and who was not fully appreciated for his contribution to American literature until after his death.

## Further Reading

Auerbach, Jonathan. *The Romance of Failure: First-person Fictions of Poe, Hawthorne, and James.* New York: Oxford University Press, 1989.

Bonaparte, Princess Marie. *The Life and Works of Edgar A. Poe; a Psycho-Analytic Interpretation.* Foreword by Sigmund Freud. Translated by John Rodker. New York: Humanities Press, 1971.

Buranelli, Vincent. *Edgar A. Poe.* New York: Twayne Publishers, 1961.

Fisher, Benjamin F. *Poe and His Times: The Artist and His Milieu.* Baltimore: Edgar Allan Poe Society, 1990.

Kennedy, J. Gerald. *Poe, Death, and the Life of Writing.* New Haven: Yale University Press, 1987.

Knapp, Bettina L. *Edgar Allan Poe.* New York: F. Ungar, 1984.

Meyers, Jeffrey. *Edgar A. Poe: His Life and Legacy.* New York: Scribner's, 1992.

Nelson, Dana D. "The Haunting of White Manhood: Poe, Fraternal Ritual, and Polygenesis." *American Literature* 69, no. 3 (September 1997): 515–547.

Thomas, Dwight, and David K. Jackson. *The Poe Log: A Documentary Life of Edgar Allan Poe 1809–1849.* Boston: G. K. Hall, 1987.

# Porter, Katherine Anne
## (Callie Russell Porter)
(1890–1980)  *short story writer, novelist, journalist*

A master of the 20th-century short story, Katherine Anne Porter led a varied and adventurous life. At different times, she made her home in Greenwich Village, Mexico, Switzerland, and Paris, among other places, and enjoyed friendships with many talented writers and artists, including Malcolm Cowley, ROBERT PENN WARREN, Barbara Harrison, and Diego Rivera. She is best known for her novel *Ship of Fools* and for her *Collected Stories*, both of which were published in the early 1960s. Both books explore Porter's signature themes—the conflict between personal freedom and the conventions of society; the tension between the traditional and mythic structures of the old South and the fast-paced chaos of the urban North; and the difficulty of living within the cultural and biological constraints placed on women. Although Porter had addressed these themes throughout her career, it was these two late publications that solidified her literary reputation and ensured her ultimate financial success.

Born Callie Russell Porter on May 15, 1890, on a farm in Indian Creek, Texas, Porter changed her name to Katherine Anne in early adulthood, taking her paternal grandmother's name as her own. She was in fact raised by her grandmother Katherine after her mother, May Alice, died in March 1892. Porter's father, Harrison, moved Katherine and her three siblings to the small town of Kyle, just outside Austin, where they lived with their grandmother until her death in October 1901. Following the grandmother's death, Harrison moved his family to San Antonio, where the children completed their formal educations. Porter attended the Thomas School, a respected Christian private girls' school. Following her graduation from the Thomas School, Katherine and her older sister Gay gave lessons in music, physical culture, and dramatic reading, in Victoria, Texas, where the family had moved.

Porter married John Henry Koontz, the first of her husbands, on June 20, 1906. The marriage lasted nine years, during which time the couple lived in Louisiana, Houston, and Corpus Christi, Texas.

Porter's first published work, a poem entitled "Texas by the Gulf of Mexico," appeared in 1912 in a trade journal to which her husband subscribed. Koontz often traveled for his work, which gave Porter time to write. When the couple separated in 1914, Porter moved to Chicago, hoping to find employment in motion pictures. She appeared in at least two movies before returning to Texas about six months later. She received a divorce from Koontz in June 1915 and a short time later found out that she had contracted tuberculosis. She spent much of the next two years recuperating, confined to a sanitarium.

In September 1917, Porter was hired as a journalist at the *Fort Worth Critic*. From this position, she moved to the *Rocky Mountain News* in Denver about a year later. She became the resident theater and art critic for the paper and also suffered a nearly fatal case of the flu, during one of the worst flu epidemics to sweep the country.

After a couple of years in Denver, Porter moved to Greenwich Village to pursue a career as a writer. Surrounded by artists and writers, she turned her focus away from journalism in favor of writing fiction. She published three short stories in early 1920 in a magazine for children called *Everyland*.

At the prompting of several Mexican friends, Porter moved to Mexico, where she became the editor of the English-language section of *El Heraldo de Mexico* and, ultimately, the managing editor and a contributor to the English language *Magazine of Mexico*, whose mission was to promote U.S. business and development south of the border. Porter traveled back and forth between the United States and Mexico for several years, all the time gathering material for three short stories that came out in 1923 in *Century* magazine—"Maria Concepción," "The Martyr," and "Virgin Violeta." During this time she also worked as a freelance editor and wrote book reviews. Her social circle began to revolve more and more around other artists and writers.

In 1927, Porter signed a contract to write a biography of COTTON MATHER, but despite conducting extensive research and spending nearly 50 years, on and off, in the effort to complete the book, she never finished it. In 1930, *Flowering Judas* was published and Porter returned to Mexico for an extended stay, during which time she received a Guggenheim fellowship of $2,000, which she used to travel to Europe in 1931 with Eugene Pressly, who eventually became her husband. Pressly had received a lifetime appointment in the American Foreign Service, so the couple spent time in Berlin, Paris, and Madrid, before settling in Basel, Switzerland. They later moved to Paris for four years, when Pressly was posted to the U.S. Embassy there. Porter wrote, or at least began, many of her most important works during the years in Paris, including *Hacienda* (1934) and *Flowering Judas and Other Stories* (1935), which contained four more stories than the 1930 edition.

Pressly and Porter returned to the United States in 1936, and Porter settled in Pennsylvania, where she wrote two of the pieces found in *Pale Horse, Pale Rider* (1939). That same year, Pressly took a position in South America, which led eventually to their divorce in April 1938. Meanwhile, Porter had met her next husband, Albert Erskine, a graduate student in Louisiana. The two were wed in 1938 but separated in less than two years, following which Porter took up residency at Yaddo, an artists' colony in upstate New York. She enjoyed life there so much that she bought a house near Saratoga Springs, but after living there barely a year, she decided her life was too isolated and began a period of almost constant movement. She lived in Cold Spring, New York, the Georgetown neighborhood of Washington, D.C., and Hollywood for a while. *The Leaning Tower and Other Stories* was published in 1944 in the midst of these moves and was followed eight years later by *The Days Before*, a book of critical essays.

In 1947, Porter embarked on yet another adventure when she taught a summer class at Stanford University. In the following decade, she held teaching positions at Stanford; the University of Michigan; the University of Liège, where she was a Fulbright fellow; the University of Virginia; and Washington and Lee University. During these years, she supplemented her income by reading, lecturing, and making public appearances on radio and television. Between stints at these universities, she lived in New York City (1949–53); Southbury, Connecticut (1955–58); and Washington, D.C. (1959–69).

Porter worked on her novel *Ship of Fools* during her three years in Connecticut and completed the novel after receiving a Ford Foundation grant in 1959. The novel was published in 1962 and became a best-seller, bringing Porter fame and financial security. *Ship of Fools* takes place in 1931 aboard a German passenger ship, which affords Porter the opportunity to explore a mixture of cultures and personalities thrown together at sea. Germans, Americans, Spaniards, Gypsies, and Mexicans form a microcosm of humanity through which Porter explores the origins of human evils, such as jealousy, hatred, and duplicity. Abby Mann wrote a screenplay, and the movie was filmed in 1965, starring Vivien Leigh and Elizabeth Ashley. When Porter's *Collected Stories* appeared in 1965, it won the National Book Award and the Pulitzer Prize, capping a decade of much success.

Although Porter continued to write and publish throughout her life, her health gradually began to deteriorate. She received several honorary degrees, including one from the University of Maryland in 1966. Shortly thereafter, she announced that she would donate her papers, personal library, and other personal effects to the University of Maryland Library, which dedicated the Katherine Anne Porter Room on May 15, 1968. The following year, Porter moved to College Park, Maryland, to be closer to the university and her papers.

Porter's *Collected Essays and Occasional Writings* appeared in 1970, and *The Never-Ending Wrong*, a book about the Sacco-Vanzetti affair, came out in 1977. Just prior to this book's publication, Porter suffered several strokes, from which she never recovered. She lived her last years with round-the-clock nursing care and died on September 18, 1980.

**Further Reading**

Givner, Joan. *Katherine Anne Porter: A Life.* New York: Simon and Schuster, 1982.

Kiernan, Robert F. *Katherine Anne Porter and Carson McCullers: A Reference Guide.* Boston: G. K. Hall, 1976.

Stout, Janis P. *Katherine Anne Porter: A Sense of the Times.* Charlottesville: University Press of Virginia, 1995.

## Pound, Ezra
### (Ezra Loomis Pound)
(1885–1972)  *poet, literary critic, editor*

Most commonly associated with developing the modernist aesthetic in poetry, Ezra Pound was also responsible for cultivating an exchange of ideas between British and American writers in the early 20th century. Acting as a kind of literary sponsor, Pound frequently provided financial support and professional expertise to promising young writers in order to advance their skill and careers. The list of Pound's protégés includes such major writers as W. B. Yeats, ROBERT FROST, WILLIAM CARLOS WILLIAMS, MARIANNE MOORE, H. D., James Joyce, ERNEST HEMINGWAY, and especially T. S. ELIOT. Pound's most significant contributions to poetry center on imagism, a movement in poetry that derived its technique from classical Chinese and Japanese poetry—stressing clarity and precision, instead of rhyme and meter, in order to, in Pound's words, "compose in the sequence of the musical phrase, not in the sequence of the metronome."

Ezra Loomis Pound was born in Hailey, Idaho, in 1885 as an only child. When Ezra was four, his mild-mannered father, Homer Loomis Pound, a civil servant who ran the government land office at Hailey, moved his family to Philadelphia when he took a job as an assistant assayer at the U.S. Mint. Ezra's mother, who had hated Hailey, was the former Isabel Weston of Washington, D.C. He would later say that his mother was a "prude" who rarely agreed with him on any matter and that his father was overly naive but easy to live with. At 12 years old, Pound entered Cheltenham, a military college two miles from home. A neighbor recollected that "he was all books" and that the other boys made fun of him. He had already written his first poem, which was about William Jennings Bryan and his populist "Free Silver" campaign. Bryan, like the older Pound, had the fruitless ambition of defeating bankers. The boy showed promise at Cheltenham and was able to enlist at the University of Pennsylvania at the young age of 15. He completed two years of college there then transferred to Hamilton College in upstate New York, from where he graduated in 1905. At Hamilton, Pound was again considered eccentric and unpopular, but he

discovered Dante and the troubadours. By now he had acquired a curiosity about foreign languages. He was known to have read Chinese characters upside down, which enabled him to make rough, invented translations from them. Following his graduation from Hamilton, Pound returned to the University of Pennsylvania to work on English literature and romance poetry. He gained an M.A. degree in 1906 and then visited Spain on a fellowship during the summer of that year.

In 1907, while Pound was simultaneously courting both Hilda Doolittle and a girl named Mary Moore (whose father was president of a railroad company), he was appointed instructor in French and Spanish at Wabash College, a small Presbyterian school in Crawfordsville, Indiana. In January 1908, after a woman was discovered in his quarters, which was strictly forbidden, he was dismissed in disgrace (although with pay) until the end of the semester. The following month Pound left for London, via Italy, with a grievance against all universities that would last for the rest of his life. In London he befriended his hero, W. B. Yeats. Between 1908 and 1911, Pound published six collections of verse, most of them dominated by a passion for Provençal and early Italian poetry. Under the influence of Ford Madox Ford and T. E. Hulme, he modernized his style and in 1912, in response to a style of poetry Doolittle (whom he renamed H. D.) had created, he launched the imagist movement, advocating concreteness, economy, and free verse. The oriental delicacy of his brief imagist lyrics soon gave way to the more dynamically avant-garde manner of vorticism. Association with vorticist visual artists such as Henri Gaudier-Brzeska and Wyndham Lewis helped him to see how poems could be composed, like post-Cubist sculptures, of juxtaposed masses and planes.

In 1914, Pound married Dorothy Shakespear. He became the London editor of the *Little Review* in 1917. In 1922, he began a lifelong relationship with the violinist Olga Rudge. Two years later he moved to Italy where, during a period of voluntary exile, Pound became involved in Fascist politics and grew to support openly the discrimination against Jews. He did not return to the United States until 1945, when he was arrested on charges of treason for broadcasting fascist propaganda by radio to the United States during World War II. In 1946, he was acquitted, but declared mentally ill and committed to St. Elizabeth's Hospital in Washington, D.C. During his confinement, the jury of the Bollingen-Library of Congress Award (which included a number of the most eminent writers of the time) decided to overlook Pound's political career in the interest of recognizing his poetic achievements, and awarded him the prize for the *Pisan Cantos* (1948), which were written during his incarceration in a prison camp near Pisa following his World War II collaboration with Mussolini's Fascist regime. This period sparked a bitter controversy that was eventually summed up by ALLEN TATE, who argued that even if Pound had been convicted of treason, he had in his revitalization of language performed an "indispensable duty to society." And, at least as a critic and as the poet of *Hugh Selwyn Mauberley*, Pound had been a central figure in modernism, and had—although not single-handedly—revived poetry in England. Pound also exercised great influence as an editor and supporter of other writers. In the 1920s in Paris, he edited Eliot's *The Waste Land* and helped ensure its publication.

Continuous appeals from writers won his release from the hospital in 1958. Once out of the institution, he started his most ambitious poetry projects, collectively known as the *Cantos*, which was intended to be a compilation of historical accounts in poetry form. These works clearly show his creativity and eccentricity. He created hundreds of cantos, covering history from the United States to faraway China. His lyrics here were noted for their elusive allusions, complicated structure, and usage of many languages from ancient Greek to Chinese ideograms. Pound eventually returned to Italy and settled in Venice, where he died, a semi-recluse, in 1972.

## Further Reading

Carpenter, Humphrey. *A Serious Character: The Life of Ezra Pound.* Boston: Houghton Mifflin, 1988.

Coyle, Michael. *Ezra Pound, Popular Genres, and the Discourse of Culture.* University Park: Pennsylvania State University Press, 1995.

Fraser, G. S. *Ezra Pound.* New York: Grove Press, 1960.

Heymann, C. David. *Ezra Pound, the Last Rower: A Political Profile.* New York: Viking Press, 1976.

Kenner, Hugh. *The Pound Era.* Berkeley: University of California Press, 1971.

Stock, Noel. *The Life of Ezra Pound.* New York: Pantheon Books, 1970.

Wallace, Emily M. "Some Friends of Ezra Pound: A Photographic Essay," *Yale Review* 75, no. 3 (1986).

Wilhelm, J. J. *Ezra Pound in London and Paris: 1908–1925.* University Park: Pennsylvania State University Press, 1990.

## Price, Reynolds
## (Edward Reynolds Price)
### (1933–  ) *novelist, poet, essayist*

The author of more than 20 books, including poetry, plays, stories, essays, and biblical translations, Reynolds Price is most widely known as a novelist. He has often been referred to as a southern writer, working in the tradition of WILLIAM FAULKNER and setting much of his fiction in the small towns and countryside of the South during the 1940s and 1950s, when he was a boy growing up in North Carolina.

Born on February 1, 1933, in Macon, North Carolina, to Elizabeth and William Price, Reynolds Price grew up in several small North Carolina towns, surrounded by tobacco and cotton farms. He attended Broughton High School in Raleigh, then received a full scholarship to Duke University, in Durham. He began writing fiction in high school and has often spoken of the encouragement he received from teachers who recognized his talent for writing as well as for painting. By the time he graduated from high school, Price knew that his career would be in writing and teaching. He continued writing while at Duke. When he met EUDORA WELTY, a visiting professor at Duke one year, she read his stories and encouraged him. She even sent one of his short stories to her agent. It was this agent who got Price's first novel published, some years later. Price graduated first in his class at Duke, then went to Oxford as a Rhodes Scholar to study English literature. Price made friends with several influential writers while at Oxford, including Stephen Spender and W. H. AUDEN. After spending three years in Oxford and earning a B. Litt. degree, he returned to the United States to begin his teaching career at Duke, where he has taught for more than 40 years and is now James B. Duke Professor of English.

Price's first book publication, *A Long and Happy Life*, appeared in 1961 and received the William Faulkner Award for a notable first novel. It has never been out of print. Among his other publications are *Kate Vaiden*, which won the National Book Critics Circle Award in 1986 and has been Price's most commercially successful work. *Kate Vaiden* recounts Kate's struggle to escape the demons of her childhood, and even of her ancestors' childhoods. Kate is left parentless when her father fatally shoots her mother and then himself. As Kate grows up, she seeks stability over and over again, only to let it slip from her grasp when she gets within its reach. Steeped in Christian themes of guilt, salvation, and shame, and set in the richly textured South, *Kate Vaiden* established Price's gift for storytelling and for writing from a woman's point of view.

Other works include *Collected Stories* (1993), *Collected Poems* (1997), *Roxanna Slade* (1998), and two memoirs, *Clear Pictures* (1989) and *A Whole New Life: An Illness and a Healing* (1995), the latter of which recounts Price's struggle with spinal cancer. In addition to these, he has published essays, plays, and a novel for children, as well as translations of the Bible. He also regularly broadcasts essays on National Public Radio, and some of these were collected and published in 2000 in *Feasting the Heart*. His plays, including a trilogy entitled *New Music*, have been produced throughout the country. *Learning a Trade: A Craftsman's Notebooks, 1955–1997* was published in 1998 and contains his observations on the craft of writing.

Despite this prolific writing and publishing life, Price has continued to teach at Duke University, usually just one semester a year. His normal schedule includes a course on writing and one on literature, often on Milton.

In addition to the National Book Critics Circle Award and the William Faulkner Award, Price was a finalist for the Pulitzer Prize for *Clear Pictures*. In 1994, documentary filmmaker Charles Guggenheim completed a film about Price entitled *Reynolds Price: Clear Pictures*, which was shown nationally on PBS. Reynolds Price is a member of the American Academy of Arts and Letters, and his books have been translated into 16 languages.

### Further Reading

Humphries, Jefferson, ed. *Conversations with Reynolds Price.* Jackson: University Press of Mississippi, 1991.

Ruhlman, Michael. "A Writer at His Best," *The New York Times Book Review.* September 20, 1987. Available online. URL: http://www.nytimes.com/books/98/07/12/specials/price-writer.html.

"Reynolds Price." Seattle Arts: Lectures. Available online. URL: http://secure3.zipcon.net/~lectures/price.html. Downloaded June 14, 2003.

## Proulx, E. Annie
### (Edna Annie Proulx)
(1935–   ) *novelist, essayist, short story writer*

The first woman to receive the prestigious PEN/Faulkner Award, E. Annie Proulx is known for her idiosyncratic characters and forbidding landscapes. A practitioner of the contemporary gothic novel, she has created tough, often rural characters who are usually struggling to adapt to some set of tragic circumstances. Despite the bleakness of these characters' lives, readers and critics alike love her books. In the short time that she has been writing novels, Proulx has also received the National Book Award and a Pulitzer Prize for Fiction, among other honors. JOHN UPDIKE included one of her stories, "Half-Skinned Steer," in *The Best American Short Stories of the Century,* which he edited for Houghton Mifflin, and Proulx herself was selected to edit the 1997 *Best American Short Stories.*

Born in Norwich, Connecticut, on August 22, 1935, Proulx grew up in small towns across New England and North Carolina. Her father, George N. Proulx, began work as a bobbin boy in a textile mill and worked his way up to vice president of the company. The family moved from town to town as his jobs changed. Proulx's mother, Lois Gill, is a painter who Proulx credits with teaching her to look and really see. Proulx wrote her first story when she was 10 years old and sick in bed with chicken pox. She continued to write a story every once in a while and published her first in *Gourmet* magazine when she was in her 20s.

Proulx attended Colby College, in Maine, and the University of Vermont, where she graduated with a B.A. degree in 1969. She later attended Sir George Williams University (now called Concordia University) in Montreal, where she received her M.A. degree in 1973. Proulx has been married and divorced three times and has raised three sons on her own. For most of her career, she did it by working as a freelance journalist to pay the bills and by involving herself in the back-to-the-land movement. She wrote dozens of articles for numerous publications, on topics such as gardening, cooking, canoeing, and building your own fences and gates. She also wrote "how-to" books on similar subjects. It was not until she was in her 50s that Proulx began to publish fiction.

Her first book, *Heart Songs and Other Stories*, appeared in 1988. *Postcards* followed in 1992, and both received considerable critical acclaim. Proulx's best-selling book, *The Shipping News*, came out in 1993 and won the Pulitzer Prize and the National Book Award. The story of a repressed man who returns to his ancestral homeland in Newfoundland and finds redemption as he becomes part of the community, *The Shipping News* is a story of self-discovery that emphasizes the importance of family. The novel's isolated seaside setting in Newfoundland made a picturesque spot for a later film adaptation, which starred Kevin Spacey, Julianne Moore, and Judi Dench. Her next book, *Accordion Crimes*, appeared in 1996, following the author's move to Wyoming. Since that move, her books have been set in the West. Her novella *Brokeback Mountain* appeared in 1998 and has also been produced as a film; the following year the story collection *Close Range: Wyoming Stories* was published, full of ranchers, cowboys and cowgirls, rodeo riders, and farmers, all coping with hard times in a hard place. In *That Old Ace in the Hole: A Novel* (2002) Proulx explores the life of her protagonist, Bob Dollar, a 25-year-old land swindler, while telling the story of the Texas Panhandle region along the way. She has often been hailed for the originality of her voice and for her descriptive and historical accuracy. She is a relentless researcher and has said that research is the best part of writing. She has also stated that she wishes more writers would ask questions about what they do not know, instead of writing about their own lives and what they already know. In addition to her penchant for detail, Proulx is known for weaving her novels around some kind of unusual motif. In *The Shipping News*, she included drawings of knots at the beginning of each chapter, along with a snippet of philosophy from *The Ashley Book of Knots*. In *Accordion Crimes*, it is the movement of a special musical instrument through the hands of several generations of American immigrants that creates another layer of connection and intrigue.

In addition to the awards already mentioned, Proulx won the *New Yorker* Book Award for Best Fiction in 1999 for *Close Range: Wyoming Stories* and the *Irish Times* International Fiction Prize for *The Shipping News*, among many others.

**Further Reading**

"E. Annie Proulx." *Contemporary Novelists*. Detroit: Gale Group, 2000.

"Imagination Is Everything: A Conversation with E. Annie Proulx." The Atlantic Online. Available online. URL: http://www.theatlantic.com/unbound/factfict/eapint.htm. Posted November 12, 1997.

Fein, Esther B. "Shutout Ends: It's Men 12, Women 1." *The New York Times Book Review*. April 21, 1993. Available online. URL: http://www.nytimes.com/books/99/05/23/specials/proulx-pen.html.

## Pynchon, Thomas
### (Thomas Ruggles Pynchon, Jr.)
(1937–  ) *novelist, short story writer*

Thomas Pynchon's writing combines fantasy and black humor to depict human alienation. Pynchon has shunned public exposure despite success as a novelist and short story writer. His first novel, *V.* (1963), won the William Faulkner Foundation Award for best first novel of the year. The novel that is considered Pynchon's masterwork, *Gravity's Rainbow* (1973), was a cowinner of the National Book Award.

Thomas Ruggles Pynchon, Jr., was born on May 8, 1937, in Glen Cove, New York, one of three children of Thomas Ruggles Pynchon, Sr., and Katherine Frances Bennett Pynchon. The family moved when Pynchon was a child. His father became town supervisor of Oyster Bay, New York, and later an industrial surveyor. Pynchon graduated from Oyster Bay High School in 1953 at age 16 with distinction in English. He received a scholarship to Cornell University and took engineering and physics classes until he left school during his sophomore year, in 1955, for service in the navy. He returned to Cornell two years later and took classes in English, including a course taught by VLADIMIR NABOKOV. Pynchon was on the editorial staff of the *Cornell Writer*, which published his first short story, "The Small Rain," in 1959. He graduated with distinction that year.

Pynchon had several options after graduating, including pursuing a number of fellowships, teaching creative writing at Cornell, becoming a disk jockey, or working as a film critic for *Esquire*. He published many short stories, including "Mortality and Mercy in Vienna" in *Epoch* (Spring 1959), "Low-lands" in *New World Writing* (1960), and "Under the Rose" in *The Noble Savage* (May 1961). He also began work on his first novel, *V.*, while in New York and in Seattle, where he worked writing technical documents for the Boeing Company until 1962. He finished *V.* in California and Mexico, and it won the William Faulkner Foundation Award for best first novel of the year. *V.* is a whimsical, cynically absurd tale of a middle-aged Englishman's search for an elusive, adventuresome, supernatural woman. The object of the Englishman's search appears in various guises at critical periods in European history.

Pynchon then published a short story, "The Secret Integration," in *The Saturday Evening Post* (December 19, 1964) and parts of a work in progress, "The World (This One), the Flesh (Mrs. Oedipa Maas), and the Testament of Pierce Inverarity" in *Esquire* (December 1965). Of his few short stories, most notable are "Entropy" (1960), a neatly structured tale in which Pynchon first used extensive technical language and scientific metaphors, and "The Secret Integration" (1964), a

story in which Pynchon explored small-town bigotry and racism.

His second novel, *The Crying of Lot 49* (1966), won the Richard and Hilda Rosenthal Foundation Award of the National Institute of Arts and Letters. In the book, Pynchon described a woman's quest to discover the mysterious, conspiratorial Tristero System in a futuristic world of closed societies. The novel served as a condemnation of modern industrialization. Pynchon wrote "A Journey into the Mind of Watts" for the *New York Times Magazine* (June 12, 1966). He worked on *Gravity's Rainbow* for several years and in 1974 that novel shared the National Book Award for fiction with ISAAC BASHEVIS SINGER's *Crown of Feathers*. Many critics deemed *Gravity's Rainbow* a visionary apocalyptic masterpiece. Judges unanimously selected *Gravity's Rainbow* for the Pulitzer Prize in literature, but the Pulitzer advisory board overruled the selection, saying the book was "unreadable," "turgid," "overwritten," and "obscene." No prize was given that year. *Gravity's Rainbow* was set in an area of post–World War II Germany called "the Zone." It centered on the wanderings of a U.S. soldier who is one of many odd characters looking for a secret V-2 rocket that will supposedly break through the Earth's gravitational barrier when launched. The narrative is filled with descriptions of obsessive and paranoid fantasies, grotesque imagery, and esoteric mathematical and scientific language. *Gravity's Rainbow* was also awarded the William Dean Howells Medal of the American Academy of Arts and Letters in 1975, but Pynchon declined the award, suggesting that it be given to another author. In a letter, he wrote, "The Howells Medal is a great honor, and, being gold, probably a good hedge against inflation, too. But I don't want it. Please don't impose on me something I don't want. It makes the Academy look arbitrary and me look rude. . . . I know I should behave with more class, but there appears to be only one way to say no, and that's no."

Pynchon has remained elusive to his fans. Many of his early short stories were collected in 1984 under the title *Slow Learner* with the autobiographical notes by the author. Pynchon was awarded the John D. and Catherine T. MacArthur Foundation Fellowship in 1989. His novel *Vineland* was published in 1990 and *Mason & Dixon,* another novel, appeared in 1997.

**Further Reading**

Bloom, Harold, ed. *Thomas Pynchon.* New York: Chelsea House Publishers, 1986.

Eddins, Dwight. *The Gnostic Pynchon.* Bloomington: Indiana University Press, 1990.

Horvath, Brook, and Irving Malin, eds. *Pynchon and 'Mason & Dixon.'* Newark: University of Delaware Press, 2000.

Pearce, Richard, ed. *Critical Essays on Thomas Pynchon.* Boston: G. K. Hall, 1981.

Stonehill, Brian. *The Self-Conscious Novel: Artifice in Fiction from Joyce to Pynchon.* Philadelphia: University of Pennsylvania Press, 1988.

# R

## Rand, Ayn
### (Alisa Rosenbaum)
(1905–1982) *novelist*

In 1991, Ayn Rand's *Atlas Shrugged* was named the second most influential book for Americans, following the Bible. Although she is easily remembered as a staunch and overtly oppositional force against collectivist doctrines of the Soviet system, her most valuable contribution to American literature may be her philosophical perspectives on objectivism.

Alisa Rosenbaum (later self-renamed Ayn Rand) was born in St. Petersburg, Russia, on February 2, 1905. Her father was a pharmacist. At age six she taught herself to read; at age nine she chose a career in writing fiction. Thoroughly opposed to the socialist thought prevalent in Russian culture at the time, she deemed herself a European writer, especially after encountering authors such as Walter Scott and her most admired writer, Victor Hugo.

During high school, Rand was eyewitness to both the Kerensky Revolution, which she supported, and the 1917 Bolshevik Revolution, which she denounced from the outset. Her family moved from St. Petersburg in 1918 to escape the communist regime and settled on the Crimean Peninsula, where her father opened a second pharmacy. The final communist victory and the establishment of Soviet Russia, however, resulted in the confiscation of her father's business, which led to frequent periods of near-starvation for her family. When introduced to U.S. history during her last year of high

school, Rand immediately considered the United States to be a showcase of a nation of free men.

When Rand's family returned to St. Petersburg (then called Petrograd), she entered the University of Petrograd to study philosophy and history. Graduating in 1924, she experienced the disintegration of free thought and the takeover of the university by communist doctrine. Amidst an increasingly bleak life and outlook, one of Rand's greatest pleasures was watching Western films and plays. She entered the State Institute for Cinema Arts in 1924 to study screenwriting.

In late 1925 Rand obtained permission to leave Soviet Russia for a visit to relatives in the United States. Although she told Soviet authorities that her visit would be short, she was determined never to return to Russia. She arrived in New York City in February 1926, spent the next six months with her relatives in Chicago, then, with a letter of recommendation and a small loan, she boarded a train in August, bound for Hollywood. In Hollywood, Rand rented a room at the Studio Club apartments, a residence for young women who hoped to make careers in the film industry, such as Ginger Rogers, Marilyn Monroe, and Kim Novak.

On Rand's second day in Hollywood, Cecil B. DeMille saw her standing at the gate of his studio, offered her a ride to the set of his movie *The King of Kings,* and gave her a job, first as an extra, then as a script reader. During the next week at the studio, she met an actor, Frank O'Connor, whom she married in 1929; they were married until his death 50 years later.

DeMille was forced to close his studio in 1929; Rand was hired as a filing clerk in the RKO wardrobe department, where a year later she became head of the department. Frank was working steadily at the time, and thus the O'Connors bought their first automobile, and Rand her first portable typewriter. She began work on several screenplays and short stories in her spare time; she then sold a story, "The Red Pawn," to Universal Studios for $1,500, which enabled her to quit her job at RKO to write full time.

The O'Connors moved to New York in 1934 and two years later *We the Living* was published. The theme of this novel, in Rand's words, is "the right of the individual to the pursuit of his own happiness. It portrays the impact of the Russian Revolution on three people who demand the right to live their own lives." During this time Rand tried unsuccessfully to bring her family to the United States, an endeavor that had become virtually impossible under Stalin's rule. Many years later her sister Nora did come to America, but returned to Russia after just a short visit.

Rand's next overtly anticollectivist work, *Anthem*, was written in 1937, published in England in 1938, then in America in 1945. She published one of her most popular novels, *The Fountainhead* (originally named *Second-hand Lives*) in 1943, which she then turned into a screenplay. It was not until after World War II, however, that a film version, starring Gary Cooper and Patricia Neal, was released. In 1946 Rand began writing her major novel, *Atlas Shrugged* (originally named *The Strike*); she completed and published the novel 11 years later. *Atlas Shrugged* was her greatest achievement and her last work of fiction. In this novel she integrated her unique philosophies concerning ethics, metaphysics, politics, economics, and sex into an intellectual mystery story that she felt was crucial in order to understand the true essence of a fictional hero. She believed she needed to formulate "a philosophy for living on earth."

Thereafter, Rand wrote and lectured on her philosophy—objectivism, which holds as its center the notion of the primacy of existence, or that existence *is*. This belief means that existence requires no explanation and thus that it makes no sense to require an explanation for existence. Existence, in

Rand's philosophy, is "simple, irreducible, and foundational." She published and edited her own periodicals from 1962 to 1976, which were composed of her viewpoints on objectivism and its application to culture. During this time Rand also spoke annually at the Ford Hall Forum in Boston to full houses; she even made a handful of television appearances with such notables as Mike Wallace, Phil Donahue, and Tom Snyder.

In 1978 O'Connor began showing signs of arterial sclerosis with some memory loss; one year later he died at age 82. The loss of O'Connor devastated Rand and she sank into a deep depression. Her last lecture was in New Orleans in late 1981. Ayn Rand died at her home in New York from heart failure on March 6, 1982, at age 78.

### Further Reading

Branden, Nathaniel. *My Years with Ayn Rand*. San Francisco: Jossey-Bass Publishers, 1999.

Den Uyl, Douglas J. *The Fountainhead: An American Novel*. Boston: Twayne, 1999.

Gladstein, Mimi Reisel. *Atlas Shrugged: Manifesto of the Mind*. Boston: Twayne, 2000.

Gladstein, Mimi Reisel, and Chris Matthew Sciabarra. *Feminist Interpretations of Ayn Rand*. Philadelphia: Pennsylvania State University Press, 1999.

Paxton, Michael. *Ayn Rand: A Sense of Life*. Salt Lake City: Gibbs-Smith, 1998.

Walker, Jeff. *The Ayn Rand Cult*. Chicago: Open Court, 1999.

## Ransom, John Crowe
(1888–1974)  *poet, literary critic*

One of the early Fugitives at Vanderbilt University, along with ALLEN TATE and ROBERT PENN WARREN, John Crowe Ransom was one of the first academics to legitimize the role of the poet and critic in English departments, which historically had favored scholars focused on the study of language and the history of literature. Although he has been considered one of the most important "minor" poets of the 20th century, his work holds a secure position in the American literary cannon. Ransom is also known as the founder of the renowned literary journal *The Kenyon Review* and one of the most influential American literary theorists. The "New Criticism" most often associated with T. S. ELIOT and ROBERT PENN WARREN, among others, actually took its name from Ransom's book of essays by the same title.

John Crowe Ransom was born on April 30, 1888, in Pulaski, Tennessee, to John James Ransom, a Methodist minister, and Ella Crowe. His upbringing was heavy on religion, but his parents maintained an open-minded household. An excellent student, Ransom entered Vanderbilt University in Nashville at age 15. Following graduation in 1909 and a stint as a high school teacher, he went on to study classics as a Rhodes Scholar at Oxford from 1910 to 1913. Ransom accepted an instructorship in Vanderbilt's English department in 1914 and, apart from service as an artillery officer in France during World War I, remained there until his departure for Kenyon College, in Ohio, in 1937. In 1920, Ransom married Robb Reavill; the couple had three children.

Ransom was inspired to begin writing poetry when he joined the Fugitive literary group, which met often to discuss philosophy and literature and eventually to critique one another's poems. He completed his first book, *Poems about God* (1919), during his military service. He quickly became disillusioned with his early work, however, and refused to ever let it be republished in subsequent volumes, even though both ROBERT FROST and Robert Graves had praised his early poems. His work that was first published in *The Fugitive*, the group's literary magazine, from 1922 through 1925 is more representative of Ransom's mature style and can be found in his books *Chills and Fever* (1924) and *Two Gentlemen in Bonds* (1927). His best-known poem is probably "Bells for John Whiteside's Daughter," which is included in *Chills and Fever*. It is indicative of his style in which he uses short lyrics to explore the ironies of human existence as they make themselves known in everyday life. By 1927 Ransom believed he had exhausted his poetic themes. In 1951, many years after he had given up writing poetry, he won the Bollingen Prize for Poetry, and in 1964 he received the National Book Award for his *Selected Poems*, which had been published the previous year.

As a critic, Ransom was quite influential throughout his long teaching career. His early work

with the Fugitives focused on defending the agrarian South and preserving traditional aesthetics that were rooted in classical forms. As he grew older, however, he came to see flaws in some of his early arguments and turned his attention toward a defense of poetry itself. He worked to encourage the study of the actual texts of poems as opposed to the biographies of the poets and the specific details surrounding their composition, an approach that came to be known as "New Criticism." Ransom believed strongly that poetry offered a unique knowledge that science could not and wrote numerous essays on the subject. The best known of these is probably "Wanted: An Ontological Critic," which was published in 1941. In addition to the titles already mentioned, Ransom's books include *Grace after Meat* (1924), *Poems and Essays* (1955), and the following books of essays: *God without Thunder* (1931), *The World's Body* (1938), *The New Criticism* (1941), *Poetic Sense: A Study of Problems in Defining Poetry by Content* (1971), and *Beating the Bushes: Selected Essays, 1941–1970* (1997), among others.

When Ransom moved to Kenyon College in 1937, he brought with him three distinguished students—RANDALL JARRELL, Peter Taylor, and ROBERT LOWELL. He founded *The Kenyon Review* and served as its editor from 1939 to 1959. He also founded the Kenyon School of English, designed to gather distinguished critics and students together to develop a more critical approach to literature along the lines he had already outlined, though by no means confined to them.

Following his retirement from teaching and from editing the *Kenyon Review* in 1959, Ransom remained active in the academic world. He wrote new essays, lectured, collected honors and recognition, and continued to revise the poems from his early career. Near the end of his life, he suffered from numerous recurring ailments that left him withdrawn and silent much of the time. Ransom died in his sleep at his home on the Kenyon campus on July 3, 1974.

### Further Reading

Buffington, Robert. *The Equilibrist: A Study of John Crowe Ransom's Poems, 1916–1963.* Nashville: Vanderbilt University Press, 1967.

Malvasi, Mark G. *The Unregenerate South: The Agrarian Thought of John Crowe Ransom, Allen Tate, and Donald Davidson.* Baton Rouge: Louisiana State University Press, 1997.

Parsons, Thornton H. *John Crowe Ransom.* New York: Twayne Publishers, 1969.

Quinlan, Kieran. *John Crowe Ransom's Secular Faith.* Baton Rouge: Louisiana State University Press, 1989.

Stewart, John L. *The Burden of Time: The Fugitives and Agrarians; The Nashville Groups of the 1920's and 1930's, and the Writing of John Crowe Ransom, Allen Tate, and Robert Penn Warren.* Princeton, N.J.: Princeton University Press, 1965.

Williams, Miller. *The Poetry of John Crowe Ransom.* New Brunswick, N.J.: Rutgers University Press, 1972.

Young, Thomas D. *Gentleman in a Dustcoat: A Biography of John Crowe Ransom.* New York: Random House, 1976.

## Reed, Ishmael
(1938–   ) *poet*

Decidedly unconventional, Ishmael Reed has enjoyed provoking controversy in his writing. As a fervent advocate of "neohoodooism," he offers trickster characters and zany rhetoric that satirizes not only suburban white culture but also African-American literature. Reed is the author of five collections of poetry, nine novels, four collections of essays, and a handful of plays. He was cofounder of Yardbird Publishing Co. in 1971 and of Reed, Cannon, and Johnson Communications in 1973. With Al Young, Reed also cofounded *Quilt* magazine. Among his honors and awards are the Richard and Linda Rosenthal Foundation Award, a Guggenheim Foundation Award, the Lewis Michaux Award, an American Civil Liberties Award, and fellowships from the National Endowment for the Arts, the American Civil Liberties Union, and the California Arts Council. Reed has lectured at numerous colleges and universities. For the past 20 years, he has been a lecturer at the University of California at Berkeley.

Ishmael Reed was born on February 22, 1938, in Chattanooga, Tennessee. When he was young, his family moved to Buffalo, New York, where he grew up. In Buffalo he attended public high school and Millard Fillmore College. Reed then transferred to the University of Buffalo with the assistance of an English teacher who was impressed with a story he had written. For financial reasons, however, he eventually withdrew from the university without taking a degree. Reed remained in Buffalo for some time, working as a correspondent for the *Empire Star Weekly,* a black community newspaper, and serving as cohost of a local radio program, which was canceled after he conducted an interview with Malcolm X, then still a controversial figure.

In 1962, Reed relocated to New York City and served as editor of a Newark, New Jersey, weekly journal while helping to establish the legendary *East Village Other,* one of the first and best-known of the region's underground newspapers. He was also a member of the Umbra Writers Workshop, an organization known for its contribution to the Black Arts movement and the Black Aesthetic.

In 1967, Reed published his first novel, *The Free-Lance Pallbearers,* and has since had a steady output of novels, poetry, and essay collections, and has edited numerous reviews and critical articles as well as two major anthologies. His novels first gained wide literary attention with the publication of *Mumbo Jumbo* (1972). *Mumbo Jumbo* depicts the struggles between black culture and Western monotheistic culture in this epic story that takes place in New Orleans and Harlem during the Jazz Age of the 1920s.

The impressive commercial success attained by some African-American authors has thus far eluded Reed. However, over the course of a distinguished and turbulent career he has received numerous critical accolades. Musician Max Roach is said to have called Reed "the Charlie Parker of American fiction," while critic Fredric Jameson has judged him to be one of the principal postmodernists. Nick Aaron Ford, in *Studies in the Novel,* referred to Reed as the "most revolutionary" African-American novelist. Reed's literary style is best known for its use of parody and satire in attempts to create new myths and to challenge the formal conventions of literary tradition. His works have alternately been criticized as incoherent and abstruse, and hailed as multicultural, revolutionary, and vivid. His novel *The Last Days of Louisiana Red* (1975) received the Rosenthal Foundation Award. *Flight to Canada* (1976) is considered by many critics to be his best novel. A slave's-eye view of the Civil War, *Flight to Canada* tackles slavery, the antebellum South, and Harriet Beecher Stowe, among other topics, with both rage and humor.

Reed and his wife, Carla Blank, a dancer and choreographer, live in Oakland, California, with their daughter, Tennessee. From his previous marriage to Priscilla Rose, Reed has a daughter named Timothy Brett. He began his teaching career at the University of California at Berkeley in 1968, where he still teaches despite being denied tenure in 1977. Reed chronicled this experience in *Shrovetide in Old New Orleans,* his first essay collection. Many other academic institutions have offered him visiting appointments, allowing Reed the opportunity to teach at Dartmouth, Harvard, Yale, Washington University in St. Louis, and the State University of New York at Buffalo, among others. A Pulitzer Prize nominee, Reed has been chosen once as a National Book Award finalist in fiction and once in poetry.

## Further Reading

Boyer, Jan. *Ishmael Reed.* Boise, Idaho: Boise State Press, 1993.

Gates, Henry. "Ishmael Reed," *The Dictionary of Literary Biography,* Volume 33. Detroit: Gale Research Group, 1984.

Mikics, David. "Postmodernism, Ethnicity and Underground Revisionism in Ishmael Reed," *Postmodern Culture.* Baltimore: Johns Hopkins University Press, 1990.

O'Brien, John. "Ishmael Reed Interview," *The New Fiction: Interviews with Innovative American Writers.* Urbana: University of Illinois Press, 1974.

Reed, Ishmael. *The Reed Reader.* New York: Basic Books, 2001.

## Rice, Anne
### (Howard Allen O'Brien, A. N. Rocquelaire, Anne Rampling)
(1941–   )  *novelist, horror fiction writer*

Anne Rice is one of the most widely read authors in America today. Her stories distinctively blend the visible and perpetual worlds and tend to incorporate elements of history, philosophy, religion, and supernatural forces, which makes them appealing to abroad range of readers. Rice has published works under three names: her own and the pen names A. N. Roquelaire and Anne Rampling. Under her own name she has published two historical novels, seven books in the Vampire Chronicles series, three books in the Mayfair Witches series, and three other novels, including her most recent, *Violin.* Rice has also published two works of erotica under the name Anne Rampling, and under the pen name A. N. Roquelaire she wrote the Beauty series, a trilogy of erotic work.

Anne Rice was born in Mercy Hospital in New Orleans on October 4, 1941. She was the second of four daughters born to Katherine and Howard O'Brien, and was given the name Howard Allen O'Brien, after her father. Of being named after her father, she has recalled that her mother "had the idea that naming a woman Howard was going to give that woman an unusual advantage in the world." The young girl officially started using the name Anne when a teacher asked her name on her first day of school. Anne yelled "Anne," and her mother did not correct her, knowing that she was deeply embarrassed by her real name.

Following her mother's death in 1956, the family moved to Richardson, Texas, where she met her husband-to-be, Stan Rice. Although the pair shared a high school journalism class and developed a close friendship, their relationship did not become official until after her graduation later that year.

In fall 1959, she left Stan behind when she enrolled at Texas Woman's College in Denton. In 1960, she moved to San Francisco, California, distancing herself even further from her family and Stan. The two continued their now long-distance relationship through letters and telephone calls. Then, in 1961, Stan proposed to Anne via telegram and the two were married later that year.

Following their wedding the Rices moved to the Haight-Ashbury section of San Francisco, and they both enrolled at San Francisco State University, from where Anne graduated in 1964 with two B.A. degrees, one in political science and one in creative writing. Two years later, on

September 22, 1966, Rice gave birth to her daughter, Michelle. During this same time, Rice moved her family to Berkeley so that she could attend graduate school there. Rice began in the Ph.D. program at Berkeley but soon abandoned her studies there for an M.A. degree in creative writing at San Francisco State University. While in Berkeley, however, Rice had completed a short story entitled "Interview with the Vampire," which was later to become her most widely recognized work of fiction.

In 1970 Rice's daughter, Michelle, was diagnosed with leukemia. She died on August 5, 1972, sending the Rices into a period of severe depression, which almost completely destroyed Rice, her marriage, and her life. In 1973, as a means of distracting herself from her grief, Rice began reworking "Interview with the Vampire" into a full-length novel. She spent a remarkably short time revising it and in 1976, Knopf published the novel. That same year, movie rights to the novel were sold to Paramount for the amount of $150,000 with a 10-year option, but the film version would not appear until 1994.

In March 1979, Rice gave birth to her son, Christopher. Christopher Rice has since gone on to become a published author himself, writing the best-selling 2001 novel *A Density of Souls*.

In following years, as Rice attempted to stay away from the vampire genre, she found that the character Lestat, her antagonist in *Interview with the Vampire*, was constantly on her mind. Of this time Rice recalls, "Almost everything I see, I ask myself 'What would Lestat think of this . . . how would Lestat react to this?' so I would say that he is the other half of me, but he is the male ruthless half of me that, thank God, does not exist, except in fiction." As a result of this obsession with her vampire character, Rice chose to continue Lestat's story, publishing her second vampire chronicle, *The Vampire Lestat* (1985), and her third, *The Queen of the Damned* (1988). Rice then published two more Vampire Chronicles—*The Tale of the Body Thief* (1992) and *Memnoch the Devil* (1995). Although these two novels were intended to end the series, Rice was unable to avoid her beloved vampires for long. In 1998, *The Vampire Armand* became the sixth installment in the series. The next novel, *Merrick* (2000), was published under tragic circum-

stances; Rice had become ill two years earlier, and at the time *Merrick* was released, she had fallen into a diabetic coma. Rice has since recovered from her crisis and has continued with her Vampire Chronicles, with the release of *Blood and Gold* in 2001. Rice currently resides with her husband and her son in the Garden District in New Orleans, Louisiana.

## Further Reading

Dickinson, Joy. *Haunted City: An Unauthorized Guide to the Magical, Magnificent New Orleans of Anne Rice*. New York: Citadel Press, 1995.

Langley, Jason Paul. *Gender Busting: Exploring Masculine and Feminine Roles in the Novels of Anne Rice*. Little Rock: Arkansas State University, 1996.

Marcus, Jana. *In the Shadow of the Vampire: Reflections from the World of Anne Rice*. New York: Thunder's Mouth Press, 1997.

Ramsland, Katherine M. *The Witches' Companion: The Official Guide to Anne Rice's Lives of the Mayfair Witches*. New York: Random House, 1994.

Roberts, Bette B. *Anne Rice*. New York: Twayne, 1995.

## Rich, Adrienne
### (Rich, Adrienne Cecile)
### (1929–   ) *essayist*

Adrienne Rich is the author of nearly 20 volumes of poetry and several books of nonfiction. In 1999, Rich received the Lifetime Achievement Award from the Lannan Foundation. Her previous awards include the Academy Fellowship, the Ruth Lilly Poetry Prize, the Lenore Marshall Poetry Prize, the National Book Award, and a MacArthur Fellowship. In 1997 Rich was awarded the Wallace Stevens Award for outstanding and proven mastery in the art of poetry.

Adrienne Cecile Rich was born on May 16, 1929, in Baltimore, Maryland. She was the older of two sisters born to an intellectual and well-off Jewish family. Rich was educated by her parents until she entered public school in the fourth grade. She graduated from Radcliffe in 1951 ("where I did not see a woman teacher for four years," and where, as she writes in the essay "When We Dead Awaken," she studied exclusively the work of male poets). That same year marked the publication of her first book of poems, *A Change of World*. W. H. AUDEN, who admired Rich's command of diction and meter, chose this volume for the Yale Series of Younger Poets Award. *A Change of World* and her next collection, *The Diamond Cutters and Other Poems* (1955), earned her a reputation as an elegant and controlled stylist.

Meanwhile, "determined to have a 'full' woman's life," Rich married Alfred Conrad, an economist at Harvard, in 1953, and had three sons before she was 30—"a radicalizing experience," as she later called it. Of this period she has said (in *Of Woman Born*), "I knew I had to remake my life; I did not then understand that we the women of that academic community—as in so many middle-class communities of the period—were expected to fill both the part of the Victorian lady of leisure, the angel in the house, and also of the Victorian cook, scullery maid, laundress, governess, and nurse." In "When We Dead Awaken," she describes the long struggle to confront for the first time her condition as a woman, which resulted in *Snapshots of a Daughter-in-Law*, the title poem of her next book, eight difficult years later.

The 1966 the Conrads moved to New York, where Alfred had taken a post at City College. There they both became increasingly involved in resistance activities against the Vietnam War. Rich taught in the SEEK Program for disadvantaged young people, and her poems as well as her view of her audience changed. Her vivid political concerns were the subject of many of the verses in *Leaflets* (1969) and *The Will to Change* (1971), while transformations in her poetic style reflected the continuing evolution of her political attitudes. Writing with a new urgency, she broke away from the tight verse forms and neat metrics that had marked much of her early work and began to produce poems that were characterized by a kind of improvisational intensity. In 1970 Rich left her marriage, "to do something very common, in my own way." Later that year, Alfred Conrad committed suicide.

Rich's works during this period, including *Diving into the Wreck* (1973) and *The Dream of a Common Language* (1978), exemplify her changing form and style; in addition to her technical evolution and now distinct improvisation, Rich began to address the experiences and aspirations of women from a strongly feminist perspective. *Diving into the Wreck* received the National Book Award in 1974. She rejected the prize as an individual but accepted it, in a statement written with AUDRE LORDE and ALICE WALKER, two other nominees, in the name of all women. That same year, Rich became professor of English at City College of New York and began the research for *Of Woman Born: Motherhood as Experience and Institution*. This prose work, published in 1976, employs personal journals, anthropology, and political and medical history as a background for meditation on a subject that, she said, she had not chosen: "It had, long ago, chosen me." The book examines the experience of motherhood, along with the myths that have been projected on that experience.

In 1977 Rich published *Twenty-One Love Poems*, which record and explore lesbian relationships. The term *lesbian*, for Rich, however, was "nothing so simple and dismissible as the fact that two women might go to bed together," as she wrote in *It Is the Lesbian in Us* (1976). Lesbianism, for her, was a sense of desiring oneself, choosing oneself; it was about an intensity between women that she felt was generally trivialized, caricatured, and invested with evil.

Recently, Rich has moved into comparatively new poetic styles and subjects. In the 1980s, her commitment to personal exploration and analysis compelled her—in *Sources* (1982) and other works—to reexamine her complex relationships with her dead father and husband, and what they represent of her Jewish heritage. In the 1990s, she produced what may be her most daring works to date, the ambitious long poem *An Atlas of the Difficult World* (1991), the historical and deeply personal *Dark Fields of the Republic* (1995), and *Midnight Salvage* (1998).

## Further Reading

Da Costa, Paulo. "Interview with Adrienne Rich." Samsära Quarterly, volume 5. Available online. URL: http://www.samsaraquarterly.net/5/rich.htm. Downloaded February 12, 2003.

Gelpi, Barbara Charlesworth, ed. *Adrienne Rich's Poetry and Prose: Poems, Prose, Reviews, and Criticism*. New York: W. W. Norton, 1993.

Klein, Michael. "A Rich Life: Adrienne Rich on Poetry, Politics, and Personal Revelation." *Boston Phoenix.* Available online. URL: http://www.bostonphoenix.com/archive/1in10/99/06/rich.html. Posted June 1999.

Prince, E. C. Ruth. "The Possibilities of an Engaged Art: An Interview with Adrienne Rich." *Radcliffe Quarterly* (fall 1998): 12–19.

## Robbins, Tom

(1936–    )  *novelist*

Writer Tom Robbins is the king of mischief and unpredictability. He writes with a distinctively rebellious but delightful tone. His themes are marked with fervent antagonism against societal norms, conformity, and abuses of natural resources. Remarkably joyful, his work carries readers along with a familiar sense of optimism and wild abandon.

Tom Robbins was born on July 22, 1936, in Blowing Rock, North Carolina, as the oldest of four children and grandson of two Baptist preachers. His mother was a nurse, a Sunday school teacher, and a writer of religious children's stories. His father was a power company executive. By age five, Robbins had taught himself to read and was already writing his own stories. Having worked a stint at the Barnes and Beers Traveling Circus at age 11, Robbins did not lack the experiences and inspirational material helpful to an early career in writing. He attended Hargrove Military Academy and then, at the age of 18, enrolled at Washington and Lee University to study journalism. While he was there, he was expelled from his fraternity for throwing biscuits at his housemother. Robbins lasted just two years at Washington and Lee before he abandoned academia for a life of transience. After leaving school in 1956, he hitchhiked around the country for a year before moving to New York City to be a poet. Shortly after settling in New York, Robbins received a draft notice and was immediately sent to Korea to work for the U.S. Air Force as a meteorologist. He spent three years in Korea during the Korean War and ventured as far as Japan, where he studied Japanese art and aesthetics.

Upon returning to the United States, Robbins finished college, tinkered in newspaper journalism, and then got a master's degree in Far Eastern studies at the University of Washington in Seattle, which included a summer trip with noted mythologist Joseph Campbell to South America. Always wildly unpredictable, he later worked as a disc jockey, wrote headlines for the Dear Abby advice column, and worked as an art critic for the *Seattle Post-Intelligencer.* When the West Coast editor of Doubleday later approached Robbins about writing a book, he was ready. He was tired of working with an editor on a day-to-day basis and relished the independence of writing a novel. He "called in well" to work: he told his newspaper editor, "I've been sick for a long time, but now I'm well so I won't be coming in again." Three years later, in 1971, *Another Roadside Attraction* hit the stands.

His next book, *Even Cowgirls Get the Blues,* came out in 1976. THOMAS PYNCHON called it "a piece of working magic, warm, funny." *Cowgirls* tells the story of Sissy Hankshaw, a beautiful, bisexual model with enormous thumbs who finds freedom by hitchhiking back and forth across the country. The quest for freedom at the expense of security is a theme that continually pops up in Robbins's books: "I encourage everyone to take chances, to court danger, to welcome anxiety, to flaunt insecurity, and always act against the grain," he has said. "The process by which the need for playfulness and liberty becomes stronger than the need for comfort and security." The book was adapted for the screen in 1993 by Gus Van Sant, but Robbins's whimsical landscapes and characters proved difficult to bring to life on the big screen. The movie attracted only small audiences and was mostly panned by critics.

Robbins published *Still Life with Woodpecker* in 1980, followed by *Jitterbug Perfume* (1984) and *Skinny Legs and All* (1990). Robbins then traveled to Timbuktu and gathered inspiration for his next novel, *Half Asleep in Frog Pajamas* (1994), which hit the *New York Times* best-seller list the following year. In addition to his written success, Robbins has also appeared on the big screen. Along with his roles in *Made in Heaven* and *Mrs. Parker and the Vicious Circle,* he was also the narrator in *Even Cowgirls Get the Blues.*

Robbins continues to gain success and loyalty with his off-the-wall stories. *Fierce Invalids Home from Hot Climates* was released in 2000 and was an immediate best-seller. *Villa Incognito* was published in 2003. Robbins currently resides in Washington in a house overlooking Skagit Bay, although he uses his other home in La Conner, Washington, as his "writing house."

### Further Reading

Harkovitch, Michael. "Living Dangerously: Tom Robbins Visits UW." The Silverfish. Available online. URL: http://students.washington.edu/aliss/silverfish/harkovitch3.shtml. Downloaded September 23, 2003.

Hoyser, Catherine E., and Lorena Laura Stookey. *Tom Robbins: A Critical Companion.* Westport, Conn.: Greenwood Press, 1997.

Whitmer, Peter O., and Bruce Vanwyngarden. *Aquarius Revisited: Seven Who Created the Sixties Counterculture that Changed America.* New York: Macmillan Publishing Company, 1987.

## Robinson, Edwin Arlington
(1869–1935) *poet*

Edwin Arlington Robinson was the first major U.S. poet of the 20th century. He was especially unique in that he devoted his life to poetry and willingly paid the price of continual poverty and obscurity. Having lived and written during an age of free verse and experimentation, Robinson is at times considered intolerably old-fashioned; however, there is no doubt that he was an absolute master of form.

Edwin Arlington Robinson was born on December 22, 1869, in Head Tide, Maine, to Edward Robinson, a timber merchant and civic leader, and Mary Elizabeth Palmer. Not long after his birth, his family moved to Gardiner, Maine, in search of a better education for their three sons. Interested in poetry from an early age, Robinson was inspired by Gardiner and wrote prolifically about the small town later in his career. "Win," as he was often called, was not encouraged by his parents to pursue poetry as a profession despite his deep interest. However, his love for poetry never diminished. "It must have been about the year 1889 when I realized finally . . . that I was doomed, or elected, or sentenced for life, to the writing of poetry."

Robinson suffered several years of hardship and discouragement during his 20s, with only minimal

accomplishment. He moved to Boston for two years to receive medical treatment and was able to attend Harvard University. He published a few poems in *The Harvard Advocate* and in other periodicals. During this time, however, Robinson's life was dominated by tragic events. Between 1889 and 1896, he lost his father to a stroke, his mother to diphtheria, the family fortune to a recession, his brother Dean to suicide, and his fiancée to his brother Herman. To make matters even worse, he had a collection of rejection slips "that must have been one of the largest and most comprehensive in literary history." Just weeks following his mother's death, he published his first book, *The Torrent and The Night Before,* which he financed out of his own pocket.

He ended up giving most of the copies to editors and authors, in hopes of reviews and recognition. In the February 1897 edition of *Bookman,* reviewer Harry Thurston Peck wrote that Robinson's "humor is of a grim sort, and the world is not beautiful to him, but a prison-house." Robinson responded ingeniously. "I am sorry that I have painted myself in such lugubrious colors. The world is not a prison house, but a sort of spiritual kindergarten, where millions of bewildered infants are trying to spell God with the wrong blocks."

Following publication of *The Children of the Night* (1897) and *Captain Craig* (1902), Robinson's creative productivity came to a standstill; eight years passed before he produced any new material. Then in 1904, President Theodore Roosevelt read *The Children of the Night* and publicly endorsed Robinson's writing. With this influential encouragement, *The Children of the Night* was republished the following year and Robinson was offered a position in the New York Customs House, which he accepted and held until 1909.

It was not until his 1910 publication of *The Town Down the River* that Robinson began to acquire a reputation as a poet. During his lifetime, he won three Pulitzer Prizes for his work. First, in 1922, Robinson was awarded for a volume called *Collected Poems.* In 1925 he won his second for *The Man Who Died Twice,* and he won his final Pulitzer in 1928 for *Tristram.* He wrote seven more books before he died, but critics compared them unfavorably to *Tristram.* Robinson's poetry was noted for its mastery of conventional forms, including the sonnet, the quatrain, and the eight-line stanza. Robinson was also known for his ability to capture the misfortunes of his characters—in works such as "Richard Cory," "Luke Havergal," "Aaron Stark," and "John Evereldown," all of whom are faced with severe failures and tragedy—with elements of compassion and respect for their inherent courage.

In January 1935, Robinson was diagnosed with terminal cancer. During his last weeks he finished *King Jasper*, then died hours after completing the book, on April 6, 1935. He had been the only living member of his immediate family.

**Further Reading**

Anderson, Wallace L. *Edwin Arlington Robinson: A Critical Introduction*. Boston: Houghton Mifflin, 1967.

Barnard, Ellsworth. *Edwin Arlington Robinson: Centenary Essays*. Athens: University of Georgia Press, 1970.

Cary, Richard. *Appreciation of Edwin Arlington Robinson: 28 Interpretive Essays*. Waterville, Maine: Colby College Press, 1969.

Coxe, Louis O. *Edwin Arlington Robinson: The Life of Poetry*. New York: Pegasus, 1969.

Franchere, Hoyt C. *Edwin Arlington Robinson*. New York: Twayne, 1968.

Joyner, Nancy Carol. *Edwin Arlington Robinson: A Reference Guide*. Boston: G. K. Hall, 1978.

Peschel, Bill. *Edwin Arlington Robinson's Life and Career*. Modern American Poetry. Available online. URL: http://www.english.uinc.edu/maps/poets/m_r/robinson/life.htm. Downloaded September 15, 2003.

## Roethke, Theodore
### (Theodore Huebner Roethke)
(1908–1963) *poet*

Theodore Roethke is considered one of the pioneers of the confessional aesthetic in poetry. His groundbreaking exploration of nature and psychology and his mastery of both traditional and free verse poetic forms secured his place in the American canon. In addition, his work exerted a significant influence over the generation of poets that followed him in the confessional school, including ANNE SEXTON, ROBERT BLY, SYLVIA PLATH, and JAMES WRIGHT.

Theodore Roethke was born on May 25, 1908, in Saginaw, Michigan, to Otto Theodore and Helen Marie (Huebner) Roethke, who owned a local greenhouse. The young Roethke attended the John Moore School, where he studied German in addition to the usual curriculum. As a freshman at Arthur Hill High School, Roethke wrote a speech on the Junior Red Cross that received much attention and was eventually published in 26 languages. In addition to being quite a successful student, Roethke played on the basketball team and was a member of the track team. In 1923, midway through his high school years, Roethke experienced two blows that would permanently alter his life when his uncle committed suicide and his father died from cancer just a few months later.

From 1925 to 1929 Roethke studied at the University of Michigan at Ann Arbor, graduating magna cum laude. He went on to law school, but dropped out after just one semester, resisting his family's desire that he pursue a law degree. From 1929 through 1931, he took graduate classes in literature at the University of Michigan and then at Harvard but was forced to leave school and take a job due to lack of funds. He began his teaching career at Lafayette College, where he worked from 1931 to 1935 and established lasting friendships with the poets LOUISE BOGAN and STANLEY KUNITZ.

In 1935, Roethke moved back to Michigan to take a teaching position at Michigan State College, but in November of that year he was hospitalized for three months for the first in a series of mental breakdowns that would affect him periodically for the rest of his life. Following his recuperation, Roethke continued to write and to publish in journals such as *Poetry*, the *New Republic*, and *Sewanee Review*. He took another teaching position, this time at Pennsylvania State University. *Open House*, his first book of poems, appeared in 1941 to excellent reviews from the major poetry critics. It established the subjective focus that would dominate Roethke's work throughout his career.

In 1942, Roethke delivered one of the prestigious Morris Gray lectures at Harvard, and in 1943, he left Pennsylvania State University to take a position at Bennington College, where he worked alongside many other well-known literary talents, including Kenneth Burke and Leonie Adams.

In 1947, Roethke accepted a teaching position at the University of Washington in Seattle. His second book, *The Lost Son and Other Poems,* was published in 1948 and contained the so-called greenhouse poems, a series of lyrics that came to be some of his most widely read and best-loved poems. These poems are known for their modern stream-of-consciousness narrative style that allows the reader to come uncomfortably close to the poet's psyche. *Praise to the End!* (1951) contained such poems as "Where Knock Is Wide Open" and "I Need, I Need," which were written from the viewpoint of a young child.

At the University of Washington, Roethke found much support from his colleague Robert Heilman, head of the English department. Heilman assisted Roethke in managing recurrent bouts of depression. As Roethke grew more famous as a poet, his ability to maintain his equilibrium worsened. Roethke also established an intimate relationship with Jerry Lee Lewis, a widow and professor in the English department.

Roethke reached the height of his career in the early 1950s. He received a Guggenheim Fellowship in 1950, *Poetry* magazine's Levinson Prize in 1951, and major grants from the Ford Foundation and the National Institute of Arts and Letters in 1952. In 1953, Roethke married Beatrice O'Connell, whom he had met during his years at Bennington. The couple spent spring 1954 in W. H. AUDEN's villa at Ischia, off the coast of Italy, where Roethke edited the final proofs for *The Waking: Poems 1933–1953.* The couple returned to Seattle later that year and settled into a house on the bank of Lake Washington.

Published in 1953, *The Waking* won the Pulitzer Prize the following year and marked the poet's return to formal verse. A Fulbright grant allowed the Roethkes to travel through Europe and England in 1955 and 1956. *Words for the Wind,* a collection of new poems mostly written in Europe, appeared in 1957 and won the Bollingen Prize, the National Book Award, the Edna St. Vincent Millay Prize, the Longview Foundation Award, and the Pacific Northwest Writers' Award. Roethke's fame meant that he traveled frequently, reading his poems throughout the United States and Europe.

Late in 1957, Roethke was hospitalized for three months when he began to show signs of another mental breakdown. He returned to teaching for a couple of years but had another breakdown in January 1959. The following year he traveled with his wife to New York and then to Europe. In 1961, Roethke published a children's book, *I Am! Says the Lamb,* and in 1963 he finished the first manuscript of *The Far Field,* which he was never able to revise. He died of a heart attack while swimming at a friend's house on Bainbridge Island, Washington, on August 1, 1963. *The Far Field* won the National Book Award when it was published posthumously in 1964. *The Collected Poems* also contained some new poems from the last part of his life and was published in 1966.

**Further Reading**

Balakian, Peter. *Theodore Roethke's Far Fields: The Evolution of His Poetry.* Baton Rouge: Louisiana State University Press, 1989.

Blessing, Richard A. *Theodore Roethke's Dynamic Vision.* Bloomington: Indiana University Press, 1974.

Bloom, Harold, ed. *Theodore Roethke.* New York: Chelsea, 1988.

Bruccoli, Matthew J., ed. *Twentieth-Century American Western Writers* Detroit: Gale, 1999.

Kalaidjian, Walter B. *Understanding Theodore Roethke.* Columbia: University of South Carolina Press, 1987.

Parini, Jay. *Theodore Roethke, an American Romantic.* Amherst: University of Massachusetts Press, 1979.

Seager, Allan. *The Glass House: The Life of Theodore Roethke.* New York: McGraw-Hill, 1968.

Stiffler, Randall. *Theodore Roethke: The Poet and His Critics.* Chicago: American Library Association, 1986.

Wolff, George. *Theodore Roethke.* Boston: Twayne, 1981.

## Roth, Philip
### (Philip Milton Roth)
(1933–   ) *novelist, short story writer*

Philip Roth has sought to depict the impact of place on American lives and has been one of the most prolific and successful American writers of the late 20th century. He achieved fame with his first book, *Goodbye, Columbus* (1959), which described the life of a Jewish middle-class family and won the National Book Award for fiction. One of his most famous works is *Portnoy's Complaint* (1969), a story about a young man's search for freedom using sex as his way of escape. Roth blended ambiguous nostalgia for his boyhood with ribald accounts of sexual adventures. One of the hallmarks of Roth's fiction is the ways in which sexual, communal, familial, ethnic, artistic, and political freedoms play themselves out in life. He has written more than 20 books, most of them novels.

Philip Milton Roth was born on March 19, 1933, in Newark, New Jersey, the son of U.S.-born Jewish parents. His father was an insurance salesman of Austro-Hungarian ethnic background. Roth grew up in Newark's lower-middle-class section of Weequahic and was educated in Newark public schools. He attended Rutgers University for a year before transferring to Bucknell University, and then received his M.A. degree in English from the University of Chicago. Roth joined the army in 1955 but was discharged after an injury during basic training and worked from 1955 to 1957 as an English teacher. He dropped out of the University of Chicago's Ph.D. program in 1959 and wrote film reviews for the *New Republic* while working on his first book.

*Goodbye, Columbus*, a novella and five stories, used irony and humor to depict Jewish life in postwar America. Although Roth received critical acclaim for the book, some in the Jewish community criticized him for depicting what they saw as the unflattering side of contemporary Jewish-American experience. Roth's first full-length novel was *Letting Go* (1962), a realistic work that explored many of the societal and ethical issues of the 1950s. He followed up with *When She Was Good* (1967), which employed a rare narrative voice for Roth: a young Midwestern female.

His third novel, *Portnoy's Complaint*, made Roth a celebrity, both at home and abroad. The book was a comic representation of Roth's middle-class New York Jewish world seen through the eyes of Alexander Portnoy. Portnoy has a possessive mother who makes him feel so guilty and insecure that he can seek relief only in elaborate masturbation and forbidden sex. *Portnoy's Complaint* was a best-seller in 1969. The novel set the tone for the straightforward, absurdist look at human sexuality that runs through many of Roth's subsequent novels. His work calls attention to desire's powerful hold on the human psyche and views with contempt efforts to repress or control that power through conventional morality.

Roth experimented with different comic modes in works including *The Breast* (1972), about a man who finds himself transformed into a massive female breast, and *The Great American Novel* (1973), a wild satire of both muckraker writer Frank Norris's quest to produce *the* "American" novel and baseball. In *My Life As a Man* (1974), Roth introduced his most developed protagonist, Nathan Zuckerman, Roth's alter ego. For the first time Roth's fiction became highly self-reflexive and postmodern. One of his most significant literary efforts was the Zuckerman trilogy: *The Ghost Writer* (1979), *Zuckerman Unbound* (1981), and *The Anatomy Lesson* (1983). It wrapped up with an epilogue, *The Prague Orgy* (1985). These novels trace Zuckerman's development from an aspiring young writer to a socially compromised and psychologically besieged literary celebrity.

In *The Counterlife* (1986), Roth probes the relationship between American and Israeli Jews. In a number of his next books, including *Operation Shylock* (1993), Roth explored the relationship between the lived world and the written world, between "fact" and "fiction." Through his protagonist in these works, also named Philip Roth, the author questioned the genres of autobiography and fiction. Fellow writer CYNTHIA OZICK called the book "the Great American Jewish Novel." In the story, Roth meets a doppelgänger, a political activist who claims to be the author. Roth's memoir of his family, *Patrimony* (1991), won the National Book Critics Circle Award in 1992. Roth's next novel, *Sabbath's Theater* (1995), told the story of an aging puppeteer through the tragicomic, psychosexual form Roth had used in *Portnoy's Complaint*.

Neither Roth's literary output nor his success has waned over time. Some critics believe that his later fiction is his best work. *American Pastoral* (1997) examined the fallout from the 1960s on one New Jersey family, specifically on the suffering father of an unrepentant terrorist daughter. *I Married a Communist* (1998), traced the effects of the anticommunist fervor in the 1940s and 1950s on a naive radio actor. *The Human Stain* (2000) cast a cold eye on political correctness that unjustly destroys a college professor's career. Each book is chronicled by an older Zuckerman, no longer the mischievous and sexually adventurous young writer he once was. In this later trilogy, the individuals represented in many ways, reflect the social, political, and psychological conflicts that define postwar America. *The Human Stain* was adapted into a film starring Anthony Hopkins and Nicole Kidman and was slated to be released in 2003.

Roth has worked as a teacher at Iowa State University, Princeton, the State University of New York, and the University of Pennsylvania. He has also been distinguished professor at Hunter College, New York. Roth has received a Guggenheim fellowship (1959), the National Book Award (1960), a Rockefeller fellowship (1966), the National Book Critics Circle Award (1988, 1992), and the PEN/Faulkner award (1993).

He retired from teaching in 1992. His home is in Connecticut, but he also has lived in Rome, London, Chicago, and New York. Roth separated from his first wife, Margaret Martinson, in 1963. She died in 1968. He is divorced from actress Claire Bloom, who wrote a scathing tell-all book about their marriage, *Leaving a Doll's House* (1996).

**Further Reading**

Baumgarten, Murray, and Barbara Gottfried. *Understanding Philip Roth.* Columbia: University of South Carolina Press, 1990.

Bloom, Harold, ed. *Philip Roth.* New York: Chelsea House, 1986.

Cooper, Alan. *Philip Roth and the Jews.* Albany: State University of New York Press, 1996.

Wade, Stephen. *Imagination in Transit: The Fiction of Philip Roth.* New York: Sheffield Academic Press, 1996.

## Rowlandson, Mary
(Mary White)
(ca. 1637–ca. 1711) *nonfiction writer, captivity writer*

Mary Rowlandson was the frontierswoman who wrote what some literary historians have called America's first best-seller. Her account of her captivity by Indians, *Narrative of the Captivity and Restoration of Mrs. Mary Rowlandson,* was originally published in 1682 and launched a new literary genre called the captivity narrative whose popularity among readers began in the early 18th century and continued well into the 19th century. Rowlandson's book has seen more than 30 editions and continues to be one of the most read and discussed captivity narratives in frontier literature.

Details of Mary Rowlandson's life are scant, but it is known that she was born in England to John and Joan White in 1637 or 1638. She set sail with her family for Salem, Massachusetts, in 1639. She was raised in Lancaster, Massachusetts, and in 1656 married Joseph Rowlandson, who had become a minister in 1654. The couple had four children. Their first child, Mary, lived just three years. The remaining three children were Joseph, who was born in 1661; Mary, born in 1665; and Sarah, born in 1669.

Rowlandson's book tells her account of the attack on Lancaster by a group of Nipmunk and Nonagansett Indians during King Philip's War and the three-month period of captivity during which the Indians held her and her children hostage. The attack occurred in 1675 while Rowlandson's husband, Joseph, was in Boston to speak with the Massachusetts General Assembly about helping the Lancaster colony fend off militant Native Americans. Joseph Rowlandson knew a major attack was imminent. When an attack came, many of Mary Rowlandson's relatives were killed, and a bullet wounded her and her daughter, Sarah. Sarah eventually died and was buried by her captives on a hilltop.

While she was a prisoner, Rowlandson traveled some 150 miles, covering ground from Lancaster to Menamaset, then north to Northfield and across the Connecticut River to meet with King Philip, the head of the Wampanoags. Following this meeting, she traveled up into southwestern New Hampshire as well. During her captivity, Rowlandson became a servant of Weetamoo, the sister-in-law of King Philip. She bartered her sewing and knitting skills for food and other supplies. When she and her two surviving children were finally ransomed back to Joseph Rowlandson for 20

This illustration, titled "The Captivity of Mrs. Rowlandson," shows Mary Rowlandson, author of *Narrative of the Captivity and Restoration of Mrs. Mary Rowlandson,* in a canoe being held captive by Indians. It was published in *Harper's Weekly* in 1857. *(Library of Congress, Prints and Photographs Division [LC-USZ62-113682])*

pounds on May 2, 1676, the family moved to Boston. They later moved, in 1677, to Wethersfield, Connecticut. Joseph Rowlandson died there on November 24, 1678, after preaching a fiery sermon. Mary Rowlandson remarried on August 6, 1679, to Captain Samuel Talcott, who died in 1691.

*The Narrative of the Captivity and Restoration of Mrs. Mary Rowlandson* was published in 1682 and received much attention from readers in the colonies and in Great Britain, as well, where people were keenly interested to learn about the dangers of life in the colonies. Rowlandson's narrative is generally considered by scholars to have been collected by Increase Mather around 1681. He had proposed to a group of Puritan ministers that they collect the stories of "special providences" of New Englanders to be sorted and eventually anthologized. Rowlandson's memoir was most likely among the providential accounts he received, but he likely suggested separate publication for the narrative due to its length. Rowlandson's accounts

are noted by contemporary critics for their uniquely sympathetic view toward her captors. Although she described them as "savages," she carefully depicted their actions realistically. Indeed, by the end of her captivity, Rowlandson was treated respectfully. In the years following the experience, she looked back on her captors with surprising compassion. Mary Rowlandson died about 1710 or 1711.

**Further Reading**

Burke, Charles. *Puritans at Bay.* New York: Exposition Press, 1967.

Drimmer, Frederick, ed. *Captured by the Indians.* New York: Dover, 1961.

Slotkin, Richard, and James Folsom. *So Dreadful a Judgment.* Middletown, Conn.: Wesleyan University Press, 1978.

Van Der Beets, Richard. *Held Captive by the Indians: Selected Narratives 1642–1836.* Knoxville: University of Tennessee Press, 1973.

# S

## Sandburg, Carl
### (Carl August Sandburg)
(1878–1967) *poet, novelist, journalist, biographer, children's writer*

A Pulitzer Prize–winning poet, Carl Sandburg has long been associated with Chicago and the American Midwest and is regarded as one of America's most essential poets. Sandburg worked as a political organizer and journalist, which helped to shape his career as a poet, and he became known for free verse poems such as "Crucible," "Dust," and "Chicago," that celebrated working-class America and the American industrial and natural landscape.

Carl August Sandburg was born to August and Clara Anderson Sandburg on January 6, 1878, in the small town of Galesburg, Illinois. His parents were immigrants from Sweden, and his father worked as a blacksmith's helper on the Chicago, Burlington, and Quincy Railroad. Carl Sandburg was the second of seven children, and he worked from the time he was a young boy. Following his graduation from eighth grade in 1891, he spent about six years working in a variety of jobs that included delivering milk, harvesting ice, laying bricks, shining shoes, and threshing wheat in Kansas.

In 1897, Sandburg took to the road as a hobo, traveling and working along the way. This experience exposed him to the harsh realities of extreme poverty and the huge differences between the lives of the rich and the poor. His distrust of capitalism began during these years and stuck with him the rest of his life, shaping his poetry and his work as

an activist and journalist, as well. It was also during his years on the road that he began to learn the folk songs that he sung later in life at speaking engagements.

Sandburg volunteered to serve in the Spanish-American War in 1898, and at the age of 20 left for Puerto Rico. He returned home later that year and entered Lombard College, where he worked as an on-call fireman and got involved in numerous organizations, including the Poor Writers' Club, whose founder was Phillip Green Wright. A talented scholar and political liberal, Wright served as a mentor to Sandburg, encouraging his talent and influencing his political views.

Sandburg left school in his senior year without a degree and wrote poetry for a couple of years before publishing his first book, *In Reckless Ecstasy*, which was printed on Wright's basement press in 1904. Two other Sandburg volumes were printed by Wright in the following years—*Incidentals* (1907) and *The Plaint of a Rose* (1908).

After college, Sandburg moved to Milwaukee, where he worked as an advertising writer, a newspaper reporter, and an organizer for the Wisconsin Social Democratic party, writing and distributing political pamphlets and literature. While there, he met Lillian Steichen (whom he called Paula) at party headquarters; she was the sister of famed photographer Edward Steichen. Sandburg and Steichen married in 1908, and Sandburg later acted as secretary to the first Socialist mayor of Milwaukee from 1910 to 1912. Prompted by the responsibility of supporting a family, the Sandburgs moved back to Illinois, where Carl worked as reporter for the *Chicago Daily News*, covering labor issues and later writing his own feature column.

In 1914, a group of Sandburg's poems appeared in *Poetry* magazine. Two years later, his book *Chicago Poems* was published, and Sandburg found himself on the verge of international celebrity. He published another volume, *Cornhuskers*, in 1918, and wrote a searching analysis of the 1919 Chicago race riots.

Sandburg continued to write poetry and branched out into children's stories with *Rootabaga Stories* (1922). That led to Sandburg's publisher suggesting he write a biography of Abraham Lincoln for children. After three years of research and writing, Sandburg produced a two-volume biography for adults. *Abraham Lincoln: The Prairie Years*, published in 1926, was Sandburg's first financial success. After moving to a new home on the Michigan dunes, he completed four more volumes of Lincoln's biography—*Abraham Lincoln: The War Years*—for which he won the Pulitzer Prize in 1940. Sandburg continued to write prolifically, publishing poems, a novel, two volumes of folk songs, and an autobiography, *Always the Young Strangers*.

In 1945, the Sandburgs moved with their herd of prize-winning goats and thousands of books to Flat Rock, North Carolina. In 1951, his *Complete Poems* won him a second Pulitzer Prize. His other awards include honorary degrees from Lombard College, Knox College, and Northwestern University. Sandburg died at his North Carolina home on July 22, 1967. As he had requested, his ashes were returned to his Galesburg birthplace and placed beneath Remembrance Rock, a red granite boulder. Ten years later, the ashes of his wife were placed there.

**Further Reading**

Callahan, North. *Carl Sandburg: His Life and His Works*. Philadelphia: Pennsylvania State University Press, 1987.

Niven, Penelope. *Carl Sandburg: A Biography*. New York: Macmillan, 1991.

Perry, Lilla. *My Friend, Carl Sandburg: The Biography of a Friendship*. New York: Scarecrow, 1981.

Salwak, Dale. *Carl Sandburg: A Reference Guide*. New York: Macmillan, 1988.

A poet of the American Midwest and of the working class, Carl Sandburg wrote poems, children's books, and autobiographies. *(Photo by Al Ravenna. Library of Congress, Prints and Photographs Division [LC-USZ62-115064])*

Sandburg, Helga. *A Great and Glorious Romance: The Story of Carl Sandburg and Lillian Steichen*. New York: Harcourt, Brace, Jovanovich, 1978.

———. *Where Love Begins: A Portrait of Carl Sandburg and His Family as Seen Through the Eyes of His Youngest Daughter*. Boston: Donald I. Fine, 1989.

Yannella, Philip R. *The Other Carl Sandburg*. Jackson: University Press of Mississippi, 1996.

## Saroyan, William
### (William Stonehill Saroyan)
(1908–1981) *playwright, short story writer, novelist, memoirist, essayist*

An Armenian-American author of more than 60 books in just about every genre except poetry,

William Saroyan achieved his greatest fame as a playwright in the 1930s. In 1939, he was the first American writer to win both the Drama Critics Circle Award and the Pulitzer Prize for his play *The Time of Your Life.*

William Stonehill Saroyan was born on August 31, 1908, in Fresno, California, to Armenak Saroyan, a preacher and poet, and Takoohi Saroyan, Armenian immigrants from Bitlis. When he was just three years old, William's father died and the young boy was sent to an orphanage, where he remained for four years. He left school at the age of 15, determined to become a writer. His first big break came in 1934, when he published the short story "The Daring Young Man on the Flying Trapeze," which met with critical and popular acclaim. In 1939, Saroyan's play *My Heart's in the Highlands* opened to great critical acclaim only to be followed later that year by the even more successful *Time of Your Life.* Although Saroyan refused to accept the Pulitzer Prize he was awarded for the play—on the grounds that art should not be given awards—he did accept the Drama Critics Circle Award that same year.

Saroyan returned to the short story form in 1940 with the publication of his collection entitled *My Name Is Aram.* Also in 1940, Saroyan's novel *The Human Comedy* was made into a major motion picture of the same name and won the Academy Award for best picture and original story for the screenplay.

In 1943 at the age of 35, Saroyan married 18-year-old New York debutante Carol Marcus in Dayton, Ohio. The couple had two children, Aram and Lucy, but divorced after six years. Though they remarried once, they divorced for the second time in 1951.

Saroyan joined the army during World War II and interest in his work began to decline shortly after his return to Broadway. With the notable exception of his play *Cave Dwellers,* which opened in 1957 in New York, Saroyan's career as a playwright ended with the war. He did, however, continue to write and published several memoirs in the last decades of his life, including *Bicycle Rider of Beverly Hills* (1952), *Short Drive, Sweet Chariot* (1966), and *Obituaries* (1979), which was nominated for a National Book Award.

Saroyan died on May 18, 1981, of prostate cancer at the age of 72, about a mile from where he was born in Fresno. A year after his death, half of his ashes were permanently enshrined in the Pantheon of Greats in Yerevan, Armenia, while the other half remained in Fresno. Saroyan was recognized in 1991 by the postal services of the United States and the USSR when a joint stamp was issued in his honor.

**Further Reading**

Balakian, Nona. *The World of William Saroyan.* Lewisburg, Penn.: Bucknell University Press, 1998.

Floan, Howard R. *William Saroyan.* New York: Twayne, 1966.

Foard, Elizabeth C. *William Saroyan: A Reference Guide.* Boston: G. K. Hall, 1989.

Foster, Edward H. *William Saroyan.* Boise, Id.: Boise State University Press, 1984.

Keyishian, Harry. *Critical Essays on William Saroyan.* New York: G. K. Hall, 1995.

Saroyan, Aram. *Last Rites: The Death of William Saroyan.* New York: Morrow, 1982.

## Service, Robert
### (Robert William Service)
(1874–1958) *poet*

Close to a century after the gold rush of 1898, Robert Service's poetry and stories of the Yukon Territory and its gold prospectors remain well ingrained in America's memory. By far, the most famous of Service's works are "The Shooting of Dan McGrew" and "The Cremation of Sam McGee," which has actually become the subject of many parodies, including a song by Guy Lombardo's band in the late 1940s, a biker variation in *Easyrider* magazine, Culver Pictures' *The Shooting of Dan McGrew* (1924), as well as many other versions passed down through the years.

Robert William Service was born in Preston, in the English county of Lancashire, on January 16, 1874. He was the first of 10 children born to Scottish parents Robert Service, a bank cashier, and Sarah Emil Parker, the daughter of a wealthy distillery family. At age five, Service was sent to live with three of his aunts and his paternal grandfather, a postmaster at Kilwinning, Ayrshire, Scotland. It was here that one year later, at six years old, he composed his first poem. Service was reunited with his parents and siblings in 1883, at which time they relocated to Scotland's largest city, Glasgow. As a young man, Service avidly read adventure stories and thought frequently of going off to sea. In an attempt to please his father, however, Service took a job at the Commercial Bank of Scotland, working a consistent and reliable schedule in order to focus on his writing after hours. During this time Service supplemented his bank income with money he received selling his verses. He also continued reading voraciously, with most of his interest in the English poets Robert Browning; Alfred, Lord Tennyson; William Makepeace Thackeray; and John Keats.

Service soon enrolled in the University of Glasgow, where he excelled in English language and literature and, upon his graduation, ranked fourth in a class of 200. During his time as a student, though, Service never abandoned his dreams of travel and adventure. He was fast becoming disillusioned by what he felt was a static and routine lifestyle in Glasgow, where he had recently been transferred. In 1896, his dreams finally came to fruition; that was when he arrived in Canada. He settled in British Columbia and over the next six years worked many different jobs. He even spent a few years traveling through California and exploring the Barbary Coast, San Francisco's notorious waterfront district.

By 1903, Service decided to return to Canada and found himself penniless in Vancouver. A local bank needed tellers and Service applied, finding himself doing the same work he had only a few years before disdained. New job postings came up for positions at the Bank of Commerce in Whitehorse, Yukon Territory. Service moved north and immediately found himself captivated by northern Canada's vast solitude and intrigued by the thousands of men arriving daily in search of Klondike gold. Whitehorse also provided Service with just enough social contact to keep him happy. He often recited poetry or gave readings at socials or church concerts. A close friend, impressed by Service's oratory prowess, encouraged him to write, and suggested he start with tales about the Yukon.

Service seized the opportunity and was almost immediately inspired by the bawdy celebration going on down the street at a popular saloon. These classic words popped into his head, "A bunch of the boys were whooping it up at the Malamute Saloon. . . ." And so in a frenzy of creativity, almost getting his head blown off in the process, he wrote his most famous work, "The Shooting of Dan McGrew."

This first effort unleashed in Service an almost unstoppable creative streak. Over the next few months he wrote dozens more poems, enough to fill a small volume. He intended to compile the Yukon lore and give the poems to family and friends for Christmas. However, *Songs of the Sourdough*, which contained the memorable "Shooting of Dan McGrew," became a resounding success with New York publishers and established Robert Service's career as a storyteller and poet, and finally gave him financial independence.

In 1908, Service was transferred to a new bank in Dawson City, 400 miles north of Whitehorse. He lived and worked in a rustic cabin where he finished another volume of poetry entitled *Ballads of a Cheechako*. His second book was another widespread success; the following year Service quit his bank job to write full time.

The gold rush, then in full swing, became the inspiration for his next book, *The Trail of '98*, which was published in New York and gained even more success for Service. Service then traveled to the southern United States, Cuba, and back to Canada, via canoe up the Mackenzie River. He retired to his cabin and finished another book of poetry, *Rhymes of a Rolling Stone* (1912). During this same time, Service took a job as a war correspondent during the Balkan war, then again during World War I. During his travels in Europe, he married a Parisian woman and purchased a villa in Brittany. Following the war, he travelled and wrote two volumes of poetry and several novels, including *Twenty Bath-Tub Ballads* (1939) and *Bar Room Ballads* (1940). When World War II broke out in Europe, Service left Poland, where he was then living, and moved to Hollywood until the war ended, at which time he returned to France. Robert Service died on September 14, 1958, in Monte Carlo.

## Further Reading

Klink, Carl F. *Robert Service, A Biography*. Vancouver, B.C.: McGraw-Hill Ryerson, 1976.

Mackay, James. *Vagabond of Verse*. Edinborough, Scotland: Mainstream Publishing, 1995.

Roberts, R. X. *A Bibliography of Robert William Service, 1874–1958*. Toronto, Ontario: University of Toronto, 1976.

## Sexton, Anne
### (Anne Gray Harvey)
### (1928–1974) *poet, playwright*

A poet of the same generation as ROBERT LOWELL and SYLVIA PLATH, Anne Sexton wrote confessional poetry with honesty and precision, exploring such personal themes as family, love, loss, guilt, death, and madness, which she hoped would have the "authentic stamp" to serve, as she quoted Franz Kafka, as "the axe for the frozen sea within us." Despite a prolific and esteemed career, Sexton struggled with severe depression throughout her life. She consistently fought the norms and expectations of a woman's place in U.S. society through her writing. She made the experience of being a woman a central issue in her poetry, and though she endured criticism for bringing subjects such as menstruation, abortion, and drug addiction into her work, her skill as a poet transcended the controversy over her subject matter.

Anne Gray Harvey was born November 9, 1928, in Weston, Massachusetts, to Mary Gray Staples Harvey and Ralph Churchill Harvey. The youngest of three sisters, Anne grew up watching her eldest sister, Jane, receive the lion's share of parental attention, while her other sister, Blanche, developed a reputation as the smartest of the three girls, loving to read and the only one to go to college. After her parents relocated to Wellesley, Massachusetts, Sexton attended public schools from the time she was six until she was 17. When she was 17, her parents sent her to Rogers Hall, a preparatory school for girls, in Lowell, Massachusetts, hoping to taper her wild nature and shape her into a "proper woman." At Rogers Hall, Sexton began writing poetry, and though she soon had her first work published in the school

yearbook, her new success was not without great personal disappointment, when her own mother called and accused her of plagiarism. She did not believe her daughter possessed such talent.

Despite this adversity, though, Sexton continued on with the refinement of her womanhood. She attended the Garland School in Boston, a finishing school for women, where she met and eloped with Alfred Muller Sexton II, whom everyone referred to as Kayo. The Sextons moved to Hamilton, New York, where Kayo had been attending Colgate University. Unable to earn enough of a living to support his wife, Kayo decided the newlyweds should return to Massachusetts. Upon moving back, Anne Sexton completed a modeling class at the Hart Agency and proceeded to make a short-lived career as a model for the agency. Meanwhile, Kayo had joined the naval reserve and had been shipped out on the USS *Boxer* to Korea. In 1952, due to damage sustained by the *Boxer*, Kayo returned home for one year to be with his wife. It was during this time that Sexton and Kayo conceived their first child. Sexton gave birth to Linda Gray Sexton in July 1953, just after Kayo had departed for Korea. Later that year Kayo was officially discharged and returned home where he then purchased a house for his family in Newton Lower Falls, Massachusetts, near both their parents.

In 1954, Sexton began to struggle with recurring depression and sought help in therapy. While in therapy, she gave birth to a second child, Joyce Ladd Sexton, whom they nicknamed Joy. Sexton soon began to see herself as a "victim of the American Dream, the bourgeois, middle-class dream," wanting only "to be married, to have children," and "trying [her] damnedest to live a conventional life." Beginning in 1956, as a result of her mental disintegration, Sexton made her first attempt at suicide and was soon hospitalized in a psychiatric institution. In December of the same year, under the guidance of her psychiatrist, Dr. Martin, she resumed writing poetry as a form of healing. Finding great therapeutic value in writing, she enrolled in a local poetry workshop and continued to pursue her writing talent. Yet falling into another deep depression, Sexton attempted suicide for a second time in May 1957. Again hospitalized, she continued to write poetry and in August of that year received a scholarship to the Antioch Writers' Conference, where she met W. D. Snodgrass. In 1958, Sexton enrolled in Robert Lowell's graduate writing seminar at Boston University, where she met Sylvia Plath and George Starbuck. Then in 1959, she was awarded the *Audience* Poetry Prize. With this award Sexton worked to publish the first of her books of poetry entitled *To Bedlam and Part Way Back,* for which she enjoyed national recognition and renewed creative energy. Sexton published her second book, *All My Pretty Ones,* in 1962. During autumn 1963, she toured Europe on a traveling fellowship from the American Academy of Arts and Letters. She enjoyed the trip but returned a month early due to an emotional disturbance abroad.

The year 1964 was traumatic for Sexton, as her longtime psychiatrist moved his practice to Philadelphia, and she began seeing a new psychiatrist who introduced her to the drug Thorazine in hope of controlling her ongoing depression and hospitalizations. In 1965, Sexton was elected a Fellow of the Royal Society of Literature in London. Soon after, she published her Pulitzer Prize–winning book, entitled *Live or Die,* in 1966. In June 1968, Sexton was awarded an honorary Phi Beta Kappa from Harvard, making her the first woman ever to join the 187-year-old chapter. Then in 1969, she published *Love Poems* while continuing her work on the play *Mercy Street* until the following fall when she began teaching a poetry seminar at Boston University. Her seminar's success led to her appointment as a lecturer at Boston University in 1970 and her eventual award of full professorship in 1972.

Despite her success as a writer, poet, and playwright, Sexton's personal life took a sudden plunge in 1973, when, over the course of the year, she was hospitalized three times and was divorced by her husband. Barely surviving much of the following year, she managed to bring her final works to a conclusion with the publishing of *The Death Notebooks,* a completed final editing of *The Awful Rowing toward God,* and a tentative arrangement of poems in *45 Mercy Street.* The conclusiveness of the works may have seemed to her to be a proper stopping point. Following her last poetry reading, at Goucher College in Maryland, Sexton returned home and committed suicide in her garage the morning of October 4, 1974, by way of carbon monoxide poisoning.

## Further Reading

Hall, Barnard, and Carolyn King. *Anne Sexton.* Boston: Twayne, 1989.

Furst, Arthur. *Anne Sexton: The Last Summer.* New York: St. Martin's Press, 2000.

George, Diana Hume. *Oedipus Anne: The Poetry of Anne Sexton.* Chicago: University of Illinois Press, 1987.

———, ed. *Sexton: Selected Criticism.* Urbana: University of Illinois Press, 1988.

McClatchy, J. D., ed. *Anne Sexton: The Poet and Her Critics.* Bloomington: Indiana University Press, 1978.

Middlebrook, Diane Wood. *Anne Sexton: A Biography.* London: Virago Press, 1991.

Sexton, Anne. *Anne Sexton: A Self-Portrait in Letters,* edited by Linda Gray and Lois Ames. Boston: Houghton Mifflin, 1977.

## Shange, Ntozake
### (Paulette Linda Williams)
### (1948– ) *playwright, poet, novelist*

Known primarily for her successful translation of poetry to the stage, Ntozake Shange is an accomplished playwright whose choreopoem *for colored girls who have considered suicide/when the rainbow is enuf* was produced Off-Broadway and on Broadway to great critical acclaim and was nominated for Tony, Grammy, and Emmy Awards, Known first for her work as a playwright and performance artist, Shange has gone on to establish herself as a novelist and poet of note as well.

Ntozake Shange was born Paulette Linda Williams in Trenton, New Jersey, on October 18, 1948, to Paul T. Williams, an air force surgeon, and Eloise Williams, a psychiatric social worker and educator. As the eldest of four children in an upper-middle-class family, Shange enjoyed a childhood rich with exposure to the arts. Her parents were acquainted with such musicians and writers as Dizzy Gillespie, Miles Davis, Chuck Berry, and W. E. B. DUBOIS. Williams was bussed to a German-American school while growing up in St. Louis. When she was 13, the family returned to New Jersey, where she completed high school.

In 1966, Williams enrolled at Barnard College. During her college years, she married and then separated from a law student. Despite several suicide attempts during these first years away from home, Williams graduated summa cum laude with a degree in American studies in 1970 and entered the University of Southern California at Los Angeles, where she earned a master's degree in American studies in 1973.

During her time at UCLA, Williams changed her name to Ntozake Shange (pronounced "en-toe-zah-kee shang-AY"). Her African name means "she who comes with her own things" and "she who walks like a lion" in Xhosa, the Zulu language. She has said that she changed her name in an effort to redirect her inner life.

Following completion of her graduate degree, Shange taught humanities and women's studies courses at Mills College, in Oakland, the University of California Extension, and Sonoma State College. She began to develop friendships and artistic relationships with other writers, performers, and teachers, who nurtured her talent. She and her friends began to perform their poetry, music, and dance in and around San Francisco.

During these years, Shange also danced with Halifu Osumare's company. When she left the company, she began collaborating with Paula Moss on the poetry, music, and dance that eventually became *for colored girls who have considered suicide/when the rainbow is enuf.* Shange and Moss moved to New York and performed the piece in a Soho jazz loft and in bars on the Lower East Side. Eventually it was produced by Woodie King, Jr., off-Broadway at the New Federal Theatre and later at the New York Shakespeare Company's Anspacher Public Theatre and then the Booth Theatre. The work significantly influenced the course of dramatic and dance history in America. It was radical when it first appeared in the 1970s for its claiming of space exclusively for women's pleasure and for its innovative use of language. In 1977, Shange married her second husband, musician David Murray.

Shange's books of poetry include *Melissa & Smith* (1976), *Natural Disasters and Other Festive Occasions* (1977), *Nappy Edges* (1978), *A Daughter's Geography* (1983), *From Okra to Greens* (1984), and *Ridin' the Moon in Texas: Word Paintings* (1987). Following *for colored girls* were the plays *A Photograph: Lovers-in-Motion* (1981), *From Okra to Greens/A Different Kinda Love Story* (1983), *Spell #7* (1985), and *Daddy Says* (1989).

Her books of prose include *Sassafrass, Cypress & Indigo: A Novel* (1982); *See No Evil: Prefaces, Essays & Accounts, 1976–1983* (1984); *Betsey Brown: A Novel* (1985); *The Black Book* (1986, with painter and photographer Robert Mapplethorpe); and *If I Can Cook You Know God Can* (1998). Her children's book, *I Live in Music,* came out in 1994, and *Liliane: Resurrection of the Daughter,* was published that same year.

In addition to writing, Shange has taught at California State College, the City College of New York, the University of Houston, Rice University, Yale, Howard, and New York University. In 1983, she became associate professor of drama at the University of Houston. Among her many awards are an Obie, a *Los Angeles Times* Book Prize for Poetry, a Pushchart Prize, and fellowships from the Guggenheim Foundation and the Lila Wallace-Reader's Digest Fund. Ntozake Shange currently resides in Philadelphia.

### Further Reading

Brown, Elizabeth. "Ntozake Shange," *Dictionary of Literary Biography: Afro-American Writers after 1955: Dramatists and Prose Writers,* volume 38, edited by T. M. Davis and T. Harris. Detroit: Gale, 1985, pp. 240–250.

Latour, Martine. "Ntozake Shange: Driven Poet/Playwright," *Mademoiselle,* September 1976, pp. 182, 226.

Metzger, Linda, et al. *Black Writers: A Selection of Sketches from Contemporary Authors.* Detroit: Gale Group, 2000, pp. 518–523.

Richards, Sandra L. "Ntozake Shange," *African American Writers,* edited by Valerie Smith, et al. Detroit: Gale, 1991, pp. 379–393.

## Shepard, Sam
### (Samuel "Steve" Shepard Rogers)
(1943– ) *playwright, screenwriter, actor, director*

Sam Shepard has written more than 40 plays, 11 of which have won Obie Awards. His play *Buried Child* was the first play ever to win a Pulitzer Prize before being produced on Broadway. His screenplay for *Paris, Texas* won the Golden Palm Award at the Cannes Film Festival in 1984. A former stable hand, orange picker, sheep shearer, and busboy, Shepard came of age in the counterculture of the 1960s, which greatly inspired his early work.

Born Samuel Shepard Rogers (and nicknamed "Steve") on November 5, 1943, in Fort Sheridan, Illinois, Sam Shepard changed his name when he began to write plays in New York City in the early 1960s—reportedly because "Steve Rogers was the name of the original Captain America." His father was a retired army pilot who moved his family frequently in his quest to become a farmer. They lived in Illinois, South Dakota, Florida, and Utah before settling in Duarte, California, a suburb of Los Angeles, where they worked an avocado farm. Steve's father was an alcoholic, and the family's home life was difficult. Steve ran away from home while still in high school, then ended up attending Mount San Antonio Junior College for three semesters, where he studied agriculture, before joining the Bishop's Repertory Company, a troupe of local actors whose mission it was to perform Christian-oriented drama. When the troupe left on a cross-country bus tour, Steve went with them. He ended up in San Francisco, where he became a playwright in residence at the Magic Theatre.

He moved to New York in 1963, where he lived with Charles Mingus, the son of the famous jazz musician. Mingus helped Shepard land a busboy job at the Village Gate, a prominent New York jazz club. Shepard was instantly immersed in the downtown Manhattan counterculture scene. His idols at the time were JACK KEROUAC, ALLEN GINSBERG, and Bob Dylan. Shepard wrote poetry, acted in plays, and began to write his own plays when a friend, Ralph Cook, then headwaiter at the Village Gate, decided to open Genesis Theatre. The first two plays Shepard gave Cook were *Cowboys* and *The Rock Garden.* They were performed as a double bill in October 1964 and won rave reviews from *Village Voice* writer Michael Smith, who called Shepard "full of promise." Uptown critics were much less impressed with the unconventional structure and long, chaotic monologues of these plays, but Shepard's career had already been set in motion.

Buoyed by his initial success, Shepard, who was just 22 at the time, asked EDWARD ALBEE, one of the most famous playwrights working in New York, to consider producing one of his plays. Albee chose to produce *Up to Thursday,* a play based on Shepard's own experience of dodging the draft by claiming to be a heroin addict. The play was successfully produced in February 1965 at the Cherry Lane Theater. Critics remained divided over Shepard's work for some time. The Beat influence did not sit well with everyone, but when Shepard's play *Chicago* won an Obie, more and more people began to take his work seriously.

Shepard married the actress O-Lan Johnson in 1969, and soon their son, Jesse Mojo, was born. The couple moved to England, where they spent three years and where Shepard enjoyed great success, one summer producing as many as five plays for London audiences. These plays included *The Tooth of Crime,* a rock drama that was staged in its American premiere at Princeton University in 1972. Shepard returned to New York in 1974, and in 1979 he won a Pulitzer Prize for his play *Buried Child.*

Shepard made his feature film acting debut in 1978 in Terence Mallick's *Days of Heaven* and in 1980 won an Oscar nomination for his role in *The Right Stuff.* His film career has also included *Renaldo and Clara* (1978, which he also cowrote), *Country* (1984), *Crimes of the Heart* (1986), *Baby Boom* (1987), *Steel Magnolias* (1989), *The Pelican Brief* (1993), and *Safe Passage* (1994) among others. He has appeared in numerous television shows and directed two pictures—*Far North* (1988) and *Silent Tongue* (1992).

Shepard's major themes include "buried enmities, porous identities, falls from grace, talk of bloodlines, and troubled male bonds," as one critic put it when reviewing the film *Simpatico* (1999).

Shepard's life and career took a big turn in 1983, when he left his wife to move in with actress Jessica Lange, whom he had met on the set of the movie *Frances,* in which they were costars. The couple eventually settled on a ranch in Minnesota with their two children. In 1986, he was elected to the American Academy of Arts and Letters, and in 1992 he received the Gold Medal for Drama from the academy. He was inducted into the Theatre

Hall of Fame in 1994. His recent work includes *Simpatico*, which was published in 1995 and made into a film in 1999. He also published a book of stories, *Cruising Paradise, Tales*, in 1997.

## Further Reading

Bottoms, Stephen J. *The Theatre of Sam Shepard*. Boston, Mass.: Cambridge University Press, 1998.

DeRose, David J. *Sam Shepard*. New York: Twayne, 1992.

McGhee, Jim. *True Lies: The Architecture of the Fantastic in the Plays of Sam Shepard*. New York: Peter Lang, 1993.

Tucker, Martin. *Sam Shepard*. New York: Continuum, 1992.

Wade, Leslie A. *Sam Shepard and the American Theatre*. Westport, Conn.: Greenwood Press, 1997.

## Shields, Carol
### (Carol Warner)
(1935–2003) *novelist, playwright, poet, literary critic*

Often referred to as a "woman's writer," whose books delve skillfully into the domestic side of life, Carol Shields is probably best known for her novel *The Stone Diaries*, which won the Pulitzer Prize, as well as numerous other awards. She wrote more than 15 novels, a handful of plays, and several collections of poetry and short stories. She was also a professor of English literature and chancellor of Winnipeg University.

Carol Shields was born Carol Warner in Oak Park, Illinois, just outside Chicago, on June 2, 1935. The youngest of three children—her siblings were a twin brother and sister—she grew up in a loving, supportive home. Her father managed a sweets factory, and her mother was a schoolteacher. Always an avid reader, she recalled favoring many British writers, including Graham Greene, Virginia Woolf, and Jane Austen, about whom she wrote a biography. Following her graduation from high school, Carol graduated from Hanover College in Indiana with a B.A. degree, studied at the University of Exeter in England, and finally earned her master's degree in English at the University of Ottawa.

Carol Warner met her husband, Donald Hugh Shields, an engineering student in Scotland, while she was on a student exchange trip to Britain in 1956. The couple, whose famously content 40-year marriage was much celebrated, married in 1957 and settled in Canada, where Don was raised. The couple had five children—John, Anne, Catherine, Meg, and Sarah—and 10 grandchildren. In addition to raising her five children, Shields worked as an editorial assistant for the journal *Canadian Slavonic Papers* and as a professor at the University of Ottawa, the University of British Columbia, and the University of Manitoba. In 1996, she became chancellor of the University of Winnipeg. Her husband became a professor of civil engineering.

Shields's first book was not published until she was 40. She was often quoted as saying that while raising her children in Winnipeg, she noticed that there were not many novels written about women and their lives and decided that she would make women her subject. Her first novel, *Small Ceremonies*, appeared in 1976 and established Shields as a skilled chronicler of daily life and of women's friendships. Her next novels were *The Box Garden* (1977), *Happenstance* (1980), *A Fairly Conventional Woman* (1982), *Various Miracles* (1985), *Swann* (1987), *The Orange Fish* (1989), *A Celibate Season* (1991), *The Republic of Love* (1992), and *The Stone Diaries* (1993). Although Shields stuck with the chosen themes of domesticity and women's relationships, she did experiment considerably with form in these novels. *A Celibate Season* was an epistolary novel, cowritten with Blanche Howard; *Swann* is a literary mystery; and quite a few of her books are told from more than one point of view.

Although Shields enjoyed moderate commercial success and a generally warm critical reception with her early works, it was *The Stone Diaries* that made her internationally famous. In addition to winning the Pulitzer Prize and Canada's Governor General Award, it was nominated for the National Book Critics Circle Award and the 1993 Booker Prize. It was also named one of the best books of the year by *Publishers Weekly* and a "Notable Book" by the *New York Times Book Review*. Her books have been translated into many other languages and several have become international best-sellers.

Shields published *Larry's Party*, winner of the 1998 Orange Prize, just before learning that she had stage-three breast cancer. After receiving that life-changing news, she underwent a barrage of cancer treatments, including a mastectomy, radiation, and chemotherapy, but her cancer did not go into remission. Despite the difficulty of living with the disease, she wrote and published a collection of short stories, a biography of Jane Austen, and a novel entitled *Unless,* which was a finalist for the 2002 Giller Prize.

In addition to the many awards already mentioned, Shields's books have won a Canada Council Major Award, two National Magazine Awards, the Canadian Author's Award, and a CBC short story award. Carol Shields died of complications from breast cancer in Victoria, British Columbia, on July 16, 2003.

## Further Reading

De Roo, Harvey. "A Little Like Flying: An Interview with Carol Shields." *West Coast Review* 23, no. 3 (December 1988): 38–56.

Duncan, Sandy. "Open Letter." *Room of One's Own* 13, no. 1–2 (1989): 77–81.

"Shields as Chancellor." *Globe & Mail Metro Edition,* May 29, 1996, pp. E1.

"The Shields Diaries." *Chatelaine,* April 1996, pp. 110–115.

Thomas, Clara, Carol Shields, and Donna E. Smyth. "'Thinking Back through Our Mothers': Tradition in Canadian Women's Writing." *Re(Dis)covering Our Foremothers: Nineteenth-Century Canadian Women Writers,* edited by Lorraine McMullen. Ottawa: University of Ottawa Press, 1990, pp. 5–21.

Werlock, Abby H. P. "Canadian Identity and Women's Voices: The Fiction of Sandra Birdsell and Carol Shields." *Canadian Women Writing Fiction,* edited by Mickey Pearlman. Jackson: University Press of Mississippi, 1993, pp. 126–41.

"Writer Named University of Winnipeg Chancellor." *Winnipeg Free Press.* May 29, 1996, p. A7.

## Silko, Leslie Marmon

(1948–  ) *poet, novelist, short story writer, essayist*

Known for weaving her mixed-ethnicity family history with the traditional stories of Native American cultures, Leslie Marmon Silko is considered by readers and critics alike to be one of the most significant Native American writers. Her work has won numerous awards, including a "genius grant" from the MacArthur Foundation and a Rosewater Foundation grant. She was the youngest writer to be included in the *Norton Anthology of Women's Literature,* for her short story "Lullaby."

Leslie Marmon was born in Albuquerque, New Mexico, on March 5, 1948. Virginia, her mother, was originally from Montana, and Lee Howard Marmon, her father, had just left the army to pursue a career as a professional photographer. He was also managing the Marmon Trading Post in the village of Old Laguna, about 50 miles outside of Albuquerque. Her father also became the Tribal Council Treasurer at the time when uranium was beginning to be mined in the Laguna area. She grew up primarily in Laguna, just a few houses away from the store, which attracted interstate travelers as well as the residents of local Pueblo villages. At this cultural crossroads, she was influenced by both Anglo culture and the culture of her Keresan forebears. Of mixed ancestry herself—Laguna, Pueblo, Mexican, and white—she grew up in a house full of books and stories, surrounded by her extended family. As she said in one interview, "I grew up at Laguna Pueblo, I am of mixed breed ancestry, but what I know is Laguna. This place I am from is everything I am as a writer and a human being."

In addition to the education she received informally from her family, she attended the Bureau of Indian Affairs school in Laguna through the fifth grade, then went to Catholic schools in Albuquerque through high school. She received her B.A. degree in English in 1969 from the University of New Mexico in Albuquerque. From there, she went on to study in the American Indian law program at the University of New Mexico Law School but eventually transferred in the creative writing program, where she received her master's degree.

She had been writing stories since her childhood, but the publication of her first story, "The Man to Send Rain Clouds" in *New Mexico Quarterly* in 1969, inspired her to focus on this work. By 1971, she had decided to pursue writing instead of law. Following her master's program in creative writing, she taught for two years at Navajo Community College. Her first book, *Laguna Woman,* a collection of poetry, was published in 1974, as was Kenneth Rosen's anthology of Native American short stories, *The Man to Send Rain Clouds,* which featured seven of her stories, including the title story. She also published a short story in *Chicago Review* that year and was awarded a National Endowment for the Arts fellowship.

Following publication of her first book, she then spent two years in Ketchikan, Alaska, during which time she completed her first novel. *Ceremony* was published in 1977. When she returned home to the Southwest, she continued to write while teaching first at the University of New Mexico and later at the University of Arizona. After her marriage to John Silko ended in 1981, Leslie Silko finished her autobiographical collection of stories and poems, *Storyteller,* which was published in 1983. That same year, she was awarded a MacArthur Foundation fellowship worth $176,000, which enabled her to work full time on her writing. She embarked on what would become the novel *Almanac of the Dead.*

During this period, Silko began to explore her interest in the visual arts, specifically filmmaking. Influenced by her father's career as a photographer and by some of the work she had done in graduate school, Silko founded the Laguna Film Project and began shooting a video version of her story "Arrowboy and Witches." She has continued to work on film projects and to write about the intersection of visual arts and storytelling.

Other books by Silko include *Delicacy and the Strength of Lace: Letters,* an edited version of her correspondence with poet JAMES WRIGHT, which was published in 1986. *Yellow Woman,* originally published in 1974, was followed by *Yellow Woman and a Beauty of the Spirit,* published in 1996. Both works are inspired by oral narratives and stories of the Laguna society before Christian missionaries arrived. In 1999 Silko published her third novel, *Gardens in the Dunes.*

Silko lives on a ranch in the mountains a few miles northwest of Tucson, Arizona, where she has been living since the publication of *Ceremony.* She was named a Living Cultural Treasure by the New Mexico Humanities Council. In 1994, she also received the Native Writers' Circle of the Americas

lifetime achievement award, an honor she now shares with N. SCOTT MOMADAY (1992), SIMON ORTIZ (1993), and JOY HARJO (1995).

**Further Reading**

Allen, Paula Gunn, ed. *Song of the Turtle: American Indian Literature, 1974–1994.* New York: Ballantine Books, 1996.

Coltelli, Laura. *Winged Words: American Indian Writers Speak.* Lincoln: University of Nebraska Press, 1990.

Niatum, Duane, ed. *Carriers of the Dream Wheel: Contemporary Native American Poetry.* New York: Harper & Row, 1975.

Ortiz, Simon J., ed. *Speaking for the Generations: Native Writers on Writing.* Tucson: University of Arizona Press, 1998.

Riley, Patricia, ed. *Growing up Native American: An Anthology.* New York: Morrow, 1993.

Salyer, Gregory. *Leslie Marmon Silko.* New York: Twayne, 1997.

Seyersted, Per. *Leslie Marmon Silko.* Boise, Idaho: Boise State University, 1980.

Velie, Alan R. *Four American Indian Literary Masters: N. Scott Momaday, James Welch, Leslie Marmon Silko, and Gerald Vizenor.* Norman: University of Oklahoma Press, 1982.

Wiget, Andrew, ed. *Dictionary of Native American Literature.* New York: Garland, 1994.

## Simic, Charles
(1938–  ) *poet, translator, essayist*

Charles Simic is known for ironic, philosophical poems that are rich with images and what one interviewer described as a sense for the "built-in absurdity of everything." The poet himself acknowledged that perhaps this was one of the outcomes of his childhood experience, growing up in war-torn Belgrade, Yugoslavia. The author of more than 60 books of poetry, translations, and essays, including *The World Doesn't End: Prose Poems* (1990), for which he received the Pulitzer Prize for poetry, Simic is a prolific writer and translator, as well as a longtime teacher.

Charles Simic was born in Belgrade, Yugoslavia, on May 9, 1938. His childhood environment was shaped greatly by World War II and the bombing of Belgrade. He told an interviewer stories of how the Germans and the Allies took turns dropping bombs on his city while he played with his collection of lead soldiers on the floor of his house. "I would go boom, boom, and then they would go boom, boom. Even after the war was over, I went on playing war. My imitation of a heavy machine gun was famous in my neighborhood in Belgrade."

In 1953, Simic, his mother, and his brother joined his father in New York City and then moved with them to Oak Park, Illinois, on the edge of Chicago, in 1955, where they remained until 1962. Simic attended Oak Park River Forest High School and graduated in 1956. Following graduation, he took a full-time job as an office boy with the *Chicago Sun-Times*, while he went to college in the evenings. In 1961 he was drafted into the U.S. Army, and in 1964 he got married. He and his wife eventually had two children. In 1966, Simic earned his B.A. degree from New York University. He became a naturalized citizen of the United States in 1971 and since 1973 has lived in New Hampshire, where he is a professor of English and creative writing at the University of New Hampshire.

Simic's first poem was published in 1959, when he was 21; his first book, *What the Grass Says*, came out in 1967. Since that time, he has published many books in the United States and abroad. His most noted poetry collections are probably *Jackstraws*, which appeared in 1999 and was named a Notable Book of the Year by the *New York Times*; *Walking the Black Cat*, which appeared in 1996 and was a finalist for the National Book Award in poetry; and *The World Doesn't End: Prose Poems*, which won the Pulitzer Prize for Poetry in 1990. Some of his other collections include *Return to a Place Lit By a Glass of Milk* (1974), *Brooms: Selected Poems* (1978), *Weather Forecast for Utopia and Vicinity: Poems 1967–1982* (1983), *Selected Poems 1963–1983* (1990), and *The Book of Gods and Devils* (1990). His essays are collected in several volumes. *The Uncertain Certainty: Interviews, Essays, and Notes on Poetry* was published by the University of Michigan Press in 1985, and *Wonderful Words, Silent Truth* appeared in 1990. His memoir, *A Fly in the Soup*, was published in 2000.

Simic once described in an interview the significance of images in his poetry. He said, "Images have always been very important to me—movies, you know, I'm a twentieth-century kid. I wanted to be a painter when I was young, loved the movies, art, photography—it was images, images, images. And I really think of my life, my experience, as a story of images. Images juxtaposed. Images that tell their story by being brought side-by-side." While his poetry makes the most of imagery and can be quite dreamlike, even phatasmagorical at times, his prose tends to stick close to his own autobiography of immigration and exile.

In addition to the books he has written, Simic has also translated numerous volumes of French, Serbian, Croatian, Slovenian, and Macedonian

Yugoslavian-born poet Charles Simic won the Pulitzer Prize in poetry for his book of prose poems entitled *The World Doesn't End. (Photo by Philip Simic. Courtesy Charles Simic.)*

poetry and four books of essays, including *Orphan Factory*, which came out in 1998. He has been awarded fellowships from the Guggenheim Foundation, the MacArthur Foundation, and the National Endowment for the Arts. He was elected to the American Academy of Arts and Letters in 1995. Simic lives with his wife, Helen, in a house overlooking Bow Lake, near Strafford, New Hampshire.

## Further Reading

Hulse, Michael. *Charles Simic in Conversation with Michael Hulse*. London: Between the Lines, 2002.

Thurley, Geoffrey. *The American Moment: American Poetry in the Mid-Century*. New York: St. Martin's, 1978.

Weigl, Bruce, ed. *Charles Simic: Essays on the Poetry*. Ann Arbor: University of Michigan Press, 1996.

## Simon, Neil
### (Marvin Neil Simon)
(1927–  ) *playwright*

Neil Simon is the only playwright ever to have four Broadway productions running simultaneously. He has written 28 plays and holds the record for the greatest number of hits in the American theater. He has had more plays adapted to film than any other playwright and has written nearly a dozen original film comedies. He helped define television comedy during the medium's early days. Simon's career has sparred more than 40 years, and he has been rewarded with four Tony Awards, two Emmys, a Screen Writers Guild Award, and a Pulitzer Prize. His plays have been produced in dozens of languages and have been blockbuster hits worldwide. Described by his longtime producer Emanuel Azenberg as "a shrewd observer of human foibles and a master of the one-line gag," Simon has, via his zany characters and touching stories, transformed the lives and tribulations of everyday people into humor.

Marvin Neil Simon was born in the Bronx on July 4, 1927, and grew up in Washington Heights, near the northern tip of Manhattan. Growing up, Simon attended public schools, followed by a brief stint at New York University (1944–45) and at the University of Denver (1945–46), before joining the U.S. Army where he began his writing career working for an army camp newspaper. The war ended one week after Simon joined the army. Thus, following his discharge, he returned to New York and became a mailroom clerk for Warner Bros.' East Coast office. Simon was soon writing comedy revues with his brother Danny in the Poconos, then for radio, providing material for such stars as Tallulah Bankhead, and finally for television, where he scripted for such comedians as Phil Silvers, Jackie Gleason, Red Buttons, Garry Moore, Sid Caesar, and Imogene Coca.

Caesar and Coca were the stars of *Your Show of Shows*, the popular weekly variety show from 1950 to 1954. Simon and his brother toiled for the show alongside such budding talents as Woody Allen, Mel Brooks, and Larry Gelbart. The theater was Simon's destiny, however, and that was where he and his brother continued their partnership, contributing sketches to a couple of Broadway musicals in the mid 1950s. Neil Simon eventually broke out on his own and, after countless drafts, completed a comedy about two brothers who do not want to take over their father's fruit business. *Come Blow Your Horn* (1961) racked up 677 performances on Broadway and hinted at a promising career for the writer. Two years later, the play *Barefoot in the Park* fulfilled Simon's promise and launched a legend.

Throughout the 1960s and 1970s, Simon turned out hit after hit for the stage and screen, most of them depicting life in and about areas of New York City—Manhattan, Brighton Beach, Yonkers, Riverside Drive, Second Avenue, and Central Park West. The Simon canon—early works *The Odd Couple* (1965), *Sweet Charity* (1966), *Plaza Suite* (1968), *The Out-of-Towners* (1970), *Promises, Promises* (1968), *The Prisoner of Second Avenue* (1971), *The Goodbye Girl* (1973), and *Chapter Two* (1977)—provides a clear, sharp, and very funny picture of the people crazy and lucky enough to call New York their home.

In 1973, following the death of his wife, Simon reached a low point in his career with two failures: *The Good Doctor* (1973) and *God's Favorite* (1976). A move to California, however, reinvigorated him and he produced a much more successful play later that year in *California Suite*. After marrying actress Marsha Mason, Simon went on to write *Chapter Two* (1977), which was considered by many critics to be his finest play to that date. His fourth musical, *They're Playing Our Song*, proved fairly successful in 1979, but his next three plays (*I Ought to Be in Pictures, Fools*, and a revised version of *Little Me*) all proved unsuccessful at the box office. Then, in 1983, Simon began to win over many of his critics with the introduction of his autobiographical trilogy—*Brighton Beach Memoirs* (1983), *Biloxi Blues* (1985) and *Broadway Bound* (1986)—which chronicled his stormy childhood, his brief army time, and the beginning of his career in television. Suddenly the critics began taking him seriously. During this time, Simon was not only getting laughs, he was also getting awards. He crowned this streak with *Lost in Yonkers*, which won the Pulitzer Prize for drama in 1991. Perhaps the secret to Simon's success is his ability, brilliantly displayed in those four plays but evident from the very beginning, to depict the pain, aspiration, and sheer panic behind his unforgettable characters.

During the course of his career, Simon has won three Tony Awards for Best Play for *The Odd Couple, Biloxi Blues*, and *Lost in Yonkers*. He has had more plays adapted to film than any other American playwright and, in addition, has written nearly a dozen original screenplays himself. He received Academy Award nominations for his screenplays *The Odd Couple* (1968), *The Sunshine Boys* (1975), and *California Suite* (1978). He has also been the recipient of the Writers Guild Award, the Evening Standard Award, the New York Drama Critics Circle Award, the Shubert Award, the Outer Circle Award, and a 1978 Golden Globe Award for his screenplay *The Goodbye Girl*.

Simon's most recent play, *London Suite*, was a hit in New York. And the city that has figured so prominently in his life and work has honored him by making him the only living playwright for whom a Broadway theater is named.

## Further Reading

Johnson, Robert K. *Neil Simon*. Boston: G. K. Hall & Company, 1983.

Kerr, Walter. "What Simon Says." *New York Times Magazine*, March 22, 1970, pp. 6–16.

McGovern, Edythe M. *Not-So-Simple Neil Simon: A Critical Study*. New York: Frederick Ungar, 1979.

Rooney, Terrie M., ed. *Contemporary Theatre, Film, & Television*. Vol. 13. Detroit: Gale Research, 1995, pp. 372–375.

Zimmerman, Paul D. "Neil Simon: Up from Success." *Newsweek*, February 2, 1970, pp. 52–56.

## Simpson, Mona
## (Mona Elizabeth Simpson)
(1957– ) *novelist*

Known for her deft portrayals of families torn apart by divorce and abandonment, Mona Simpson became a major voice in contemporary fiction before she was 30 years old. The publication of her first novel, *Anywhere But Here*, launched her career quickly when it became an instant best-seller in 1987. She has won the Whiting Prize and was named one of *Granta* Magazine's 20 Best American Writers under 40.

Mona Simpson was born on June 14, 1957, in Green Bay, Wisconsin. Her mother's family were German-American, and her father was from the Middle East. When she was 12, she and her divorced mother left Green Bay for Los Angeles, where she attended Beverly Hills High School. Simpson received her B.A. degree in creative writing from the University of California, Berkeley, in 1979 and her M.F.A from Columbia University in 1983. Following her studies, Simpson worked at *The Paris Review*, where among other things, she championed the early work of writer Susan Welch. She was in her mid-20s when she first met her biological brother, Apple Computer tycoon Steve Jobs, whom her parents had put up for adoption as a baby just a couple of years before she was born.

Critics and fans have made much of the way Simpson's novels resemble her own life, but Simpson tends to be reticent about the extent to which her fiction borrows from the autobiographical details of her life. She has said, "What I'd finally say about truth and autobiography is that all writers are probably trying to get at some core truth of life, at some configuration that is enduring and truthful. I just haven't found the truth to be my vehicle."

*Anywhere But Here* tells the story of a mother and daughter, Adele and Ann August, who move from Bay City, Wisconsin, to Beverly Hills in hopes that the daughter will become a child star. Ann suffers much as a result of her impulsive mother's lifestyle, and their relationship deteriorates as Ann grows up and eventually moves away. The book was a bestseller and was later made into a movie starring Susan Sarandon as Adele and Natalie Portman as Ann.

*The Lost Father* is a continuation of Simpson's first novel and includes many of the same characters. The daughter Mayan (Ann) Atassi, is now living in New York City as a medical student. Her life becomes complicated when she becomes obsessed with finding her Egyptian father, who abandoned the family when she was a young girl. She squanders her savings when she hires a sleazy detective who never gets her any closer to finding her father. Her studies, friendships, and health soon deteriorate as her search spans the globe from Egypt to Wisconsin.

Simpson's third book, *A Regular Guy*, introduces Jane, who was brought up in a commune by her flaky mother, Mary. Her father, Tom Owens, is a college dropout who abandons Mary after making her pregnant, then goes on to create a small fortune for himself when he launches Genesis, an extremely successful biotech company. Tom's life is forever changed when Jane shows up on his doorstep one day.

*Off Keck Road* was published in 2000. The book follows the life of Bea, a woman who cannot quite get the hang of relationships with men, from adolescence into middle age, while also chronicling her changing habitat. Keck Road starts as a semi-rural place but by the novels end has become an American "everywhere," full of fast food chains and superstores.

In addition to the previously mentioned awards, Simpson is the recipient of a fellowship from the Guggenheim Foundation, the Hodder Fellowship at Princeton University, and a grant from the Lila Wallace–Reader's Digest Foundation. Since 1988, she has taught at Bard College, where she is the Sadie Samuelson Levy Professor of Languages and Literature.

In 1994, Simpson moved with her husband, Richard Appel, back to Southern California,

returning to New York each fall to teach at Bard College. A former New York City prosecutor, Appel had always wanted to write television comedy. Working nights and weekends on scripts, he won a 10-week tryout with *The Simpsons* that turned into a four-year stint, after which he wrote for *King of the Hill*. He hopes to develop his own series next. Simpson and her husband now live with their son, Gabriel, and daughter, Grace, in New York City and in Santa Monica, California.

**Further Reading**

"A Conversation with Mona Simpson," MPR Books. Available online. URL: http://www.mpr.org/books/features/ganda_monasimpson.shtml. Posted October 17, 2000.

Kline, Christine Baker. *Child of Mine: Writers Talk about the First Year of Motherhood*. New York: Hyperion, 1997.

"Mona Simpson: Off Keck Road." StarTribune.com. Talking Volumes Past Authors. Available online. URL: http://www.startribune.com/stories/1437/675605.html. Posted on September 6, 2001.

## Sinclair, Upton
(1878–1968) *novelist, essayist, playwright, short story writer, children's writer*

Known as one of the "muckrakers," Upton Sinclair wrote nearly 100 books—novels, essays, short stories, plays, and children's books that were primarily concerned with social and industrial reform. His most famous novel, *The Jungle*, a graphic and horrifying portrayal of the Chicago stockyards, appalled the public and led to major reforms in food inspection laws. He also wrote a series of novels dealing with world events since 1914, the first of which was published in 1940 and the third of which, *Dragon's Teeth*, won the Pulitzer Prize in 1942. An avid socialist, Sinclair was active politically and was defeated as the Socialist candidate for governor of California in 1934.

Upton Sinclair was born in Baltimore, Maryland, on September 20, 1878, to a family descended from the ruined southern aristocracy. His grandparents were wealthy, but his own life with his parents was impoverished. His father was a liquor salesman and alcoholic. When Sinclair was 10, the family moved to New York, and Sinclair, who had always done well in school, entered New York City College at the age of 14. He began writing dime novels and hack fiction for pulp magazines shortly thereafter to pay his tuition bills. In 1897, Sinclair enrolled at Columbia University and managed to complete one novelette per week to finance his studies. During those years he wrote Clif Faraday stories and Mark Mallory stories for various weekly boys' magazines. He was a prolific writer and successful student. By the time he was 17, Sinclair was earning enough money to afford an apartment of his own while also supplementing his parents' income.

In 1900 Sinclair married his first wife. Soon thereafter he wrote *Springtime and Harvest*, a story based on this relationship. The couple divorced in 1911. He followed this novel with *The Journal of Arthur Stirling* (1903), *Prince Hagen* (1903), *Manassas* (1904), and *A Captain of Industry* (1906), but none of these were commercially successful. At this same time, Sinclair was developing his political views and becoming active as a socialist. He was a founding member of the Intercollegiate Socialist Society and was significantly inspired by the work of FRANK NORRIS.

Sinclair was an avid reader of the socialist journal *Appeal to Reason*, and was commissioned by its editor, Fred Warren, in 1904 to write a novel about immigrant workers in the Chicago meatpacking houses. The owner of the journal provided Sinclair with a $500 advance, and after seven weeks of research, Sinclair wrote *The Jungle*. It was serialized in the journal and responsible for greatly increasing its circulation. The novel, however, was rejected by six publishers before Sinclair decided to publish it himself. He advertised his decision in the *Appeal to Reason* and received 972 orders for the book. When he told Doubleday of these orders, they changed their mind and decided to publish it. The book was a huge and immediate success, selling more than 150,000 copies. It was soon translated into 17 languages.

When President Theodore Roosevelt read *The Jungle*, he requested an investigation of the meatpacking industry. Ultimately, these efforts resulted in the passing of the Pure Food and Drug Act of 1906 and the Meat Inspection Act of 1906. The impact of the novel on politics and law concerned politicians, who feared investigative journalism, and inspired Roosevelt to coin the term "muckraking."

With the notoriety he had won, Sinclair launched his career in politics and became the Socialist Party candidate for Congress in New Jersey. He lost the election in a landslide defeat, winning just 750 out of 24,000 votes. Sinclair also used some of the profits from his book to found a socialist community called Helicon Home Colony in Englewood, New Jersey. A suspicious fire destroyed it just four months after it opened.

Despite his fame, Sinclair's novels in the next few years were commercially unsuccessful. He published *The Overman* (1907), *The Metropolis* (1908), *The Moneychangers* (1908), *Love's Pilgrimage* (1911), and *Sylvia* (1913) before taking a break from writing novels and moving to Croton-on-Hudson, then a radical enclave north of New York City, with his second wife, whom he had married in 1913.

In 1915, Sinclair edited an anthology of social protest called *Cry for Justice*. His socialist friends were all quite supportive of his efforts, but when Sinclair began arguing with Max Eastman, editor of *The Masses*, and John Reed, the famous socialist war reporter, within the pages of *The Masses*, the Socialist Party became divided and Sinclair resigned from its membership. He moved to Pasadena, California, in 1915. Sinclair eventually rejoined the Socialist Party and became its unsuccessful candidate for governor of California in 1926. He ran again in California in 1934 and lost again, but his program, EPIC (End Poverty in California), found significant support.

Sinclair's other political novels included *King Coal* (1917), based on an industrial dispute; *Oil* (1927); *Boston* (1928), which was about the Sacco-Vanzetti affair; and *Little Steel* (1938). *World's End* was published in 1940 and commenced Sinclair's 11-volume "Lanny Bud" series of novels on U.S. government and history, the third of which won a Pulitzer Prize. Sinclair moved in 1953 to the remote village of Buckeye, Arizona. His second wife died in 1961. Sinclair's third wife died in 1967, just one year before him.

Upton Sinclair died on November 25, 1968, having published more than 90 books. These included an autobiography, *American Outpost* (1962), a collection of essays on his life that appeared in 1932, and *My Lifetime in Letters* (1960).

## Further Reading

Biggers, Jeff. "Qué Viva Mexico! The Folly of Upton Sinclair and Sergei Eisenstein." *Brick* 65–66 (fall 2000): 142–152.

Bloodworth, William A. *Upton Sinclair.* Boston: Twayne, 1977.

Gottesman, Ronald. *Upton Sinclair: An Annotated Checklist.* Kent, Ohio: Kent State University Press, 1973.

Harris, Leon A. *Upton Sinclair, American Rebel.* New York: Crowell, 1975.

Herms, Dieter, ed. *Upton Sinclair: Literature and Social Reform.* Frankfurt, Germany: Peter Lang, 1990.

Mookerjee, R. N. *Art for Social Justice: The Major Novels of Upton Sinclair.* Metuchen, N.J.: Scarecrow, 1988.

Yoder, Jon A. *Upton Sinclair.* New York: Ungar, 1975.

## Singer, Isaac Bashevis
### (1904–1991) *novelist, short story writer, essayist, children's writer*

A Polish Jew who immigrated to the United States in 1935, Isaac Bashevis Singer wrote prolifically until his death at age 87. Known as a writer whose stories have Jewish roots but universal appeal, Singer was the Yiddish writer of his generation who most successfully captured the American imagination. His translated works include 12 books of short stories, 13 children's books, three collections of essays, and four books of memoir. Sometimes criticized as profane by Orthodox Jews and as antifeminist by young American readers, Singer was not always popular, but he did manage to bridge the gap between the traditional Yiddish culture of his upbringing and the secular culture of contemporary America. His work enjoyed a wide and diverse audience. Singer received the 1978 Nobel Prize in literature.

Born on July 14, 1904, in Radzymin, Poland, Isaac Bashevis Singer grew up the second son of a poor Hasidic rabbi, who considered secular writing to be heretical. His mother, a rabbi's daughter, was more skeptical and rational in her outlook. During his childhood, Singer lived in the tiny Jewish villages of Leoncin and Bilgoray. His upbringing was poor in material opportunities but rich with imagination and dreams. Singer loved to listen to his older brother, Isaac Joshua Singer (who also became a major Yiddish writer) tell stories. He later moved to Warsaw, following his brother, who lived there and worked for a magazine. Although Isaac B. Singer attended Tachkemoni Rabbinical Seminary in Warsaw for several years starting in 1921, he eventually left to take a job as a proofreader at the Yiddish magazine where his brother worked and to begin writing stories of his own.

Singer's stories were concerned with Jewish folklore and the occult. He often wrote about witches, devils, and prostitutes, for which he was consistently criticized. Singers' parents' two perspectives collided in the early stories he wrote in Warsaw and then in New York, where he followed his brother in 1935. One reviewer described this tension well: "The clash between tradition and renewal, between other-worldliness and faith and mysticism on the one hand, and free thought, secularization, doubt and nihilism on the other, is an essential theme in Singer's short stories and novels."

Although he was expected to become a Hasidic rabbi like his father, Singer started freelancing in New York City for the *Jewish Daily Forward,* the city's biggest Yiddish daily. His wife, Alma, was the refugee daughter of a rich German Jewish weaver. When Singer met her in the Catskills in the late 1930s, she was already married. She divorced in 1939, the same year Singer's mother and younger brother were killed by Nazis in Poland. Five years later, Joshua died of a heart attack at age 51. Whatever Singer's grief was at all these losses, it did not slow his productivity. He wrote his big family novels during this period—*The Family Moskat, The Manor,* and *The Estate.* Most of his fiction is set in the shtetls of Eastern Europe that were destroyed by the Nazis, but the stories he tells are the universal stories of men, women, and children everywhere.

These big novels were followed by collections of short stories, more novels, and his memoirs, as well as numerous books of children's fiction. In all, Singer published about 12 collections of short stories that were translated into English. Some of the most notable titles include *Gimpel the Fool* (1953), *The Spinoza of Market Street* (1961), *A Friend of Kafka* (1970), and *A Crown of Feathers and Other Stories* (1973), which won the National Book Award.

It was in these short stories that Singer's most fantastical characters came to life. Passions are personified as demons, ghosts, and all kinds of supernatural powers derived from the Jewish popular imagination. Singer almost always wrote in Yiddish. (His works were translated into English.) He once said, "Yiddish contains vitamins that other languages don't have."

Singer once explained that he began writing children's books because "children are the best readers of genuine literature." He went on to describe how adults are affected by big names and advertising, but children are truly independent readers who rely on nothing but their own taste. *Schlemiel Went to Warsaw and Other Stories* (1968) is one of his most popular children's books. Some of the most notable books written in the latter part of Singer's career were *The Penitent* (1974) and *Shosha*, which was published in 1978, the same year that Singer was awarded the Nobel Prize. From then, Singer's reputation grew to heroic proportions. Although this degree of fame was somewhat troubling to him, he continued to write into the 1980s, publishing his last book the same year that he died.

Several of Singer's books were made into films. *The Magician of Lublin*, (1978) starred Alan Arkin and was based on Singer's novel of the same name. Barbara Streisand's movie *Yentl* (1983) was based on Singer's short story "Yentl, The Yeshiva Boy." When questioned about the film, Singer claimed he saw no artistic merit in the production or directing and believed there was too much singing.

This type of sharp criticism gained Singer a reputation as a sometimes contentious character. In addition, many Jews found his writing too profane, and some even argued against him receiving the Nobel Prize. There was a story that circulated about some of the religious Linotype operators at the *Jewish Daily Forward* refusing to handle his texts when he was a frequent contributor at the paper because the words so offended their sensibilities.

Despite this, his is a deep and original body of work that will forever be part of literary history. In 1989, Ron Silver and Anjelica Huston starred in *Enemies: A Love Story*, which was also based on a Singer novel. The novel, a comedy-drama, tells the story of a Jewish immigrant, Herman, who escapes the horrors of World War II and settles in New York, where he struggles to make a life for himself while working as a ghostwriter for a rabbi. Herman lives a double life, hiding his work and his mistress from his wife, and all the time believing that the wife and children he lost in Germany are dead. When his first wife turns up in New York, Herman must face the sadness of his past and the deceptions and hurt of the present.

Singer lived most of his life on the Upper West Side of Manhattan, though he kept a house in Florida, as well. Isaac Bashevis Singer died on July 24, 1991, in Surfside, Florida.

## Further Reading

Farrell, Grace, ed. *Critical Essays on Isaac Bashevis Singer.* Boston: Twayne, 1996.

Green, Norman. "Master in the Shadows: Isaac Bashevis Singer." Salon.com. Available online. URL: http://www.salon.com/books/int/1998/04/cov_si_28int.html. Posted April 28, 1998.

Hadda, Jante. *Isaac Bashevis Singer: A Life.* Madison: University of Wisconsin Press, 2003.

Kresh, Paul. *Isaac Bashevis Singer: The Magician of West 86th Street.* New York: Doubleday, 1979.

———. *Isaac Bashevis Singer: The Story of a Storyteller.* New York: E. P. Dutton, 1984.

## Smiley, Jane
(1949–   ) *novelist*

Jane Smiley has covered a wide range of subjects in her novels, spanning from incest to horse racing to academia. Despite her diverse body of work, she has been labeled a Midwestern writer, but she probes America deeper, both its inner and outer landscapes. Many of her novels and novellas begin with the description of what appears to be an idyllic life in a pastoral setting, and then Smiley introduces darker themes. Despite this, she tends to present loving portrayals of families, individual family members, and the interactions among them. *A Thousand Acres* (1991), for which Smiley won a Pulitzer Prize, weaves the plot of William Shakespeare's *King Lear* through the story of an Iowa farm woman who was sexually abused by her father. Smiley has written more than a dozen novels and short story collections.

Jane Smiley was born on September 26, 1949, in Los Angeles, but her family lived there for only one year before moving to St. Louis, Missouri. She attended grammar school and the John Burroughs School before heading to Vassar College. She graduated with a B.A. degree from Vassar in 1971. Smiley then traveled in Europe for a year, sightseeing and working on an archeological dig before going to graduate school at the University of Iowa, where she received her M.F.A. and Ph.D. degrees.

Smiley's first books were *At Paradise Gate* (1981), *Duplicate Keys* (1984), *The Age of Grief* (a collection of stories) (1987), *The Greenlanders* (1988), *Ordinary Love and Good Will: Two Novellas* (1989), and *Life of the Body* (a collection of stories) (1990). *Duplicate Keys* was different from many other Smiley novels in that it took place in New York City instead of the Midwest. However, the story revolves around a group of friends from the Midwest in the late 1960s who cluster around a marginally successful rock band and move to New York. Alice Ames, the main character, is a librarian. She finds two members of the band sitting in their apartment, shot to death.

Her later novels include *A Thousand Acres* (1991), *Moo* (1995), *The All-True Travels and Adventures of Lidie Newton* (1998), and *Horse Heaven* (2000). *Moo* centered on academic life at an agricultural university and *Horse Heaven* on the horse racing community. Smiley owns several horses. She has called *The All-True Travels and Adventures of Lidie Newton* a look at the intersection of ideology and violence in America. In the novel, Lidie Newton, a young widow, recalls all that happened a year ago, in 1855. It begins when Lidie meets Thomas Newton, an abolitionist passing through on his way to his claim in the Kansas Territory. Lidie has no strong moral feelings about slavery but is intrigued by Thomas, who declares it to be "evil incarnate." When he proposes marriage, she agrees. Lidie's sense of "why not" defines her.

Marrying a man she barely knows and moving to a strange, dangerous place seems no more to her than an adventure.

Smiley's work is not autobiographical. She has aimed to write each one of the four major narrative forms—epic (*The Greenlanders*), tragedy (*A Thousand Acres*), comedy (*Moo*), and romance (*The All-True Travels and Adventures of Lidie Newton*). "She's constantly looking for a new challenge, some new project that makes her have to do something differently," says Neil Nakadate, author of *Understanding Jane Smiley*. Smiley has written on politics, farming, horse training, child rearing, literature, impulse buying, getting dressed, Barbie dolls, marriage, and many other topics. She is also the author of a book on craftspeople living in the Catskills.

Of her writing, Smiley has said that she is more of an outward than an inward-looking writer and that although she has written about many subjects her concerns have remained the same over the years. "I'm interested in how people relate to the groups that they're in (whether those groups are families or communities), in how power is negotiated among people, in character idiosyncrasies, and in the relationship of power to love," she has said. "I'm always interested in the concerns of the natural world—in capitalism and how it fails, mostly, but also in how it sometimes succeeds. I'm always interested in broader historical forces. Most of my books are in some sense historical novels, because they all draw on an analysis of what happened at a particular historical moment."

Smiley's work has been influenced by William Shakespeare, as well as by Virginia Woolf, George Eliot, and Charles Dickens. In addition to her novels, she has written many essays for *U.S. News & World Report,* the *New York Times,* and other publications. Smiley won the Pulitzer Prize as well as the National Book Critics Circle Award for *A Thousand Acres*. She has also won the American Academy of Arts and Letters Award.

Smiley taught for 15 years at Iowa State University, leaving in 1996 to live and write full time in northern California. She has been married three times, to John Whiston, William Silag, and Stephen M. Mortensen. She lives with her three children.

## Further Reading

"The Adventures of Jane Smiley." Atlantic Unbound. Available online. URL: http: www.theatlantic.com/ unbound/bookauth/ba980528.htm. Posted May 28, 1998.

Nakadate, Neil. *Understanding Jane Smiley.* Columbia: University of South Carolina Press, 1999.

Random House. Jane Smiley Website. Available online. URL: http://www.randomhouse.com/features/smiley/. Downloaded March 18, 2003.

## Snyder, Gary
(1930–  )  *poet*

Gary Snyder was one of the original Beat poets, who helped to shape modern poetry and to fuel the cultural revolution of the 1960s along with fellow writers ALLEN GINSBERG and JACK KEROUAC. Snyder's spiritual and literary explorations led him to study Zen Buddhism, which became a lifelong practice. His spirituality and a reverence for nature are reflected in his work, and he has been an advocate of community living. Having expanded far beyond the Beat poems that first brought attention to his work, Snyder has produced a broad-ranging body of work. His book *Turtle Island* (1974) won the Pulitzer Prize for poetry. He has published more than 15 books of poetry and prose.

Gary Snyder was born on May 8, 1930, in San Francisco, California, and was brought up in Oregon and Washington State. His early love of nature led him to mountaineering. At 15 he had climbed Mount St. Helens and by 17 he had ascended most of the major peaks in the Northwest. Snyder attended Reed College, in Portland, and was part of a bohemian group that later joined him in San Francisco. Snyder received his B.A. degree in anthropology from Reed College in 1951. After graduation, he embarked on a life of academia mixed with spiritual study and physical labor. He worked as a logger, a trail-crew member, and a seaman on a Pacific tanker. He entered the Asian language program of the University of California at Berkeley, where he lived in a small cottage near the Young Buddhist Association and saved his money to study Buddhism in Japan.

Snyder's experiences as a logger and ranger were inspirations for his first two collections of poetry: *Riprap* (1959) and *Myths and Texts* (1960). "Simplicity, distance, accuracy of atmosphere: these are hallmarks of the work throughout," wrote Glyn Maxwell. "The laid-back, jotted-down tone masks an acute sensitivity to rhythm and, in particular, assonance." *Riprap* specifically reflected Snyder's time in Yosemite National Park in 1955 as a trail crew laborer laying "riprap," a kind of rock pavement set into an eroding trail. "Mid-August at Sourdough Mountain Lookout" and "Milton by Firelight" were inspired by his earlier summer jobs as a lookout ranger in the mountains of Washington. Snyder met Jack Kerouac and Allan Ginsberg at a poetry reading in 1955 that marked one of the first readings of Ginsberg's *Howl.* "Night Highway Ninety-nine" described various trips hitchhiking from Seattle to San Francisco early in 1956, accompanied at times by Allen Ginsberg. It was while Snyder was climbing Matterhorn Peak in the Sierra Nevada with Jack Kerouac that Kerouac decided to use Snyder as the semimystical poet in his autobiographical *Dharma Bums* (1958).

In 1956, Snyder left for Japan, where he spent 12 years studying Rinzai Zen Buddhism, researching and translating Zen texts. He spent six months traveling throughout the Far East and India. Snyder returned to the United States in 1969 and established a farmstead on the San Juan Ridge in the foothills of the northern Sierra Nevada. It is from there that Snyder became a major figure in the ecology movement.

Much of his writing has demonstrated the influence of WALT WHITMAN and EZRA POUND, as well as intimations of mysticism exemplified in Far Eastern forms. Many of Snyder's later works focused on alternatives to city living and showed a reverence for nature and a deep interest in the philosophies of the East. "I hold the most archaic values on earth . . . the fertility of the soul, the magic of the animals, the power-vision in solitude . . . the love and ecstasy of the dance, the common work of the tribe," Snyder has said.

His poetry in the 1975 Pulitzer Prize–winning *Turtle Island* spoke of a sense of place, specifically Turtle Island. Snyder wrote of the land and the planet being a living being along with the varied people of the Earth, sharing an ancient solidarity. "I pledge allegiance to the soil of Turtle Island and to the beings who thereon dwell one ecosystem in diversity under the sun," he wrote.

Snyder's other volumes include *The Black Country* (1967), *Regarding Wave* (1969), *Axe Handles* (1983), *The Old Ways* (1977), and *No Nature: New and Selected Poems* (1992). *No Nature* was a finalist for the National Book Award in 1992. When his long poem cycle, *Mountains and Rivers without End,* was published in 1996, Snyder received the Bollingen Poetry Prize and the Robert Kirsch Lifetime Achievement Award from the *Los Angeles Times.* He has also received an American Academy of Arts and Letters Award, a Guggenheim Foundation fellowship, the Bess Hokin Prize, the Levinson Prize from *Poetry,* and the Shelley Memorial Award.

Since 1985 Snyder has spent half of each year at the University of California at Davis, teaching ethno-poetics, creative writing, and the literature of wilderness. He is married to Carole Koda and has two sons, both by his previous wife, Masa Uehara, and two stepdaughters.

**Further Reading**

Dean, Tim Dean. *Gary Snyder and the American Unconscious.* New York: St. Martin's Press, 1991.

Halper, John, ed., *Gary Snyder: Dimensions of a Life.* San Francisco: Sierra Club Books, 1991.

Snyder, Gary. *Gary Snyder Reader: Prose, Poetry, and Translations 1952–1998.* Boulder, Colo.: Counterpoint Press, 2000.

White, Kenneth. *The Tribal Dharma: An Essay on the Work of Gary Snyder.* New York: Unicorn, 1975.

## Stegner, Wallace
### (Stegner, Wallace Earle)
(1909–1993) *novelist, short story writer, essayist*

An internationally renowned figure in American letters, Wallace Stegner won both the Pulitzer Prize and the National Book Award for his fiction. He was also a member of the prestigious National Institute and Academy of Arts and Letters, Phi Beta Kappa, and the American Academy of Arts

and Sciences, as well as a teacher whose student protégés include other American literary greats such as EDWARD ABBEY, WENDELL BERRY, and ROBERT HAAS. In addition to his career as a writer and teacher, Stegner was active as an environmentalist and historian of the West. His legacy lives on in several different environmental centers named in his honor and in Stanford University's creative writing program, which he founded in 1947 and led until his retirement in 1971.

Wallace Stegner was born in Lake Mills, Iowa, on February 18, 1909. His family led a somewhat nomadic life during his childhood, living in Iowa, Utah, North Dakota, Washington, Montana, Wyoming, and Saskatchewan. Stegner did his undergraduate work at the University of Utah and received both his M.A. and his Ph.D. in literature from the University of Iowa in 1932 and 1935 respectively. He married Mary Stuart Page, a fellow graduate student at the University of Iowa, in 1934. Their son, Page Stegner, is today a writer and a professor at the University of California at Santa Cruz.

Following his education, Stegner traveled the country again, moving to take academic appointments at Augustana College in Rock Island, Illinois, the University of Utah in Salt Lake City, the University of Wisconsin in Madison, Harvard University in Cambridge, and finally Stanford University. Stegner's wife has told how the couple was in Southern California for the winter when her husband got the offer from Stanford to come and teach. When Stanford agreed to meet his terms— appointment as full professor with tenure, no morning classes, and no committee work—the Stegners called back to Cambridge and had some of their furniture shipped out. The decision was made very quickly, and the Palo Alto area in California became the couple's home in 1945 and the place they would remain the rest of their lives.

Stegner's vast body of work includes many prizewinning novels and short stories, as well as historical and political nonfiction. His work in all genres has focused largely on the people and history of the American West and the social issues faced there. His first major novel, *The Big Rock Candy Mountain,* was published in 1943 to wide critical acclaim. It was followed by *The Preacher and the Slave* (1950; reprinted as *Joe Hill* in 1969); A

*Shooting Star* (1961); *All the Little Live Things* (1967); *Angle of Repose* (1971), which won the Pulitzer Prize; *The Spectator Bird* (1976), which won the National Book Award; and *Crossing to Safety* (1987), among others.

In addition to his many novels and collections of short stories, Stegner wrote books of history on the Mormons, a biography of Bernard De Voto, and collections of essays on writing and the environment, among other topics. Some of these titles include *Mormon Country* (1942), *Beyond the Hundredth Meridian: John Wesley Powell and the Second Opening of the West* (1954), *The Gathering of Zion* (1964), *Where the Bluebird Sings to the Lemonade Springs: Living and Writing in the West* (1992), a collection of anecdotes and essays, and *On the Teaching of Creative Writing* (1997).

As founder of the creative writing program at Stanford in 1946, Stegner exercised an important influence over two generations of writers. He directed the program until 1971, when he retired from teaching, citing the antiwar movement and the disruptions caused on campus as his main reason for retiring. He was staunchly opposed to the Vietnam War, but he was just as staunchly opposed to the trashing of college campuses and the disregard for classes and study that went on in the name of the protest movement. Stanford still offers a fellowship in Stegner's name.

Stegner's influence has also been great in the conservation movement in the West. In the 1950s he fought construction of a dam on the Green River in order to preserve Dinosaur National Monument, which sits along the border of Colorado and Utah and contains numerous prehistoric fossils. His involvement led to his serving on the National Parks Advisory Board in the 1960s and working as an assistant to Secretary of the Interior Stuart Udall during the Kennedy Administration. His so-called Wilderness Letter, which spoke of the "geography of hope," served as the introduction to the 1964 bill establishing the National Wilderness Preservation System and is considered one of the early manifestos of the environmental movement. It was written in 1960 to David Pesonen of the University of California's Wildland Research Center, which was conducting a national wilderness inventory.

In the 22 years following Stegner's retirement from teaching in 1971, he wrote two of his best-known novels—*Angle of Repose* and *The Spectator Bird*, as well as the novel he considered his most personal work, *Crossing to Safety*. Wallace Stegner died on April 13, 1993, from complications resulting from a car accident in Santa Fe, New Mexico, that he was involved in two weeks earlier.

### Further Reading

Benson, Jackson J. *Wallace Stegner: His Life and Work.* New York: Penguin, 1997.

Etulain, Richard. *Conversations with Wallace Stegner.* Salt Lake City: University of Utah Press, 1983.

*The Geography of Hope: A Tribute to Wallace Stegner.* Washington, D.C.: Sierra Club Books, 1996.

Rankin, Charles. *Wallace Stegner: Man and Writer.* Albuquerque: University of New Mexico Press, 1996.

## Stein, Gertrude

(1874–1946) *poet, memoirist, novelist, biographer, literary critic, playwright*

One of the most influential writers of the 20th century, Gertrude Stein is known for her playful experimentation with language, which included an emphasis on sound over sense and the use of words separate from their conventional meanings. Her Paris apartment, which she shared with her companion, Alice B. Toklas, was the salon of choice for writers and artists in the early 20th century.

Born on February 3, 1874, in Allegheny, Pennsylvania, Gertrude Stein was the fifth and youngest child of Daniel Stein and Amelia Keyser Stein. Her father was vice president of a steel railway, and the family lived a comfortable upper-middle-class life. When Gertrude was three years old, the Steins moved to Europe, living for a time in Vienna and then Paris before returning to the United States in late 1878, when Gertrude was five years old. Soon after their return, the family settled in Oakland, California, where most of her childhood was spent.

Stein was quite close to her brother Leo, who was two years older. They shared many interests in common and forged a bond in childhood that

Known for her experimentation with the sound and sense of language, Gertrude Stein lived most of her adult life in France. *(Library of Congress, Prints and Photographs Division, Carl Van Vechten Collection [LCPP005A-52655])*

would last well into their adult years. Gertrude was an omnivorous reader; she read Shakespeare and books on natural history beginning at an early age. She began to try her hand at writing at the age of eight.

In 1891, Stein's father died suddenly, and her oldest brother, Michael, took responsibility for supporting the family. The Steins moved to San Francisco at this time, and Gertrude had her first real exposure to opera and theater, with which she became obsessed. In 1892, she moved to Baltimore to live with a wealthy aunt, and in 1893 Stein entered Radcliffe College in Boston, where she studied under William James, a noted philosopher and writer and the brother of HENRY JAMES. Stein studied at Radcliffe from 1893 to 1897, during which time she published a paper about her

experiments with automatic, spontaneous writing in a psychological journal. She wanted to be a writer throughout college, but according to her, she received little support, except from William James.

Stein went on to study medicine at Johns Hopkins University, where she focused on brain anatomy, but never completed her degree. From there, she moved to London where she studied Elizabethan prose for a year, lived with her brother Leo, and traveled throughout England, Italy, and Germany. She returned to New York for a brief time where she wrote her first novel, *Q.E.D.*, which was lost for 30 years and published posthumously in 1950 under the title *Things as They Are.* When Leo settled in Paris, Stein followed him there in 1904 and moved into his apartment. The pair lived together for more than a decade before Leo moved on. Gertrude remained in that first Paris apartment for nearly 40 years.

Leo and Gertrude collected paintings by Pablo Picasso, Auguste Renoir, Paul Gauguin, and Paul Cézanne. Their apartment became known for its walls covered in contemporary art. Some of these artists became personal friends, visiting the apartment often, where one could almost be sure to run into other artists, writers, and critics. Picasso, Henri Matisse, and Georges Braque were among her circle of friends, as were ERNEST HEMINGWAY and SHERWOOD ANDERSON in the 1920s.

In 1907, Stein met Alice B. Toklas, who became her lifelong companion and secretary. Toklas helped with the proofreading of Stein's first published book, *Three Lives*, which was published in 1909 and became a best-seller. In 1910, Toklas moved in with Gertrude and Leo. Gertrude Stein's first periodical publications occurred around this time as well in Alfred Steiglitz's *Camera Works* magazine.

In 1912, Stein began working on the material that would eventually become *Tender Buttons*, which was published in 1914. As her style became more abstract and difficult to follow, Stein's work began to receive lots of criticism.

Stein's relationship with Leo began to deteriorate around this time, and in 1913 Leo moved out of the apartment they had shared in Paris. The two had little contact with one another from that time on.

In March 1914, Stein and Toklas left Paris following a series of bombing alerts. When they returned in 1916, they joined the American Fund for French Wounded. Stein and Toklas's job was to drive a Ford around Paris, delivering supplies to hospitals. Following the war, Stein and Toklas returned to their country home in Bilignin, France, where Stein wrote many of her best-known books. At this time, she had developed a name for herself, but her work was not yet widely read. All this changed in 1933 with the publication of *The Autobiography of Alice B. Toklas*, which became a best-seller in the United States after *The Atlantic Monthly* printed a serialization of the book. Stein became much wealthier than she had ever been. *Everybody's Autobiography* was published in 1938 and contained fascinating portraits of artists and writers in Paris.

Stein's other primary publications include *Geography and Plays* (1922); *The Making of Americans* (1925); *Four Saints in Three Acts* (1929), an opera on which she collaborated with composer Virgil Thompson; *The Geographical History of America* (1936); *Ida, A Novel* (1941); *The Mother of Us All* (1949); and *Patriarchal Poetry* (1953). The opera *Four Saints* is notable in that it was the first opera written for an all-black cast, preceding *Porgy and Bess* by a couple of years.

Although she had resisted returning to the United States, for fear that she would not be well received, she and Toklas did sail back to America following her sudden success. They were given a tremendous welcome by the press when their ship docked in New York on October 24, 1934. The pair traveled cross-country on their book tour, making more than 40 appearances and visiting with many other writers and celebrities.

In the spring of 1935, Toklas and Stein returned to their country home in France to rest and recuperate from all the publicity they had received on their tour. In 1937, they were forced to give up the Paris apartment they had kept for more than three decades. They moved their belongings to another apartment but by June 1940, the Germans occupied Paris, and Stein and Toklas were unable to return to the city until 1944. The war years were frightening for both women, who were of Jewish descent and narrowly escaped being transported to a concentration camp in Germany. Their neighbors actively protected their identities.

Stein and Toklas returned to Paris and found to their great relief that the paintings they had left in their Paris apartment were unharmed. In December 1945, Stein began to complain of abdominal pains while on a trip to Brussels. She was diagnosed a few months later with colon cancer. On July 19, 1946, she was rushed to the hospital. She made out her will on July 23, leaving most of her estate to Toklas. She underwent emergency surgery at the American Hospital in Neuilly, a suburb of Paris, but did not survive. Gertrude Stein died on July 27, 1946.

### Further Reading

Adams, Timothy D. *Telling Lies in Modern American Autobiography.* Chapel Hill: University of North Carolina Press, 1990.

Benstock, Shari. *Women of the Left Bank: Paris, 1900–1940.* Austin: University of Texas Press, 1986.

Bridgman, Richard. *Gertrude Stein in Pieces.* New York: Oxford University Press, 1970.

Caramello, Charles. *Henry James, Gertrude Stein, and the Biographical Act.* Chapel Hill: University of North Carolina Press, 1996.

Hobhouse, Janet. *Everybody Who Was Anybody: A Biography of Gertrude Stein.* New York: Putnam, 1975.

Knapp, Bettina L. *Gertrude Stein.* New York: Continuum, 1990.

Simon, Linda, ed. *Gertrude Stein Remembered.* Lincoln: University of Nebraska Press, 1994.

### Steinbeck, John
### (John Ernst Steinbeck)
(1902–1968) *novelist, short story writer*

John Steinbeck combined the themes of social protest with a benign view of human nature in his novels, gaining wide popularity during the Great Depression of the 1930s. He also used a biological interpretation of the human experience. Steinbeck is best remembered for *The Grapes of Wrath* (1939), a novel widely considered to be a 20th-century classic. The epic about the migration of the Joad family, driven from their land in Oklahoma to

California, sparked a wide debate about the hard life of migrant laborers and helped to trigger agricultural reform. Steinbeck received the Nobel Prize for literature in 1962.

John Ernst Steinbeck was born in Salinas, California, on February 27, 1902, the only son of four children. His father, John Steinbeck, Sr., was the county treasurer and his mother, Olive Hamilton Steinbeck, was a former schoolteacher. His native region of Monterey Bay was later the setting for most of his fiction. As a youth, he worked as a ranch hand and fruit picker to help support his family during the summer months, descriptions of which he would later write about. He attended Salinas High School, contributed to the school newspaper, and graduated in 1919. He attended Stanford University sporadically between 1920 to 1925. Originally an English major, he pursued a program of independent study but never finished a degree. Several of his poems and short stories appeared in university publications. During this time he worked periodically at various jobs and left Stanford permanently to pursue his writing career in New York City. He supported himself working as a laborer and a reporter for the *American*. However, he was unsuccessful in getting any of his creative writing published and finally returned to California.

His first novel, *Cup of Gold* (1929), a story that romanticized the life and exploits of the famous 17th-century Welsh pirate Sir Henry Morgan, attracted no attention. His two subsequent novels, *The Pastures of Heaven* (1932) and *To a God Unknown* (1933), were also poorly received. They dealt with the cost of pursuing the American dream. To support himself, Steinbeck continued to work as a manual laborer so that he could spend his evenings writing. He married Carol Henning in 1930 and moved to Pacific Grove, California. Often writing firsthand about the quiet dignity he saw in the poor and the oppressed, whom he had seen growing up, Steinbeck became a master at depicting characters who were trapped in an unfair world. In Pacific Grove, Steinbeck met Edward Ricketts, a marine biologist, whose views on the interdependence of all life deeply influenced Steinbeck. In *To a God Unknown*, Steinbeck depicted a farmer, Joseph Wayne, who builds a farm for himself in a distant valley. He develops his own

beliefs of death and life, and to bring an end to a drought he sacrifices himself on a stone, becoming "earth and rain."

*Tortilla Flat* (1935) marked the turning point in Steinbeck's literary career. It received the California Commonwealth Club's Gold Medal for best novel by a California author. It was an episodic, humorous tale of pleasure-loving Mexican Americans. Their lives are given the air of legend and likened to the tales of King Arthur's Round Table. *In Dubious Battle* (1936) was a novel about a migratory fruit pickers' strike and its defeat by the landowners with their vigilantes.

In 1937, Steinbeck published *Of Mice and Men*, a tragic story of two itinerant farm laborers yearning for a small farm of their own. It was a story of shattered dreams and became Steinbeck's first big success. The novella *The Red Pony* was released the same year and is considered among many critics to be among Steinbeck's finest works. The first two sections of the story sequence, "The Gift" and "The Great Mountains," were published in the *North American Review* in 1933, and the third section, "The Promise," did not appear in *Harper's* until 1937. With "The Leader of the People," the four sections are connected by common characters, settings, and themes. *The Red Pony* functions as a symbol of the main character's innocence and maturation. A movie version, for which Steinbeck wrote the screenplay, was made in 1949.

Steinbeck published what is considered his masterwork in 1939 with *The Grapes of Wrath*. It won the Pulitzer Prize and was made into a notable movie starring Henry Fonda. For *The Grapes of Wrath*, Steinbeck traveled around California migrant camps in 1936. Fleeing publicity followed by the book's success, Steinbeck went to Mexico in 1940 to film the documentary *Forgotten Village*. During World War II, Steinbeck was a war correspondent for the *New York Herald Tribune* in Great Britain and the Mediterranean area. Some of his dispatches were later collected and made into *Once There Was a War* (1958). He also wrote government propaganda in the form of *The Moon Is Down* (1942), which depicted a resistance movement in a small town occupied by the Nazis.

In 1943, Steinbeck moved to New York City, his home for the rest of his life. His marriage to Carol

Henning ended in 1942. The next year he married the singer Gwyndolyn Conger and they had two sons, Thom and John. However, the marriage was unhappy and they were divorced in 1949. His immediate postwar work—*Cannery Row* (1945), *The Pearl* (1947), and *The Wayward Bus* (1947)—reflected a bitterness against the greedy elements of society that Steinbeck felt had made the war possible. *Cannery Row* returned to the world of *Tortilla Flat*. The novel was an account of the adventures and misadventures of workers in a California cannery and their friends. Its sequel, *Sweet Thursday*, appeared in 1954. *The Pearl* was about a Mexican pearl diver who finds a valuable pearl that changes his life, but not in the way he expected. Steinbeck wrote the script for the film version of *The Pearl* (1948), as well as the scripts for *Forgotten Village* (1941), *The Red Pony* (1949), and *Viva Zapata!* (1952).

In 1950, Steinbeck married Elaine Scott. His son John was hospitalized for codeine addiction at age seven, and he also had many problems in later years with drugs and alcohol until his death in 1991. *East of Eden* (1952), Steinbeck's long family novel, was based partly on the story of Cain and Abel. The story is set around the start of the 20th century and explores the saga of two families whose history reflects the formation of the United States. The second half of the book focuses on the lives of the twins, Aron and Caleb, and the woman between them. This novel also was adopted into a film starring James Dean in 1955.

Steinbeck spent a year in England and when he returned to the United States he traveled around his country with his poodle, Charley, and published *Travels with Charley in Search of America* (1962), a memoir of the trip. *The Winter of Our Discontent* (1961), set in contemporary America, was Steinbeck's last major novel, and continued his exploration of the moral dilemmas involved in being fully human. The book was not well received. However, Steinbeck was awarded the Nobel Prize for literature in 1962 ". . . for his realistic as well as imaginative writings, distinguished by a sympathetic humor and a keen social perception." In his Nobel acceptance speech, Steinbeck said, ". . . the writer is delegated to declare and to celebrate man's proven capacity for greatness of heart and spirit—for gallantry in defeat, for

courage, compassion and love. In the endless war against weakness and despair, these are the bright rally flags of hope and of emulation. I hold that a writer who does not passionately believe in the perfectibility of man has no dedication nor any membership in literature."

In later years, Steinbeck spent time abroad, including reporting on the Vietnam War. His modernization of the Arthurian legends, *The Acts of King Arthur and His Noble Knights*, was published posthumously in 1976. Throughout his life John Steinbeck remained a private person who shunned publicity. He died December 20, 1968, in New York City.

### Further Reading

Benson, Jackson J., ed. *The Short Novels of John Steinbeck: Critical Essays with a Checklist to Steinbeck Criticism.* Durham, N.C.: Duke University Press, 1990.

French, Warren, ed. *A Companion to The Grapes of Wrath.* New York: Penguin, 1989.

French, Warren G. *John Steinbeck.* Boston: Twayne, 1975.

Lisca, Peter. *John Steinbeck, Nature and Myth.* New York: Crowell, 1978.

Steinbeck, John, IV, and Nancy Steinbeck. *The Other Side of Eden: Life with John Steinbeck.* Amherst, N.Y.: Prometheus Books, 2001.

## Stevens, Wallace
(1879–1955) *poet*

Regarded by critics as one of the most significant American poets of the 20th century, Wallace Stevens was concerned with portraying the imaginative mind at work. He tried throughout the course of his career to capture "with language the imagination in the act of imagining." He pursued very separate careers as an insurance executive and a poet and rarely participated in the literary world. His work was largely ignored by the general public until the publication in 1954 of his *Collected Poems*. Stevens was the recipient of two National Book Awards, the Bollingen Prize in Poetry, and the Pulitzer Prize.

Wallace Stevens was born in Reading, Pennsylvania, on October 2, 1879. His father, Garrett Barcalow Stevens, was a wealthy country lawyer. Stevens's mother taught school. Stevens attended Reading Boys' High School, then continued his studies at Harvard College from 1893 to 1900. Stevens began writing during his years at Harvard and published his work in the *Harvard Advocate, Trend,* and *Poetry* magazine. Although Stevens never graduated from Harvard, he graduated from a New York law school in 1903 and was admitted to the New York bar the following year.

In 1904, Stevens met Elsie Kachel Moll, a shopgirl who was also from Reading. In 1908, after working at several different law firms, Stevens went to work at the American Binding Company. He married Elsie in 1909 and their one child, Holy Bight, was born in 1924, following the publication in 1923 of Stevens's first book of poems, *Harmonium.* Discouraged by negative reviews, Stevens wrote very little through the 1920s, focusing instead on his budding business career. In 1914, he had taken a position as the vice president of the New York Office of the Equitable Surety Co. of St. Louis. He changed jobs again in 1916 and moved his family to Connecticut, when he went to work as a specialist in investment banking at the Hartford Accident and Indemnity Company, where he worked for the rest of his life. In 1934, he was named a vice president of the company. He has been seen as both odd and ordinary for the unusual way he lived as both an insurance executive and a great poet.

Stevens and his family lived in an upper-middle-class neighborhood in Hartford and took regular vacations to Florida and Cuba. He collected art from abroad and was a gourmand who imported foods from around the world. He also visited New York City frequently, often socializing with Barbara and Henry Church, who encouraged numerous artists and writers during the 1930s and 1940s.

In 1935, *Ideas and Order,* Stevens's second collection of poems, was published to mixed reviews. Some of its critics disliked what they saw as indifference to political and social concerns of the day. His next book, *Owl's Clover* (1937), contained meditations on art and politics in response to his critics. *The Man with the Blue Guitar and Other Poems* also came out in 1937.

Beginning in the early 1940s, Stevens became more creative and more prolific. Some of his most acclaimed poems were written in the latter part of his career. They include "Notes toward a Supreme Fiction," "The Auroras of Autumn," "An Ordinary Evening in New Haven," and "The Planet on the Table." Some of his other book publications include *Parts of a World* (1942), *Notes toward a Supreme Fiction* (1942), *The Auroras of Autumn* (1950), *Selected Poems* (1952), and *The Collected Poems of Wallace Stevens* (1954). In 1946, Stevens was elected to the National Institute of Arts and Letters. His essays on writing were collected in 1951 as *The Necessary Angel.*

Wallace Stevens died in Hartford from complications of cancer on August 2, 1955, the same year that he won the Pulitzer Prize. A rise in interest in his work continued for many years following his death, producing quite a few important critical studies of Stevens and securing his place in American literature.

**Further Reading**
Bates, Milton J. *Wallace Stevens: A Mythology of Self.* Berkeley: University of California Press, 1985.
Burney, William A. *Wallace Stevens:* New York: Twayne Publishers, 1968.
Deese, Helen, and Steven G. Axelrod, eds. *Critical Essays on Wallace Stevens.* Boston: G. K. Hall, 1988.
Dickie, Margaret. *Lyric Contingencies: Emily Dickinson and Wallace Stevens.* Philadelphia: University of Pennsylvania Press, 1991.
Filreis, Alan. *Wallace Stevens and the Actual World.* Princeton, N.J.: Princeton University Press, 1991.
Fisher, Barbara. *Wallace Stevens: The Intensest Rendezvous.* Charlottesville: University Press of Virginia, 1990.
Kermode, Frank. *Wallace Stevens.* New York: Grove Press, 1961.
Sharpe, Tony. *Wallace Stevens: A Literary Life.* New York: Palgrave Macmillan, 2000.
Weston, Susan B. *Wallace Stevens: An Introduction to the Poetry.* New York: Columbia University Press, 1977.

## Stowe, Harriet Beecher
## (Stowe, Harriet Elizabeth Beecher)
(1811–1896) *novelist, nonfiction writer, essayist, poet*

Best known for her antislavery novel *Uncle Tom's Cabin,* Harriet Beecher Stowe was a prolific and popular writer whose work was published in the leading magazines of the day, including *The Atlantic Monthly*, *The Independent*, and *The Christian Union*. She published nearly a book a year between 1862 and 1884 on topics ranging from slavery to religious faith, domesticity, and family life.

The daughter of Congressional minister Lyman Beecher and Roxana Foote Beecher, Harriet Elizabeth Beecher was born on June 14, 1811, in Litchfield, Connecticut. She had one sister and six brothers, and her mother died when she was four years old. Beecher was brought up in a strict, puritanical household. At the age of 11, she entered the seminary at Hartford, Connecticut, that was kept by her older sister, Catherine. At 15, Beecher became an assistant teacher there. Her father remarried about this time and became the president of Lane Theological Seminary. Beecher and

Harriet Beecher Stowe wrote the famous antislavery novel *Uncle Tom's Cabin*. (Library of Congress, Prints and Photographs Division [LC-USZ62-11212])

her sister, Catherine, eventually founded the Western Female Institute, a new seminary.

Beecher's writing career began when she won a prize contest in 1834 of the *Western Monthly Magazine*. Soon thereafter she was a regular contributor of stories and essays. In 1836, she married Calvin E. Stowe, a professor at her father's seminary. Stowe went on to have seven children in the next 14 years. The family lived in poverty until 1850, when Calvin Stowe accepted a position as a professor at Bowdoin College and moved his family to Brunswick, Maine. Despite the pressures of her growing family, Stowe published her first book, *The Mayflower*, in 1843.

Stowe's most famous book, *Uncle Tom's Cabin*, was first published in serial form in the antislavery newspaper *The National Era* in 1851–52. Written in response to the Fugitive Slave Act of 1850, which made it a crime to assist an escaped slave, the novel decried the institution of slavery for its destructive effects on both blacks and whites. The book was translated into 37 languages, smuggled into Russia in Yiddish, and sold in the first five years following publication more than 500,000 copies in the United States alone. It also became one of the most popular plays of the 19th century.

Stowe became an overnight celebrity, and she began to publish her work in some of the most prestigious magazines of the time. She was undoubtedly the most famous female writer publishing in *The Atlantic Monthly* for some time. With this commercial success, Stowe traveled to Europe in 1853, 1856, and 1859, where she became friends with other women writers, including George Eliot, Elizabeth Barrett Browning, and Lady Byron.

In 1953, Stowe published *The Key to Uncle Tom's Cabin*, in which she presented the source material upon which she had based the original novel as a response to critics who questioned the veracity of her portrayal. Another antislavery novel came out in 1856. *Dred: A Tale of the Great Dismal Swamp* told the story of an attempted slave rebellion. Though *Dred* was generally well received, none of Stowe's later works earned the praise and readership of *Uncle Tom's Cabin*, but she continued to write well into her older age.

In 1862, Stowe met President Abraham Lincoln, who is famously quoted as having said to her, "So you are the little woman who wrote the book that started this great war!" Stowe and her husband spent the summers in New England and the winters in an elaborate house in Florida during their latter years. She continued to write, publishing studies of social life, essays, a volume of poems, and more novels, including several that were based on her husband's childhood. *The Pearl of Orr's Island* (1862), *Old-Town Folks* (1869), and *Poganuc People* (1878) incorporated her husband's reminiscences about his youth and stand as one of the first examples of regional writing in New England. During this time, she also befriended Mark Twain and other writers and artists in Hartford.

Stowe's husband died in 1886, and two years later her mental faculties began to fail. She died on July 1, 1896, in Hartford, Connecticut. Her home in Hartford has been rebuilt (across from MARK TWAIN's house) and restored and is now a National Historic Site.

## Further Reading

Adams, John R. *Harriet Beecher Stowe: Updated Version.* Boston: Twayne, 1989.

Ashton, Jean W. *Harriet Beecher Stowe: A Reference Guide.* Boston: G. K. Hall, 1978.

Berkson, Dorothy. "'So We All Became Mothers': Harriet Beecher Stowe, Charlotte Perkins Gilman, and the New World of Women's Culture." *Feminism, Utopia, and Narrative.* Edited by Libby Falk Jones and Sarah Webster Goodwin. Knoxville: University of Tennessee Press, 1990.

Coultrap-McQuin, Susan. *Doing Literary Business: American Women Writers in the Nineteenth Century.* Chapel Hill: University of North Carolina Press, 1990.

Johnston, Norma. *Harriet: The Life and World of Harriet Beecher Stowe.* New York: Beech Tree Press, 1996.

Kelley, Mary. *Private Woman, Public Stage: Literary Domesticity in Nineteenth-Century America.* New York: Oxford University Press, 1984.

Romines, Ann. *The Home Plot: Women, Writing and Domestic Ritual.* Amherst: University of Massachusetts Press, 1992.

Wagenknecht, Edward. *Harriet Beecher Stowe, the Known and Unknown.* New York: Oxford University Press, 1965.

## Strand, Mark
(1934–   ) *poet, translator*

A former poet laureate of the United States, Mark Strand has published nine volumes of poetry, a novel, several books on realism in art, three books for children, and numerous translations. His work is known for its sparseness and general sense of foreboding, its occupation with the surreal, and the precision of its language.

Mark Strand was born in Summerside, Prince Edward Island, Canada, on April 11, 1934, and spent his childhood living in Halifax, Montreal, New York, Philadelphia, and Cleveland. During his teenage years, his family moved around South America, living at different times in Columbia, Peru, and Mexico. He graduated from Antioch College and then went to Yale University, where he studied painting with Joseph Albers and received a B.F.A. degree. About his shift from painting to poetry, Strand said, "I woke up and found that's what I was doing. I don't think these kinds of lifetime obsessions are arrived at rationally." He went on to get his M.A. at the Iowa Writers' Workshop.

Strand has worked as a teacher during most of his career. He taught at Mt. Holyoke College in 1967, and at Brooklyn College from 1970 to 1972. Since then he has held visiting professorships at various places, including Columbia University, the University of Virginia, Yale, the University of Utah, the Iowa Writers' Workshop, and Harvard. He was the Elliott Coleman Professor of Poetry at Johns Hopkins University, where he taught in the Writing Seminars until 1998. Strand now teaches at the University of Chicago as a member of the Committee on Social Thought.

Strand has published 10 books of poems, including *Blizzard of One*, which appeared in 1998 and won the Pulitzer Prize; *Dark Harbor* (1993); *The Continuous Life* (1990); *Selected Poems* (1980); *The Story of Our Lives* (1973); and *Reasons for Moving* (1968). He has also published a book of short stories, *Mr. and Mrs. Baby* (1985), several volumes of translation of works by Rafael Alberti and Carlos Drummond de Andrade, and books on contemporary artists William Bailey and Edward Hopper, as well as three books for children. His collection of critical essays, *Weather of Words: Poetic*

*Invention,* was published in 2000, as was *The Making of a Poem,* which he cowrote with Eavan Boland. In addition to his writing, he has edited several anthologies, among them *The Golden Ecco Anthology* (1994) and *The Best American Poetry 1991.*

Strand's honors and awards include two Fulbright awards, three fellowships from the National Endowment for the Arts, and fellowships from the Ingram Merrill Foundation, the Guggenheim Foundation, and the Rockefeller Foundation. In 1979, Strand was awarded the Fellowship of the Academy of American Poets, and in 1982 he was writer-in-residence at the American Academy in Rome. The very prestigious John D. and Catherine T. MacArthur Foundation "genius" award was given to Strand in 1987. He was the U.S. Poet Laureate in 1990–91, the 1993 recipient of Yale's Bollingen Prize for Poetry, and the 1999 recipient of the Pulitzer Prize for poetry.

**Further Reading**

Infante, Victor D. "Stranded: Poet Mark Strand Preaches Political Indifference at UCI," About.com Poetry. Available online. URL: http://poetry.about.com/library/weekly/aa031400a.htm. Downloaded January 30, 2003.

Maio, Samuel. *Creating Another Self: Voice in Modern American Personal Poetry.* Kirksville, Mo.: Thomas Jefferson University Press, 1995.

PBS Online NewsHour. "The Pulitzer Poet." Available online. URL: http://www.pbs.org/newshour/bb/entertainment/jan-june99/pulitzer_4-15.html. Posted April 15, 1999.

## Styron, William
(1925–   ) *novelist, memoirist*

William Styron is known for setting his fiction, especially the novels *Sophie's Choice* (1979) and *The Confessions of Nat Turner* (1967), in the context of actual historical events and for addressing some of the most fundamental and unresolved moral dilemmas of modern times. For this, he has been both praised and criticized. In addition to publishing several highly acclaimed novels, Styron won an even larger audience when he published his memoir of crippling depression and recovery, *Darkness Visible,* in 1990.

William Styron was born on June 11, 1925, in Newport News, Virginia, to William and Pauline Styron. His father was a shipyard engineer who suffered with depression, and his mother died when Styron was 13. His ancestors were Scandinavian and had settled in Virginia in the early 1700s. Although they were not slaveowners, Styron's grandfather fought in the Confederate army during the Civil War and as a young boy, Styron loved to hear stories about his wartime adventures.

Styron was rather rebellious as a young boy. He was sent to boarding school after his mother's death, but he never focused very well on his studies, though he knew from an early age that he wanted to write. When Styron graduated from high school, World War II was being fought, and he joined the marines. When the war ended, Styron, who had become a first lieutenant, left the marines and enrolled at Duke University, where he graduated in 1947. He moved from North Carolina to New York and worked briefly as an assistant editor at McGraw-Hill. Styron also began studying with Hiram Haydn at the New School for Social Research. In 1951, at age 26, Styron published his first novel, *Lie Down in Darkness.* The book, which tells the wartime story of a young Virginia woman's troubled family and her eventual descent into suicide, was well received by critics, won the American Academy's Prix de Rome, and launched Styron's literary career.

Styron lived in Paris for a short time in the early 1950s and helped launch *The Paris Review.* In 1953, he married Rose Burgunder, a published poet, and the couple moved to Roxbury, Connecticut, where they settled into an old farmhouse. They had four children—Susanna, Paola, Thomas, and Alexandria, and eventually acquired a summer house on Martha's Vineyard.

Styron published his second novel, *The Long March,* in 1957. It was followed by *Set This House on Fire* (1960) and then by what is perhaps Styron's most famous work, *The Confessions of Nat Turner* (1967). This novel, which won the Pulitzer Prize, was both praised by literary critics and despised by many in the African-American community for what they saw as a clichéd portrayal of an important figure in black history. Some went so far as to accuse Styron of racism. About the reception of his book, Styron said at a forum in 1998, "I was especially lacerated and hurt that it was labeled racist. That was hard to take for a writer who attempted to expose the horrors and evils of slavery. . . . Basically it is a very politically incorrect book written by a white man trying to seize his own interpretation and put it into the soul and heart of a black man."

It was more than 10 years before Styron published another book. *Sophie's Choice* appeared in 1979 and again put the author in the spotlight, with a compelling story that is deeply engaged in 20th-century world history. The book was well received in general, but there were critics who argued that Styron was exploiting the tragedy of yet another ethnic community, this time Jews after the Holocaust. *Sophie's Choice* was made into a prize-winning film, starring Meryl Streep and Kevin Kline, that appeared in the early 1980s. Styron's book of essays, *The Quiet Dust and Other Writings*, appeared in 1979, as well.

Styron's 1990 memoir, *Darkness Visible: A Memoir of Madness*, tells the story of his struggle with depression and alcoholism. A short and eloquent book, it became extremely popular and introduced Styron to many new readers. Styron continued to write and publish throughout the 1990s. *A Tidewater Morning: Three Tales from Youth* appeared in 1993, and *Fathers and Daughters: In Their Own Words* came out the following year, coedited with Mariana Ruth Cook.

Styron's many awards include the Howells Medal of the American Academy of Arts and Letters for *The Confessions of Nat Turner*; an American Book Award and National Book Critics Circle Award nomination, both in 1980, for *Sophie's Choice*; a Connecticut Arts Award in 1984; the Cinco del Duca prize in 1985; the Edward MacDowell Medal in 1988; the Bobst Award in 1989; a National Magazine Award in 1990; a National Medal of Arts in 1993; a Medal of Honor from the National Arts Club in 1995; and a Common Wealth Award in 1995. He also has honorary doctorates from Duke University and Davidson College in Davidson, North Carolina.

Styron has developed quite a few friendships over the years with other writers, including PHILIP ROTH, JAMES BALDWIN (who lived in Styron's guesthouse at one point), Art Buchwald, and Peter Matthieson. Styron still lives with his wife of more than 50 years. His daughter, Susanna Styron, made a feature-length film from Styron's short story "Shadrach."

## Further Reading

Clarke, John Henrik, ed., *William Styron's "Nat Turner": Ten Black Writers Respond.* Boston: Beacon Press, 1968.

Duff, John B., and Peter M. Mitchell, eds., *The Nat Turner Rebellion: The Historical Event and the Modern Controversy.* New York: Harper and Row, 1971.

Friedman, Melvin J., and Irving Malin, eds., *William Styron's "The Confessions of Nat Turner": A Critical Handbook.* Belmont, Calif.: Wadsworth, 1970.

Ratner, Marc L., *William Styron.* New York: Twayne, 1972.

Tischler, Nancy M., ed., "*The Confessions of Nat Turner:* A Symposium," *Barat Review,* 6 (1971): 3–37.

West, James. *William Styron: A Life.* New York: Random House, 1998.

# T

## Tan, Amy
### (Amy Ruth Tan)
(1952– )  *novelist, children's fiction writer*

The author of one of the most popular and critically acclaimed novels of the late 20th century, Amy Tan has gone on from her debut success with *The Joy Luck Club* to pen several other best-selling works of fiction, including *The Kitchen God's Wife, The Hundred Secret Senses,* and *The Bonesetter's Daughter.* She has also written two books for children, *The Moon Lady* and *The Chinese Siamese Cat.* Tan is often considered part of a movement of Asian-American women writers that includes MAXINE HONG KINGSTON and Wakako Yamauchi. Her work has been highly praised for its fresh treatment of universal themes and its thorough exploration of the lives of Chinese-American women.

Amy Ruth Tan was born in Oakland, California, on February 19, 1952, the only daughter of three children of John Yuehhan Tan and Daisy Tu Ching Tan. Her parents had left China in 1949, the year of the communist takeover, and moved to California. Both her parents were professionals—her father worked as an electrical engineer and was also a Baptist preacher in China; Tan's mother was a vocational nurse. Tan became a published writer at the age of eight, when her essay on the local public library was published in her hometown newspaper, but her path to becoming a novelist was rather long and circuitous.

When Tan was 14, her father and one of her brothers died of brain tumors. In 1968, amidst the emotional turmoil and sadness of the family's losses, Tan moved with her mother and surviving brother to Switzerland, where she completed high school. The family returned to California the year after Tan's high school graduation and settled in Santa Clara. Tan attended eight different colleges before graduating from San Jose State University with a B.A. degree in English and linguistics in 1973 and an M.A. degree in linguistics in 1974. Tan married Louis DeMattei, an attorney, in 1974, and did graduate work at the University of California at Berkeley from 1974 to 1976. She then became a consultant to the Alameda County Association for the Mentally Retarded, a job she held from 1976 to 1981. From 1981 to 1983, she worked as a reporter, managing editor, and associate publisher for *Emergency Room Reports.* After 1983, she worked as a freelance technical writer, working around the clock to craft speeches for her high-paying business clients. But Tan took no joy in the work, and began writing fiction as a diversion, hoping it would curb her workaholic tendencies. *The Joy Luck Club* (1989) was the result.

The novel, which deals with the relationships between Chinese-born mothers and U.S.-born daughters, won the Bay Area Book Reviewers Award for best book of fiction and the American Library Association Award for best book for young adults, and was a nominee for the prestigious National Book Critics Circle Award. A best-seller, it was made into a major motion picture in 1993.

Tan cowrote the screenplay for the film, which enjoyed a great deal of popular and critical success as well.

*The Kitchen God's Wife,* Tan's second novel, appeared in 1991. Covering much of the same ground as the first novel, this book also won rave reviews. A more mixed response greeted the third novel, *The Hundred Secret Senses,* which came out in 1993. Instead of addressing a mother-daughter relationship, this book follows the cultural conflicts endured by a pair of sisters and employs an emphasis on mysticism and even surrealism. *The Bonesetter's Daughter,* another story that follows a second-generation Chinese-American woman and is concerned with the nature of storytelling, was published in 2001 to excellent critical reviews and the popular success that Tan's other works have enjoyed.

In addition to her fiction for adults, Tan has found much success writing for children, too. *The Chinese Siamese Cat,* a folktale in which a mother cat tells her kittens the true story of their ancestry, has been made into a PBS cartoon series, *Sagwa,* with Tan supervising the writing and production. Tan lives in San Francisco with DeMattei, her husband of 27 years. Her books have been translated into 23 languages.

## Further Reading

Hawley, John C. "Assimilation and Resistance in Female Fiction of Immigration: Bharati Mukherjee, Amy Tan, and Christine Bell." *Rediscovering America 1492–1992: National, Cultural and Disciplinary Boundaries Re-Examined.* Edited by Leslie Bary, Janet Gold, Marketta Laurila, Arnulfo Ramirez, Joseph Ricapito, and Jesus Torrecilla. Baton Rouge: Louisiana State University Press, 1992, pp. 222–234.

Heung, Marina. "Daughter-Text/Mother-Text: Matrilineage in Amy Tan's *Joy Luck Club.*" *Feminist Studies* 19, no. 3 (1993), pp. 597–616.

Kramer, Barbara. *Amy Tan, Author of* The Joy Luck Club. Springfield, N.J.: Enslow, 1996.

Wong, Sau-ling Cynthia. "'Sugar Sisterhood': Situating the Amy Tan Phenomenon." *The Ethnic Canon: Histories, Institutions, and Interventions.* Edited by David Palumbo-Liu. Minneapolis: University of Minnesota Press, 1995, pp. 174–210.

## Tate, Allen
### (John Orley Allen Tate)
(1899–1979) *poet, literary critic, essayist, novelist*

A master poet and literary critic, Allen Tate was an influential figure not only of the so-called Southern Renaissance, but also of the modernist movement in literature. His essays articulated the framework for southern cultural achievement and his poems stretched the limits of formal verse. He is remembered as one of the founding members of the Fugitives, the group of writers at Vanderbilt University in the 1920s that included JOHN CROWE RANSOM and ROBERT PENN WARREN, among others.

Allen Tate was born on November 19, 1899, near Winchester in Clarke County, Kentucky, to John Orley Tate, a businessman, and Eleanor Parke Custis Varnell. His two brothers were more than 10 years older than he. Tate's father's business interests in lumber, real estate, and stocks kept the family moving. Sometimes they lived in as many as three different places in one year. When his father's business and his parents' marriage failed around 1911, Tate lived with his mother, who continued to move frequently.

Tate became a serious student of music as an adolescent. From 1916 to 1917, he studied the violin at the Cincinnati Conservatory of Music. His poem "The Buried Lake" implies that Tate felt "the death of youth" when he failed to fulfill his musical ambitions. He enrolled in Vanderbilt University in Nashville, Tennessee, in 1918. At the beginning of his senior year, he was invited by English professor Donald Davidson to join a group of men, including Professor John Crowe Ransom, in their regular meetings to discuss literature. The group became known as the Fugitives, when they began publishing a literary magazine by that name in 1922 and that was instrumental in signaling a rebirth in Southern literature.

By the time he was 20 years old, Tate had immersed himself in reading the French symbolist poets, W. B. Yeats, and T. S. ELIOT, about whom he once wrote, "This man, though by no means famous at that time, was evidently so thoroughly my contemporary that I had been influenced by him before I had read a line of his verse."

Tate withdrew from Vanderbilt in 1922, when he came down with a slight case of tuberculosis. After recuperating in the North Carolina mountains for several months, he returned to the university in 1923, where he spent his final semester sharing a room with Robert Penn Warren, who would remain Tate's close friend throughout his life.

During this time, Tate worked with Ridley Wills, another of the Fugitive poets, on *The Golden Mean,* which was a parody of Eliot's *The Waste Land.* He graduated magna cum laude from Vanderbilt in 1923, though his diploma was dated 1922. In 1924, Tate moved to New York City, where he met and became friends with HART CRANE. On a visit home to Kentucky that year to see Warren, he began a relationship with Caroline Gordon, a novelist, and the couple married in New York in May 1925. Their daughter, Nancy, was born in September but lived with her maternal grandparents in Kentucky for the first three years of her life. Tate and Gordon remained in New York, where Tate wrote freelance articles and reviews for publications such as the *Nation* and the *New Republic,* did editorial work for pulp romance magazines, and performed janitorial duties in the building where they lived. Gordon worked for English novelist Ford Madox Ford during this time. It was during these first years in New York that Tate established many of the literary relationships that would remain important to him throughout his life. Some of his friends included Edmund Wilson, John Peale Bishop, Malcolm Cowley, and Kenneth Burke. He shared a house with Hart Crane in rural Patterson, New York, during the winter of 1925. In 1926, Tate wrote the introduction to Crane's first collection of poems, *White Buildings,* which came out in 1926.

Tate's first book publications appeared in 1928: *Mr. Pope and Other Poems* and a biography entitled *Stonewall Jackson: The Good Soldier.* The first book of poems contained several well known Tate poems, including his often-anthologized "Ode to the Confederate Dead." The biography was to be the first of three biographies of Confederate heroes from the Civil War. The second, *Jefferson Davis: His Rise and Fall,* was published in 1929, but the third book, *Robert E. Lee,* was never completed, and Tate eventually abandoned the project.

Tate won a Guggenheim Fellowship in 1928, which allowed him to travel to London and Paris. In London, he met Eliot, and in Paris, he met GERTRUDE STEIN, became friends with ERNEST HEMINGWAY, and visited with several other writers. He returned to the United States in 1930 and settled with his family on the Cumberland River near Clarksville, Tennessee, in an old farmhouse named "Benfolly" for Tate's older brother, who had become a successful businessman and purchased the house for his younger brother.

Tate's life and work embraced agrarianism. His contribution to the seminal collection of southern writers, *I'll Take My Stand* (1930) was an essay entitled "Remarks on Southern Religion." The book stood in defense of the agriculturally based rural South and championed the traditional way of life as opposed to the industrialized urban life of the North.

*Poems: 1928–1931* (1932) and *The Mediterranean and Other Poems* (1936) were collected into Tate's first *Selected Poems* in 1937. This book brought together all of the shorter poems on which Tate's literary reputation still stands. Tate's one novel, *The Fathers,* was published in 1938 and featured Pleasant Hill, his mother's homeplace in Fairfax County, Virginia. The novel firmly secured Tate's place in American literature. Many accolades followed. He became a poet-in-residence at Princeton University in 1939 and remained there until 1942. In 1943, he was named consultant in poetry at the Library of Congress. He became editor of the *Sewanee Review* in 1944 and editor of belles lettres at Henry Holt publishers in New York in 1946. He returned to academia in 1948, when he accepted a three-year appointment at New York University. In 1948, two collections of Tate's essays and poems were published—*On the Limits of Poetry: Selected Essays, 1928–1948* and *Poems, 1922–1947.* The book of poems included one of Tate's most famous long poems from his later career, "Seasons of the Soul."

In 1951, Tate became a tenured professor at the University of Minnesota, where he taught until his retirement in 1968. During the latter part of his career, he frequently traveled abroad as a Fulbright lecturer, visiting England, France, Italy, and India. He published *The Man of Letters in the Modern*

*World* in 1952, which collected some of his most influential essays. He also wrote a sequence of autobiographical poems in the 1950s—"Our Cousin, Mr. Poe" and "The Angelic Imagination."

In his last two decades, Tate's personal life underwent much change. He and his first wife, Caroline Gordon, divorced in 1959, the same year that he married the poet Isabella Gardner. Gardner and Tate eventually divorced, and Tate married Helen Heinz, a former student of his at Minnesota, in 1966. In 1967, Heinz gave birth to twin sons, one of whom died in an accident in 1968 following the family's move to Sewanee, Tennessee. A third son was born in 1969. Tate died in Nashville on February 9, 1979.

### Further Reading

Bishop, Ferman. *Allen Tate*. New York: Twayne, 1967.

Buffington, Robert. "Allen Tate: Society, Vocation, Communion." *Southern Review* 18, no. 1 (winter 1982): 62–72.

Chabot, C. Barry. "Allen Tate and the Limits of Tradition." *Southern Quarterly* 26, no. 3 (spring 1988): 50–66.

Doreski, William. *The Years of Our Friendship: Robert Lowell and Allen Tate*. Jackson: University Press of Mississippi, 1990.

Dunaway, John M., ed. *Exiles and Fugitives: The Letters of Jacques and Raissa Maritain, Allen Tate, and Caroline Gordon*. Baton Rouge: Louisiana State University Press, 1992.

Hemphill, George. *Allen Tate*. Minneapolis: University of Minnesota Press, 1964.

Rubin, Louis D., Jr. "Allen Tate 1899–1979." *Sewanee Review* 87 (1979): 267–273.

Squires, Radcliffe. *Allen Tate: A Literary Biography*. New York: Pegasus, 1971.

Underwood, Thomas A. *Allen Tate: Orphan of the South*. Princeton, N.J.: Princeton University Press, 2000.

## Teasdale, Sara
### (Sarah Trevor Teasdale)
(1884–1933) *poet*

Known for the understated elegance of her poetry, Sara Teasdale wrote at the very beginning of the 20th century in what is considered to be the femi-nine school. Her highly personal lyric poems rose from the life of her emotions and most often explored the subjects of love and nature. Like the 19th-century poets EMILY DICKINSON and Christina Rossetti, Teasdale found reclusiveness to be the answer to the difficulties of pursuing the writing life. By the time of her suicide at the age of 48, Teasdale had published five volumes of poetry, one of which, *Love Songs*, was awarded the annual prize of the Columbia University Poetry Society (the forerunner of the Pulitzer Prize) in 1918.

Born Sarah (she dropped the "h" when she published her first poetry) Trevor Teasdale on August 8, 1884, in St. Louis, Missouri, to well-educated, middle-aged parents, she was the youngest child in a prominent family. Her father was John Warren Teasdale, a well-known businessman with a fine stable. Her mother, Mary Elizabeth Willard Teasdale, was socially prominent in St. Louis, and both parents were staunch Baptists.

Teasdale received a typical Victorian upbringing. She was tutored at home before attending private local girls' schools. She graduated from high school in 1903, and then traveled to Europe a couple years later. Her first book of poems *Sonnets to Duse, and Other Poems*, was published in 1907. *Helen of Troy and Other Poems* appeared in 1911 and brought her considerable recognition within the literary community. She became lifelong friends at this time with Louis Untermeyer and his wife, Jean, who were great supporters of her writing. Teasdale first entertained thoughts of suicide in 1913 when a relationship she depended upon failed. One year later, on December 19, 1914, Teasdale married Ernst B. Filsinger. *Rivers to the Sea* came out in 1915, with *Flame and Shadow* following in 1920, and *Rainbow Gold: Poems Old and New Selected for Boys and Girls* (1922), followed by *Stars To-night: Verses New and Old for Boys and Girls* (1930), and *A Country House* (1932). The award-winning *Love Songs* was published in 1926. *Strange Victory* did not appear until 1933, several years following her divorce from Filsinger and just a few months after her suicide.

Teasdale's work has always been noted for its simplicity and clarity. She wrote almost solely in classical forms, and her subjects were romantic love and nature. Some of her most often cited poems include "There Will Come So It Rains," "Barter," and "The Metropolitan Tower."

From early childhood until her death, Teasdale suffered a number of health problems that were associated with emotional stress. She often experienced sudden chills, fatigue, nervousness, and weakness, symptoms very similar to those experienced by modern sufferers of chronic fatigue syndrome. Teasdale struggled with what she saw as an internal struggle between her Puritan, Christian upbringing and her artistic, pagan leanings. Teasdale lived at home until her marriage at age 30, and despite her Christian background, she reportedly created an altar to Aphrodite in her room and recited prayers before it. She once wrote in a letter that the goddess had been more real to her "than the virgin."

Sara Teasdale committed suicide on January 29, 1933, in New York. *Mirror of the Heart*, a posthumous collection of her poems, was published by Macmillan in 1984.

## Further Reading

Drake, William. *Sara Teasdale, Woman and Poet*. New York: Harper & Row, 1979.

Sara Teasdale. Available online. URL: http://community2.webtv.net/desertstreams/TEASDALEHOME MENU. Downloaded January 30, 2003.

Tribute to Sara Teasdale. Available online: http://home.att.net/~Teasdale/sara.html. Downloaded January 30, 2003.

## Thompson, Hunter S.
### (Hunter Stockton Thompson)
(1937– ) *novelist, essayist, journalist*

Known as the inventor of "gonzo journalism," in which the reporter's personal thoughts and beliefs are considered essential components of news reporting, Hunter S. Thompson was a central figure in the countercultural revolution of the 1960s. He is most famous for *Fear and Loathing in Las Vegas*, an autobiographical novel that became a film in 1998 with director Terry Gilliam and star Johnny Depp.

Hunter S. Thompson was born on July 18, 1937, in Louisville, Kentucky. Although he was quite athletic as a young boy, Thompson's interests and abili-

ties leaned more toward sports reporting as a teenager. He organized a sports league for children under 14 years of age and began writing sports columns for the *Southern Star*, a mimeographed paper edited by a similarly precocious adolescent. Just before he was scheduled to graduate from high school, Thompson and several friends found themselves in trouble with the law. Thompson was sentenced to 60 days in juvenile detention—ultimately reduced to 30 days for good behavior—to be followed immediately by enlistment in the U.S. Army. Thompson joined the air force instead and following boot camp was stationed at Eglin Air Force Base and assigned to electronics school, which he reportedly despised. His early experience with journalism served him well when he learned that the base's newspaper needed an editor. The *Command Courier* became Thompson's new post, and he remained there until he managed to get out of the air force with an honorable discharge in the fall of 1957.

Following his discharge, Thompson traveled to South America, where he spent the remainder of the 1950s working for various newspapers. When he returned to the United States, Thompson wrote the novel *Rum Diary* during a period in Puerto Rico in 1959, then moved to San Francisco, where he began to hang out with other writers, including KEN KESEY, Tom Wolfe, and ALLEN GINSBERG. He began a legendary relationship with the Hell's Angels, chronicled in *Hell's Angels: A Strange and Terrible Saga*, and immersed himself fully in 1960s counterculture. He also participated in the Chicago Democratic Convention demonstrations, where he was assaulted by police while working as a freelance reporter for a magazine.

Thompson's first book publication was *Hell's Angels: A Strange and Terrible Saga*, which appeared in 1967 and was based on Thompson's relationship with the Hell's Angels in San Francisco during the early 1960s. By 1970, Thompson was living in Aspen, Colorado, where he ran for sheriff. His article about his campaign, "The Battle of Aspen," appeared in *Rolling Stone* magazine and initiated a long and fruitful relationship between the two. This relationship was further strengthened when *Fear and Loathing in Las Vegas* appeared in *Rolling Stone* in two parts. Shortly after the book's publication in 1971, *Rolling Stone* decided to make Thompson its political correspondent. He was the magazine's reporter during the Nixon-McGovern presidential campaign of 1972. He reported from the heart of the McGovern campaign and went on to write many more articles over the years.

Thompson's other major publications include *Fear and Loathing: On the Campaign Trail '72* (1973), which was originally published as a series of articles in *Rolling Stone*. *The Curse of Lono* appeared in 1984, and *Rum Diary* was first published in 1999, 40 years after it was written. Thompson's other books are compilations of articles and essays. They include *Generation of Swine: Tales of Shame and Degradation in the '80s* (1989), *Songs of the Doomed* (1990), *The Great Shark Hunt* (1991), *Screwjack* (1991), *Better Than Sex* (1995), *The Proud Highway: Saga of a Desperate Southern Gentleman* (1998), and *Fear and Loathing in America: The Brutal Odyssey of an Outlaw Journalist, 1968–1976* (2000).

Hunter S. Thompson lives in Woody Creek Canyon in western Colorado, down the valley from the town of Aspen. Owl Farm, the name of his home, is a rustic ranch and rod and gun club, where shooters can practice hitting clay pigeons. He continues to contribute articles to national and international publications.

**Further Reading**

Burns, Alex. "Hunter S. Thompson." Disinformation. Available online. URL: http://www.disinfo.com/pages/dossier/id361/pg1.html. Posted on March 4, 2001.

Carroll, E. Jean. *Hunter: The Strange and Savage Life of Hunter S. Thompson*. New York: Dutton, 1993.

McKeen, William. *Hunter S. Thompson*. Boston: G. K. Hall, 1991.

Perry, Paul. *Fear and Loathing: The Strange and Terrible Saga of Hunter S. Thompson*. New York: Thunder's Mouth Press, 1993.

Whitmer, Peter. *When the Going Gets Weird: An Unauthorized Biography*. New York: Hyperion, 1993.

## Thoreau, Henry David
(1817–1862) *essayist, poet*

Known as one of the leading personalities in New England transcendentalism, Henry David Thoreau was an essayist of the first order, a sometime poet, and a practical philosopher. His autobiographical book about life at Walden Pond, where he went to live in close contact with nature, is still his most famous work, but his essay "Civil Disobedience" made a significant impact on the world, influencing the passive resistance campaign of Mohandas K. Gandhi in India as well as the civil rights politics of Martin Luther King, Jr., in America.

Born in Concord, Massachusetts, on July 12, 1817, to John and Cynthia (Dunbar) Thoreau, Henry David Thoreau studied at the Concord Academy from 1828 through 1833, and then enrolled at Harvard University, where he graduated in 1837. He taught for a brief period during his last year at Harvard and following his graduation. His first position was in Canton, Massachusetts, in 1835–36, the same year that he contracted the tuberculosis that would plague him off and on for the rest of his life. Thoreau worked at Center School in 1837 but resigned after just two weeks on the job because he did not believe in the use of corporal punishment.

When he left Center School, Thoreau returned to Concord and took a job in his father's pencil factory from 1837 until 1838, then again in 1844 and in 1849–1850. In 1838, Thoreau and his brother, John, opened a school in Concord, and Thoreau taught there from 1838 through 1841, when his brother became fatally ill. He died that year from tetanus. Starting in 1848, Thoreau lectured regularly at Concord Lyceum. He also worked as a land surveyor. Thoreau met RALPH WALDO EMERSON in Concord and went to live in his house from 1841 to 1843 and again from 1847 to 1848, working as a handyman. He also tutored William Emerson's sons in Staten Island, New York, in 1843.

In 1845, Thoreau built a home on the shores of Walden Pond, where he lived until September 6, 1847. As wrote in his book *Walden*, an account of his life there, "I went to the woods because I wished to live deliberately, to front only the essential facts of life, and see if I could learn what it had to teach, and not, when I came to die, discover that I had not lived." He began construction of the cabin early in the year and moved in on July 4, 1845. Although his aim was to be as self-sufficient

Henry David Thoreau is often credited with inspiring the civil disobedience of Mohandas K. Gandhi and Martin Luther King, Jr. *(Library of Congress, Prints and Photographs Division [LC-USZ61-361])*

as possible, Thoreau took a number of things with him when he moved to Walden Pond, including seed, lumber, clothes, nails, and other practical supplies. He also received help from his friends when it came time to put the roof on his cabin. He spent his time there reading and writing in his journal, growing his own food, and walking the woods. *Walden*, published in 1854, was crafted largely from his many journal entries.

Thoreau's first book, however, was *A Week on the Concord and Merrimack Rivers*, which came out in 1849 and tells a story based on a canoe trip Thoreau and his brother, John, took in 1839. His most famous essay, "Civil Disobedience," was published in 1849 as well. It was a response to a night Thoreau spent in jail when he refused to pay his taxes, citing his opposition to the Mexican War and the institution of slavery.

Following his time at Walden, Thoreau lectured frequently and traveled a few times to Maine and once to Minnesota. He wrote prolifically and published numerous essays during the 1850s. Some of these include "A Yankee in Canada," "Slavery in Massachusetts," "Chesuncook," "A Plea for Captain John Brown," and "The Succession of Forest Trees." In addition to his writing, Thoreau was a pioneer conservationist, one of the first Americans to write about his understanding of the country's limited resources. He distrusted institutions, including government and religion.

Thoreau died having published just two books, both of which were out of print at his death. Although Thoreau never achieved any commercial success as a writer, his works now fill 20 volumes. He wrote almost constantly throughout his life and did prepare some of his journals for publication shortly before his death. Emerson edited his letters, and they were published posthumously in 1865. *Poems of Nature* appeared in 1895, and *Collected Poems* in 1943. His 14-volume collection of journals was published in 1906. In 1999, *Wild Fruits* was published. Written in the last decade of his life, when Thoreau resided in the third-floor attic of his parents' house, the book records his observations of the vegetation around Concord and argues against the destruction of the wilderness. Henry David Thoreau died in Concord from tuberculosis on May 6, 1862.

**Further Reading**

Bridges, William E. *Spokesmen for the Self: Emerson, Thoreau, Whitman.* Scranton, Pa.: Chandler, 1971.

Bridgman, Richard. *Dark Thoreau.* Lincoln: University of Nebraska Press, 1982.

Cain, William E., ed. *A Historical Guide to Henry David Thoreau.* New York: Oxford University Press, 2000.

Harding, Walter. *The Days of Henry Thoreau: A Biography.* New York: Knopf, 1965.

Neufeldt, Leonard. *The Economist: Henry Thoreau and Enterprise.* New York: Oxford University Press, 1989.

Richardson, Robert D., Jr. *Henry Thoreau: A Life of the Mind.* Berkeley: University of California Press, 1986.

Schneider, Richard J. *Henry David Thoreau.* Boston: Twayne, 1987.

# Thurber, James

(1894–1961) *short story writer, cartoonist, playwright*

James Thurber was a short story writer who is considered one of America's greatest humorists. He focused on the small events of life and the frustrations of the modern world, using a wry humor that showed great sensitivity to human fears and follies. Thurber's stories influenced later writers such as KURT VONNEGUT and Joseph Heller. Thurber's work consisted mostly of shot stories, fables, and cartoons, and is collected in more than 30 volumes. In addition to his fame as a writer, mainly for The *New Yorker*, Thurber was a well-known artist and cartoonist as well. His surreal, minimalist sketches were a regular feature of the magazine, where they became prototypes of its modern, sophisticated cartoons.

James Thurber was born on December 8, 1894, in Columbus, Ohio, the son of Charles Thurber and Mary Fisher Thurber. His father was a minor politician and his mother was a strong-minded woman and a practical joker. Thurber was shot in the eye while playing a bow-and-arrow game with his brothers as a child, causing blindness in one eye. As a result, he was unable to participate in games and sports with other children, and developed a rich fantasy life that became the basis of his writing. Thurber was elected class president in his senior year at East High School and graduated with honors. He entered Ohio State University (OSU) in 1913 and struggled with the required gym courses, as well as in science labs, partly because of his poor eyesight. Thurber reported for the college paper, the *Lantern*, and was editor-in-chief of the *Sundial* humor and literary magazine. He left OSU in 1918 without taking a degree.

Thurber then worked for the State Department as a code clerk in Washington, D.C., and at the U.S. Embassy in Paris. In 1921, he returned to Columbus and began working as a reporter for the *Columbus Dispatch*. He also wrote and directed musical comedies for the Scarlet Mask Club at OSU. Thurber married Althea Adams, an Ohio State beauty with a dominant personality, in 1922. They later had a daughter. In 1925, Thurber went to Paris to write for the *Chicago Tribune*, then to New York City the following year to report for the *New York Evening Post*. He joined the *New Yorker* in 1927, which was newly established, and it was there that he found his clear, concise prose style.

Thurber's first book, *Is Sex Necessary?* (1929), which was cowritten with his *New Yorker* colleague E. B. White, was a parody of the popular sex and psychology books of the day. The book contained Thurber's drawings on the subject and instantly established him as a true comedic talent. Thurber occasionally looked to his background for his work. He depicted his comedic mother in *My Life and Hard Times* (1933) and reportedly based on his father, who had dreams of being an actor or lawyer, the typical small, slight men of many of Thurber's stories. During his career, Thurber experimented with many types of writing. He said that his ideas were influenced by the Midwestern atmosphere he grew up in, movies, and comic strips. After several years of difficulty and separations, Thurber and his wife divorced in 1935 and he married Helen Wismer, an editor.

Thurber reduced his role at the *New Yorker* in 1933 from staff member to contributor. In 1939, he collaborated with college buddy Elliot Nugent on *The Male Animal*, a play about OSU, which was an enormous success on Broadway. Thurber published two collections of fables during his lifetime, *Fables for Our Time* (1940) and *Further Fables for Our Time* (1956). Fantasy was his forte, and some critics consider these two works among Thurber's best. In them, he gives age-old wisdom a new and humorous twist. JOHN UPDIKE has said that "Thurber's genius was to make of our despair a humorous fable." In the fable "The Shrike and the Chipmunk," a female chipmunk leaves her husband and says that he will never survive on his own, but he gets along fine until she returns and gets them both killed during a morning walk she insists on taking. Its moral: "Early to rise and early to bed makes a male healthy and wealthy and dead."

One of Thurber's most famous works was his 1947 story "The Secret Life of Walter Mitty." The title character is a meek, mild-mannered, henpecked husband who escapes his everyday existence through heroic fantasies. "Humour is emotional chaos remembered in tranquillity," Thurber said. It was taken up by a psychologist and "Walter Mitty Syndrome" was put forward in a British medical journal as a clinical condition, which manifested itself in compulsive fantasizing.

Thurber's failed first marriage and his declining health steadily darkened his outlook as he aged. Ten of the 47 pieces in *Further Fables for Our Time* consisted of lightly veiled essays supporting free speech. The *New Yorker* refused to publish some of these fables, although the collection had just won the American Library Association's Liberty and Justice Award for 1956, because of political pressure. Thurber was blacklisted by the House Un-American Activities Committee.

By the 1950s, Thurber was almost completely blind, but he continued to work. He published modern fairy tales for children, *The 13 Clocks* (1950) and *The Wonderful O* (1957), which were both quite successful. His children's tales displayed a cynical undercurrent and showed at times a great deal of bitterness. Despite his poor eyesight, Thurber continued to compose stories in his head, and he played himself in 88 performances of the play *The Thurber Carnival* (1945). Thurber published his memoirs under the title *The Years with Ross* (1959), which referred to his former boss at the *New Yorker*, Harold Ross. Thurber's writing continued to appear in the *New Yorker* until his death.

During his life, he received a number of honorary degrees, including doctorates from Kenyon College, Williams College, and Yale University, among others. In later years, Thurber and Helen Wismer Lived at West Cornwall, Connecticut. He collapsed one evening after a theater opening and lingered a month before finally succumbing to respiratory failure on November 2, 1961.

**Further Reading**

Grauer, Neil A. *Remember Laughter: A Life of James Thurber.* Omaha: University of Nebraska Press, 1994.

Kinney, Harrison. *James Thurber: His Life and Times.* New York: Henry Holt and Company, 1995.

Thurber, James. *My Life and Hard Times.* New York: Harper & Row, 1973.

## Toomer, Jean
### (Jean Nathan Eugene Toomer)
(1894–1967) *short story writer, poet*

Jean Toomer was credited as an early writer of the Harlem Renaissance era, although he mainly associated with progressive white writers. After the publication of *Cane* (1923), black writers considered Toomer to be the most promising black writer of that time. *Cane* was considered his masterwork. It was composed of poetry, short stories, drama, and prose that covered African-American culture in the rural South and urban North. Toomer's friends were members of the Lost Generation of writers intent on reforming American literature. He saw the loss of some of the strongest elements of African-American culture in the move toward modernization and technology.

Jean Nathan Eugene Toomer was born on December 26, 1894, in Washington, D.C., the son of Nathan Toomer, a planter, and Nina Pinchback. Like his parents, Toomer could easily pass for white, his heritage comprising several European and African bloodlines. Indeed, throughout his formative years until age 18, he lived alternately as white and as African American. In 1895, Nathan Toomer abandoned his family, forcing Nina and her son to live with her father, Pinckney Benton Stewart (P. B. S.) Pinchback, governor of Louisiana during Reconstruction and the first U.S. governor of African-American descent. The family lived in a white neighborhood, but Toomer attended the all-black Garnet Elementary School. His mother remarried in 1906 and the family moved to New Rochelle, New York, where they also lived in a white neighborhood, but this time Toomer attended an all-white school. He returned to Washington, D.C., three years later after his mother died and attended the all-black Dunbar High School. After graduation in 1914, he sought to live not as a member of any racial group but as an American.

For the next three years, Toomer studied agriculture, psychology, and literature at several colleges and universities, including the University of Wisconsin, the University of Chicago, and New York University, although he never took a degree. He attended off-campus lectures on naturalism, atheism, psychology, evolution, and socialism.

Three articles, "Ghouls," "Reflections on the Race Riots," and "Americans and Mary Austin" that Toomer wrote for the *New York Call* in 1919 and 1920 were his most militant public statements about racial issues. He prophesied the race movement of the 1960s and showed a subtle understanding of how American prejudice spilled over lines of race or class identity, political party, or regional affiliation. It was these articles and other writing which gave Toomer entry into a circle of friends that included HART CRANE and SHERWOOD ANDERSON.

In 1920, Toomer studied Far Eastern philosophy, which would influence his writing. He wrote short stories, the plays *Natalie Mann* (1922) and *Balo* (1922), and poems, including "The First American," a lyrical expression of his racial and democratic idealism. As an idealist, Toomer proposed the power of the mind to reconcile and transcend the self and the world. He traveled to Sparta, Georgia, in 1921 and served for two months as interim principal of the Sparta Agricultural and Industrial Institute. Living as an African American in the rural South prompted Toomer to create the poems, lyrical narratives, and short stories in his lyrical novel and masterwork, *Cane* (1920). One part of the book presents portraits of six women of the rural South, in a style reminiscent of Sherwood Anderson's gallery of characters in *Winesburg, Ohio* (1919). *Cane* also used settings in Washington, D.C., and Chicago to depict the modern world as a postwar wasteland. He wrote that nature nurtured African Americans, while the desire for money, material positions, and sex could unbalance the soul and cause destruction.

Shortly after the publication of *Cane*, Toomer began studying the austere idealism of George Ivanovitch Gurdjieff, and he attended the Gurdjieff Institute for Harmonious Development in France. In 1925, the symbolist sketch "Easter" was published in *Little Review*, and in 1927, Toomer completed a burlesque novel, *The Gallonwerps*, and a modern morality play, *The Sacred Factory*. His poems "White Arrow" and "Reflections" appeared in the *Dial*. In 1929, *York Beach*, a psychological novella set in Maine, was published in *The New American Caravan*. In 1931, Toomer completed his long poem *The Blue Meridian*, a lyrical affirmation of democratic idealism modeled partly on WALT WHITMAN's "Song of Myself."

Also in 1931, Toomer conducted a Gurdjieffian summer workshop in psychological and social development in Portage, Wisconsin. He married author Margery Latimer and they lived in an artists' colony in Carmel, California. Latimer died while giving birth to a daughter, and in 1934 Toomer married Marjorie Content, daughter of a Wall Street banker. Because both of Toomer's marriages were interracial, they were highly publicized.

In 1935, Toomer fell out with Gurdjieff, but did not reject his philosophy. When the Toomers moved to Doylestown, Pennsylvania, in 1936, Toomer established a Gurdjieff center and gave lectures on spiritual self-development. During this time he published three monographs: "Living Is Developing" (1937), "Work-Ideas I" (1937), and "Roads, People, and Principles" (1939). Toomer developed an interest in Quaker religious philosophy and wrote numerous essays on it. Toomer toured India in 1939, but later admitted that this new quest for spiritual enlightenment was unsuccessful. When he returned to Doylestown in January 1940, he became involved in various Quaker activities. However, he continued his devotion to Gurdjieffian idealism.

Between 1940 and 1950 Toomer continued to write, but his work shifted more toward lectures, essays, and pamphlets on Quaker religious philosophy. Many of his essays were published in the Quaker journal *Friends Intelligencer*. As his health declined, Toomer produced less and withdrew from public life. He died in Doylestown at age 71 on March 30, 1967.

## Further Reading

Byrd, Rudolph P. *Jean Toomer's Years with Gurdjieff: Portrait of an Artist, 1923–1936.* Athens: University of Georgia Press, 1990.

McKay, Nellie Y. *Jean Toomer, Artist: A Study of his Literary Life and Work, 1894–1936.* Chapel Hill: University of North Carolina Press, 1984.

O'Daniel, Therman B., ed. *Jean Toomer: A Critical Evaluation.* Washington, D.C.: Howard University Press, 1988.

Jones, Robert B., and Margery Toomer Latimer, eds. *The Collected Poems of Jean Toomer.* Chapel Hill: University of North Carolina Press, 1988.

## Truth, Sojourner
### (Isabella Baumfree)
(1797–1883) *nonfiction writer, autobiographer, slave narrative writer*

Sojourner Truth was primarily a tireless campaigner against slavery and for the rights of freedmen. But she was also a powerful figure in several other national social movements, such as women's rights and suffrage, temperance, prison reform, and the abolishment of capital punishment. She was known for her wit and originality of phrasing. Straight-talking and unsentimental, Truth became a national symbol for strong black women in particular and all strong women in general. A former slave herself, Truth traveled the country preaching and lecturing. Although she was illiterate, Truth dictated articles and her memoirs, *The Narrative of Sojourner Truth: A Northern Slave* (1850).

Sojourner Truth was born Isabella Baumfree in 1797 in Ulster County, a Dutch settlement in upstate New York. She was one of 13 children born to enslaved parents, James and Betsey. She spoke only Dutch until she was sold from her family at about age 11. Because of the cruel treatment she suffered at the hands of her new master, she learned to speak English quickly but would continue to speak with a Dutch accent for the rest of her life. She was sold several times and relied on her Christian faith to endure the hardships she suffered under slavery.

Forced to submit to the will of her third master, John Dumont, Truth married an older slave named Thomas and had five children with him. She stayed on the Dumont farm until a few months before the state of New York ended slavery in 1828. When Dumont reneged on his promise to grant her freedom, Truth ran away with her infant daughter. She had to leave the other children behind because they were not legally freed in the emancipation order until they had served as bound servants until their 20s.

She eventually settled in New York City, working as a domestic for several religious communes. In 1843, Truth was inspired by a spiritual revelation to change her name to Sojourner Truth. She walked through Long Island and Connecticut, preached, and worked against injustice. After months of travel, she settled in Northampton, Massachusetts, and joined a utopian community known as the Northampton Association for Education and Industry, where she met and worked with such abolitionists as Frederick Douglass. Her dictated memoirs, written by abolitionist and feminist Olive Gilbert, were published in 1850 as *The Narrative of Sojourner Truth: A Northern Slave.* She eventually added abolitionism and women's suffrage to her

Primarily an antislavery activist and writer, Sojourner Truth also campaigned for women's suffrage, prison reform, and other causes. *(Library of Congress, Prints and Photographs Division [LC-USZ62-119343])*

oratory, often giving personal testimony about her experiences as a slave.

As an abolitionist and a feminist, Truth once said "If the first woman God ever made was strong enough to turn the world upside down all alone, these women together ought to be able to turn it back and get it right-side up again. And now that they are asking to do it, the men better let them," she said.

In 1851, Truth delivered her famous "Ain't I a Woman" speech at the Women's Rights Convention in Akron, Ohio, which was later recorded on paper by Frances Gage. Truth stood in front of the audience and pointed to one of the ministers at the convention and said: "That man over there says that women need to be helped into carriages, and lifted over ditches, and to have the best place everywhere. Nobody helps *me* any best place. And ain't I a woman?"

Truth later settled in Battle Creek, Michigan, with two of her daughters and continued her national human rights crusade. A second edition of her memoirs was published in 1855 with an introduction by HARRIET BEECHER STOWE. A third edition was published in 1875. Truth worked at Freedman's Village and for the Freedman's Bureau trying to improve the living conditions of thousands of freed former slaves who had fled to Washington, D.C., seeking safety and jobs in the 1860s. Truth attempted to petition Congress to give the ex-slaves land in western states such as Kansas.

She continued preaching and lecturing until ill health forced her to retire. She died at her home on November 26, 1883.

## Further Reading

Fitch, Suzanne P., and Roseann M. Mandziuk. *Sojourner Truth as Orator: Wit, Story, and Song.* Westport, Conn.: Greenwood Press, 1997.

Mabee, Carleton, and Susan M. Newhouse. *Sojourner Truth—Slave, Prophet, Legend.* New York: New York University Press, 1993.

Rockwell, Anne F. *Only Passing Through: The Story of Sojourner Truth.* New York: Alfred A. Knopf, 2000.

Yellin, Jean F. *Woman & Sisters: The Anti-Slavery Feminists in American Culture.* New Haven, Conn.: Yale University Press, 1989.

# Twain, Mark
## (Samuel Langhorne Clemens)
(1835–1910) *novelist, short story writer, essayist, journalist, poet, autobiographer*

Known for his humor and stories of youthful adventure, Mark Twain introduced colloquial speech into American fiction and laid the foundation for the modern American novel with his best-selling book *Adventures of Huckleberry Finn.*

Born Samuel Langhorne Clemens in Florida, Missouri, on November 30, 1835, he was the son of John Marshall Clemens, a lawyer who worked as a merchant. He had moved his family from Jamestown, Tennessee, to Florida as a speculative venture, anticipating the town's growth into a major metropolis on the Salt River. Clemens established a small business in the tiny town, but by 1839 he had lost faith in Florida's future promise and moved his family to the Mississippi River town of Hannibal, Missouri, where Samuel spent most of his boyhood.

Samuel attended school until he was about 12, when his father died. It was necessary that each child in the family contribute to the family income, so Samuel was apprenticed to a local printer named Ament, who provided his board and clothing as wages. Meanwhile, his older brother, Orion, was working as a printer. When he saved up money to buy a small newspaper in Hannibal in 1850, Samuel left his apprenticeship to work with his brother on the paper, the *Hannibal Journal.* This provided his first writing and publishing experience.

He worked with his brother until 1853, when he grew weary of the limitations of Hannibal and set out for the big city. Telling his family he was headed for St. Louis, the young man—he was not yet 18—ended up in New York City, where the World's Fair was taking place. He found work as printer but after a short time moved on to Philadelphia, where he worked briefly before heading West. He wound up in Keokuk, Iowa, where Orion had landed and remained there until the winter of 1856–57, when he headed South, determined to go to Brazil. He made it as far as New Orleans, where his dreams of South American travel were eclipsed by another sort of adventure when he took a job as a riverboat pilot on the Mississippi.

He remained at this post from 1857 to 1861, when the Civil War effectively put an end to riverboat travel. His boat was put into service by the Confederate army and sent up the Red River.

He sympathized with the South at this time and decided to head to Hannibal, Missouri, to join the Confederates. He enlisted but was discouraged by the conditions and resigned after two weeks. Orion, who was a Union abolitionist, had been appointed secretary of the new territory of Nevada, so Samuel decided to travel west with him. *Roughing It* (1872) tells the story of the brothers' travels and of what they found when they arrived in Virginia City. It was while living there, on February 3, 1863, that Samuel adopted the pseudonym by which the world would always know him. "Mark twain" was actually a riverboat call, meaning "by

Mark Twain was the pen name chosen by Samuel Langhorne Clemens, author of *Adventures of Huckleberry Finn* and numerous other works of fiction. *(Library of Congress, Prints and Photographs Division [LC-USZ62-5513])*

the mark of two fathoms," that was used when sounding river shallows.

At this time, Twain was writing occasional humorous accounts of his travels and newspaper pieces for the Virginia City *Enterprise,* as well as working as a miner in Aurora, California. When Joe Goodman, editor and owner of the *Enterprise,* asked Twain to take the position as local editor, Twain walked 130 miles back to Virginia City in the late summer of 1862 to take the job.

Twain stayed in Virginia City until 1864, when he moved to San Francisco to work as a newspaper reporter. He traveled to Hawaii as a correspondent for the *Sacramento Union* and then left for a world tour. Twain published his accounts of traveling in France and Italy in *The Innocents Abroad,* which appeared in July 1869 and received rave reviews. By the end of three years, the book had sold nearly 100,000 copies.

Twain's success allowed him the financial security necessary to marry. On February 2, 1870, he married Olivia Langdon and the couple moved to Buffalo, New York, where Olivia's father had bought them a house. Their first year of married life was a difficult one, however. Their first baby, Langdon Clemens, was born in November 1870, but he was never a strong child. The family moved to Hartford, Connecticut, in 1871, and in 1872, the baby died. Twain continued to lecture, travel, and write. *Roughing It* appeared in 1872 and later that year a daughter, Susy, was born. The family traveled back and forth between England and the United States several times.

In fall 1874, Twain moved his family into a new house in Hartford, the home they would stay in for 17 years. In Hartford, they entertained almost constantly, hosting other writers, such as HARRIET BEECHER STOWE, and foreign visitors of all sorts, including Rudyard Kipling. The Clemenses spent their summers at Quarry Farm, the country home of Mrs. Clemens's sister. Twain had a study there and accomplished much of his writing in the summers.

*The Prince and the Pauper* was published in 1881 as was *Adventures of Tom Sawyer,* which recounts the youthful adventures of a schoolboy named Tom Sawyer, whose reputation for mischief precedes him wherever he goes. The novel captures the idylls of boyhood and small-town life in preindustrial

America and is still Mark Twain's best-selling work, though critics generally favor *Huckleberry Finn*. *Life on the Mississippi* appeared in 1883. *Huckleberry Finn*, which was intended as a sequel to *Tom Sawyer*, appeared in 1884 and became famous for its artful exploration of racial tensions, its unaffected portrayal of life through the eyes of children, and its use of both black and white vernacular speech. Although Twain's novels were quite successful, he never believed in himself as a novelist and felt more comfortable writing travel pieces.

Twain's latter years were difficult. The death of his first daughter, Susy, while he was traveling, and of his wife in 1904 darkened his life. In addition, Twain throughout his life had found money-making schemes hard to resist, and the immense commercial success he found early in his career made him vulnerable to all those who proposed such schemes. By the 1890s, Twain had lost most of his wealth in failed financial speculation and in the downturn of his own publishing firm. He and his family lived abroad in order to live more cheaply and closed their house in Hartford. Twain also decided during this period to launch a world lecture tour as a means of recovering financially. He toured New Zealand, Australia, India, and South Africa and continued writing books. His last published books included *The Tragedy of Pudd'nhead Wilson* (1884), *Personal Recollections of Joan of Arc* (1885), and the travel book *Following the Equator* (1897).

In addition to the many books he published during his long career, Twain wrote numerous essays for magazines such as *The Galaxy*, *Harper's*, *The Atlantic Monthly*, and *North American Review*. Some of the more famous essays include "Sandwich Islands" (1873), "Queen Victoria's Jubilee" (1897), "King Leopold's Soliloquy" (1905), and "To the Person Sitting in Darkness" (1901). Mark Twain also wrote dozens of short stories that ranged from humorous frontier tales, such as "The Notorious Jumping Frog of Calaveras County," to the biting satire of such later stories as "The Man That Corrupted Hadleyburg."

Late in his life, Mark Twain also received significant recognition from the academic world, including doctoral degrees from Yale University, the University of Missouri, and in 1907 Oxford University. His final trip across the Atlantic to receive his doctorate from Oxford was a joyous one, with people recognizing and applauding him everywhere he went.

Twain lived the last part of his life at Stormfield, his home in Redding, Connecticut, where he continued to write and enjoy the company of friends and family. His daughter, Jean, who suffered from epilepsy throughout her life, died the day before Christmas in 1909, when she was struck with a convulsion while in the bath. Twain died just a few months later, on April 21, 1910.

Twain had dictated his autobiography to his secretary, A. B. Paine, during his last years, and it was published posthumously in 1924. A final book of fiction, *The Mysterious Stranger*, was published after Twain's death as well, in 1916. His old house in Hartford has been restored and stands as a National Historic Site.

## Further Reading

Budd, Louis J. *A Listing of and Selections from Newspaper and Magazine Interviews with Samuel L. Clemens, 1874–1910.* Arlington: University of Texas at Arlington Press, 1977.

Camfield, Gregg. *The Oxford Companion to Mark Twain.* New York: Oxford University Press, 2003.

Fatout, Paul, ed. *Mark Twain Speaking.* Iowa City: University of Iowa Press, 1976.

Gribben, Alan. *Mark Twain's Library: A Reconstruction.* 2 vols. Boston: G. K. Hall, 1980.

Lampton, Lucius. *The Genealogy of Mark Twain.* Jackson, Miss.: Diamond L Publishing, 1990.

LeMaster, J. R., and James D. Wilson, eds. *The Mark Twain Encyclopedia.* New York: Garland Publishing, 1993.

Rasmussen, R. Kent. *Mark Twain A to Z: The Essential Reference to His Life and Writings.* New York: Oxford University Press, 1996.

Tenney, Thomas A. *Mark Twain: A Reference Guide.* Boston: G. K. Hall, 1977.

## Tyler, Anne
(1941–   ) *novelist, short story writer*

Known as an expert chronicler of the ups and downs of family life, Anne Tyler won the Pulitzer

Prize for her 11th novel, *Breathing Lessons*, in 1988. She is considered by many of her fans to be a modern-day Jane Austen, combining a sense of tradition with a cast of quirky characters in novels loved by both readers and critics.

Anne Tyler was born in Minneapolis, Minnesota, on October 25, 1941, but grew up in a Quaker community in Raleigh, North Carolina. Her father, Lloyd Parry Tyler, was an industrial chemist. Her mother, Phyllis Mahon Tyler, was a social worker. The family moved several times when Tyler was very young, living in several rural southern Quaker communities before settling in 1948 in the Celo Community, near Burnsville, in the mountains. The Tylers lived in their own private house at Celo, raised some livestock, and used organic farming techniques. Children at Celo studied art, carpentry, and cooking. Tyler also attended a small public school in Harvard, North Carolina. She began writing stories at age seven and telling stories to help herself fall asleep at night, although she has said that she never intended to become a writer when she was young.

In 1961, at age 19, she graduated Phi Beta Kappa from Duke University with a degree in Russian. She had taken a required English course with the prolific writer and critic REYNOLDS PRICE, who encouraged her writing and introduced her to his agent. She also twice won the Anne Flexner Award for creative writing at Duke. Her first published short story, "Laura," appeared in Duke University's literary magazine, the *Archive*.

Tyler then went on to do graduate work in Russian studies at Columbia University from 1961 to 1962. Following her studies at Columbia, Tyler held several library jobs, including a post as a bibliographer at Duke and another position at McGill University in Montreal. In 1963, she married Taghi Mohammad Modarressi, an Iranian psychiatrist.

During the early and mid-1960s, Tyler published the occasional story in the *Saturday Evening Post*, *Harper's*, and the *New Yorker*. Although Tyler wrote and published novels in her 20s, she did not take writing seriously until 1967, when she began to write full time. Her two children, Mitra and Tezh, were born in the late 1960s. In one of her rare interviews, she described the writing process she used while raising her children. She would write from precisely 8:05 A.M. until 3:30 P.M., when school let out. According to one reporter who interviewed her in her home, she also relied heavily on unlined white index cards, where she would jot down thoughts that could be filed away and used later. Tyler writes her novels in longhand with a Parker ballpoint pen on white paper attached to a clipboard.

Although her earliest work was generally well received, Tyler has said that she dislikes her first two novels—*If Morning Ever Comes* (1964) and *The Tin Can Tree* (1965). She once named *Dinner at the Homesick Restaurant* (1982) as the favorite among her own books. Indeed, this was Tyler's breakthrough novel, bringing her both commercial success and fame when it was published in 1982. It was followed by two more immensely successful novels. *The Accidental Tourist*, published in 1986, won the National Book Critics Circle Award. A subtle comedy that traces the efforts of its protagonist, Maconheary, a middle-aged travel writer, to rebuild his life following the death of his son and his wife's decision to leave him. *Breathing Lessons* appeared just two years later and won the Pulitzer Prize. This novel takes place in a single day as its main characters, Maggie and Ira Moran, drive to a funeral, where they reunite with several old classmates from high school and consider stopping in to visit their ex-daughter-in-law. The day inspires the couple to take stock of their lives in a new way as they reexamine their family's life. Other titles by Tyler include *Celestial Navigation* (1974), *Searching for Caleb* (1975), *Earthly Possessions* (1977), *Saint Maybe* (1991), *Ladder of Years* (1996), *A Patchwork Planet* (1998), and *Back When We Were Grownups* (2001).

Several of Tyler's novels have been adapted for television and film, including *The Accidental Tourist*, an award-winning 1988 movie directed by Lawrence Kasdan and starring Kathleen Turner, William Hurt, and Geena Davis. *Earthly Possessions* was also made into a film starring Susan Sarandon, in 1999.

When interviewed once about the influence of EUDORA WELTY on her own writing, Tyler responded, "She taught me there were stories to be written about the mundane life around me."

Indeed, Tyler has been quite prolific and successful, writing about the everyday lives of families. She lives in the same house she has lived in for more than 30 years in Baltimore's Roland Park neighborhood, which also appears as the setting for many of her stories.

## Further Reading

Bail, Paul. *Anne Tyler: A Critical Companion*. Westport, Conn.: Greenwood, 1998.

Croft, Robert W. *An Anne Tyler Companion*. Westport, Conn.: Greenwood, 1998.

Evans, Elizabeth. *Anne Tyler*. New York: Twayne, 1993.

Linton, Karen. *The Temporal Horizon*. Philadelphia: Coronet Books, 1989.

Petry, Alice Hall. *Understanding Anne Tyler*. Columbia: University of South Carolina Press, 1990.

Voelker, Joseph C. *Art and the Accidental in Anne Tyler's Major Novels*. St. Louis: University of Missouri Press, 1989.

# U

## Updike, John
### (John Hoyer Updike)
#### (1932– ) *novelist, short story writer, poet*

John Updike has been considered one of America's most distinguished and prolific writers. He observes the ordinary life he sees around him and frequently asks the reader to recognize and reconsider one's preconceptions. Updike is best known for his "Rabbit" novels *Rabbit, Run* (1960); *Rabbit Redux* (1971); *Rabbit Is Rich* (1981); and *Rabbit at Rest* (1990). They follow the life of Harry "Rabbit" Angstrom, a star athlete, from his youth through the social and sexual upheavals of the 1960s, to later periods of his life, and to final decline. *Rabbit Is Rich* and *Rabbit at Rest* both won Pulitzer Prizes. Updike also won the National Book Award for his novel *The Centaur* (1963). Updike's body of work is large, consisting of more than 50 books, including novels, collections of poems, short stories, and essays. He also has written much literary criticism.

John Hoyer Updike was born on March 18, 1932, in Reading, Pennsylvania, the only child of Wesley Russell and Linda Grace (Hoyer) Updike. His father was a math teacher and farmer, and his mother was an aspiring writer. His grandparents lived with them on the isolated farm as the family suffered in the Great Depression. As a child Updike was afflicted by psoriasis and stammering, but his mother encouraged his literary ambitions. He went to Shillington High School, near Reading, and was a voracious reader. In 1950, he won a full scholarship to Harvard, majoring in English, and con-

tributed to and later edited the *Harvard Lampoon*. He initially dreamed of being a cartoonist. He married Mary Pennington, a fine arts student at Radcliffe, in 1953.

After graduating with a B.A. degree in 1954, Updike and Pennington spent a year in England at the Ruskin School of Drawing and Fine Arts in Oxford. In 1955, Updike joined the staff of the *New Yorker*, writing editorials, poetry, stories, and criticism. During this time he wrote two unpublished novels. In 1957, Updike left the *New Yorker* to devote himself to writing. He moved to Ipswich, Massachusetts, which became the setting for his novel *Couples* (1968), a portrait of sexual passion and adultery among a group of young suburban married couples. In his office in Ipswich, Updike set himself a target of writing three pages a day, reserving the morning for producing fiction and the afternoon for poetry, reviewing, and other business. His first book, *The Carpentered Hen and Other Tame Creatures*, a collection of poetry, appeared in 1958. Updike's first novel, *The Poorhouse Fair* (1959), was about the residents of an old people's home.

A Guggenheim fellowship supported Updike while he worked on *Rabbit, Run*. It was published only after changes were made to the manuscript to avoid possible lawsuits for obscenity. It was the first book about his famous hero, Harry "Rabbit" Angstrom, a sexually magnetic natural athlete. *Rabbit, Run* (1960) shows him trying to escape from his town, his job, and his wife and child. In *Rabbit Redux* (1971), Harry is a middle-aged bourgeois, who finds his life shattered by the infidelity of his wife. *Rabbit at Rest* (1991), the fourth and final (so far) volume in the series, is set in the late 1980s and parallels the decay of the society.

*The Centaur* (1963), which some critics consider Updike's most ambitious novel, used a mythological framework to explore the relationship of a schoolmaster father and his son. It won the National Book Award. Updike traveled to Russia and eastern Europe in 1964 and 1965, and to Africa in 1973. *The Coup* (1979) was an exotic first-person narration by an ex-dictator of a fictitious African state. In 1974, Updike and Pennington divorced. They had four children. Updike married Martha Bernhard in 1977. He published *The Witches of Eastwick,* a comic novel about the lives of three single women who are going crazy with boredom in small-town America, in 1984. A movie based on the book came out three years later.

Although Updike's plots have focused on the commonplace, his themes have centered on existential questions. He has also read theologians for guidance and regularly attends church for worship.

As a writing critic, Updike has looked for felicity in style, accuracy in presenting one's subject, precision in describing external and inner worlds, and humanistic values. His latest novel, *Seek My Face,* was published in 2002.

Updike has received numerous honors and awards, including the National Book Award, the American Book Award, the National Book Critics Circle Award, a National Arts Club Medal of Honor, and the O. Henry Prize. At 32, he was the youngest member of the National Academy of Arts and Letters when he was elected in 1964. He became a member of American Academy of Arts and Letters in 1976. He lives in Massachusetts with his wife.

**Further Reading**

Detweiler, Robert. *John Updike.* Boston: Twayne, 1984.

Plath, James, ed. *Conversations with John Updike.* Jackson: University Press of Mississippi, 1994.

Schiff, James A. *John Updike Revisited.* Boston: Twayne, 1998.

## Vonnegut, Kurt
### (Kurt Vonnegut, Jr.)
(1922–    )  *novelist, short story writer*

Kurt Vonnegut has used fantasy and science fiction to examine the horrors and absurdities of 20th-century civilization with a tone that is both moral and irreverent. Vonnegut, a mentor for young pacifists, is best known for his novel *Slaughterhouse-Five* (1969), which was based on his experiences in Dresden, Germany, where he was a prisoner of war during the town's destruction in 1945. His novels are known for their dark humor, as well as for their serious moral vision and cutting social commentary. *Cat's Cradle* (1963) explored the destructive rationality of Western science and the turn toward mysticism. Vonnegut has published more than a dozen novels.

Kurt Vonnegut, Jr., was born on November 11, 1922, in Indianapolis, Indiana, to Kurt Vonnegut, Sr., an architect, and Edith Lieber. Vonnegut, Jr., wrote for his high school newspaper before he enrolled at Cornell University in 1940. He studied biochemistry, but did poorly. He did, however, enjoy a position working for the *Cornell Sun,* and wrote antiwar articles. In 1942, Vonnegut left Cornell; the university had been preparing to ask him to leave because of poor academic performance. He enrolled at the Carnegie Institute of Technology (now Carnegie-Mellon) in 1943, but stayed there only briefly before enlisting in the army. His mother committed suicide in 1944.

Later that year, Vonnegut was sent to Europe as a battalion scout. Captured in the Battle of the Bulge, he was held as a prisoner of war in Dresden. When the city was bombed by Allied forces, Vonnegut and some of the other prisoners were in a meat cellar deep under a slaughterhouse. They were among the few who survived the destruction. The Germans later employed Vonnegut to scout for corpses. In *Slaughterhouse-Five,* Vonnegut used historical facts and fantasy to depict the firebombing of Dresden, seen through the eyes of Billy Pilgrim. He finds peace of mind after being kidnapped by the extraterrestrial Tralfamadorians, and learns that the secret of life is to live only in the happy moments. Vonnegut was awarded a Guggenheim fellowship to complete the book.

He returned to the United States in 1945 and married Jane Marie Cox, a childhood friend. They eventually had two daughters and a son, and also adopted the three children of Vonnegut's sister, who died of cancer. Vonnegut studied anthropology at the University of Chicago, but the department unanimously rejected his M.A. thesis. The university allowed a high-quality piece of writing to substitute for a dissertation. Years later, Vonnegut showed the department *Cat's Cradle* and received his degree in 1971.

He worked various jobs, including those of a reporter and public relations writer for General Electric in 1947. His first published short story, "Report on the Barnhouse Effect," was published in *Collier's Weekly* in 1950. His first novel, *Player Piano* (1952), was a futuristic story that depicted human beings becoming less useful as scientists and engineers of large corporations made greater use of machines. Although much of Vonnegut's writing deals with technology, science, and fantasy, he does not consider himself a science fiction writer. Often using his frequent protagonist, Kilgore Trout, Vonnegut has combined fantastic plots with dark humor and social commentary. *The Sirens of Titan* (1959) features a character for whom the events of history take place simultaneously. *Cat's Cradle* was about a scientist who creates a chemical that turns all water into ice. Vonnegut was virtually anonymous before his success with *Slaughterhouse-Five*. Although some critics have accused him of recycling his ideas, he has developed a cult following over the years, partly because of his pacifism. In 1965, Vonnegut accepted an appointment to the University of Iowa's Writers' Workshop.

*Breakfast of Champions* (1973) was a commercial success, but it was not well received by critics. Subsequent works by Vonnegut have included *Jailbird* (1979) and *Deadeye Dick* (1983). *Hocus Pocus* (1990) was set in the years following the Vietnam War. *Timequake* (1997), which took Vonnegut 10 years to write, has fragments of auto-biography. Vonnegut has also written plays, essays, criticism, and television plays.

Vonnegut was elected vice president of the PEN American Center in 1972, and elected vice president of the National Institute of Arts and Letters in 1975. Vonnegut and Cox divorced in 1979, and he married photographer Jill Krementz. He attempted suicide in 1985. In recent years, he has taught advance writing at Smith College in New York. He has taught at several other universities, including Harvard, New York University, and the City University of New York.

## Further Reading

Bloom, Harold, ed. *Kurt Vonnegut*. Philadelphia: Chelsea House Publishers, 2000.

Goldsmith, David H. *Kurt Vonnegut, Fantasist of Fire and Ice*. Bowling Green, Ohio: Bowling Green University Popular Press, 1972.

Klinkowitz, Jerome. *Kurt Vonnegut*. London: Methuen, 1982.

———. *Vonnegut in Fact: The Public Spokesmanship of Personal Fiction*. Columbia: University of South Carolina Press, 1998.

Merrill, Robert, ed. *Critical Essays on Kurt Vonnegut*. New York: Chelsea House, 1990.

# W

## Waldman, Anne
(1945–   )  *poet, editor*

Known as one of the most influential performance poets of the 20th century, Anne Waldman has dedicated her life to returning poetry to its rightful place as an oral and public art form. Both a teacher and a poet, she has been instrumental in organizing forums for poetry and in helping to promote the work of other poets. One of the most prolific members of the post-Beat poetry community, Waldman has published more than 30 books and produced dozens of sound recordings, as well as films and videos. She cofounded with ALLEN GINSBERG the Jack Kerouac School of Disembodied Poetics at Naropa Institute in Boulder, Colorado, in 1974.

Anne Waldman was born on April 2, 1945, in Millville, New Jersey. Growing up in New York City's Greenwich Village, she experienced the rich cultural diversity of the city. According to Waldman, her mother, Frances, "scrimped to send [her] to art classes at the Museum of Modern Art" and made sure that they regularly had tickets to ballet, modern dance, and classical music concerts. Her parents, she has said, were "sufficiently original" and supportive of her early interest in literature. Waldman and her younger brother, Carl, attended Grace Church School in Greenwich Village starting in seventh grade. She became involved in the school's literary activities and began meeting with other like-minded students after school in the home of the Hourwich twins, who were classmates. The friends read Shakespeare and

Molière aloud, argued politics with Mr. Hourwich, and admired the beautiful woven tapestries Mrs. Hourwich created on her loom.

Waldman went to high school at Friends Seminary, a Quaker school, where she edited the school newspaper, the *Oblivion*, and contributed to *Stove*, the literary magazine. Her best friend in high school, Jonathan Cott, also became a journalist, poet, and critic. During high school, Waldman subscribed to *Evergreen Review*, read the *Village Voice* faithfully, and even submitted her poems to the *New Yorker* and other magazines.

After high school, Waldman attended Bennington College, where she studied with Howard Nemerov and first began her struggle to determine a place for her own poetic voice within the largely male canon of American poetry. In the summer of 1965, she traveled with her brother and a friend to California. She ended up in Berkeley, where she was eager to attend the poetry readings of poets such as Jack Spicer and Robert Duncan. The night of a Robert Duncan reading, Waldman was introduced to a young poet and novelist from New York, Lewis Warsh. A highly disciplined writer, who had written several novels in high school, Warsh and Waldman became, in her words, "romantic cohorts." They hitchhiked to Mexico together, then hitched back to New York City, where they founded *Angel Hair* magazine and book company and lived together until 1970. The couple married in 1967 at St. Mark's Church.

After graduating from Bennington, Waldman moved into an apartment on St. Mark's Place. She was hired as a poetry assistant to Joel Oppenheimer, who was directing the poetry program for the St. Marks Church-in-the-Bowery arts project. Following two years in that position, from 1966 to 1968, Waldman became the director of the poetry project, a position she held until 1978. Many of the Beat poets read and performed their work at St. Mark's and Waldman began to read her own work during these years as well.

Waldman's long chant poem, *Fast Speaking Woman*, attracted much attention from fellow poets. ALLEN GINSBERG, KENNETH KOCH, and LAWRENCE FERLINGHETTI were among the writers who praised Waldman's work. Ferlinghetti went on to publish a City Lights Pocket Poets edition of 10 Waldman poems in 1975, an event that Waldman has said put her work and its performance into a larger context, as City Lights was the publisher of Ginsberg, DIANE DI PRIMA, Gregory Corso, and other Beat poets she admired.

Waldman became a Buddhist, guided by the Tibetan Chogyam Trungpa Rinpoche, who would also become Allen Ginsberg's guru. In summer 1974, Ginsberg, Waldman and others gathered in Boulder, Colorado, where the Naropa Institute, founded by Trungpa, was holding its first summer program. Ginsberg and Waldman were invited to "design a poetics department in which poets could learn about meditation and meditators could learn about poetry." They founded the Jack Kerouac School of Disembodied Poetics.

Waldman was invited in the fall of 1976 to join Bob Dylan on his "Rolling Thunder Revue" tour as a poet-in-residence. Ginsberg was invited as well. A caravan of rock musicians, poets, and others traveled across the country, stopping periodically to give impromptu concerts. Singer/songwriter Joni Mitchell and SAM SHEPARD were among her cohorts on the tour. In addition to their concerts and performances on the tour, the crew worked on the film *Renaldo and Clara*, for which Sam Shepard was writing the script.

By the late 1970s, Waldman had met Reed Bye, a poet and roofer, working in Boulder. The couple married in 1980 and worked together on a magazine, *Rocky Ledge*, and a press they founded, Rocky Ledge Cottage Editions. Bye became a serious Buddhist, as well as a teacher of poetry at Naropa. Their child, Edwin Ambrose, was born on October 21, 1980.

Waldman has published more than 30 books over the years, including *First Baby Poems* (1982), *Skin Meat Bones* (1985), and *Helping the Dreamer: New and Selected Poems: 1966–1988* (1989). More recent titles include *Vow To Poetry: Essays, Interviews & Manifestos* (2001) *Marriage: A Sentence* (2000), *Kill or Cure* (1996), and *Iovis: All Is Full of Jove: Books I & II* (1993, 1997). Her books have been translated into Italian, German, French, Turkish, and Czech, among other languages.

Waldman is also the editor of *The Beat Book* (1996) and coeditor of *Disembodied Poetics: Annals of the Jack Kerouac School* (1993), and with Lewis Warsh, *The Angel Hair Anthology* (2001).

Her film and video credits include feature roles in *Battle of the Bards* and *Eye in All Heads*. She has collaborated with visual artists such as Elizabeth Murray and Susan Rothenburg, and with musicians, including Steven Taylor and Mark Miller, on a number of projects. In 2001, Waldman released a CD entitled *Alchemical Elegy: Selected Songs and Writings*. Her other sound recordings include *Jazz Poetry* and *Beat Poetry*, both produced in London in 1999. As a performance artist, Waldman has twice won the International Poetry Championship Bout in Taos, New Mexico. She performed at Town Hall in New York City in a tribute for Bob Dylan's 60th birthday, and in 2002, she received a grant from the Foundation for Contemporary Performance Arts.

In addition to her position at Naropa, where she still directs the Naropa Abroad Program to Bali, she has taught at the Institute of American Indian Arts in Santa Fe, New Mexico, and served as adviser to the Prazska Skola Projekt in Prague. She was also the director of curriculum for the Schule fur Dichtung in Vienna in the fall of 1999. Waldman's many awards include the Shelley Memorial Award for poetry, and grants from the National Endowment for the Arts and the Poetry Foundation. Anne Waldman lives in Boulder, Colorado, and New York City.

**Further Reading**
Ash, Mel. *Beat Spirit: The Way of the Beat Writers as a Living Experience*. New York: Putnam, 1997.

Charters, Ann. *Beats and Company, Portrait of a Literary Generation.* New York: Doubleday, 1986.

Knight, Brenda. *Women of the Beat Generation.* Berkeley, Calif.: Conari Press, 1996.

McDarrah, Fred and Gloria McDarrah. *The Beat Generation: Glory Days in Greenwich Village.* New York: Schirmer Books, 1996.

Watson, Steven. *Birth of the Beat Generation.* New York: Pantheon Books, 1995.

# Walker, Alice
## (Alice Malsenior Walker)
(1944–   ) *novelist, poet, short story writer, nonfiction writer, essayist, screenwriter, memoirist, poet*

Alice Walker became the first African American to win a Pulitzer Prize. She received the award in 1983 for her novel *The Color Purple* (1982), a story about the struggles of African-American women in the South. Walker has been credited for her insightful treatment of African-American culture, as well as for her struggle for women's rights. She was active in the Civil Rights movement of the 1960s. Heavily influenced by Harlem Renaissance writer ZORA NEALE HURSTON, Walker was among the first to introduce a university course on African-American women writers. She has published novels as well as collections of poems, short stories, and essays.

Alice Malsenior Walker was born on February 9, 1944, in Eatonton, Georgia, the eighth and youngest child of Willie Lee Walker and Minnie Tallulah Grant Walker, who were sharecroppers. When she was eight years old, Walker was blinded in one eye when one of her brothers accidentally shot her with a BB gun. She was self-conscious about the large white scar tissue left in her eye. When she was 14 years old, one of her brothers had the tissue removed by a doctor, but Walker never regained her vision in that eye. She was class valedictorian and prom queen when she graduated from high school in 1961. Walker left home to attend Spelman College, an African-American women's institution, in Atlanta, Georgia, on scholarship. Before leaving, her mother gave her a sewing machine for self-sufficiency, a suitcase for independence, and a typewriter for creativity.

While at Spelman, Alice participated in civil rights demonstrations. She was invited to Martin Luther King, Jr.'s, home in 1962 at the end of her freshman year in recognition of her invitation to attend the Youth World Peace Festival in Helsinki, Finland. After attending the conference, Walker traveled to Europe for the summer.

After spending two years at Spelman, Walker transferred to the more liberal Sarah Lawrence College in New York, and during her junior year traveled to Uganda as an exchange student. After she received her B.A. degree from Sarah Lawrence College in 1965, she returned to the South, registering voters door-to-door in Mississippi. She met Mel Leventhal, a young Jewish law student, and returned to New York with him and they were later married. She won first place in the *American Scholar* annual essay contest for "The Civil Rights Movement: What Good Was It?", which was her first published article. Walker won a writing fellowship to work at the prestigious MacDowell Colony in New Hampshire, but she gave it up to marry Leventhal in 1967.

While still working on her novel, Walker and Leventhal returned to Mississippi where he could pursue civil rights litigation. They were the first legally married interracial couple in the state and received threats. Walker accepted a teaching position at Jackson State University, published her first volume of poetry, *Once* (1968), and gave birth to a daughter. Her first novel, *The Third Life of Grange Copeland,* was published in 1970. The book, which involved the murder of a woman by her husband, centered on the effects of economic, political, and social powerlessness upon the lives of Grange and Brownfield Copeland. Many African-American critics said Walker dealt too harshly with the black male characters in her book. Walker said the characters were based on people she had known and did not care what critics thought about her not portraying the "correct image" of African-American people in her work.

Walker accepted a teaching position at Wellesley College in 1972 and began one of the first women's studies courses in the nation, a course on the literature of African-American women such as Zora Neale Hurston. In 1973, Walker embarked on a search for Hurston's grave. She eventually found it and marked it with a tombstone. Her article about this endeavor, "In Search of Zora Neale Hurston," was published in *Ms.* magazine in 1975 and resurrected literary interest in Hurston's work. Walker's first collection of short stories, *In Love & Trouble: Stories of Black Women*, and her second volume of poetry, *Revolutionary Petunias and Other Poems*, were published in 1973. Her second novel, *Meridian*, was published in 1976 and chronicled a young woman's struggle during the Civil Rights movement. Some critics hailed it as one of the best novels to come out of that era. Meanwhile, her marriage to Leventhal ended. Walker accepted a Guggenheim Fellowship to concentrate full time on her writing and moved to San Francisco. Her second book of short stories, *You Can't Keep a Good Woman Down*, was published in 1981.

In 1982, *The Color Purple*, was published. The novel went on to win the Pulitzer Prize and the American Book Award and brought fame to Walker. She thought it would take at least five years to write, but she wrote it in less than a year. It tells the story of Celie, an African-American woman in the South who writes letters to God in which she tells about her life. In the course of her story, Celie meets a series of other African-American women who shape her life. The book was written in what Walker described as "black folks' English." Despite the success of *The Color Purple*, Walker again received criticism for her portrayal of African-American men. The story was made into a successful film in 1986.

Walker published her third volume of poetry, *Horses Make a Landscape Look More Beautiful* in 1984. She followed this in 1988 with her second book of essays, *Living By the Word*. The next year, she published her epic novel, *The Temple of My Familiar*, followed by her fifth novel, *Possessing the Secret of Joy*. It chronicles the psychic trauma of one woman's life after forced genital mutilation. Her interest in ending genital mutilation took her on a journey to Africa with filmmaker Pratibha Parmar to make a documentary called "Warrior Marks: Female Genital Mutilation and the Sexual Blinding of Women." Walker also wrote a companion book, *Warrior Marks*, chronicling her experiences.

In 1996, Walker published *The Same River Twice: Honoring the Difficult*, in which she describes through essays and journal entries the loss of her mother, the break-up of a 13-year relationship with Robert Allen, her battle with Lyme disease and depression, and her awakening sense of bisexuality. Walker published her first novel in six years in 1998 with *By the Light of My Father's Smile*, which explores the relationships of fathers and daughters. As in previous fiction, Walker weaves back and forth through time and individual perspectives, her characters seeking redemption, forgiveness, and peace. *The Way Forward Is with a Broken Heart* (2000), a collection of autobiographical short fiction, explores the ambiguities of intimate relationships.

Among Walker's other numerous awards and honors are the Lillian Smith Award from the National Endowment for the Arts, the Rosenthal Award from the National Institute of Arts and Letters, a Radcliffe Institute Fellowship, a Merrill Fellowship, a Guggenheim Fellowship, and the Front Page Award for Best Magazine Criticism from the Newswoman's Club of New York. She also has received the Townsend Prize and a Lyndhurst Prize. Walker lives in Mendocino, California.

### Further Reading

Awkward, Michael. *Inspiring Influences: Tradition, Revision, and Afro-American Women's Novels.* New York: Columbia University Press, 1991.

Bloom, Harold, ed. *Alice Walker.* Boston: Chelsea, 1989.

Christian, Barbara T., ed. *Alice Walker: "Everyday Use."* Princeton, N.J.: Rutgers University Press, 1994.

Johnson, Maria V. "'You Just Can't Keep a Good Woman Down': Alice Walker Sings the Blues." *African-American Review* 30, no. 2 (summer 1996): 221–236.

Winchell, Donna H. *Alice Walker.* Boston: Twayne, 1992.

### Warren, Robert Penn
(1905–1989) *poet, novelist, biographer, literary critic*

Like any successful writer who lives to a great age, Robert Penn Warren grew to be an institution. He was highly distinguished in the academic world and successful in numerous genres, including fiction, poetry, biography, history, social commentary, and textbooks. His long list of literary awards includes three Pulitzer Prizes; he was the only writer at the time to have won the Pulitzer in both fiction and poetry. Known as a southern writer, and specifically as one of the early Fugitives at Vanderbilt University, Warren easily transcended regionalism in his work as he explored universal themes with the craft and insight of a master.

Robert Penn Warren was born in Guthrie, Todd County, Kentucky, on April 24, 1905. He was the oldest of three children. Warren's parents were Robert Franklin Warren, a banker, and Anna Ruth Penn Warren, who taught school. Warren grew up on a tobacco farm and lived amidst his extended family, including his two grandfathers, who had fought for the Confederacy during the Civil War and who told countless stories of their adventures. Warren acknowledged after he was an established writer that his grandfathers' stories had provided a rich source of images for his writing.

Warren's early education was at the Guthrie school, from which he graduated at the age of 15. His mother thought he was too young to go to college, so in 1920 he enrolled in Clarksville High School in Clarksville, Tennessee, and graduated in just one year. He suffered an injury to his eye in the spring of 1921, when his younger brother threw a rock at him, that resulted eventually in his losing his left eye, an event that shaped him forever.

Warren had obtained an appointment to the U.S. Naval Academy and went in the summer of 1921 for six weeks to Citizens Military Training Corp in Fort Knox, Kentucky. He published his first poem, "Prophecy," in *The Messkit*. Due to his eye injury, however, his appointment to the Naval Academy was canceled and Warren went instead to Vanderbilt University in fall 1921. He was 16 years old.

At Vanderbilt, Warren found himself among a group of other young men who were interested in poetry and attached to the disappearing culture of the agrarian South. Although these men never set out to start an intellectual movement, the magazine they published, *The Fugitive*, linked them and their writing forever. Members of this group included ALLEN TATE, who was Warren's roommate, and JOHN CROWE RANSOM, who was one of their teachers. Both were at the beginning of what would become quite distinguished careers. Referred to as

the Fugitives, these writers exercised considerable influence on the early writing of Warren. In the summer of 1925, he graduated from Vanderbilt summa cum laude, Phi Beta Kappa, and was a Founder's Medalist. By this time he was determined to make his career as a writer.

Warren went on to do graduate study, following the example of his Vanderbilt teachers who supported their literary aspirations with teaching careers. Warren studied at the University of California, where he received his master's degree in 1927, before entering Yale University on a fellowship. In the fall of 1928, he went to Oxford University in England as a Rhodes Scholar. In 1930, Warren returned to the United States with a degree in English literature and took a position teaching English at Southwestern College in Memphis, Tennessee. In summer 1929, he secretly married Emma "Cinina" Brescia, whom he had met during his brief stint at the University of California.

Warren's career in academia was impressive. After teaching just one year at Southwestern, he accepted an offer from Vanderbilt, where he taught for three years before moving to Louisiana State University in Baton Rouge. During his eight years in Louisiana, he became one of the most influential academics of his generation. He founded and edited, along with Cleanth Brooks and Charles W. Pipkin, a literary quarterly, *The Southern Review*. The magazine was an immediate success, boasting a list of contributors and subscribers that testified to its national scope. When the magazine suspended publication during the changed economy of World War II, Warren left Louisiana State University and took a position as director of creative writing at the University of Minnesota in Minneapolis.

In 1950, Warren made radical changes in his life. He left the University of Minnesota to take a professorship of playwriting at Yale University in New Haven, Connecticut. In 1951, his marriage to Emma Brescia Warren ended in divorce, and in 1952 he married Eleanor Clark, with whom he had two children—Rosanna Phelps Warren and Gabriel Penn Warren. Although there was much upheaval in his life at this time, Warren managed to begin writing poems again.

He had collected his early work in *Selected Poems, 1923–1943* (1944) but after that had been unable to write poetry. Although he did complete and publish one long narrative poem, *Brother to Dragons* (1953), he could not finish any lyric poems until after his new marriage. When *Promises: Poems 1954–1956* came out in 1957, it featured his new family, and it was clear that Warren had found a new voice and a new source of inspiration.

Warren was a prolific writer who worked successfully in numerous genres. He published 10 novels, including *All the King's Men*, which won the Pulitzer Prize and was made into a play, a motion picture, and an opera. Inspired by the life of Louisiana governor Huey Long, *All the King's Men* tells the story of a charismatic southern politician whose ruthless lies and cut-throat deals belie his populist roots. The novel was eventually translated into 20 languages. *Band of Angels*, another of his novels, was also made into a film. He published 16 volumes of poetry, two of which won Pulitzer Prizes—*Promises: Poems, 1954–1956* and *Now and Then: Poems, 1976–1978*. He is the only writer to have won the Pulitzer Prize for both fiction and poetry. In addition to his novels and poems, he published one collection of short stories, two collections of critical essays, a biography, three historical essays, a study of HERMAN MELVILLE, a critical book on THEODORE DREISER, and two studies of race relations in America.

Warren's career as a novelist began with *Night Rider*, a story that examines his boyhood but is also about the tobacco war of 1905–08 in Kentucky between independent tobacco growers and large tobacco companies. It was published in 1939. It was the first of seven novels he wrote that span the time period of his life. *At Heaven's Gate*, published in 1943, is set in Nashville during Warren's college years. *All the King's Men* (1946) is informed by Warren's years as a university professor in Louisiana. *The Cave* (1959), *Flood* (1964), and *Meet Me in the Green Glen* (1971) take place in the South during the years from World War II into the 1960s. *A Place to Come To* (1977), Warren's last novel, serves as a kind of summary of his life. In the novel, the main character closely resembles Warren. Among his other 10 novels are *World Enough and Time* (1950) and *Wilderness* (1961), historical novels that, like *Band of Angels*, were set in the pre–Civil War South.

In addition to his poetry and fiction, Warren wrote numerous academic and critical works. He collaborated with colleague Cleanth Brooks on several textbooks that served an important role in introducing New Criticism to the literature classroom. These texts include *Understanding Poetry*, which came out in 1938, and *Understanding Fiction*, published in 1943.

As his reputation grew weightier, Warren found that his readers were interested in his opinion on many different topics. He wrote several books of social commentary, including *Segregation: The Inner Conflict in the South* (1956), an analysis of the dilemma southerners faced in dealing with entrenched attitudes toward race. In 1965, he published a collection of interviews with civil rights leaders called *Who Speaks for the Negro?*

In addition to the many prizes already mentioned, Warren won the Bollingen Prize, the National Medal for Literature, the Sidney Hillman Award, the Edna St. Vincent Millay Memorial Award, the Presidential Medal of Freedom, and served as a chancellor of the Academy of American Poets from 1972 until 1988 and as the first U.S. Poet Laureate, in 1985.

Although his imagination always seemed rooted in the South, Warren remained in Connecticut, where he had moved in the 1950s, for the rest of his life. His summer home was in Vermont. He is buried at Stratton, Vermont, but as he requested before his death, on September 15, 1989, there is also a memorial marker in the Warren family gravesite in Guthrie, Kentucky.

## Further Reading

Bedient, Calvin. *In the Heart's Last Kingdom: Robert Penn Warren's Major.* Cambridge: Harvard University Press, 1984.

Blotner, Joseph L. *Robert Penn Warren: A Biography.* New York: Random House, 1997.

Bohner, Charles H. *Robert Penn Warren.* New York: Twayne, 1964, 1965.

Justus, James H. *The Achievement of Robert Penn Warren.* Baton Rouge: Louisiana State University Press, 1981.

Nakadate, Neil. *Robert Penn Warren, A Reference Guide.* Boston: G. K. Hall, 1977.

Ruppersburg, Hugh M. *Robert Penn Warren and the American Imagination.* Athens: University of Georgia Press, 1990.

Snipes, Katherine. *Robert Penn Warren.* New York: Ungar, 1983.

Walker, Marshall. *Robert Penn Warren, A Vision Earned.* New York: Barnes & Noble, 1979.

## Washington, Booker T.
### (Booker Taliaferro Washington)
### (1856–1915) *memoirist, nonfiction writer*

A leading black educator of the late 19th and early 20th centuries, Booker T. Washington exerted tremendous influence on race relations in the South and dominated black public affairs from the turn of the 20th century until his death in 1915. His skill as a politician and his accomodationist philosophy served him well in both these roles and became the hallmarks of his career. Booker T. Washington is best remembered for helping black Americans rise up from the economic slavery that held them down long after they were legally free citizens.

Born on April 5, 1856, on a small tobacco farm owned by the Burroughs family in Franklin County, near Roanoke, Virginia, Booker T. Washington was the son of a slave named Jane, who worked as a cook, and a white man who lived on a nearby farm. It was illegal to educate slaves, so Washington did not attend school until after emancipation. Instead, he carried the books for one of James Burroughs's daughters. He wrote in his autobiography, "I had the feeling that to get into a schoolhouse and study would be about the same as getting into paradise."

When the Emancipation Proclamation was issued, someone came to read the document to the slaves on the Burroughs farm. Soon after, Washington's family left Virginia and moved to Malden, West Virginia, where his stepfather lived. Washington went to work in a salt mine there, in a job that began at 4 A.M. so that he could attend school after work. After a few years, a wealthy woman in the town took him in as a houseboy and encouraged his education. When Washington was 16, he set off back to Virginia on foot. Washington

had heard about the Hampton Institute and knew that he would be able to work his way through the school. He finished his secondary education there, then dabbled in the ministry and in law before taking a position as a teacher at Hampton. This job as an educator changed the course of his life forever.

Washington went on to become president in 1881 of Tuskegee Normal and Industrial Institute, which was modeled after Hampton Institute, in Alabama. Although the school was barely operating when he became its president, within a decade it became one of the leading facilities for black education in America. Washington became one of the country's most influential black leaders. His influence grew even larger following his delivery of the Atlanta Compromise Address at the Cotton States Exposition in 1895. He became one of the chief black advisers to Presidents Theodore Roosevelt and William Howard Taft and to various business leaders.

Washington wrote his autobiography, *Up from Slavery,* once he had reached the height of his career. It was published in 1891 and became a huge popular and commercial success, both nationally and internationally. The account of his life focuses on his walk from West Virginia back to Virginia to attend the Hampton Institute and on his founding of the Tuskegee Institute. Proceeds from the book provided much-needed funds for the operation of Tuskegee Institute.

Washington's other works of literature include *The Future of the American Negro* (1899); *Working with the Hands* (1904); and *My Larger Education: Being Chapters from My Experience* (1911). An edition of his autobiography entitled *The Story of My Life and Work* was published in 1970 with an introduction by J. L. M. Curry and numerous illustrations by Frank Beard.

Although his influence was powerful, Washington had an ongoing feud with W. E. B. DuBOIS, who resented Washington's willingness to exercise his political muscle in what DuBois and his supporters referred to as the "Tuskegee Machine." Many charged that his conservative accomodationist politics undermined the effort toward racial equality. Washington was always aware of the need for support from powerful white people, so he

Booker T. Washington was an extremely influential educator and politician, as well as a writer. *(Library of Congress, Prints and Photographs Division [LC-USZ62-49568])*

modulated his rhetoric to avoid inflaming potential supporters. But by the last years of his life, Washington had grown weary of this approach and had begun speaking more frankly about racism. Booker T. Washington died on November 14, 1915, at the age of 59.

**Further Reading**

Gibson, Donald B. "Strategies and Revisions of Self Representation in Booker T. Washington's Autobiography." *American Quarterly* 45, no. 3 (September 1993): 370–393.

Harlan, Louis R. *Booker T. Washington in Perspective: Essays of Louis R. Harlan.* Jackson: University of Mississippi Press, 1988.

———. *Booker T. Washington: The Making of a Black Leader, 1856–1901.* New York: Oxford University Press, 1972.

———. *Booker T. Washington: The Wizard of Tuskegee, 1901–1915.* New York: Oxford University Press, 1983.

Meier, August. *Negro Thought in America, 1880–1915: Racial Ideologies in the Age of Booker T. Washington.* Ann Arbor: University of Michigan Press, 1963.

Perry, John. *Unshakable Faith: Booker T. Washington: George Washington Carver.* Sisters, Oreg.: Multnomah Publishers, 1999.

Thornbrough, Emma L. *Booker T. Washington.* Englewood Cliffs, N.J.: Prentice Hall, 1969.

## Wasserstein, Wendy
(1950–  ) *playwright, essayist*

Best known for *The Heidi Chronicles*, which won the 1989 Pulitzer Prize, a Tony Award, and the New York Drama Critics Circle Award, among others, Wendy Wasserstein has written screenplays, books, and essays, and is a contributing editor for *New York Woman* and *Harper's Bazaar*.

Wendy Wasserstein was born in Brooklyn, New York, on October 18, 1950, to Morris Wasserstein and Lola Scheifer Wasserstein. The youngest of four children, she was raised on Manhattan's Upper East Side. Her father was a textile manufacturer. Wasserstein's secondary education took place at the Calhoun School, an exclusive private school. She went to college at Mount Holyoke, in western Massachusetts where she earned her bachelor's degree in history in 1971.

Wasserstein began writing plays while still in college. The summer following her sophomore year, she enrolled in a summer playwriting course and decided she wanted to pursue playwriting as a career. When she graduated from college, Wasserstein moved back to New York and began to study creative writing at the City College of the City University of New York. Her first play, *Any Woman Can't*, was produced off Broadway in 1973 by Playwrights Horizon, a nonprofit theater group that nurtured her talent as a young playwright. The success of this first production encouraged Wasserstein to continue her study of drama. She enrolled in Yale University's School of Drama, where she met and worked with other new playwrights, including David Hollister, with whom she worked on a musical, *Mont Pelier Pa-Zazz*, which Playwrights Horizons produced in 1975. Wasserstein earned her master's degree from Yale in 1976. The following year she wrote for the Yale cabaret group, working with well-known playwright Christopher Durang.

Wasserstein's first major success was *Uncommon Women and Others* (1978), which opened at the Marymount Manhattan Theater in a full-scale off-Broadway production by the Phoenix Theater Company. It tells the story of eight Mount Holyoke women approaching adulthood at the height of the women's movement. Next came *Isn't It Romantic*, which opened in May 1981 at the Phoenix Theater but received mixed reviews that prompted Wasserstein to revise the play. It reopened at the Phoenix Theater in December 1983, and this time both critics and Wasserstein were happy. It eventually moved to a large off-Broadway theater where it ran for 733 performances.

By the late 1970s, Wasserstein turned her attention to producing two teleplays for the Public Broadcasting System (PBS). She produced *The Sorrows of Gin* (1979) by JOHN CHEEVER for PBS's Great Performances Series, and she wrote a short play called *Drive She Said* (1986) for the series *Trying Times*.

Wasserstein began work on her most famous play, *The Heidi Chronicles*, in 1986. The play follows its central character, Heidi Holland, from the early 1960s into the 1980s, when Heidi, influenced by the women's movement, begins to feel the full impact of the choices she has made. Produced by Playwrights Horizons, it opened to excellent reviews in 1988 and went on to win the Tony Award, the Pulitzer Prize for Best Play of the 1988–89 season, and the New York Drama Critics Circle Award, among others. It eventually moved to the Plymouth Theater, where it enjoyed a long Broadway run.

Wasserstein's other plays include *The Sisters Rosensweig*, which opened at Lincoln Center in October 1992 and moved to Broadway in March 1993. She also wrote the screenplays for the films *The Object of My Affection* (1998) and *Uncommon Women and Others* (2002).

Wasserstein is also the author of two books, *Bachelor Girls* (1991), a collection of essays, and

*The Heidi Chronicles and Other Plays* (1990). She has served on the Council of the Dramatists Guild, on the Board of the British American Arts Association, and as a member of Playwrights Horizons' artist board. She has taught at Columbia University and New York University.

Her other awards include the Drama Desk Award, the Susan Smith Blackburn Prize, and the Outer Critics Circle Award. She was the recipient of the William Inge Award for Distinguished Achievement in the American Theatre in 1993, and she holds an Honorary Doctorate from Mt. Holyoke College. Wendy Wasserstein lives in New York City with her daughter, Lucy Jane.

## Further Reading

Balakian, Jan. *Wendy Wasserstein. Speaking on Stage: Interviews with Contemporary American Playwrights.* Tuscaloosa: University of Alabama Press, 1996.

Cohen, Esther. "Uncommon Women: An Interview with Wendy Wasserstein" *Women's Studies: An Interdisciplinary Journal* 15, nos. 1–3 (1988): 257–270.

Franklin, Nancy. "The Time of Her Life." *New Yorker*, April 14, 1997, pp. 62–68, 70–71.

Jacobson, Leslie. "Wendy Wasserstein." In *The Playwright's Art: Conversations with Contemporary American Dramatists.* Edited by J. R. Bryer. New Brunswick, N.J.: Rutgers University Press, 1995, pp. 257–276.

## Welch, James
(1940–2003) *poet, novelist, essayist*

Part of the Montana Renaissance of the 1970s, James Welch has written four novels, a collection of poems, and a nonfiction book on the Battle of Little Big Horn. Less well known than other Native American writers of his generation, such as N. SCOTT MOMADAY, LESLIE MARMON SILKO, and LOUISE ERDRICH, Welch is a writer's writer, whose work is best known by those who seek out books on Indian subjects. Nevertheless, his achievement as a writer easily rivals those whose celebrity exceeds his.

Born on November 18, 1940, in Browning, Montana, James Welch is the son of a Blackfeet father and a Gros Ventre mother, who raised him primarily on the Fort Belknap Reservation. When he was young, Welch thought he wanted to be a writer, although he really had no idea what that might mean. He attended school on the Blackfeet and Fort Belknap reservations, graduating from high school in Minneapolis, Minnesota, in 1958. He studied at the University of Montana and Northern Montana State University at Havre before ultimately earning his B.A. degree from the University of Montana in 1965. He then spent two years studying with the poet Richard Hugo in the M.F.A. program in creative writing at the University of Montana.

Hugo urged Welch to write about what he knew—the reservation, the landscape of Montana, and the Indian people—and throughout his career, he has taken Hugo's advice to heart. He writes almost solely about the Blackfeet and is the author of six books, including *Riding the Earthboy 40* (1971), one of the first books of poetry published by a Native American author, and *Fools Crow* (1986), for which he won the American Book Award. The novel follows the life of a member of the Love Eaters band of Pikuni (Blackfeet) Indians, revealing the group's complex political structure and passing on important legends. His novel *Winter in the Blood* (1974), is considered one of the groundbreaking novels of Native American literature. His other books include the novels *The Death of Jim Loney* (1987), *The Indian Lawyer* (1990), and *The Heartsong of Charging Elk: A Novel* (2000), as well as *Killing Custer: The Battle of Little Bighorn and the Fate of the Plain Indians* (1994), a book of nonfiction.

Welch has pursued an academic career in addition to his writing. He has taught at the University of Washington and Cornell University, as well as the University of Montana. He has served on the Parole Board of the Montana Prisons Systems and on the Board of Directors of the Newberry Library D'Arcy McNickle Center.

His many awards include the Los Angeles Times Book Prize for fiction, a Chevalier de L'Ordre des Arts et des Lettres from France, the Pacific Northwest Booksellers's Association Award, and the Native Writer's Circle lifetime achievement award. He has also been awarded honorary doctorates from Rocky Mountain College and the University of Montana.

Welch died on August 4, 2003.

**Further Reading**

Bevis, William W. "James Welch." *Western American Literature* 32, no. 1 (spring 1997): 33–53.

McFarland, Ron. *James Welch*. Columbia: University of South Carolina Press, 2000.

McFarland, Ron, ed. *James Welch*. Lewiston, N.Y.: Confluence, 1986.

Velie, Alan. *Four American Indian Literary Masters: N. Scott Momaday, James Welch, Leslie Marmon Silko, and Gerald Vizenor*. Norman: University of Oklahoma Press, 1982.

Wild, Peter. *James Welch*. Boise, Idaho: Boise State University, 1983.

## Welty, Eudora Alice

(1909–2001) *short story writer, novelist, autobiographer*

Eudora Welty was considered a master of the short story and a leading figure in the literature of the South. She probed small-town eccentricities and the intricacies of relationships to depict the lives and emotions of her characters. She contended that character is brought out by strong sense of place. All of her works reflect the life and manners of the people in her native South, but Welty did not consider herself a regional writer. She won the Pulitzer Prize for the *The Optimist's Daughter* (1972), a tale of coming to terms with one's family and one's past.

Eudora Alice Welty was born on April 13, 1909, in Jackson, Mississippi, to Christian Webb, an insurance executive, and Chestina Andrew Welty, an avid reader. Welty was the oldest of three children and the only daughter. Her early interests were in painting and photography. She attended Central High School and then the Mississippi State College for Women (now the Mississippi University for Women) from 1925 to 1927. She transferred to the University of Wisconsin, where she studied English and graduated in 1929. She then went to New York City to attend the Columbia University School of Business for a short time before returning to Jackson in 1931.

During the Great Depression, Welty worked at a radio station in Jackson and for the Works Progress Administration (WPA), writing articles and advertisements. An amateur photographer, she also took pictures of Mississippi life, some of which were published in the WPA's *Guide to Mississippi*. A collection of her photographs was published in 1989. Her first short story was published in 1936 when "Death of a Traveling Salesman" appeared in the literary magazine *Manuscript*. The story established the photographic technique and the subject matter that would become the foundation for much of Welty's work. Many of her stories are set in small towns or rural Mississippi. She focused on characters that are psychotic, mentally retarded, senile, suicidal, or suffering from other afflictions as she developed her themes, often with humor. Some themes included the fulfillment of marriage or the satisfactions and the constraints of domestic rituals, imbued with undercurrents of death, violence, and degradation. "I'm not any kind of prophet, but I think it's in our nature to talk, to tell stories, appreciate stories," she said in a 1991 interview. "I think you write about whatever's current. . . . They won't be the same kind of stories, but they'll be about human beings."

After publishing stories in a number of other magazines, including the *New Yorker* and the *Atlantic Monthly*, Welty's publication of the story collection *A Curtain of Green* (1941) brought her a widespread audience. It contained two of her most anthologized stories, "The Petrified Man," which dealt with illicit sexuality, and "Why I Live at the P.O.," which focused on an odd, solitary young woman in a small town. Welty drew on her experiences traveling across Mississippi for the WPA to write the stories in *A Curtain of Green*.

In 1942, her short novel *The Robber Bridegroom* was published, followed by her first full-length novel, *Delta Wedding* (1946). *The Robber Bridegroom* was an extended fantasy, a folktale mixing elements of fairy tales, Celtic tales, and ancient classical myths. The story deals with self-deception, self-discovery, and the ambiguity of love. But just as Welty was gaining national recognition she had to put her writing on hold to help her ailing two brothers and mother. She spent most of the next decade caring for them.

Her next novels included *The Ponder Heart* (1954), *Losing Battles* (1970), and *The Optimist's*

*Daughter*, a semiautobiographical novel that won the Pulitzer Prize in 1973. *The Optimist's Daughter* explores the bonds between parents and children, and the complexities of love and grief. It tells the story of a young southern woman who travels to New Orleans to take care of her dying father. After his death, she returns to the small Mississippi town where she was raised and, while living in her old family home, comes to terms with her past and her relationship with her family.

"It is easy to praise Eudora Welty," ROBERT PENN WARREN wrote, "but it is not easy to analyze the elements in her work that make it so easy—and such a deep pleasure—to praise. To say that may, indeed, be the highest praise, for it implies that the work, at its best, is so fully created, so deeply realized, and formed with such apparent innocence that it offers only itself, in shining unity."

*The Wide Net and Other Stories* (1943), *The Golden Apples* (1949), and *The Bride of Innisfallen and Other Stories* (1955) are collections of short stories, and *The Eye of the Story* (1978) is a volume of essays. *The Collected Stories of Eudora Welty* was published in 1980. One of her most popular books, *One Writer's Beginnings*, was published in 1984. This autobiography explored what Welty called her "sheltered life" in Jackson and how her early fiction grew out of it. "As you have seen, I am a writer who came of a sheltered life. A sheltered life can be a daring life as well. For all serious daring starts from within," Welty wrote.

Welty received numerous awards, including the Pulitzer Prize, the National Book Critics Circle Award, the American Book Award, four O. Henry Awards, the Gold Medal of the National Institute of Arts and Letters, the Medal of Freedom, and the Howells Gold Medal for Fiction of the Academy of Arts and Letters. She lectured and taught at many colleges. Welty avoided the role of a public literary figure and always returned to her childhood home in Mississippi. She never married. She died at the age of 92 on July 22, 2001.

## Further Reading

Bloom, Harold, ed. *Eudora Welty*. New York: Chelsea, 1986.

Carson, Barbara H. *Eudora Welty: Two Pictures at Once in Her Frame*. Troy, N.Y.: Whitston, 1992.

Waldron, Ann. *Eudora: A Writer's Life*. New York: Doubleday, 1998.

Weston, Ruth D. *Gothic Traditions and Narrative Techniques in the Fiction of Eudora Welty*. Baton Rouge: Louisiana State University Press, 1994.

## West, Nathanael
**(Nathan Weinstein)**
(1903–1940) *novelist*

Nathanael West attempted to reveal what he saw as the absurdity and fraudulence of the American dream. He was fascinated by the power of unfulfilled desires. His best-known novel, *The Day of the Locust* (1939), presented a gallery of horrifying misfits living in a vacuous, surreal Hollywood atmosphere. Many consider it to be the most scathing attack on Hollywood ever written. Although West was never a commercial success, nor much of a critical success, in his lifetime, his popularity rose after World War II, first in France. West wrote four novels before he was killed in an automobile accident at the age of 37.

Nathanael West was born Nathan Weinstein on October 17, 1903, in New York City, the son of Max Weinstein, a construction contractor, and Anna (Wallenstein) Weinstein. His parents were well-off immigrant Jews from Lithuania. West gained admission to Tufts University, but quickly flunked out, and forged admissions records to gain admittance to Brown University. He edited a campus literary magazine and tried to cultivate the manner and dress of the gentile Ivy League elite. He graduated in 1924 and changed his name to Nathanael West. He had not had a traditional Jewish upbringing and was embarrassed by his Jewish heritage.

West went to Paris for two years and led a bohemian life among the Lost Generation there. When he returned to New York, he managed small hotels from 1927 to 1932. West assisted other writers with housing at these hotels, including Dashiell Hammett and ERSKINE CALDWELL. His first novel, *The Dream Life of Balso Snell* (1931), was a garish satire about Western civilization set in the innards of the Trojan horse. The book was a critical and commercial failure. West coedited the literary jour-

nal *Contact* with WILLIAM CARLOS WILLIAMS and edited the magazine *Americana* briefly as well. Although he was a communist sympathizer, he never joined the party or made political ideology prominent in his fiction.

West worked as a journalist in the early 1930s, drawing on his experiences to write his second novel, *Miss Lonelyhearts* (1933). It depicted the painful life of a male columnist for the lovelorn, who goes by the pen name Miss Lonelyhearts. He becomes tragically involved with one of his suffering correspondents—a 16-year-old girl who was born without a nose. Although the book was a critical success it sold poorly. A movie version of the book debuted in 1958.

West's next novel, *A Cool Million* (1934), was an attack on the optimistic rags-to-riches ideal, the same ideal that his father had pushed on him as a child, hoping he would enter the family business. West moved to Hollywood in the mid 1930s, struggling as a scriptwriter and gathering material for his next novel. *The Day of the Locust* (1939) was a study of the fragility of illusion. "Amid Hollywood-dominated Los Angeles, West found a realm so imbued by consumer culture and its 'dream factories,' as to be wholly unaware of its vapid and ironical absurdities," wrote critic Jim Tejani. "The cityscape unfolds as an unending film reel where the central difficulty is discerning where charade ends and reality begins." *The Day of the Locust* received mixed reviews—some believed its theme was too dark for depression-era America—and it did not sell well. *The Complete Works of Nathanael West* was published in 1957.

West was killed in an automobile accident on December 22, 1940, in California, with his wife, Eileen McKenney, while returning from a trip to Mexico. They were recently married. West's good friend, F. SCOTT FITZGERALD, died the previous day, overshadowing press coverage of West's own death.

### Further Reading
Barnard, Rita. *The Great Depression and the Culture of Abundance: Kenneth Fearing, Nathanael West, and Mass Culture in the 1930s*. New York: Cambridge University Press, 1995.

Long, Robert Emmet. *Nathanael West*. New York: Ungar Publishing Company, 1985.

Martin, Jay. *Nathanael West: The Art of His Life.* New York: Carroll & Graf, 1984.

## Wharton, Edith
### (Edith Newbold Jones)

(1862–1937)  *novelist, short story writer, poet, essayist, travel writer, letter writer, journalist, memoirist*

The author of more than 40 books, Edith Wharton was the first woman to win the Pulitzer Prize, which she was awarded in 1921 for her novel *The Age of Innocence.* Wharton chronicled the lives of women within society's upper echelons, giving particular attention to the limitations that social conventions placed on individual fulfillment.

Born Edith Newbold Jones in New York City on January 24, 1862, Wharton was raised with her two older brothers in a wealthy and socially prominent family. Her parents, George Frederic and Lucretia Jones, were descendants of English and Dutch colonists who had made fortunes in shipping, banking, and real estate. Her family lived on inherited wealth and traveled frequently in Europe, spending six years there, from the time Edith was four until she was 10. When the Joneses returned to the United States and settled in Manhattan, she did not attend school but read voraciously on her own from her father's library and was instructed in various subjects by a governess.

In 1885, when she was 23, she married Edward ("Teddy") Robbins Wharton, an attractive and kind man, who came from a similar social background. A banker from Boston, Teddy Wharton was 12 years her senior and not at all interested in the intellectual pursuits that captivated his wife. Edith Wharton's first book, *The Decoration of Houses,* appeared in 1897. Written with Ogden Codman, a friend and architect, the book denounced lavish Victorian decorating practices, proposing instead a look based on classical design principles of symmetry, proportion, and balance in architecture. The book was quite successful and encouraged the emergence of a new era in professional decorating.

In the 1890s, Wharton began contributing stories to *Scribner's Magazine.* Her first collection of short stories appeared in the late 1890s, but it was her first novel, *The House of Mirth* (1905), that made her famous. The story of an unforgettable character, Lily Bart, who is trying to survive as a woman alone in New York City at the turn of the 20th century, the book became an overnight success. It was followed by *The Custom of the Country* (1913), which tells the story of a young, ambitious upper-class woman. *The Age of Innocence,* which won the Pulitzer Prize, appeared in 1920 and told the story of one man's frustrated love for a woman outside his social standing.

Not long after, her husband began to spend money on younger women and to show increasing signs of mental instability. Wharton's role as a wife with social responsibilities and her writing ambitions resulted in nervous collapse. On hearing that she had composed poems as a teenager, her doctor advised her to resume her writing, believing it would aid in her recovery. In 1902, Wharton built her own country house, The Mount, in Lenox, Massachusetts, but beginning in 1906 the Whartons spent much of their time in Europe. While residing in Paris, in the historic Faubourg Saint-Germain area, where she had begun spending winters in 1907, Wharton met Morton Fullerton, a journalist on the *London Times* and a friend of HENRY JAMES. Their affair began in 1908 and lasted until 1909. He was the great love of her life, but judging from letters she wrote to Fullerton that were published in 1988 in *The Letters of Edith Wharton,* he often toyed with her affection.

Edith Wharton divorced her husband in 1913 and remained in France, where she spent the rest of her life, even though she always maintained a residence in the United States. At her garden home in the south of France and at her Paris apartment, she became a literary hostess to young writers. Her circle of friends included Henry James, Walter Berry, Bernard Berenson, Paul Bourget, Jacques-Émile Blanche, Anna de Noailles, André Gide, and Jean Cocteau. She also enjoyed on occasion the company of Theodore Roosevelt when he visited Paris.

Wharton was a prolific writer, completing nearly a book a year starting in 1902. Among her best known works are *The Valley of Decision* (1902), *The House of Mirth* (1905), *Madame de Treymes* (1907), *Ethan Frome* (1911), *The Reef* (1912), *The*

*Custom of the Country* (1913), *The Age of Innocence* (1920), *Old New York* (1924), *A Backward Glance* (1934), and *The Buccaneers* (1938), which was completed by Marion Manwaring following Wharton's death.

Wharton became fiercely dedicated to the Allied cause during World War I. She helped to organize the American Hostel for Refugees and the Children of Flanders Rescue Committee, which took care of 600 Belgian children who had to leave their orphanage when the Germans began their advance across Europe. She also helped establish

The first woman to win the Pulitzer Prize, Edith Wharton became the grande dame of American letters, though she spent most of her adult life in Europe. *(Library of Congress, Prints and Photographs Division [LC-USZ62-29408])*

jobs for women who were left with no means of support during the war years. She also traveled to the front lines of war and reported for newspapers and other publications in America, urging the United States to join the war. Wharton also helped produce an anthology of war writings by prominent writers and artists of the time.

By the end of her career, Wharton had become a grande dame of American letters. In addition to the Pulitzer Prize, Wharton was a member of the National Institute of Arts and Letters and the American Academy of Arts and Letters. She was the first female recipient of the Gold Medal of the National Institute of Arts and Letters and was nominated for the Nobel Prize in literature in 1927. She was also a recipient of the French Legion of Honor for her philanthropic work during World War I. She returned to the United States in 1913 and then in 1923 for the final time in order to receive an honorary degree from Yale University, the first woman ever awarded an honorary doctorate by Yale. The last years of her life were spent gardening in France. In the summer her home was at Pavillon Colombe, a small village north of Paris. Winters were spent at Château Sainte-Claire at Hyères, an estate perched over the Mediterranean Sea. She had many visitors in these years and continued to write and travel. She died in France on September 11, 1937.

### Further Reading

Bell, Millicent, ed. *The Cambridge Companion to Edith Wharton.* New York: Cambridge University Press, 1995.

Benstock, Shari. *No Gifts from Chance: A Biography of Edith Wharton.* New York: Scribner's, 1994.

Goodwyn, Janet. *Edith Wharton: Traveller in the Land of Letters.* New York: St. Martin's, 1990.

McDowell, Margaret. *Edith Wharton.* Boston: Twayne, 1991.

### Wheatley, Phillis
### (Phillis Peters)
(ca. 1753–1784) *poet*

Phillis Wheatley's poems were the first published work by an African American. Her poems, whose themes were moral or religious, were considered to be among the best of 18th-century America. Wheatley was among the first to address such issues as slavery in verse, as in the poem "On Being Brought from Africa to America." However, her poems were not political. In the 1830s, abolitionists reprinted her poetry and the powerful ideas contained in her verse stood against the institution of slavery. Her most well-known poems are "To the University of Cambridge in New England" and "To the King's Most Excellent Majesty."

Phillis Wheatley was born in about 1753 and was captured in Africa and sold in the Boston slave market in 1761. She was bought by John Wheatley, a pious and wealthy tailor, and Susanna Wheatley. Phillis Wheatley was welcomed more as a new member of the Wheatley household than as a slave. They recognized Wheatley's remarkable intelligence and, with the help of their daughter, Mary, Phillis learned to read and write. She quickly learned English and Latin. Her earliest surviving poem was written when she was 12 or 13 years old. She imitated popular poets of the day, such as Alexander Pope and Thomas Gray.

Wheatley's first poem was published when she was 17 years old. "On Messrs. Hussey and Coffin" appeared in the *Newport Mercury* in 1767. In the following years, a number of poems appeared in various publications in and around Boston. "On the Death of the Rev. Mr. George Whitefield, 1770," a tribute to the great evangelical preacher who frequently toured New England, was published in at least 10 separate editions in cities such as Boston, Newport, and Philadelphia. The poem made her a sensation in Boston. In 1770, the poem appeared in London and served to cement Wheatley's growing international reputation as a talented poet.

She tried to sell newspaper advertisements to solicit enough subscribers to publish a collection of her poems, but when skepticism over her racial background made this impossible, Susanna Wheatley helped arrange for the poems to be published in London in 1773. *Poems on Various Subjects, Religious and Moral* is the first book known to be published by an African American. Wheatley was 20 years old. Wheatley traveled to London with a member of the Wheatley family to promote the

Phillis Wheatley was likely the first African American to be published in the United States. *(From Wheatley's book* Poems on Various Subjects, *1773. Library of Congress, Prints and Photographs Division [LC-USZ62-40054])*

book and to recuperate from the frigid New England winters. There were at least four printings of the book in London the first year, but the publication sold poorly in Boston, again because of resistance to Wheatley's race.

Around the same time Wheatley's first poetry collection was published she was formally freed by the Wheatley family. But she chose to remain with them until her marriage to John Peters, a free black man, in 1778. Wheatley struggled to support her family as a poet and as a seamstress. Peters was having little luck in business. Wheatley could no longer rely on the support of the Wheatleys because they had passed away. Peters put Phillis and their children into a black boardinghouse where poor sanitary conditions resulted in the children's deaths and a drastic decline in Wheatley's health.

Wheatley continued, however, to write poetry. In 1779, she advertised in the *Boston Evening Post* and *General Advertiser*, in hopes of finding a publisher for a volume of 33 poems and 13 letters. But the volume was never published. In 1784, several poems celebrating the end of the Revolution were published under the name Phillis Peters. Although Wheatley addressed issues such as slavery in her poetry, she was also a patriot and admirer of George Washington. The only indication of injustice found in her poems is in the line "Some view our sable race with scornful eye." It would take nearly 100 more years for another African American to write openly about the African-American experience. Another theme in Wheatley's poetry was the salvation message of Christianity—that all men and women, regardless of race or class, are in need of salvation. Among Wheatley's best-known poems is "To S.M., a Young African Painter, on Seeing His Works." The poem praised and encouraged another talented black artist and both confronts white racism and asserts spiritual equality.

On December 5, 1784, Wheatley died in Boston. After her death, Peters went to a woman who had provided temporary shelter for Wheatley and the children and demanded the manuscripts of the proposed second volume. But the manuscripts disappeared with Peters and have never been recovered.

**Further Reading**

Derounian, Kathryn Zabell, and William H. Robinson, eds. *Critical Essays on Phillis Wheatley*. New York: Hall, 1982.

Shields, John, ed. *The Collected Works of Phillis Wheatley*. New York: Oxford University Press, 1988.

Watson, Marsha. "A Classic Case: Phillis Wheatley and Her Poetry." *Early American Literature* 31, no. 2 (1996): 103–132.

# Whitman, Walt
(1819–1892) *poet*

Walt Whitman is one of America's most celebrated poets and was an early campaigner for human rights. His work reflected a 19th-century America that he often considered cruel, discriminating, and unfair. In Whitman's era, such views were thought of as unpatriotic, and Whitman was often chided. Only after his death was his work reevaluated. Whitman is best known for the poetry collection *Leaves of Grass* (1855), which was occasionally banned, and for the poems "I Sing the Body Electric" and "Song of Myself." Whitman published more than 500 poems, but he lived his entire life in poverty.

Walt Whitman was born on May 31, 1819, in Long Island, New York, the son of Walt Whitman, Sr., a Quaker carpenter and farmer, and Louisa Van Velsor. The elder Whitman was never very successful at either of his trades, and moved his wife and nine children to Brooklyn in 1823 to pursue a career as a house builder. Young Walt, had a great love of nature early in his life that was later reflected in his poetry. He attended elementary school in Brooklyn, and when he was 11 years old he began to work as a clerk in a local office. He left school early to become a printer's apprentice, although he remained an avid reader. In 1836, at the age of 17, Whitman began teaching in the one-room schoolhouses of Long Island. He turned to journalism as a full-time career in 1841 and founded his own weekly newspaper, *The Long Islander*. Through poetry and prose, Whitman began to express and publish his views on democracy and American society. He also edited and wrote for several other periodicals, including *The Brooklyn Eagle*.

In 1848, he took an editing job at a newspaper called *Crescent* in New Orleans, but returned within six months to Brooklyn to edit the *Brooklyn Freeman*. However, Whitman's trip to New Orleans changed his life and his art. After witnessing the conditions of slavery, he began to write about the abuses he saw. The Mexican-American War further prompted him to write about oppression, poverty, honor, and compassion. These became the central themes of Whitman's poetry. Whitman set out to write a collection of poems based on his experiences and his views of American democratic idealism and the country's hopeful expectations.

The first edition of *Leaves of Grass* appeared in 1855, printed at Whitman's expense because no respected publisher would consider the work. The book consisted of 12 untitled poems and a preface. It was followed by five revised and three reissued editions during the author's lifetime. *Leaves of Grass* spoke of compassion for slaves, respect for prostitutes, and opposition to the draft. The collection includes a group of poems entitled "Calamus," which Whitman said celebrated the "beautiful and sane affection of man for man." The poems have been considered to reveal Whitman as homosexual. He reportedly had only one abortive attempt at a sexual relationship, presumably with a man. *Leaves of Grass* also referred to Adam and Eve as myths, which prompted some Americans to accuse Whitman of blasphemy. He was also considered a traitor and immoral. RALPH WALDO EMERSON, however, was among Whitman's early admirers and wrote of *Leaves of Grass* in 1855: "I am very happy in reading it, as great power makes us happy."

Whitman's poems were written to be spoken. They have a great variety in rhythm and tonal volume. He maintained that a poet's style should be simple and natural, without orthodox meter or rhyme. His use of free verse had a profound influence on poetry, and would be an inspiring example for the Beat generation of the 1950s. Whitman's second edition of *Leaves of Grass* (1856) contained 33 poems, a letter from Emerson praising the first edition, and a long open letter by Whitman in response. "Song of Myself" has been considered by many to be Whitman's most important work. Its message is that everyone carries something of the divine within and that the holiest thing people can do for themselves and society is to listen and learn.

> I have said that the soul is not more
>     than the body,
> And I have said that the body is not
>     more than the soul,
> And nothing, not God, is greater to one
>     than one's self is,
> And whoever walks a furlong without
>     sympathy walks to his
> Own funeral drest in his shroud . . .

Revisions to the third edition of *Leaves of Grass* were made to include references to the Civil War, which had broken out in 1861. Whitman traveled to Washington, D.C., where he ended up staying for 11 years, to care for his brother after he was

wounded. He also cared for other Union and Confederate soldiers and worked as a clerk for the Department of the Interior. His job there ended, however, when the secretary of the interior, James Harlan, discovered that Whitman was the author of *Leaves of Grass*. Harland found the work offensive and fired Whitman. Whitman published *Drum-Taps* in 1865, which contained poems about the war. The assassination of President Abraham Lincoln greatly affected Whitman because he felt that Lincoln was the ideal democratic figure. *Sequel to Drum-Taps* (1865–66) included the famous elegy on Lincoln, "When Lilacs Last in the Dooryard Bloom'd." The blooming lilacs of April, which was the month Lincoln died, reminded Whitman of the

Walt Whitman published more than 500 poems during his lifetime. *(Library of Congress, Prints and Photographs Division [LC-USZ62-79934])*

slain president. The lilacs also served as a metaphor for the eternal renewal of life. Another famous Whitman poem about the death of Lincoln was "O Captain! My Captain!"

By the 1870s, although most Americans continued to criticize Whitman, *Leaves of Grass* had been translated into French and German. The French, German, English, and Spanish were much greater fans of his poetry. Few American writers have had a greater influence in as many parts of the world as Whitman. *Leaves of Grass* has been translated in complete editions in Spain, France, Germany, Italy, China, and Japan, and partial translations have appeared in all major languages but Arabic. His importance stems not only from his literary qualities but also from his defense of liberty and revolution; he has been a major icon for socialists and communists.

Whitman settled in Camden, New Jersey, where he had gone to visit his dying mother at his brother's house in the 1870s. He continued adding poems and revising *Leaves of Grass*. In 1873, at the age of 44, Whitman suffered a stroke that left him severely paralyzed, preventing him from returning to Washington. He would never fully recover from the stroke, yet he continued to publish poetry, to give lectures on the successes of President Lincoln, and to give public readings. In 1882, Whitman published *Specimen Days* and *Collect*. In 1888, he had another severe stroke, which nearly immobilized him completely. Sick as he was, he still managed to write and publish *November Boughs* and *Complete Poems and Prose*.

His final volume of poems and prose was *Good-Bye, My Fancy* (1891). His "deathbed" edition of *Leaves of Grass* was prepared in 1892. It concludes with the prose piece "A Backward Glance O'er Travel'd Roads," in which he attempts to explain his life and work. Whitman died on March 26, 1892, in Camden.

**Further Reading**

Loving, Jerome. *Walt Whitman: The Song of Himself.* Los Angeles: University of California Press, 1999.

Reynolds, David S. *A Historical Guide to Walt Whitman.* New York: Oxford University Press, 2000.

Whitman, Walt, and Jonathan Levin. *Walt Whitman.* Boston: Sterling Publishers, 1997.

## Wideman, John Edgar

(1941–    ) *novelist, nonfiction writer, literary critic*

John Edgar Wideman's work has universal appeal. He was a Rhodes Scholar and a basketball star, as talented on the court as he was intelligent in the classroom. Wideman is the only writer to have been awarded the PEN/Faulkner Award for Fiction twice—once in 1984 for his novel *Sent for You Yesterday* and again in 1990 for *Philadelphia Fire*. The latter also won the National Book Award. Wideman has written nearly 20 works of fiction and nonfiction. His works have been translated into 11 languages, including Italian, Japanese, and Turkish. He has also written four short story collections and is a widely published essayist and social critic.

John Edgar Wideman was born on June 14, 1941, in Washington, D.C. Shortly before his first birthday, his family moved to Homewood, an African-American community in Pittsburgh, Pennsylvania. Wideman has used Homewood as a locale for much of his fiction. He attended Peabody High School, one of Pittsburgh's best secondary schools, where he excelled in his studies as well as in sports. He was awarded a Benjamin Franklin Scholarship by the University of Pennsylvania, where he not only won a creative writing prize but also earned membership in Phi Beta Kappa. Matching his scholastic achievements with his athletic ones, he won All–Ivy League status as a forward on the basketball team and successfully competed on the track team. In 1963, he graduated with a B.A. degree in English, and won a Rhodes scholarship to study philosophy at Oxford University's New College. Wideman is the second African-American Rhodes Scholar. He graduated from Oxford in 1966.

Returning to the United States in 1966, Wideman spent a year as a Kent Fellow at the University of Iowa Writers' Workshop, where he completed his first novel, *A Glance Away* (1967), at age 26. He then published *Hurry Home* (1969), *The Lynchers* (1973), the short story collection *Damballah* (1981), *The Homewood Trilogy* (1984), and *Brothers and Keepers* (1984). The latter was a memoir about his brother Robby's murder conviction and life sentence. The victim was killed by Robby's partner in a robbery in 1976. The memoir told of Wideman's struggle to come to terms with his brother's actions and their consequences. In 1986, Wideman's 16-year-old son stabbed and killed a classmate during a field trip. Reports indicated that the boy suffered from emotional trouble.

Some of Wideman's other books include *Fever* (1989), *Two Cities* (1998), and the short story collection *All Stories Are True* (1993). *Two Cities* is a redemptive, healing love story that brings to culmination the themes Wideman has developed over the years. Narrated by its three main characters, *Two Cities* recalls the gripping drama of *Philadelphia Fire* and the emotional resonance of *Fatheralong*. *All Stories Are True* is set mainly in Homewood. The 10 stories depict African Americans from all walks of life, including ancestors, family, and lovers, in the context of American history and their own demons.

"Writing of any sort consists of setting down one word after another, making something that doesn't exist until it's expressed with the medium of written language," Wideman has said. "The effort of making is at some level play, like patting clay, beating a drum, or tapping your toes, singing, or spreading paint with your fingertips—play that's a gift to the artist the artist passes on, from the one to the many to the one. Serious play that reminds us we're all in this together, this life, and what we make goes into the collective project to brighten and lighten, to glorify and transform the unavoidable pain and burden of being alive."

Wideman's *Hoop Roots* (2001) is his memoir of discovering basketball one hot summer when his grandmother was dying. It is also the story of the roots of black basketball in America, which Wideman sees as a story inextricable from American racism. In two years, two of Wideman's books were included on the list of 15 best books of the year by the *New York Times Book Review*. In 1998, Wideman won the Rea Award. In 1990, he also received the American Book Award for fiction. He was awarded a Lannan Literary Fellowship for Fiction in 1991 and the MacArthur Award in 1993. Other honors include the St. Botolph Literary Award (1993), the DuSable Museum Prize for Nonfiction for *Brothers and Keepers* (1985), the

Longwood College Medal for Literary Excellence, and the National Magazine Editors' Prize for Short Fiction (1987).

Wideman began his teaching career in the English department of the University of Pennsylvania, where he founded and chaired the African-American studies department. He is a professor of English at the University of Massachusetts, Amherst. His articles on Malcolm X, Spike Lee, Michael Jordan, and women's professional basketball, among other issues and personalities, have appeared in the *New Yorker*, *Vogue*, *Esquire*, *Emerge*, and the *New York Times Magazine*. Wideman lives in Amherst with his wife, Judy, a lawyer specializing in death penalty cases.

**Further Reading**

Byerman, Keith E. *John Edgar Wideman: A Study of the Short Fiction*. Boston: Twayne Publishers, 1998.

Coleman, James W. *Blackness and Modernism: The Literary Career of John Edgar Wideman*. Jackson: University Press of Mississippi, 1989.

Lucy, Robin. "John Edgar Wideman (1941– )." *Contemporary African American Novelists: A Bio-Bibliographical Critical Sourcebook*. Westport, Conn.: Greenwood, 1999, pp. 482–490.

TuSmith, Bonnie. *Conversations with John Edgar Wideman*. Jackson: University Press of Mississippi, 1998.

## Wilder, Thornton Niven
(1897–1975) *playwright, novelist*

Thornton Wilder is the only writer to have won the Pulitzer Prize for both literature and drama. Through his novels and plays, Wilder put humankind under a magnifying glass, often in an expansive historical context. Wilder was best known for his Pulitzer Prize–winning play *Our Town* (1938), a story that focused on the universality of human experience. In *The Skin of Our Teeth* (1943), also a Pulitzer winner, Wilder wrote of a family affected by war, disease, and poverty over thousands of years. His novel *The Bridge of San Luis Rey* (1943) also won a Pulitzer.

Thornton Niven Wilder was born in Madison, Wisconsin, on April 17, 1897, the son of Amos

Parker Wilder and Isabella Niven Wilder. His twin brother died at birth, and Wilder grew up with an another brother and three younger sisters. The family lived in China for a time, where Amos Parker Wilder was U.S. consul general to Hong Kong and Shanghai. He had also been a newspaper editor and was a strict Calvinist. Thornton Wilder began writing as a boy. He finished high school in California, and in 1915 he enrolled in Oberlin College, in Ohio, where he studied the Greek and Roman classics in translation. In 1917 the family moved to New Haven, Connecticut. Wilder transferred to Yale University. Wilder's first full-length play, *The Trumpet Shall Sound,* appeared in 1920 in the *Yale Literary Magazine,* but it was not produced until 1926. Wilder served for eight months in the Coast Artillery Corps as a corporal in World War I. He received his undergraduate degree at Yale in 1920 and went to Rome, where he studied archaeology at the American Academy. He received an M.A. degree in French literature from Princeton in 1926.

His first novel, *The Cabala,* was published the same year. It was a fantasy about U.S. expatriates in post–World War I Italian society. Wilder's second novel, *The Bridge of San Luis Rey* (1927), was a breakthrough. The story examined justice and altruism as it focused on the fates of five travelers in 18th-century Peru. As they cross a bridge, it breaks and they are killed. A scholarly monk attempts to explain the working of divine providence through the tragedy.

Wilder's next book, *The Woman of Andros* (1930) featured his archetype of the virtue of hope through the character Chrysis. From 1930 to 1937, Wilder worked as a part-time lecturer in comparative literature at the University of Chicago. Wilder's best known work, *Our Town* (1938) was inspired by *The Making of Americans* (1925), by GERTRUDE STEIN, a close friend. *Our Town* became a huge success and earned Wilder another Pulitzer. The story was set in the fictitious Grover's Corners, New Hampshire, and traced the childhood, courtship, marriage, and death of Emily Webb and George Gibbs. Most of Wilder's novels were historical, but with *Heaven's My Destination* (1934), Wilder began to focus more on contemporary America. The story was a satirical portrait of an evangelical fundamentalist traveling salesman. *The Skin of Our Teeth,* inspired by James Joyce's *Finnegans Wake,* premiered in 1942 and told of 5,000 years in the life of a suburban family.

Early in World War II Wilder enlisted in the army. He eventually became a lieutenant colonel in the air force and earned the Legion of Merit and the Bronze Star. His responsibilities included the interrogation of prisoners and the preparation of reports for the Mediterranean Air Headquarters. After his discharge, Wilder completed *The Ides of March* (1948), a historical novel about Julius Caesar, with which he had been long struggling and which was his most experimental work. Wilder's *The Merchant of Yonkers* (1938) was revised under the new title of *The Matchmaker* (1954). In 1964, the musical comedy *Hello, Dolly!,* based on the play, opened in New York.

This portrait shows Thornton Wilder as Mr. Antrobus in his play "The Skin of Our Teeth." *(Library of Congress, Prints and Photographs Division, Carl Van Vechten Collection [LC-USZ62-42494])*

Wilder received the National Medal for Literature in 1962. His last two novels were *The Eighth Day* (1967), a story about a talented inventor accused of murder, and *Theophilus North* (1973), about a young man and his many possible careers. Wilder died on December 7, 1975, in Hamden, Connecticut, where he had lived off and on for many years with his sister Isabel Wilder, who was also his secretary, business manager, and literary adviser. He never married and was believed to be homosexual, although his personal relationships were few.

## Further Reading

Blank, Martin. *Critical Essays on Thornton Wilder.* New York: G. K. Hall, 1996.

Castronovo, David. *Thornton Wilder.* New York: Ungar, 1986.

Kuner, Mildred C. *Thornton Wilder: The Bright and the Dark.* New York: Crowell, 1972.

Wilder, Amos N. *Thornton Wilder and his Public.* Philadelphia: Fortress Press, 1980.

## Williams, Tennessee
### (Thomas Lanier Williams)
(1911–1983) *playwright, autobiographer, novelist, poet, screenwriter, short story writer*

Tennessee Williams is considered one of America's greatest playwrights. Nearly all of his plays are set in the South but rise above regionalism to approach universal themes. Often drawing on his own life for inspiration, Williams examined turbulent emotional and sexual forces and physical and spiritual needs. He won the Pulitzer Prize three times, for *A Streetcar Named Desire* (1947), *Cat on a Hot Tin Roof* (1955), and *Night of the Iguana* (1961). He also won four New York Drama Critics' Circle Awards. In addition to more than two dozen full-length plays, Williams produced dozens of short plays and screenplays, two novels, a novella, 60 short stories, more than 100 poems, and an autobiography.

Tennessee Williams was born Thomas Lanier Williams in Columbus, Mississippi, on March 26, 1911, the second of three children of Cornelius

Coffin Williams and Edwina Dakin Williams. His mother, the daughter of a minister, was of genteel upbringing, while his father, a shoe salesman, came from a prominent Tennessee family, which included the state's first governor and first senator. The Williams household was often full of tension and despair, owing in part to the father's gambling and drinking. The family lived for several years in Clarksdale, Mississippi, before moving to St. Louis, Missouri, in 1918. Williams's schoolmates ridiculed him for his poverty and deep southern accent, which earned him the nickname "Tennessee" from his university classmates. At age 16, Williams won third prize for an essay, "Can a Good Wife Be a Good Sport?," in *Smart Set*. A year later, he published "The Vengeance of Nitocris" in *Weird Tales*. In 1928, Williams traveled with his grandfather to Europe and was inspired by its atmosphere and culture to write poetry. He entered the University of Missouri in 1929. His chances for success there were dubious and the family's lack of funds forced him to leave. In 1931, Williams began work for the same shoe company that employed his father. There he worked with a young man named Stanley Kowalski whom he would later adapt into a character in *A Streetcar Named Desire*.

Williams returned to school, transferring to the University of Iowa. Two of his plays, *Candles to the Sun* and *The Fugitive Kind*, were produced by Mummers of St. Louis in 1937. The following year he graduated from the University of Iowa. After failing to find work in Chicago, he moved to New Orleans and changed his name from "Tom" to "Tennessee." As World War II loomed, Williams found a bit of fame when he won the Group Theater prize of $100 for *American Blues. Battle of Angels* was produced in Boston in 1940. Among the writers he admired were Federico Garcia Lorca, Arthur Rimbaud, Rainer Maria Rilke, HART CRANE, and D. H. Lawrence.

Near the close of the war in 1944, what many consider to be Williams's finest play, *The Glass Menagerie*, had a very successful run in Chicago. A year later it received critical acclaim after appearing on Broadway. The play tells the story of Tom, his disabled sister Laura, and their controlling mother Amanda. Amanda tries to make a match between Laura, a withdrawn crippled girl who collects glass animal figures, and a gentleman caller. During a quarrel with his mother, Tom smashes Laura's menagerie. Laura was modeled after Williams's beloved sister Rose, his muse, who spent most of her life in mental hospitals and was lobotomized. Williams cared for Rose throughout much of her adult life. *The Glass Menagerie* won the New York Drama Critics' Circle Award for best play of the season. Williams, at age 34, had made his mark.

Shortly after *The Glass Menagerie* closed, the playwright was already at work on a new piece that contained the image of a young woman who had just been stood up by the man she was planning to marry. He saw her sitting alone in a chair by a window in the moonlight. By 1947, this piece was finished and performed on the stage as *A Streetcar Named Desire*. The fading southern belle Blanche DuBois and the oafish and cruel Stanley Kowalski became household names nearly overnight. The play won a Pulitzer Prize and was made into a successful movie directed by Elia Kazan and starring Vivien Leigh and Marlon Brando.

"There are no 'good' or 'bad' people. Some are a little better or a little worse but all are activated more by misunderstanding than malice. A blindness to what is going on in each other's hearts," Williams was quoted as saying in Kazan's autobiography *A Life* (1988). "Stanley sees Blanche not as a desperate, driven creature backed into a last corner to make a last desperate stand—but as a calculating bitch . . . Nobody sees anybody truly but all through the flaws of their own egos. That is the way we all see each other in life."

Over the next eight years Williams wrote *Summer and Smoke* (1948), *The Rose Tattoo* (1951), and *Camino Real* (1953), which all appeared on Broadway. Although his reputation on Broadway continued to grow, Williams reached a larger, worldwide public after *The Glass Menagerie* and *A Streetcar Named Desire* were made into films. Williams had achieved a fame few playwrights of his day could equal. Later plays that were also made into motion pictures include the Pulitzer Prize–winning *Cat on a Hot Tin Roof*, which dramatizes the conflicts of a Mississippi family following the diagnosis of their father's cancer. It became a popular film starring Elizabeth Taylor, Paul Newman, and Burl Ives. Williams's reputation continued to grow with plays such as *Orpheus Descending* (1947) and *Night of the Iguana* (1961) which also won a Pulitzer.

*Night of the Iguana* was Williams's last great success. Among Williams's own screenplays, the most notable was *Baby Doll* (1956). It was the first film he wrote and it was directed by Elia Kazan. The story tells of a man who attempts to seduce an older man's child bride, who refuses to consummate their marriage. The Legion of Decency railed against the film and *Time* magazine wrote that it was "just possibly the dirtiest American-made motion picture that has ever been legally exhibited."

Williams often used his own life, including his alcoholism and homosexuality, and his family and friends to provide subjects and characters for his plays, stories, and novels. Much of his work reflects the romantic southern gothic tradition as exemplified in the works of CARSON McCULLERS and WILLIAM FAULKNER, or sexual freedom as in the novels of D. H. Lawrence. Elia Kazan, who directed many of Williams's greatest successes, said of Williams: "Everything in his life is in his plays, and everything in his plays is in his life." Exceptionally, Williams set the story of his novel *The Roman Spring of Mrs. Stone* (1950) in Rome.

Williams divided his time between homes in Key West, New Orleans, and New York. In 1961, Williams's longtime companion, Frank Merlo, died of lung cancer and Williams went into a deep depression that lasted for 10 years. He had struggled with depression throughout most of his life and lived with the constant fear of having a mental breakdown as did his sister Rose. Williams died on February 24, 1983, at the Hotel Elysée in New York City. He had choked to death on a bottle cap.

## Further Reading

Devlin, Albert J., ed. *Conversations with Tennessee Williams.* Jackson: University Press of Mississippi, 1986.

Gunn, Drewey Wayne. *Tennessee Williams: A Bibliography.* New York: Scarecrow, 1980.

Leverich, Lyle. *Tom: The Unknown Tennessee Williams.* New York: Crown Publishers, 1995.

Spoto, Donald. *The Kindness of Strangers: The Life of Tennessee Williams.* New York: Little, Brown, 1985.

## Williams, Terry Tempest
(1955–   ) *essayist, memoirist, nonfiction writer, editor, nature writer*

Best known for her book *Refuge: An Unnatural History of Family and Place*, which was published in 1991 and is considered a classic in American nature writing, Terry Tempest Williams is the author of more than a dozen books. She has also been one of the most influential environmental activists of her generation and a naturalist-in-residence at the Utah Museum of Natural History.

Terry Tempest was born on September 8, 1955, to John Henry Tempest III and Diane Dixon Tempest. The oldest child, she had three younger brothers and grew up in sight of the Great Salt Lake in Utah. A native of that region, she is the sixth generation of a Mormon family whose history is deeply rooted in that environment. On June 2, 1975, she married Brooke Williams in the Mormon Temple in Salt Lake City, following in the tradition of her parents.

Williams earned both a B.A. (1979) and an M.S. (1984) from the University of Utah. Her most famous book, *Refuge*, chronicles the rise of the Great Salt Lake and the flooding of the Bear River Migratory Bird Refuge in 1983 against the backdrop of her mother's struggle with ovarian cancer, believed to have been caused by radioactive fallout from nuclear tests conducted in the Nevada desert in the 1950s and 1960s.

Williams's other books include *Pieces of White Shell: A Journey to Navajoland* (1984), *Coyote's Canyon* (1989), *An Unspoken Hunger* (1994), *Desert Quartet: An Erotic Landscape* (1995), *Leap* (2000), and *Red: Patience and Passion in the Desert* (2001). She is also the author of two children's books—*The Secret Language of Snow* (1984) and *Between Cattails* (1985). Her work has been widely anthologized and has appeared in periodicals such as the *New Yorker*, the *Nation, Outside, Audubon, Orion*, the *Iowa Review*, and the *New England Review*. She has collaborated with other writers and editors on *Great and Peculiar Beauty: A Utah Reader*, edited with Thomas J. Lyon (1995); *Testimony: Writers of the West Speak on Behalf of Utah Wilderness*, edited with Stephen Trimble (1996); and *The New Genesis: Mormons Writing on*

Terry Tempest Williams is best known for *Refuge: An Unnatural History of Family and Place. (Photo by Ann P. Tempest. Courtesy Terry Tempest Williams.)*

*Environment*, edited with William Smart and Gibbs Smith (1998).

In addition to her writing, Williams is extremely active as an environmentalist. She has twice testified before the U.S. Congress regarding women's health issues and environmental links associated with cancer. She served on the Governing Council of the Wilderness Society and was a member of the western team of the President's Council for Sustainable Development. She also has served on the advisory board of the National Parks and Conservation Association, the Nature Conservancy, and the Southern Utah Wilderness Alliance. *Newsweek* magazine named Williams in 1991 as someone who would likely make "a considerable impact on the political, economic, and environmental issues facing the western states this decade."

Williams has been the Shirley Sutton Thomas Visiting Professor of English at the University of

Utah. She has also worked as a naturalist at the Bear River Migratory Bird Refuge and the Utah Museum of Natural History. Her list of awards is numerous and includes fellowships from the John Simon Guggenheim Memorial Foundation and the Lannan Foundation. She was inducted into the Rachel Carson Institute's Honor Roll and has received the National Wildlife Federation's Conservation Award for Special Achievement. *Utne Reader* named Terry Tempest Williams as one of their "Utne 100 Visionaries," and called her "a person who could change your life." Physicians for Social Responsibility honored Williams for "distinguished contributions in literature, ecology, and advocacy for an environmentally sustainable world." Williams resides in Castle Valley, Utah, just outside Salt Lake City, with her husband.

## Further Reading

Blake, Catherine S. "Mormon Author Draws Inspiration from Land and Life." *The Los Angeles Times,* December 9, 2001, page B11.

Leaf, C. "Body of Evidence." *Harper's Bazaar,* January 1992, p. 32.

Mencimer, Stephanie. "A Fierce Responsibility." *Mother Jones,* March/April 1994, p. 17.

Pearlman, Mickey. *Listen to Their Voices: Twenty Interviews with Women Who Write.* New York: W. W. Norton, 1993.

Petersen, David. "Memory Is the Only Way Home: A Conversational Interview with Terry Tempest Williams." *Bloomsbury Review,* November/December 1994, p. 12.

Shauffler, F. Marina. *Turning to Earth: Stories of Ecological Conversion.* Charlottesville: University of Virginia Press, 2003.

## Williams, William Carlos
(1883–1963) *poet, playwright, novelist, short story writer, autobiographer*

One of the most influential and accessible modernist poets, William Carlos Williams was a principal figure in the imagist school, which included EZRA POUND and T. S. ELIOT. Williams eventually distinguished himself, however, from these other poets with his interest in portraying everyday circumstances and ordinary folks in his poetry. Although his influence spread slowly in the early part of the 20th century, he eventually had a significant impact on the Beat poets, who admired the simplicity of his language and his focus on common subjects.

William Carlos Williams was born on September 17, 1883, in Rutherford, New Jersey. His father, William George Williams, was British and chose to retain his British citizenship though he lived most of his life in the United States. He worked as a manufacturer and distributor of eau de cologne. His work gave the family many opportunities for travel, and they often traveled for months at a time. Williams helped to found the Unitarian society in Rutherford and considered himself a socialist.

Williams's mother, Elena, grew up in Martinique and Puerto Rico, and her ancestry was a mixture of French, Dutch, Spanish, and Jewish. She had studied art in Paris before meeting and marrying Williams's father. At home, she spoke mostly Spanish, French whenever she could, and English only when necessary. Her family and friends from Paris and the Caribbean visited the home often.

In 1897, Williams and his brother, Edgar, accompanied their mother to Europe, where they spent a good deal of time in Paris. They had attended public schools in Rutherford, but in Europe the boys attended a private school in Switzerland and a French school in Paris, as well. Neither boy was fluent in French, however, so the experience was somewhat difficult. When he returned to the United States, Williams attended a private school in New York City, where he first studied American poetry and became a fan of WALT WHITMAN. Williams began writing poetry and decided to become both a writer and a doctor.

Following his secondary education, he attended the University of Pennsylvania, entering the medical school there in 1902, where he met and became good friends with Ezra Pound. Williams completed his medical internship in pediatrics in New York City from 1906 to 1909. Following the internship, he moved back to New Jersey, where he established a practice in Rutherford and worked as a pediatrician for the rest of his life. His first published book, titled simply *Poems*, was published in 1909.

In Rutherford, Williams regularly worked on poems between appointments. He published frequently in small magazines. When he completed his second collection of poems, *The Tempers* (1913) Pound helped arrange the London publication of the book. Although Pound exercised a significant influence over Williams's work, Williams eventually developed his own poetics, experimenting with line and meter and focusing on everyday subjects and what he came to refer to as the "American idiom." He sought to make poems that were fresh and distinctively American, and he is remembered for having achieved this. Two of his most famous poems, "The Red Wheelbarrow" and "This Is Just to Say," attest to his achievement of these goals.

His major works include *Kora in Hell* (1920), *Spring and All* (1923), *The Complete Collected Poems of William Carlos Williams 1906–1938* (1938), *Pictures from Brueghel and Other Poems* (1962), the five-volume epic *Paterson* (1963, 1992), and *Imaginations* (1970), which was published posthumously. *Paterson* was probably Williams's most memorable achievement. His choice of the town of Paterson, New Jersey, as the subject for his epic work exemplified his poetic values and gave him the opportunity to experiment freely with form.

By the 1950s and 1960s, the Beat poets had begun to discover Williams's work and he became a more prominent figure in American poetry than he had been. Williams was ALLEN GINSBERG's pediatrician, so the two had a relationship that leant itself to Williams's mentoring of Ginsberg in his early career. Williams wrote the introduction for Ginsberg's first book of poetry, *Howl and Other Poems*, in 1955. Other poets influenced by Williams include DENISE LEVERTOV and ROBERT CREELEY. Williams's health began to decline after a heart attack in 1948 and a series of strokes that left him partly paralyzed, but he continued writing until his death on March 4, 1963. Later in 1963, he was posthumously awarded the Pulitzer Prize in poetry for *Pictures from Brueghel* (1962).

**Further Reading**

Breslin, James E. B. *William Carlos Williams, An American Artist.* New York: Oxford University Press, 1970.

Coles, Robert. *William Carlos Williams: The Knack of Survival in America.* New Brunswick, N.J.: Rutgers University Press, 1983.

Duffey, Bernard I. *A Poetry of Presence: The Writing of William Carlos Williams.* Madison: University of Wisconsin Press, 1986.

Morris, Daniel. *The Writings of William Carlos Williams: Publicity for the Self.* Columbia: University of Missouri Press, 1995.

Simpson, Louis A. *Three on the Tower: The Lives and Works of Ezra Pound, T. S. Eliot, and William Carlos Williams.* New York: Morrow, 1975.

Tapscott, Stephen. *American Beauty: William Carlos Williams and the Modernist Whitman.* New York: Columbia University Press, 1984.

Wagner-Martin, Linda. *William Carlos Williams: A Reference Guide.* Boston: G. K. Hall, 1978.

Whitaker, Thomas R. *William Carlos Williams.* New York: Twayne Publishers, 1965.

Whittemore, Reed, *William Carlos Williams, Poet from Jersey.* Boston: Houghton Mifflin, 1975.

Williams, William Carlos. *Autobiography.* New York: W. W. Norton, 1967.

## Wilson, August
## (Frederick August Kittel)
### (1945– ) *playwright*

The author of a renowned series of plays exploring African-American heritage, decade by decade, over the 20th century, August Wilson is an award-winning playwright whose work has been hailed by critics and adored by theatergoers since the 1980s. One critic called his body of work "the most complete cultural chronicle since Balzac wrote his *Human Comedy.*"

August Wilson was born Frederick August Kittel on April 27, 1945, in Pittsburgh, Pennsylvania. His father, Frederick August, was a baker, and his mother, Daisy Wilson Kittel, was a house cleaner. His stepfather was David Bedford. Wilson grew up in poverty in Pittsburgh, where he lived with his parents and five siblings. Although his childhood was difficult, he has often said that his parents, like many other black parents of that generation, shielded him from the truly great hardships they endured. It has been his goal in his series of plays covering each decade of the 20th century to shed light on the struggles of his parents and others in their generation. Wilson has been married twice. His first wife was Judy Oliver, a social worker, with whom he had a daughter, Sakina Ansari. They divorced in 1981, and Wilson later married Constanza Romero, a costume designer, with whom he has one daughter, Azula Carmen.

Wilson attended school until the age of 16, when he dropped out and began educating himself at the local library and working at menial jobs. He has said that he left school due largely to the racist treatment he endured there. After leaving school, he began to pursue a literary career, writing poems and submitting them to the black publications at the University of Pittsburgh.

In 1968, Wilson founded Black Horizons on the Hill, a theater in Pittsburgh. Wilson did not write his first play, however, until 1978, after he moved to St. Louis, Missouri. *Jitney,* a realistic drama set in Pittsburgh, had a successful run at a small theater in Pittsburgh and was noted for its truthful portrayal of black urban speech and life. *Jitney* was followed by *Fullerton Street* (1980), then *Ma Rainey's Black Bottom* (1984), which earned Wilson a spot at the O'Neill Theatre Center's National Playwrights Conference. Director Lloyd Richards from the Yale Repertory Theatre was impressed by Wilson's play and worked with him to refine it and present it at Yale in 1984. When the play was produced, a *New York Times* review hailed Wilson as "a major find for the American theater." The play came to Broadway later in 1984, where it also enjoyed exceptional reviews. From this point on, Wilson's work has drawn significant attention.

His subsequent plays include *Fences* (1986), which won the Pulitzer Prize; *Joe Turner's Come and Gone: A Play in Two Acts* (1988); and *The Piano Lesson* (1990), which garnered Wilson a second Pulitzer Prize. Wilson later adapted *The Piano Lesson* for a Hallmark Hall of Fame television production. *Two Trains Running* was produced on Broadway in 1992 and continued Wilson's 10-play cycle on black American history. Next was *Seven Guitars*, which was produced at the Goodman Theatre in Chicago in 1996 and *King Hedley II* (1999).

Wilson's other awards include a Tony Award for *Fences*, Great Britain's Olivier Award for *Jitney*, and seven New York Drama Critics Circle Awards. In addition, the recording of *Ma Rainey's Black Bottom* received a 1985 Grammy Award. Wilson is also the recipient of many fellowships and awards, including Rockefeller, Bush, and Guggenheim fellowships and the Whiting Writers' Award. He received a National Humanities Medal from the president of the United States and numerous honorary degrees, including the only high school diploma ever issued by Pittsburgh's Carnegie Library. Wilson is a member of the American Academy of Arts and Letters. August Wilson lives in Seattle, Washington.

**Further Reading**

Carroll, Rebecca. *Swing Low: Black Men Writing.* New York: Crown, 1995.

DiGaetani, John L. *A Search for a Postmodern Theater: Interviews with Contemporary Playwrights.* New York: Greenwood Press, 1991.

Elkins, Marilyn, ed. *August Wilson: A Casebook.* New York: Garland, 1994.

Grant, Nathan L. "Men, Women, and Culture: A Conversation with August Wilson." *American Drama* 5, no. 2 (spring 1996): 100–122.

Nadel, Alan, ed. *May All Your Fences Have Gates: Essays on the Drama of August Wilson.* Iowa City: University of Iowa Press, 1994.

Pereira, Kim. *August Wilson and the African-American Odyssey.* Carbondale: University of Illinois Press, 1995.

Wolf, Peter. *August Wilson.* New York: Twayne Publishers, 1999.

## Wolfe, Thomas
### (Thomas Clayton Wolfe)
(1900–1938) *novelist, short story writer*

One of the great writers of the 20th century, Thomas Wolfe had a short but powerful career. His work is known for its unique literary style, its autobiographical tendencies, and its largesse of vision and language.

Thomas Wolfe was born on October 3, 1900, in Asheville, North Carolina, where he grew up. He was the youngest of eight children, six of whom survived to adulthood. His father, William Oliver

Thomas Wolfe is remembered for the grandeur of his prose in such novels as *Look Homeward, Angel.* (Library of Congress, Prints and Photographs Division, Carl Van Vechten Collection [LC-USZ62-87328])

study playwriting at Harvard University. He was part of the renowned 47 Workshop under the leadership of Professor George Pierce Baker. Wolfe completed a master of arts degree in literature after two years but remained at Harvard for a third year in order to gain more experience in the workshop. Wolfe's book *Of Time and the River* (1935), satirized life at Harvard with its many pretensions. Although Wolfe's talent was applicable to the theater, his temperament was not. He had a difficult time getting his plays produced and ended up taking a position as an English instructor at New York University in 1924. He would teach there intermittently between 1924 and 1930.

These were turbulent years for Wolfe, who began a love affair with Aline Bernstein in August 1925. Wolfe had spent the summer of 1925 in Europe and was returning home by ship when he met Bernstein, a successful set and costume designer who was 20 years older than he, married, and the mother of two grown children. The two had much in common artistically, but they were at totally different places in their lives.

In June 1926, while on vacation in England with Bernstein, Wolfe began to write what would become *Look Homeward, Angel.* With the emotional and financial aid of Mrs. Bernstein, he was able to continue his writing in New York. *Look Homeward, Angel* was published in 1929, just nine years before his death. It bore a dedication to Bernstein, although Wolfe was already feeling trapped in the relationship. In March 1930, Wolfe received a Guggenheim fellowship that allowed him to travel to Europe for almost a year. He took this opportunity to end the relationship with Bernstein. She did not disappear, however, from his work. The character of Esther Jack in Wolfe's posthumous novels is clearly based on Bernstein and illustrates the love he always felt for her. Later in her life, Aline Bernstein recounted her love affair with Wolfe in two books—*Three Blue Suits* (1933) and *The Journey Down* (1938).

Wolfe went on to complete his second novel when he returned from the year in Europe. He rented an apartment in Brooklyn and began to look to his editor, Max Perkins, for the support he no longer had from Bernstein. *Of Time and the River,* the second novel, was published in 1935 and was followed

Wolfe, was a tombstone maker whose vigorous spirit inspired his son's own eager approach to life. His mother, Julia E. Wolfe, was a real estate speculator at a time when few women participated in such business ventures. After the age of 11, Wolfe attended a private school in Asheville, where he received much encouragement and personal attention. He went on from there to the University of North Carolina at Chapel Hill shortly before he turned 16. While studying at Chapel Hill, Wolfe worked on the school magazines and newspapers. He became editor of the college newspaper, the *Tar Heel.* He also did some work with the Carolina Playmakers while in college, which influenced him initially to pursue a career in theater.

Following his graduation in 1920 from the University of North Carolina, Wolfe went on to that same year by a collection of short stories, *From Death to Morning*. Perkins was a legendary editor who worked with such writers as ERNEST HEMINGWAY and F. SCOTT FITZGERALD. He took Wolfe in as the son he never had—Perkins was the father of five daughters—and the two became very close. Wolfe went on to complete his final publication before his death, an autobiographical essay on writing called *The Story of a Novel* (1936). In 1937, Wolfe severed his relationship with Perkins, perhaps feeling that his dependence on Perkins was limiting.

In addition to these book publications, Wolfe published many short stories over the years in magazines. Three posthumous works—*The Web and the Rock* (1939), *You Can't Go Home Again* (1940), and *The Hills Beyond* (1941)—were constructed from Wolfe's manuscripts following his death.

Wolfe signed a new contract with Harper's in 1937 and began working with a young editor, Edward Aswell. When Wolfe fell ill with pneumonia during a trip out West, doctors were confused by the unusual complications he developed. He was admitted to Johns Hopkins Hospital in Baltimore, Maryland, in September 1938. His doctor was Walter Dandy, the foremost brain surgeon in the country at the time. He believed that Wolfe had tuberculosis that had spread to his brain. When he operated on him on September 12 in a final effort to save his life, the doctor found that the entire right side of Wolfe's brain was indeed covered with tubercles. The disease, which Wolfe had contracted as a boy, had been activated by the pneumonia. Wolfe never regained consciousness and died on September 15, 1938, in Baltimore. He was buried in Riverside Cemetery in Asheville, North Carolina, and his boyhood home remains a memorial to his life and is preserved as a state historic site.

### Further Reading

Brodin, Pierre. *Thomas Wolfe*. Asheville, N.C.: Stephens Press, 1949.

Evans, Elizabeth. *Thomas Wolfe*. New York: Frederick Ungar Publishing Co., 1984.

Holman, C. Hugh. *Thomas Wolfe*. Minneapolis: University of Minnesota Press, 1960.

Johnston, Carol Ingalls. *Of Time and the Artist: Thomas Wolfe, His Novels, and the Critics*. Columbia, S.C.: Camden House, 1996.

Tattoni, Iginia. *The Unfound Door: Innovative Trends in Thomas Wolfe's Fiction*. Rome: Bulzoni Editore, 1992.

## Wouk, Herman
(1915– ) *novelist*

Herman Wouk is a best-selling novelist whose work is best known for themes encompassing the moral dilemmas of the Jewish experience. Wouk's epic war novels have been especially popular. Several of them have been filmed, including *The Caine Mutiny* (1951) and *Marjorie Morningstar* (1955). Wouk's two-volume historical novel set during World War II, *The Winds of War* (1971) and *War and Remembrance* (1978), also gained success as television miniseries. His books have been translated into more than 30 languages.

Herman Wouk was born in New York City on May 17, 1915, into a family of Jewish immigrants from Russia. His upbringing was marked by his father's and grandfather's unyielding devotion to Judaism and the Talmud. Wouk once complained to his father about the countless hours he was expected to study the Talmud with his grandfather, and his father replied, "I understand . . . but if I were on my deathbed, and I had breath to say one more thing to you, I would say 'Study the Talmud.'" Thus, except for "a brief interlude after college which had been all chase and no thought," Wouk heeded his father's advice and embraced an observant religious life.

Wouk studied at Columbia University, where he worked as the editor of the college's humor magazine. After completing his undergraduate work at Columbia, he became a radio scriptwriter and worked on and off in this profession from 1936 to 1946, when he began to dedicate himself full time to writing. In 1941, Wouk briefly served the U.S. government, producing radio broadcasts to sell war bonds. He then joined the U.S. Navy and served in the Pacific during World War II on two destroyer-minesweepers, the USS *Zane* and the USS *Southard*. It was during this time period that Wouk began his first novel, during his off-duty hours while at sea.

When he returned from the war in 1945, he married Betty Sarah Brown, with whom he would have three sons. The year after their marriage he began to work as a full-time writer, his occupation to this day. A visiting professor at Yeshiva University from 1953 to 1957, Wouk also served as scholar-in-residence from 1973 to 1974 at Aspen Institute in Colorado. He also was a trustee of the College of Virgin Islands between 1961 and 1969.

Published in 1947, Wouk's first novel, *Aurora Dawn*, satirizes the advertising industry in New York. He followed his first novel with *City Boy* (1948), a partly autobiographical story of a boy growing up in the Bronx, New York.

His next novel, *The Caine Mutiny*, was published in 1952 and won the Pulitzer Prize for fiction that same year. The novel was adapted as a film starring Humphrey Bogart as Captain Queeg in 1954 by Columbia and a hit Broadway play featuring Henry Fonda in the role. *The Caine Mutiny* addresses the events surrounding a crew mutiny aboard a minesweeper, which is captained by an incompetent and cowardly tyrant. The main character is Willie Keith, a rich New Yorker, who matures as he witnesses the events that take place aboard the *Caine*. However, the work is best known for its portrayal of Captain Queeg, who suffers from paranoia, incompetence, and cowardice.

Critics considered Wouk's fourth novel, *Marjorie Morningstar*, reactionary in tone. Marjorie, the title character, is a Jewish New Yorker with great ambitions. She rebels against her parents' middle-class values in pursuit of her dream of becoming an actress. She fails to achieve her dream, surrenders her illusions, marries and lives as a conventional suburban housewife. In *Youngblood Hawke*, Wouk continued to expand his subject matter by depicting one writer's obsessions in the publishing world, events based in part on the life of THOMAS WOLFE. Wouk's 1959 novel *This is My God* includes discussion of Orthodox Judaism.

Wouk continues to write prolifically today. A thorough researcher, he has received praise for his novels' historical accuracy, in addition to the satire, humor, and narrative skill they contain.

His recent works include *The Hope* (1993), an account of the establishment of the state of Israel and its struggle through three wars in the first two decades, and two epic historical novels of World War II—*Winds of War* (1992) and *War and Remembrance* (2002). He has received several awards for his writing, including the Pulitzer Prize in 1952, the Columbia University Medal of Excellence in 1952, the Hamilton Medal in 1980, the American Academy of Achievement Golden Plate Award in 1986, and the U.S. Navy Memorial Foundation Award in 1987, to name just a few. Wouk has also received several honorary degrees from universities in the United States and Israel.

**Further Reading**

Beichman, Arnold. *Herman Wouk: The Novelist as Social Historian.* Somerset, N.J.: Transaction Publishers, 1984.

Mazzeno, Laurence W. *Herman Wouk.* Boston: Twayne, 1994.

Paulson, Barbara A. *The Historical Novel: A Celebration of the Achievements of Herman Wouk.* Washington, D.C.: Library of Congress, 1999.

# Wright, Charles
(1935–   ) *poet, literary critic*

A lyric poet whose work has earned him two Pulitzer Prizes among a host of other awards, Charles Wright is the author of more than a dozen books of poems, including three trilogies of verse. His work is known for its musicality and its groundedness in the visual world.

Charles Wright was born in Pickwick Dam, Tennessee, in 1935. He grew up in Kingsport, Tennessee, and went to Davidson College as an undergraduate, where he majored in history and considered pursuing a career in law or advertising. Following his graduation in 1957, Wright joined the army in 1957 and was sent to Verona, Italy, as a member of a counterintelligence unit. Wright fell in love with the Italian landscape and began reading poetry, carrying EZRA POUND's *Cantos* with him everywhere he went. Although he had tried writing fiction while in high school, he had experienced little success in creating narratives and found the lyric poem much more to his liking.

When he left the army, Wright returned to the United States and enrolled in the Writers' Workshop at the University of Iowa, where he received his M.F.A. degree in 1963. He then settled into a position at the University of California at Irvine in 1966, where he stayed until 1968 when he returned to Italy as a Fulbright lecturer at the University of Rome and the University of Padua. He taught at various universities, including the University of Iowa, before moving to Charlottesville, Virginia, in 1983 to teach at the University of Virginia.

Wright's books of poetry include *The Grave of the Right Hand* (1970), *Hard Freight* (1973), *Bloodlines* (1975), *China Trace* (1977), *The Southern Cross* (1981), *Country Music: Selected Early Poems* (1982), *The Other Side of the River* (1984), *Zone Journals* (1988), *The World of the Ten Thousand Things: Poems 1980–1990* (1990), *Chickamauga* (1995), *Black Zodiac* (1997), *Appalachia* (1998), *Negative Blue* (2000), and *A Short History of the Shadow: Poems* (2002). He has also published translations, including Eugenio Montale's *The Storm and Other Poems* (1978), and two volumes of criticism—*Halflife* (1988) and *Quarter Notes* (1995). Wright is known for poems with long, symmetrical, musical lines that meditate, often in a Taoist way, on the fleeting nature of all things. His works often acknowledge the influence of other poets, especially Chinese and Italian poets. He has said that he thinks of himself as a kind of landscape painter, a poet writing from what he sees rather than from an idea.

Wright's many awards and honors include a National Endowment for the Arts grant (1974), a Guggenheim fellowship (1975), the Academy of American Poets' Edgar Allan Poe Award (1976), an Academy Institute grant from the American Academy and Institute of Arts and Letters (1977), the National Book Award in poetry (1983), and the Brandeis Creative Arts Citation for poetry (1987). He was also awarded the PEN Translation Prize for his translation of *The Storm and Other Things. Chickamauga* won the Academy of American Poets' Lenore Marshall Poetry Prize in 1996, and in 1997 Wright won the Pulitzer Prize and the *Los Angeles Times* book prize for *Black Zodiac.* Wright is also the recipient of the American Academy of Arts and Letters Award of Merit Medal and the Ruth Lilly Poetry Prize. In 1999, he was elected a Chancellor of the Academy of American Poets.

Wright lives in Charlottesville, Virginia, with his family and is Souder Family Professor of English at the University of Virginia.

### Further Reading

Gussow, Mel. "Charles Wright: A Good Ear for the Music of His Own Life." *New York Times.* Available online. URL: http://www.nytimes.com/library/books/041698 wright-poetry.html. Posted April 16, 1998.

Riggs, Thomas, ed. "Charles Wright." *Contemporary Poets.* Detroit: St. James Press, 2000.

Schuldt, Morgan. "An Interview with Charles Wright." *Sonora Review.* Available online. URL: http://www.coh.arizona.edu/sonora/43/interview.html. Downloaded on June 17, 2003.

## Wright, James
## (James Arlington Wright)
### (1927–1980) *poet*

Widely recognized as one of the finest American poets of the 20th century, James Wright is remembered for his sad but hopeful vision in poems often set in the industrial and natural landscapes of his Ohio River Valley childhood. Wright was one of the early poets in the confessional school, but his work showed how the new free verse could be employed to address social justice themes and the world beyond the poet's personal life.

Born on December 13, 1927, in Martin's Ferry, Ohio, James Wright was the middle son in a working-class family. His father worked for more than 50 years in the Hazel-Atlas glass factory, and his mother had quit school at age 14 to work in a laundry. Neither parent went beyond the eighth grade in school. From an early age, Wright was determined to avoid factory work and see the world beyond Martin's Ferry.

While in high school, Wright wrote an autobiography that described his life as a "visionary" beginning in the second grade. When he was 16,

Wright missed a year of school due to a nervous breakdown, but he returned the next year and graduated in 1946. His nervous breakdowns would eventually be diagnosed as bipolar disorder and would affect him the rest of his life. In 1946, just following his graduation, Wright was drafted into the army and stationed in Japan during the American occupation. When he returned home, he enrolled in Kenyon College on the G.I. Bill, where he was able to study under JOHN CROWE RANSOM. Wright graduated cum laude and Phi Beta Kappa in 1952 from Kenyon and married his Martin's Ferry high school sweetheart, Liberty Kardules, that same year.

The couple moved to Austria when Wright won a Fulbright fellowship to the University of Vienna, where he studied the work of poet Georg Trakl and others. His first son, Franz, was born in Vienna in 1953. When the couple returned to the United States in 1954, they moved to Seattle, where Wright enrolled at the University of Washington and eventually earned his master's and doctoral degrees under the guidance of THEODORE ROETHKE and STANLEY KUNITZ. His first book, *The Green Wall*, was selected for publication in the Yale Younger Poets Series by W. H. AUDEN in 1954 and appeared in 1957, the same year that Wright joined the faculty at the University of Minnesota, alongside fellow poets ALLEN TATE and JOHN BERRYMAN. Marshall, Wright's second son, was born in 1958, just one year before Wright and his wife separated. Their divorce became final in 1962. In 1959 Wright completed his dissertation on Charles Dickens, was awarded his Ph.D., and published his second book, *Saint Judas*.

Although Wright was active as a critic, publishing frequently in such journals and magazines as the *New Yorker*, *Sewanee Review*, and *New Orleans Poetry Review*, the University of Minnesota denied him tenure and he took a position at nearby Macalester College. It was during these years that Wright and ROBERT BLY began their lifelong friendship that included collaborating on translations of European and Latin American poets, such as Georg Trakl and Cesar Vallejo.

*The Branch Will Not Break*, Wright's third book, appeared in 1963 and became one of the most widely read and influential collections of poetry in the 1960s. Its free verse poems and personal voice foreshadowed the work of later poets in the Confessional school and signaled a move away from formalism and tradition.

In 1966, Wright took a position teaching at Hunter College of the City University of New York. The following year, he married his second wife, Annie Crunk, and published *Shall We Gather at the River*, a book that some critics have called his most important work. His *Collected Poems* appeared in 1971 and received the Pulitzer Prize. His work throughout this time period continued to extend beyond the realm of the autobiographical and merely personal to address questions of social justice and community. His other collections include *Two Citizens* (1973), *I See the Wind* (1974), *Old Booksellers and Other Poems* (1976), *Moments of the Italian Summer* (1976), and *To a Blossoming Pear Tree* (1978). *This Journey* (1982), *The Temple in Nimes* (1982), and *Above the River: The Complete Poems* (1992), were all published posthumously.

Wright's awards include fellowships from the Guggenheim Foundation, the *Kenyon Review*, and the Academy of American Poets, as well as the Ohiona Book Award in 1960 for *Saint Judas*, the Creative Arts Award from Brandeis University in 1970, and the Melville Cane Award from the Poetry Society of America in 1972, among others. In 1979, a chronic sore throat was diagnosed as cancer of the tongue. Wright died on March 25, 1980, in New York City.

## Further Reading

Barillas, William. "James Wright and the Native American Spirit of Place." *Midamerica* 21 (1994): 132–142.

Dougherty, David C. *James Wright*. Boston: Twayne, 1987.

Elkins, Andrew. *The Poetry of James Wright*. Tuscaloosa: University of Alabama Press, 1991.

Graves, Michael. "Crises in the Career of James Wright." *Hollins Critic* 22, no. 5 (December 1985): 1–9.

Graziano, Frank, and Peter Stitt, eds. *James Wright: A Profile*. Durango, Colo.: Logbridge-Rhodes, 1988.

Lense, Edward. "This Is What I Wanted: James Wright and the Other World." *Modern Poetry Studies* 11, nos. 1–2 (1982): 19–32.

# Wright, Richard
(1908–1960) *novelist, autobiographer*

Richard Wright was among the first African-American writers to achieve literary fame and fortune. Many, however, believe that his most significant contribution to African Americans was his effort to accurately portray blacks to white readers, thereby destroying the white myth of the patient, humorous, subservient black man. His two most important works were *Native Son* (1940), a novel, and his autobiography, *Black Boy* (1945). *Native Son* was the first best-selling novel and the first Book-of-the-Month Club selection by an African-American writer. The novel earned Wright the National Association for the Advancement of Colored People's prestigious Spingarn Medal in 1941.

Richard Wright was born on September 4, 1908, on a plantation near Natchez, Mississippi, the son of Nathaniel Wright, an illiterate sharecropper, and Ella Wilson, a well-educated schoolteacher. Poverty forced the family to move to Memphis. Soon after, Wright's father abandoned the family and his mother was forced to work as a cook to support her children. Wright and his brother briefly stayed in an orphanage during this period. The family later moved in with relatives in Arkansas, but they moved again, to another place in Arkansas, after Wright's uncle was murdered by whites. Wright left school early, by 1919, to help support the family. At age 13, Wright returned to school, delivered newspapers, and worked briefly with a traveling insurance salesman. In the meantime, he read pulp novels, magazines, and anything he could find. His first story, "The Voodoo of Hell's Half Acre," was published in 1924 in the *Southern Register*, a local black newspaper. Wright graduated as valedictorian of his ninth-grade class in 1925 but soon dropped out of high school to help support the family again. He then worked several menial jobs in Jackson and Memphis while he continued writing.

Wright moved to Chicago in 1927 and worked as a post office clerk until the Great Depression forced him to take on various temporary positions. He also attended meetings of black literary groups and became involved with the Communist Party, writing articles and stories for both the *Daily*

Richard Wright's *Native Son* was the first best-selling novel by an African American. *(Library of Congress, Prints and Photographs Division, Carl Van Vechten Collection [LC-USZ62-42502])*

*Worker* and *New Masses*. He published his first major story, "Superstition," in *Abbot's Monthly*, a black journal, in 1931. Wright moved to New York in 1937 and became the Harlem editor of the *Daily Worker* and helped edit a short-lived literary magazine, *New Challenge*. He unsuccessfully tried to sell his first novel, *Cesspool*, which was published posthumously as *Lawd Today!* (1963). The novel reflected his experiences in the post office. Wright was hired by the Federal Writers' Project to research the history of Illinois and of African Americans in Chicago. His short story "Big Boy Leaves Home" (1936) appeared in *The New Caravan* anthology, where it attracted mainstream critical attention. His short story "Fire and Cloud" won first prize in a contest sponsored by *Story* magazine in 1937. It also won the O. Henry Memorial Award. In 1938, four of Wright's stories were collected as *Uncle Tom's Children,* which received good reviews.

He then received a Guggenheim fellowship, which allowed him to complete his first novel, *Native Son* (1940), which became a best-seller and received many favorable reviews. Bigger Thomas, the central figure of *Native Son,* is a murderer, but his situation prompted African Americans to further consider confronting racism and to determine their own future. Wright had become deeply interested in the case of Robert Nixon, an 18-year-old black man accused of murdering a white woman and used it as a documentary parallel to characters and events in *Native Son.* The book was banned in Birmingham, Alabama, libraries, but Wright received international acclaim. The story was staged successfully as a play on Broadway by Orson Welles in 1941.

In 1939, Wright married Dhimah Rose Meadman, a white dancer, but the two separated shortly thereafter. In 1941, he married Ellen Poplar, a white member of the Communist Party, and they had two daughters. Wright broke with the Communist Party in 1944 but continued to follow liberal ideologies. His autobiography, *Black Boy,* became a best-seller and received good reviews, although the U.S. Senate denounced the book as "obscene." The section about Wright's life in Chicago and experience with the Communist Party was not published until 1977 under the title *American Hunger.* In 1945, Wright's publishers had wanted only the story of his life in the South.

Wright moved to Paris with his family in 1947 and established friendships with the existentialist writers Jean-Paul Sartre and Albert Camus. At the time, Wright was going through an existentialist phase, which was best depicted by his second novel, *The Outsiders* (1953), a story about a white psychopathic murderer, which received mixed reviews. Wright refused to return to the United States, citing risk of subpoena by an anticommunist congressional investigating committee. In 1954, he published a minor novel, *Savage Holiday.* Wright traveled throughout Europe, Asia, and Africa, and these experiences led to a number of nonfiction works. In *The Color Curtain: A Report on the Bandung Conference* (1956), Wright emphasized race as the crucial factor in resolving the problems of Western and Third World cultures. Another of his polemical writings of that period was *White Man, Listen!* (1957), which was originally a series of lectures given in Europe. In his later years, Wright fell ill and suffered financial hardship. Throughout this period he wrote approximately 4,000 English haiku and another novel, *The Long Dream* (1958). He also prepared another collection of short stories, *Eight Men,* which was published after his death on November 28, 1960, of an apparent heart attack, in Paris.

## Further Reading

Fabre, Michel. *The Unfinished Quest of Richard Wright.* New York: Morrow, 1993.

Gayle, Addison, Jr. *Richard Wright—Ordeal of a Native Son.* New York: Doubleday, 1980.

Rampersad, Arnold, ed. *Richard Wright: A Collection of Critical Essays.* Englewood Cliffs, N.J.: Prentice Hall, 1995.

Williams, John A., and Dorothy Sterling. *The Most Native of Sons: A Biography of Richard Wright.* New York: Doubleday, 1970.

# Young Bear, Ray Anthony
(1950–  )  *poet, autobiographer, novelist*

Native American poet Ray A. Young Bear is revered for his unique and masterful blend of traditional and modernist voices. An enrolled member of the Meskwaki tribe in Iowa, Young Bear still lives on the land where he was raised. He has published both poetry and prose to critical and popular acclaim.

Ray A. Young Bear was born in 1950 in Marshalltown, Iowa, and raised on the Meskwaki Tribal Settlement near Tama, Iowa, where he still lives with his wife, Stella, and nephew, Jesse. Young Bear and his wife are in the process of adopting five Meskwaki children who are currently in the state's custody.

Although his first language is Meskwaki, Young Bear began writing in English as a teenager. When asked by an interviewer about the influences on his writing, he still cites his grandmother, Ada Kapayou Old Bear, as the first: "From her I learned mythology, the language and customs." Other influences included the Upward Bound program at Luther College in Decorah, Iowa, and the poet ROBERT BLY, whom Young Bear met in 1969.

Before Young Bear went out into the world and encountered these influences, it was his grandmother's encouragement that kept him writing. In the beginning, he wrote by thinking in Meskwaki and then translating into English. While he no longer does this, his style still reflects the patterns of traditional, formal Meskwaki speech that he heard so often growing up.

Young Bear's great-great grandfather, Maminwanike, was a sacred chieftain who purchased the tribal settlement land in 1856 from the U.S. government. Consequently, these ancestral lands along the Iowa River are not a reservation, a situation that makes the Meskwaki unique among other area tribes.

From 1969 to 1971, Young Bear attended Pomona College in California. He has also attended the University of Iowa, Grinnell College, Northern Iowa University, and Iowa State University. Young Bear's poetry was first published in 1968 in the *South Dakota Review.* At about that time, the poet Robert Bly had taken an interest in Young Bear's work and helped introduce him to various literary magazines where his poems began to be published. Since that time, Young Bear's work has appeared in numerous magazines, including *American Poetry Review, Gettysburg Review,* the *Georgia Review,* the *Kenyon Review, Michigan Quarterly Review, Parnassus, Ploughshares, Solo, Virginia Quarterly Review,* and *Witness.* His work has also been widely anthologized in such collections as *The Best American Poetry 1996,* edited by ADRIENNE RICH; *Against Forgetting: Twentieth-Century Poetry of Witness,* edited by Carolyn Forché; and *Harper's Anthology of 20th-Century Native American Poetry.*

Young Bear's books of poems include *Waiting to Be Fed* (1975), *Winter of the Salamander: The Keeper of Importance* (1980), *The Invisible Musician: Poems* (1990), and *The Rock Island Hiking Club* (2001). He has also published several books of prose. His autobiographical trilogy, *Black Eagle Child: The Facepaint Narratives* appeared in 1997. *Remnants of the First Earth* came out in 1997 as well.

Young Bear has described the sources of his poetry as myth, history, and especially dreams. In his work, he is most interested in illuminating the places where dreams and other realities converge. He sees the writing process, he has said, as a delicate negotiation of those meetings that occur within contested spaces. Robert Gish, an expert on Native American literature at the University of New Mexico, has called Young Bear "a great modern poet." In speaking about his book *The Rock Island Hiking Club*, Gish said, "he combines the power of indigenous voice with a modernist voice."

Young Bear received a creative writing grant from the National Endowment for the Arts in 1976. He has also received an honorary doctorate in letters from Luther College in 1993 and the Ruth Suckow Award for *Remnants of the First Earth* as an outstanding work of fiction about Iowa in 1997.

Throughout his career, Young Bear has occasionally taken positions teaching creative writing and Native American literature. He has taught at the Institute of American Indian Art (1984), Eastern Washington University (1987), Meskwaki Indian Elementary School (1988–89), the University of Iowa (1989), and at Iowa State University (1993 and 1998).

In addition to his work as a writer, Young Bear and his wife cofounded a cultural performance group called Black Eagle Child that has toured the Midwest and the Netherlands. His readings of poems often begin with Meskwaki songs, accompanied by a hand drum and English translations. The group recorded one album in 1987 called *The Woodland Singers: Traditional Mesquakie Songs*.

## Further Reading

Bataille, Gretchen M. "Ray A. Young Bear: Tribal History and Personal Vision," *Studies in American Indian Literatures* 5 (summer 1993): 17–20.

Gish, Robert F. "Mesquakie Singer: Listening to Ray A. Young Bear," in *A Journal of Contemporary Literature* 4 (1979): 24–28.

McAdams, Janet. "We, I, 'Voice,' and Voices: Reading Contemporary Native American Poetry," *Studies in American Indian Literatures*, 7, no. 3 (fall 1995): 7–16.

Roemer, Kenneth M. *Native American Writers of the United States*. Vol. 175. Dictionary of Literary Biography. Detroit: Gale, 1999.

# Z

## Zitkala-Sa
### (Gertrude Simmons Bonnin)
(1876–1938) *short story writer, essayist, memoirist*

Zitkala-Sa was the first Native American woman to write her story without help from an editor, interpreter, or ethnographer. A devoted social reformer, she was not afraid of supporting unpopular positions. Both her writing and her activism were informed by a concern for gender expectations, the struggle between traditional culture and the pressure to assimilate, and the conflict between traditional spirituality and Christianity, among others. She was one of the first writers to experiment with literary art as a form of protest.

Zitkala-Sa was born on February 22, 1876, on the Pine Ridge Reservation in South Dakota. Raised in a tipi on the Missouri River until the age of 12, she was the third child of Ellen Tate 'I yohiwin Simmons, a full-blood Yankton Nakota Sioux, and a white man named Felker, who deserted the family. Zitkala-Sa's mother remarried John Haysting Simmons, who gave his name to the girl, calling her Gertrude Simmons. Sources disagree about when she began to be called Zitkala-Sa, which means Red Bird, but it probably was a name she gave herself sometime after her graduation from college. Following in the tradition of her mother, who attended the same boarding school, Zitkala-Sa left the reservation at age 12 to attend a Quaker missionary school for Indians, White's Manual Institute, which was located in Wabash, Indiana.

When she returned to the reservation three years later, Zitkala-Sa struggled with her identity, experiencing the ambivalence toward her heritage that was so common among Native American children who were sent away to boarding school. She wrote about this feeling in "The School Days of an Indian Girl," which was published in 1900, describing herself as "neither a wild Indian, nor a tame one."

Zitkala-Sa returned to school four years later at Santee Normal Training School in Nebraska in an attempt to remain close to her mother, but she found the school very limited and accepted scholarships to attend Earlham College in Indiana in 1895, where she studied until her graduation in 1897. Although she was a loner in school, she excelled in her studies and received many honors for her performance in oratory contests. She was also a violinist of note and won a scholarship to the Boston Conservatory of Music following her graduation from Earlham. She even went to Paris in 1900 with the Carlisle Indian Industrial School as a violin soloist for the Paris Exposition. Throughout, she struggled with a sense of alienation from her culture, feeling that she did not fit in anywhere. Gradually, she began to identify the need to use the oral traditions of her people to revitalize their culture.

Zitkala-Sa taught at the Carlisle Indian Industrial School in Pennsylvania. She began publishing autobiographical essays and traditional Native American legends in such prominent national magazines as the *Atlantic Monthly* and *Harper's*. Her feelings of estrangement and anger at the treatment of her people became part of the public discourse on Native American relations. Her essay "Why I Am a Pagan" appeared in 1902, when it was still common for Native Americans to humbly describe their conversion to Christianity. Zitkala-Sa insisted on the importance of traditional Native American spirituality and the right of Native Americans to choose for themselves.

Zitkala-Sa returned to her reservation where she met Captain Raymond Bonnin, who was of mixed Nakota heritage like herself, and who was working for the Bureau of Indian Affairs. They were married in 1902, and their son, Ohiya, meaning Winner, was born in 1903. Zitkala-Sa and her husband moved to the Ute Reservation in Utah, where they lived for 14 years, and she worked in various capacities. Her career as an activist included fighting for government reform, law codification, employment for Native Americans with the Bureau of Indian Affairs, the redress of land settlements with the Court of Claims, and the preservation of Native American history. Later in her career, her ideas evolved and she advocated assimilation, citizenship, and abolishing the Bureau of Indian Affairs.

In 1913, Zitkala-Sa collaborated with classical music composer William Hanson on an opera, *Sun Dance,* for which she wrote the libretto and songs. She also contributed substantially to the music, playing it for Hanson on her violin, so that he could score it. The opera was performed by a few rural amateur groups but only once, in 1937, by a professional music company. It premiered in New York with the New York Light Opera Guild, which selected it as its only American opera for that year. *Sun Dance* remains the only opera ever authored or coauthored by a Native American. It has not been performed since 1937 and has no published score or libretto. Although her health had already declined significantly, Zitkala-Sa did hear the opera performed in New York the year before she died.

In 1916, Zitkala-Sa and her husband moved to Washington, D.C., following her election as secretary of the Society for American Indians, a position that greatly supported her work as a reformer. She served as editor of the organization's publication, *American Indian Magazine,* which gave her the freedom to publish on controversial topics, such as corruption within the Bureau of Indian Affairs and

Native American military service in World War I. Zitkala-Sa also lectured frequently on these and other topics.

Zitkala-Sa's first book, *Impressions of an Indian Childhood,* appeared in 1899. It was followed by *American Indian Stories* in 1921, a unique blend of autobiography and fiction. Her political book, *Oklahoma's Poor Rich Indians: An Orgy of Graft, Exploitation of the Five Civilized Tribes, Legalized Robbery,* appeared in 1924 with two white coauthors. Its revelations of the robberies and murders of Native Americans in Oklahoma led to the Indian Reorganization Act of 1934. She also continued to publish political essays throughout her career. As an activist, she influenced a generation of policy makers in Washington, D.C., and helped to persuade Native American people to use their right to vote to support political candidates whose policies were favorable.

In response to Zitkala-Sa's advocacy, President Herbert Hoover appointed two Indian Rights Association representatives to the Bureau of Indian Affairs. In 1930, she formed the National Council of American Indians and served as president of the organization until her death in 1938. She also secured support from the General Federation of Women's Clubs, which, along with the Indian Rights Association and the Indian Welfare Committee, investigated government tribal treatment and abuse.

Zitkala-Sa died January 26, 1938, at the age of 61 and was buried in Arlington National Cemetery, beside her husband, who had served in World War I. Her book *Old Indian Legends* was published posthumously in 1985, as was a new edition of *American Indian Stories.*

## Further Reading

Fischer, Dexter. "Zitkala-Sa: The Evolution of a Writer." *American Indian Quarterly* 5 (1979): 229–238.

Lauter, Paul. "Zitkala-Sa." *The Heath Anthology of American Literature.* Lexington, Mass.: D. C. Heath and Company, 1994, pp. 925–940.

Warrior, Robert Allen. "Reading American Indian Intellectual Traditions." *World Literature Today* 66 (1992): 236–240.

Willard, William. "Zitkala-Sa, A Woman Who Would Be Heard." *Wicazo Sa Review* 1 (1995): 11–16.

# Bibliography and Recommended Sources

Alton, R. C. *A Checklist of Women Writers, 1801–1900: Fiction, Verse, Drama.* Boston: G. K. Hall, 1990.

Arata, Esther Spring. *Black American Playwrights, 1800 to the Present: A Bibliography.* Metuchen, N.J.: Scarecrow Press, 1976.

———. *More Black American Playwrights: A Bibliography.* Metuchen, N.J.: Scarecrow Press, 1978.

Bailey, Brooke. *The Remarkable Lives of 100 Women Writers and Journalists.* Holbrook, Mass.: Bob Adams, 1994.

Bain, Robert, Jr., Louis D. Rubin, and Joseph M. Flora, eds. *Southern Writers: A Biographical Dictionary.* Baton Rouge: Louisiana State University Press, 1979.

Bataille, Gretchen M. *Native American Women: A Biographical Dictionary.* New York: Garland, 1991.

*Black Writers: A Selection of Sketches from Contemporary Authors.* 2d ed. Detroit: Gale Research, 1994.

Bloom, Harold. *American Women Poets.* New York: Chelsea House, 1986.

Brumble, H. David. *An Annotated Bibliography of American Indian and Eskimo Autobiographies.* Lincoln: University of Nebraska Press, 1981.

Bryer, Jackson R., ed. *Sixteen Modern American Authors: A Survey of Research and Criticism.* New York: Norton, 1973. Volume 2, 1989.

Burke, W. J., and Will D. Howe. *American Authors and Books: 1640 to the Present Day.* Revised by Irving Weiss and Anne Weiss. 3d rev. ed. New York: Crown, 1972.

Cahill, Susan, ed. *Writing Women's Lives: An Anthology of Autobiographical Narratives of Twentieth-Century American Women Writers.* New York: HarperCollins, 1994.

Chapman, Dorothy Hilton. *Index to Poetry by Black American Women.* New York: Greenwood Press, 1986.

Cline, Cheryl. *Women's Diaries, Journals, and Letters: An Annotated Bibliography.* New York: Garland Publishers, 1989.

Colonnese, Tom. *American Indian Novelists: An Annotated Critical Bibliography.* New York: Garland Publishers, 1985.

Coltelli, Laura. *Winged Words: American Indian Writers Speak.* Lincoln: University Press of Nebraska, 1990.

Drake, William. *The First Wave: Women Poets in America, 1915–1945.* New York: Macmillan, 1987.

Foster, Mamie Marie Booth. *Southern Black Creative Writers, 1829–1953: Biobibliographies.* New York: Greenwood, 1988.

Gallagher, Edward J., and Thomas Werge, eds. *Early Puritan Writers: A Reference Guide.* Boston: G. K. Hall, 1976.

Halio, Jay L., and Ben Siegel, eds. *Women of Valor: Contemporary Jewish American Women Writers.* Newark: University of Delaware Press, 1997.

Harris, Trudier. *Afro-American Writers Before the Harlem Renaissance. Dictionary of Literary Biography.* Vol. 50. Detroit: Gale, 1986.

Hedgepeth, Chester M. *Twentieth-Century African-American Writers and Artists.* Chicago: American Library Association, 1991.

Helterman, Jeffrey, and Richard Layman, eds. *American Novelists Since World War II.* Detroit: Gale, 1978.

Holte, James Craig. *The Ethnic I: A Sourcebook for Ethnic-American Autobiography.* New York: Greenwood, 1988.

Huggins, Nathan Irvin, ed. *Voices from the Harlem Renaissance.* New York: Oxford University Press, 1976.

James, Edward T., ed. *Notable American Women.* Cambridge, Mass.: Belknap Press of Harvard University Press, 1971.

Kanellos, Nicolas. *Biographical Dictionary of Hispanic Literature in the United States.* Westport, Conn.: Greenwood, 1989.

Kunitz, Stanley J., and Howard Haycraft, eds. *American Authors 1600–1900: A Biographical Dictionary of American Literature.* New York: H. W. Wilson, 1981.

Leary, Lewis G. *Soundings: Some Early American Writers.* Athens: University of Georgia Press, 1975.

Levernier, James A., and Douglas R. Wilmes, eds. *American Writers before 1800: A Biographical and Critical Dictionary.* 3 vols. Westport, Conn.: Greenwood, 1983.

Lindfors, Bernth. *Black African Literature in English: A Guide to Information Sources.* Detroit: Gale, 1979.

Ling, Amy. *Between Worlds: Women Writers of Chinese Ancestry.* New York: Pergamon, 1990.

Magil, Frank N., ed. *Great Women Writers: The Lives and Works of 135 of the World's Most Important Women Writers.* New York: Henry Holt, 1994.

Mainiero, Lina, ed. *American Women Writers: A Critical Reference Guide from Colonial Times to the Present.* 4 vols. New York: Ungar, 1979–1982.

*Notable Asian Americans.* New York: Gale Research, 1995.

*Notable Native Americans.* New York: Gale Research, 1995.

Parker, Peter, ed. *Reader's Companion to Twentieth-Century Writers.* New York: Oxford University Press, 1996.

Peck, David R., ed. *American Ethnic Literatures: Native American, African American, Chicano/Latino, and Asian American Writers and Their Backgrounds.* Pasadena, Calif.: Salem Press, 1992.

Peterson, Bernard L. *Early Black American Playwrights and Dramatic Writers: A Biographical Directory and Catalog of Plays, Films, and Broadcasting Scripts.* New York: Greenwood, 1990.

Popkin, Michael, and Steven Serafin, eds. *Modern Black Writers.* New York: Ungar Publishing Company, 1982.

Roses, Lorraine Elena, and Ruth Elizabeth Randolph, eds. *Harlem Renaissance and Beyond: Literary Biographies of 100 Black Women Writers, 1900–1945.* Boston: G. K. Hall, 1990.

Shapiro, Ann R. *Jewish American Women Writers: A Bio-Bibliographical and Critical Sourcebook.* Westport, Conn.: Greenwood, 1994.

Shatzky, Joel, and Michael Taub, eds. *Contemporary Jewish-American Novelists: A Bio-Critical Sourcebook.* Westport, Conn.: Greenwood, 1997.

Showalter, Elaine, consulting ed., Lee Baechler and A. Walton Litz, eds. *Modern American Women Writers.* New York: Scribner, 1991.

Sinnott, Susan. *Extraordinary Hispanic Americans.* Chicago: Children's Press, 1991.

Smith, V., L. Baechher, and A. W. Litz, eds. *African American Writers.* New York: Scribner, 1991.

Sonneborn, Liz. *A to Z of Native American Women.* New York: Facts On File, 1998.

Unger, Leonard, ed. *American Writers: A Collection of Literary Biographies.* 4 vols. New York: Scribner, 1974.

Straub, Deborah Gillian, ed. *Voices of Multicultural America: Notable Speeches Delivered by African, Asian, Hispanic, and Native Americans, 1790–1995.* Detroit: Gale Research, 1996.

Whitson, Kathy J. *Native American Literatures: An Encyclopedia of Works, Characters, Authors, and Themes.* Santa Barbara, Calif.: ABC-CLIO, 1999.

Williams, Ora. *American Black Women in the Arts and Social Sciences.* Metuchen, N.J.: Scarecrow Press, 1994.

Yellin, Jean Fagan, and Cynthia D. Bond, eds. *The Pen Is Ours: A Listing of Writings by and about African-American Women Before 1910.* New York: Oxford University Press, 1991.

# ENTRIES BY LITERARY GENRE

**ADVENTURE FICTION**
Burroughs, Edgar Rice
Dorris, Michael
Erdrich, Louise

**AUTOBIOGRAPHER**
Angelou, Maya
Baraka, Amiri
Bruchac, Joseph
Dillard, Annie
Johnson, James Weldon
Truth, Sojourner
Twain, Mark
Welty, Eudora
Williams, Tennessee
Williams, William Carlos
Wright, Richard
Young Bear, Ray

**BIOGRAPHER**
Buck, Pearl S.
Burroughs, John
Chesnutt, Charles Waddell
Irving, Washington
Lowell, Amy
Mowat, Farley
Sandburg, Carl
Stein, Gertrude
Warren, Robert Penn

**CHILDREN'S WRITER**
Alcott, Louisa May
Alger, Horatio
Atwood, Margaret

Barthelme, Donald
Baum, L. Frank
Berry, Wendell
Bontemps, Arna
Bruchac, Joseph
Cullen, Countee
Dorris, Michael
Erdrich, Louise
Hall, Donald
Hawthorne, Nathaniel
Jarrell, Randall
Le Guin, Ursula
Mowat, Farley
Sandburg, Carl
Sinclair, Upton
Singer, Isaac Bashevis
Tan, Amy

**DETECTIVE/MYSTERY WRITER**
Chandler, Raymond
McMurtry, Larry
Oates, Joyce Carol

**DIARIST/JOURNAL WRITER**
Nin, Anaïs

**EDITOR**
Ashbery, John
Bly, Robert
Bruchac, Joseph
Bryant, William Cullen
Davies, Robertson
DuBois, W. E. B.
Emerson, Ralph Waldo

Fuller, Margaret
Gilman, Charlotte
Hall, Donald
Hawthorne, Nathaniel
Jarrell, Randall
Masters, Edgar Lee
Pound, Ezra
Waldman, Anne
Williams, Terry Tempest

**ESSAYIST**
Abbey, Edward
Ackerman, Diane
Alcott, Louisa May
Baldwin, James
Baraka, Amiri
Bellow, Saul
Berry, Wendell
Bly, Robert
Bradbury, Ray
Brooks, Gwendolyn
Burroughs, John
Burroughs, William
Chesnutt, Charles Waddell
Davies, Robertson
DeLillo, Don
Didion, Joan
Dillard, Annie
Dorris, Michael
DuBois, W. E. B.
Ellison, Ralph
Emerson, Ralph Waldo
Fitzgerald, F. Scott
Freneau, Phillip

Fuller, Margaret
Hall, Donald
Hansberry, Lorraine
Harrison, Jim
Hawthorne, Nathaniel
Jackson, Laura Riding
Johnson, Charles
Jong, Erica
Kincaid, Jamaica
King, Stephen
Kingsolver, Barbara
Kunitz, Stanley
Levertov, Denise
Lopez, Barry
Lorde, Audre
Mencken, H. L.
Momaday, Scott
Morrison, Toni
Mowat, Farley
Oates, Joyce Carol
O'Brien, Tim
Oliver, Mary
Olsen, Tillie
Ortiz, Simon
Ozick, Cynthia
Percy, Walker
Price, Reynolds
Proulx, E. Annie
Rich, Adrienne
Saroyan, William
Silko, Leslie Marmon
Simic, Charles
Sinclair, Upton
Singer, Isaac Bashevis
Stegner, Wallace
Stowe, Harriet Beecher
Tate, Allen
Thompson, Hunter S.
Thoreau, Henry David
Twain, Mark
Walker, Alice
Wasserstein, Wendy
Welch, James
Wharton, Edith Newbold Jones
Williams, Terry Tempest
Zitkala-Sa

### FOOD/TRAVEL WRITER
Abu-Jaber, Diana
Harrison, Jim
Irving, Washington
Wharton, Edith

### HORROR FICTION WRITER
King, Stephen
Rice, Anne

### JOURNALIST
Agee, James
Bryant, William Cullen
Capote, Truman
Davis, Rebecca Harding
Didion, Joan
Freneau, Phillip
Fuller, Margaret
Haley, Alex
Irving, Washington
Johnson, James Weldon
Kingsolver, Barbara
Mencken, H. L.
Porter, Katherine Anne
Sandburg, Carl
Thompson, Hunter S.
Twain, Mark
Wharton, Edith

### LETTER WRITER
Agee, James
Alcott, Louisa May
Dickinson, Emily
Wharton, Edith

### LITERARY CRITIC
Agee, James
Aiken, Conrad
Algren, Nelson
Allen, Paula Gunn
Bell, Madison Smartt
Berryman, John
Bogan, Louise
Dickey, James
DuBois, W. E. B.
Eliot, T. S.
Fuller, Margaret
Glück, Louise

Jackson, Laura Riding
Jarrell, Randall
Johnson, James Weldon
Levis, Larry
Mencken, H. L.
Parker, Dorothy
Percy, Walker
Pound, Ezra
Ransom, John Crowe
Shields, Carol
Stein, Gertrude
Tate, Allen
Warren, Robert Penn
Wideman, John Edgar
Wright, Charles

### MEMOIRIST
Ansay, A. Manette
Buck, Pearl S.
Bukowski, Charles
di Prima, Diane
Dorris, Michael
Erdrich, Louise
Gibbons, Kaye
Hellman, Lillian
Jong, Erica
Kincaid, Jamaica
Kingston, Maxine Hong
Lorde, Audre
Mencken, H. L.
Merrill, James Ingram
Nin, Anaïs Antolina
O'Brien, Tim
Plath, Sylvia
Saroyan, William
Stein, Gertrude
Styron, William
Walker, Alice
Washington, Booker
Wharton, Edith
Williams, Terry Tempest
Zitkala-Sa

### NATURE WRITER
Abbey, Edward
Ackerman, Diane
Berry, Wendell
Burroughs, John

Dillard, Annie
Lopez, Barry
William, Terry Tempest

**NONFICTION WRITER**
Agee, James
Algren, Nelson
Asimov, Isaac
Baldwin, James
Berry, Wendell
Bly, Robert
Capote, Truman
Dillard, Annie
Dorris, Michael
DuBois, W. E. B.
Emerson, Ralph Waldo
Fuller, Margaret
Gilman, Charlotte Perkins
Lindsay, Vachel
Lopez, Barry
Mather, Cotton
Mowat, Farley
Olsen, Tillie
Rowlandson, Mary
Stowe, Harriet Beecher
Truth, Sojourner
Walker, Alice
Washington, Booker T.
Wideman, John Edgar
Williams, Terry Tempest

**NOVELIST**
Abbey, Edward
Abu-Jaber, Diana
Agee, James
Aiken, Conrad
Alcott, Louisa May
Alexie, Sherman
Algren, Nelson
Allen, Paula Gunn
Anderson, Sherwood
Angelou, Maya
Ansay, A. Manette
Ashbery, John
Asimov, Isaac
Atwood, Margaret
Baldwin, James
Bambara, Toni Cade

Banks, Russell
Baraka, Amiri
Barthelme, Donald
Baum, L. Frank
Bell, Madison Smartt
Bellow, Saul
Berry, Wendell
Bontemps, Arna
Boyle, T. Coraghessan
Bradbury, Ray
Brautigan, Richard
Bruchac, Joseph
Buck, Pearl S.
Bukowski, Charles
Burroughs, Edgar Rice
Burroughs, William
Caldwell, Erskine
Capote, Truman
Cather, Willa
Chandler, Raymond
Chávez, Denise
Cheever, John
Chesnutt, Charles Waddell
Chopin, Kate
Cisneros, Sandra
Cooper James Fenimoore
Crane, Stephen
Creeley, Robert
Cullen, Countee
cummings, e. e.
Davies, Robertson
Davis, Rebecca Harding
DeLillo, Don
Dickey, James
Didion, Joan
Dillard, Annie
Doctorow, E. L.
Dorris, Michael
Dos Passos, John
Dove, Rita
Dreiser, Theodore
Ellison, Ralph
Erdrich, Louise
Faulkner, William
Fitzgerald, F. Scott
Ford, Richard
Freeman, Mary Wilkins
Gibbons, Kaye

Gilchrist, Ellen
Gilman, Charlotte Perkins
Glasgow, Ellen
Green, Paul
Haley, Alex
Hamilton, Jane
Harrison, Jim
Harte, Bret
Hawthorne, Nathaniel
H. D.
Hemingway, Ernest
Hijuelos, Oscar
Hughes, Langston
Hurston, Zora Neale
Irving, Washington
Jackson, Laura Riding
Jackson, Shirley
James, Henry
Jarrell, Randall
Jewett, Sarah Orne
Jin, Ha
Johnson, Charles
Johnson, James Weldon
Jong, Erica
Kerouac, Jack
Kesey, Ken
Kincaid, Jamaica
King, Stephen
Kingsolver, Barbara
Kingston, Maxine Hong
Kinsella, W. P.
Koch, Kenneth
Lee Chang-rae
Le Guin, Ursula
Lewis, Sinclair
London, Jack
Lopez, Barry
Mailer, Norman
Malamud, Bernard
McCarthy, Cormac
McCullers, Carson
McMurtry, Larry
Melville, Herman
Merrill, James Ingram
Michener, James
Miller, Henry
Momaday N. Scott
Morrison, Toni

Mowat, Farley
Mukherjee, Bharati
Munro, Alice
Nabokov, Vladimir
Nin, Anaïs
Oates, Joyce Carol
O'Brien, Tim
O'Connor, Flannery
Ondaatje, Michael
Ozick, Cynthia
Percy, Walker
Plath, Sylvia
Porter, Katherine Anne
Price, Reynolds
Proulx, E. Annie
Pynchon, Thomas
Rand, Ayn
Rice, Anne
Robbins, Tom
Roth, Philip
Sandburg, Carl
Saroyan, William
Shange, Ntozake
Shields, Carol
Silko, Leslie Marmon
Simpson, Mona
Sinclair, Upton
Singer, Isaac Bashevis
Smiley, Jane
Stegner, Wallace
Stein, Gertrude
Steinbeck, John
Stowe, Harriet Beecher
Styron, William
Tan, Amy
Tate, Allen
Thompson, Hunter S.
Twain, Mark
Tyler, Anne
Updike, John
Vonnegut, Kurt
Walker, Alice
Warren, Robert Penn
Welch, James
Welty, Eudora
West, Nathanael
Wharton, Edith
Wideman, John Edgar

Wilder, Thornton
Williams, Tennessee
Williams, William Carlos
Wolfe, Thomas
Wouk, Herman
Wright, Richard
Young Bear, Ray

## PLAYWRIGHT

Albee, Edward
Anderson, Sherwood
Angelou, Maya
Ashbery, John
Baldwin, James
Baraka, Amiri
Baum, L. Frank
Bellow, Saul
Bontemps, Arna
Bradbury, Ray
Burroughs, William S.
Capote, Truman
Chávez, Denise
Cullen, Countee
Davies, Robertson
DeLillo, Don
Dove, Rita
Eliot, T. S.
Freeman, Mary Eleanor Wilkins
Green, Paul
Hansberry, Lorraine
H. D.
Hellman, Lillian
Hwang, David Henry
Inge, William
James, Henry
Koch, Kenneth
Lewis, Sinclair
Mamet, David
McNally, Terrence
Millay, Edna St. Vincent
Miller, Arthur
Odets, Clifford
Ondaatje, Michael
O'Neill, Eugene
Saroyan, William
Sexton, Anne
Shange, Ntozake
Shepard, Sam

Shields, Carol
Simon, Neil
Sinclair, Upton
Stein, Gertrude
Thurber, James
Wasserstein, Wendy
Wilder, Thornton
Williams, Tennessee
Williams, William Carlos
Wilson, August

## POET

Ackerman, Diane
Agee, James
Ai
Aiken, Conrad
Alcott, Louisa May
Alexie, Sherman
Alger, Horatio
Algren, Nelson
Allen, Paula Gunn
Ammons, A. R.
Anderson, Sherwood
Angelou, Maya
Ashbery, John
Atwood, Margaret
Auden, W. H.
Baldwin, James
Banks, Russell
Baraka, Amiri
Berry, Wendell
Berryman, John
Bishop, Elizabeth
Bly, Robert
Bogan, Louise
Bontemps, Arna
Bradbury, Ray
Bradstreet, Anne
Brautigan, Richard
Brooks, Gwendolyn
Bruchac, Joseph
Bryant, William Cullen
Buck, Pearl S.
Bukowski, Charles
Burroughs, John
Capote, Truman
Carver, Raymond
Chávez, Denise

Chin, Marilyn
Cisneros, Sandra
Clifton, Lucille
Crane, Hart
Crane, Stephen
Creeley, Robert
Cullen, Countee
cummings, e. e.
Dickey, James
Dickinson, Emily
Dillard, Annie
di Prima, Diane
Dove, Rita
Eliot, T. S.
Emerson, Ralph Waldo
Erdrich, Louise
Ferlinghetti, Lawrence
Freeman, Mary Eleanor Wilkins
Freneau, Phillip
Frost, Robert
Ginsberg, Allen
Giovanni, Nikki
Glasgow, Ellen Anderson
Glück, Louise
Green, Paul Eliot
Hall, Donald
Harjo, Joy
Harrison, Jim
Harte, Bret
H. D.
Hughes, Langston
Irving, Washington
Jackson, Laura Riding
Jarrell, Randall
Jeffers, Robinson
Jin, Ha
Johnson, James Weldon
Jong, Erica
Koch, Kenneth
Kunitz, Stanley
Levertov, Denise
Levine, Philip
Levis, Larry
Lindsay, Vachel
Longfellow, Henry Wadsworth
Lorde, Audre
Lowell, Amy
Lowell, Robert

Masters, Edgar Lee
Melville, Herman
Merrill, James
Millay, Edna St. Vincent
Momaday, N. Scott
Moore, Marianne
Nabokov, Vladimir
O'Hara, Frank
Oliver, Mary
Ondaatje, Michael
Ortiz, Simon
Paley, Grace
Parker, Dorothy
Plath, Sylvia
Poe, Edgar Allen
Pound, Ezra
Price, Reynolds
Ransom, John Crowe
Reed, Ishmael
Rich, Adrienne
Robinson, Edwin Arlington
Roethke, Theodore
Sandburg, Carl
Service, Robert
Sexton, Anne
Shange, Ntozake
Shields, Carol
Silko, Leslie Marmon
Simic, Charles
Snyder, Gary
Stevens, Wallace
Stowe, Harriet Beecher
Strand, Mark
Tate, Allen
Teasdale, Sara
Thoreau, Henry David
Toomer, Jean
Twain, Mark
Updike, John
Waldman, Anne
Walker, Alice
Warren, Robert Penn
Welch, James
Wheatley, Phillis
Whitman, Walt
Williams, Tennessee
Wright, Charles

Wright, James
Young Bear, Ray

## SCIENCE FICTION/HISTORICAL FANTASY WRITER
Asimov, Isaac
Bradbury, Ray
Burroughs, Edgar Rice
Doctorow, E. L.
Le Guin, Ursula

## SCREENWRITER
Agee, James
Alexie, Sherman
Algren, Nelson
Bell, Madison Smartt
Bradbury, Ray
Bukowski, Charles
Capote, Truman
Chandler, Raymond
Didion, Joan
Dorris, Michael
Faulkner, William
Fitzgerald, F. Scott
Haley, Alex
Harrison, Jim
Hwang, David Henry
Johnson, Charles
King, Stephen
Mamet, David
Parker, Dorothy
Shepard, Sam
Walker, Alice
Williams, Tennessee

## SHORT STORY WRITER
Aiken, Conrad
Alcott, Louisa May
Algren, Nelson
Anderson, Sherwood
Ansay, A. Manette
Asimov, Isaac
Atwood, Margaret
Baldwin, James
Bambara, Toni
Banks, Russell
Barthelme, Donald
Bell, Madison Smartt
Bellow, Saul

Berryman, John
Bishop, Elizabeth
Bontemps, Arna
Boyle, T. Coraghessan
Bradbury, Ray
Brautigan, Richard
Buck, Pearl S.
Bukowski, Charles
Burroughs, William
Caldwell, Erskine
Carver, Raymond
Cather, Willa
Chandler, Raymond
Chávez, Denise
Cheever, John
Chesnutt, Charles Waddell
Chopin, Kate
Cisneros, Sandra
Clifton, Lucille
Crane, Stephen
Creeley, Robert
Davis, Rebecca Harding
DeLillo, Don
Dove, Rita
Ellison, Ralph
Erdrich, Louise
Faulkner, William
Fitzgerald, F. Scott
Ford, Richard
Freeman, Mary Wilkins
Gibbons, Kaye
Gilchrist, Ellen
Gilman, Charlotte Perkins
Glasgow, Ellen
Green, Paul
Hamilton, Jane
Harrison, Jim

Harte, Bret
Hemingway, Ernest
Henry, O.
Hursten, Zora Neale
Irving, Washington
Jackson, Laura Riding
Jackson, Shirley
James, Henry
Jewett, Sarah Orne
Jin, Ha
Johnson, Charles
Kincaid, Jamaica
King, Stephen
Kingsolver, Barbara
Kingston, Maxine Hong
Kinsella, W. P.
Levis, Larry
London, Jack
Lopez, Barry
Malamud, Bernard
McCullers, Carson
Melville, Herman
Momaday, N. Scott
Mukherjee, Bharati
Munro, Alice
Nabokov, Vladimir
Nin, Anaïs
Oates, Joyce Carol
O'Brien, Tim
O'Connor, Flannery
Olsen, Tillie
Ortiz, Simon
Ozick, Cynthia
Paley, Grace
Parker, Dorothy
Poe, Edgar Allen

Porter, Katherin Anne
Proulx, E. Annie
Pynchon, Thomas
Roth, Philip
Saroyan, William
Silko, Leslie Marmon
Sinclair, Upton
Singer, Isaac Bashevis
Stegner, Wallace
Steinbeck, John
Thurber, James
Toomer, Jean
Twain, Mark
Tyler, Anne
Updike, John
Vonnegut, Kurt
Walker, Alice
Welty, Eudora
Wharton, Edith
Williams, Tennessee
Wolfe, Thomas
Zitkala-Sa

## SLAVE OR CAPTIVITY NARRATIVE WRITER

Rowlandson, Mary
Truth, Sojourner

## TRANSLATOR

Bly, Robert
Buck, Pearl S.
Kunitz, Stanley
Nabokov, Vladimir
Simic, Charles
Strand, Mark
Wright, Charles

# ENTRIES BY LITERARY MOVEMENT/ REGION/SUBJECT/STYLE

This index of writers by literary movement, region, subject, and style is intended to provide an additional means of searching for writers in the book. Some categories, however, may need explanation. The regional categories, such as California, New England, and the South, include writers commonly associated with these regions. They do not include all writers born in these regions. Thus, one will find Joan Didion and Jack London under "California"—they both were born there and wrote often about their home state. However, one will also find Nathanael West, who hailed from New York but wrote about Hollywood. Other terms, such as "Deep Image," "Agrarian," "Naturalist," and "New York School," refer to particular styles or movements about which much has been written. For definitions and further information, please consult one of the following reference sources:

## Further Reading

Baldick, Chris. *Concise Dictionary of Literary Terms.* Oxford: Oxford University Press, 2001.

Cuddon, J. A., and Claire Preston. *Penguin Dictionary of Literary Terms and Literary Theory.* 4th ed. New York: Penguin, 2000.

### ABOLITION MOVEMENT
Stowe, Harriet Beecher
Truth, Sojourner
Washington, Booker T.

### AGRARIAN/FUGITIVE
Ransom, John Crowe
Tate, Allen
Warren, Robert Penn

### AMERICAN REVOLUTION
Freneau, Phillip
Wheatley, Phillis

### BEAT
Baraka, Amiri
Brautigan, Richard
Bukowski, Charles
Burroughs, William S.
di Prima, Diane
Ferlinghetti, Lawrence
Ginsberg, Allen
Kerouac, Jack
Kesey, Ken
Waldman, Anne

### BLACK ARTS
Bambara, Toni Cade
Baraka, Amiri
Giovanni, Nikki
Lorde, Audre
Reed, Ishmael
Walker, Alice

### BLACK MOUNTAIN
Creeley, Robert
Levertov, Denise

### CALIFORNIA
Brautigan, Richard
Didion, Joan
Ferlinghetti, Lawrence
Harte, Bret
Levis, Larry
London, Jack
Steinbeck, John
Twain, Mark
West, Nathanael

### CARIBBEAN
Kincaid, Jamaica

### CHICAGO
Anderson, Sherwood
Brooks, Gwendolyn
Cisneros, Sandra
Hughes, Langston

Lindsay, Vachel
Mamet, David
Masters, Edgar Lee
Sandburg, Carl
Sinclair, Upton

### CHINA
Buck, Pearl S.
Chin, Marilyn
Hwang, David Henry
Jing, Ha
Lee, Chang-Rae
Tan, Amy

### CIVIL RIGHTS

#### African American
Baraka, Amiri
Bontemps, Arna Wendell
Brooks, Gwendolyn Elizabeth
DuBois, W. E. B.
Ellison, Ralph
Green, Paul
Haley, Alex
Hansberry, Lorraine
Johnson, James Weldon
Morrison, Toni
Stowe, Harriet Beecher
Truth, Sojourner
Washington, Booker T.

#### Native American
Alexie, Sherman
Allen, Paula Gunn
Bruchae, Joseph
Erdrich, Louise
Silko, Leslie Marmon
Young Bear, Ray A.
Zitkala-Sa

#### Women's
Angelou, Maya
Atwood, Margaret
Buck, Pearl S.
Chávez, Denise
Chin, Marilyn
Chopin, Kate
Freeman, Mary Wilkins

Fuller, Margaret
Gilman, Charlotte Perkins
Jong, Erica
Kincaid, Jamaica
Kingston, Maxine Hong
Lorde, Audre
Morrison, Toni
Mukherjee, Bharati
Nin, Anaïs
Rich, Adrienne
Stowe, Harriet Beecher
Tan, Amy
Truth, Sojourner
Walker, Alice
Wasserstein, Wendy
Zitkala-Sa

### CONFESSIONAL POETRY
Berryman, John
Lowell, Robert
Plath, Sylvia
Sexton, Anne

### DEEP IMAGE
Bly, Robert
Roethke, Theodore
Strand, Mark

### ENVIRONMENTAL MOVEMENT
Abbey, Edward
Ackerman, Diane
Alexie, Sherman
Berry, Wendell
Dillard, Annie
Jewett, Sarah Orne
Kingsolver, Barbara
Lopez, Barry
Oliver, Mary
Snyder, Gary
Stegner, Wallace
Thoreau, Henry David
Williams, Terry Tempest

### EXPATRIATE BACKGROUND
Aiken, Conrad
Ashbery, John
Baldwin, James Arthur
Buck, Pearl S.

Eliot, T. S.
Fitzgerald, F. Scott
Hemingway, Ernest
Irving, Washington
James, Henry
Miller, Arthur
Miller, Henry
Nin, Anaïs
Parker, Dorothy
Plath, Sylvia
Pound, Ezra
Stein, Gertrude
Twain, Mark
Wharton, Edith

### FOLKLORISTS
Hurston, Zora Neale
Zitkala-Sa

### FRONTIER
Cather, Willa
Cooper, James Fenimore
Twain, Mark

### GAY AND LESBIAN
Bishop, Elizabeth
H. D.
Ginsberg, Allen
Lorde, Audre
Millay, Edna St. Vincent
Nin, Anaïs
O'Hara, Frank
Rich, Adrienne
Stein, Gertrude

### GOTHIC WRITERS
Alcott, Louisa May
Atwood, Margaret
Bradbury, Ray
Hawthorne, Nathaniel
Irving, Washington
Jackson, Shirley
James, Henry
King, Stephen
Melville, Herman
Morrison, Toni
Oates, Joyce Carol
Poe, Edgar Allan

Rice, Anne
Shepard, Sam
Wharton, Edith

## HARLEM RENAISSANCE
Bontemps, Arna
Cullen, Countee
DuBois, W. E. B.
Hughes, Langston
Hurston, Zora Neale
Johnson, James Weldon
Toomer, Jean

## IMAGISM
H. D.
Lowell, Amy
Moore, Marianne
Pound, Ezra
Williams, William Carlos

## IMMIGRANT OR CROSS-CULTURAL EXPERIENCE

### African American
Ai
Angelou, Maya
Baldwin, James
Bambara, Toni Cade
Baraki, Amiri
Bontemps, Arna
Brooks, Gwendolyn
Chesnutt, Charles W.
Clifton, Lucille
Cullen, Countee
Dove, Rita
DuBois, W. E. B.
Ellison, Ralph
Giovanni, Nikki
Green, Paul
Haley, Alex
Hansberry, Lorraine
Hughes, Langston
Hurston, Zora Neale
Johnson, Charles
Johnson, James Weldon
Lorde, Audre
Morrison, Toni
Reed, Ishmael

Shange, Ntozake
Toomer, Jean
Truth, Sojourner
Walker, Alice
Washington, Booker T.
Wheatley, Phillis
Wilson, August
Wright, Richard

### Arab American
Abu-Jaber, Diana

### Asian American/South Asian
Chin, Marilyn
Hwang, David Henry
Jin, Ha
Lee, Chang-rae
Kingston, Maxine Hong
Mukherjee, Bhareti
Ondaatje, Michael
Tan, Amy

### Cajun/Creole
Chopin, Kate

### Caribbean
Kincaid, Jamaica

### Eastern European/Jewish
Asimov, Isaac
Bellow, Saul
Jong, Erica
Malamud, Bernard
Nabokov, Vladimir
Odets, Clifford
Rand, Ayn
Singer, Isaac Bashevis

### Hispanic American
Chávez, Denise
Cisneros, Sandra
Dos Passos, John
Hijuelos Oscar
Lopez, Barry Holstun

### Native American
Alexie, Sherman
Allen, Paula Gunn

Bruchac, Joseph
Dorris, Michael
Erdrich, Louise
Harjo, Joy
Momaday, N. Scott
Ortiz, Simon
Silko, Leslie Marmon
Young Bear, Ray
Zitkala-Sa

## LOST GENERATION
Anderson, Sherwood
Baldwin, James
Crane, Hart
Dos Passos, John
Fitzgerald, F. Scott
Hemingway, Ernest
Stein, Gertrude

## MIDWEST
Anderson, Sherwood
Ansay, A. Manette
Cather, Willa
Harrison, Jim
Henry, O.
Inge, William
Levine, Philip
Shepard, Sam
Smiley, Jane

## MODERNISTS
Anderson, Sherwood
Auden, W. H.
Baldwin, James
Bishop, Elizabeth
Bogan, Louise
Brooks, Gwendolyn
Crane, Hart
cummings, e. e.
Dos Passos, John
Dreiser, Theodore
DuBois, W. E. B.
Eliot, T. S.
Ellison, Ralph
Faulkner, William
Fitzgerald, F. Scott
Frost, Robert
Gilman, Charlotte Perkins

Glasgow, Ellen
H. D.
Hemingway, Ernest
Hughes, Langston
Hurston, Zora Neale
Jackson, Laura Riding
James, Henry
Johnson, James Weldon
Lewis, Sinclair
Lindsay, Vachel
Lowell, Amy
Mencken, H. L.
Milley, Edna St. Vincent
Moore, Marianne
O'Neill, Eugene
Parker, Dorothy
Pound, Ezra
Ransom, John Crowe
Roethke, Theodore
Sandburg, Carl
Stein, Gertrude
Steinbeck, John
Stevens, Wallace
Tate, Allen
Teasdale, Sara
Thurber, James
Toomer, Jean
Warren, Robert Penn
Welty, Eudora
West, Nathanael
Wharton, Edith
Wilder, Thornton
Williams, William Carlos
Wolfe, Thomas
Wright, Richard

**MUCKRAKERS**
Davis, Rebecca Harding
Sinclair, Upton

**NATURALISTS**
Crane, Stephen
Dreiser, Theodore
London, Jack

**NEW ENGLAND**
Alcott, Louisa May
Banks, Russell

Bryant, William Cullen
Dickinson, Emily
Emerson, Ralph Waldo
Freeman, Mary Wilkins
Frost, Robert
Hall, Donald
Hawthorne, Nathaniel
Jewett, Sarah Orne
King, Stephen
Kunitz, Stanley
Lowell, Amy
Oliver, Mary
Peoulx, E. Annie
Thoreau, Henry David

**NEW YORK CITY**
Ashbery, John
Cheever, John
Crane, Hart
Doctorow, E. L.
Dos Passos, John
Hijuelos, Oscar
Jong, Erica
Mailer, Norman
Paley, Grace
Simon, Neil
Wasserstein, Wendy

**NEW YORK SCHOOL**
Ashbery, John
Koch, Kenneth
O'Hara, Frank

**PACIFIC NORTHWEST**
Alexie, Sherman
Carver, Raymond
Leverton, Denise
Lopez, Barry
Roethke, Theodore
Snyder, Gary

**POSTMODERNIST**
Albee, Edward
Ammons, A. R.
Ashbery, John
Barthelme, Donald
Boyle, T. Coraghessan
Brautigan, Richard

Carver, Raymond
Chin, Marilyn
DeLillo, Don
Glück, Louise
Johnson, Charles
Morrison, Toni
Nabokov, Vladimir
Pynchon, Thomas
Roth, Philip
Shepard, Sam
Thompson, Hunter S.
Vonnegut, Kurt

**PURITAN**
Bradstreet, Anne
Mather, Cotton
Rowlandson, Mary

**REALIST**
Cather, Willa
Chesnutt, Charles Waddell
Chopin, Kate
Crane, Stephen
Davis, Rebecca Harding
Gardner, John
Gilman Charlotte Perkins
Harte, Bret
James, Henry
Lindsay, Vachel
Masters, Edgar Lee
Morrison, Toni
Sandburg, Carl
Twain, Mark
Walker, Alice
Wharton, Edith

**THE SOUTH**
Agee, James
Aiken, Conrad
Caldwell, Erskine
Faulkner, William
Gibbons, Kaye
Gilchrist, Ellen
Glasgow, Ellen
Jarrell, Randall
McCullers, Carson
O'Connor, Flannery
Ransom, John Crowe

Tate, Allen
Warren, Robert Penn
Welty, Eudora

## SOUTHERN GOTHIC WRITERS
Capote, Truman
Faulkner, William
McCarthy, Cormac
McCullers, Carson
O'Connor, Flannery
Rice, Anne
Williams, Tennessee

## SOUTHWEST
Abbey, Edward
Chávez, Denise
Cisneros, Sandra
Kingsolver, Barbara
McCarthy, Cormac
McMurtry, Larry
Ortiz, Simon
Silko, Leslie Marmon

## TRANSCENDENTALISTS
Alcott, Louisa May
Dickinson, Emily
Emerson, Ralph Waldo
Fuller, Margaret
Thoreau, Henry David
Whitman, Walt

## VIETNAM
O'Brien, Tim

## VIRGINIA
Davis, Rebecca Harding
Glasgow, Ellen

## THE WEST
Lopez, Barry
Snyder, Gary
Stegner, Wallace
Twain, Mark
Welch, James

## WOMEN'S LITERATURE
Alcott, Louisa May
Ansay, A. Manette
Atwood, Margaret
Chopin, Kate
Glasgow, Ellen
Gibbons, Kaye
Gilchrist, Ellen
Hamilton, Jane
Jewett, Sarah Orne
Munro, Alice
Price, Reynolds
Shields, Carol
Simpson, Mona
Smiley, Jane
Tan, Amy
Tyler, Anne
Updike, John

# ENTRIES BY YEAR OF BIRTH

**1600–1699**
Bradstreet, Anne
Mather, Cotton
Rowlandson, Mary

**1700–1799**
Bryant, William Cullen
Cooper, James Fenimore
Freneau, Phillip
Irving, Washington
Truth, Sojourner
Wheatley, Phillis

**1800–1849**
Alcott, Louisa May
Alger, Horatio
Burroughs, John
Davis, Rebecca Harding
Dickinson, Emily
Emerson, Ralph Waldo
Fuller, Margaret
Harte, Bret
Hawthorne, Nathaniel, Jr.
James, Henry
Jewett, Sarah Orne
Longfellow, Henry Wadsworth
Melville, Herman
Poe, Edgar Allan
Stowe, Harriet Beecher
Thoreau, Henry David
Twain, Mark
Whitman, Walt

**1850–1859**
Baum, L. Frank
Chesnutt, Charles W.
Chopin, Kate
Freeman, Mary Wilkins
Washington, Booker T.

**1860–1869**
DuBois, W. E. B.
Gilman, Charlotte Perkins
Henry, O.
Masters, Edgar Lee
Robinson, Edwin Arlington
Wharton, Edith

**1870–1879**
Anderson, Sherwood
Burroughs, Edgar Rice
Cather, Willa
Crane, Stephen
Dreiser, Theodore
Frost, Robert
Glasgow, Ellen
Johnson, James Weldon
Lindsay, Vachel
London, Jack
Lowell, Amy
Sandburg, Carl
Service, Robert
Sinclair, Upton
Stein, Gertrude
Stevens, Wallace
Zitkala-Sa

**1880–1889**
Aiken, Conrad Potter
Chandler, Raymond
Eliot, T. S.
H. D.
Jeffers, Robinson
Lewis, Sinclair
Mencken, H. L.
Moore, Marianne
O'Neill, Eugene
Ransom, John Crowe
Teasdale, Sara
Williams, William Carlos

**1890–1899**
Bogan, Louise
Buck, Pearl S.
Crane, Hart
cummings, e. e.
Dos Passos, John
Faulkner, William
Fitzgerald, F. Scott
Green, Paul
Hemingway, Ernest
Hurston, Zora Neale
Millay, Edna St. Vincent
Miller, Henry
Nabokov, Vladimir
Parker, Dorothy
Porter, Katherine Anne
Tate, Allen
Thurber, James
Toomer, Jean
Wilder, Thornton

**1900–1909**

Agee, James
Algren, Nelson
Auden, W. H.
Bontemps, Arna
Caldwell, Erskine
Cullen, Countee
Hellman, Lillian
Hughes, Langston
Jackson, Laura Riding
Kunitz, Stanley
Michener, James
Nin, Anaïs
Odets, Clifford
Rand, Ayn
Roethke, Theodore
Saroyan, William
Singer, Isaac Bashevis
Stegner, Wallace
Steinbeck, John
Warren, Robert Penn
Welty, Eudora
West, Nathanael
Wolfe, Thomas
Wright, Richard

**1910–1919**

Bellow, Saul
Berryman, John
Bishop, Elizabeth
Brooks, Gwendolyn
Burroughs, William S.
Cheever, John
Davies, Robertson
Ellison, Ralph
Ferlinghetti, Lawrence
Inge, William
Jackson, Shirley
Jarrell, Randall
Lowell, Robert
Malamud, Bernard
McCullers, Carson
Miller, Arthur
Olsen, Tillie
Percy, Walker
Williams, Tennessee
Wouk, Herman

**1920–1929**

Abbey, Edward
Albee, Edward
Ammons, A. R.
Angelou, Maya
Ashbery, John
Asimov, Isaac
Baldwin, James
Bly, Robert
Bradbury, Ray
Bukowski, Charles
Capote, Truman
Creeley, Robert
Dickey, James
Ginsberg, Allen
Haley, Alex
Hall, Donald
Kerouac, Jack
Koch, Kenneth
Le Guin, Ursula
Levertov, Denise
Levine, Philip
Mailer, Norman
Merrill, James
Mowat, Farley
O'Connor, Flannery
O'Hara, Frank
Ozick, Cynthia
Paley, Grace
Rich, Adrienne
Sexton, Anne
Simon, Neil
Styron, William
Vonnegut, Kurt
Wright, James

**1930–1939**

Allen, Paula Gunn
Atwood, Margaret
Bambara, Toni Cade
Baraka, Amiri
Barthelme, Donald
Berry, Wendell
Brautigan, Richard
Carver, Raymond
Clifton, Lucille
DeLillo, Don
Didion, Joan

di Prima, Diane
Doctorow, E. L.
Gilchrist, Ellen
Hansberry, Lorraine
Harrison, Jim
Kesey, Ken
Kinsella, W. P.
Lorde, Audre
McCarthy, Cormac
McMurtry, Larry
McNally, Terrence
Momaday, N. Scott
Morrison, Toni
Munro, Alice
Oates, Joyce Carol
Oliver, Mary
Plath, Sylvia
Price, Reynolds
Proulx, E. Annie
Pynchon, Thomas
Reed, Ishmael
Robbins, Tom
Roth, Philip
Shields, Carol
Simic, Charles
Snyder, Gary
Strand, Mark
Thompson, Hunter S.
Updike, John
Wright, Charles

**1940–1949**

Ackerman, Diane
Ai
Banks, Russell
Boyle, T. Coraghessan
Bruchac, Joseph
Chávez, Denise
Dillard, Annie
Dorris, Michael
Ford, Richard
Giovanni, Nikki
Glück, Louise
Johnson, Charles
Jong, Erica
Kincaid, Jamaica
King, Stephen
Kingston, Maxine Hong
Levis, Larry

Lopez, Barry
Mamet, David
Mukherjee, Bharati
O'Brien, Tim
Ondaatje, Michael
Ortiz, Simon
Rice, Anne
Shange, Ntozake
Shepard, Sam
Silko, Leslie Marmon
Smiley, Jane
Tyler, Anne
Waldman, Anne
Walker, Alice

Welch, James
Wideman, John Edgar
Wilson, August

**1950–1959**
Abu-Jaber, Diana
Bell, Madison Smartt
Chin, Marilyn
Cisneros, Sandra
Dove, Rita
Erdrich, Louise
Hamilton, Jane
Harjo, Joy
Hijuelos, Oscar

Hwang, David Henry
Jin, Ha
Kingsolver, Barbara
Simpson, Mona
Tan, Amy
Wasserstein, Wendy
Williams, Terry Tempest
Young Bear, Ray Anthony

**1960–1969**
Alexie, Sherman
Ansay, A. Manette
Gibbons, Kaye
Lee, Chang-rae

# INDEX

Locators in **boldface** indicate main entries. Locators in *italics* indicate photographs.

Pinter, Harold 9, 221, 222
*The Pioneers* (James Fenimore Cooper) 86
Pipkin, Charles W. 356
Pitt, Brad 151
*Plain Song* (Jim Harrison) 152
*The Plaint of a Rose* (Carl Sandburg) 301
"Planes of Personality: Two Speak Together" (poetry series, Amy Lowell) 215
"The Planet on the Table" (Wallace Stevens) 327
*The Planets: A Cosmic Pastoral* (Diane Ackerman) 4
*The Plant* (electronic book, Stephen King) 192
Plath, Sylvia xv, **275–276**
  Robert Lowell 216
  Theodore Roethke 296
  Anne Sexton 305, 306
*Player Piano* (Kurt Vonnegut) 350–351
*Playing in the Dark: Whiteness and the Literary Imagination* (Toni Morrison) 247
*Play It As It Lays* (Joan Didion) 102
*Plaza Suite* (Neil Simon) 313
Poe, Edgar Allan xi, xii, **276–278,** 277
  Conrad Aiken 7
  Donald Hall 147
  Stephen King 191
*Poems, 1923–1954* (e. e. cummings) 93
*Poems about God* (John Crowe Ransom) 289
*Poems* (Marianne Moore) 244
*Poems on Various Subjects, Religious and Moral* (Phillis Wheatley) 366
Poetic Justice (band) 150, 151
*A Poetry Handbook* (Mary Oliver) 263
*Poetry: A Magazine of Verse*
  Louise Bogan 48
  Gwendolyn Brooks 57
  Robert Creeley 89
  Stanley Kunitz 198
  Vachel Lindsay 206–207
  James Merrill 235
  Edna St. Vincent Millay 238
  Theodore Roethke 296
  Wallace Stevens 327
*A Poet's Alphabet: Reflections on the Literary Art and Vocation* (Louise Bogan) 48
The Poets Press 106
*Poganuc People* (Harriet Beecher Stowe) 329
*The Poisonwood Bible* (Barbara Kingsolver) 193

*Poland* (James Michener) 236
*Political Fictions* (Joan Didion) 103
*Popo and Fifina* (Langston Hughes and Arna Bontemps) 164
*The Portable Faulkner* (William Faulkner) 124
Porter, Katherine Anne xvi, 87, 228, 250, **279–280**
*Portnoy's Complaint* (Philip Roth) 298
*Portrait of the Artist as a Bad Character and Other Essays on Writing* (Cynthia Ozick) 270
*Postcards* (Annie E. Proulx) 284
*The Postman Always Rings* (David Mamet) 222
postmodernism
  Donald Barthelme 36
  Don DeLillo 97–98
  Vladimir Nabokov 252, 253
*Post Office* (Charles Bukowski) 62, 63
Pound, Ezra xiv, **281–282**
  Conrad Aiken 7
  John Berryman 43
  e. e. cummings 92, 93
  Diane di Prima 105
  T. S. Eliot 116, 117
  H. D. 155
  Ernest Hemingway 158
  Ha Jin 181
  Amy Lowell 215
  Marianne Moore 244
  Gary Snyder 320
  William Carlos Williams 375, 376
  Charles Wright 380
*The Prague Orgy* (Philip Roth) 298
*Praise to the End!* (Theodore Roethke) 297
*The Preacher and the Slave* (Wallace Stegner) 321
*Preface to a Twenty-Volume Suicide Note* (Amiri Baraka) 34
*Pretty Boy Floyd* (Larry McMurtry) 229
Price, Reynolds xvii, **282–283,** 346
*Prince Hagen* (Upton Sinclair) 316
*The Prisoner of Second Avenue* (Neil Simon) 313
*The Prisoner of Sex* (Norman Mailer) 219
*Prison Project Newsletter* 58
"The Promise" (John Steinbeck) 325
*Promises: Poems 1954–1956* (Robert Penn Warren) 357
*Promises, Promises* (Neil Simon) 313
*Proofs & Theories* (Louise Glück) 143
Proulx, E. Annie **283–284**
Proust, Marcel 235
Provincetown Fine Arts Workshop 263

Provincetown Players 267
*Prufrock and Other Observations* (T. S. Eliot) 117
Pueblo of Acoma Press 269
Puritanism 53, 100, 101, 153, 224–225, 300
Pynchon, Thomas xvi, **284–286,** 294

## Q

*Q.E.D.* (Gertrude Stein) 323
*The Queen of the Damned* (Anne Rice) 292
*Questions of Travel* (Elizabeth Bishop) 46
*The Quiet Dust and Other Writings* (William Styron) 331
*Quilt* magazine 290

## R

*Rabbit at Rest* (John Updike) 349
*Rabbit Redux* (John Updike) 348–349
*Rabbit Run* (John Updike) 348
*Ragged Dick* (Horatio Alger) 13
*Ragtime* (E. L. Doctorow) 106, 107
*Ragtime* (libretto, Terrence McNally) 229, 230
*A Raisin in the Sun* (Lorraine Hansberry) 149, 150
Rand, Ayn **287–288**
Random House 265
Rank, Otto 254, 255
Ransom, John Crowe xv, **288–290**
  Laura Riding Jackson 172
  Allen Tate 333
  Robert Penn Warren 356
  James Wright 382
"The Ransom of Red Chief" (O. Henry) 161
*Rational Meaning: A New Foundation for the Definition of Words* (Laura Riding Jackson and Schuyler Brinckerhoff Jackson) 173
*Rat Jelly* (Michael Ondaatje) 266
Rattigan, Terence 222
*Ravelstein* (Saul Bellow) 41
*The Raven and Other Poems* (Edgar Allan Poe) 278
"The Raven" (Edgar Allan Poe) 277, 278
*The Real Life of Sebastian Knight* (Vladimir Nabokov) 253
*Reasons for Moving* (Mark Strand) 329
*Recitative* (James Merrill) 235
*Recollections of My Life As a Woman* (Diane di Prima) 105
*The Red Badge of Courage* (Stephen Crane) 88
Redford, Robert 221